LONDON

D0558751

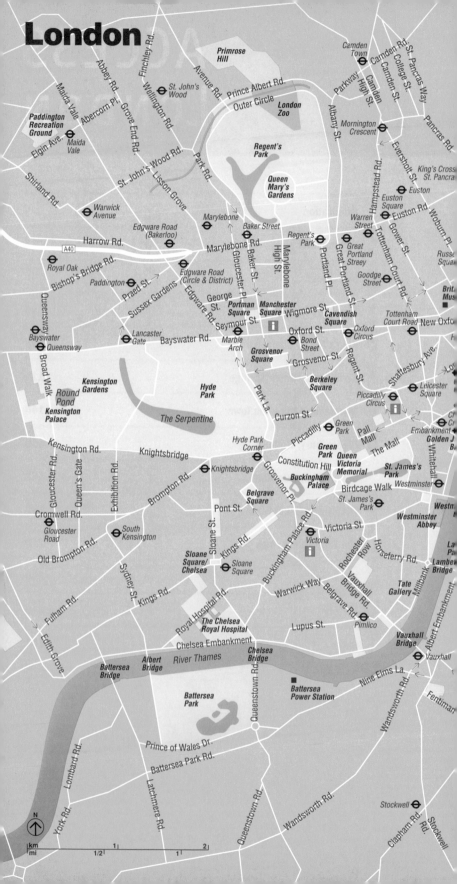

ORIENTATION

A provincial settlement on the edge of the civilized world; a trading district dominated by merchants and aldermen; a royal stronghold; a center of politics, power, and culture ... London has had almost as many faces as it has years of history. England's capital and Britain's seat of government has evolved over the centuries from an area covering just 677 acres into a vast 620-square-mile metropolis along the north and south banks of the River Thames, home to seven million citizens. Indeed, London is not one but several cities existing in the same space. Look up at Big Ben on a bright autumn morning or stroll along the Embankment on a warm summer evening at sunset and you'll find the London of film sets, complete with red double-decker buses, chunky black cabs, and umbrella-toting politicians. Look closer and catch a glimpse of local London, comprising 32 highly individual boroughs, each with its own mayor and council, not to mention its own special quirks and charms. An elegant town-house atmosphere permeates Mayfair, for example, whereas the literary legacy of Virginia Woolf's era clings to Bloomsbury. To the east, finance still dominates the original City, or Corporation, of London; meanwhile, law and politics rule sober Westminster. Of course, there is also historic London, seat of cathedrals and kings. The city was established roughly 2,000 years ago, first as a Celtic settlement, then as Londinium, a lonely Roman outpost that eventually grew into the hub of an empire extending around the globe. The city is a survivor, having weathered the brazier of history: Queen Boadicea of the Celts burned the city to the ground in AD 61, but within a few years it had risen from the ashes; the Great Plague swept through in 1665, followed by the Great Fire of 1666, but neither disaster nor the 20th-century Blitz, centuries later, could annihilate the city's collective soul or the souls of its inhabitants past and present. Famous ghosts from every epoch cohabit here—in just one day you may happen upon Henry VIII or Anne Boleyn in the Tower of London, William Shakespeare in Southwark, and Charles Dickens in Tavistock Square. Even modern redevelopment plans have failed to tarnish London's grandeur: St. Paul's Cathedral retains its majesty, despite the cheerless and now derelict glass-and-steel structures that crowd it on Paternoster Square.

The great thing for me, living in London, is its glorious mix of races and cultures. Nowadays this is even reflected architecturally. If you venture outside the center as far as Neasden you will see a stunning Hindu temple, the Shri Swaminarayan Mandir—the largest outside India. Nearly 3,000 tons of Bulgarian limestone and 2,000 tons of Italian marble were shipped to India, carved by more than 1,500 craftsmen into 26,300 separate pieces, and then shipped back to London, where they were put together by 1,000 workers from the various Hindu communities to create this marvel in less than 3 years. This is a paradigm of London: it doesn't have fabulous natural resources, it no longer has the amazing and dedicated traditional craftsmen it once did, and it lacks the kind of indigenous laboring task force that will work to achieve something like this out of love and pride. But somehow everything ends up in London, because London is the place to be. So you will find much that is wonderful here, but while there is much that is *in* London, there is less that is *of* London. The same goes for cuisine and wines and theater and even shopping. But a visit to London could save you a fortune in airfares to the rest of the world! And it goes without saying that London is no more England than Paris is France or New York is the USA. London is a great, fascination-filled place for a vacation. So much to see, so much to do. If you have the time, and can even bear to think about wandering "off Access," then venture outside the center and find some of London's villages . . . Chiswick and Barnes, Richmond and Stoke Newington. They are almost all accessible by the tube. And each has its own character. However, unlike other cities I love and write about, including Venice, Florence, and Rome, I would advise against getting lost in London. It is not really a "wanderer-friendly" place.

To call London from the US, dial 001-44, followed by the city code and local number. When calling from inside Great Britain, dial the city code and the local number. The city code for inner London is 0207; for outer London, 0208. Dialing from within London, you are required to add the 7 or the 8 to the front of the three-figure local code. Unless indicated, all the codes in this book are 7.

Getting to London

Two major airports serve London from North America: Heathrow, roughly 15 miles west of the city's center, and Gatwick, some 28 miles to the south.

Airports

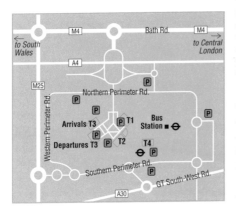

Heathrow Airport

Heathrow is the world's busiest airport, and the closest to London proper. Most major North American airlines (with the exception of Delta) fly into Heathrow's four terminals; there are information desks in each terminal. Transport information desks are in terminals 1 and 3 and outside terminal 4. There is also a Hotel and Traveler Center in terminal 3.

Currency exchange and ATMs are available in all terminals, as are public telephones and fax machines, lost luggage facilities, fast-food outlets, coffee shops, bars, pharmacies (terminal 1 for prescriptions), bookshops, and news agents . . . pretty much like home, really! Post offices are located in terminals 2 and 4.

There are also a chapel, showers, and a health center (0208/745.7047). Lost property can be

reclaimed (one hopes!) by calling 0208/745.7727. Information for passengers with disabilities is available from Heathrow Travel-Care counters or by calling 0208/745.7495. Information for the hard of hearing is available at 0208/745.7950, and there are wheelchair-accessible phones and fax machines, text telephones, and induction loops in all terminals. Help with baggage can be booked through Skycaps at 0208/745.6011, and accessible transportation to and from the airport can be had on the Help Bus (0208/745.6261). Heathrow's new terminal—terminal 5—is currently under construction. While construction is in progress, underground trains will not be stopping at terminal 4. A bus service is provided from Hatton Cross.

AIRPORT SERVICES

Each of the four terminals has its own facilities and services, so to minimize confusion there is one number to call that will connect you to the right department (specify which terminal), no matter what information you require, from parking to immigration control: 0870/000.0123.

AIRLINES

Air Canada	0208/897.1331,	800/776.3000
American Airlines	0345/789789,	800/433.7300
British Airways	0208/759.2525,	800/247.9297
KLM Royal Dutch Airlines		0208/750.9820
United	0028/990.9900,	800/241.6522
Virgin Atlantic	01293/511581,	800/862.8621

Getting to and from Heathrow Airport

BY BUS

Airbus (0171/222.1234) offers two buses that connect **Heathrow** with central **London**: the **A1** goes to **Victoria Station** via **Hyde Park Corner**, and the **A2** goes to **Russell Square** via **Euston Station**. Both buses run daily between 6AM and 11:50PM, depart every 30 minutes, and stop at each terminal. Bus transport costs more than the tube (subway) and usually takes a lot longer (75 to 100 minutes, depending on traffic), but if you can keep from nodding off after the long flight, you can sightsee along the way.

National Express (0870/580.8080; www.nationalexpress.com) offers frequent service to central London. Should your flight arrive at night, the N9 service will take you to central London (Traveline 0870/608.2608).

How to Read This Guide

ACCESS® LONDON is arranged so you can see at a glance where you are and what is around you. The numbers next to the entries in the following chapters correspond to the numbers on the maps. The text is color-coded according to the kind of place described:

Restaurants/Clubs: Red

Hotels: Purple | Shops: Orange

🇵 **Outdoors/Parks: Green** | Sights/Culture: Blue

RATING THE RESTAURANTS AND HOTELS

The restaurant star ratings take into account the quality, service, atmosphere, and uniqueness of the restaurant. An expensive restaurant doesn't necessarily ensure an enjoyable evening; a small, relatively unknown spot could have good food, professional service, and a lovely atmosphere. Therefore, on a purely subjective basis, stars are used to judge the overall dining value (see the star ratings at right). Keep in mind that chefs and owners often change, which sometimes drastically affects the quality of a restaurant. The ratings in this guidebook are based on information available at press time.

The price ratings, as categorized at right, apply to restaurants and hotels. These figures describe general price-range relationships among other restaurants and hotels in the area. The restaurant price ratings are based on the average cost of a dinner entrée for one person, including tax (Value Added Tax, or VAT) but excluding tip. Hotel price ratings reflect the base price of a standard room for two people for one night during the peak season. At press time, the exchange rate was $1.86 to £1.

RESTAURANTS

★	Good
★★	Very Good
★★★	Excellent
★★★★	An Extraordinary Experience
$	The Price Is Right (less than $15)
$$	Reasonable ($15–$22)
$$$	Expensive ($23–$30)
$$$$	Big Bucks ($31 and up and up)

HOTELS

$	The Price Is Right (less than $150)
$$	Reasonable ($150–$220)
$$$	Expensive ($220–$360)
$$$$	Big Bucks ($360 and up and up)

MAP KEY

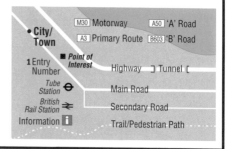

Speedlink (0990/747777), a luxury bus company, provides service between Heathrow and Gatwick Airports daily, every 15 minutes, between 6:15AM and 11:30PM; travel time is about 1 hour.

BY CAR

To get to London from **Heathrow Airport**, take the **M4** east to the **A4**, which leads into the center of the city. To get to the airport from the city, take the **A4** west to the **M4**. There is long- and short-term parking at each terminal. There are no tolls in either direction; depending on the traffic, the drive takes between 30 and 45 minutes.

RENTAL CARS

The following rental car companies have counters at Heathrow Airport:

Alamo.....................0800/272300 (toll-free in Britain),
....800/327.9633

Avis.............................0990/900500, 800/331.1212

Budget........................00/626063 (toll-free in Britain),
....800/527.0700

Eurodollar..0208/897.3232,
....800/800.4000

Europcar..0208/897.0811,
....800/227.7368

Hertz..0345/555888,
....800/654.3131

BY SUBWAY

The **Underground** system has two tube (subway) stations at the airport: one serving **Heathrow Central** (**terminals 1** through **3**), the other serving **terminal 4**. Heathrow's new terminal—terminal 5—is currently under construction. While construction is in progress, underground trains will not be stopping at terminal 4. A bus service is provided from Hatton Cross. Both tube stations are on the **Piccadilly Line** and are the quickest and cheapest way to go between central London and the airport. Trains leave approximately every 10 minutes Monday through Saturday, between 5:08AM and 11:49PM (5:26AM–11:33PM in terminal 4), and on Sunday from 5:58AM to 10:57PM (5:52AM–10:46PM in terminal 4); operation is more frequent during peak hours (weekdays, 7-9:30AM and 4:30–7PM). The trip takes 40 to 55 minutes, depending on the destination. For more information about schedules and fares, call 0207/222.1234.

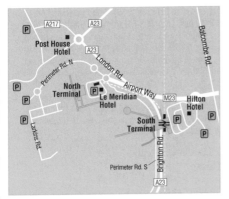

There is now the option of the **BAA Heathrow Express**, which runs from **Paddington Station** to all four terminals every 15 minutes between 5:10AM and 11:40PM. The last express coming back from Heathrow leaves at 11:52PM. The journey takes around 15 minutes, and luggage may be checked in at Paddington. For more information or to book by credit card, call 0845/600.1515. www.heathrowexpress.com

By Taxi

Taxis wait for passengers at the authorized ranks located outside each terminal; it takes about 50 minutes to travel from the airport to the center of town. Fares can be steep, however ($150 to Piccadilly, for example), so it's best to share a cab with other travelers. An alternative option is the Airport MiniCab Service, bookable at www.lastminutecarz.com; look out for a good minicab service to bring you back. Black cabs are unacceptably expensive for everything but short-hop rides.

Gatwick Airport

Besides serving many major North American airlines, Gatwick also receives the bulk of charter flights into its North and South Terminals, which are linked by a free rapid-transit system that runs every 3 minutes. Both terminals have 24-hour information desks located in the international arrivals concourse. Both terminals have currency exchange and ATMs, restaurants, shops . . . what can I say, they're almost as good as in America. The South Terminal has a post office and a 24-hour Internet café. Lost luggage facilities are available in both terminals, and lost luggage can be found through Excess Baggage Company, 01293/502104 (South Terminal) or 01293/502013 (North Terminal). There are also baby changing rooms, a children's play area, and a medical center that offers vaccinations (01293/507 400). There are extensive facilities for disabled travelers (Travel-Care can be contacted in the South Terminal, 01293/504 823).

Airport Services

Airport information/emergencies (specify which terminal)...0870/000.2468

Parking (short term) 01293/502390

Parking (long term) ... 0800/626671 (toll free in Britain)

Police..01293/531122

Business Service Centers

Meridien London Gatwick Hotel, North Terminal
....01293/567070

Gatwick Hilton Hotel, South Terminal
....01293/518080

Airlines

American Airlines 0345/789789, 800/433.7300

British Airways............0208/759.2525, 800/776.3000

Canadian Airlines................................0207/745.5000

Continental 01293/776464, 800/231.0856

Delta.......................0800/414767 (toll-free in Britain),
.... 800/221.1212

Northwest 01293/561000, 800/447.4747

Virgin Atlantic..............01293/562345, 800/862.8621

Getting to and from Gatwick Airport

By Bus

Flightline 777 (0208/668.7261) operates a daily bus service between **Gatwick** and **Victoria Coach Station**; buses run between 5:20AM and 11PM and leave both terminals approximately every hour; travel takes at least 1 hour and 20 minutes. Unlike the other transportation options from the airport, Flightline accepts American and Canadian dollars as payment. **Speedlink** (0990/747777) offers luxury bus service to the center of London; travel time is about 90 minutes.

By Car

To get from **Gatwick** to **London**, take the **M23** north to the **M25**, which circles the city and links with several roads leading into the center, including the **A23**, the **A316**, and the **A20**. To get to the airport from the city, take the **M25** to the **M23** heading south. There is long- and short-term parking at the **North** and **South Terminals**. The drive takes between 1 hour and 90 minutes, depending on traffic.

Rental Cars

The following rental car companies have counters at **Gatwick Airport**:

Alamo...................... 0800/272300 (toll free in Britain),
....800/327.9633

Avis 01293/529721, 800/331.1212

Budget..................... 0800/626063 (toll free in Britain),
....800/527.0700

Eurodollar..................01293/513031, 800/800.4000

Europcar....................01293/531062, 800/227.7368

Hertz...........................01293/530555, 800/654.3131

By Train

The fast, convenient **Gatwick Express** (0845/850.1530, www.gatwickexpress.co.uk) train leaves the **South Terminal** for **Victoria Station** every 15 minutes between 5:20AM and 9:50PM (then every 30 minutes until 12:50PM); travel time runs about half an hour. The Gatwick

Express is by far the best and most efficient train link to any London airport. So, of course, the rail authorities are thinking of stopping it. Pray it is still running when you get there. Certain airlines will allow you to check in baggage at **Victoria Station**. Another option is the **Thameslink** (0345/484950) train service, which runs from **Gatwick** to **London Bridge**, **Blackfriars**, and **King's Cross** stations every 15 minutes between 3:34AM and 12:05PM. Unless masochism is your religion of choice, take the Gatwick Express.

BY TAXI

Gatwick Airport Taxi Service is provided by Checker Cars (0800/747 737, www.checkercars.com). If you are going into London, you can kiss good-bye to your first $150 at least.

If you are thinking of traveling around Europe using London as a base, London's other airports are **Stansted**, **Luton**, and **London City**. Most of the cheaper bargain airlines fly from these airports. **Stansted** is reached by the Stansted Express from **Liverpool Street**; **Luton**, by Thameslink from **Kings Cross**; and **London City**, by taxi or bus.

Getting Around London

A word of advice for surviving urban London: Don't hesitate to carry a map—even Londoners do, partly because Londoners are not renowned for their friendliness and helpfulness and it is much easier to look at a map than to attempt to persuade your average Londoner to give you directions. The *A-Z* series (National Geographers A-Z Ltd., in various sizes and prices) is by far the best; you can pick up a copy at most newsstands and bookstores.

The best sources for tourist information are the **London Tourist Board Information Centre** in **Victoria Station** and the **British Travel Centre** (see **Visitors' Information Centers**, page 14).

Public Transport

Welcome to my world! When it works, the **London Underground** is good—albeit obscenely overpriced and oblivious to the fact that some people like to stay out later than midnight. The main problem is that it so often doesn't work. It is frequently dirty, the staff is often rude, and one lives in hope of finding someone to inject some genuine contrition into their "London Underground regrets to inform you" announcement, because it gets used so often. If you are traveling with companions, you will frequently find that it is cheaper and much more pleasant to get a cab and split the fare. Tube stations are marked by circular red and blue London Transport signs. There are 11 lines (or routes), each designated by a different name and color. Large-scale maps of the Underground network are displayed in each station, and each compartment of the train should have a map of the train's route. You can also pick up a free map at any tube station. Be fore-warned: Some trains, such as those on the District and Circle Lines, use the same platforms, so check the lighted platform signs and the destination board on the front of the train before boarding. Smoking is not permitted anywhere on the Underground.

Service runs between 5:30AM and sometime between 12:30 and 1AM, Monday through Saturday (depending on which line you are on and how far you are hoping to get) and between 7AM and around midnight on Sunday and bank holidays. Be sure to hold on to your ticket: You'll need it to pass through the entry/exit turnstiles, and once in a while, a plainclothes inspector may ask to see it during your journey. If you cannot show a valid ticket, you are liable for an on-the-spot fine. In London, 24-hour travel information about the Underground is available at 0207/222.1234.

BUSES

TRAVELCARDS

A bit of a minefield in London. Staff in Underground stations and on buses can be less than helpful. There are machines in all Underground (known as "the tube") stations, but you need to know what zone you are traveling from and to before you can buy the right ticket. Buying the wrong ticket can result in an on-the-spot fine. Free maps of the Underground, with all the lines marked in different colors and the zones delineated, are available at most Underground stations, free of charge.

The cheapest way to travel is to buy an **Oystercard**. These are travel smartcards that you touch to a yellow pad at the start and finish of your journey. They are available for set periods (7 days, monthly, or longer) or as Pay as You Go (exactly like a Pay as You Go phone), and you can fill out the form and get traveling at any tube station. The cards work on tube, bus, and DLR (Docklands Light Railway). I resent being forced into "the system" with these cards, but when you see that traveling a single stop on a ticket bought from the office at the point of travel will now cost you $8 (read it and weep—$8!) while the same journey on an Oystercard will cost $3, you will understand that sometimes you have to give in to blackmail.

Individual tickets are still available at all stations (but be aware that some stations close their ticket offices unexpectedly and that you have to have cash for the machines). Single-day travel cards are also still available. Just be sure you know which zones you are traveling out of and in to. London Transport staff live to fine you!

Many bus routes now demand that you buy a ticket before boarding, and ticket machines are also now installed at many bus stops, demanding exact fare (generally £1.20).

Buses are no longer the user-friendly Routemasters with the open platforms at the back and the helpful conductor in the aisle. Now London has the curse of "the bendy bus," double-length, multiple-entry, single-decker nightmares with concertina sections in the middle that make the roads much scarier places. There are still double-deckers, however, on many routes, and if speed is not a priority, the view from the top can be entertaining.

Because many routes are handled by private companies, some buses may not be the traditional red color; however, all have "London Transport Board Service Bus" written on the side. All stops have signs indicating the numbers of the buses that stop there, and most show outlines of the route. The destination is written in the window at the front of the bus, and you need to know which direction you are going. Hang on to your bus ticket, as inspectors make occasional spot checks.

SCENIC BUS ROUTES

Route numbers are displayed on the front of the bus.

8—Victoria, Mayfair, Oxford Circus, Holborn, Bank, Liverpool Street. This bus affords views into **Buckingham Palace** gardens and includes most of the **Oxford Street** shopping area. It's the only bus that goes through **Berkeley Square** and **Bond Street**.

11—King's Road, Sloane Square, Victoria Coach Station, Victoria, Westminster Cathedral, Westminster Abbey, Westminster, Whitehall, Horse Guards, Trafalgar Square, National Gallery, The Strand, Law Courts, Fleet Street, St. Paul's Cathedral.

12—Bayswater, Hyde Park, Marble Arch, Oxford Street, Oxford Circus, Regent Street, Piccadilly Circus, Trafalgar Square, National Gallery, Horse Guards, Whitehall, Westminster, Millbank, Tate Gallery, Vauxhall Bridge.

15—Paddington, Marble Arch, Oxford Street, Oxford Circus, Regent Street, Piccadilly Circus, Trafalgar Square, The Strand, Aldwych, Fleet Street, St. Paul's Cathedral, Tower of London.

53—Oxford Circus, Regent Street, Piccadilly Circus, National Gallery, Trafalgar Square, Whitehall, Horse Guards, Westminster, Westminster Bridge, Imperial War Museum, Elephant and Castle.

NIGHT BUSES

Special night buses (marked with an *N*) run from London to the suburbs all night until 6AM (unlike ordinary buses, which run until midnight or 1AM). Buses leave from **Trafalgar Square** and the restaurant, theater, and cinema districts in central London. The **London Visitor Travelcard** is not valid on these buses; exact change is required.

DRIVING

If you can avoid driving in London, by all means do so. If you're determined to try it, however, remember that driving in the UK is a left-hand/left-lane experience. The Congestion Charge imposed on all vehicles (with a few exceptions) by London Mayor Ken Livingstone has extended its zone outward to cover just about everywhere in the Access Guide. It will cost you $16 per day (weekdays, 7AM-6PM) for the privilege of driving into central London to move at an average of 11.8 miles per hour and spend $8 per hour to park (if you can). The perimeters of the Congestion Charge Zone are clearly marked with big *C*'s, and cameras operate within it to check that you are not there on the sly. The charge can be paid at many shops, garages, news agents, etc. (look for the big *C*) or online at www.cclondon.com. But it must be paid before or on the day of travel to avoid fines. On the web site, there is information about FastTrack payments and paying by text message. There are fines imposed on a sliding scale for nonpayment and cameras everywhere checking license plates of the cars within the Congestion Charge Zone. In case you were wondering, no, the lord mayor himself doesn't drive. Who'd have

guessed? There is a great new and very user-friendly site called www.kenbuster.com that will also take care of all your Congestion Charge payments, once you have signed up. Bear in mind that gasoline (called petrol on this side of the Pond) is much more expensive than it is in the US.

That said, here are some tips to make the ride smoother: As long as you have been driving for at least a year and are over the age of 18 (21 in some cases), your US or Canadian driver's license is valid for 12 months in the UK. However, getting an **International Driving Permit**—available for a small fee through the **American Automobile Association (AAA)** or the **Canadian Automobile Association (CAA)**—isn't a bad idea because it could help placate the police if you're unlucky enough to have an accident. It is mandatory in Britain to wear seat belts—both in the front seat and the backseat. Speed limits in urban areas are technically 30 mph, but most Londoners tend to ignore this. When approaching a roundabout, a circular junction that is the bane of those who are unfamiliar with it, *always, always* yield to the traffic approaching from *your right*.

CAR RENTAL

Renting a car in Britain isn't cheap (£169 and up per week for a midsize car), but rental companies such as **Avis**, **Budget**, and **Hertz** frequently offer sizable discounts if you arrange to rent a car when purchasing your airline ticket. The cheapest option is **easyRentacar**, whose fleet of small but handy Mercedeses costs £9.00 per day.

The charges usually include unlimited mileage, insurance, and temporary **Automobile Association (AA)** membership, but be sure you understand exactly what type of insurance is included in the package (and waive the coverage if your credit card already provides rental car insurance). If you want a car simply to take you out of London, then hold off and rent one from a local company rather than from the bigger, more expensive names at the airports.

PARKING

Unless you want to carry a hefty supply of change and risk having your wheel clamped or your car towed away, look for one of the multistory National Car Parks (NCPs) sprinkled around central London; some are marked on the larger-scale city maps. These car parks may be more expensive than meters, but they save hassles, headaches, and a lot of precious time.

CHAUFFEUR SERVICES

For the fainthearted (and the wise), chauffeur-driven cars may be an appealing alternative. Most major car-rental agencies, including those listed below, offer this service.

Avis	0208/899.1035
Carey Camelot	0207/235.0234
Europcar	0207/834.6701
Hertz	0207/284.9900

TAXIS

London black cabs are famous all over the world . . . safe, reliable, capacious, and driven by "salt of the earth" Londoners who know every nook and cranny of the capital. Well, sort of. They are flaggable in the street when the yellow light is on. Taxi ranks are more or less everywhere, and drivers are usually knowledgeable, although if your journey is to a tiny, obscure street, you may have to help them, and journeys are metered, so there is no arguing over the fare. But for my money (which it frequently is), London cabs are no more impressive than New York cabs—and a lot more expensive. London's lord mayor has slapped an evening surcharge to your fare, so be aware that costs take a hike after 8:00PM.

For an extra fee (of course), they can be booked in advance (272.0272). Black cabs are a terrific value if there are four or five of you. But there are alternatives. Registered minicab companies are a much better value if you are going any distance. Their drivers are usually reasonably knowledgeable. Just get a fare quoted before you get in the car. You will find numbers in the Yellow Pages and on cards distributed everywhere. Most bars and restaurants will have their own pet companies. Even unregistered minicab companies can be useful. Clusters of drivers collect under little lit "Cab Office" signs in all parts of the city. Trust your instincts. Get a price. And be prepared for no rear suspension.

Alternative Cab Rides

Texting HOME to 60835 will get you one black cab and two local, licensed minicab numbers to choose from wherever you are in London.

Karma Kabs (from £50 per hour) is nirvana in a cab. Lovely soft furnishings in glowing colors, soothing music, delightfully exotic perfume, and drivers who are "ambassadors" and the very embodiment of charm. If you consider the journey itself as important as the destination, this is your kind of transport—an experience (0208/933.7052; www.karmakabs.com).

Rickshaws now provide short-haul, soft-top travel in the city center at about £5 per person per mile. Fun on a summer evening and available 7PM–4AM. Choose your rider his or her powerful thighs and you'll be all right. They congregate around **Soho** and on **Old Compton St** (www.bugbugs.co.uk).

Black Taxi Tours of London: Book yourself a personalized tour of the capital, day or night, in one of the city's black cabs. The taxi will pick you up at your hotel or apartment and take you on a 2-hour drive, with your cabbie providing a running commentary (935.9363).

Ladycabs (272.3300) employ only female cabdrivers.

Tours

The best way to see London (especially on a warm, sunny day) is by boat. You can cover 28 twisting miles of the Thames from **Hampton Court** to **Greenwich Palace** on one of the passenger boats that spend their days cruising up- and downstream from central London, with the pilot providing commentary along the way. For general information, call 0891/505471 (premium rate call); for information on trips from **Westminster Pier** to **Greenwich**, call 0207/930.4097; for the **Tower of London**, 0207/930.9033; to the **Thames River Barrier**, 0207/930.3373; to **Hampton Court**, 0207/930.4721; and to **Kew Gardens**, 0207/930.2062. There are also boats from **Charing Cross Pier** to the **Tower** and **Greenwich** (0207/987.1185).

A good way to get a sense of the city on dry land is via bus tour. There are two basic types: the panorama, which is an 18- to 20-mile nonstop sightseeing excursion, and full- or half-day guided tours, which typically cover **Westminster Abbey** and the **Changing of the Guard** (if it's being held) in the morning, and **St. Paul's** and the **Tower of London** in the afternoon. The grande dame of coach excursions is the **Original London Sightseeing Tour** (operated by **London Coaches**; 0208/877.1722), which runs a 1.5-hour tour through the city on a traditional red double-decker bus (open-topped in summer).

Between 10AM and 5PM Easter–October (10AM–4PM, November–Easter), tours depart every half hour from **Piccadilly Circus**, **Victoria**, and **Baker Street Stations**. There's no need to book; just show up and wait. **Harrods** offers 2-hour bus tours that include tea, coffee, biscuits, and commentary (given daily at 10:30AM, 1:30PM, and 4PM), as well as an extensive, full-day excursion (given Thursday only) that features **Westminster Abbey**, **St. Paul's Cathedral**, the **Changing of the Guard**, and the **Tower of London**. Lunch, tea, coffee, and biscuits are included in the full-day trips. The tours leave the store at approximately 8:45AM; 0207/581.3603.

Note: For those who love castles, abbeys, palaces, stately homes, gardens, and historic sites, a **Great British Heritage Pass** will give you access to 600 of them dotted around the country—many of which are accessible on day trips from London (see **Day Trips**, page 230). Available for 3-, 7-, and 15-day lengths, the pass can be purchased at the **British Travel Centre** (see **Visitors' Information Centers**, page 14), at the **Tourist Information Centres** at **Heathrow** and **Gatwick Airports**, at the **London Tourist Information Centre** at **Victoria Station**, or through your travel agent or **British Tourist Authority** (**BTA**) offices in the US and Canada. The **London White Card**, a 3-day or 7-day pass (for individuals and families) to 15 major attractions in the city, mostly museums, is also sold at BTA offices in the US and Canada, at top London hotels, at tourist information centers, or at the attractions themselves.

Trains

The whole country is linked to London via a rail network that used to be called **British Rail**; however, the railways and their related services have been privatized, so you will now see many different logos at the various rail stations. A circular network of stations (including **Charing Cross**, **Euston**, **King's Cross**, **Liverpool Street**, **Paddington**, **Victoria**, and **Waterloo**) fans out into the suburbs (and some lines go farther out into the English countryside as well). If you want to get to the continent from London, either take the train from **Victoria Station** to the ferry at **Folkestone** or head to **Waterloo Station**, where you can pick up the **EuroStar** (0345/303030) train that goes to **Paris** or **Brussels** via the **Channel Tunnel**.

Most long-distance trains have buffet or restaurant facilities, but check when you buy your ticket. All have toilets and all are at least somewhat accessible to those with disabilities, but some of the stations are more difficult to negotiate than others. On some routes, you might need to change trains (which can be nightmarish), so find out beforehand.

One of the best ways to enjoy cheap train fares is to get a **BritRail** pass (available from travel agents), which you must purchase before you arrive in Britain. Both first-class and standard tickets are valid for periods of 4, 8, 15, and 22 days and for 1 month. They include versions for 16- to 25-year-olds (Youth Pass) and over-60-year-olds (Senior Pass). Railway personnel maintain that if you take three trips out of London to big cities or major attractions, you will cover the cost of the pass. BritRail passes allow you to travel on any train, although on busy routes, such as London to Edinburgh, you should reserve a seat. Check when you book the ticket.

On long-distance intercity journeys, book **Apex** tickets from rail stations (7 days before departure) or buy a **Saver** or **Super Saver** ticket if you book in advance and travel on any day except Friday, a summer Saturday, Easter, or on a bank holiday weekend. Those who buy Savers or Super Savers will find there are early morning and some evening travel restrictions. Children under 16 pay half price, and those under 5 ride free when accompanied by an adult.

Even without a pass or a discount ticket, however, you can sometimes find good train fares. To get the cheapest fare (this depends on how full the train is likely to be, not on your bargaining skills) for rail travel in Britain, and for rail and sea journeys to the continent and Ireland, visit the **British Travel Centre** (see **Visitors' Information Centers**, page 14) or one of these main line station travel centers: **Charing Cross**, **Euston**, **King's Cross**, **Liverpool Street**, **Paddington**, **Waterloo**, or **Victoria**. London has nine major rail train stations, each of which serves a different part of Britain and is accessible by tube or bus. For information about trains and schedules, there is one number to call: 08457/484950 (24-hour service).

WALKING

You can really get to know and love a city only through your eyes and feet, and London offers marvelous rewards to the walker. Such distinguished feet as those of Daniel Defoe, Samuel Johnson, James Boswell, John Gay, Thomas Carlyle, and Sir Anthony Hopkins have made walking the streets of London part of their life's work. Some advice: In addition to regular traffic, there's the hazard (and one not to be underestimated) of cyclists cutting swaths through pedestrians on the pavement. Walking tours are listed in the *Times* and in the weekly *Time Out* magazine and include such topics as "The City," "The Great Fire and Plague," and "The London of the Romans, Victorians, Shakespeare, and Dickens." It is now possible to walk from the **Thames Flood Barrier** back to the river's source in the **Cotswolds**—a very long walk, indeed! Pick up a special free leaflet, *The Thames Path*, at the main tourist information centers.

FYI

ACCOMMODATIONS

In addition to hotels, there are other kinds of accommodations in London. Bed-and-breakfast establishments are available in a variety of price ranges, and staying in one allows visitors to make contact with local people and get a sense of the city's everyday life. The organization

Uptown Reservations (0207/351.3445) puts visitors in touch with stylish host homes in **Chelsea**. Another option is to rent an apartment (which the British call a flat) or cottage. The cheapest lodgings (probably best suited to young people) are at youth hostels. They offer only the most basic accommodations, and you must be prepared to share rooms and facilities. These fill up quickly; call ahead to check if there is space. The best two (in terms of location) are **Holland House** (Holland Walk, between Kensington High St and Holland Park Ave, 0207/937.0748), in **Holland Park** in **Kensington**, and **City of London** (36 Carter La at Deans Ct, 0207/236.4965), right by **St. Paul's**. London is a popular place to visit year-round, so it is always a good idea to make reservations before you come (and reservations are absolutely necessary during high season—between April and October).

BUSINESS SERVICES

Almost every hotel and an increasing number of shops and newsstands offer fax and photocopy services for a charge. Sending a fax to the US, however, will cost a minimum of £3.50 per page. **Chesham Executive Centre** (150 Regent St, between Regent's Pl and Beak St, 0171/439.6288) has fax, telex, and photocopy facilities. easyEverything (Tottenham Court Rd, Trafalgar Square, Oxford St, and Victoria) are open 24 hours a day and offer e-mail and online services from £1.00 for 6 hours.

CLIMATE

Believe it or not, London's climate is relatively moderate and mild, although it is prone to change at a moment's notice. Whatever the season, you'd be well advised to bring sweaters and jackets for evenings, as well as raincoats, umbrellas, and, above all, shoes that are kind to the feet and can endure the occasional puddle.

MONTHS	AVERAGE TEMPERATURE (°F)
January–March	36–45
April–June	40–56
July–September	56–72
October–December	45–58

CUSTOMS AND IMMIGRATION

All foreign visitors to the UK must have a valid passport, which will be stamped by immigration officials at each entry point. Although there is rarely a problem, it might help speed things along if you can provide the address where you'll be staying while in the UK.

DRINKING

The pub (short for *public house*) is to Britain what cafés are to France. To complete the British experience, you should have at least one drink, and preferably a meal, in a pub. The minimum age for drinking in the UK is 18. Pubs are usually open between 11AM and 11PM. Bars and pubs can remain open 24 hours. It is up to individual landlords what hours they open, so it's best to check, if you are making a night of it. Ten minutes before closing time, you'll usually hear the bartender call for "last orders." Many pubs are getting more adventurous with food—indeed, the "gastropub" is the big growth area in eating. Even at the bottom of the pub food chain, there are terms to learn: Bangers are sausages; bangers and mash are sausages with mashed potatoes; chips are french fries, whereas crisps are potato chips; Cornish pasties consist of meat and vegetables wrapped in dough; a ploughman's lunch is a cheese-and-salad plate; a pork pie is chopped spiced pork wrapped in dough; sausage rolls are tiny sausages rolled up in dough; and shepherd's pie consists of ground lamb covered in mashed potatoes.

EMBASSIES AND CONSULATES

Australian High Commission (Australia House, Strand, at Aldwych, 0207/379.4334).

Canadian High Commission (Macdonald House, Grosvenor Sq, between Grosvenor and Brook Sts, 0207/258.6600).

US Embassy (24 Grosvenor Sq, between Upper Grosvenor and Upper Brook Sts, 0207/499.9000).

HOURS

Most shops and businesses in London are open Monday through Saturday between 9AM and 5 or 6PM; more and more shops now operate on Sunday, usually between noon and 5 or 6PM. Opening and closing times for shops and attractions are listed by day(s) only if they open between 8 and 11AM and close between 4 and 7PM. In all other cases, specific hours will be given (e.g., 6AM–2PM, daily 24 hours, noon–5PM).

MEDICAL CARE

Because the US and the UK have no reciprocal health agreement, be sure to take out medical insurance before leaving home. If you should become ill, you will be treated at a London hospital or doctor's office without question, but you'll be charged at the private patient rate, which can be expensive. In emergencies, dial 999, and you will be connected to an operator who will inquire about the nature of the problem, then arrange for an ambulance, police, or a fire engine. Although patients who arrive at a hospital by ambulance get priority, horror stories about delays abound. If possible, head for the nearest hospital casualty department (i.e., emergency room), then be prepared to have someone make a fuss on your behalf until you're seen by a doctor; otherwise, you could be in for a long wait. The following London hospitals have 24-hour emergency rooms: **Charing Cross Hospital** (Fulham Palace Rd at St. Dunstan's Rd, 0208/846.1234), **Royal Free Hospital** (Pond St, between Fleet Rd and Rosslyn Hill, 0207/794.0500), and **University College Hospital** (Gower St at University St, 0207/387.9300). **St. Bartholomew's Hospital** (W Smithfield, between Little Britain and Giltspur St, 0207/601.8888) treats patients (for minor injuries only) between 8AM and 8PM.

There is only one 24-hour pharmacy (chemists, in Britspeak) in London. It is **Zafash Pharmacy** (235 Old Brompton Rd SW5; Tube: Earls Court; 0207/373.2798); other than that, night duty rotates, and the places that are closed display the name and address of the evening's all-night drugstore in the window. **Bliss Chemist** (5-6 Marble Arch, between Cumberland Pl and Edgware Rd, 0207/723.6116) is open daily 9AM–midnight. **Boots** has two locations that keep long hours: one in the center of Piccadilly Circus (0207/734.6126), which is open Monday through Friday 8:30AM–8PM, Saturday 9AM–8PM, and Sunday noon–6PM; and one at 114 Queensway, between Inverness Pl and Porchester Gardens (0207/229.1183), which is open Monday through Saturday 9AM–10PM and Sunday noon–6PM.

MONEY

The basic unit of British currency is the pound sterling. There are 100 pence to the pound. Pound coins are small, thick, and golden; £2 coins are a larger, but similar, version; 50-pence coins are silver and hexagonal, whereas the 20-pence coin is similar but smaller; the 10-pence coin is small, silver, and round; and the 5-pence coin is minuscule; tuppences (two-penny pieces) and pennies are both copper. The color of £5 notes is greenish blue; £10, orange; £20, light purple; and £50, greenish gold. Credit cards are used as in the US, the most popular being VISA and MasterCard (which used to be known in Britain as Access).

Banks are open Monday through Friday, 9AM to 4:30PM, and many branches are open on Saturday between 9AM and noon as well. Traveler's checks in US dollars can be exchanged for British currency at large banks (such as **Barclays, Lloyds, Midland,** and **National Westminster**) during their normal operating hours, or at the **American Express Travel Service Office** (103 Victoria St, between Artillery Row and Carlisle Pl, 0208/828.4567), Monday through Friday, 9AM–5:30PM, and Saturday, 9AM–4PM. This office also allows you to cash personal checks for up to $1,000, depending on the type of American Express card you have. In addition, many post offices now change traveler's checks. Avoid changing your money at exchange bureaus and hotel cashiers, as they charge a higher commission.

PERSONAL SAFETY

Keep a close eye on your bags and valuables at all times. Many pickpockets operate around the Underground system, in the main rail stations, and on the busiest tourist streets. If possible, women should use a closed or zipped purse—and hang on to it. Some pickpockets travel in gangs during the summer, so be particularly careful when people are crowding onto buses or tubes.

Steer clear of the many accommodations hustlers who work the areas around the main train stations, especially **Victoria**; most of the places offered by these room touts are overcrowded and uninsured and have little or no fire protection—and they're usually pretty dreadful as well. It's better to consult the **Tourist Information Centre** at the station or find your own accommodations.

POST OFFICE

The **Trafalgar Square Post Office** (24 William IV St, between Adelaide St and St. Martin's La, 0207/930.9580) offers full postal service and collectors' items, such as stamps, coins, and cards; it also changes traveler's checks. General post office inquiries: 0845/722.3344, M, W, Th, F, 8:30AM–6:30PM; Tu, 8:45AM–6:30PM; Sa, 9AM–5:30PM. Local post offices, which are often within newsstands or corner grocery shops, are usually open Monday through Friday, 9AM–5PM, and Saturday, 9AM–noon.

PUBLICATIONS

Of London's many newspapers, the *Times*, the *Guardian* (especially its Saturday supplement *The Guide*, a pocket-sized treasury of what is on in the capital in every way), the *Independent*, and the *Daily Telegraph* (all dailies) and the *Sunday Times* and the *Observer* (Sunday only) are most useful to visitors. They are all national newspapers. Most helpful of all is the *Evening Standard*—London's local paper, available around lunchtime each weekday and carrying an accurate listings section. *Time Out* (published each Wednesday) is absolutely invaluable, no matter whether you fancy eating, art galleries, rugby matches, or holistic massages. All are available at news agents and bookstores throughout the city. *Time Out* and the *Evening Standard* also have excellent web sites (www.timeout.com and www.thisislondon.com, respectively).

PUBLIC HOLIDAYS

In addition to the Christmas and Easter holidays, Britain rests on Boxing Day (26 December), Easter Monday, May Day (first Monday in May), Spring Bank Holiday (last Monday in May), and August Bank Holiday (last Monday in August). These are called bank holidays because banks close on those days. Many other businesses stay open, but you'll never know which ones unless you call ahead or happen to wander past.

RESTAURANTS

Increasingly, reservations are advisable except at the most casual restaurants. Many more expensive restaurants will ask for a phone number and credit card number on booking and will ask you to phone and confirm your booking. Most of the time, casual dress is acceptable, although some of the more elegant places do require that men wear jackets and ties.

REST ROOMS

As in many cities around the world, there never seem to be enough public toilets (or loos, as they're often called here), especially when you need one. However, all public buildings, including museums and department stores, have them, and if you're poised and surreptitious, you can take advantage of those in the larger hotels. Pubs and restaurants generally expect you to be a customer for the privilege. For the daring, there are automated, French-style toilets, located in public parks; these, however, can often be a chilling experience.

SERVICES FOR TRAVELERS WITH DISABILITIES

Artsline (54 Chalton St, London NW1 1HS, 0208/388.222; fax 0207/383.265) advises on theater, cinema, museum, and other arts and entertainment center access for those with disabilities and special needs. Most cinemas, theaters, and public places try to accommodate disabled patrons, although doing so is not mandated by law as it is in the US. Always call and check when booking or visiting, as this ensures special help when you arrive and an appropriate seat. A monthly magazine, *Disability Arts in London*, is available free to any disabled person in the UK; call 0207/916.6351. Free at theaters is the *Disabled Access Guide to London's West End Theatres*,

published by the **Society of London Theatre** (**SOLT**) (Bedford Chambers, The Piazza, Covent Garden, London WC2E 8HQ, 0207/836.0971; fax 497.2543).

Evan Evans (26–28 Paradise Rd, Richmond, Surrey TW9 1SE, 0207/930.2377), which runs daily coach tours of London, takes a number of disabled passengers as long as each one is accompanied by an able-bodied person. Tours leave from its office (26 Cockspur St on the southwest side of Trafalgar Sq). Call ahead to book a reservation, specifying the nature of the disability.

Holiday Care Service (second floor, Imperial Buildings, Victoria Rd, Horley, Surrey RH6 7PZ, 01293/774535; fax 01293/784647) is a charity offering free information and advice on vacations for people with special needs, such as the elderly and the disabled. Call or write explaining your special needs and what sort of holiday you are looking for, and provide a rough estimate of your budget. Though it is not a booking service, the organization has details on inclusive or specialized holidays, accommodations, transportation, publications, and guides for UK destinations. In addition, it can connect you with car and driver hire services, if desired. **Tripscope** (0208/994.9294; fax 0208/994.3618) is another service that offers free advice about local and long-distance journeys from London.

London Transport (55 Broadway, London SW1H 0BD, 0207/918.3312) runs a daily **Stationlink** bus service catering to people with disabilities. Beginning at 8:30AM, two circular routes cover all the main line rail stations (except **Charing Cross** and **Cannon Street**). **SL1** goes clockwise; **SL2** goes counterclockwise; both connect with the wheelchair-accessible **Airbus** services to **Heathrow Airport** at **Victoria** and **Euston**. These are fully accessible, low-fly buses, and the drivers are well trained in handling the needs of people with disabilities. You also can call **London Transport** for advice on public transport.

The National Trust (36 Queen Anne's Gate, between Petty France and Dartmouth St, 0207/222.9251; fax 0208/809.1754), which owns places of historic interest or natural beauty all over the country, publishes a free annual booklet, *Information for Visitors with Disabilities*, showing those sights accessible to people with disabilities, including scented gardens for the blind. And for further information, contact the **Royal Association for Disability Rehabilitation** (**RADAR**; 250 City Rd, London EC1V 8AF, 0207/250.3222; fax 0207/250.0212).

SHOPPING

London is truly a shopper's paradise, whether you're a serious buyer or just looking. Some of the city's most upscale shopping streets, with a mixture of tony department stores, antiques shops, and high-fashion clothiers, include **Old** and **New Bond Street**; **St. Christopher's Place**; **Regent**, **Sloane**, and **Jermyn Streets**; **Knightsbridge**; and **King's Road**. **Burlington Arcade**, **Piccadilly Arcade**, and **Princes Arcade** offer a wide selection of fashionable stores as well, and **Savile Row** is *the* place to go for custom-made menswear.

Oxford Street is the main shopping place for a mixed variety of shops and department stores, mostly midrange and low-cost. Also be sure to check out at least one of London's many street markets, which offer everything from kitschy collectibles to priceless antiques; the best are **Portobello Road**, **Camden Passage**, **Petticoat Lane**, **Piccadilly Market**, and the **Covent Garden** area.

SMOKING

Smoking is now banned indoors in all public places in London, as you will see from the sad, damp, freezing little huddles of smokers who can no longer hang out with their friends over a meal or a drink, but are exiled to the pavement. Even our fabulous, deluxe cigar bars have been stubbed out. Your high-priced five-star hotel *might* allow you to smoke in the room you are paying so much for . . . but not necessarily.

TELEPHONE

Telephone boxes accept a variety of change: 10 pence, 20 pence, 50 pence, and £1 coins. British Telecom (BT) cards, which are used like credit cards to make calls at specially marked phone boxes, can be obtained from most newsstands and sweet shops in units of 10 to 200. If you'll be making a lot of calls, dial after 6PM or during weekends, when the rates are cheapest. Some numbers are referred to as "premium rate"; this means that you'll pay up to 50 pence per minute for a call, usually for recorded information (similar to 900 numbers in the US). Most premium-rate numbers have a special prefix, such as 0891. Telephoning from hotels is expensive, and unless your cell-phone service provider is really sticking it to you, it's probably better to use it, making sure you have a handset. If you come here a few times, it is also a good idea to buy a UK pay-as-you-go phone card to use for local calls. Saves a fortune! Direct-dial calls to the US can be made by dialing 001, followed by your area code and number.

Directory assistance has now been privatized and there are many numbers to dial. Most are not particularly efficient. The best is 118247, but it is still not great.

TICKETS

Beware of the ubiquitous ticket touts (scalpers) who operate along theater queues and from supposedly reputable ticket offices scattered throughout the city. Most of the time, the tickets they sell are grossly overpriced—and some may not even be genuine. Aim instead to get standby tickets directly from theater box offices, your hotel, or the **Society of London Theatre** half-price ticket booth in **Leicester Square**; at the latter, you'll have to stand in line on the day of the performance, but it's worth it to get a legitimate seat at a reasonable price. Also, be adventurous: Some excellent performances at lower prices can be found at smaller theaters outside the **West End**, as well as in the larger arts complexes such as the **Barbican** or **South Bank**; check *Time Out* for details.

Tickets for concerts and sporting events can be ordered by phone from **Ticketmaster** (0207/344.4444) and **First Call** (0207/420.0000), as well as from the individual box offices.

TIME ZONE

London is in the Greenwich Mean Time zone, which is 5 hours later than New York and 8 hours later than Los Angeles. Like the US, Britain observes daylight savings time, turning clocks ahead an hour in the spring and back an hour in the fall, although the two countries don't do it on the same date. British timetables use a 24-hour clock to denote time; for example, 1:30PM would be written as *13:30*.

TIPPING

In restaurants, check whether service is included, especially if you find the amounts you are expected to pay left blank on the credit card slip (as it quite often is) because they just want a bit more money. If service is not included and the service and food have been good, then go ahead and tip between 10% and 15%. When you collect your bill at your hotel, again check whether service has been included. Taxi drivers hope for between 10% and 15%. Porters, cloakroom attendants, and hairdressers also expect a small tip. But don't give what is not warranted—watch the Londoners; they don't.

VALUE ADDED TAX

At 17.5% of the marked price, the Value Added Tax (VAT) can be substantial. But if you are leaving the UK within 3 months, you can claim back the VAT on many of the items you buy if you have spent more than a certain amount in one shop (the total varies). Make sure the store operates the over-the-counter export scheme, which involves filling out a VAT 707 form. (The shop will give it to you along with a stamped, addressed envelope.) You must carry as hand luggage the goods for which you intend to collect a VAT refund and present them to UK customs as you leave the country. Customs will stamp the forms, which you will then mail back to the shop before leaving the country. If you forget and pack the goods or simply cannot carry them, then you have to show them to the officials when you arrive in the US, get the form stamped there, and mail it to the shop. You can get your refund as a check in pounds sterling (which can cost a lot to process through your bank) or, if you've paid with a credit card, as a credit to your account. The refund process takes about 6 weeks.

VISITORS' INFORMATION CENTERS

The **London Tourist Board** (**LTB**) **Information Centre** in the front court of **Victoria Station** (Terminal Pl, between Wilton and Buckingham Palace Rds; daily) offers free information on travel within London and the UK; theater, concert, and tour bookings; and accommodations. It also has good maps and guidebooks for sale. It charges a nominal fee for arranging a place to stay.

Other information centers are at the **Liverpool Street Underground Station**, at **Waterloo International Terminal** (inside **Waterloo** rail station), at **Hay's Galleria** (Tooley St, at Battle Bridge La, 403.8299; daily, mid-Mar–Oct; M-Sa, 11AM–4PM, and Su, noon–4PM, Nov–mid-Mar), at **Heathrow Airport** (at the Underground station concourses for **terminals 1, 2,** and **3** and at the arrivals concourse for **terminal 4**), and at **Gatwick Airport** (at the arrivals concourse of the **South Terminal**). For hotel and bed-and-breakfast reservations, call 0208/824.8844 (credit card holders only).

The **British Tourist Authority** (**BTA**) (British Travel Centre, 12 Regent St, at Carlton St) also runs an information center that gives free comprehensive information for all of Britain.

Phone Book

Ambulance/Police/Fire 999
Dental Emergencies 0208/677.6363
Drugstores
    Bliss Chemist....................................0207/723.6116
    Boots.................0207/734.6126, 0207/229.1183
Emergency Road Services (for members)
    Automobile Association (AA) 0800/919595
    ....(toll-free in Britain)
    RAC ....0800/550550 (toll-free in Britain)

HOSPITALS

    Charing Cross Hospital....................0208/846.1234
    Chelsea & Westminster..............................746.8000
    Guy's Hospital..................................0207/188.7188
    Guy's Hospital Dental Emergencies......M-F, 9AM-5PM
    Royal Free Hospital 0207/794.0500
    St. Mary's Hospital..........................0207/886.6666
    University College Hospital 0845/155.5000

LOST OR STOLEN CREDIT CARDS

    American Express.............................01273/696933
    MasterCard..0800/964767
    VISA....................0800/895082 (toll-free in Britain)

VISITORS' INFORMATION

British Hotel Reservation Centre........... 0207/828.2425
Directory Information 192
Disabled Visitors' Information 01293/774535,
.... 0181/994.9294

International Operator..155
International Telegrams 0800/190190
....(toll-free in Britain)

LONDON TRANSPORT

    Lost Property 0207/486.2496
    Travel Information............................ 0207/222.1234
    Travel Update (traffic flow).............. 0207/222.1200
Operator Services 100
Recorded tourist information, premium rate
(dial 0891/505, then the following numbers):
    Changing of the Guard.. 452
    Current Exhibitions... 441
    Day Trips 469
    Museums.. 462
    Palaces... 466
    River Trips/Boats for Hire.................................... 471
    Sporting Events.. 442
    Sunday in London... 444
    What's on This Week... 440
Time check 123
US and International Directory Information.............. 153
US Customs/US Passport Office 0207/499.9000
Weather 0839/500951

YOUTH HOSTELS

    Central London Booking Service 0207/248.6547
    City of London Youth Hostel............. 0207/236.4965
    Holland House Youth Hostel 0207/937.0748

THE LONDON LEDGER OF ANNUAL EVENTS

For the traveler who wishes to take in more than just the sights, the following is a calendar of the most interesting events in London. For more information about what's happening in the city, consult listings in magazines or visit any tourist information center.

January

Lord Mayor of Westminster's New Year's Day Spectacular Beginning at noon on 1 January, a parade complete with marching bands, floats, classic cars, and clowns makes its way from **Parliament Square** along **Whitehall** to **Trafalgar Square**, then west along **Cockspur Street** and **Pall Mall**, north along **Regent Street** to **Piccadilly Circus**, west along **Piccadilly**, then north along **Berkeley Street** to finish in **Berkeley Square**. A gala performance is usually held at the **Royal Albert Hall, Kensington Gore**, in conjunction with the festivities.

International Boat Show This 10-day display of all types of boats and boating equipment, including a specially created indoor harbor, takes place at the

Earl's Court Exhibition Centre the first week of January. For details, call 0207/385.1200.

Commemoration Ceremony of Charles the Martyr At 11:30AM on the last Sunday of the month, the **King's Army** (members of the English Civil War Society in period dress) progresses from **St. James's Palace** to **Banqueting House**. There, at noon, a wreath is laid beneath the window through which Charles I stepped onto the scaffold. The parade continues to **Trafalgar Square** to the base of the statue of the ill-fated king, then returns through **Admiralty Arch** to **St. James's Palace**.

February

Chinese New Year In late January or early February, usually on the Sunday closest to the actual date of Chinese New Year, celebrations, including the famous Lion Dance (where three or four performers wear a huge, brightly colored dragon costume and dance through the streets), take place mostly in **Chinatown**. The best places to watch the festivities include the areas around **Gerrard Street** in **Soho**, where streets are decorated with streamers and garlands, and **Leicester Square**.

Fine Art and Antiques Fair   This is held annually at the end of the month at **Olympia** exhibition halls in **Earl's Court**. About 350 antiques and fine art dealers from all over Britain and Europe display their wares. For details, call 0207/603.3344.

March

Head of the River Race   Held on the **Thames** around 20 March, this race is a processional contest for eight-oared racing shells. The course extends from **Mortlake** to **Putney**; 420 crews—one behind the other—start at 10-second intervals, and the one that returns in the fastest time wins. The best place for viewing is from the **Surrey** bank, just above **Chiswick Bridge**. Arrive about 30 minutes before the race begins (approximately 3:45PM), then walk along the towpath toward Putney.

Oxford and Cambridge Boat Race   The two universities first raced on the **Thames** in 1829 and have competed annually since 1845. The race takes place around the last week of March, and its course is from the **University Stone**, Putney, to Mortlake. It starts at 4PM. Good views can be had from the **Putney** and **Chiswick Bridges**, from the **Dove Inn** (19 Upper Mall between Rivercourt and Weltje Rds, Hammersmith), or from the **Ship Inn** (Ship La, between Lower Richmond Rd and Thames Bank, Mortlake).

April

London Harness Horse Parade   Easter Monday presents a rare opportunity to see working horses of all kinds compete for prizes at **Battersea Park** in south London. Festivities begin around 10:30AM with a veterinary inspection, followed by a parade, a judging of classes (such as Heavy Horses and Single-Horsed Commercial Vans), and a Grand Parade of Winners between noon and 1PM. For other Easter events, call 0891.505455.

London Marathon   More than 25,000 runners compete in this grueling 26-mile race, which takes place in mid-April. It begins 9–9:30AM at **Blackheath/Greenwich** and ends at the **Mall**. For details, call 0207/620.4117.

May

Football Association Cup Final   The top prize event in the soccer world, it takes place in midmonth at **Wembley Stadium**. For details, call 0208/900.1234.

Chelsea Flower Show   The event for gardeners the world over takes place at the **Royal Hospital Grounds**, **Chelsea**, for four days during the last week of May. Plants, flowers, garden furniture, tools, theme gardens, and greenhouses are all on display. The first 2.5 days are reserved for members of the **Royal Horticultural Society** only; the last 2 are for the public (excluding children under 5 years of age). Advance tickets may be purchased by phone with a credit card (call 0207/344.4343).

June

Derby Day   Held on the first Saturday of the month at **Epsom Racecourse**, Epsom, Surrey, this is one of the greatest horse-racing events in the world. The main race, called the Derby, is held at 3:45PM. Tickets can be ordered starting in January by writing to the Racing Department, Sandown Park Racecourse, Esher, Surrey, KT10 0AJ; call 01372/470047 for more information.

Beating the Retreat   Mounted bands, trumpeters, massed bands (several bands performing as one group), and pipes and drums of the Household Division display their marching and drilling prowess at 9:30PM at **Horse Guards Parade**. The event occurs at the beginning of the month. Tickets go on sale at the end of February; call 0207/839.5323.

Sounding Retreat: Light Division   During the second week of the month, **Horse Guards Parade** stages a follow-up to **Beating the Retreat**. The **Sounding Retreat** display takes place over three consecutive nights beginning at 6:30PM. See **Beating the Retreat** for ticket details.

Royal Academy Summer Exhibition   The **Royal Academy of Arts** hosts the largest contemporary art show in the world, featuring works by painters, sculptors, printmakers, and architects—well-knowns alongside the undiscovered. The show begins in early June and lasts through mid-August.

Trooping the Colour   Also known as the **Queen's Birthday Parade**, this ceremony celebrates the sovereign's official (but not actual) birthday on the second or third Saturday. The queen leaves **Buckingham Palace** at around 10:30AM and travels down the **Mall** to **Horse Guards Parade**, where massed bands greet her with the national anthem and a gun salute in **Green Park**. After the queen's troop inspection, the parade begins. At 12:30PM, Her Royal Highness returns to **Buckingham Palace**, where she appears on the balcony to witness the Royal Air Force fly past at 1PM. Tickets for outdoor seats on **Horse Guards Parade** (behind the **Horse Guards Building**) are available by ballot only and are limited to two per person. If you can't get ceremony tickets, try for tickets to one of the two rehearsals (without the queen). Apply in writing before the end of February to the Brigade Major (Trooping the Colour), Household Division, Horse Guards, Whitehall, London SW1A 2AX. Do not send money—instead, include a self-addressed envelope with two international reply coupons (the equivalent of British stamps). For recorded information, call 0891/505453.

Royal Ascot   This famous mid-June horse race at **Ascot Racecourse** in **Berkshire** (roughly 25 miles west of London), immortalized in *My Fair Lady*, is well known for the fashions—especially the hats—of those who attend. The queen and other members of the royal family arrive from **Windsor** each day in open carriages. They then drive down the course at 2PM before the first race begins. Admission to the Grandstand for the 4-day event is by ticket only; write well in advance to the Secretary, Grand Stand, Ascot Racecourse, Berkshire SL5 7JN; call 01344/22211 for details.

Wimbledon Lawn Tennis Championships   Top players from all over the world converge on the **All England Club** in **Wimbledon** (about 6 miles southwest of central London) from the last week of June to the beginning of July to compete for one of the most coveted titles in tennis. Though some tickets are available on the day of play, it's advisable to apply for them between August and December. Send a self-addressed envelope with international reply coupons to the All England Lawn Tennis & Croquet Club, P.O. Box 98, Church Road, Wimbledon, SW19 5AE, or call 0208/946.2244. The **London Tourist Board** provides information starting in June; call 0839/123417.

July

Hampton Court Palace International Flower Show   Almost as well established as the show at Chelsea, this one is held during the second week in July at **Hampton Court**. The show also features musical entertainment and crafts displays. Call 0207/344.4333 for details.

BBC Henry Wood Promenade Concerts   The "Proms" have taken place at the **Royal Albert Hall** every year since they were begun in 1895 by Sir Henry Wood. The nightly concerts, which range from jazz to classical music, begin in mid-July and run until mid-September. Season and individual tickets are available in advance from the **Royal Albert Hall**; call 0207/589.8912 for details. In addition, inexpensive standing-room tickets may be had on the day of the performance. You can purchase the *Proms Guide*, available early May, at major newsstands.

August

Notting Hill Carnival   The carnival—a sort of midsummer Mardi Gras—takes place on the Sunday and Monday of the last weekend of August (a bank holiday) in **Notting Hill**, a London area with a strong Caribbean tradition. Lovers of steel bands and *soca* (a fusion of soul and Calypso music that originated in the West Indies) will be in their element. There are fabulous costume parades, and hundreds of street vendors sell food and crafts from all over the globe. Festivities kick off at 11AM.

September

Great River Race   At the end of the month, more than 150 traditional boats sail 22 miles on the **Thames**, from **Richmond** to the **Docklands**. The flotilla includes gigs, skiffs, Chinese dragon boats, Hawaiian war canoes, Irish curraghs, and whalers. The race begins just below **Ham House**, **Richmond**, at 10AM and finishes at **Greenwich Pier** around 1PM.

October

Pearly Kings and Queens Harvest Festival   Cockney fruit and vegetable hawkers, known as costermongers, have a reputation for being snappy dressers. The leading costermongers were once called the Pearly Kings and Queens, in recognition of their characteristic pearl-button- studded outfits. This religious service, held around 3 October at 3PM at **St. Martin-in-the-Fields Church** (0207/930.1862), is probably the only place you'll see their sartorial splendor. The altar is arrayed with fruits and vegetables, and a Pearly King or Queen reads from the Bible.

Horse of the Year Show   Top names in equestrian circles compete in show jumping, dressage, shire, hunter, and hacks at **Wembley Arena, Wembley**, in northwest London. The event is usually held during the first week of the month. Call the box office at 0181/900.1234 for ticket information.

Trafalgar Day Parade   On or around 21 October, the anniversary of Lord Nelson's victory at the Battle of Trafalgar in 1805 is commemorated with a parade and service performed by Sea Cadets (boys and girls aged 12–18) from all over the country. A wreath is laid at the foot of **Nelson's Column**, and Nelson's Prayer is read by a young cadet. The ceremony starts at 11AM in **Trafalgar Square**.

November

Bonfire Night   On 5 November 1605, Guy Fawkes was arrested as one of the conspirators in the Gunpowder Plot to kill King James I and blow up Parliament. Since then, fireworks and bonfires have been lit throughout the country on this date. For details of displays in the London area, call 0839/123410.

London to Brighton Car Run   Held on the first Sunday of November, this gathering attracts more than 400 entrants from all over the world who subject their veteran and classic cars to a grueling 58-mile stretch of road. Cars leave from **Hyde Park Corner** between 8 and 9AM and follow the **A23** to **Brighton**, where they begin arriving at **Madeira Drive** around 10:45AM.

Lord Mayor's Show   This tradition, which dictates that the lord mayor ride in the gilded State Coach to the **Law Courts** for the declaration of office, dates from the 13th century. Today, there's also a parade featuring floats, military bands, and units of the armed services, and fireworks on the **Thames**. The event is usually slated for the second Saturday of the month. For more information, call 0891/505453.

Remembrance Sunday   On a date near 11 November, a memorial service is held at the **Cenotaph, Whitehall**, to honor all those in the military who gave their lives in the two world wars and other conflicts. The queen arrives at 10:59AM, and a 2-minute silence begins at 11AM, ended by the firing of a gun from **Horse Guards Parade**. The queen lays a wreath at the **Cenotaph**, and the Bishop of London conducts a short service.

Christmas Lights   Christmas lights are switched on daily from dusk to midnight on **Bond**, **Jermyn**, **Oxford**, and **Regent Streets** from mid-November until Twelfth Night (6 January). For more information, call the London Tourist Board's Christmas Service at 0891/505455.

December

Trafalgar Square Christmas Tree   Since 1947, the city of Oslo, Norway, has presented London with a Norwegian Christmas spruce in gratitude for help given by the British during World War II. The tree is set up in **Trafalgar Square** in early December and decorated with white lights. It is lit daily between 3PM and midnight until Twelfth Night (6 January), and carols are sung each evening until Christmas Eve.

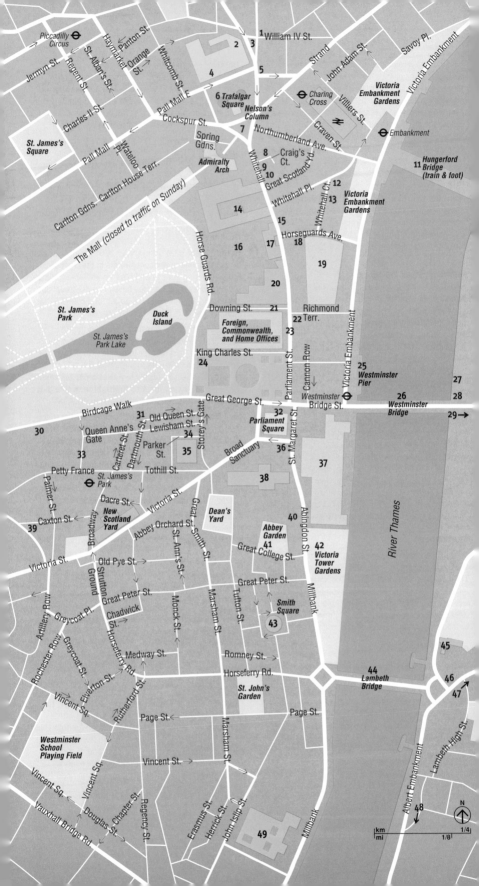

WESTMINSTER

A walk through the City of Westminster forms a kind of pilgrimage, a journey that parallels the **River Thames**, covers one and a half acres of hallowed ground, embraces 900 years of history, and provides a first-rate view of history in the making. Westminster is Britain's seat of power: Kings and queens are still crowned here, and the process of democracy continues to unfold before public scrutiny. The **Palace of Westminster**, better known as the **Houses of Parliament**, is where the **House of Commons** and the **House of Lords** conduct the sometimes tempestuous, sometimes snoozy day-to-day business of government. Neighboring **Westminster Abbey** occupies the seat of spiritual power and, with its sepulchres of famous Britons, serves as a reminder of the ultimate end to all struggles—death. Your tour of **Westminster Abbey** could be delayed by a wedding or a funeral, as this is not a museum; people make vows, pray, and mourn the dead here.

About a mile north of Westminster Abbey is **Trafalgar Square**, where London's citizens regularly gather (like so many excitable pigeons) to celebrate or protest; through it all, this English *grande place* casts an impartial eye on the legislation passed down the road by Parliament and administered next door by officials in **Whitehall**.

The **National Portrait Gallery** is a who's who of English history, the **National Gallery** surveys European art dating from the 1200s to the turn of this century, and the splendid **Tate Gallery** revels in British art. After perusing the collections, contemplate the Thames with London as a backdrop, a scene that could have been painted by the pre-Raphaelites or Whistler. You may also decide to stop for a concert at **St. John's** in **Smith Square** or sample English ale in a pub next to an MP or two.

The ideal time to visit this area is Monday through Friday, when Parliament is in session. On weekends, Westminster and Whitehall are all but abandoned—MPs return to their constituencies; civil servants stay home; and many of the restaurants, pubs, and shops that exist primarily to serve the governing elite are closed. On Sunday, the most interesting parts of Westminster Abbey are closed.

For the best views of Westminster, cross over the Thames to **Lambeth**, a south London district whose main attractions, **Lambeth Palace** and the **Museum of Garden History**, cluster beside the river.

City code 0207 unless otherwise noted.

1 THE CHANDOS

★★$ A handsome pub across the street from the **Trafalgar Square Post Office**. The eatery offers the usual pub grub. It serves cottage pie in winter only—the steak pie is better. ♦ Pub ♦ Food served F-Su. 29 St. Martins La (at William IV St). 836.1401. Tube: Charing Cross, Leicester Sq

2 NATIONAL PORTRAIT GALLERY (NPG)

The National Portrait Gallery celebrated her 150th birthday in 2006. Like many ladies of "a certain age," she has had a fair amount of work done, and at the moment is looking very, very good.

Above the entrance are busts of three men: Philip Henry (1805-1875), fifth Earl of Stanhope who was principally responsible for founding the gallery, and his two main supporters, Thomas Carlyle and Thomas Macauley. It took Stanhope 10 years to persuade Parliament to establish "a gallery of original portraits, such portraits to consist as far as possible of those persons who are most honorably commemorated in British history as warriors or as statesmen, or in arts, in

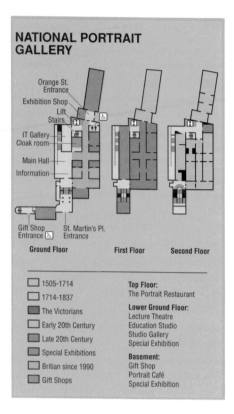

NATIONAL PORTRAIT GALLERY

Orange St. Entrance
Exhibition Shop
Lift
Stairs
IT Gallery
Cloak room
Main Hall
Information

Gift Shop Entrance | St. Martin's Pl. Entrance

Ground Floor　　　**First Floor**　　　**Second Floor**

- 1505-1714
- 1714-1837
- The Victorians
- Early 20th Century
- Late 20th Century
- Special Exhibitions
- Britian since 1990
- Gift Shops

Top Floor:
The Portrait Restaurant

Lower Ground Floor:
Lecture Theatre
Education Studio
Studio Gallery
Special Exhibition

Basement:
Gift Shop
Portrait Café
Special Exhibition

---

literature or in science." With an initial grant of £2,000 from Parliament, the gallery was established on the basis that the important thing was history, not art; the stature of the person, not the quality of the painting.

Originally the trustees allowed only paintings of the great and the good if they had been dead for more than 10 years, the only exception being the reigning monarch and his or her consort. Since 1969, you no longer need to die to get into the National Portrait Gallery. For the first 40 years of its existence the collection moved all over London, but in 1889, William Henry Alexander (1832–1905) offered to pay for a permanent home with the proviso that the government donate a site for the building within a mile and a half of St. James's. Prime Minister Lord Salisbury agreed. If only negotiating with governments were still so straightforward! For his initial £60,000, Alexander was also allowed to engage his architect of choice: **Ewan Christian**.

The gallery was created in three linked but individual blocks: the **East Block**, the **North Block**, and the central **Entrance Block**. They were designed in Florentine Renaissance style, faced with Portland stone, and decorated with stone portraits of eminent artists, historians, and writers created by Frederick C. Thomas. Sadly, Christian died of

a chill in 1895 before his new building was opened at 10AM on 4 April 1896. Its opening day drew 4,200 visitors. For most of its 150 years the gallery was a quiet, scholarly place. But, at the age of 71, in 1967, it got a new director. Roy Strong did for the National Portrait Gallery what Steven Spielberg did for extraterrestrial life forms. (Well, maybe not quite!) He curated Cecil Beaton's photographic exhibition in 1968 and attracted 75,000 visitors to the gallery, and opened the Department of Film and Photography. The gallery commissioned Annigoni to paint the Queen in 1970 (and, like it or not, 250,000 came to see the portrait in the first two months). When Strong moved on to the Victoria & Albert in 1974, John Hayes took over and began the policy of commissioning portraits. He also established the BP Portrait Award.

If not exactly the gallery that offers the greatest emotional bang for your buck (actually, entrance is free!), this is a fascinating place that puts faces to names such as Jane Austen (the only known portrait of her, by her sister Cassandra), the Brontë sisters, Keats, Byron, Elizabeth and Robert Browning, and Charles Darwin. The oldest portrait is one of Henry VII painted in 1505; the tallest is by Sir James Guthrie and stands (or hangs, to be precise) nearly 4 meters tall; and the widest (which, like the tallest, is of statesmen from the First World War) is nearly 5.3 meters wide, making it 52,000 times larger than the gallery's smallest portrait (of Henrietta Anne, Duchess of Orleáns, 1644–1670), which is about the size of a man's thumbnail. There are 65 portraits of Gladstone and 50 of HM Queen Elizabeth II. And there is a portrait of the entire House of Commons with 400 people in it, 320 of which have been identified!

If you are around for a few days and want more out of a gallery than a wander around and a tick in the "have visited" column on your London To Do list, you might be interested to know that the gallery hosts lots of events, talks, and lectures (both evening—usually Thursday or Friday—and daytime), workshops for kids, and Friday music evenings and film nights. Almost all of them are free. And fascinating!

The ground floor houses changing special exhibitions and displays, as well as the IT Gallery. Here you have access to the Portrait Explorer, funded by the Woodward Trust. Ten large flat-screen viewers let you see 31,500 portraits in the National Collection. The gallery lends out parts of its collection, so not every portrait is actually there every month of the year. However, this virtual viewing is a good option. The first floor has the **Victorian Galleries**, **Early 20th Century** and **Late 20th Century Galleries**, and Alison Watt's famous and much-debated portrait of the Queen

Mother. On the second floor you will find the **Tudor Galleries, 17th- and 18th-century collections**, and occasional special exhibitions.

Before the gallery was even open, it was too small to house the National Collection. By 1924 it had doubled in size, and World War I put a dent in the "buy a new wing for the National Portrait Gallery fund," so it wasn't until 1928 that the gallery found a sugar daddy in the form of Sir Joseph Duveen, who donated £40,000 to build a three-story extension along Orange Street. King George V and Queen Mary opened the new wing on 30 March 1933, since which time it has had a further makeover, and it now tends to house temporary exhibitions. The web site will keep you up to date with what is coming up.

Galleries. ♦ Free; occasional charge for special exhibitions. M–W, Sa, Su, 10AM–6PM; Th, F, 10AM–9PM. 2 St. Martin's Pl (at Trafalgar Sq). 306.0055. Tube: Charing Cross, Leicester Sq. www.npg.org.uk

Within the NPG:

GIFT SHOP

If you know anyone with a coffee table, this place has the books for it! There's a great range of books, postcards, and gifts, and a marvelous new facility in The Portrait Printer—which will (for a reasonable price) print out your choice from over 42,000 paintings in four sizes. Okay, so it is only digital. But it saves you the jail sentence that goes with trying to take the real thing back home

THE PORTRAIT CAFÉ

$ Tucked in beside the gift shop and designed by leading London architects **Dixon Jones,** the café offers light meals, snacks, fresh salads, terrific panini and freshly made sandwiches, good coffee, and yummy cakes (if the raspberry and chocolate is available, try it; it is something of a masterpiece in itself). ♦ Sa–W, 10AM–5:30PM; Th, F, 10AM–8:30PM

THE PORTRAIT RESTAURANT

★★$$ The restaurant has hugely benefited from the arrival of Swedish-born Katarina Todosijevic and her culinary skills. But although the asparagus in season is delicious and the whole plaice in shrimp butter a lovely lunch, the real feast up here is for the eyes. You are sitting on the roof of London—92 feet above ground level—with a view hitherto enjoyed only by pigeons: Trafalgar Square (with a unique view of Nelson's bottom), Westminster, and beyond. There is a 25-seater bar area adjacent to the restaurant. You could do worse than put the "high" in highball up here! ♦ Daily, lunch; Th, F, dinner. 312.2490

THE HEINZ ARCHIVE AND LIBRARY

No, not ketchup, but rather the prime center for research in the field of British portraiture. It dates back to the foundation of the gallery in 1856 and was set up to assist research on the gallery's collection of portraits of eminent men and women. It contains extensive files of engravings, photographs, and other reproductions of portraits, arranged by sitter and artist. The library has a reference section of 35,000 books, catalogues, and periodicals, the sketchbooks of the gallery's first director (Sir George Sharf), several sitters' notebooks, a set of Gillray caricatures, and autograph letters. The archive and library are open by appointment.

3 STATUE OF EDITH CAVELL

Behind **Trafalgar Square** stands a monument to Edith Cavell, a nurse accused by the Germans of spying and helping some 200 Allied prisoners to escape to neutral Holland during World War I; she was executed in 1915. The statue was created by Sir George Frampton and unveiled in 1920 by Queen Alexandra. Four years later, Cavell's famous last words were added: "Patriotism is not enough." ♦ St. Martin's Pl and William IV St

4 NATIONAL GALLERY

Built in 1838 by **William Wilkins**, the most important building in **Trafalgar Square** anchors the north side. Architects complain that the scale of the neoclassical building is weak in relation to the square, but the blame should fall on a parsimonious Parliament, which compelled Wilkins to use columns from the demolished Carlton House in the portico. The original building was only one room deep, more a façade than a gallery. But the gallery's size at its debut had little effect on its destiny: today, it is home to one of the most comprehensive surveys of Western European art in the world.

Unlike most of the great national galleries of Europe, this one is not built on the foundations of a former royal collection, nor did it inherit a nationally based collection. In fact, it began late; in 1824, George IV persuaded the government to buy 38 paintings from the collection of Russian émigré and marine insurance underwriter John Julius Angerstein. The government paid £57,000 for the pictures—which included five paintings by Claude Lorraine, Hogarth's *Marriage à la Mode* series, and works by Raphael, Reynolds, and Van Dyck—then opened the gallery to the public in Angerstein's former town house at 100 Pall Mall. Two other collectors, Sir George Beaumont and the Reverend William Holwell Carr, promised important paintings to the nation if a suitable building were provided to house them. In 1838, the National Gallery opened, and the Beaumont and Holwell Carr paintings, along with Angerstein's, formed the nucleus of the national collection.

As the gallery's collection grew, so did its building. The dome and additional rooms were added in the 1870s, followed by the central staircase and further additions in 1911. In 1975, the excellent northern extension was added, and the innovative **Sainsbury Wing** opened in 1991. The 2,200-plus pictures in the gallery are predominantly by the Old Masters. They represent one of the finest histories of Western European painting in existence, from Duccio in 14th-century Italy to Cézanne in the early 20th century, from 1260 to 1900. The masterpieces of Holbein, Van Dyck, and Velázquez displayed here are finer than those that can be seen in their native countries. The cutoff date that divided the two collections was originally 1920, but an agreement recently made between the National Gallery and the **Tate** changed the date to 1900. This has resulted in an exchange of relevant 19th- and 20th-century works between the two galleries.

It's not the first time such an exchange has taken place. When the **Tate Gallery** opened in 1897, it took on the dual role of modern art museum and home of British art. Many British paintings in the National Gallery were transferred to the Tate, leaving the National with a small but choice collection that consists of 2 paintings by Stubbs, *The Milbanke* and *Melbourne Families*; 6 by Reynolds, including *General Banastre Tarleton*, a portrait of the general during the American War of Independence; 5 by Constable, including *The Hay Wain*; 10 by Gainsborough, including *Mr. and Mrs. Andrews* and *The Morning Walk*; and 7 by Hogarth, 6 of which are part of the *Marriage à la Mode* series.

There is no substitute for beholding the original paintings, and one of the bonuses of a free museum is being able to look at only a few works at a time, guiltlessly. No one has to see it all in one visit, and no one should try. A lifetime spent looking at these paintings seems to be about right, starting with old favorites and acquiring new loves along the way. If you are daunted by the size of the collection, use a portable "Gallery Guide" on CD (available for a donation), which provides an introduction to each section of the gallery and commentary on each work. Free 1-hour guided tours are offered twice daily; three times on Wednesday.

The gallery has also made a kind of "Hit Parade" of the 20 most famous pictures. The *Twenty Great Paintings* booklet, available in

the **National Gallery Shops** (see page 23), describes them and is worth the price. The National Gallery's main building was undergoing major refurbishment as late as 1998, so paintings will inevitably have been moved around; check with room guards or the information desks if you can't find a painting listed here. (Also, the top 20 may change to include Hans Holbein's *Ambassadors*, now returned after conservation treatment.) The 20 masterpieces:

The Wilton Diptych, English or French school (ca. 1395). ♦ Room 53

The Battle of San Romano, Paolo Uccello (1397-1475). ♦ Room 55

The Arnolfini Marriage, Jan Van Eyck (1395?-1441). ♦ Room 56

The Baptism of Christ, Piero Della Francesca (1420?-92). ♦ Room 66

Cartoon: The Virgin and Child with Saint John the Baptist and Saint Anne, Leonardo Da Vinci (1452-1519). ♦ Room 51

The Doge Leonardo Loredan, Giovanni Bellini (1430?-1516). ♦ Room 61

A Lady with a Squirrel and a Starling, Hans Holbein the Younger (1498-1543). ♦ Room 4

Bacchus and Ariadne, Titian (1488?-1576). ♦ Room 9

Le Chapeau de Paille (*The Straw Hat*), Peter Paul Rubens (1577-1640). ♦ Room 28

Equestrian Portrait of Charles I, Anthony Van Dyck (1599-1641). ♦ Room 30

The Toilet of Venus (*The Rokeby Venus*), Diego Velázquez (1599-1660). ♦ Room 29

Self Portrait Aged 63, Rembrandt (1606-1669). ♦ Room 27

Landscape with Psyche Outside the Palace of Cupid (*The Enchanted Castle*), Claude Gellée (Le Lorrain) (1604/5-1682). ♦ Room 19

A Young Woman Standing at a Virginal, Johannes Vermeer (1632-1675). ♦ Room 16

The Stonemason's Yard, Canaletto (1697-1768). ♦ Room 38

The Fighting Temeraire, J.M.W. Turner (1775-1851). ♦ Room 34

The Hay Wain, John Constable (1776-1837). ♦ Room 34

Madame Moitessier, Jean-Auguste-Dominique Ingres (1780-1867). ♦ Room 41

Bathers at La Grenouillère, Claude Monet (1840-1926). ♦ Room 45

Bathers at Asnières, Georges Seurat (1859-1891). ♦ Room 44

On the lower floor of the gallery, stacks of minor masterpieces sit alongside paintings by great artists as an overflow from the main displays above.

The *National Gallery Mosaics*, by Russian-born artist Boris Anrep, on the floors of the vestibules and halfway landing, are works of art that usually go unnoticed. In the west vestibule, the theme is *The Labors of Life*, with 12 mosaics completed in 1928, including *Art*, which shows a sculptor at work; *Sacred Love*, which depicts a father, mother, child, and dog; and *Letters*, which shows a child's slate with two favorite children's books, *Robinson Crusoe* and *Alice in Wonderland*. In the north vestibule, the theme is *The Modern Virtues*, with 15 mosaics completed in 1952. *Compassion* shows the Russian poet Anna Akhmatova being saved by an angel from the horrors of war; *Compromise* has actress Loretta Young filling a cup with wine to symbolize American and British friendship; *Defiance* portrays Winston Churchill on the cliffs of Dover, confronting an apocalyptic beast in the shape of a swastika; and *Leisure* is T.S. Eliot contemplating both the Loch Ness monster and Einstein's formula.

In the east vestibule are 11 mosaics completed by Boris Anrep in 1929 representing *The Pleasures of Life*, including *Christmas Pudding*; *Conversation*, with two girls gossiping; *Mudpie*, with mud pies, a bucket, and a spade; and *Profane Love*, showing a man and two girls with a dog. In the landing is *The Awakening of the Muses*, illustrating London's beau monde in the 1930s. It portrays the Honorable Mrs. Bryan Guinness (one of the Mitford girls and later Lady Diana Mosley) as Polyhymnia, Muse of Sacred Song; Christabel, Lady Aberconway as Euterpe, Muse of Music; Clive Bell as Bacchus, God of Wine; Virginia Woolf as Clio, Muse of History; Sir Osbert Sitwell as Apollo, God of Music; and Greta Garbo as Melpomene, Muse of Tragedy.

Special exhibitions include the *Making and Meaning* series, which provides an in-depth analysis and presentation of a major work in the collection. Guided tours leave twice a day Monday through Saturday; also Wednesday evening. There are free lunchtime lectures Tuesday through Friday at 1PM and on Saturday at noon. Free films are shown Monday at 1PM. ♦ Free. Daily, 10AM–6PM; W, till 9PM. On the north side of Trafalgar Sq (between St. Martin's Pl and Whitcomb St). 839.3321. Tube: Charing Cross, Leicester Sq

Within the National Gallery:

SAINSBURY WING

Though from the outside it may appear to be a separate building, it is in fact linked with the main gallery, and often has excellent current exhibitions for a charge. When the wing was first proposed, Prince Charles, always outspoken about architecture, complained that the designs for this extension, incorporating an office block, were "a monstrous carbuncle on the face of a much-loved and elegant friend." People listened; plans were dropped. Enter the supermarket barons **Lord Sainsbury of Preston Candover** and **Simon** and **Timothy Sainsbury**, who funded this new design and construction. A second architectural

competition was held and won by the Philadelphia firm **Venturi, Scott Brown & Associates**. The result is a modern architectural success. (Charles himself laid the foundation stone in 1988.) The Sainsbury Wing is also faced with Portland stone so that the façade evolves before your eyes from the neoclassical architecture of the original gallery to a clean, ultramodern style that suits Trafalgar Square perfectly. Displayed here is the **National Gallery**'s early collection. The 250 Early Renaissance paintings from 1260 to 1510 include Duccio's *The Virgin and Child* triptych (room 52), *The Battle of San Romano* by Uccello (room 55), Van Eyck's *The Arnolfini Marriage* (room 56), and *The Ansidei Madonna* by Raphael (room 60). ♦ M, Tu; W, 10AM–8PM; Th–Sa; Su, noon–6PM.

Within the Sainsbury Wing:

MICRO GALLERY

Don't miss this free and fascinating computerized visual information system that offers background information on every painting in the collection as well as on the artists, periods, subjects, and genres. The system is easy to use and requires no particular knowledge of computers or art history.

NATIONAL GALLERY SHOPS

The main shop, in the **Sainsbury Wing**, carries a full range of gallery publications, a splendid collection of art books, and specially commissioned gifts from top designers, including picture frames, velvet scarves, and fancy hats inspired by artists. In full color and reasonably priced, *The National Gallery Companion Guide*, by Erika Langmuir, is excellent. The gallery also publishes short, introductory guides exploring such major themes as *The Care and Conservation of Paintings*, *Frames*, *Still Life*, and *Allegory*. Also for sale are color slides and black-and-white photographs. The smaller **Room 3 Shop**, at the top of the entrance to the main gallery, carries a more limited selection. ♦ M–Sa, Su, 10AM–5:30PM. 839.3321

THE NATIONAL CAFÉ

★★★$ This is a terrific addition to the National Gallery. It is actually a brasserie rather than a café, and a very good one.

Designed by David Collins and serving the terrific, gutsy food of Shaun Gilmore, it is an Oliver Peyton restaurant. Which is a bit like saying "a Valentino gown"—you just know the guy isn't going to make a bad one. Best of all is breakfast, which extends till a very civilized 11AM. They have eggs Benedict, eggs Norwegian, French toast with banana and maple syrup, and good coffee down to a fine art. And if that all sounds like a recipe for a Rubenesque waistline, they also do an egg white and fresh herb omelette. Lunch might offer a home-cured gravlax, a smoked haddock fish cake with poached egg, or the succulent Farmer Sharp's aged Galloway beef. Or there are "boards"—mixed plates of excellent charcuterie or cheese to share, served with salad, olives, and pickle. As you are in England, perhaps you should try an afternoon tea (very good) or a cream tea (really shouldn't be missed). And if you last till dinner, the Café does specials, like a whole roast *poulet noir* (black chicken) for two people to share, or a grilled chateaubriand, also for two. Even if you don't have time to linger in the chic interior, there is a take-out section that does some of the best portable edibles in town. It is worth a trip here just to try their made-to-order bags of potato chips. If you are feeling brave, then you really should try the café's National Catastrophe—freshly churned vanilla ice cream, marshmallow, hazelnuts, caramel, meringue, cookie crumbs, fresh raspberry sauce, whipped cream, and chocolate sauce. Oh, go on! You're on vacation!
♦ Daily, 8AM-11PM. East Wing, National Gallery. 747.5942. www.thenationalcafe.com

THE NATIONAL GALLERY DINING ROOMS

★★★$$$ This place opened to the kind of reviews that make your mouth water and won the *Time Out* Best British Restaurant award for 2007. "As English as the sound of leather on willow and absolutely divine," said their critic. It is another Oliver Peyton creation, and his expertise and passion for great British produce really shows. The flavors bursting across the main menu pack enough punch to fight at Madison Square Garden and win. They have a fabulous selection of expertly kept and presented British cheeses, a great Sunday lunch menu (yes, they do a great roast beef and Yorkshire pudding), a children's menu that is the best argument for being young since Father Christmas, and an in-house bakery where, as well as one of London's most delicious bread selections, you can have salads, homemade quiches, pots of delicious pâtés, and unbelievably delicious gooey delights like traditional treacle tart. Just when you think it can't get any better, you find the dining room

sundaes—your wildest dreams in a tall glass topped with a cherry. The wine list is a joy, generously priced, and there are even some properly interesting beers on tap. ♦ Daily, 10AM-5PM; W, 10AM-8:30PM. 747.2525. www.thenationaldiningrooms.co.uk

5 ST. MARTIN-IN-THE-FIELDS

John Nash's design for **Trafalgar Square** was never realized, but his role in it endures because of his idea to open up the vista that brings this church into the square. The church, where Charles II was christened and his mistress, Nell Gwyn, was buried, is not actually part of the square but is its single source of pure loveliness. Built in 1726 by **Sir Christopher Wren**'s disciple, **James Gibbs**, the church boasts a steeple that soars to 185 feet, almost the same height as **Nelson's Column**. The steeple, which was added in 1824, has been an inspiration for many American churches. The interior is light and airy, with a lovely ceiling of Italian plasterwork. The porch offers shelter to passsersby on rainy days, and the steps provide a resting place for tired tourists. On Monday, Tuesday, and Friday at 1:05PM, you can enjoy free concerts of chamber or choral music in the church. Tu, Th, F, Sa, 7:30PM, concert price is £6–18. ♦Daily. Trafalgar Sq and Duncannon. Concert bookings, 839.8362. Tube: Charing Cross

Within St. Martin-in-the-Fields:

CAFÉ IN THE CRYPT

★★$ Hidden within the church's crypt is this restaurant still known by the cognoscenti as **Fields**. It's used by actors for private parties and by office workers to meet their friends for lunch. Try the spinach and cheese pancakes. The floors (gravestones), the walls (16th-century stone), and the black furniture are made less sepulchral by the strains of Bach.
♦ Café ♦ M-Sa, lunch and snacks to 8PM; Su, lunch and snacks. 839.4342

BRASS RUBBING CENTER

Here, you can rub effigies of medieval brasses (facsimiles), creating your own knight in shining armor or damsel in a gown. If you feel pressed for time, buy one ready-made. Children love creating effigies, and the center adjoins the **Café in the Crypt**, so you can enjoy a coffee while keeping an eye on the kids. ♦ M-Sa, 10AM-6PM; Su, noon-6PM. 930.9306

6 TRAFALGAR SQUARE

A testament to the Battle of Trafalgar, England's decisive victory over Napoléon's fleet off the coast of Spain in 1805, Trafalgar Square is one of London's most impressive squares. Recently it was the subject of an attempt to improve the ghastly crush of traffic that swirled around the fountains and monuments like a polluted moat around a lovely old castle. The square has now opened out and looks the best it ever has, but the multiple lanes of traffic are still there, just in a much more complicated routing. If this were Paris, Haussmann's ruthlessness would have you looking down heart-stopping vistas of **Buckingham Palace** and **Westminster Abbey**; broad avenues would connect the square to Regent Street and the **British Museum**; and the square itself, instead of sunken and treeless, would be green, elevated, and uniform. But I guess that's what you get for beating Napoléon!

Until 1830, the site was occupied by the **Royal Mews**, when mews were reserved for mewing: the molting of birds of prey. Edward I (ruler between 1272 and 1307) kept his hawks here, and Richard II (who reigned between 1377 and 1399) kept his falcons and goshawks, a rather distinguished legacy for the famous pigeons and starlings who mew monotonously in the square today. Unfortunately, for those who come to feed the pigeons, London's mayor has banned their feeding in an attempt to rid the square of the birds.

By the reign of Henry VII (1485 to 1509), horses were kept in the Royal Mews. In 1732, landscape gardener, architect, and painter **William Kent** built the **Royal Stables** on this site, then known as Great Mews, Green Mews, and Dunghill Mews. The stables stood until 1830, when the site was leveled to construct the square and **Nelson's Column**.

The original idea of the square came from architect **John Nash**, who had already brought elegance and grandeur to London with Regent Street, **Regent's Park**, and **Marble Arch**, under the aegis of the prince regent, later George IV. With Regent Street, Nash provided the first north–south axis to connect London's three main east–west routes (Oxford Street, Piccadilly, and the Strand). In his early sketches of Trafalgar Square, Nash saw the site as the medieval turning point in the road leading from **Westminster Abbey** to **St. Paul's Cathedral**. There was no open space, only a widening where the bronze statue of Charles I had stood since 1675, marking the spot where the three roads met. Nash designed the area as a grand axis connecting government (Parliament), finance (the City), and aristocracy (St. James's and the Royal Parks).

Parliament accepted Nash's site but unfortunately rejected his designs.

Trafalgar Square, as it appears today, is largely the work of **Sir Charles Barry**, the distinguished architect of gentlemen's clubs, including the **Reform Club** and the **Traveller's Club** in Pall Mall, and that club of clubs, the **Houses of Parliament**. Barry favored the Italian palazzo style for this war memorial. Four octagonal oil lamps, which have been converted to electricity, occupy the corners of the square; they are reputedly from Nelson's flagship, HMS *Victory*. Every year on 21 October, the anniversary of the Battle of Trafalgar, a parade and service are held in the square by members of the Royal Navy. Officers from modern ships of the fleet lay wreaths at the bottom of the column, and descendants of those who fought at Trafalgar contribute an anchor of laurels. Nelson, a genius for naval battle, was a hero with a gift for inspiring devotion.

The highlights of the year in the square are Christmas and New Year's Eve. An enormous Christmas tree, a gift from Norway, is erected, and carols are sung most December evenings. On New Year's Eve, thousands used to congregate in the square and welcome in the New Year to the chimes of nearby **Big Ben**. London's lord mayor has recently banned celebrations in the square, which can now look really rather sad as the rest of the world celebrates. ♦ Bounded by the Strand and Pall Mall E and by Whitehall and Charing Cross Rd. Tube: Charing Cross

At Trafalgar Square:

NELSON'S COLUMN

Born in 1758, Horatio Nelson entered the service of his country at the age of 12, suffered from seasickness all his life, and lost his right eye at the Battle of Calvi, his right arm at Santa Cruz, and his life at Trafalgar. The hero now stands atop William Railton's 170-foot-high granite column, erected in 1843. The statue of Lord Nelson by E.H. Bailey is 17 feet high, and his sword measures 7 feet 9 inches. Altogether, the monument is as tall as an 18-story building, a fine tribute to a man who stood just 5 feet 4 inches in real life.

Almost 40 years went by after Nelson's funeral at **St. Paul's** in 1805 until his column was raised in Trafalgar Square. Railton's design of a massive Corinthian column won the competition for the monument in 1837. The capital is of bronze cast from cannons recovered from the wreck of the *Royal George*. On the sides of the pedestal are four bronze bas-reliefs cast from the metal of captured French cannons, representing incidents in the battles of St. Vincent, Aboukir, Copenhagen, and Trafalgar.

Restaurants/Clubs: Red | Hotels: Purple | Shops: Orange | Outdoors/Parks: Green | Sights/Culture: Blue

Guarding the column are four vast (20 feet by 11 feet) and lovable lions by Queen Victoria's favorite animal painter, Sir Edwin Landseer. Late arrivals (they were installed in 1868), these magnificent, tender-faced creatures give the square its vitality. When Landseer died in 1871, the public put wreaths around the lions' necks.

STATUE OF GEORGE IV

Standing out among the statues is George IV (king between 1820 and 1830), who worshiped Nelson (though the feeling was not mutual) and under whose auspices **John Nash** first conceived the square. After the Battle of Trafalgar had established Britain's command of the seas, George IV commissioned Turner's great battle piece, *The Battle of Trafalgar* (hanging in the **National Maritime Museum** in Greenwich). But George IV's obsession was architecture. As prince regent, he built the **Brighton Pavilion**; as king he rebuilt **Buckingham Palace** and transformed **Windsor** into the finest of all the royal castles. An expert horseman, he commissioned most of the equestrian paintings by George Stubbs in the **Royal Collection**. Although it seems odd that this statue by Sir Francis Chantrey shows the king in Roman dress, riding a horse bareback without stirrups, it is in keeping with the 18th-century predilection for classical poses and costumes.

STATUES OF JAMES II AND GEORGE WASHINGTON

Facing the square from the north are two contrasting statues: On the west is James II, in Roman dress, sculpted by 17th-century artist Grinling Gibbons; on the east is George Washington, a 1921 bronze replica of Jean Antoine Houdon's original, which stands in Richmond, Virginia. (Perhaps Washington is honored because he had an English grandfather.) James II, who reigned between 1685 and 1688, was impulsive and bullheaded. He annoyed Parliament because of his pro-Catholic wife and politics, was succeeded by his Protestant daughter, Queen Mary II, and spent the last 11 years of his life in exile in France.

OTHER STATUES

The naval influence in Trafalgar Square includes busts in the terrace walls of Admirals Beatty and Jellicoe of World War I and Admiral Cunningham of World War II. Carved into the stone of the north wall between Jellicoe and Cunningham are the Imperial Standards for length, showing the exact measurements of an imperial inch, foot, yard, rod, chain, pole, and perch.

THE FOURTH PLINTH

After protracted discussion, the long-empty fourth plinth in the square was first filled by Marc Quinn's beautiful white alabaster portrait of artist Alison Lapper, naked, pregnant, and disabled. Since then there has been a rolling program of statues filling the plinth, usually for a year each. The current one is a multicolored glass creation by Thomas Schutte entitled *Model for a Hotel*. Yes, it is just as exciting as it sounds. The occupant for 2008 is currently being chosen . . . so who knows what you might see!

FOUNTAINS

In a city famous for rain, fountains are few. **Sir Charles Barry**'s original fountains and their large pools were part of a design to break up the large, unruly crowds that the government of the day was perceptive enough to realize would meet in the square. Even with the fountains and their pools, however, 50,000 people can and do congregate here when the cause of democracy calls. The original fountains designed by Barry now face Parliament in Ottawa, Canada; the fountains in the square today were designed by **Sir Edwin Lutyens** to honor Admirals Jellicoe and Beatty. They have first-rate water power, and every morning at 10AM the mermaids and mermen respond to the repetitive booms of **Big Ben** by democratically christening nearby Londoners and visitors, people and pigeons.

BUILDINGS

The late Sir John Betjeman, poet laureate and passionate defender of Victorian architecture, saw the weighty stone buildings that surround Trafalgar Square as a historic backdrop. Looking left in the direction of Whitehall are **Herbert Baker**'s **South Africa House**, built in 1935, its somber classical façade indifferent; the rounded **Grand Buildings** and **Trafalgar Buildings**, designed by **Frederick** and **Horace Francis** and built in 1878 and 1881, respectively; **George Aitchison**'s **Royal Bank of Scotland**, erected in 1885; **Reginald Blomfield**'s **Uganda House**, built in 1915; and **Canada House,** the most handsome building on the square, designed by **Sir Robert Smirke** and completed in 1827. Originally the **Royal College of Physicians**, this building of warm Bath stone has suffered from conversion and extension of the upper parts; nonetheless, it remains a dignified presence.

7 STATUE OF CHARLES I

Whitehall physically begins on the south side of **Trafalgar Square** with this equestrian statue of Charles I, who reigned between 1625 and 1649. The statue, created in 1633 by **Hubert Le Sueur**, shows the monarch gazing toward the scene of his tragic execution at **Banqueting House** on 30 January 1649, with **Parliament** looming in the distance. It was his quarrel with Parliament that led to his downfall. In 1642, civil war erupted between the Parliamentarians (the Roundheads, led by Oliver Cromwell) and the Royalists (known as the Cavaliers) over Parliament's demand to approve the king's choice of ministers. Charles was tried for treason to the realm and died on the scaffold.

Now stranded in an islet, unreachable except by the most intrepid pedestrian, this is the oldest, finest, and most poignant statue in London. The horse's left hoof bears the date 1633 and the sculptor's signature. When the Civil War broke out in 1642, the statue was hidden in the churchyard of **St. Paul's**, **Covent Garden**. After the king's execution, Cromwell sold the statue for scrap to a resourceful brazier named John Rivett, who kept the statue intact but enjoyed a brisk trade in candlesticks, thimbles, spoons, and knife handles supposedly created from it. This Charles I souvenir shop thrived until the Restoration, when the statue miraculously reappeared. Charles II rewarded the brazier with £1,600. The statue finally found its home here in 1675. Note that Whitehall is the name of the street and of the immediate area, as well as a nickname for governmental bureaucracy and red tape (thanks to all the official ministries and departments here).
♦ Trafalgar Sq and Whitehall. Tube: Charing Cross

7 THE TRAFALGAR LONDON HOTEL

$$$$ The façade of this "style" hotel is a historic landmark right on Trafalgar Square. It is all historical building outside and 21st-century cool inside. There are 129 bedrooms with all the modern conveniences, including CD and DVD players, high-speed Internet access, and—should you have a "player" in tow—a PlayStation. Be aware that standard rooms do not come with that Trafalgar Square view. There are huge baths in some of the rooms—big enough for two! The hotel offers what they describe as "modern cuisine" in both their **Rockwell** restaurant and in their gorgeous sixth-floor Roof Terrace with an incredible panoramic view. The terrace can be booked for private parties.
♦ 2 Spring Gardens. 870.2900; fax 870.2911. Tube: Charing Cross. www.thetrafalgar.hilton.co.uk
Within the Trafalgar London Hotel:

ROCKWELL

London's first bourbon bar. If the juice of the rye is your tipple, then you will be in heaven with over 100 to choose from and—for London—reasonably knowledgeable bar staff. Despite the fact that service can be somewhat less than instantaneous, this place has won both the *Evening Standard* and *Time Out* "Best New Bar" awards.

8 WALKERS OF WHITEHALL

★$$ To find a civilized setting for a drink, lunch, or snack, turn into tiny Craig's Court and enter this pub/wine bar on the left. You can try cask-conditioned ales or premium lagers with bangers and mash, or, if you prefer, a glass of wine with one of the chef's specials—for example, broccoli and cheese bake. ♦ Pub/Wine bar ♦ M-Sa, lunch and dinner. Craig's Ct (off Whitehall). 925.0090. Tube: Charing Cross

9 SILVER CROSS

★★$$ Charles I licensed this establishment as a brothel and pub in 1647. The façade is Victorian, but the building dates to the 13th century, with a barrel-vaulted ceiling, ancient walls sheathed in lead, and, in the bar, a plaster ceiling embossed with vine leaves, grapes, and hops made while Charles I was still living down the street. A warm, special place, it serves home-cooked food. On its upper floors purportedly lives a ghost, said to be of the Tudor maiden whose portrait hangs over the fireplace. ♦ Pub ♦ Daily, lunch and dinner. 33 Whitehall (between Great Scotland Yd and Craig's Ct). 930.8350. Tube: Charing Cross

10 CLARENCE

★★$ A Whitehall institution since the 18th century, this pub has great atmosphere: leaded windows, oak beams overhead, and wooden tables and pews. This is also a good choice for connoisseurs of real ale, which can be enjoyed with full bar meals. ♦ Pub ♦ Daily, lunch and dinner. 53 Whitehall (between Great Scotland Yd and Craig's Ct). 930.4808. Tube: Charing Cross

11 HUNGERFORD BRIDGE

What was once a dingy iron-sided walkway alongside the railway bridge into Charing Cross is now an impressive example of modern architecture. £40 million transformed the pedestrian bridge, which is particularly impressive at night when it is atmospherically lit up. A great way to approach the South Bank. Tube: Embankment

Restaurants/Clubs: Red | Hotels: Purple | Shops: Orange | Outdoors/Parks: Green | Sights/Culture: Blue

12 ROYAL HORSE GUARDS HOTEL

$$$$ Now part of Thistle group and once the apartments of the influential, the 280 rooms and suites, some featuring panoramic views of the Thames, are now for the affluent. The reception rooms and restaurant have the feel of an elegant country house, the lobby is light and airy, and the guest rooms are grand—some of them even have marble bathrooms! The outdoor courtyard overlooks an ornamental garden. ◆ 2 Whitehall Ct (at Whitehall Pl). 0870/333.9222; fax 925.2263. Tube: Embankment

At the Royal Horse Guards Hotel:

ONE TWO ONE TWO

★★$$$$ Just off the lobby, this dining room is decorated in traditional English style, with comfortable leather armchairs, dark wallpaper, and mahogany tables. The menu is, as you would expect, full of five-star ingredients: pâté of duck confit comes with a foie gras center, carpaccio of beef fillet comes with a lime truffle marinade, and monkfish comes on skewers with scallops and tiger prawns on mango and celeriac salad and a lime coriander marinade. The restaurant is a popular lunchtime choice with civil servants from the nearby **Ministry of Defence**. In summer, there's outdoor seating overlooking the **Victoria Embankment Gardens**, and in the evenings there is a piano bar. ◆ Modern British ◆ Daily, lunch and dinner. 451.9333

13 WHITEHALL COURT

This massive Victorian attempt at a French château was originally a grand apartment building, constructed in 1887 by **Archer and Green**. It was designed by the great Victorian architect **Alfred Waterhouse**, who also built the cathedral-like **Natural History Museum**. Both H.G. Wells and George Bernard Shaw had flats here, and it was the home of several clubs, including the **Farmers'** and the **Liberal Clubs**. It still houses the **National Liberal Club**, but after recent refurbishment, much of the building is now rented for functions. ◆ Whitehall Ct (at Horseguards Ave). Tube: Embankment

14 OLD ADMIRALTY

The **Robert Adam** stone screen adorned with sea horses that leads into the cobbled courtyard is all that can be seen of the place that ruled the waves for 200 years. The building was designed in 1725 by **Thomas Ripley**. In the **Board Room** upstairs is a wind dial dating from 1708 that still records each gust over the roof, even though no one waits here anymore for a sign that the wind will carry the French across the English Channel. The present Admiralty, or Royal Navy, still meets in the building. Smoking has never been allowed here, a rule even Winston Churchill humbly obeyed. Here Nelson both took his orders and returned 5 years later to lie in state, awaiting his funeral at **St. Paul's**. Bailey's original model for Nelson's statue in Trafalgar Square is kept here. ◆ Whitehall (between Downing St and The Mall). Tube: Charing Cross

15 MINISTRY OF DEFENCE

In this more peaceful age, the **Old War Office**, built in 1898 by **William Young & Son**, is now called the **Ministry of Defence**. Inevitably, it lacks the romance of the **Old Admiralty** across the street, but the Baroque domes above its corner towers, visible from **Trafalgar** and **Parliament Squares** as well as from **St. James's Park,** have a certain grandeur. ◆ Whitehall (at Horseguards Ave). Tube: Charing Cross

16 HORSE GUARDS PARADE

Go through the arch at **Horse Guards** to enter this parade ground with its splendid white-stone Palladian building boasting arches, pediments, and wings, architecturally one of the finest buildings in London. The parade ground used to be the **Whitehall Palace** tiltyard. In 1540, Henry VIII invited knights from all over Europe to compete in a tournament on this site.

Every year on the second or third Saturday in June, the queen leaves **Buckingham Palace** in her carriage to drive down Horse Guards Parade in the Trooping the Colour ceremony. This is the most spectacular military display of the year in a country that has no rival in matters of pomp. An annual event dating back to medieval times, it was originally an exercise to teach soldiers to recognize their regimental flags, called "the colours." Now it marks the sovereign's official birthday—ceremonial acceptance that English weather does not guarantee a successful outdoor occasion before June. Crowds line The Mall to watch the procession, but it is possible to get tickets, which are allocated by ballot, by writing to the Brigade Major (Trooping the Colour), Household Division, Horse Guards, Whitehall, London SW1A 2AX. Do not send money—instead, include a self-addressed envelope with two international reply coupons (the equivalent of British stamps). ◆ Behind Horse Guards. Tube: Charing Cross

17 HORSE GUARDS

William Kent, George II's chief architect, designed this long, picturesque—if uninspired—building as the headquarters of the king's military General Staff. It replaced a similar dilapidated structure, dating from the reign of Charles II, which had been built on the site of Henry VIII's tiltyard. Begun in 1750, the building was completed in 1758 by **John Vardy**, who took over the design project after Kent's death. Today, it's a favorite attraction for young visitors, who come to watch the pair of mounted sentries within the central archway.

The two troopers, who change duty every 2 hours, are drawn from the Cavalry Regiments of the Household Division, which protects the sovereign, better known to military buffs as the Life Guards, and the Blues and Royals. They sit, magnificent and impassive, on their horses, their uniforms elegant compositions of tunics and plumes. (The red tunics and white plumes belong to the Life Guards; the blue tunics and red plumes belong to the Blues and Royals.)

In addition to the sentries in the archway, the entire Household Division is on daily duty, and the guards are changed each day in a ceremony many Londoners and visitors prefer to that which takes place at **Buckingham Palace**. At approximately 10:30AM (9:30AM on Sunday), the new guard of the Household Division leaves **Hyde Park Barracks** to ride down Pall Mall, arriving at Horse Guards about half an hour later, at which point the old guard returns. This was an entrance to the long-gone **Whitehall Palace**. The soldiers are not allowed to talk, but once they are in position—if you don't touch their swords or their mounts—you can take photos or be photographed with them. ♦ Whitehall (between Downing St and The Mall). Recorded information 0891/505.452 (premium rate call). Tube: Charing Cross

18 BANQUETING HOUSE

On a bitter winter's day in 1649, a small procession left **St. James's Palace** and walked through the park to Whitehall. The king of England was going to his execution. Crossing Whitehall, Charles I may have had his first glimpse of the scaffold built outside the central windows of this building, which is now all that is left of the fabulous **Whitehall Palace** on this site. It would be his last look at the perfectly proportioned Palladian building commissioned by his father, James I, for grand dining occasions. Banqueting House and the fate of Charles I are inextricably bound. The proportions of the hall, one of the grandest rooms in England, create a perfect double cube at 110 feet long and 55 feet high. This design, created by **Inigo Jones** in 1622, represents the harmony of the universe, of peace, order, and power—the virtues of divine kingship instilled in Charles I by his father.

The building, possibly London's first with a façade of Portland stone, so inspired writer Horace Walpole that he dubbed it

"the model of the most pure and beautiful taste." The magnificent ceiling, which Charles commissioned from Peter Paul Rubens, represents the glorification of James I, a statement of James's belief in the absolute right and God-given power of kings. If you follow the panels from the far end of the room, you see James rising up to heaven, having created peace on earth by his divine authority as king: Peace reigns; the arts flourish; and the king is defender of his realm, the faith, and the church.

When Charles I tried to impeach five members of Parliament, civil war broke out between the Parliamentarians and the Royalists. Seven years later, he was tried in **Westminster Hall** and convicted of treason against the realm. On the day of the execution, Charles wore a second shirt so that he would not shiver in the cold and have his subjects believe he was afraid. He was a sad and courageous king in death: "I go from a corruptible to an incorruptible crown where no disturbances can be."

With one blow, England was without a king, and severed with Charles's head was the belief in the divine right of kings. Until that moment, kings were considered the chosen representatives of God on earth. But after that point, monarchs were just men and women—powerful, perhaps, but not all-powerful.

Despite being one of the most important buildings in English architecture, Banqueting House is almost always empty—but not haunted; there is no feeling that the ghost of Charles I lingers in the place where he was executed. A bust of Charles I over the staircase entrance (added by Wyatt in 1798) marks the site of the window through which he climbed onto the scaffold. ♦ Admission. M-Sa, 10AM-4:30PM; closed bank holidays. Whitehall (at Horseguards Ave). 930.4179. Tube: Embankment

19 NEW MINISTRY OF DEFENCE

Designed by **Vincent Harris** just after World War II and completed in 1959, these vast buildings were placed behind Whitehall on Horseguards Avenue out of respect for the scale and proportions of the **Banqueting House**. This ministry is where the real problems of war and peace are handled— with a few exceptions. In the basement is all that survives of the original **Whitehall Palace**: Henry VIII's wine cellar. The Tudor brick-vaulted roof is 70 feet long and 30 feet wide and weighs 800 tons. Because the wine cellar interfered with the line of the new building, it was moved 43 feet to one side, lowered 20 feet, and then pushed

---

Restaurants/Clubs: **Red** | Hotels: **Purple** | Shops: **Orange** | Outdoors/Parks: **Green** | Sights/Culture: **Blue**

back to its original site. A huge excavation was made, a mausoleum of concrete and steel was built around the cellar to protect it, and a system of rollers was devised to shift the cellar a quarter of an inch at a time until it had completed its journey. The whole operation cost £100,000, a vast sum at the time. ♦ Horseguards Ave (off Whitehall). Tube: Embankment

20 CABINET OFFICE

From 1733 to 1844, several great architects had a hand in the design of this building, including **William Kent, Sir John Soane,** and **Sir Charles Barry**. The lengthy façade exudes Victorian self-confidence and weightiness. At the north end is the office of the Privy Council, the queen's private council comprising "princes of the blood," high officers of the state, and members of Parliament appointed by the Crown. It seems fitting that a statue of Sir Walter Raleigh, created in 1959 by William Macmillan, looks on from across the road. Once a member of Elizabeth I's Privy Council, Raleigh was executed at Whitehall for conspiring against James I. Raleigh exhibited a very stiff upper lip on the scaffold. Testing the sharpness of the ax, he remarked, "This is a sharp medicine, but it will cure all diseases." The building is not open to the public. ♦ Whitehall (between Downing St and The Mall). Tube: Westminster

21 DOWNING STREET

History and television have made this street one of the most famous and familiar in the world. But politics and terrorism have caused it to be shut off from the public; it can be viewed only through a wrought-iron gate. Named after its first owner, Sir George Downing, the street retains a quiet, residential air. In 1735, **No. 10** became the official residence of the first prime minister, Sir Robert Walpole. (The prime minister now also has an official country house called Chequers.) **No. 11** is the residence of the Chancellor of the Exchequer. **No. 12** is the office of the Chief Party Whip, the title for the member of Parliament responsible for stirring up party support for bills and issues. ♦ Between Whitehall and Horse Guards Rd. Tube: Westminster

22 RICHMOND HOUSE

This building, which houses the Department of Health and Social Security, was built in 1988 by **William Whitfield** and is an example of how a clever architect can create a modern structure that blends into a historic area. Note the stone-mullioned windows and the cluster effect of the yellow brick-and-gray granite columns, neatly set back from the street. Like other government buildings, it is not open to the public. ♦ 79 Whitehall (at Richmond Terr, facing the Cenotaph). Tube: Westminster

22 RED LION

★★$ This is the MPs' pub. The original was built in 1733 and visited by Dickens when he was only 11—the author found it memorable enough to bear mention in *David Copperfield*. After being torn down, the pub was rebuilt in 1899 and has hardly changed since. The bar walls are covered with drawings, cartoons, and photographs of famous politicians. There's a nice old-fashioned dining room upstairs serving old-fashioned English food; the bar serves typical pub food such as baguettes and toasted sandwiches. Both bar and restaurant have division bells (these signal a vote is taking place on a bill being debated in Parliament), and the Parachute Regiment has its annual reunions here. ♦ Pub ♦ Pub: daily, lunch. Dining room: daily, lunch. 48 Parliament St (at Derby Gate). 930.5826. Tube: Westminster

23 CENOTAPH

Rising in the center of Whitehall is **Sir Edwin Lutyens**'s austere memorial to "The Glorious Dead" of World Wars I and II. Erected in 1920, the simple structure of Portland stone shows no sign of imperial glory or national pride or religious symbolism; it is a monument not to victory but to loss. Between the wars, men would take off their hats whenever they passed. Now hats have gone out of style and memories have faded, but once a year, on Remembrance Sunday (the second Sunday of November), an impressive service and parade is held to remember the dead of these wars. It is attended by the queen and the royal family, the prime minister, representatives of the army and navy, and leading statesmen and leaders of Commonwealth countries and the colonies. Wreaths are placed, and at 11AM, a 2-minute silence is observed. ♦ Whitehall (between King Charles and Downing Sts). Tube: Westminster

24 CABINET WAR ROOMS

Winston Churchill masterminded the British war effort from this complex 10 feet underground. The public can visit 21 of these rooms, including the one where the War Cabinet met in 1940 and 1945. The control room is still crammed with phones and maps covered with marker pins showing the positions of military defenses. Churchill made many of his stirring wartime broadcasts from the room marked "Prime Minister." It is amazing to think that he brilliantly conducted a global war from these cramped underground rooms. ♦ Admission. Apr-Sept, 9:30AM-6PM; Oct-Apr, 10AM-

WESTM

6PM. Clive Steps, King Charles St (at Horse Guards Rd). 930.6961. Tube: Westminster

25 WESTMINSTER PIER

Perhaps the only thing better than seeing London by foot is seeing London from the river. This pier is the main launching point for boat trips, either downstream to the **Tower**, Greenwich, and Thames Barrier, or upstream to the delights of **Kew Gardens**, Richmond, and **Hampton Court Palace**. There are daily cruises upstream between April and October, and downstream year-round; call the pier for more information. ◆ Victoria Embankment (just north of Westminster Bridge). 930.4097; fax 930.1616. Tube: Westminster

25 QUEEN BOADICEA

This symbol of liberty, depicting the Celtic queen looking out onto the **Houses of Parliament** from her chariot, is well placed. In AD 61, a savage revolt broke out in the newly conquered province of Britain when Roman soldiers forced their way into her palace in east England. They flogged the recently widowed queen for refusing to surrender the lands of the Iceni and raped her two daughters. In her fury, Boadicea led a fierce rebellion, massacring the inhabitants of the Roman capital at Colchester, then turning southeast to the undefended port of Londinium. No mercy was shown, and the flourishing town was quickly destroyed. Some 70,000 people lost their lives. But the revenge of the Queen of Iceni was short-lived. The Romans annihilated the tribe. Boadicea is alleged to have poisoned herself. In this bronze statue, erected in 1902 by Thomas Thorneycroft, Boadicea has her two half-naked daughters at her side. ◆ Westminster Bridge and Victoria Embankment. Tube: Westminster

26 WESTMINSTER BRIDGE

Designed by **Thomas Page**, who rebuilt it to complement **Sir Charles Barry**'s **Houses of Parliament**, this bridge is one of the best-loved vantage points in the whole of

London. You really must enjoy the greatest view of government. The Gothic almost vertically from the Thames, inspiration for poets and painters alike. The 810-foot cast-iron bridge is not the one that inspired Wordsworth to write his sonnet, but the view surpasses by far what Wordsworth noted that early morning in 1803. He would not have seen the highly wrought **Houses of Parliament** with the imposing **Victoria Tower**, nor could he have set his watch by the clock lovingly, if inaccurately, called **Big Ben**. ◆ Between York Rd and Bridge St. Tube: Westminster

27 BRITISH AIRWAYS LONDON EYE

London's hugely popular viewing point for the city is easier to get to than the Statue of Liberty in New York and more fun than the Eiffel Tower in Paris. Conceived and designed by architects **David Marks** and **Julia Barfield**, the Eye stands 450 feet high. The pods are spacious and feel totally safe—even for those nervous about heights. When the weather is really hot, owing to the fact that it is not allowable to open a window (for obvious reasons), the pods do have a tendancy to overheat. Of course the weather in London rarely gets really hot. Each "flight" (as they are called) takes 30 minutes—meaning that your pod revolves at 26cm per minute. So it's not one for speed freaks! One of the pods has just seen its first wedding ceremony take place as the wheel went around. If you want something extra, there are Champagne Flights and Mince Pie and Mulled Wine Flights at Christmas. The Eye is unbelievably popular, so book in advance. ◆ Daily, (June-Sept) 10AM-9PM, (Oct-May) 10AM-8PM. Fee: adults £15 (£14.50 if pre-booked), children 5-15 years £7.50. South Bank SE1 (right alongside County Hall). 0870/500.0600. Tube: Westminster. www.londoneye.com

28 COUNTY HALL

Look across the Thames from **Westminster Pier**, and you're sure to be taken aback by the palatial sweep of crescent-shaped County Hall—well, the former County Hall. Designed by **Ralph Knott** for the London County Council and built between 1911–1922 and 1931-1933, the building eventually formed the headquarters of the Greater London Council (known as the GLC) in 1965. In 1986, the GLC was abolished by the Tory government, and the 2,390 rooms and 10 miles of corridors became empty.

Restaurants/Clubs: Red | Hotels: Purple | Shops: Orange | Outdoors/Parks: Green | Sights/Culture: Blue

Now there are various attractions, a couple of hotels, and a plethora of eateries.

Trivia buffs will be interested to learn that in the early 18th century, a stoneworks on the site of County Hall took out a patent on a particular type of terra-cotta, which was later improved by a woman named Eleanor Coade and thus was named Coade stone. Strong, appealing, and amazingly weather-proof, Coade stone was used to build the **Royal Opera House**, **Somerset House**, and the **Bank of England**, among other structures. Yet when the stone yard closed in 1840, the secret of Coade stone died with it, and subsequent attempts to analyze its composition failed. ♦ Belvedere Rd (at Westminster Bridge). Tube: Westminster

Within County Hall:

London Aquarium

Lurking underneath the County Hall is £25 million worth of Europe's largest aquatic exhibition: 9 millimeters of acrylic is all that stands between you and 1 million liters of water in which live 3,000 examples of marine life from coral reefs to sharks. The Aquarium is divided into 14 zones, each one representing the different kinds of waters in the world—streams to oceans, fresh to salt, tropical to Arctic. There are talks and demonstration dives, and you can even get up close and personal in the ray pool at feeding time. ♦ Daily, 10AM-6PM. Fee: adults $13.25, children $11.25 (25% discount if you book online). Shop: daily until 9PM. 967.8000. Tube: Westminster/Waterloo

Dalí Universe

This marvelous gallery is dedicated to the outrageous **Salvador Dalí**. It was created by **Bernard Levi**, a personal friend of the artist. The Spanish surrealist's cultivated eccentric-ity and rampant exhibitionism are explored in a collection of about 500 works, catalogued in themes, which makes for illuminating viewing. It also boasts the largest existing collection of Dalí's sculpture.

County Hall Gallery

There are three major spaces in the County Hall Gallery, one of which houses the permanent Dalí exhibition (see above). The other two house temporary exhibitions, but always of great works and well-chosen cutting-edge stuff. ♦ Daily, 10AM-6PM. Fee: adults $12, children $10. 0870/744.7485. www.countyhallgallery.com

THEBOOKSTORE@COUNTY HALL GALLERY

This great little shop, a treasure trove for Dalí fans, sells books, posters, desk toys, T-shirts, and the whole surreal thing. ♦ Daily, 10AM-6:30PM. 450.7601

28 London County Hall Premier Inn

$$ This hotel represents pretty good value in a city where there is not much bang for the US buck. Its location alone should double its price, but it doesn't. Rooms are decent-sized, beds are spacious and comfy, and all are en-suite and nicely kitted out. There are also family rooms, which are an even better value. There is Wi-Fi Internet access here, a decent enough restaurant that does breakfast best, and a fully licensed bar. Neither restaurant nor bar is exactly a "destination," but then, you'll be out sightseeing and trying other restaurants in your Access Guide, won't you? ♦ Belvedere Road. 0780/238.3300. www.premierinn.com

28 South Bank Lion

The 12-foot-high lion that guards the southern end of **Westminster Bridge** was originally created for the long-gone **Lion Brewery**. The regal beast weighs in at 13 tons of Coade stone. ♦ Westminster Bridge Rd (at Westminster Bridge). Tube: Westminster

29 London Marriott Hotel County Hall

$$$$ Superior accommodations plus an enviable location on the River Thames opposite the **Houses of Parliament** put this hotel high on the list of London's great places to stay if you're in town on a holiday. Many of the 200 rooms (five of which are suites) have river views. Beds are dressed in Egyptian cotton-rich linen, rooms have individual climate control, there is high-speed Internet and personal voice mail, and guests are provided comfy slippers and a fluffy bathrobe. There is a good business center for those who are not here just for fun, a secretarial service, limousine service, 24-hour room service, and the largest and most extensive pool and gym facilities of any London hotel. The Marriott has **Leader's Bar** (fine wines, premier spirits), the **Library Lounge** (which does a decent afternoon tea with a great view of Big Ben), the **Rotunda Lounge** (for breakfast with views you will never forget), and the **County Restaurant** (five-star international dining). ♦ Westminster Bridge Rd. 928.5200; fax 928.5300. Tube: Westminster. www.marriott.com

29 Florence Nightingale Museum

Devoted to the famous "lady of the lamp" who transformed nursing into a proper, disciplined profession, this museum is appropriately sited at **St. Thomas's Hospital**, where Florence Nightingale inspired the founding of Britain's first school of nursing, in 1860. (The hospital is still in use, having been rebuilt after suffering damage during World War II.) The museum has tableaux of her time in the Crimea, plus personal belongings, including her medicine bag and the famous lamp. There are also photographs and documents portraying the development of health care as pioneered by this illustrious lady, who died, aged 90, in 1910. ♦ Admission. M–Sa, 10AM–5PM. 2 Lambeth Palace Rd (at Westminster Bridge Rd). 620.0374. Tube: Westminster/Waterloo

30 GUARDS MUSEUM

If you would like to learn more about the five regiments of foot soldiers who take part in the Changing of the Guard ceremony, this is the place to visit. You'll find lots of memorabilia, the scarlet uniforms and bushy helmets, tableaux, and displays explaining the history of the regiments and their duties. There's also a shop. ♦ Admission. Daily, Feb–mid-Dec. Wellington Barracks, Birdcage Walk (between Queen Anne's and Buckingham Gates). 930.4466 ext 3271. Tube: St. James's Park

31 THE TWO CHAIRMEN

★★$$ The 18th-century pub takes its name from the chair carriers who brought customers to the Royal Cockpit (where cockfights were staged for the entertainment of the king and his court), and stood on the adjacent Cockpit Steps until 1810. (To reach the pub, climb up Cockpit Steps off Birdcage Walk to Dartmouth Street.) In the Sedan Room (the chairs were called sedans) you can lunch on steak-and-ale pie or fish and chips. ♦ Pub ♦ Daily, lunch. 39 Dartmouth St (at Queen Anne's Gate). 222.8694. Tube: St. James's Park

32 PARLIAMENT SQUARE

Sir Charles Barry conceived this square as a kind of garden foreground to his new **Houses of Parliament**, and it was thus laid out in 1850. Today, it forms an open-air sculpture gallery for prime ministers and other statesmen, although they suffered in the interests of progress. (The square was a construction site for the Jubilee Underground line, which was completed in 2000.) A 12-foot bronze sculpture by Ivor Robert Jones shows a determined-looking Winston Churchill standing on the corner gazing at the **House of Commons**, where he was once a leader. Among the many other brooding statesmen here are Disraeli (Lord Beaconsfield), erected in 1883 by Raggi, and Abraham Lincoln, tall and rumpled. His statue is a copy of the one by Augustus St.-Gaudens in Lincoln Park, Chicago. ♦ Bounded by Bridge and Great George Sts and by St. Margaret and Parliament Sts. Tube: Westminster

33 QUEEN ANNE'S GATE

This lovely street is lined with wonderful 18th-century houses; note that the doors are wide enough to allow passage of the popular sedan chairs of the period, as well as crinolined ladies. You'll also see boot scrapers, the occasional torchlight snuffer, and a statue of Queen Anne at **No. 15**. Beyond the statue, the houses (dating from 1704) have doorways topped by lacy-looking wooden canopies. ♦ Between Petty France and Dartmouth St. Tube: St. James's Park

34 WESTMINSTER ARMS

★★$ Home-cooked steak, kidney pie, and real ale make this pub popular with MPs, journalists, and young clerics in the neighborhood who are summoned to lunch by bells—in the past, by the Division Bell in the pub, and nowadays, by the church bells next door. ♦ Pub ♦ M–F, lunch and dinner; Sa, Su, lunch. 9 Storey's Gate (between Parker and Lewisham Sts). 222.8520. Tube: St. James's Park

35 WESTMINSTER CENTRAL HALL

This domed historic hall, an international headquarters for Methodism, was built by **E.A. Rickards** and **H.V. Lancester** in 1912; the dome is the third largest in London, after those of **St. Paul's** and the **Reading Room** of the **British Library**. In addition to being a place of worship, the hall hosts concerts and exhibitions. ♦ Chapel: daily. Services: Su, 11AM, 6:30PM. Storey's Gate and Tothill St. Tube: St. James's Park

Within Westminster Central Hall:

THE CAFÉ

★$ Head to this downstairs eatery for a full English breakfast. Soup and sandwiches are offered for lunch. It's a simple but welcome respite from the abbey crowds. ♦ Café ♦ M–Sa, breakfast and lunch. 222.8010

36 ST. MARGARET'S

A few of this church's historical highlights: Sir Walter Raleigh, who was beheaded out

---

Restaurants/Clubs: Red | Hotels: Purple | Shops: Orange | Outdoors/Parks: Green | Sights/Culture: Blue

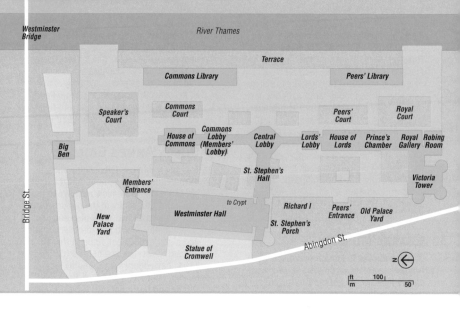

Westminster Bridge

River Thames

Terrace

Commons Library

Peers' Library

Speaker's Court

Commons Court

Peers' Court

Royal Court

House of Commons

Commons Lobby (Members' Lobby)

Central Lobby

Lords' Lobby

House of Lords

Prince's Chamber

Royal Gallery

Robing Room

Big Ben

Members' Entrance

St. Stephen's Hall

Victoria Tower

to Crypt

Richard I

Peers' Entrance

Old Palace Yard

New Palace Yard

Westminster Hall

St. Stephen's Porch

Bridge St.

Statue of Cromwell

Abingdon St.

ft 100
m 50

front in 1618, is actually buried beneath the altar; Samuel Pepys married a vivacious 15-year-old here in 1655 (he was 22); John Milton married here a year later; and Winston Churchill married here in 1908. The structure was designed in 1523 by **Robert Stowell** (the tower was added in the 18th century) and has been the parish church of the **House of Commons** since 1614. The magnificent Flemish glass window was commissioned by King Ferdinand and Queen Isabella of Spain to celebrate the engagement of their daughter Catherine of Aragon to Prince Arthur, the older brother of Henry VIII. By the time the window arrived, Henry had become king and married Catherine—by then his brother's widow. Only Henry VIII is depicted in the window. Almost anywhere else, all this would be quite enough to get one's attention, but this church has the bad luck of being wedged in between the **Houses of Parliament** and **Westminster Abbey**, which steal its thunder a bit. Treasures in the church include the font, created by Nicholas Stone in 1641; stained-glass windows in the south aisle, done by artist John Piper in 1967; the west windows, given to the church by Americans; and the Milton window, with the blind poet dictating to his daughter. A memorial window to Sir Walter Raleigh, the colonizer of Virginia, quotes American poet John Greenleaf Whittier: "The New World honours him whose lofty plea for England's freedom made her own more sure." A tablet near the altar urges: "Reader—Should you reflect on his errors Remember his many virtues And that he was a mortal." William Caxton, the father of modern printing, is buried somewhere here; ironically, his grave is unmarked. ♦ M–F 9:30AM–3:30PM, Sa 9:30AM–1:30PM, Su

2–5PM. St. Margaret St (at Parliament Sq). Tube: Westminster

37 HOUSES OF PARLIAMENT

To the modern world, no single view so powerfully symbolizes democracy as this assemblage of Gothic buildings, which look as if they have been here throughout the 900 years that this area has served as the site of British government. In fact, these buildings have been standing for less than 170 years, but their Gothic style powerfully represents the aspirations and traditions of those nine centuries. The "Symbol of Democracy" and the "Mother of Parliaments" remains a royal palace; it is officially called the **New Palace of Westminster**, a name that goes back to the 11th century, when this was the site of the **Palace of Westminster**. First occupied by Edward the Confessor, the building was the principal London residence of the monarchs until 1512, when Henry VIII moved down the street to **Whitehall Palace**. Now the resident is a commoner, the Speaker of the **House of Commons**, who has a grand apartment here. Parliament sat here until the palace burned to the ground in the disastrous fire of 1834. All that is left of the ancient Palace of Westminster is the crypt and cloisters of **St. Stephen's Chapel**, the **Jewel Tower**, and **Westminster Hall**, the long Norman hall that is the greatest window into the history of Britain's parliamentary heritage. After the fire, **Sir Charles Barry** and **Augustus Pugin** won a design competition for a new and enlarged Houses of Parliament building (to occupy the same site) in either the Gothic or Tudor style. Barry gave the buildings an almost classic body; Pugin created a meticulous and exuberant Gothic design. Built between 1840 and 1860, the Houses of Parliament are laid out on an axial plan that reflects the hierarchical nature of British society: **House of Commons**, **Commons Lobby**, **Central Lobby**, **Lords' Lobby**, **House of Lords**, **Prince's Chamber**, and **Royal Gallery** (a detailed map of the area is depicted on page 34). The complex of buildings covers an area of eight acres and has 11 courtyards, 100 staircases, almost 1,200 rooms, and two miles of passages. The House of Commons is in the northern end (MPs enter from New Palace Yard on the corner of Bridge Street and Parliament Square), and the House of Lords is in the southern end. (The Peers' entrance is in Old Palace Yard, where Guy Fawkes was hanged, drawn, and quartered in 1606 for trying to blow up the king and Parliament, and where Sir Walter Raleigh was beheaded in 1618.) ♦ Bridge St and Parliament Sq. Tube: Westminster

Within the Houses of Parliament:

WESTMINSTER HALL

Built in 1097 by William Rufus, son of William the Conqueror, this vast, barnlike room is where Parliament began and where Simon de Montfort marched in and enforced it. At the end of the 14th century, Richard II had the hall rebuilt by **Henry Yevele**, who added the massive buttresses that support 600 tons of oak roof. The hall contains the oldest surviving example of an oak hammer beam roof, created by Hugh Herland; it was a miracle of engineering in its day, marking the end of supporting piers. The austere and venerable room has witnessed earthshaking moments of history almost since its beginning. Under the benevolent eyes of the carved angels in the arches of the beams, Richard II was deposed the year the work was completed, and Henry IV was declared king. In 1535, Sir Thomas More, former Speaker of the **House of Commons**, stood trial here for treason against his former friend and tennis partner, Henry VIII, and was beheaded on Tower Hill. Seventy years later, on 5 November 1605, England's most famous terrorist, Guy Fawkes, was captured and subsequently tried and convicted for the crime of trying to blow up King James I and Parliament. Charles I stood trial in his own hall in 1649 and was convicted of treason. Oliver Cromwell, the most formidable parliamentarian who ever lived, signed the king's death warrant and had himself named Lord Protector here in 1653. After the restoration of Charles II to the throne, Cromwell was brought back to the hall—or

rather his skull was cut from his skeleton and stuck on a spike on one of the oak beams, where it rattled in the wind for 25 years before finally blowing down in a storm. And it was here that Churchill lay in state while a grateful nation paid its last respects.

CRYPT/ST. MARY'S UNDERCROFT

Though once abused and desecrated, and even used as the Speaker's coal cellar, the chapel was richly restored by **E.M. Barry** and has a wonderful pre-Raphaelite feeling. The main walls, vaulting, and bosses have withstood at least five fires. Members of both Houses of Parliament use the chapel for weddings and christenings.

ST. STEPHEN'S PORCH

The public enters the **Houses of Parliament** through this porch and hall. Be prepared for the airport-style security check, with metal-detecting arches right next to **Westminster Hall**, an understandable though inglorious entrance to the **Central Lobby**.

CENTRAL LOBBY

The crossroads of the **Palace of Westminster** connects the **House of Commons** with the **House of Lords**. Citizens meet their MPs in this octagonal vestibule. The ceiling, 75 feet above the floor, contains 250 carved bosses with Venetian mosaics that include the patron saints of England, Ireland, Scotland, and Wales. Above the ceiling is the central spire of the palace, a feature imposed on **Sir Charles Barry**'s original plans by one Dr. Reid, a ventilation expert who insisted that it be built as a shaft to expel "vitiated" air.

MEMBERS' LOBBY

Off the **Central Lobby** is the Piccadilly Circus of Commons life, where members gossip and talk to the lobby journalists. Also known as the **Commons Lobby**, it is architecturally rather bleak (most often described as neo-Gothic) and was never fully restored after the 1941 German bombing that left it in ruins. A moving reminder of the destruction is the **Churchill Arch**, made from stones damaged in the fire of 1941. Churchill proposed that it be erected in the lobby in memory of those who kept the bridge during the dark days of the war. Above the main door of the **Commons Chamber** hangs the family crest of Airey Neave, placed here after he was assassinated by terrorists in New Palace Yard in 1979.

HOUSE OF COMMONS

Each day the House opens with a procession in which the Speaker enters

(wearing a long black gown), preceded by the sergeant-at-arms, who carries a mace (the symbol of authority), and followed by the train-bearer, chaplain, and secretary. The day begins with prayers, and no strangers (journalists or visitors) are ever admitted. When praying, MPs face the seats behind them—an extraordinary sight—because in the days when they wore swords it was impossible to kneel on the floor; therefore, they turned to kneel on the benches behind them. Every member has to swear loyalty to the Crown (a problem for the occasional MP from Northern Ireland), although no monarch has been allowed to enter the House of Commons since 1642, when Charles I burst in to arrest his parliamentary opponents. The House of Commons was completely destroyed in the air raid of 10 December 1941, and was rebuilt in 1950 by **Sir Giles Gilbert Scott**, simply and without decoration and, under Winston Churchill's influence, in the exact proportions of the prewar building. It is impressively small: Only 436 of the 659 members can actually sit down at any one time; the rest often can be seen crowding around the door and the Speaker's chair or sitting on the steps. The lack of space is considered to be fundamental to the sense of intimacy and conversational form of debate that characterize the House. Equally important is the layout of the Chamber, with the party in office (called the Government) and the Opposition facing each other, their green leather benches two sword lengths apart and separated by two red lines on the floor, which no member is allowed to cross while addressing the Chamber. The **Press Gallery** and the **Public Gallery** are located at opposite ends of the Chamber.
◆ Sessions: M–Th, 2:30PM–closing (often late); W, 9:30AM–2PM; F, 9:30AM–3PM. Prime Minister's question time: W, 3–3:30PM. Tours of the building for overseas visitors are possible, generally on Friday afternoon. Write at least 2 weeks in advance to the Public Information Office. 219.4272; fax 219.5839

HOUSE OF LORDS

This is the most elaborate part of **Sir Charles Barry**'s design and **Augustus Pugin**'s ultimate masterpiece: Victorian, romantic, and stunning. At 80 feet long, it is not grand in size, but it is extravagantly ornate. Stained-glass windows cast a dark red light, and 18 statues of the barons of the Magna Carta stare down from the walls. Their saintlike demeanor emphasizes the sacred look of the room, but the long red-leather sofas on either side suggest a chapel of sorts. Between the two sofas is the "Woolsack" (the traditional seat of the

Lord Chancellor), a huge red pouffe stuffed with bits of wool collected from all over the Commonwealth. Under an immense gilded canopy is the ornate throne reserved for the queen. ◆ Sessions: M–W, 2:30PM–closing; Th, 3PM–closing; F, 11AM–midafternoon (occasionally). 219.3107; fax 219.5979

Outside the Houses of Parliament:

BIG BEN

Here is the most beloved image in all of London, towering 320 feet over the Thames and lighting up the sky. Every guidebook will tell you that Big Ben refers to the bell, not the clock; however, in people's hearts, the **Clock Tower** (officially known as **St. Stephen's Tower**), is, and always will be, Big Ben. The clock's four dials are 23 feet wide. The hands are each as tall as a red London double-decker bus. The pendulum, which beats once every 2 seconds, is 13 feet long and weighs 685 pounds. Besides being endearing, the clock is a near-perfect timekeeper. After an extensive restoration a few years ago, the Clock Tower emerged several shades lighter and glistening—4,000 books of gold leaf were used to regild the gold surfaces. The initial plan had been to restore the hands to their original color, but when it was found that they were blue (the color of the Conservative party), it was felt that Big Ben could not be partisan, so they were painted black instead (or so some people say). The hours are struck on the 13.5-ton bell, which was named Big Ben allegedly after Sir Benjamin Hall, the first Commissioner of Works, when the bell was hung. Since 1885, a light has been shining in the tower at night when Parliament is sitting.

VICTORIA TOWER

Sir Charles Barry saw the **Palace of Westminster** as a legislative castle, and this was to be its keep, its great ceremonial entrance. When it was built in 1860, the 336-foot tower was the tallest in the world—taller than early American skyscrapers—and it is still the world's highest square masonry tower. The tower's gateway is the entrance the queen uses for the richly ceremonial State Opening of Parliament each November. It is now an archive of more than three million parliamentary documents dating back to 1497, including the death warrant of Charles I and a master copy of every act of Parliament since 1497. During the day, the Union Jack flies when Parliament is sitting, and the Royal Standard is raised when the queen is present.

STATUE OF CROMWELL

The godlike statue of Oliver Cromwell caused so much controversy when Sir Hamo

Thornycroft finished it in 1899 that Parliament refused to pay for it (mainly owing to protests from the Irish Party). Eventually, Lord Rosebery, who was prime minister at the time, paid for the statue personally. An interesting speculation is why Cromwell has been placed in exactly this spot: He looks straight across the street at the bust of the man he helped do away with—the executed Charles I, whose face is sculpted into the top of the doorway of St. Margaret's church.

38 WESTMINSTER ABBEY

This is one of the finest French-English Gothic buildings in the world. Officially called the **Collegiate Church of St. Peter**, it is also the most faithful and intimate witness of British history. The abbey has survived the Reformation, the Blitz, and, requiring even more miraculous tenacity, nine centuries of visitors, pilgrims, worshipers, wanderers, and tourists.

It is almost impossible to see the abbey without being surrounded by thousands of tourists, either moving aimlessly down the aisles or purposefully following a raised umbrella beneath which a voice reels off abbey highlights. If possible, come here for a service, when the abbey empties of gawkers and regains some of its serenity. (Note that visitors may not walk around the abbey during services.) In any case, try to avoid it in the morning—unless you attend the blissfully quiet 8AM communion service—when all the guided bus tours in London visit Westminster Abbey (even more hectic because they combine a stop here with the Changing of the Guard spectacle).

Once upon a time, this really was an abbey, a monastic community designed for a life of self-sufficient contemplation, with cloisters, refectory, abbot's residence, orchards, workshops, and kitchen gardens. According to legend, the first church was built in the seventh century by Sebert, King of the East Saxons, and St. Peter himself appeared at the consecration. A Benedictine abbey was also founded; it was called **Westminster** ("west church") because it was west of the City of London. The existence of the abbey as it appears today is credited to the inspired determination of Edward the Confessor, who in 1050 set to work on a great monastery to promote the glory of God. To supervise the progress of the abbey and efficiently preside over his kingdom of England, he moved his palace next door—hence, the **Palace of Westminster**—and established the bond between church and state that has endured ever since.

Edward the Confessor was brought up in Normandy and built his abbey in a Norman style, advanced far beyond anything that had ever been seen in England. [...] to attend the consecration [...] which took place on 28 De[...] king died a week later. No one knows if his successor, Harold, was crowned here or at St. Paul's, but after Harold's death at the Battle of Hastings, William the Conqueror was crowned here on Christmas Day 1066—the ceremony procedure was written down in the 14th century and remains unchanged. Since 1066, the kings and queens of England have all been crowned here, with two exceptions: Edward V, presumed murdered; and Edward VIII, who ascended to the throne on his father's death but was never crowned, having abdicated because of his relationship with the divorced Wallis Simpson.

In 1245, Henry III rebuilt the now-canonized **St. Edward's Church** in a more magnificent style. Influenced by the French Gothic style of the cathedrals of Amiens and Reims (La Sainte Chapelle in Paris was being built at the same time), Henry started to build, at his own expense, the soaring and graceful church that is here today. The king's architect, **Henry de Reyn** (i.e., "of Reims"), worked with great speed in cathedral terms. By 1259, the chancel, transepts, part of the nave, and the chapter house were complete, giving the medieval church a remarkable unity of style. The nave, continued in the late 14th century by **Henry Yevele** (the master mason who built **Westminster Hall**), was built in the style originally planned by Henry de Reyn. The only important additions to Henry III's church have been the Henry VII Chapel, begun in 1503 and believed by many to be the most beautiful and most perfect building in England, and the towers on the west front, built in the 18th century from the designs of **Christopher Wren** and **Nicholas Hawksmoor**.

The best way to enter the abbey is under the towers by the **West Door**, where you can take in the majestic height of the roof: 102 feet to the exalted vault, the pale stone touched with gold and tinted by the colored glass of the aisle windows. The eye is pulled upward by the sheer beauty of it all, then immediately distracted by the white-marble figures. (For a general floor plan of the abbey, see page 38.)

Standing at the entrance, you see the impressive length of the stone-flagged nave and the decorated choir screen in front of the nave (some say too gold, too gaudy, too late; it was created by Edward Blore in 1834). Above are 16 Waterford chandeliers presented by the Guinness family in 1965 to mark the 900th anniversary of the consecration of the abbey.

Immediately in front of you, beside the green marble slab honoring Winston Churchill, is the **Tomb of the Unknown Warrior**, a nameless British soldier brought to the abbey

---

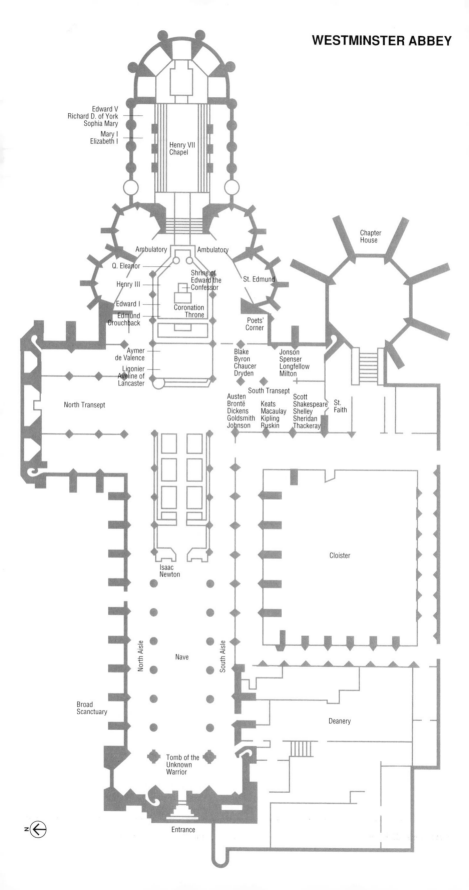

WESTMINSTER ABBEY

Edward V
Richard D. of York
Sophia Mary
Mary I
Elizabeth I

Henry VII
Chapel

Ambulatory   Ambulatory

Chapter
House

Q. Eleanor

Henry III

Edward I

Edmund
Crouchback

Shrine of
Edward the
Confessor

St. Edmund

Coronation
Throne

Poets'
Corner

Aymer
de Valence

Ligonier
Aveline of
Lancaster

Blake   Jonson
Byron   Spenser
Chaucer   Longfellow
Dryden   Milton

St.
Faith

North Transept

South Transept

Austen   Scott
Brontë   Keats   Shakespeare
Dickens Macaulay Shelley
Goldsmith Kipling Sheridan
Johnson Ruskin Thackeray

Isaac
Newton

Cloister

North Aisle

South Aisle

Nave

Broad
Scanctuary

Deanery

Tomb of the
Unknown
Warrior

z⊙

Entrance

from France on 11 November 1920. The flag that covered the coffin hangs nearby, alongside the Congressional Medal of Honor. The poppy-covered coffin contains earth and clay from France, a terrible and moving reminder of a whole generation lost. His was the last full-bodied burial in the abbey.

To your right is **St. George's Chapel**, the **"Warrior's Chapel,"** with an altar by Sir Ninian Comper and a tablet on the west wall commemorating the one million men from the Empire and the Commonwealth who died in World War I. A memorial to Franklin D. Roosevelt hangs here. Just outside the chapel is a haunting portrait of the young Richard II. It is the first genuine portrait of a king painted in his lifetime. The sad brevity of Richard's life seems to show in his face. Looking toward the abbey center, Blore's choir screen jolts a bit. Its bright gold drains the color from Lord Stanhope and Sir Isaac Newton, who are framed within the arches. Near Newton, a bevy of Nobel scientists are gathered, including Charles Darwin, who used science to destroy the myth of creation, and Lord Rutherford, who unsettled creation by splitting the atom.

Behind the screen is the choir. The choir stalls are Victorian, but the choir itself has been in this position since Edward the Confessor's own abbey stood on the site. The organ was installed in 1730, but it has been uplifted, rebuilt, and enlarged. Organists at the abbey have been quite distinguished, including Orlando Gibbons, John Blow, and his pupil, English composer Henry Purcell.

Because the **North Transept** has **Solomon's Porch**, one of the main entrances to the abbey, it is usually thronging with people. Still, persevere until you reach **St. Michael's Chapel** in the east aisle and Roubilliac's monument to Lady Elizabeth Nightingale (no relation to Florence). The poor woman was frightened by lightning and died of a miscarriage. She collapses into her husband's arms, while he, frantic and helpless with fear, watches Death, a wretched skeleton, aim its spear at her. A little beyond this chapel, beside the Blore screen, is the paying entrance to the rest of the abbey, including the royal chapels, the sanctuary, the **Lady Chapel**, and **Poets' Corner**. Kings and queens have been crowned in the sanctuary itself since the time of Richard II in 1377. A platform is created under the central space (the lantern) between the choir and the sanctuary. The **Coronation Chair** is brought from the **Confessor's Chapel** and placed in front of the high altar. Since the coronation of Charles I, the anthem "I was glad when they said unto me/We will go into the House of the Lord" is begun as soon as the sovereign enters the **West Door**. When Queen Elizabeth entered the choir for her coronation in 1953, under the eyes of God and the television cameras, a chorus of "Vivat, vivat, vivat regina Elizabetha" rang out from the voices of **Westminster School**'s scholars. There was an elaborate ceremony of oath taking, a service of holy communion, and anointment with special oil. Then, robed in gold and delivered with ring, scepter, and orb, the queen was crowned by the archbishop.

To the north are the three finest medieval tombs in the abbey: Edmond Crouchback, Earl of Lancaster and youngest son of Henry III; his wife, the rich and pretty Aveline of Lancaster (theirs was the first marriage in the new abbey in 1269); and Amyer de Valence, Earl of Pembroke.

Behind the high altar is the **Shrine of Edward the Confessor**. This is the most sacred part of the abbey, the destination of pilgrims, particularly on St. Edward's Day (13 October). The Purbeck marble tomb contains the body of the king-turned-saint. Beside him lie Henry III, who built the church in homage to the Confessor; Henry's son Edward I, the first king to be crowned in the present building; and his beloved Queen Eleanor, for whom he set up what became known as the Eleanor Crosses (the original Charing Cross was one). The crosses marked the places where her funeral cortège stopped to rest along the way from Lincoln to the abbey.

The Coronation Chair, when not in use for coronations, stands behind the high altar. Built in 1300, the wooden chair was designed to incorporate the **Stone of Scone** (pronounced *Skoon*) but there is an empty space there now. In 1996, the stone—which had been part of the Scottish throne since the 9th century but was spirited out of Scotland by Edward I in 1297 and placed in the chair—was ceremoniously returned and is now on display in Edinburgh Castle. The Stone in the Throne represented the union of the two countries, a union that, even 600 years later, is not without resistance. (The stone was even stolen from the abbey for a few weeks by Scottish nationalists in 1952.) The graffiti on the throne is blamed on 18th-century schoolboys from **Westminster School**. A truly wonderful part of the abbey is the **Henry VII Chapel** (officially, the **Lady Chapel**). Except in high summer, the chapel is quieter and less crowded than the rest of the building—a blessing, as this is one of the most beautiful places you may ever see. Notice the exquisite tracery of the fan vaulting, intricacies, and ecstasies of stone, Matisse-like in their exuberance; the high, wooden choir stalls that line the nave—and their misericords (carvings located beneath the seats), including a woman beating

---

her husband, and mermaids, mermen, and monkeys; the black-and-white marble floor; and throughout, the royal badges, a kind of illustrated Shakespeare of Tudor roses, leopards of England, the fleur-de-lys of France, the portcullis of the Beauforts, greyhounds, falcons, and daisy roots. This is the Renaissance in England, and heaven is on earth in a world alive with confidence, harmony, beauty, and art. The chapel is the grand farewell to the great Gothic style and forms the perfect setting for flags of the Order of the Bath, the chivalrous knights whose tradition dates back to 1399.

In the aisles on both sides of the chapel are a few unforgettable tombs. In the south aisle rests the effigy of Lady Margaret Beaufort, created by Torrigiani. The mother of Henry VII, she was a remarkable Renaissance woman devoted to education, the arts, and the journey of her soul. Her effigy, one of the finest in the abbey, shows a delicately lined face with gentle sensitivity. "Having restored religion to its original sincerity, established peace, restored money to its proper value. . . ." Most world leaders would give anything to merit an epitaph like that, but it seems rather an understatement for Queen Elizabeth I. Her four-poster tomb in the north aisle reflects Gloriana gloriously, although ironically she is buried with her half-sister, Mary I, who imprisoned her in the **Tower of London**. (And if that weren't enough, Mary, Queen of Scots, who was beheaded at Elizabeth's order, is buried nearby too. Her tomb is directly across the way on the south side of the chapel.)

In **Innocents' Corner**, at the end of the aisle, are effigies of the two infant daughters of James I: Sophia, under her velvet coverlet, died at birth; and Mary, leaning on one elbow, died at age 2. Both look like small dolls. Close by lie the bones of two children found in the Tower and brought here by order of Charles II in 1674. They are believed to be Edward V and his brother Richard, sons of Edward IV and allegedly murdered by their uncle Richard III in 1483.

In 1889, Henry James came to Westminster Abbey for the memorial service of Robert Browning, whose ashes were being consigned to Poets' Corner. Afterward he wrote that Browning stood for "the thing that, as a race, we like best—the fascination of faith, the acceptance of life, the respect for its mysteries, the endurance of its charges, the vitality of will, the validity of character, the beauty of action, the seriousness, above all, of the great human passion." James's testimony to Browning seems a perfect testimony to Anglo-Saxon England, Westminster Abbey, and above all, to its Poets' Corner, where the recognition is the greatest a generous nation has to confer. Despite its name, this section is not a corner (it fills an entire transept on the south side of the nave), nor is it exclusively devoted to poets (it pays tribute

to other writers, musicians, and performing artists).

All those honored here are not buried here, although Charles Dickens is (against his wishes), as is Thomas Hardy (but his heart is buried in his beloved Dorset). The honored include Geoffrey Chaucer, Edmund Spenser, Ben Jonson (who is buried upright elsewhere in the abbey!), William Shakespeare, John Milton, John Dryden, Dr. Samuel Johnson, Thomas Gray, Richard Brinsley Sheridan, Oliver Goldsmith, William Blake, William Wordsworth, Samuel Taylor Coleridge, Percy Bysshe Shelley, John Keats, Thomas Babington Macaulay, Jane Austen, the Brontë sisters, Sir Walter Scott, William Makepeace Thackeray, Henry Wadsworth Longfellow, John Ruskin, Rudyard Kipling, Lord Byron, George Eliot, Dylan Thomas, W.H. Auden, D.H. Lawrence, Lewis Carroll, Gerard Manley Hopkins, and Henry James. One of the newest stones, a memorial to the writers of World War I, was unveiled on 11 November 1985. Among those mentioned are Rupert Brooke, Robert Graves, Herbert Read, Siegfried Sassoon, and William Owen. Above the dates 1914–1918 is a quotation from Owen: "My subject is War, and the pity of War. The poetry is in the pity." And the ashes of Lord Olivier, one of the finest British actors, were interred in 1990—a fitting tribute to this well-loved artist.

Ninety-minute Supertours of the nave, choir, **Statesman's Aisle**, Poets' Corner, **Royal Chapels**, and Coronation Chair are offered Monday through Friday at 10AM, 11AM, 2PM, and 3PM and on Saturday at 10AM, 11AM, and 12:30PM. (The **Jericho Parlour** and **Jerusalem Chamber** can be seen only on this tour.) Reservations should be made in the south aisle of the nave. Note: Photography is not allowed anywhere in the abbey. ♦ At press time, there were plans to charge admission; the nave will remain free. Nave and cloisters: daily. Royal Chapels (including Poets' Corner): M-Sa. Services: M-F, 7:30AM, 8AM, 12:30PM, 5PM; Sa, 8AM, 9:20AM, 3PM; Su, 8AM, 10AM, 11:15AM, 3PM, 6:30PM. The Sanctuary (off Broad Sanctuary). 222.7110. Tube: Westminster, St. James's Park

Within Westminster Abbey:

ABBEY BOOKSHOP

Just inside the main entrance, to the right, is the official abbey shop, where you can buy books, postcards, drawings—and even **Westminster Abbey** fudge. ♦ M-Sa, 9:15AM-4:45PM. 654.4900

CHAPTER HOUSE

From 1257 until Henry VIII's reign, this exquisite octagon with a Purbeck marble roof (completed in 1250) served as the Parliament House for the Commons. ♦ Admission. Daily. 654.4900

PYX CHAMBER

Built circa 1090 and once the monastery treasury, this structure passed to the Crown during the Dissolution. Today, it contains the oldest altar in the abbey, dating from circa 1240. The word *pyx* referred to the large wooden chests that once held the standard gold and silver pieces against which coins were annually tested. ♦ Admission. Currently closed for renovation. 223.0019

GREAT CLOISTER

The courtyard offers a breathtaking view of the flying buttresses on the south side of the **Lady Chapel**. There is a coffee stall and a brass-rubbing center. ♦ M–Sa. 654.4900

WESTMINSTER ABBEY MUSEUM

The museum is housed within the vaulted undercroft beneath the former monks' dormitory. The centerpiece of the exhibition is the abbey's collection of royal and other effigies, which includes the effigy of Charles II (died 1685), dressed in his own garter robes, recently restored and cleaned in the textile conservation workshop of the Victoria and Albert Museum. There is also the funeral effigy of Henry VII (died 1509), taken from a death mask, and an effigy of Admiral Nelson with his famous hat and eye patch. There are replicas of the coronation regalia, the funeral armor of Henry V, alabaster carvings by Grinling Gibbons, and some lovely medieval glass panels.

Beside Westminster Abbey:

DEAN'S YARD

This is the point where Parliament meets public school. You can go through the iron gate to the charming tree-shaded yard behind the abbey. The yard and the buildings of **Westminster School** are also in **Little Dean's Yard**, which can be viewed through an arch on the square's east side, and are not normally open to the public; however, visits may be arranged (but are limited during term time). Write well in advance to The Domestic Bursar, Westminster School, Dean's Yard, London SW1P 3PF. The gate at the back of Dean's Yard leads to tranquil Great College Street, dating from 1722.

BROAD SANCTUARY

The west entrance of Westminster Abbey (the usual entrance for visitors) faces an area known as Broad Sanctuary. This takes its name from the section surrounding the west side of the abbey, which gave fugitives a safe haven from civil law in the Middle Ages. The most famous asylum seeker was probably Elizabeth Woodville, wife of Edward IV, who came here with her sons, the sad and tragic Little Princes. ♦ Between Parliament Sq and Victoria St. Tube: Westminster

39 BLEW COAT SCHOOL NATIONAL TRUST

This delightful shop is chock-full of English country-house accessories and gifts, such as tea towels, tea cozies, diaries, candles, fragrances, and books. Many items display designs inspired by the palatial properties under the care of the National Trust, the organization that maintains stately homes as well as much of the English countryside and coastline. This building is historic in its own right. Erected in 1709, it once served as a school for poor children. Notice the little statues of a boy and girl at the back of the building. ♦ M–F, 10AM–5PM, with late closing Th—open till 7PM. 23 Caxton St (at Buckingham Gate). 222.2877. Tube: St. James's Park. A smaller range of items is available at 1a St. Christopher's Pl (at Barrett St). 224.0488. Tube: Bond St

40 JEWEL TOWER

In 1365-1366, Edward III had the tower built, probably by **Henry Yevele**, to hold his jewels, silver and gold vessels, clothes, and furs—a sort of glorified warehouse. This surviving part of the original royal **Palace of Westminster** has a chunky look, with narrow, round-arched windows—this is also how the abbey looked before it was rebuilt in the Gothic style we see today. ♦ Admission. Daily. Abingdon St (at Old Palace Yd). 222.2219. Tube: Westminster

41 ABBEY GARDEN

This quiet and simply laid out 900-year-old garden (it claims to be the oldest cultivated garden in England) is known for its lavender. In July and August, there are lunchtime band concerts. ♦ Nominal admission. Tu, Th. Great College St and College Mews. Tube: Westminster, St. James's Park

42 VICTORIA TOWER GARDENS

These gardens overlooking the Thames are ideal for a picnic lunch or an afternoon nap. Two varying principles of heroism can be found in the sculpture: A.G. Walker's statue of Emmeline Pankhurst, the leader of the women's suffrage movement, who lived from 1858 to 1928 and was often imprisoned for her beliefs; and a replica (1915) of Rodin's *Burghers of Calais* (1895), a monument to those who surrendered to Edward III in 1347 rather than see their town destroyed. ♦ Off Millbank (between Lambeth Bridge and Abingdon St). Tube: Westminster

---

Restaurants/Clubs: Red | Hotels: Purple | Shops: Orange | Outdoors/Parks: Green | Sights/Culture: Blue

43 ST. JOHN'S, SMITH SQUARE

Itzhak Perlman and Yo-Yo Ma have given lunchtime concerts in this church, along with the **Allegri**, **Endymion**, and **Amadeus Quartets** and the **Academy of London Orchestra**. The musical reputation is high indeed, partly because each Monday the concerts are broadcast live on BBC Radio 3. The church was built in 1728 by **Thomas Archer** and is original, idiosyncratic, and personal. After near destruction by bombs in 1941, it was rebuilt in 1965-1969 by architect **Marshall Sisson**. ♦ Smith Sq (bounded by Dean Stanley and Dean Trench Sts and by Dean Bradley and Lord North Sts). 222.2168, box office 222.1061. Tube: St. James's Park, Westminster

44 LAMBETH BRIDGE

Built in 1929-1932, this ornate bridge replaced the one erected in 1861. Before any bridge spanned the Thames here, there was a ferry to carry horses across the river, with the money going to the Archbishop of Canterbury. However, his little moneymaker came to a halt when the first **Westminster Bridge** opened downriver in 1750, and by an act of Parliament, he was compensated for his loss of income in the amount of £2,205.
♦ Between Lambeth Palace Rd and Millbank. Tube: Westminster

45 LAMBETH PALACE

The London home of the Archbishop of Canterbury, the religious head of the Church of England for 800 years, the palace is mostly hidden behind high walls. However, visible from the riverfront are some 14th- and 15th-century towers. The most important, **Lollard's Tower**, was where, during the reign of Cromwell, the royalist poet Sir Richard Lovelace was imprisoned and wrote the famous line "Stone walls do not a prison make, nor iron bars a cage." Facing **St. Mary's** church nearby is **Morton's Tower and Gate**, dating from 1485 and an outstanding example of an early Tudor brick building; it is still used as the main entrance to the palace. The palace is not open to the public. ♦ Lambeth Palace Rd (between Lambeth Rd and Royal St). Tube: Westminster, Lambeth North

46 MUSEUM OF GARDEN HISTORY

This unusual museum, which opened in 1979 in the deconsecrated 14th-century church of **St. Mary's-at-Lambeth**, next to **Lambeth Palace**, features an exhibition on the origins of domestic, decorative gardening. The subject is of avid interest to most English householders, whether they have a flower-bedecked London balcony or a country cottage garden. During the 17th century, plant pioneers John Tradescant and his son brought back such specimens as spiderwort, larch, and jasmine among rare beauties gathered during their world travels. Father and son are buried in the graveyard, which boasts a knot garden devoted to the plants they acquired. As it happens, Captain William Bligh of *Bounty* fame, who was a local resident, is also buried here; it seems appropriate because he too searched for plants—his ship was carrying breadfruit when the mutiny occurred in 1789.
♦ Free. Museum of Garden History: daily, 10AM-5PM. Lambeth Palace Rd (at Lambeth Rd). 401.8865. Tube: Westminster, Lambeth North

47 IMPERIAL WAR MUSEUM

Despite its formidable name, this huge museum devoted to the warfare of the 20th century also features interesting exhibits about the social and domestic aspects of the wars: fashions, cooking, morale boosting, and propaganda. The Blitz Experience lives up to its name, re-creating the noise, smoke, and blaring searchlights during the bombings as Londoners sheltered in the Underground. Aircraft, tanks, and artillery are on display plus photographs and paintings. There's an airy, cheerful café and a shop with some amusing cards and souvenirs. ♦ Daily. Lambeth Rd (between St. George's and Kennington Rds). 416.5000. Tube: Lambeth North

48 VAUXHALL CROSS

As you leave the **Tate Gallery**, if you look diagonally across the Thames, next to Vauxhall Bridge, you'll see an extraordinary yellow-and-green building that appears to be a modern fortress. It is, in fact, the headquarters of MI6, one of the government's secret service departments (James Bond was MI5). Notice how well its concrete façade fits its role, from the bunker effect of the lower floors to the menacing spiked windows higher up. Designed by **Terry Farrell** and completed in 1993, it has an impenetrable look with no hint of human activity inside. The building is closed to the public.
♦ Albert Embankment (at Vauxhall Bridge). Tube: Pimlico

49 TATE BRITAIN

This wonderful gallery remains accessible and welcoming despite its vast collection of more than 4,000 paintings, 50,000 prints and unique works on paper, more than 1,000 sculptures, not to mention 200 new acquisitions annually. Unable to show all its works at once, the Tate rotates the displays so that those in storage are made available and there is always something different to discover. Since the opening of its sister gallery—the **Tate Modern**—the gallery's name has been changed to Tate

THE BEST

Adele D. Evans
Freelance Radio Broadcaster/Writer

Harrods Food Hall—a feast for all the senses. Still the biggest authentic foods paradise in the metropolis with impeccable service, and the sale bargains are definitely worth a detour.

Beauchamp Place—a little road in Knightsbridge full of designer boutiques—from **Deliss** and its bespoke shoe service to **Janet Reger** with her stunning lingerie—and where it's always fun to watch the men shamefacedly returning their purchases for up- *and* downsizing.

Haymarket, Theatre Royal—catch a glimpse of the infamous "woman in white" resident ghost in London's most magnificent auditorium, complete with ceiling paintings. One of London's most elegant theaters—but then we are spoiled for choice!

Globe Theatre—not the original Shakespeare one, of course, but a wonderful testament to Sam Wanamaker's tenacity and vision.

The **National Theatre** on the **South Bank**—anything!

Eurostar to Paris in 3 hours—go there for lunch and back to London, the theater capital of the world, for a play/comedy/musical.

Chelsea Flower Show—considered to be the first event of the English summer social season. Originally held in 1888 in the **Temple Gardens** on the **Embankment**; moved to the present site of **Sir Christopher Wren**'s **Royal Hospital, Chelsea**, in 1913. Chat with the red-uniformed Chelsea Pensioners and be there on the last day, Friday, at 5PM when the plants are sold and the **Chelsea Bridge Road** becomes a sea of moving flowers.

Witness the massacre at **Sloane Square** station as delphiniums get trapped in the tube doors!

Lamb & Flag pub, **Covent Garden**—authentic, tiny, spit-and-sawdust 16th-century hostelry—don't forget to breathe in!

Walk everywhere—especially along **Pimlico Road** (just south of Sloane Square) to covet the contents of all the antiques and designer shops.

Lunch at the **National Gallery**, new **Sainsbury Wing**'s brasserie—a bird's-eye view across **Trafalgar Square** and excellent food—don't miss the fresh strawberry sabayon. If you run out of time because lunch is just too enjoyable, you can always claim, with reason, that you've "done a gallery." Or linger even longer and cross the road to **St. Martin-in-the-Fields** for a 7:30PM concert.

Do go to the **Royal Academy**—2001 saw the 233rd summer exhibition—the largest contemporary art exhibition in the world with work by new and living artists.

Visit the **Royal Parks**—the lungs of London, with more open spaces than any other capital in the world. **St. James's** is very romantic and the most ornamental—ducks, geese, and pelicans swim on the lake. You can feed them and have a bird's-eye view of "Buck House" too!

Take a boat to **Greenwich** and stand astride the Greenwich meridian.

Visit **Edward Stanford**'s bookshop in **Covent Garden** with its wonderful collection of travel guides and maps to plan your next trip, but always remember "when a man is tired of London, he is tired of life; for there is in London all that life can afford" (Samuel Johnson). I'm sure that he meant women too!

Britain, and its collection comprises British art from 1550 through the present, and the **Turner Bequest** or **Collection**. Tate Britain began life as the **Tate Gallery**, through the generosity of Sir Henry Tate (of the sugar manufacturer Tate & Lyle), who donated his collection of 70 "modern" British paintings and sculptures and offered to pay for a building to house it. A vacant lot on the River Thames at Millbank was acquired (it had been previously occupied by the Millbank Penitentiary, a so-called model prison based on the ideas of the philosopher and social reformer Jeremy Bentham). The wedding-cake building with a majestic entrance, designed by **Sidney J.R. Smith**, opened in 1897. Its formative years were spent as a kind of annex of the **National Gallery**, but a formal, albeit friendly, divorce took place in 1955, and the Tate became independent. In 1979, the northwest extension was created by **Michael Huskstepp**. Although the Tate's collection used to overlap with that of the National Gallery, that problem was solved with a formal agreement in September 1996. The directors of the two galleries decreed that the principal dividing date between their respective collections of foreign art would be 1900, and the galleries exchanged the relevant paintings to reflect this dateline. Now the entire **International Collection** has been moved to the Tate Modern.

The best way to locate what you want to see in the huge, rotating collection is to avail yourself of the free floor plans provided by the gallery. There are 35 rooms, all on the

---

Restaurants/Clubs: Red | Hotels: Purple | Shops: Orange | Outdoors/Parks: Green | Sights/Culture: Blue

THE BEST

Mark Taylor

Director, Museums Association

As the global village gets smaller, the experiences available in the world's greatest cities are disturbingly similar. Here are a few suggestions that are uniquely British and leave you in no doubt you are in London:

Happy visitors march on their stomachs—London does high-class food very well:

Lunch at the **Design Museum** at **Butler's Wharf**—great food and an even better view of the **River Thames** and **Tower Bridge**.

The food halls at **Fortnum & Mason** in **Piccadilly** and **Harrods** in **Knightsbridge**—specialist food beautifully presented and horrifyingly priced. Get there early in the morning.

Even earlier in the morning, visit **Smithfields Market**, a fascinating hive of activity with pubs, shops, and cafés surrounding the market and all jumping at 5AM. A great venue for a proper English breakfast—not for vegetarians.

Take tea, as only the English can, at the **Basil Hotel** in **Knightsbridge** or the **Cadogan Hotel** in **Sloane Street**.

For art galleries that present art in an intelligent but unpatronizing way, try the **National Gallery** in **Trafalgar Square** (the evening openings are fun) or the **Tate Gallery** on **Millbank**. For a more noisy, interactive time visit the **Science** and **National History Museums** in **South Kensington** or the **Museum of the Moving Image** at **Waterloo**.

Residents forget it, but London is beautiful—particularly the River Thames and its parkland. First thing on a summer morning, the following places can do nothing but raise your spirits:

The view of the Thames from **Blackfriars Bridge**.

Canary Wharf and the new business center at the **Isle of Dogs**.

The north end of **Regents Park**.

The view toward **Buckingham Palace** from **St. James's Park**.

Hampden Court from the river.

The climb to the **Royal Observatory** and the view from the top.

---

ground floor, showing works chronologically. The Linbury Galleries—nine newly refurbished spaces—were unveiled by Prince Charles as part of the Tate Britain's centennial development in November 2001.

The Turner Bequest is among the great treasures London offers its citizens and visitors and is one of the truly remarkable collections of the work of a single artist. At his death in 1851, J.M.W. Turner left his personal collection of nearly 300 paintings and 20,000 watercolors and drawings to the nation, with the request that they be kept together. His wish was only partially fulfilled, with some rooms devoted to his oil paintings. Now the entire collection is housed in the **Clore Gallery**, designed in 1987 by **James Stirling** and **Michael Wilford & Associates** and situated next door to the main building. The paintings are top-lit with natural daylight—the kind of light, with all its varied and changeable qualities, in which the artist expected his pictures to be exhibited. Works on paper (watercolors and drawings) hang in galleries where daylight is kept out to prevent the fading of the images. Not only have the architects taken great care to see that the art is sympathetically displayed and scientifically preserved, but they have also made it possible for visitors to glimpse the River Thames as they stroll past the pictures. The Thames played a prominent part in Turner's life and art—he painted it, and he lived and died on its banks in Chelsea.

The Tate's British collection will always include the great names: William Blake, William Hogarth, Joshua Reynolds, Thomas Gainsborough, John Constable, George Stubbs, David Hockney, and the Pre-Raphaelites, who are the most popular painters here. The large, elegant central galleries, which usually contain sculpture, draw crowds when the exhibits for the Turner Prize are on display. Featuring primarily controversial young artists, works include sculpture, painting, and photography. Audio guides to new displays and to the Turner Collection are available. *Tate Gallery: An Illustrated Companion*, by Simon Wilson, describes 300 works. The Tate's 1997 centenary sparked off other publications, including *An Illustrated History of the Tate Gallery* by Frances Spalding. ♦ Free, but a donation is usually expected. Admission for certain exhibitions. ♦ Daily, 10AM-6PM. Also, first Friday of every month till 10PM for "Late at the Tate," events relating to specific exhibitions. Millbank (at Atterbury St). 887.8000. Tube: Pimlico. www.tate.org.uk

Within the Tate Gallery:

REX WHISTLER RESTAURANT AT TATE BRITAIN

★★$$ Two artists impress here: **Rex Whistler**, who decorated the restaurant and whose specially commissioned mural *The*

A Year in the Cotswolds

February: Cheltenham Folk Festival—all the best of national and local folk singing, dancing, and arts.

March: Bath Shakespeare Festival.

April: Shakespeare Birthday Celebrations in Stratford-upon-Avon with strolling players and musicians, Shakespeare morris dancing, RSC Performance, and Charity Ball.

May: Tetbury Woolsack Races. Join in if you think you can carry a 60-pound woolsack up and down Gumstool Hill!

Cheese Rolling on Cooper's Hill, Gloucester: the ancient tradition of chasing a whole Gloucester cheese down a ridiculously steep hill. Vegetarians beware—it gets bloody!

Bampton Day of Dance: traditional English golf and morris dancing through the ages. Weird but wonderful!

June: Bath International Music Festival.

Burford Dragon Parade, commemorating the victory of King Cuthbert of Wessex over King Ethelbad of Murcia in AD 752. Yes, there is a dragon. No, it's not real.

July: The Joust at Berkeley Castle, near Stroud. A week of medieval mayhem including jousting and medieval games. BYO armor and maiden!

Royal International Air Tattoo, Fairford: the world's biggest military air show.

July/August: Roman Baths by Torchlight at Bath. During these months the baths remain open till 10PM and are lit by torches.

Living Heritage Oxfordshire Craft Fair at Blenheim Palace: more than 100 stalls with traditional and unusual crafts and activities.

September: Painswick Ancient Clypping Ceremony, an ancient folk tradition reconsecrating the local church, St. Mary's.

Jane Austen Festival at Bath.

October: Cheltenham Literary Festival—10 days of readings, performances, and other live events.

November: Bath Christmas Market. If this traditional market with its carolers and mulled wine doesn't make your bells jingle, nothing will.

December: Carols By Candlelight in the gorgeous Georgian Pump Room in Bath. The choir does most of the work, but you are allowed to join in.

Expedition in Pursuit of Rare Meats, painted in 1926–1927, makes an impressive setting for any meal, and chef Richard Oxley. His menu is packed with great contemporary British delights. Jersey royal and spinach soup with wild garlic leaf is a delicious taste experience, as is the equally inventive white chocolate and rhubarb trifle with Champagne jelly. Oxley even treats vegetarians as proper diners! His Neal's Yard goat's cheese and red pepper polenta cake with buttered baby vegetables stands up to that mural rather well. The wine list continues to win awards. If you like your art early in the day, the restaurant also does a good breakfast on Saturday and Sunday. ◆ M-Su, lunch 11:30AM-4PM; Sa, Su, breakfast 10AM-11:30AM. Reservations recommended. 887.8825. britain.restaurant@tate.org.uk

Tate Gallery Shop

On sale here are superbly printed postcards, excellent books, T-shirts with depictions of the museum's masterpieces, canvas bags, prints, posters, and framing facilities, plus specially commissioned items. ◆ M-Sa, 10:30AM-5:30PM. 887.8876

Tate Café

★★$ The self-service café offers light meals, soups, sandwiches, and freshly baked pastries. They will also do children's packed lunches. ◆ Daily, 10AM-5:30PM

Tate Boat

Without doubt the most marvelous way to get from one major art gallery to another. It makes you think of the Thames almost like London's Grand Canal. Even if you don't want to visit the galleries—and you should—you cannot fail to be delighted to board the Tate Boat at Tate Britain and make your way downriver, past the Houses of Parliament, the London Eye, the newly revamped South Bank Center, The National Theatre (okay, it is unbelievably ugly), The Savoy . . . to Tate Modern. The boat is a state-of-the-art 220-seat catamaran, and the specially commissioned interior and exterior designs are by Damien Hirst. The Tate Boat runs every 40 minutes during gallery hours. ◆ Fee: adults £4, children £2, family tickets £10. Tickets available from Tate Modern, Tate Britain, online, or by calling 887.8888

Restaurants/Clubs: Red | Hotels: Purple | Shops: Orange | Outdoors/Parks: Green | Sights/Culture: Blue

ST. JAMES'S

St. James's (pronounced, by Londoners, with two syllables—as *Jameses*) is all about mystery and history, royalty and aristocracy, pomp and civilized circumstance, and kings, queens, gentlemen, and ladies. In this elegant, anachronistic enclave, time seems to have stood still. Gentlemen still go to their clubs, an unchallenged English custom; shoes are still made with painstaking care for royal feet and hats sewn seamlessly for aristocratic heads; and when the queen is home at **Buckingham Palace**, the royal standard flies. This neighborhood provides one of the most agreeable walks in London, where visitors can gaze around at a portrait of

England and Englishness utterly unchanged by war, development, mass production, pollution, the weak pound, or the European Community. It's the England of history books and literature, heroes and heroines, George Meredith and Oscar Wilde, and fashionable Edward VII. Amid the Champagne and syllabub, however, egalitarians and feminists will perceive two ancient phenomena: the segregation of the classes and the segregation of the sexes (although a few enlightened "gentlemen's clubs" have begun accepting women as members).

You can begin the journey at a monument to the uppermost echelon of society, **Admiralty Arch**, designed as a tribute from Edward VII to his mother, Queen Victoria. Proceed to **Jermyn Street**, where window shopping is like viewing museum exhibits—the prices can reach Old Master figures. In an area no larger than a football field, you can have a pair of shoes especially made to fit your feet, purchase the most handsome and most expensive pipe you'll ever own, and have a tailor take your measurements for custom-made shirts (with a minimum order of six and a minimum wait of 6 weeks). You can buy cheddars, Stiltons, Wensleydales, and Caerphillys in **Paxton & Whitfield**, a shop that may convince you the French are only the second-best cheese producers in the world. You can choose wild hyacinth bath oil from a famous perfumery (**Floris**) or Ajaccio Violet cologne from a regal perfumery/barbershop (**Trumper's**), drink excellent ale in a truly Victorian pub (the **Red Lion**), or dine in one of the trendy restaurants that have infiltrated this bastion of tradition (**Quaglino's, The Avenue**). You'll see where kings and queens lived before they moved to **Buckingham Palace** and gaze at the windows of **St. James's Palace**, where Prince Charles resides. Afterward, have a look at some of the treasures from the **Royal Collection** (displayed at Buckingham Palace and the **Queen's Gallery**), check out the royal horses and coaches, and end the day beside the shimmering lake in **St. James's Park**, London's oldest and perhaps most romantic greensward, where Charles II walked his spaniels.

A Saturday in St. James's feels like a Sunday. The streets are empty, despite the fact that most of the shops are open. If you want to watch the Changing of the Guard ceremony at Buckingham Palace, call for the schedule (0839/123411) and get there half an hour early. There are few places for visitors to wait out drizzles near the royal palaces, so bring your umbrella if the sky looks threatening. The ceremony is canceled in very rainy weather.

City code 0207 unless otherwise noted.

1 ST. JAMES'S STREET

The elegant street serves as a compass for this royal and aristocratic quarter. At the bottom of the street is Henry VIII's gatehouse to **St. James's Palace**, with a sentry or two on duty. Pall Mall joins the street just in front of the palace, where the tradition of gentlemen's clubs continues, although the 18th-century clubs here are considered even more social, snobbish, and arrogant than the clubs farther along Pall Mall. There are no signs to indicate which club is which—if you're a member, you know, and if you aren't, you don't need to know. ♦ Between Pall Mall and Piccadilly. Tube: Green Park

1 WHITE'S

London's oldest, most famous, and still most fashionable club was founded in the 1690s as **White's Chocolate House** (a meeting place where bitter hot chocolate was drunk). Built by **James Wyatt** in 1788, this is where Evelyn Waugh sought "refuge from the hounds of modernity" and where

Prince Charles had his stag party the night before he married Diana. The gaming room here was called Hell in the previous century. This club is exclusive indeed: Even if you are sufficiently well connected to be proposed and accepted for membership, there is a waiting list of 8 years (though Prince Charles probably didn't have to wait that long). Not surprisingly, it is not open to the public. ♦ 37–38 St. James's St (between Jermyn St and Piccadilly). 493.6671. Tube: Green Park

2 JERMYN STREET

Named after the Earl of St. Albans, Henry Jermyn, this narrow street is only a few blocks long and the architecture isn't remarkable. (The west end of the street was badly damaged during the 1940 raids, when all but one of the buildings between Duke and Bury Streets were destroyed.) But it's the essence of St. James's, an exclusive shopping enclave for well-to-do Englishmen who dress as the Duke of Edinburgh and Prince Charles do. ♦ Between Haymarket and St. James's St. Tube: Green Park, Piccadilly Circus

3 FAVOURBROOK

Fabulous-looking silks, velvets, and damasks are used in fashioning the waistcoats (vests), luxurious smoking jackets, frock coats, and tasseled fez-style smoking hats sold here. In fact, the character played by Simon Callow in the film *Four Weddings and a Funeral* wore one of the shop's creations—a waistcoat hand-painted with an angel. Although the decadent English fop look is at odds with the conservative tastes reflected in the rest of the street, the style has become so popular that Favourbrook moved its menswear collection to these premises from its Piccadilly Arcade location around the corner. ♦ M-Sa. 55 Jermyn St (between Piccadilly Arcade and St. James's St). 493.5060. Tube: Green Park. Womenswear only is sold at 18 Piccadilly Arcade (between Jermyn St and Piccadilly). 491.2331. Tube: Green Park

3 WILTONS

★★$$$$ If you are looking for tradition with your supper, you could do worse than dine here. Wiltons has been in St. James's since 1742. Its current owners have been in charge for 60 years. The restaurant itself has been at its current address since 1982. Wiltons recently had an impressive facelift and some of the more twee decorative idiosyncrasies have gone. The place is now very elegant. And so is the food. Marvelously English delicacies like gull's eggs (in season) are rarely found—but you will find them here. Chef Jerome Ponchelle MCA is a protégé of Michel Boudain, and it shows. His menu offers braised fillet of wild Scottish salmon in champagne sauce, or lobster, crab, and truffle omelette. His wine list is intelligent and expensive. **Wiltons Oyster and Seafood Bar** is legendary. Should your holiday budget balk at the cost of a full meal, the bar offers a cut-down menu of Ponchelle's elegant delights. And a plate of oysters, or some Colsten Bassett cheddar with a glass of one of the house's excellent ports, is a delicious and very London experience. ♦ M-F, lunch and dinner. Reservations generally required. 55 Jermyn St. 629.9955. Tube: Green Park. www.wiltons.co.uk

4 DUNHILL

It was on this very site in 1907 that Alfred Dunhill opened his small tobacconist shop; his philosophy was that everything must be "the best of its kind"—which, coincidentally, is also the motto of a new generation of consumers. The shop has expanded to include leather goods, pens, watches, fragrances, umbrellas, and all sorts of accessories to complement men's and women's clothes and complete the ever-so-smart Dunhill look. There is still a tobacconist area, a humidor room, and a wall display of "museum" pieces. ♦ M-F, 9:30AM-6PM; Sa, 10AM-6PM. 30 Duke St (at Jermyn St). 499.9566. Tube: Green Park. Also at 21 New Bond St. 355.9505. Tube: Bond St

5 DAVIDOFF

Using three recipes for flavor, Zino Davidoff has created a cigar and pipe smoker's heaven. He purveys the finest Havana cigars, and there is a walk-in humidor. The shop has an ineffably masculine pull, with the handmade wooden humidors, the matchboxes, the cigar cases in leather, the cigar holders, and many other smoking accessories, as well as cognacs. The sweet smell of unsmoked cigars evokes a sense of prosperity and sedate virility. ♦ M-Sa. 35 St. James's St (at Jermyn St). 930.3079. Tube: Green Park

6 TURNBULL & ASSER

The name is familiar to Americans who wear English custom-made shirts, especially now that there's a Turnbull & Asser club in New York as well as department stores in the States that take appointments with their tailors. But those experiences aren't the same as coming into this solemn, dark, wood-paneled shop where you can't be certain if the person next to you is a duke or the salesperson. The store's made-to-measure service takes 6 weeks, with a minimum order of six shirts after you approve the first. There are a lot of decisions to make: the shape of the collar; the length of the points, pockets, and monograms; the shape and color of the buttons; a two- or three-button cuff. You also must be patient—

and it helps if you're as much a stickler for detail as the shirtmakers themselves. First you are measured; then a sample shirt is made and sent to you. Next you must write a set of fastidious notes and return the shirt, which is then remade and again returned to you for approval. This routine can go on for quite some time before you get a shirt that is perfect. The shop truly reflects Jermyn Street's Beau Brummell legacy faithfully: The famous Regency dandy could not resist fine craftsmanship, simple lines, and daring colors. The store also has a large selection of ready-mades, and it sells blouses and shirts to women, including Candice Bergen, Lauren Bacall, Jacqueline Bisset, and model Naomi Campbell. ◆ M–Sa. 71–72 Jermyn St (at Bury St). 930.0502. Tube: Green Park. Also at 23 Bury St (between Ryder St and King St). 930.0502. Tube: Green Park

7 QUAGLINO'S

★★★$$$ "Tables to kill for" was the verdict of food critics when Sir Terence Conran opened this beautiful restaurant in 1993 (named for a smart-set club that flourished here in the 1930s). This opulent place is a welcome addition to his restaurant empire (four places at Butler's Wharf and **Bibendum** in Kensington, among the 41 in his empire, which now stretches to New York!) and a further tribute to his talents. On the street level, the discreet Q logo seems to adorn a minimalist delicatessen; there's a bar inside (overlooking the main attraction below) with a small eating area and a snack menu offering Thai-spiced tuna salad and grilled tuna. However, a sweeping grand staircase leads to a huge subterranean restaurant that's as large and resplendent as a luxury ocean liner. Romantically lit with an artificial skylight ceiling, it has walls of mirrors and large urns filled with fresh lilies. And the food lives up to the surroundings. Appetizers include a rich chicken and foie gras terrine, grilled quail with figs, and, on a lighter note, artichoke and ricotta tart. That is, of course, unless you want to choose from Quaglino's enormous and justifiably famous seafood bar with its several varieties of oyster, its lobster, langoustine, and crab all heaped up on glistening hillocks of ice. Main courses cover a delicious lamb shank with sweet potato purée, veal with anchovies and capers, and—enough to turn anyone vegetarian—pea and mint tort with samphire. There are nearly 20 Champagnes to choose from, as well as an intelligent carte of reds and whites. Mr. Conran's signature Cigarette Girls patrol, so almost all your vices can be satisfied at your table. There are almost always bargain-priced promotions available on set lunches and, should you wish

to soak up the atmosphere but not eat a full meal, there is a short menu in the delightful mezzanine-level bar. Jazz trios play there on weekends, and there is frequently a pianist on other nights. ◆ Daily, lunch and dinner. Reservations recommended. 16 Bury St (between Ryder and Jermyn Sts). 930.6767. Tube: Green Park. www.conran.com

8 GREEN'S RESTAURANT AND OYSTER BAR

★★★$$$ Here is a dining spot that has the ambience of a gentlemen's club and seems to be filled with typical Bertie Wooster clones (however, the serving staff aren't as deferential and all-knowing as Jeeves). It has a bar with booths for the secretive and an open eating area for rubberneckers. Choose from a mountain of lobsters, crabs, oysters, and salmon, all fresh, simply prepared, and outstanding. During the season you can get grouse, pheasant, wild duck, and partridge, hung properly and roasted perfectly. The desserts include treacle tart and gooseberry fool. If you come here for lunch, resign yourself to eating in a very crowded room. The oyster bar is cheaper. ◆ British ◆ Restaurant: daily, lunch and dinner, Oct–Easter; M–Sa, lunch and dinner, and Su, lunch, Easter–Sept. Oyster Bar: daily, lunch and dinner. Reservations required. 36 Duke St (between Ryder and Jermyn Sts). 930.4566. Tube: Green Park

9 PAXTON & WHITFIELD

At any one time you can find 200 cheeses from Britain and Europe inside this shop, which occupies a house built in 1674. Mr. Paxton and Mr. Whitfield opened the shop 200 years ago, when the public predilection was for French cheeses. Now English cheeses are finally being acknowledged for their outstanding quality and for being ideal partners with wine. The salespeople here are generous with samples, so go ahead and taste the golden cheddars, the peach- and ivory-colored Cheshires, the russet Leicester, the marbled green sage Derby, and the blue-veined Stilton. Also available are fabulous game pies, hams, and pâtés, plus crackers and bread to accompany the cheese. The shop also sells wine. ◆ M–Sa. 93 Jermyn St (between Duke of York and Duke Sts). 930.0259. Tube: Green Park, Piccadilly Circus

9 FLORIS

Since 1730, members of the Floris family, now in its eighth generation, have been creating aromatic perfumes, bath oils, and soaps from the flowers of the English garden. In this pretty, evocative shop, the jasmine, rose, gardenia, lily of the valley, and wild hyacinth all smell fresh and clean and as close to the real thing as you can imagine. New scents are continually being developed as well. You will also find large natural sponges, fine English brushes, antique objects for *la toilette*, and a line of scents for men. Both Queen Elizabeth and Prince Charles have bestowed their Royal Warrants on the shop, and it's popular with other famous people as well, including Nancy Reagan. ♦ M–Sa. 89 Jermyn St (between Duke of York and Duke Sts). 930.2885. Tube: Green Park, Piccadilly Circus

10 HILDITCH & KEY

The shop specializes in made-to-measure shirts for men and women, including royals and politicians—but of course these tailors are far too discreet to name names. All shirts are cut by hand: the bodies with shears, the collars with a knife. The collars, considered the most important part of a shirt, are turned by hand and have removable stiffeners that must be taken out before laundering. The buttons are never synthetic—they're made from real shells. Besides the fine English cotton poplins, there's a solid selection of Viyella, a soft, warm equal mix of cotton and wool. The women's shirts come in many of the same colors and fabrics as the men's but with additional choices of bright colors created by the shop's own designers. The nightshirts (for men and women) and pajamas are wonderful. ♦ M–Sa. 37 Jermyn St (at Princes Arcade). 930.5336. Tube: Green Park, Piccadilly Circus. Also at 88 Jermyn St (at Bury St). 930.2329; 131 Sloane St. 823.5683. Tube: Knightsbridge

11 RED LION PUB

★★★$ Dating from around 1880, this Victorian jewel has mahogany paneling and beautiful old mirrors, each engraved with a different British flower. Have a sandwich with your pint of bitter. Note that this small pub can be crowded and smoky. ♦ Pub ♦ M–Sa, lunch. 2 Duke of York St (at Ormond Yd). 321.0782. Tube: Green Park, Piccadilly Circus

11 HARVIE & HUDSON

These third-generation shirtmakers use the finest cotton poplin, which is designed, colored, and woven just for them. Their tweed jackets and overcoats are reasonably priced. ♦ M–Sa. 97 Jermyn St (at Duke of York St). 930.3949. Tube: Green Park, Piccadilly Circus. Also at 55 Knightsbridge (at Wilton Pl). 235.2651. Tube: Knightsbridge

12 22 JERMYN ST.

$$$$ This rather impressively opulent boutique "townhouse" hotel, owned and run by the Togna family since 1915, offers 13 suites (some with one bedroom, some with two) and five double rooms. Sofa beds are available on request (and at additional charge!). Rooms have absolutely everything you could want, including broadband and DSL, a video library, and popcorn. There is 24-hour portering, a concierge, a personal shopper, and a business office, and mobile phones and computers are available on loan. The hotel will not only babysit for you, but dog or catsit too. Room service is extensive and runs from sandwiches and drinks to full meals, such as braised lamb knuckle served with a choice of accompaniments. Full English breakfast is available, or simply a Bloody Mary, if that is your preference. Traditional afternoon tea and high tea are also on offer. ♦ 22 Jermyn St (between Regent and Duke of York Sts). 734.2353. Tube: Green Park

13 TRUMPER'S

With a lovely atmosphere and a legendary reputation, this shop offers top-quality hairbrushes, shaving brushes, soaps, hair tonics, and aftershaves. The Ajaccio Violet men's cologne smells like violets, comes in old-fashioned bottles, and is used by both sexes. There is also a traditional barbershop on the premises. ♦ M–Sa, 9AM–5PM. 20 Jermyn St (between Regent St and Eagle Pl). 734.1370. Tube: Piccadilly Circus. Also at 9 Curzon St (between Clarges and Queen Sts). 499.1850. Tube: Green Park

13 BATES THE HATTER

This tiny gentlemen's hat shop is undaunted by the bareheaded 20th century, and time seems to be on its side. Hats are beginning to reappear. You will pay less here than at **Lock & Co.** (see page 56). Be sure to admire Binks, the huge tabby cat who lived here between 1921 and 1926; he was so beloved that a taxidermist was enlisted after his death to preserve him for all time. ♦ M–Sa. 21A Jermyn St (between Regent St and Eagle Pl). 734.2722. Tube: Piccadilly Circus

13 JERMYN STREET THEATRE

This tiny subterranean gem of a theater, offering a range of drama, musicals, and cabaret, has only 90 seats, recently refurbished to a good level of comfort. Terrible wine served from a little hatch but great atmosphere. This is about as close as the West End gets to some of what Off-Broadway offers. Happily, it is within a stone's throw of **Eros.** ♦ Jermyn St (at Lower Regent St). 287.2875. Tube: Piccadilly Circus

13 HERBIE FROGGS

These two shops side by side offer the would-be well-dressed man-about-town all he could want. The larger shop (at Nos.18/19) offers Herbie Froggs' own line of suits and shirts in quality fabrics (the swiss cotton shirts feel

CELLULOID LONDON

With its long history, an abundance of architectural masterpieces, and an atmosphere that suggests mystery, tragedy, and comedy all at the same time, London makes an ideal film location. And over the years, many motion pictures have been set in this city—from historical dramas to Hollywood musicals to the great Ealing Studios comedies to grittier contemporary films. The following movies can start you on your cinematic tour of the English capital.

Alfie (1966) Michael Caine became a major star acting the title role of a callous Cockney playboy cruising the streets of 1960s London to pick up girls. Also a photographer, Alfie uses such background settings as **Big Ben**, the **Houses of Parliament**, and **Tower Bridge**.

An American Werewolf in London (1981) In a queasy mix of horror and satire, an American student is transformed into a werewolf after a gory attack in the Yorkshire moors. Some of the action takes place in London locations, including **Regent Park**, the **Tottenham Court Road** tube station, **Trafalgar Square**, and **Piccadilly Circus**.

A Christmas Carol (1956) There have been many film adaptations of this most famous Dickens tale, but none has been as highly acclaimed as this one. In a memorable performance, Alastair Sim plays the miserly, ill-tempered, misanthropic Scrooge, and again, Victorian London is evocatively portrayed.

A Fish Called Wanda (1988) Jamie Lee Curtis, Kevin Kline (who won the Best Supporting Actor Oscar), John Cleese, and Michael Palin star in this funny farce about double- and triple-crossing jewel thieves. Several scenes of the film, directed by Charles Crichton, were shot in the **Law Courts**, the **Hatton Garden** diamond district, and the **Docklands** area.

Four Weddings and a Funeral (1994) Hugh Grant became an international star thanks to this stylish romantic comedy about a confirmed English bachelor who falls for a freewheeling American.

Gaslight (1944) The archetypical fog and mist of Victorian London provides an eerie backdrop for the classic tale of a man (Charles Boyer) trying to drive his wife insane. Angela Lansbury, playing a surly housemaid, makes her film debut.

Great Expectations (1946) One of several Dickens novels to be adapted to the screen. Director David Lean expertly tells the story of a poor orphan boy in Victorian London who is elevated in society by a mysterious patron.

The Krays (1990) This atmospheric, sometimes shockingly violent biography tells the story of Ronnie and Reggie Kray, the psychotic twins who dominated London gangland in the 1960s, virtually running everything in the East End.

The Lavender Hill Mob (1951) Timid bank clerk Alec Guinness dreams up the perfect way to rob his employers of a fortune in gold—and then everything goes hilariously wrong in this classic Ealing comedy directed by Charles Crichton.

Looking for Richard (1996) In a witty and incisive documentary, Al Pacino describes his quest to produce a meaningful film version of Shakespeare's *Richard III*. His research includes visits to the Tower of London and the construction site of the rebuilt **Globe Theatre**.

The Madness of King George (1994) The film version of Alan Bennett's play *The Madness of George III* deals with the struggle for power in the court of King George as he begins to exhibit strange behavior. Several scenes were filmed in London area locations, including **Eton College**, **Syon House**, **Kew**, and the **Royal Naval College**, **Greenwich** (but not **Windsor Castle**, where much of the action is set).

The Man Who Knew Too Much (1956) This Alfred Hitchcock thriller about a man whose son is kidnapped to prevent him from revealing an assassination plot stars James Stewart and Doris Day. The climactic scene takes place in the **Royal Albert Hall**.

Mona Lisa (1985) Small-time hood Bob Hoskins, hired to drive a call girl around, begins to fall for her in this movie about London gangland. Michael Caine costars as a vicious mob boss. London locations include the neighborhoods of **Soho** and **Hampstead** and the **Ritz Hotel**.

My Fair Lady (1964) In a lavish cinematic version of the Lerner and Loewe musical, Professor Henry Higgins (Rex Harrison) bets that he can turn Cockney flower girl Eliza Doolittle (Audrey Hepburn) into a well-mannered, upper-class lady within a month. The first scene is set in front of the **Royal Opera House**, **Covent Garden**.

Oliver Twist (1948) Another David Lean interpretation of a Dickens tale, this film about a down-and-out lad who gets involved with a gang of thieves features Alec Guinness as Fagin and Anthony Newley as the Artful Dodger. In 1968, the story was made into the Oscar-winning musical *Oliver!*

101 Dalmatians (1996) The live-action remake of the famous Disney cartoon feature stars Glenn Close as the delightfully malevolent Cruella De Vil, who wants to skin a litter of puppies so she can have a fur coat. The movie was filmed on location in central London. One dazzling sequence shows a cyclist careening through the **Burlington Arcade** in **Mayfair** and ending up in **Trafalgar Square**.

Restaurants/Clubs: Red | Hotels: Purple | Shops: Orange | Outdoors/Parks: Green | Sights/Culture: Blue

lovely!) and a nice range of ties, cufflinks, and other accessories. Their staff are happy to come to your hotel to measure you, daytime or evenings. The smaller shop (at No. 21) carries mainly Hugo Boss designs. Very smart stuff. Staff are charming. ♦ 18/19 and 21 Jermyn St (near Regent St). M-Sa, 9:30AM-6PM. Tube: Piccadilly Circus

14 COMEDY THEATRE

Built in 1881 by **Thomas Verity** and extensively restored in 1955, this little 800-seater is almost never dark. It is not one for claustrophobes, and if you want to make a quick exit at the end, get yourself a seat in the circle, as it is actually at street level, while the stalls are in the basement. The bars are tiny, hence the spillage of its audience out onto Panton Street at intermission. The pub across the road is very welcoming, should you be unable to go without an intermission drink. It also offers an alternative to the endless queue for the ladies'! ♦ Panton St (at Oxendon St). 321.5305. Tube: Piccadilly Circus

14 STOCKPOT

★$ For years this restaurant has been the salvation of hungry students and penurious travelers looking for agreeable, generous meals at low prices. The lunchtime rush is not for the fainthearted, but service tends to be genial, if frantic. (Expect to share tables with strangers.) Typical filling meals are spaghetti, chicken casserole, Spanish omelettes, and vegetarian dishes. Old-fashioned desserts include golden syrup sponge pudding and apple crumble. ♦ International ♦ M–Sa, breakfast, lunch, and dinner; Su, lunch and dinner. ♦ No credit cards accepted. 40 Panton St (between Oxendon St and Haymarket). 839.5142. Tube: Piccadilly Circus. Also at 18 Old Compton St (between Charing Cross Rd and Greek St). 287.1066. Tube: Leicester Square; 50 James St (between Barrett and Wigmore Sts). 486.1086. Tube: Bond St; 6 Basil St (between Hans Crescent and Sloane St). 589.8627. Tube: Knightsbridge

15 AL DUCA

★★★$$ A smart, friendly restaurant in the heart of St. James's. You know by the marvelous smells wafting around you that it is good. The house Prosecco is excellent, and the entire wine list admirably Italian; there is a good selection of half bottles, and

There's actually a serious organization in London called the Society of Psychical Research that lists 1,000 ghosts that people claim to have seen in stately homes, manor houses, and inns.

you can, should you wish, choose one of 16 excellent grappe as a *digestivo*. The menu is modern Italian and there is a terrific choice in all courses. Marinated salmon on mixed herbs, or gently poached egg with a Parmesan crust with a salad of potatoes and wild mushrooms? Pasta includes a delicious *conchigliette* (ear-shaped pasta) with purple broccoli and Italian sweet sausage. Main courses offer red bream escalope or baby chicken served with spinach and garlic cloves, and the restaurant's excellent beef comes braised in Barolo. ♦ M-Sa, lunch and dinner. 4/5 Duke of York St. 839.3090. Tube: Piccadilly Circus

16 LONDON LIBRARY

"It is not typically English. It is typically civilized," wrote E.M. Forster in an essay on this private subscription library, founded in 1841 by Thomas Carlyle but built in the 1760s by James Stuart. The interior looks rather run down, with worn leather chairs in the reading room, Victorian portraits on the walls, and high windows overlooking the square. Past members include Lord Tennyson, W.E. Gladstone, Henry James, Thomas Hardy, H.G. Wells, Aldous Huxley, Virginia Woolf, and Edith Sitwell. Current members are historians, biographers, critics, novelists, philosophers, playwrights, and scriptwriters, who all come to use some of the library's million-plus books; however, memberships are hard to obtain. The library is not open to the general public, but its windows give a fine glimpse inside. ♦ 14 St. James's Sq (between King and Duke of York Sts). 930.7705. Tube: Green Park, Piccadilly Circus

17 ST. JAMES'S SQUARE

This fine square was begun in 1665 by Henry Jermyn, first Earl of St. Albans and allegedly the secret husband of Henrietta Maria, widow of Charles I and mother of Charles II. While Charles II was in exile in France, he gave the land to the earl in gratitude for his "faithful devotion." The square was designed with mansions on all sides for the nobility who wanted or needed to be near the palace.

The gardens in the square's center are open to the public (which is unusual in London, where only residents may use most neighborhood squares). The handsome bronze statue by John Bacon the Younger of William III on horseback includes the molehill on which the horse stumbled, throwing the king in a fatal accident. During World War I, a rustic building resembling a country inn was erected at the square's center to quarter American officers. Called the **Washington Inn**, it stood until 1921. At **No. 32**, the allied commanders under General Eisenhower launched the invasions of North Africa in 1942 and of northwest Europe in 1944. On the north side of the square is **Chatham House**, the residence of three prime ministers: the Earl of Chatham, otherwise known as Pitt the Elder; the Earl of Derby; and W.E. Gladstone. Wellington's dispatch announcing his victory at Waterloo was delivered to **No. 16** by the bloodstained Major Percy to the prince regent, who was dining with his foreign secretary, Lord Castlereagh. Included with the dispatch were the captured French eagle standards, now in Wellington's **Apsley House** at **Hyde Park Corner**.

St. James's Square became famous overnight when the Libyan People's Bureau at **No. 5** was besieged on 17 April 1984. Gunmen within the building fired on demonstrators outside, killing a young police officer named Yvonne Fletcher. Because diplomatic immunity made it impossible for police to enter the building, the siege went on for 10 days, and the suspects were deported instead of arrested. Fresh flowers are placed on a memorial opposite No. 5 year-round in honor of Fletcher. ♦At Charles II, King, and Duke of York Sts. Tube: Green Park, Piccadilly Circus

18 HAYMARKET THEATRE

It has been officially named the **Theatre Royal, Haymarket** since the 1760s, when it acquired its royal license, but it's always listed as the Haymarket (probably because there is another Theatre Royal in Drury Lane, Covent Garden). Built in 1720, it was known affectionately as the "Little Theatre in the Haymarket" in the 1730s. Henry Fielding, whose first satire, *Tom Thumb*, ran here in 1730, was one of its managers—and the principal reason Lord Chamberlain instituted powers of censorship in 1737, some of which were not lifted until 1968. After **John Nash** rebuilt it in 1820, the theater hosted performers such as Ellen Terry and Samuel Phelps. Nash's exterior remains fairly intact, but the interior, redesigned first in 1904 by **C. Stanley Peach**, has been altered several times since and seats 888 people today. This is one of London's most jaw-droppingly lovely theater interiors. ♦ Haymarket (between Suffolk Pl and Orange St). 930.8800. Tube: Piccadilly Circus, Charing Cross

19 HER MAJESTY'S THEATRE

This 1,219-seat theater changes its name to fit the gender of the sovereign—hence it's Her Majesty's, for now. The current building was erected in 1897 for Sir Herbert Beerbohm Tree by **C.J. Phipps** (who also built the **Savoy**), but a theater has stood on this site since 1705. The first opera by Handel to be produced in England was performed here, as was the first Handel oratorio. Jenny Lind made her English debut here; so did Beethoven's *Fidelio*. And the **Royal Academy**

of Dramatic Art (**RADA**) started here. Now the theater is best known as the venue for Andrew Lloyd Webber's *Phantom of the Opera*, playing here since 1986. Seats are always sold out, but it's worth standing in line at the box office on the day of the show to see if anyone has turned in tickets. ♦ Haymarket (at Charles II St). 494.5400. Tube: Piccadilly Circus, Charing Cross

20 NEW ZEALAND HOUSE

This 18-story glass-and-concrete building is a veritable skyscraper in this area and among the first to represent London's move toward modern architecture. It was built in 1963 by **Robert Matthew** for the New Zealand government. Note the interesting plaque, which says that Ho Chi Minh worked at the **Carlton Hotel**, which opened in 1899 and closed in 1939. ♦ 80 Haymarket (between Pall Mall and Charles II St). Tube: Piccadilly Circus, Charing Cross

21 HAYMARKET

A 17th-century market that supplied the horses of the **Royal Mews**, when the mews were on Trafalgar Square, gave this street its name. The market was placed here after Lord St. Albans was ordered to move it from Mayfair because of the filth that resulted from the cattle and sheep for sale. A market of some kind remained at Haymarket until the early 1800s. ♦ Between Pall Mall and Coventry St. Tube: Piccadilly Circus, Charing Cross

22 ECONOMIST BUILDING

Alison and **Peter Smithson**'s complex is considered a fine example of successful modern architecture in London. In 1964, the architects designed a group of buildings that are compatible with the 18th-century scale of St. James's Street but still maintain their 20th-century integrity. The complex provides a public open space, offices for *The Economist* magazine, a bank, and apartments. In the front court and in the foyer are sculptures as part of changing exhibitions of modern works. The building is not open to the general public. ♦ 25 St. James's St (at Ryder St). 830.7000. Tube: Green Park

23 LONGMIRE

Acclaimed as "the king of custom cufflinks," Mr. Longmire boasts the world's largest selection, whether new, antique, gold, enameled, or set with precious gems. Initials, corporate logos, heraldry, racing colors, cars, and dogs, among many other subjects, can be immortalized in made-to-order enamel designs. He maintains a heraldic reference library and has two Royal

Warrants. The shop also makes brooches, pendants, earrings, and buttons; contemporary jewelry is also available. ♦ M–F, Jan–Aug; M–Sa, Sept–Dec. The shop is closed for 1 week in August. 12 Bury St (at Ryder St). 930.8720. Tube: Green Park

24 JAMES J. FOX & ROBERT LEWIS

Discerning cigar smokers flock to this Dickensian tobacco shop in droves. They follow in the footsteps of Robert Lewis's most famous customer, Sir Winston Churchill; he opened an account here on 9 August 1900 and placed his last order on 23 December 1964, a month before his death. James Fox also runs the tobacco departments at **Harrods** and **Selfridges**. ♦ M–Sa. 19 St. James's St (between King and Ryder Sts). 930.3787. Tube: Green Park

25 STAFFORD HOTEL

$$$$ This elegant, Englishly lavish hotel is one of the few in London to boast the AA's Red Star Status. Its 81 rooms boast all the usual five-star mod cons, including a full valet service and US-style electrical plugs. All televisions are also tuned to US news channels. In its self-styled "World Famous Carriage House," there are another 12 generously proportioned rooms created out of their original 18th-century stables. All these rooms have original timber beams thought to have been reclaimed from sailing ships in the 1750s. The "Guv'nor's Suite" is a deluxe two-story suite with all the olde worlde charm you can take. The hotel's restaurant has a shelf groaning with the awards it has won, and its **American Bar** has been voted the second best bar in the world by *Gourmet* magazine. Its Stafford Dry Martini is the perfect pick-me-up. If fine wine is your tipple, the hotel's 350-year-old cellars house a range of more than 800 top labels and rare vintages. ♦ 16-18 St. James's Pl (off St. James's St). 493.0111. Tube: Green Park. www.thestaffordhotel.co.uk

26 SPENCER HOUSE

The entrance to this remarkable Palladian mansion faces St. James's Place, but its finest façade is opposite **Green Park**. The house was begun in 1756 by **John Vardy**, who designed it for John, Earl of Spencer, an ancestor of Princess Diana. **James Stuart** took over its (mainly interior) construction in 1758; Stuart was nicknamed "the Athenian" for his love of classical architecture, and his anglicized Greek influence can be seen throughout. When completed in 1766, the house was considered one of the finest London residences. "I know not of a more beautiful piece of architecture," wrote Arthur Young after seeing it in 1772. The J. Rothschild Group of Companies acquired the

building in 1985 and has restored its original splendor. On Sunday, visitors may enter (by guided tour only) to see Vardy's dining room with its elaborate gilt-wood furniture, Stuart's neoclassical state rooms, and Lady Spencer's private drawing room. Tours are given every 20 minutes. Before going in, look across the road at the building's austere neighbor, a concrete apartment block built by **Sir Denys Lasdun** in 1959–1960 in the stark style he also used to design the **National Theatre**. Although not harmonious with its graceful surroundings, this apartment house has been lauded for its strong, modern design on a human scale. ♦ Admission. £6. Su, Feb–July, Sept–Dec. 27 St. James's Pl (off St. James's St). 499.8620. Tube: Green Park

26 DUKES HOTEL

$$$ This hotel is situated in the very heart of St. James's, in its own flower-filled courtyard where the original Edwardian gas lamps are lit by hand every evening. The privately owned Dukes has 89 rooms and suites, all serviced by elevator and boasting marble bathrooms, private bar, and twin phone lines with dataport and voice mail. The Penthouse Suite has spectacular views over Green Park, and all the suites have large south-facing drawing rooms. The hotel bar is famous for its martinis and its huge collection of fine cognacs—some over 150 years old. The hotel now has its own health club, with every kind of training machine you can imagine, and is open 8AM–8PM. If you are a relaxing kind of a guest as opposed to a working-out kind of a guest, the hotel has its own resident beauty therapist. ♦ 35 St. James's Pl (off St. James's St). 491.4840; fax 493.1264; US toll-free telephone 800/381.4702. Tube: Green Park. www.dukeshotel.com

27 LUCIANO'S

★★★$$$$ The latest addition to the Marco Pierre White empire is named after his eldest son. It marks his return to his Italian roots after years of producing the sexiest French food in town. The restaurant's Johnny Walker Bar makes for an impressive entrance, with its marble mosaic floor, pressed tin ceiling, and red leather banquettes. The main space is roomy and impressively unfussy—like a good Northern Italian restaurant. The menu is a sort of Ital-English mix, but the influences are definitely Italian. You can start with Cornish crab with *pane carasau* (more commonly known as *carta di musica*—the thin crispy bread of Sardinia) or carpaccio of tuna with artichoke, followed by papardelle with Tuscan veal ragu and excellent *bistecca ai porcini* (beef served with wonderful meaty wild mushrooms), and the dessert to go for is definitely the *semifreddo al torrone* with chocolate sauce. The wine list is very smart and very Italian with lots of interesting choices, which are all the easier to make with the expertise of sommelier Livio Italiani. "French food is too rich to eat every day of the week, but you can eat Italian and never get bored," says Marco. You certainly couldn't get bored here! ◆ Daily, lunch and dinner. 72/73 St James's St. 408.1440. Tube: Green Park

28 KING STREET

This street's claim to fame was once **St. James's Theatre**, completed in 1835, which premiered Oscar Wilde's *Lady Windermere's Fan* and *The Importance of Being Earnest*, Arthur Pinero's *The Second Mrs. Tanqueray*, and, later, Terence Rattigan's *Separate Tables*. Unfortunately, the theater was demolished in 1959, even though Vivien Leigh interrupted a Parliamentary session in an attempt to save it. It stood at the passageway to Angel Court. Note the other narrow passages opening onto this street, vestiges of a bygone era when streets were no more than pedestrian thoroughfares. Saunter down Crown Passage, which leads to Pall Mall and has some interesting shops, cafés, and restaurants. ◆ Between St. James's Sq and St. James's St. Tube: Green Park

29 CHRISTIE, MANSON & WOODS LTD.

Better known simply as **Christie's**, this is one of the world's leading auction houses. In the art and antiques trade, **Sotheby's**, the largest auction house, is said to be run by businessmen trying to be gentlemen, whereas Christie's is run by gentlemen trying to be businessmen. Founded in 1766 on Great Castle Street, this firm has been located here since 1823, except for a period during and after World War II when the building was damaged during the Blitz. If you arrive in the morning (when sales are generally held), you may see millionaires battling over a van Gogh or Picasso, an emerald necklace, or a famous pop star's worldly goods. If very important paintings are being auctioned, representatives from the world's museums will be here, and the atmosphere will resemble a cross between a Broadway opening and an operating room, with the auctioneer as leading actor and surgeon. Items to be sold are on view in the rooms and galleries around the auction room; perusing them is like exploring an informal museum, with the bonus that if you lose your head over the 17th-century carpet or the sentimental Victorian watercolor of the girl and the rabbit, you can attend the sale and bid on it. This auction house also offers wine for sale, and it purveys vintage motorcars, tribal art, photographs, and stamps. Its many experts specialize in

icons, nonmasterpiece artwork, furniture, and carpets. Glossy catalogs are for sale in the front shop. ◆ M–F; during a sale, also Tu, 9AM–8PM, and Su, 2PM–5PM. 5–8 King St (at Bury St). 839.9060. Tube: Green Park. Also at 85 Old Brompton Rd (between Sumner and Cranley Pls). 581.7611. Tube: South Kensington

30 THE GOLDEN LION

★$ The heavy theatrical curtains reflect this cozy pub's close links with the old **St. James's Theatre**; the upstairs bar had been connected to it and was patronized by theatergoers. Though the pub has been licensed since 1732, it was rebuilt in 1898 and given a flamboyant façade. There is still an upstairs bar, where you'll find such typical pub fare as lamb stew. ◆ British ◆ M–F, lunch and sandwiches, noon–2:30PM. 25 King St (at Angel Ct). 925.0007. Tube: Green Park

31 LOBB'S

Five generations of Lobbs have shod the rich and famous since John Lobb walked from Cornwall to London to set himself up as a shoemaker. The list of distinguished feet served here is considerable: those of Queen Victoria, Mountbatten, King George VI, the current royals, Cecil Beaton, Winston Churchill, Laurence Olivier, Groucho Marx, Frank Sinatra, Cole Porter, and Katharine Hepburn. In the basement of the shop, 15,000 wooden lasts of customers' feet are kept until they die—and some for long after that. The shoemakers draw an outline of each of your feet in their book, examine it from every angle in search of peculiarities, and then, on a long slip of paper, take a series of measurements, which are marked by snips in the paper. This is translated into wooden models of your feet, around which the leather is molded. After you've been walking the streets of London for a few days, the four-figure price may even sound appealing because it'll get you shoes that fit perfectly. ◆ M–Sa. 9 St. James's St (between Pall Mall and King St). 930.3664. Tube: Green Park

31 THE AVENUE

★★$$$ Chic minimalist décor has finally arrived in staid St. James's with this showy restaurant (formerly a bank). Attracting a well-heeled, trendy clientele, the restaurant creates imaginative dishes with a Mediterranean flair, such as endive tart with green-herb mustard for an appetizer, and such entrées as brill in bacon broth with white beans and juniper-cured salmon with horseradish crème fraîche. For dessert, there's a Port-glazed fig tart with praline ice cream. ◆ Modern British ◆ Daily, lunch and dinner. Reservations suggested. 7–9 St. James's St (between Pall Mall and King St). 321.2111. Tube: Green Park. www.theavenue.co.uk

31 LOCK & CO.

The house of Lock has been covering heads since 1676; it moved into this building in 1759. Lord Nelson's cocked hats were made here, and the Duke of Wellington, Beau Brummell, and all the American ambassadors to the Court of St. James's also purchased hats from this shop. The first bowlers were produced here in 1850 for the gamekeepers of a man named William Coke, and the shop still refers to the style as a Coke. There are about 16,000 hats in stock, but you can have one custom-made with the French *conformateur* that has been used to determine head measurements for 150 years. The flat tweed caps are popular with English country-lovers such as J.P. Donleavy and Prince Philip. The shop has extended its services to selling women's hats and even has a designer on the premises for custom-made commissions. It has two Royal Warrants. Paul McCartney shops here! ◆ M–F; Sa, 9:30AM–12:30PM. 6 St. James's St (between Pall Mall and King St). 930.8874. Tube: Green Park

31 L'ORANGER

★★★$$$ A lovely restaurant with lots of polished wood on the floors and wall panels. The rear of the room is a lovely place to sit . . . carpeted, glass-ceilinged, and overlooking a sweet courtyard. The chef is from Provence, where he held a trio of Michelin stars. His cooking is still pretty starry. There is a set lunch menu (with an admirable number of choices in each course), an à la carte menu, and a degustation menu. All are peppered with ingredients like Scottish blue lobster, foie gras, Dover sole, fillet of beef, and the like. The blood orange and lemon confit with caramel ice cream is toothachingly good. The wine list is masterful, and the restaurant organizes monthly wine tasting and "meet the producer" evenings. ◆ Modern European ◆ Daily, lunch and dinner; Su, dinner. Reservations recommended. 5 St. James's St (between Pall Mall and King St). 0871/332.0853. Tube: Green Park

32 BERRY BROS. AND RUDD

A wonderful, Dickensian structure with exquisite, strangely shaped black windows, this wine shop looks much as it did in the 18th century. The long, dark room contains a large oval table, chairs, antique prints, a few bottles of wine, and a pair of enormous scales embossed with "The Coffee Mill," acquired from the grocer who originally occupied the site. Starting in the 1760s, clients used to weigh themselves on the huge scales, and their weights are recorded in the shop's ledgers. Weight watching was serious business even in the days when corpulence signified prosperity. The Duke of York, who led his men up the hill and down again, weighed 14.5 stone (1 stone is 14 pounds), but the weight of his brother, King George IV, famous for his large girth, is not recorded. The wine, however, is what marks this shop for posterity. The distinctive black-and-white labels have been appearing on bottles of claret for more than 200 years, and the cellars contain bottles that would fill many a French citizen with awe. The shop also offers a wide selection of single-malt whiskeys (including its own Cutty Sark brand). ◆ M–Sa. 3 St. James's St (at Pickering Pl). 396.9600. Tube: Green Park

32 PICKERING PLACE

Timber wainscoting still lines this 18th-century alleyway. Halfway along the street is a plaque, "The Republic of Texas Legation 1842–45," commemorating the days when Texas was an independent republic and this was its embassy. It was rented to the Texans by the **Berry Bros. and Rudd** wine shop during a serious slump in the business of vintners. At the end of the alley is a court surrounded by houses that looks more like a cul-de-sac in a cathedral town than in the center of London. ◆ Between Crown Passage and St. James's St. Tube: Green Park

33 FARLOW'S

Hunting and fishing enthusiasts come to this upmarket shop for its reels, rods, game guns, and accessories as well as the weatherproof country clothes that go with them. It's located in the **Royal Opera Arcade**, London's first shopping mall, which still boasts pure Regency shop fronts from 1816, including the shop itself. The arcade's name harks back to the era when opera was being produced around the corner at **Her Majesty's Theatre**. ◆ M–Sa. 61 Pall Mall (between Crown Passage and St. James's St). 839.2423. Tube: Green Park

34 RED LION

★★$$ Dating back 400 years, this picturesque, timber-fronted pub was once used for the assignations of Nell Gwyn and Charles II. There is a small wood-paneled bar where you can order sandwiches and a pleasant upstairs room in which to partake of hearty home-cooked food. Tuck into fish-and-chips or a steak-and-ale pie. ◆ Pub ◆ M–Sa, lunch. Crown Passage (between Pall Mall and King St). 930.4141. Tube: Green Park

35 OXFORD AND CAMBRIDGE CLUB

This club is more democratic and less misogynistic than the others on Pall Mall, although true equality has not yet arrived. Out

CROWN COMMODITIES: THE ROYAL FAMILY TALKS SHOP

Although it may be hard to picture them doing so, members of Britain's royal family have been known to go shopping. Whether the baskets and bags are filled by the sovereigns or their servants is a matter for speculation; however, finding out where the ruling class spends its cash is simple—look for a Royal Warrant, a coat of arms that represents one of four members of the royal family: the queen, the queen mother, the Duke of Edinburgh, or the Prince of Wales. When a supplier holds a Royal Warrant, it means that it provides goods to one of the "Big Four" by appointment. The privilege is worth having, because the supplier can then advertise to all and sundry that "royalty shops here"—not a bad way to drum up business. Like much of English heritage, the tradition began in the Middle Ages. Henry VIII gave his approval to a "King's Laundresse"; his daughter, Elizabeth, had her own "Operator for the Teeth." To qualify for royal approval today, a business must have supplied goods or services to the royal household for 3 years running. At last count, there were around 1,000 Royal Warrant holders.

Some are easy to identify and fairly obvious. There is **Harrods**, of course, with all four Royal Warrants;

Hatchards, the bookseller, and **Lobb's**, the shoemaker, both hold three. **Twinings**, on the Strand, has the honor of supplying all the royal tea, the **House of Hardy** claims to have sold fishing rods to every Prince of Wales in the 20th century, and **Lock & Co.** serves as hatter to the Duke of Edinburgh. You can play "spot the Warrant" throughout **St. James's** and **Piccadilly** (the insignia are usually displayed over or near the shop's door)—because these two areas are convenient to **Buckingham Palace**, they contain possibly the largest concentration of Royal Warrant holders in London.

The other way to find out what the royals use is simply to look at the goods. With this method, you can tell which marmalade the queen prefers (it's probably sold at **Fortnum & Mason**, "the Queen's Grocer") and what cologne Prince Charles uses (from **Floris**). Every roll of Andrex brand toilet paper proudly displays the Royal Warrants of the queen and the queen mother, an advertising coup for Scott Limited, the supplier that proclaims itself "by appointment . . . manufacturer of disposable tissues" to these two royal shoppers.

of a total membership of 4,500, women number only 550. This is a private club for people who have been admitted as members of a college at the Universities of Oxford or Cambridge. It has arrangements with some 125 clubs overseas, including many university clubs in the US, and lodging in one of the club's 42 rooms costs a fraction of the rates at hotels. Behind the impressive façade, the rooms are decorated and arranged as for a large town house of the early 19th century. The dining rooms aren't fancy, but the wine lists are. Sir Robert Smirke and Sydney Smirke built this headquarters in 1837. ♦ 71 Pall Mall (between St. James's Sq and Pall Mall Pl). 930.5151. Tube: Green Park

36 SCHOMBERG HOUSE

A rare example of Queen Anne architecture, this house was built around 1698. The warm brown-red brick, tall Dutch windows, and human scale come as a relief from the imposing Italianate stones and stucco that dominate this area. Gainsborough spent his last years here, dying in 1788 after finally reconciling with his old friend and rival Joshua Reynolds. His parting words were, "We are all going to Heaven and Van Dyck is of the company." After World War II, the

house was gutted and filled with modern offices. Next door is the site of a house that was owned by the charming actress Nell Gwyn, mistress of Charles II. All the property on Pall Mall belongs to the Crown, with the exception of **No. 79**, because Gwyn refused to live in a house she didn't own. The blue plaque here spells her name as *Gwynne*, but it appears as *Gwyn* or even *Gwynn* in the many references to this memorable royal mistress. Neither of the premises is open to the public. ♦ 82 Pall Mall (between Carlton Gardens and Marlborough Rd). Tube: Green Park

37 PALL MALL

Americans pronounce it like the brand of cigarettes, but the upper-class English who have their clubs here say "Pell Mell." Named after *paille maille*, the ball game that was played in The Mall, which runs parallel, this is part of the ancient route from the City to St. James's. Pall Mall is lined with gentlemen's clubs and a few appropriately exclusive shops, but its residential character has given way almost entirely to offices. It is a stately boulevard by day, a windy, monumental wasteland by night. ♦ Between Haymarket

---

Restaurants/Clubs: Red | Hotels: Purple | Shops: Orange | Outdoors/Parks: Green | Sights/Culture: Blue

and St. James's St. Tube: Piccadilly Circus, Charing Cross

38 ATHENAEUM CLUB

This most august of the gentlemen's clubs occupies one of the most distinguished buildings in London. Completed in 1830, it was designed by **Decimus Burton**, the man who gave **London Constitution Arch** and the screen at the entrance to **Hyde Park**. The cream stucco façade has pure architectural dignity. A Wedgwood-like frieze wraps around the building above the first-floor windows; it is worth noting because it is a reconstruction of the one that adorned the Parthenon. (The extraordinary original remnants are in their own display room at the **British Museum**.) A large gilded figure of Pallas Athena, goddess of wisdom, practical skills, and prudent warfare, graces the porch and accurately sets the standards for those who enter—bishops, scientists, and the top brains of the Civil Service and Foreign Office. Inside, the atmosphere is one of intimidating sagacity. A portrait of member Charles Darwin broods over the living. The Royal Society's Dining Society, an elite group within the formidably elite Royal Society, meets here, and those within that clever and select circle are de facto members of the **Athenaeum**, which was named after the emperor Hadrian's university in Rome. The club is not open to the public. ♦ 107 Pall Mall (at Waterloo Pl). 930.4843. Tube: Charing Cross, Piccadilly Circus

39 CRIMEAN WAR MEMORIAL

Florence Nightingale is one of the few women represented in this masculine part of London; in this statue, she holds her famous lamp. Standing next to her is Sidney Herbert, secretary of war during the Crimean campaign. *Honor* is cast from captured Russian cannons. The memorial was created by John Bell in the 1850s. ♦ Waterloo Pl and Pall Mall. Tube: Charing Cross, Piccadilly Circus

40 INSTITUTE OF DIRECTORS

The **United Service Club**, known as the **Senior**, was founded in 1815 for the triumphant officers of the Napoleonic wars and inhabited this structure for 150 years. The first building commissioned by a club, it was originally designed by **John Nash** in 1828, but most noticeable are the alterations carried out by **Decimus Burton**: the Doric columns and the Corinthian portico. The granite mounting block outside on Waterloo Place was put there by Wellington to help short men mount their horses. The Senior collapsed in 1974. Today it is a business center for the Institute of Directors, but it still has the 19th-century furniture designed for the club (including a 15-foot chandelier

presented by George IV to commemorate the Battle of Waterloo), and it retains an inimitably masculine atmosphere of mahogany and leather. It too is closed to visitors. ♦ 116 Pall Mall (at Waterloo Pl). 839.1233. Tube: Charing Cross, Piccadilly Circus

41 LANCASTER HOUSE

In 1825, **Benjamin Dean Wyatt** started construction of this house in light Bath stone for the Duke of York, who commissioned the extravagant home but died before paying for it, whereupon it was sold to the Marquess of Stafford (hence the structure was first called **York House** and then **Stafford House**). **Sir Robert Smirke** completed it in 1840, and **Sir Charles Barry** designed the interior. Chopin played for Queen Victoria in the **Music Room**, and the Duke of Windsor lived here when he was the Prince of Wales (between 1919 and 1930). Since being restored from war damage, the building has been a venue for state banquets and conferences. The Louis XV interiors are sumptuous. It is closed to the public. ♦ Stable Yard Rd (at Stable Yd). Tube: Green Park, St. James's Park

42 CLARENCE HOUSE

This house was built for the Duke of Clarence, later King William IV. Until Queen Elizabeth's accession to the throne in 1952, she and Prince Philip lived here. Then it became the dwelling of the queen mother, who came to the gate to greet the public on her birthday, 4 August. On that day a lone bagpiper played in the garden at 9AM, a gentle Scottish alarm clock for one of the best-loved members of the royal family. Diana Spencer and Sarah Ferguson stayed here on the eves of their weddings. Now it is home to Prince Charles and Camilla, Duchess of Cornwall. Parts of the house are open to the public in the summer—5 rooms and a small art collection, which belonged to the late queen mother and which includes the 1945 portrait of her by Sir James Gunn. The collection also contains works by Sir Noël Coward, W.S. Sickert, and Augustus John. Tickets *must* be pre-booked. ♦ Daily, Aug–mid-Oct. 776.7303. Stable Yard Rd (off the Mall). Tube: Green Park, St. James's Park. www.royal.gov.uk

43 ST. JAMES'S PALACE

The whole St. James's area owes its development to the **Palace of St. James's** (whose name comes from the Augustinian hospital for leprous women that stood on this site in the 13th century). Henry VIII purchased the land in 1532 to build a small royal palace—initially a hunting lodge (he also enclosed some 300 acres to the south) and later his third royal residence. After the fall of Cardinal Wolsey, Henry switched his allegiance to **Whitehall Palace**. Even so, he regarded with affection the rambling brick mansion called St. James's Palace. Feminine appreciation for the palace is suggested in its history of royal births—Charles II, James II, Mary II, and Queen Anne were all born here in the 1600s. Charles II never liked Whitehall, so he spent time, energy, and money building up this palace; however, it did not become the official residence of the sovereign until 1698, when Whitehall Palace burned down. It remained the monarch's London residence until Queen Victoria ascended to the throne in 1837 and moved the court to **Buckingham Palace**. Yet St. James's maintains a presence in modern British life; not only does Prince Charles have his office here but he also now resides in rooms here during the week. To this day, all foreign ambassadors present their "credentials" to the **Court of St. James's** before riding in the Glass Coach to Buckingham Palace. The palace originally had four courts, but fire, rebuilding, and time have cut the number in half. The state rooms, which can be glimpsed over the wall facing The Mall, were rebuilt by **Sir Christopher Wren** in 1703. The most charming surviving part of the Tudor palace is the gatehouse, with its octagonal clock tower, which faces St. James's Street. This four-story building of worn redbrick sits astride a pair of vast old gates. The turrets crowned with battlements and the sentry box staffed by a soldier from the Guards seem too "Gilbert and Sullivan" to be true but are reminders of the pomp for which this palace exists. ♦ Pall Mall (at St. James's St). Tube: Green Park

At St. James's Palace:

Chapel Royal

This lovely chapel, west of the gatehouse at St. James's Palace, was built by Henry VIII in 1532. It is one of the great gems of Tudor London, with a coffered ceiling painted by Hans Holbein. Married beneath it were William III and Mary II (1677), Queen Anne (1683), George IV (1795), Queen Victoria (1840), and George V (1893). But what stirs the heart most is not the royal weddings, but Charles I, the sad, brave king who received communion in the chapel on the morning of his execution, 30 January 1649. This is one of five **Chapels Royal** in London, and as such, it is not subject to a bishop but owes its allegiance directly to the sovereign. Visitors can attend services in the chapel every Sunday between October and Easter. Because the chapel is within the palace complex, there is strict security, with a police officer on duty at a sentry box. Services start

promptly. ♦ Su, 8:30AM, 11:15AM, Jan–Easter and Oct–Dec. Ambassadors' Ct (at Stable Yard Rd)

43 Friary Court

Every new sovereign is proclaimed from the balcony in this courtyard, and it was from here that the cheers of her subjects reached the ears of 18-year-old Queen Victoria, causing her to weep. The **State Apartments**, reached through the door in the northeast corner, are open only on special occasions, usually when royal gifts are on display, and the wait can be considerable. The **Armoury Room** is lined with ancient weapons, and the **Tapestry Room** is filled with pictorial textiles woven for Charles II. The last person to have a hand at decorating these rooms was William Morris in the 1860s. ♦ Off Marlborough Rd

44 Queen's Chapel

This 17th-century architectural gem by **Inigo Jones** was the first church built in the classical style; like **Banqueting House** in **Whitehall**, also by Jones, the interior is a perfect cube. The chapel was built for the Spanish Infanta Maria, the intended bride of Charles I. The arrangement didn't work out, however, and Charles eventually married another woman, Henrietta Maria, here. Now it is one of five **Chapels Royal** in the city. The gold-and-white coffered ceiling is original. On summer Sundays, the chapel is marvelously lit by the sun through the wide Venetian window, which occupies the entire east wall. Visitors can enter the church for Sunday services. ♦ Su, 8:30AM, 11:15AM, Easter–July. Marlborough Rd (between The Mall and Pall Mall). Tube: Green Park

45 Marlborough House

Sir Christopher Wren built this residence for John Churchill, first Duke of Marlborough, between 1709 and 1711—though it was more for the duchess than for the duke. Formidable, turbulent, brilliant, and beautiful, Sarah Churchill, first duchess of Marlborough and lady-in-waiting as well as intimate friend of Queen Anne, laid the inscribed foundation stone that survives within the house. The duchess hated the monumental palace of Blenheim (which Queen Anne had created for the duke after his victory at the Battle of Blenheim), so she instructed Wren to make her London mansion strong, plain, and convenient. The Crown acquired the house in 1817. Unfortunately, the house's pure simplicity has been disguised by the additions and enlargements made in the

Restaurants/Clubs: Red | Hotels: Purple | Shops: Orange | Outdoors/Parks: Green | Sights/Culture: Blue

early 1860s by **Sir James Pennethorne**. Edward VII lived here while he was Prince of Wales, George V was born in the house, and his consort, Queen Mary, lived here during her widowhood. In 1959, Queen Elizabeth presented the house to the nation so that it could become the **Commonwealth Conference Center** in London; it is used for meetings. The house is closed to the public. ♦ Pall Mall (at Marlborough Rd). 839.3411. Tube: Green Park

46 CARLTON GARDENS

During World War II, the Free French occupied **No. 4**, where Charles de Gaulle's message to his compatriots is inscribed on a plaque. ♦ Off Pall Mall. Tube: Charing Cross, Piccadilly Circus

47 WATERLOO PLACE

One of the few pieces of town planning in London is also one of the most impressive. **John Nash** designed it in 1816 to commemorate the Duke of Wellington's triumph over the French the previous year. It marks the beginning of Nash's triumphal route to **Regent's Park**. **Carlton House Terrace** frames Waterloo Place, which intersects Pall Mall on its way north into lower Regent Street and Piccadilly Circus. ♦ Between Carlton House Terr and Pall Mall. Tube: Charing Cross, Piccadilly Circus

At Waterloo Place:

DUKE OF YORK STEPS AND DUKE OF YORK MONUMENT

Benjamin Dean Wyatt's dramatic column, built in 1834, dominates Waterloo Place. The 7-ton bronze monument here, dedicated to Frederick, the second son of George III, was financed by withholding a day's pay from all soldiers. Made by Sir Richard Westmacott, the statue of the duke stands on a pedestal that soars 137 feet into the sky; because the duke died owing £2 million, some quipped that the pink-granite column was meant to keep him out of reach of his creditors.

STATUE OF EDWARD VII

In front of the Duke of York Steps and facing Waterloo Place is Edward VII, looking hale and beefy, as Sir Bertram MacKennal immortalized him in 1921. Because of the long life of his mother, Queen Victoria, the king reigned for only 9 of his 69 years, but in that short time he inspired the Edwardian Age: a secure, elegant period for the rich and aristocratic, a world where to amuse and be amused were raisons d'être. He contributed color and pageantry to the monarchy, but he also brought a sense of serious commitment to such issues as the quality of workers' lives and the treatment of Indians by English officials. Edward was aware that beyond Europe lay his empire, the largest the world had ever known. As king, he created the *entente cordiale* with France and used his considerable diplomatic skill and charm to ease the conflicts between Germany and England, conflicts that were tragically too deep for any monarch to resolve. However, he is best remembered for his voracious appetite: At his last formal dinner at **Buckingham Palace**, on 5 March 1910, he made his way through nine dishes, including salmon steak, grilled chicken, saddle of mutton, and several snipe stuffed with foie gras. He died 2 months later, yet souvenirs of the Edwardian Age are still tucked away in the small streets nearby.

48 CARLTON HOUSE TERRACE

These creamy white, glossy buildings on this little street parallel to the Mall are among the last contributions **John Nash** made to London before his death in 1835. Actually, it's the graceful backs of the buildings that face The Mall. The 1,000-foot-long terrace is a stately confection of Corinthian columns and human-scale arches; the former were evidently inspired by **Jacques-Ange Gabriel**'s buildings in the Place de la Concorde. The clean outline, intercepted in the center by the **Duke of York Steps**, is a splendid contribution to The Mall: an impressive backdrop for royal processions by day, a royal wedding cake when floodlit at night. Erected between 1827 and 1832, Carlton House Terrace replaced **Carlton House**, the palatial home purchased in 1732 by Frederick, Prince of Wales, who died before his father, George II. It was subsequently owned by George III, and then by his son, the prince regent, who transformed it at staggering expense into what was considered the most beautiful mansion in England. But after he became King George IV, he and Nash agreed to demolish it and convinced Parliament to allocate funds for the conversion of **Buckingham House** into **Buckingham Palace**. The columns were saved and recycled into the portico of the **National Gallery**, and Nash was asked to design the buildings seen today. Originally, the terrace was to line both sides of The Mall, providing grand town houses for the aristocracy; only one side was built, leaving **St. James's Park** on view. ♦ The Mall (between Trafalgar Sq and Duke of York Steps). Tube: Charing Cross, Piccadilly Circus

Within Carlton House Terrace:

MALL GALLERIES

These rooms exhibit traditional paintings by members of the Royal Society of Portrait Painters and the Federation of British Artists. Here is one of the few London venues to show work by well-established British artists such as Tom Coates and Claire Spencer alongside that of up-and-coming students and young unknown painters. There are regular workshops and demonstrations. ◆ Admission. Daily. 930.6844

INSTITUTE OF CONTEMPORARY ARTS (ICA)

Founded in 1947, this lively arts center has an industrious, avant-garde atmosphere. Its three galleries exhibit British and foreign photography, architectural drawings, paintings, and event art, among other shows. In the evening, interesting foreign and cult movies are shown in the cinema, whereas experimental films, videos, and works by new filmmakers are screened in the **Ciné-mathèque** and cutting-edge plays are performed in the theater. There is always a buzz of artistic activity here, although some of the programs have been cut back because of budget constraints. Even if you don't take in a performance here, visit the first-rate bookshop, which has all the latest art books as well as magazines, postcards, and recent works by avant-garde novelists. The exhibitions are known for highlighting new, provocative artists; the galleries featured the first solo show of Damien Hirst well before he won the **Tate**'s Turner Prize. ◆ Admission. Arts center: M, noon–11PM; Tu-Sa, noon–1AM, including the bar; Su, noon–10:30PM. Galleries: M-Su, noon–7:30PM. Bookshop: M-Sa, noon–10PM; Su, noon–8PM. 766.1452; box office, 930.3647

Within the Institute of Contemporary Arts (ICA):

ICA CAFÉ

★$ Enjoy an Italian or vegetarian meal or a selection of bar snacks with a trendy beer (such as Rolling Rock, Becks, or Pils) at the bar upstairs while you indulge in a spot of people watching or listen to the arty talk from the nearest table. ◆ Italian/Vegetarian ◆ Daily, lunch, dinner, and afternoon tea with homemade cakes and biscuits. 930.8619

ROYAL SOCIETY

Formed in the 1640s and formalized by King Charles II in 1660, this society is one of the most distinguished scientific bodies in the world. In the 17th century it was a hub of scientific discovery, where Newton, Halley, Dryden, and Pepys chatted about inventions, although Pepys, then president, never understood Newton's *Principia*. Past presidents include Sir Christopher Wren, Davy, Huxley, Thomson, Rutherford, and

Fleming. Today, the society gives medals annually for original research in many scientific fields; however, it is closed to the public. ◆ 6 Carlton House Terr. 839.5561

49 ADMIRALTY ARCH

The inglorious car race around **Trafalgar Square** doesn't prepare you for this grand Corinthian structure in Portland stone, which is actually a screen with five arches: the center arch, whose iron gates open only for ceremonial processions; two side arches for automobile traffic; and two smaller arches for pedestrians. Created by **Sir Aston Webb** in 1910, its very monumentality is a surprise because it is so un-London. This structure marks the first part of the royal processional route from **Buckingham Palace** to **St. Paul's Cathedral**. The structure was part of Edward VII's tribute to his mother, Queen Victoria, although the king himself died before the memorial was completed. ◆ The Mall (between Trafalgar Sq and Horse Guards Rd). Tube: Charing Cross

50 THE MALL

Two double rows of plane trees line this royal processional road (pronounced to rhyme with *pal*), which sweeps theatrically to a monumental climax. Laid out after the Restoration in 1660, the stretch from **Trafalgar Square** to **Buckingham Palace** was originally an enclosed alley for playing *paille maille* (a French game similar to croquet, called "pell mell" by the English). It was transformed to give a formal vista of **Buckingham Palace** by **Sir Aston Webb** in 1910 as part of a memorial to Queen Victoria. The present Mall runs just south of the original promenade, now used as a bridle path. On Sunday, the Mall partially closes to traffic, so strolling is more pleasant. ◆ Between Trafalgar Sq and Buckingham Palace. Tube: Charing Cross, Piccadilly Circus

51 THE CITADEL

The enveloping ivy generates an air of mystery around what is actually a bomb shelter, built in 1940 for naval officers and never demolished. Scrupulously maintained by the Parks Department, which mows the acre of grass on top, it serves as a reminder of the past era, before bomb technology made shelters like this obsolete. ◆ The Mall (at Horse Guards Rd). Tube: Charing Cross, Piccadilly Circus

52 ST. JAMES'S PARK

In the 16th century, Henry VIII enclosed this, the oldest and most perfect of royal parks.

Restaurants/Clubs: **Red** | Hotels: **Purple** | Shops: **Orange** | Outdoors/Parks: **Green** | Sights/Culture: **Blue**

THE BEST

Andrew Currie

Owner, Nomad Books/Whiskey Distiller

Waterloo Bridge, October—walking across at sunset to the **National Theatre**.

Royal Opera House, **Crush Bar**—best bar staff in Europe.

Zen Central—best Chinese food.

Putney Towpath—running to **Hammersmith Bridge** past **Harrods Depository**.

Soho, summer, 6AM Sunday—last night's detritus with new day.

Stamford Bridge, August—watching new football season. Clean grass, clean shirts, bright hope.

Paddington Station, November, 7AM—good cappuccino. Leaving town as commuters arrive.

Today it comprises 93 acres and is an enchantment of water, birds, views, gaslights, and Englishness. It is a royal park in the best sense of the word: Monarchs have lavished their wealth and ingenuity on it, making it a graceful, contemplative place. Henry VIII drained the marshland between **St. James's** and **Whitehall Palaces** to make a forest and deer-hunting park. Charles I created the ceremonious walks, and he strode bravely across the park to his execution. His son, Charles II, created what you see today; he hired French landscape gardener André Le Nôtre and, shortly after the Restoration, opened this exotic oasis of trees, flowers, ducks, geese, and pelicans to the public. In 1827, George IV enlisted **John Nash** to reshape the canal and create the meandering lake, spanned by a bridge that grants a magical view of **Buckingham Palace**. Daily at 3PM the distinguished pelicans appear for an afternoon tea of whiting and other aquatic delicacies; they are direct descendants of the pair given to Charles II by a Russian ambassador. On the south side of the park runs **Birdcage Walk**, named for the aviaries Charles II established here for his amusement. ♦ Bounded by Horse Guards and Spur Rds and by Birdcage Walk and The Mall. Tube: St. James's Park

53 BUCKINGHAM PALACE

The royal palace is the most looked-at building in London, not because of its magnificence (it is not very magnificent) and not because of its age (there are plenty of older buildings to see). The wistful gazes are inspired by the appealing mystique of the monarchy—and as Maude declared to her young lover in *Harold and Maude*, "We [Americans] may not believe in monarchy, but we miss the kings and queens."

This is the oldest monarchy in the world, and it resides in the last country where monarchy exists on a grand and sanctified scale, with religious processions and backed up by a titled aristocracy that transcends nationality, social class, and party affiliation.

Her Most Excellent Majesty Elizabeth the Second, by the Grace of God, of the United Kingdom of Great Britain and Northern Ireland and of her Realms and Territories Queen, Head of the Commonwealth, Defender of the Faith, Sovereign of the British Orders of Knighthood, is the 40th monarch since the Norman Conquest, descended from Charlemagne and King Canute. Her accession in 1952 coincided with the beginning of the end of the British Empire, and she has presided over its dissolution with noble leadership. She is probably one of the best-informed diplomats alive today, having had continuous access to world leaders for more than 40 years. She has known Nikita Khrushchev, Dwight Eisenhower, Charles de Gaulle, John F. Kennedy, Leonid Brezhnev, Ronald Reagan, and Mikhail Gorbachev, and is acquainted with every current major head of state around the globe. On Tuesday nights when Queen Elizabeth is in London, the prime minister goes to Buckingham Palace for a talk with her. The queen's concern, excellent memory, and sharp insight have been appreciated by almost all the prime ministers of her reign.

Will she retire and turn the business over to her eldest son? The answer is no. Elizabeth is queen for life, having been anointed during what is considered to be the sacrament of coronation; the monarchy's continuity and survival depend on adherence to its spiritual laws. Under the hereditary system, the last intake of breath by the dying sovereign coincides with the next intake by the living sovereign, hence the ancient cry, "The king is dead. Long live the king."

When the queen is in residence at Buckingham Palace, the royal standard flies overhead. The tourist's viewpoint is the rather dour eastern façade, completely rebuilt by **Sir Aston Webb** in 1913. The front western façade, visible only to visitors to the palace, is by **John Nash**, the palace's first architect (Nash began the building in 1820, and **Edmund Blore** finished it). The main building is flanked by two classical pavilions and overlooks an immense sweep of lawn, 45 acres of private gardens, woodlands, giant trees, more than 200 species of wild plants, a lake graced with pink flamingos, a leafy border, and tennis courts. This is where the queen's garden parties are held each summer.

The original redbrick house, built for the Duke and Duchess of Buckingham in 1702-1705, was bought by George III some 60 years later for his beloved Queen Charlotte, who filled it with children and made it into a family home, which became known as Queen's House. George IV commissioned Nash to make it into a residence worthy of a monarch, but the plans became grander and more difficult to execute with time. The transformation process had many of the elements of a Laurel and Hardy film, not the least being the scheme to surround the palace with scaffolding to disguise the fact that a new palace was being constructed, as Parliament had granted permission only for renovations and repairs. When the king died, an investigation into the palace's spiraling costs revealed financial irregularities. Nash, who had transformed London into an elegant city, was dismissed by an outraged Parliament. Publicly disgraced, he died 5 years later, in 1835. George IV died before the palace was finished, and his successor, William IV, preferred to live in **Kensington Palace** until his death.

Buckingham Palace became the official London residence of the sovereign in 1837, when Queen Victoria moved in. Building work began soon after: There were not enough bedrooms or nurseries, and the kitchens were old-fashioned and badly planned. Yet the royal standard flew as repairs were made, and the queen and her consort, Prince Albert, extended the palace, also building the **State Supper Room** and the **Ball Room**. The queen had the **Marble Arch** removed from the front of the palace and placed at its present site on the north side of **Hyde Park**. By 1843, Victoria had written in her diary that she was very happy here. Webb, architect for George V and his popular wife, Mary of Teck, transformed the palace's façade, replacing the flaking Caen stone with Portland stone and adding the French-inspired pilasters. George V also saw the 1911 unveiling of the **Victoria Memorial** in front of the palace: A wedding cake of a sculpture by Sir Thomas Brock, it shows a seated, 13-foot-high Queen Victoria facing **The Mall**, surrounded by the figures of Truth, Justice, and Motherhood—all dear to her heart. At the top, Victory is attended by Constancy and Courage.

Buckingham Palace is open to the public during August and September (when the royals are vacationing). Tickets can now be bought in advance—they go on sale at 9AM in a ticket office erected each summer beside **Green Park** in The Mall. Beginning at 9:30AM, time-specific tickets (for that day only) gain visitors entry to a palace entrance on Buckingham Palace Road. The admission price goes toward the restoration of the fire-damaged **Windsor Castle**. The 18 rooms on view include the **State Rooms**, the **Throne Room**, the **State Dining Rooms**, and the **Music Room**. Many works in the nonpareil **British Royal Collection** can be seen as well (also see the **Queen's Gallery**, below). A gift shop in a hut at the garden exit sells specially commissioned gifts that are available only here. The Changing of the Guard ceremony is held inside the palace gates at 11:30AM between early April and early August, usually every 48 hours (call for information about the schedule or check the *Times*) and varies the rest of the year. ◆Daily, Aug–Sept. At the end of The Mall. 839.1377. Information on the Changing of the Guard ceremony: 0839/123411 (premium rate call). Tube: St. James's Park, Victoria, Green Park. www.royal.gov.uk

54 QUEEN'S GALLERY

This royal treasure chest, built by **John Nash** in 1831, was originally a conservatory and in 1843 became a chapel. In 1962, Her Majesty established it as a gallery to show artworks from the **Royal Collection**, one of the world's greatest art collections. Only a small fraction of the hundreds of paintings, sculptures, furnishings, and drawings in the collection can be shown at any one time. Exhibits (which change every 18 months) focus on a particular subject or theme, such as royal children, animal paintings, British soldiers, specific Old Masters such as Gainsborough or Leonardo, or heirloom silver, cutlery, and furniture. There is also a gift shop, excellent for souvenirs from the royal homes, such as pungent lavender scent from Prince Charles's country house Highgrove. ◆ Admission; one admission ticket to both the Queen's Gallery and the **Royal Mews** (see below) is also available. Daily. Buckingham Gate (between Birdcage Walk and Buckingham Palace Rd). 839.1377. Tube: Victoria, St. James's Park

55 ROYAL MEWS

All seven state carriages and coaches from all periods are on display in this circa-1826 building by **John Nash**; this is probably the finest and most valuable collection of state coaches in the world. Here is the State Coach acquired by George II in 1762 that is still in use today. It looks like the enchanted coach from *Cinderella*, with elaborate carvings representing eight palm trees, branching at the top and supporting the roof, and three cherubs, representing England, Scotland, and Ireland. It is 24 feet long, 8 feet wide, and 12 feet high; it weighs 4 tons. This is also the home of the royal horses, which may sometimes be seen pulling carriages in **Hyde Park**. ◆ Admission. W, noon–4PM, Oct–Mar;

Restaurants/Clubs: Red | Hotels: Purple | Shops: Orange | Outdoors/Parks: Green | Sights/Culture: Blue

Tu–Th, noon–4PM, Apr–July; M–Th, noon–4PM, Aug–Sept. Buckingham Palace Rd (at Lower Grosvenor Pl). 839.1377. Tube: Victoria

56 41

$$$$ A unique little hotel. It has been awarded five stars from the American Association of Hospitality Sciences. It was ranked No. 2 in England in *Travel & Leisure's World's Best 500 Hotels of 2008.* It is one of the Red Carnation Group, which means you will never have been anywhere like it. Red Carnation president Bea Tollman oversees the interior design of every room in each hotel herself, and no two are the same. No. 41 has a chic, metropolitan feel. All the rooms have iPod docking systems as standard (phew!), and most have working fireplaces. The suites come with almost too many amenities to use in one stay. But you will probably be able to enjoy your personal butler, your use of the Bentley, and your personal assistant (9AM–5:30PM). The Master Suite (start saving now) has a cupola over the bedroom, and so, in the heart of London, you can sleep gazing up at the stars. The level of attention and care is incredible. There are two members of staff to every guest. You get a drink to welcome you, complimentary canapés each evening, and a pantry to plunder for snacks and nibbles throughout the day. Breakfast can be taken in The Executive Lounge under a glass ceiling (all the better to see the rain). They also have a relaxed all-day menu here, so you can have piri piri chicken or a burger anytime you like. You just might cry when you have to leave. ♦ 41 Buckingham Palace Rd, SW1. 300.0041; fax 300.0141. Tube: Victoria. www.redcarnationhotels.com

56 THE RUBENS AT THE PALACE

$$$ Checking into this luxurious and well-appointed hotel, rated Four Star Deluxe, is guaranteed to set your pulse quickening. The building was originally constructed, in 1911, as accommodation for debutantes attending parties at the palace, and the place still has a way of making you feel you could be part of that world. Let's face it, how many hotels have a pet concierge? The marvelously decorated rooms—all plush velvet, chintz, and silk—offer a level of comfort and decadence lacking in most London hotels, while the business-ready suites make working a breeze. The sumptuous "Royal Wing" takes things to another level by featuring eight rooms, each themed to a specific English monarch, and all equipped with DVD players, printers, scanners, and everything modern royalty could possibly want in a home away from home. I should warn you that the décor in some of the historically named suites is not to be viewed with even the mildest of headaches. This is "Extreme Décor." But you kind of have to love it. Dining choices (should you opt not to take advantage of the hotel's 24-hour room service) include the intimate and cozy **Library Restaurant** (see below); the all-day dining room, **Old Masters** (justly famed for its traditional English roasts and boasting quite possibly the most nationalistic table linen in the world); and the Cavalry Bar and Palace Lounge, with views of the **Royal Mews** across the street, a fantastic afternoon tea service, and live piano music nightly. All of this is held together by a staff that truly knows what it is doing—the uniformly attentive and warm service is excellent and proof-positive that Red Carnation president Bea Tollman must be the most gracious employer around; only an eager and well-appreciated staff can offer this level of pampering and royal treatment to everyone! ♦ 39 Buckingham Palace Rd. 834.6600; fax 828.5401. Tube: Victoria. www.rubenshotel.com

Within The Rubens:

LIBRARY RESTAURANT

★★★$$$ The Library has just been included in the prestigious *Tatler Restaurant Guide.* As sumptuously decorated as it is possible for a library to be, it is gloriously over-the-top. The menu is less overwrought, including watercress and sorrel soup (although you can opt for the foie gras with fried onion, apple crisp, and Muscat-soaked grapes); the restaurant's signature dish of whole-grilled Dover sole with chive and butter sauce will lead you perfectly to Madagascan vanilla panna cotta with golden kiwi and crystallized vanilla pod. The wine list includes the restaurant's own Bouchard Finlayson collection of South African wines (ask and you will be offered a free tasting!). ♦ Daily, breakfast, lunch, and dinner

57 THE GORING

$$$$ The Goring family have run this hotel through four generations, since 1910, making it one of the oldest privately owned hotels in London; it also is the only one with five stars. It has recently been voted among the world's Top 100 Hotels by *Traveller Magazine.* Jeremy Goring is the man in charge now. It is still as traditionally English as gray skies and bad service, but now has an impressively redecorated restaurant. There are 71 bedrooms and suites, some of the nicest overlooking the hotel's private garden. The staff are absolutely charming and wonderfully efficient. If you really want to know you are in England, as opposed to the limbo of "five-star hotel world," this would be the place to stay. Champagne afternoon teas can be taken on The Terrace, and the luxury Weekend to Remember (two nights in a deluxe room with dinner, Champagne, full English breakfasts

The Best

John Ruler

Travel Writer and Broadcaster, Ruler Editorial Services

Watching the sun set over the **Thames** from the walkways of **Tower Bridge**, now open to the public.

Having afternoon tea and homemade cakes in the **Crypt Restaurant** at **St. Martin-in-the-Fields** close to **Trafalgar Square**; their sandwiches and hot snacks are pretty good too.

The scent of spring flowers, especially the daffodils, in the almost country-cottage setting of **Church Street, Chelsea**, still a village in so many ways.

Admiring **Buckingham Palace** from the bridge in the middle of **St. James's Park**, ready-made for photographers looking for that distinctive shot.

Browsing through the specialist bookshops on **Charing Cross Road**.

Strolling along the **South Bank** away from the traffic—and with more than its fair share of sights—in either direction. Plenty of coffee and rest room stops—also novelty shopping at the **National Film Theatre** and the **Museum of the Moving Image**.

Feeling proud that at long last **Southwark**, the genuine heart of London, is being recognized, thanks to projects like the reconstruction of **Shakespeare's Globe Theatre**, and the conversion of the old **Bankside Power Station** into the **Tate Gallery of Modern Art**.

Listening to Shakespeare during the summer at the open-air theater, **Regent's Park**; mulled wine during the interval keeps out the evening chill. If it looks like rain, bring an umbrella and book a seat for *The Tempest*.

Horse-riding in **Rotten Row**: Go early when the Horse Guards are exercising. It's as extraordinary as riding in Central Park, New York. I have done both.

Taking the riverbus to **Greenwich Park** for a picnic and a tour round the splendidly ornate **Maritime Museum**.

---

served in your room, flowers, fruit bowls, and generalized pampering) is exactly that. ♦ 17 Beeston Pl (at Eaton La). 396.9000; fax 834.4393. Tube: Victoria

Within The Goring:

The Garden Bar

A really lovely place to have a drink. *Sumptuous* is the word that springs to mind. The hotel's much-lauded wine list is available, as are premium spirits and the rest. The inventive bar team has a cocktail list that changes monthly, and there is always something on it to tempt.

The Goring Restaurant

★★$$$ This restaurant has just been named Best British Restaurant by the prestigious Tio Pepe Restaurant Awards. It has also just had a glamorous makeover by David Linley (Viscount Linley, should you wish to be formal, son of the late Princess Margaret) and is a vision in biscuit, cream, and caramel under sparkling Swarovski chandeliers. The menu is dedicately English cuisine. The lobster omelette is famous, as is the seasonal selection of game, such as venison and gray-legged partridge. Desserts are, as you might expect, something of a specialty here, and plum crumble, sticky toffee pudding, and the trio of chocolate mousse are all worth going up a dress size for! The wine list is renowned amongst the cognoscenti as one of the best in London. The Goring is one of a very few restaurants that actually buy wine to lay down, allowing their lucky diners to sip some seriously impressive bottles at very reasonable prices. ♦ Su-F, breakfast, lunch, and dinner; Sa, dinner.

58 Westminster Cathedral

Coming across this distinctive red-and-white structure is a sweet surprise amid the thundering traffic of this area. Its hidden location is a shame, because the cathedral is the principal Roman Catholic church in England. By London standards, it came on the scene relatively late—the cathedral was designed and built in 1894 by **John Bentley** at the behest of Arch-bishop Herbert Vaughan, who demanded something entirely different from **Westminster Abbey**. Bentley mixed Roman-esque and Byzantine influences, just as he mixed redbrick with white Portland stone. The result is somewhat Venetian. Within, side chapels are decked with glowing mosaics, and there is a bronze by Elizabeth Frink. The view from **St. Edward's Tower**, a 273-foot bell tower, is stunning. Every second Tuesday between mid-June and mid-September, the cathedral hosts concerts of classical music played on its organ, which is one of the finest such instruments in Europe. ♦ Admission for concerts and the bell tower. Daily. Ashley Pl (between Ambrosden Ave and Morpeth Terr). 798.9055. Tube: Victoria

---

Restaurants/Clubs: Red | Hotels: Purple | Shops: Orange | Outdoors/Parks: Green | Sights/Culture: Blue

From its risqué beginning as the site of a ribald 17th-century festival, Mayfair has grown into one of the most desirable of London addresses. Bordered to the north and east by celebrated shopping thoroughfares **Oxford Street** and **Regent Street**, to the south by charismatic Piccadilly, and to the west by frenetic but fashionable **Park Lane**, this neighborhood is a playground for the wealthy. Such affluence grew from an initial half-dozen estates. The owners, landed aristocrats, laid out the rectangular area in orderly patterns of generous avenues and stately squares and lined them with their elegant mansions—which, of course, were equipped with mews in back for horses and carriages. After the rich and famous came the suppliers to the rich and famous; soon the district contained elite merchants as well as their prosperous patrons.

Today, diplomats from **Grosvenor Square** and financial magnates from **Brook Street** have replaced the dukes and duchesses, but the aristocratic ambience lingers. Mayfair and Park Lane are still the most expensive, exclusive properties on Britain's Monopoly board, with the retail meccas of **Oxford, Bond**, and **Regent Streets** close behind. Dotted in between are some of the most luxurious hotels and restaurants the pound can buy. To the south lies the "Magic Mile" of Piccadilly, named for a fashionable 17th-century collar called a picadil. The street begins at **Hyde Park Corner** in an atmosphere of respectability, then coasts past the verdant **Green Park**; the Ritz hotel, with its "romantic getaway" mystique; and tranquil **St. James's**, Piccadilly. But as Piccadilly approaches the beloved statue of **Eros**, a popular meeting place in the center of **Piccadilly Circus**, the grandeur diminishes. Piccadilly Circus, London's answer to Times Square, has consistently defied attempts to make it dignified. Confusion, traffic, and neon characterize the scene (no wonder they call it a circus), yet Londoners and visitors fiercely defend this traffic circle–*cum*–meeting place, flocking to the feet of the God of Love (meant to represent the angel of Charity).

City code 0207 unless otherwise noted.

1 LOCANDA LOCATELLI

★★★★$$$ In February 2001, Locanda Locatelli was opened by Giorgio Locatelli after a £1.5 million refurbishment by David Collins. This venture marked Giorgio's full-time return to the kitchen since leaving **Zafferano** in 2001. The essence of Giorgio's cooking is to highlight the natural flavors of quality produce, much of which is imported directly from Italy. This is a wonderful restaurant. The front of the house is run (with an awesome combination of relaxed friendliness and incredible efficiency) by Giorgio's delightful wife, Plaxy. The food is Michelin-starred and garlanded with major awards year after year. Dishes like baby mackerel salad with saffron, fabulous pastas and risotti (including an ambrosial white truffle risotto in season), and a spiced wine polenta with pears and liquorice mousse never fail to hit the mark. The wine list is an education in Italian wines and a joy. It was put together by Giorgio with Massimo Folli, head of the Association of Italian Sommeliers. This restaurant is a delight for the tastebuds and the soul. You will want to come back. Book as you leave; the place is justifiably popular. ◆ M-Sa, lunch and dinner. 8 Seymour St (on corner of Portman Sq). 935.9088/935.8390. Tube: Marble Arch

1 HYATT REGENCY LONDON— THE CHURCHILL

$$$ After a lavish makeover, The Churchill is looking cool, sophisticated, and really very lovely. The lobby will sell the whole hotel to you.

You'll feel like a million dollars just walking into it. And the rooms don't let you down. The décor is chic, sleek, and relaxing, and the views over quiet Portman Square are as restful as a hotel this central can offer. It might not seem much to some people, but I particularly loved the fact that windows here actually open, so you don't get that "hermetically sealed" feel so many places have. Rooms come with complimentary newspapers each morning, individual heat control, and all the usual modern conveniences, plus some even more modern than usual, such as iPod iHome docking. Club Rooms are on a private floor with private concierge, and the Regency Club serving complimentary continental breakfast, evening cocktails, and canapés. Some of the suites have balconies overlooking the gardens. There is an excellent bar, a choice of restaurants, a 24-hour business center, a good fitness center, and a sauna. ◆ 30 Portman Square (at Seymour St). 486.5800; fax 486.1255. Tube: Marble Arch. www.london.churchill.hyatt.com

Within the Hyatt Regency Churchill:

THE MONTAGU

★★ $$$ This restaurant will take you through the day, from a full English breakfast through a good traditional English afternoon tea (it is a member of the Tea Guild, and the tea selection on offer—from Darjeeling 2nd Flush to Whole Rosebud China Black—is about as exciting as tea gets) through dinner. Typical dishes include Loch Fyne mussels and sun-dried tomatoes steamed in white wine, fillet of veal with stuffed baby squash and thyme jus, and sticky toffee pudding with toffee sauce and Cornish vanilla ice cream. As hotel restaurants go, it goes well. ◆ Daily, 6:30AM–10:45PM. 299.2037

THE CHURCHILL BAR

With its all-wood paneling and beige leather, this is a very relaxing place to end a day. The bar offers a selection of 86 malt whiskeys, good classic cocktails, and bar snacks. There is live music between 7PM and midnight from Tuesday through Saturday. ◆ Daily, 11AM–2AM (nonresidents will be charged a small fee after 11AM—it's a legal thing)

2 THE CUMBERLAND

$$$ Quite possibly the most impressive makeover in London. I haven't put this hotel in the guide before because it was dull and so much less than you deserve. Well, look at the old gal now! A sub-Schrager refit has turned her very sexy. The lobby is cool and huge, underlit in changing colors and peppered with artworks and sculptures. There are 1,000 rooms and suites done out in smart contemporary style. Everyone gets power showers and fluffy bathrobes, plasma-screen TVs, and original artworks on the

wall. Take a suite and you can check in at 10AM and enjoy access to the Executive Lounge for complimentary breakfasts, canapés, coffee, and pastries, as well as business facilities. A gymnasium with cool machines that have built-in TVs to watch while you work out is available to guests 24 hours a day. Should you prefer your exercise another way, the hotel's Carbon Bar offers the chance to burn off calories to the sounds of some of London's top DJs. ◆ Great Cumberland Pl. 0871/376.9014. Tube: Marble Arch. www.guoman.com

Within The Cumberland:

THE MARKET

★$ This little food hall within the hotel has five open kitchens offering 11 styles of eating, from sandwiches and soup through salads, pasta, and pizza, to rotisserie and stir-fry. ◆ Daily, breakfast, lunch, and dinner

KUA BAR

This is a great, laid-back, grown-up bar, even if you are not a resident. Kua is, the barman tells me, Thai for "smile." And I did. They have a list of 44 cocktails, including the great idea of a virgin mojito for nondrinkers and the utterly delicious Mr. Valentine (raspberry vodka, crème de framboise, fresh raspberries, and Champagne). Coffee and teas are available, as are light snacks. The staff is charming, helpful, and knowledgeable. ◆ Daily

RHODES W1

★★★ $$$$ The latest and most glitzy of Gary Rhodes's restaurants has "So, what about a Michelin star now?" written all over it. And it worked—he got one. The décor is glamorous—all cascading crystal chandeliers and muted leather. The menu is also glamorous. ◆ Daily

3 MARBLE ARCH

Built in 1827 by **John Nash**, this version of Rome's Arch of Constantine was originally a gateway to **Buckingham Palace**. When the front of the palace was redesigned, it was no longer appropriate, so the arch was moved to a corner of **Hyde Park**, which is actually on the former location of the Tyburn Gallows, London's main site for public executions until the 18th century. Only the royal family and the King's Troop Royal Horse Artillery may pass through Marble Arch. However, the incessant flow of traffic around it tends to negate its dignity. ◆ Oxford St and Park La. Tube: Marble Arch

4 OXFORD STREET

What was once a Roman road from Hampshire to the Suffolk coast was already a renowned commercial strip by the 19th century. It is said that some of the modern-day fruit and flower sellers are descended from the original traders who once pushed their barrows along this street. An estimated 464,500 square miles of selling space lines the street, although not all of it is worth looking at. Oxford Circus, at the junction of Oxford and Regent Streets, was part of **John Nash**'s grand plan, though it was rebuilt by **Sir Henry Tanner** in the early 1920s. More than ever, this is a street of two halves. From Oxford Circus east to Charing Cross Road, it is a mix of smaller outlets and discount stores with snack food outlets and an increasing number of electrical goods retailers. West from Oxford Circus, the street is dominated by a handful of giant department stores, all of which have been recently refurbished and are a sparkly enticement to all those who live to love to shop. ♦ Between Charing Cross Rd and Park La. Tube: Oxford Circus, Marble Arch, Bond St

5 MARKS & SPENCER

Marks & Spencer—or M&S, or Marks & Sparks, as it is familiarly known—has spread to over 30 countries, and this store at the Marble Arch end of Oxford Street is its largest. This most British of department stores has come a long way from finding fame for sensible underwear and sweaters. This double store holds the whole M&S range—clothing for everyone (including "Featured Collections" such as Autograph, Per Una Limited Collection, and Blue Harbour Vintage), accessories, lingerie, bedding, soft furnishings, lighting, and furniture. The Food Hall is a Great British Institution, their wines feature regularly in experts' recommendations, and their fruit gums are without a shadow of a doubt the most deliciously more-ish in the world of confectionery. ♦ M-Su. 458 Oxford St. 935.7954

5 PRIMARK

The latest phenomenon in high street-bargain fashion, this is Primark's new flagship store. There were riots when it opened—people queued overnight to get at the extraordinarily low-priced fashions inside. There is everything here, and there are new lines all the time. A top from Primark might not last you forever, but it will put you up with the fashionistas for as long as it takes for the fashion to change. Favored by wannabes and celebrities alike,

> When a proud mother said her baby looked like Winston Churchill, he replied: "Madam, all babies look like me."

this is the store that has really brought the bargains out of the basement. ♦ Daily. 470 Oxford St (between N Audley and Park Sts). Tube: Marble Arch

6 SELFRIDGES

First opened in 1909, this other Great British Institution was in fact founded by an American—a retail magnate from Wisconsin by the name of Gordon Selfridge. Its six floors cover an entire city block. The perfume department is said to be the largest in Europe, and alongside it is a fabulous beauty department that could turn any sow's ear into a silk purse. Women's fashions come from every label you can imagine, from casualwear to the store's first-ever Chanel Boutique, and the newly redesigned accessories hall, with its many glass-walled mini-stores, is just shopping nirvana. A new Ralph Lauren Boutique has opened in Selfridges' equally impressive men's fashions department, which offers over 20,000 pairs of shoes to choose from. The store offers everything for the home, from soft furnishings and designer lighting (the chandelier department is quite fabulous) to furniture. You can get anything from a spool of thread to the new $40,000 diamond Apple iPhone. The new Wonder Room is a bit of a must-see—a fabulous fantasy made real, which the store describes as "a bazaar of special things." Such things come with labels like Hermès, Tiffany, and Chanel. Take care with the credit card, because it is very tempting. The ground-floor Food Hall is a gourmet's dream! Not only does it have everything you might find in a top food hall, but a whole store cupboard full of exclusives! Top Michelin-starred chef Tom Aikens's take-out range has launched there exclusively, as has an entire deli counter devoted to The Iberico Pig. The Lola's Kitchen section is tart heaven—each fabulous fruity confection pure and handmade on the day it is sold. And the Prince of Wales's own brand of all-organic Duchy of Cornwall produce sets out its stall there too. The wine and spirits section is an alcoholic Aladdin's cave! Throughout the store you will find no less than 15 tempting opportunities for eating and drinking well. From nibbling Krispy Kreme doughnuts and Oddono's ice cream to fueling up at the fresh juice bar or snacking at Yo Sushi, the Oyster Bar, or the terrific Brass Rail Salt Beef Bar in the Food Hall, you can have anything right up to a full meal here amid the fashions, fabrics, and furnishings. There are regular events throughout the store, themed weeks in various departments, and one of the best Christmas displays in London. ♦ 400 Oxford St. 0870/837.7377. M-W, F, Sa, 9:30AM-8PM; Th, 9:30AM-9PM; Su, 11:30AM-6PM

Restaurants/Clubs: Red | Hotels: Purple | Shops: Orange | Outdoors/Parks: Green | Sights/Culture: Blue

Within Selfridges:

WONDER BAR

★★★★$$ Well named! This place *is* a wonder. It boasts one of the UK's first Enomatic Wine Systems—a marvelous dispenser that allows you to serve yourself with taster-sized glasses of any one of 52 top vintages of amazing wines. You can have just a "sip" (25ml) if you like . . . but it could be of 1996 Château Pétrus, which would retail at £940 a bottle. The food here is terrific too. Platters of charcuterie and beautifully kept cheeses are the ideal thing to enjoy with your reds . . . or top-quality lobster and seafood platters will set off your crisp white to perfection!

LAB CAFÉ

★★$ Specialties include the chop salad. Choose your ingredients, have them tossed, and munch away with chums in the airy lightness of this newly refurbished eatery in the middle of the Women's Contemporary Fashions section. If you want to risk your dress size, there's a daily hot special, good dim sum, and yummy cakes.

FOOD GARDEN CAFÉ

★★$$ If the buzz of shopping has given you the serious munchies, this is where to come—a self-service restaurant with great views over the city as far as the Tower of London and the London Eye. There are several different counters serving different cuisines: the curry is good and a great value, the basic British fish and chips is a good filler, and the roast is renowned. The fresh salad bar is terrific and a challenge to your skills as a high-rise architect.

GORDON'S BAR AND RESTAURANT

★★★$ This is a great place (and popular!) offering excellent main-course salads, terrific sandwiches and wraps, great mezze plates to share, and a carte of moreish classic cocktails. It was named after Gordon Selfridge, the store's founder, and I think he would be very happy with that.

THE MOËT BAR

Right above the new Chanel boutique, and approached up a spiral staircase, this is a place to pose. But dress to impress. Even the cocktails are designer—by such names as Alice Temperley, Julien MacDonald, and Tracey Boyd. If you want to nibble with your bubbles, the little duck spring rolls are a popular bar snack.

OBIKA MOZZARELLA BAR

★★★$$ Silvio Ursini has created little temples to mozzarella: three beautiful handmade buffalo mozzarellas, two fresh each day from Paestum and Piana del Volturna and one smoked. The cheeses are never refrigerated and are always eaten within 36 hours of being made! All the dishes here are made to order, and as well as those featuring the fabulous mozzarella, there is excellent charcuterie and terrific salads. This is a real foodie experience. ♦ 0870/837.7377

7 ST. CHRISTOPHER'S PLACE

Just off the hurly-burly noise and activity of Oxford Street, this narrow pedestrian alleyway is an oasis of smart shops and restaurants. The first little stretch is also called Gees Court. Its many boutiques include **Nicole Farhi** (see page 75), offering women's clothing by the eponymous designer, and **Buckle-My-Shoe** (935.5589), which sells designer footwear for kids up to age 10. For quality gifts, there is the small **National Trust** shop (224.0488). ♦ Between Oxford and Wigmore Sts. Tube: Bond St

On St. Christopher's Place:

PADDY CAMPBELL

Creating understated but stylish clothes for women, this designer pays great attention to detail. Her collection, primarily daywear, includes chic suits and classic wool and linen dresses; she also provides a range of flattering evening wear. ♦ M-Sa. 8 Gees Ct. 493.5646. 225.0543. Tube: Knightsbridge

7 THE AMBER CENTRE

Small but glowing with amber of every age, color, and shade, the shop sells necklaces, earrings, bracelets, and rings set in silver and gold, as well as figurines and little boxes. Most of the amber comes from the Baltic, with a little from Mexico and the Caribbean. Beautiful gifts, whether for yourself or another. Prices range from £14 to £7,000, so there is something for everyone. ♦ M-Sa, 10AM–6PM (open till 7PM Th). 24 St. Christopher's Pl. 224.2953. Tube: Bond St

7 CARLUCCIOS

The grand old mushroom-meister of the famous **Neal Street Restaurant** has branched out. These zingy, clattery, happy, relaxed cafés offer a great selection of light snacks and meals—his homemade soups, pastas, and risottos (try anything with mushrooms and you won't go wrong), wonderful plates of antipasto, taste-bomb marinated olives, and the kind of bread basket that makes you weep for anyone who is gluten intolerant. There are wonderful cheeses and a little menu of children's portions with mini pizzas and lasagna. A short but classy wine list even offers Prosecco by the glass. Gorgeous staff members make gorgeous coffee, and the atmosphere is so friendly you could stay all day. Beware on your way out, as the deli section at the front offers antipasti, ready-made meals, pastas, that wonderful bread, lethal pastries and gooey things, and a range of top-class olive oils, most of which are available for tasting. And of course, all of the great man's books! ♦ Italian ♦ M–F, 8AM–11PM; Sa, 11AM–11PM; Su, 11AM–10PM. St. Christopher's Pl. 935.5927. Tube: Bond St. Also at 8 Market Place W1. 636.2228. Tube: Oxford Circus

8 DEBENHAMS

Another revamped wallet-opener of a store. The great thing here is their Designer Floor, where top designers like Jasper Conran, Ben di Lisi, John Rochas, Julien MacDonald, and Betty Jackson all create diffusion lines exclusively for Debenhams. If there is such a thing as a designer bargain, this could well be it—with, of course, all the necessary accessories just waiting to be snapped up on the ground floor. There is all the rest here too . . . including furnishings, electricals, a good kitchenware department, and a whole hall of great beauty counters. Definitely worth a browse . . . ♦ Daily. 334-348 Oxford St. (between James St and Marylebone La). 0844/561.6161. Tube: Bond St. www.debenhams.com

9 HOUSE OF FRASER

Started in Scotland, House of Fraser is now all over the UK. This excellent newly refurbished store is good for "high street-designer" fashions (basement), its excellent beauty hall, and a great range of accessories, especially interesting costume jewelry. ♦ M–Sa. 318 Oxford St (at Old Cavendish St). Tube: Bond St

10 JOHN LEWIS

The motto of this most British of department stores is "Never knowingly undersold." It does have a pretty comprehensive stock of most decent brands of most things—from electric kettles to designer accessories and from fine fabrics to cross-trainers. The word "reliable" doesn't sound very exciting, but John Lewis makes reliable as appealing as it gets. The store is gorgeous now, and the gifts department is always worth a visit. You will find that Londoners use this place as their "default" shop, which is really quite a recommendation! The store recently picked up the *Evening Standard* Best Shopping Experience Award. More stop-press on this place is the addition of a *fabulous* food hall in the basement. It really is a class act. There is a proper cheese room, a wonderful wine section, expertly prepared butchery and fish . . . oooh, it is just lovely! ♦ Daily. 278 Oxford St (at Holles St). 629.7711. Tube: Bond St, Oxford Circus. www.johnlewis.com

11 SPEAKERS' CORNER

Oratory at the famous northeastern corner of **Hyde Park** dates back to 1872, when mass demonstrations at the site (against a proposed Sunday Trading Bill) led to the established right of assembly. The area is liveliest on Sunday afternoons, and hecklers are part of the show. ♦ Cumberland Gate (at Park La). Tube: Marble Arch

12 PARK LANE

Once a narrow strip between a green oasis and prominent grand houses, this hectic four-lane thoroughfare runs past several high-rise hotels and offices. From the 18th century onward, the street has been associated with riches, though today's version concentrates more on conglomerate wealth than the private kind. Take a taxi ride here in the evening and you're likely to come across limos dropping off debutantes for a charity ball or powerful executives for a gala dinner; at any rate, you'll see a lot of slicked hair, tailcoats, and flowing gowns. ♦ Between Hyde Park Corner and Oxford St. Tube: Marble Arch, Hyde Park Corner

13 BROWNS

Stocking top designers' labels such as Georgina von Etzdorf and Prada, this handsome store looks rather like a large house. It is divided into cozy rooms for its women's and men's departments. Other locations include **Browns Focus** (38 S Molton St, 491.7833), which offers more affordable clothing than Browns, and **Browns Labels for Less** (62 S Molton St, 495.7301), which features the creations of established designers at a discount. ♦ M–Sa. 23-27 S Molton St (at Davies St). 491.7833

14 GRAYS ANTIQUE MARKET/ GRAYS MEWS

About 180 antiques dealers display their wares at these two adjacent market areas, and if prices for the collectibles, fashion jewelry, and curios are not the lowest, they are at least reasonable. In addition, all items are backed up by a guarantee of authenticity. ♦ M–F. Market: 58 Davies St (at S

Restaurants/Clubs: Red | Hotels: Purple | Shops: Orange | Outdoors/Parks: Green | Sights/Culture: Blue

Molton St). Mews: 1–7 Davies Mews (at S Molton La). 629.7034 (for both)

15 HANOVER SQUARE

This formal square was built in 1717 to reflect the Baroque style of King George I's German house of Hanover. Early residents included two of the king's mistresses. Although the square's architect is unknown, **John James** designed the **St. George Hanover Square Church**, just south on St. George Street. Completed in 1724, it was the site of several famous weddings, including those of Percy Bysshe Shelley, Benjamin Disraeli, and George Eliot. ♦ At Hanover and Brook Sts and at St. George St and Harewood Pl. Tube: Oxford Circus

16 GODIVA

Taste some of the best chocolate truffles in Europe or simply rest your shopping-weary feet while sipping a cappuccino. ♦ M–Sa. Princes and Regent Sts. 495.2845. Tube: Oxford Circus

17 CLARIDGE'S

$$$$ Claridges began life in 1812, as a single house at 51 Brook Street. By 1854 it had expanded to fill the entire row of houses from No. 49 to No. 57 at the end of the block. In 1894, Claridges was purchased by Richard D'Oyly Carte, owner of The Savoy. He promptly demolished all the houses and created a purpose-built hotel, which opened in 1898. During both World Wars, the hotel became a refuge for aristocrats and royalty fleeing hostilities. During World War II, Winston Churchill declared Suite 212 to be Yugoslav soil, and legend has it that a spadeful of Yugoslav earth was placed there when the son of King Peter of Yugoslavia was born there in 1945. The British Royal Family have a close relationship with the hotel and hold many private family functions there. In 1996, David Collins created a new cocktail bar, and Thierry Despont, using archive photographs of the ballroom extension of 1930 as inspiration, created the glorious modern Art Deco foyer with a fabulous Dale Chihuly chandelier at its center. It really is quite something! The list of amenities and services that come with your room is also quite something: fresh flowers and complimentary shoe shine, wireless Internet access, flat-screen TVs, dual-voltage plugs, a whole menu of on-demand child-friendly possibilities, porter service, dry cleaning, a doctor on-call, personal trainers in the fully equipped gym, picnics made to order, in-room massage, chauffeur-driven cars, jogging maps, and local mobile phones to rent on request. And that is just for starters. ♦ Brook St (at Davies St). 629.8860, 800/63 SAVOY; fax 499.2210. Tube: Bond St. www.claridges.co.uk

Within Claridge's:

GORDON RAMSAY AT CLARIDGE'S

★★★$$$$ The man who makes Howard Stern look like Mary Poppins stands astride posh London nosh like Joshua over Jericho after the Battle. Of course, when we say "Gordon Ramsay at Claridge's" we don't expect Gordon will actually be *at* Claridge's, but the hugely talented Mark Sargent is. Although Gordon is there in the price tag. The food is about as evolved as food gets without turning into another life form altogether. You can start with ravioli of Dorset blue lobster and salmon poached in a lemongrass bisque, or perhaps mosaic of foie gras and Goosnargh duck, Red Pippin apple and walnut salad, or summer truffle before moving on to tenderloin of Suffolk pork with glazed crayfish, macerated peaches, French beans, bok choi, and a tarragon jus. After which you might just manage lychee and rosewater sorbet with creamed tapioca. The wine list is not for the faint of wallet and has little sympathy for anyone who might just want a glass of something interesting. ♦ Daily, lunch and dinner. 499.0099

THE READING ROOM

★★★$$$ Two Art Deco cream marble fireplaces, mahogany leather columns, and strokeable suede walls are some of the things that make this a lovely place to eat. It is most famous for its award-winning afternoon tea, with more than 30 teas to choose from and delicate finger sandwiches, pastries, and homemade raisin and apple scones with Claridge's bespoke tea-infused jam and clotted cream to nibble on. Breakfast and a light menu du jour are also available. ♦ Daily (reservations essential for afternoon tea). 409.6307

THE FOYER

★★★$$$ Even your goosebumps will have goosebumps sitting here in Art Deco splendor under the 800 individual handblown glass components of Claridge's famously fabulous chandelier. The dress code is smart—but this is the sort of place that makes you want to dress up anyway. Light snacks, terrific cocktails, and that famous afternoon tea are served here. And there is live music every afternoon and evening. ♦ Daily. 409.6307

CLARIDGE'S BAR

The **David Collins**-designed bar boasts a **Champagne Library** with many rare editions and a carte of exclusive cocktails such as the gin-based Mayfair Classic and the frothy, Champagney Flapper. The food is as chic as the surroundings, and ranges from sushi or sashimi through a warm lamb and hummus sandwich to fish and chips. ♦ Daily

THE FUMOIR

The opulent eggplant leather-clad smoking room, with its choice of 20 top-of-the-line Cuban cigars and the largest selection of Mancanudo cigars in the country, is one of the most tragic victims of the Health Police ban on smoking. Now it is—although still a beautiful place to sit—reduced to the status of a bar. You can still enjoy the Fumoir's wide range of fine cognacs, armagnacs, rums, whiskeys, and tequilas, served from its lovely marble horseshoe bar. But Fumoir it is now in name only. ♦ Daily

18 RISTORANTE SEMPLICE

★★★★$$$ One of the best additions to the London eating scene of 2007. It's not particularly *semplice*, it has to be said, but very, very good. The staff is a delight, and the intimate lacquered rosewood and Fortuny gold-swirl decorated space is always welcoming. The food is superb—from the simple spaghetti with Pecorino, Malga butter, and black Sarawak pepper (which is possibly the best pasta dish I have eaten in my life) to the highly evolved *coniglio nostrano* (the rabbit comes as a pie-sized rack of rabbit, a rabbit escalope Milanese, sautéed rabbit liver, a pastry stuffed with confit leg meat, tiny oysters of saddle, and a couple of drumsticks). I remember my dining companion making squeaking noises of joy as she ate. The beef is Fassone, hand-reared in Piedmont. The desserts are wonderful, but the cheese trolley is breathtaking. And the most delicious selection of Italian artisanal cheeses you will find in London are served by the wonderful Vito, who explains and advises as he garnishes each cheese with a little something—a dusting of dried elderberries on one, acacia honey on another. The wine list is informed and generous. You come out of this place glowing like its golden walls. ♦ M-Sa, lunch and dinner. 10 Blenheim St (off New Bond St). 495.1509. Tube: Bond St. www.ristorantesemplice.com

19 BOND STREET

This is Fifth Avenue, Rodeo Drive, and the Faubourg Saint-Honoré rolled into one. Imperturbably chic, Bond Street leads from Piccadilly to Oxford Street and appears to be paved all the way with American Express Gold cards (it might as well be, anyway). Just over a decade ago, the legendary shopping street celebrated its 300th birthday, but it cheated a little bit: Although Old Bond Street was built in 1686, New Bond Street, which begins at Clifford Street, dates back only to 1721. You can blame the confusing street numbering system on Parliament, which, in 1762, forbade the use of hanging signs to identify shops (too many customers were being clobbered in high winds) and numbered the streets separately, first up the east side toward Oxford Street and then down again on the west.

Art galleries flourish on and around Bond Street: buy a Turner at **Thomas Agnew & Son** or discover an unknown genius at **Sotheby's**, the world's largest auction house. If art is your interest, browse along Albemarle, Dover, and Grafton Streets—and don't overlook Cork Street, with its little upscale galleries that always seem to be showing works by the latest artists. Antiques lovers should turn in to Burlington Gardens, then also explore a maze of backstreets crammed with the old, the opulent, and the unusual.

You can shop at an almost endless number of international fashion boutiques—including **Gucci**, **Donna Karan**, **Nicole Farhi**, **Hermès**, **Cartier**, **Louis Vuitton**, **Ralph Lauren**, **Christian Lacroix**, and **MaxMara**. The designer district spreads into nearby streets: If Oxford Street is behind you, turn right onto Brook Street (it cuts across Bond) to find British designer **Margaret Howell**. Her shop (here and in Knightsbridge) specializes in a modern yet classic English look with well-coordinated clothes for men and women. Then stroll along South Molton Street to find many stylish shops. If you turn left onto Brook Street instead, you will come on **Halcyon Days**—a darling little gift emporium filled with enamel boxes and knickknacks by Royal Appointment. ♦ Between Piccadilly and Oxford St. Tube: Bond St, Green Park

---

Restaurants/Clubs: Red | **Hotels: Purple** | **Shops: Orange** | **Outdoors/Parks: Green** | **Sights/Culture: Blue**

reet Shopping

OXFORD STREET

clothing **Zara**
larger-size fashions **Elvi**
clothing **House of Labels**
designer clothing **Proibito**
bridalwear **Pronovias**

Next clothing

Reiss clothing
Francesco Biasia handbags

BLENHEIM STREET

menswear **Bernini**
Royal Bank of Scotland
womenswear **Doly by Dany Mizrachi**
designer menswear **Cesari**
shoes **Mephisto**
auctioneer **Bonhams**
menswear **Pellini Uomo**
shoes **Ivory**
jewelry **Flawless & Co**
clothing **Gant**
French designer menswear **Lanvin**
shoes **Russell & Bromley**

DERING STREET

NEW BOND STREET

Lionidas Belgian chocolates
Watches of Bond Street
Basler German womenswear
Timberland outdoor clothing/boots

Ventilo French womenswear
TM Lewin shirts/ties/accessories
Robina womenswear
Whole Man men's grooming
Oliver Sweeney designer shoes
Calvin Klein underwear

BROOK STREET

knitwear **Pringle**
home furnishings **Armani Casa**
fashion/accessories **Emporio Armani**
shoes **Bally**
handbags/shoes **Anya Hindmarsh**
accessories **Porsche Design**
costume jewelry **Folli Follie**
Italian menswear **Canali**

Fenwicks department store
D&G accessories/junior clothing

Emporio Armani designer clothing
Chappell of Bond Street musical instruments
Samsonite luggage/clothes/shoes
F. Pinet women's shoes

LANCASHIRE COURT

womenswear **Miu Miu**
Bond St. Antiques
menswear **Pal Zileri**
womenswear **Jigsaw**
bank **HSBC**

GROSVENOR STREET

casual designs **Diesel**
fine tailoring **Corneliani**
shoes **Church's**
artworks **Opera Gallery**
antiques **Renoir House**
crystal **Daniel Swarovski**
chocolates/dates **Bateel**
silverware **S.J. Phillips**
menswear **Zilli**
antiques **Mallett**
childrenswear **Polo/Ralph Lauren**
fine art **Partridge**
fine art **Richard Green**
The Fine Art Society
menswear **Wana**
designer clothing **Emanuel Ungaro**

MADDOX STREET

NEW BOND STREET

Avi Rossini menswear
Wempe watches/jewelry
Mulberry leather accessories
Smythson of Bond Street stationers
Ermenegildo Zegna menswear
Tavernier jewelry
Sotheby's auctioneer
Richard Green Old Master paintings
Furla Italian bags
Anne Fontaine womenswear
Halcyon Fine Arts Dealers
Longchamp luggage
Jimmy Choo shoes/bags
Lucie Campbell jewelry
Russell & Bromley shoes

BRUTON STREET

designer accessories **Hermès**
cashmere **Ballantyne**
luxury leisurewear **Loro Piana**
designer clothing **Nicole Farhi**
womenswear/accessories **Celine**
jewelry/handbags/glassware/porcelain **Lalique**

CONDUIT STREET

Burberry designer clothing
Louis Vuitton luggage/accessories

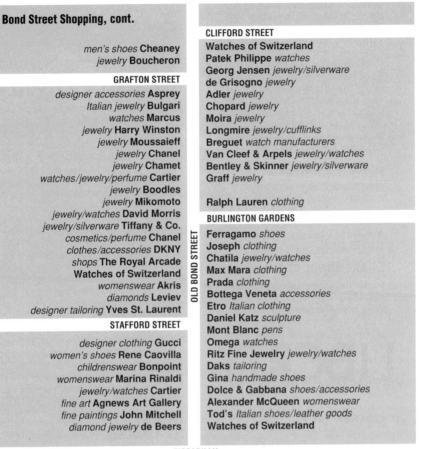

Bond Street Shopping, cont.

men's shoes **Cheaney**
jewelry **Boucheron**

GRAFTON STREET

designer accessories **Asprey**
Italian jewelry **Bulgari**
watches **Marcus**
jewelry **Harry Winston**
jewelry **Moussaieff**
jewelry **Chanel**
jewelry **Chamet**
watches/jewelry/perfume **Cartier**
jewelry **Boodles**
jewelry **Mikomoto**
jewelry/watches **David Morris**
jewelry/silverware **Tiffany & Co.**
cosmetics/perfume **Chanel**
clothes/accessories **DKNY**
shops **The Royal Arcade**
Watches of Switzerland
womenswear **Akris**
diamonds **Leviev**
designer tailoring **Yves St. Laurent**

STAFFORD STREET

designer clothing **Gucci**
women's shoes **Rene Caovilla**
childrenswear **Bonpoint**
womenswear **Marina Rinaldi**
jewelry/watches **Cartier**
fine art **Agnews Art Gallery**
fine paintings **John Mitchell**
diamond jewelry **de Beers**

CLIFFORD STREET

Watches of Switzerland
Patek Philippe *watches*
Georg Jensen *jewelry/silverware*
de Grisogno *jewelry*
Adler *jewelry*
Chopard *jewelry*
Moira *jewelry*
Longmire *jewelry/cufflinks*
Breguet *watch manufacturers*
Van Cleef & Arpels *jewelry/watches*
Bentley & Skinner *jewelry/silverware*
Graff *jewelry*

Ralph Lauren *clothing*

BURLINGTON GARDENS

Ferragamo *shoes*
Joseph *clothing*
Chatila *jewelry/watches*
Max Mara *clothing*
Prada *clothing*
Bottega Veneta *accessories*
Etro *Italian clothing*
Daniel Katz *sculpture*
Mont Blanc *pens*
Omega *watches*
Ritz Fine Jewelry *jewelry/watches*
Daks *tailoring*
Gina *handmade shoes*
Dolce & Gabbana *shoes/accessories*
Alexander McQueen *womenswear*
Tod's *Italian shoes/leather goods*
Watches of Switzerland

OLD BOND STREET

PICCADILLY

On Bond Street:

SMYTHSON

The leather address books and diaries sold here are highly coveted status symbols, and even though it's *un peu* pretentious, the address book divided into three sections and inscribed simply "London/New York/ Paris" is truly useful for fortunate vagabonds.
♦ M-Sa. 40 New Bond St (near Maddox St). 629.8558. Also at 135 Sloane St. 730.5520

MULBERRY

For the traditional British look in menswear and womenswear, with matching accessories, this handsome shop is the place to visit. It's also known for its leather goods; home furnishings are found only here, at their flagship store.
♦ M-Sa. 41-42 New Bond St (near Maddox St). 491.3900. Also at 12 Gees Ct (between Oxford and Barrett Sts). 493.2516. Tube: Bond St; 185 Brompton Rd (at Beauchamp Pl). 225.0313. Tube: Knightsbridge

NICOLE FARHI

Always popular with conservatively fashionable women in their thirties and forties, this French-born designer (married to playwright David Hare) makes beautiful

Restaurants/Clubs: Red | Hotels: Purple | Shops: Orange | Outdoors/Parks: Green | Sights/Culture: Blue

clothes for women that reflect the season's trends. The flagship store is large, cool, and relaxed, with a chic basement restaurant. There's also a menswear collection and accessories. ♦ M–Sa. 158 New Bond St (between Grafton and Bruton Sts). 499.8368. Also at 193 Sloane St (between Harriet St and Knightsbridge). 235.0877. Tube: Knightsbridge; 25–26 St. Christopher's Pl (between Barrett and Wigmore Sts). 486.3416. Tube: Bond St; 11 Floral St (between James and Garrick Sts). 497.1813. Tube: Covent Garden

ASPREY & GARRARD

Allow the doorman to welcome you to England's most luxurious jewelry and gift shop, which specializes in the finest items, from crocodile suitcases to Fabergé frames. ♦ M–Sa. 165–169 New Bond St (at Grafton St). 493.6767

CHARBONNEL ET WALKER

The fabulous chocolates come in boxes that are equally treasured. ♦ M–Sa. 28 Old Bond St (at Royal Arcade). 491.0939

LIBERTY

20 LIBERTY

Since the shop opened in 1875, its name has been synonymous with the best-quality printed fabrics money can buy. Founder Arthur Lasenby Liberty was a fan of the Orient, and his skill at importing and selling exotica actually helped foment the pre-Raphaelite movement. (Ruskin, Rossetti, and Whistler were all regular customers.) The remarkable Tudor-style building is worth experiencing for its architecture alone. Built in the 1920s, it is not authentic, but the beams and timbers came from two 19th-century ships, and the interior features linen-fold paneling, balustrades, oak staircases, stained glass, and Italian carving. A frieze on the Regent Street frontage, completed in 1925, shows goods being transported from Asia to Britain. Of course, the merchandise housed here also merits admiration. Fashions are both classic and classy for men and women; the perfumery and beauty departments are gorgeous, and offer much in the way of natural products. Rummage in the remnants section of the fabrics department for designer prints at bargain prices, then head to the basement to browse through an eccentric collection of china and gifts from all over the world. Recently expensively renovated, Liberty now has a contemporary

glow to its traditional feel. A lovely place to shop. ♦ M-W, F, Sa, 10AM-7PM; Th, 10AM-8PM; Su, noon-6PM. 210-220 Regent St (at Great Marlborough St). 734.1234. Tube: Oxford Circus

Within Liberty:

CHAMPAGNE AND OYSTER BAR

★★★ $$$ It's every bit as opulent as it sounds—Acropolis marble bar, shiny black stools, gold-plated cargo lights, chilled fizz, and everything good that comes from the sea. If you hate seafood—what is *wrong* with you?—there are always interesting salad options and homemade soups on offer. ♦ Daily, noon to closing time

TEA

A gorgeously grown-up tearoom on the ground floor, offering 48 different kinds of tea (some very rare), traditional cakes (some made to recipes dating back to the 1800s), and delicate sandwiches, all served on classic china. ♦ Daily

CAFÉ LIBERTY

★★$$ I love the cheeseboard platters, mainly for the homemade walnut bread, apple chutney, and English quince that come with them. The patterns on the upholstery and wall panels make this a dangerous place to bring a headache, but the food is good, and it is lovely and calm up here on the second floor. ♦ Daily

21 HAMLEYS

First established as the 18th-century "Noah's Ark" on High Holborn, the shop with the "infinite variety of toys, games, magical apparatus and sports goods" moved to Regent Street in 1881; shortly afterward, it introduced table tennis to London. Today, the variety of toys and games still seems limitless, spread out as it is over seven levels. Unless you have a strong constitution, avoid this store near Christmastime, when a one-way system is in operation to keep the aisles from getting jammed. Any other time of year, indulge the child in yourself. ♦ M-Sa; Su, noon-6PM. 188 Regent St (between Beak St and Foubert's Pl). 734.3161. Tube: Oxford Circus. Also at Unit 3, The Piazza, Covent Garden. 240.4646. Tube: Covent Garden

LE GAVROCHE

22 LE GAVROCHE

★★★★$$$$ The *Good Food Guide* regularly votes this among the top restaurants in London, and Michelin keeps giving it two stars. Having taken over from his father, the famous Albert Roux, the equally renowned Michel Roux produces divine dishes based on regional French recipes. Million-dollar deals are struck here as property developers bargain across the lunch table, while diplomats from the American Embassy speak softly in this opulent basement with its deep green walls edged in copper and lined with paintings. Appetizers include langoustine with pesto and balsamic vinegar, and one of the formidable main courses is pigeon on a bed of glazed turnips and rosemary-flavored risotto. The prices are just as formidable, but as in many expensive restaurants, the fixed-price lunch menu is a better value. The wines are fabulously expensive. ◆ French ◆ M–F, lunch and dinner. Reservations required; jacket and tie required. 43 Upper Brook St (between Park St and Park La). 408.0881. Tube: Marble Arch

23 AMERICAN EMBASSY

The design of **Eero Saarinen**'s bunkerlike embassy, completed in 1959, has few fans, especially because Georgian town houses were demolished for its construction. The Duke of Westminster still owns this land in the area known as Little America, so even though it is the largest embassy in Britain (with 5.85 acres of floor space), it's also probably one of the only American embassies not to stand on American soil. Note the gigantic bald eagle on top; its wingspan is approximately 35 feet. ◆ 24 Grosvenor Sq (at S Audley St). 499.9000. Tube: Bond St, Marble Arch

24 GROSVENOR SQUARE

The largest square in London after **Lincoln's Inn Fields**, this was once the grandest address the capital could offer. In 1710, Sir Richard Grosvenor procured an act allowing him to build on his property, a group of fields in the area between **Oxford Street** and **Park Lane**. The entire estate was planned as a unit, with the architecturally imposing square at its heart. **Colen Campbell** designed the east side with uniform houses, but the rest grew up in a variety of Georgian styles, all overlooking a central formal garden said to have been laid out by William Kent. Today, fancy additions and rebuilding have erased the architectural consistency, and the garden is merely a swath of pleasant green, watched over by William Reid Dick's bronze statue of Franklin Delano Roosevelt. ◆ S Audley St (between Upper Grosvenor and Upper Brook Sts). Tube: Bond St, Marble Arch

24 MAZE

★★★$$$ One of the most talked-about restaurant openings—but then, it has Gordon Ramsay behind it, and he creates a furor when he opens an envelope! This time the Rambo of the culinary world is in collaboration with head chef Jason Atherton, who has worked at the amazing El Bulli, in Spain, so the food should be inventive and exciting. It is described as French with Asian influences and comes either as a standard appetizer, main course, and dessert or as a wide variety of small "tasting" dishes, which diners can choose and mix as they please. So you could try pressed foie gras and smoked eel with baked potato foam and dill or beef tongue 'n' cheek with capers, raisins, and ginger carrots. Desserts to tempt include a coconut panna cotta with black olive caramel and chocolate granita. Cocktails here are imaginative and include the balsamic Caipirinha, honey and rhubarb Bellini, and a Brandy Blazer that does actually blaze. Gordon is currently redecorating and should be opening again—with a new restaurant added to the premises, along with three private dining rooms. ◆M–Su, lunch and dinner. 10-13 Grosvenor Square. 107.0000. www.gordonramsay.com

25 SKETCH GALLERY

★★★$$$$ Sketch is the brain—and love—child of legendary Algerian-born restaurateur Momo Mazouz and renowned French master chef Pierre Gagnaire. They took over the old RIBA headquarters and turned it into a designer's dream (or nightmare . . . depending on taste). The stairway is bright blue and scrawled with poetry, pictures transform into chairs, and the toilets are set with Swarovski crystal! The building houses a whole complex of restaurants, from the **Library** and **Lecture Room**, through the newly refurbished **Parlour** (where you can even breakfast) and the new **Glade** (light meals and snacks), to the **East Bar**. The Lecture Room is not for the faint of wallet, and its original claim to fame was as London's most expensive restaurant.

Sketch Gallery opens only for dinner. This is dinner as a sort of multimedia experience. There are wraparound video displays as well as music to distract you from what you eat—which might start with fresh corn soup with lemongrass, ricotta, toasted garlic, and popcorn, or some slow-cooked organic salmon with fruit escabeche, Japanese noodles, and a crisp apple tuile. Main courses include goose foie gras served with Gewürztraminer jelly

---

Restaurants/Clubs: **Red** | Hotels: **Purple** | Shops: **Orange** | Outdoors/Parks: **Green** | Sights/Culture: **Blue**

BOOKING IT THROUGH LONDON

Although there's no substitute for an actual visit to London, you can get a good sense of this city's history, geography, and personality from the printed page. The number of books that have been published about London in the latter half of the 20th century alone could fill several libraries, but the titles listed below are a fine place to start.

Behind the Blue Plaques of London, by Alan Symons (Polo Publishing, 1994): Throughout the city, blue plaques mark the residences of the great statesmen, writers, musicians, artists, and soldiers who lived in London. This book relates the stories behind those plaques, giving a sense of individual personalities and idiosyncrasies.

Chelsea Past, by Barbara Denny (Historical Publications, 1996): Scores of interesting characters from British history have called the **Chelsea** area home, ranging from saints (Thomas More) to sinners (Oscar Wilde) and from kings (Henry VIII) to villains (the criminal Aleister Crowley). Their stories are told in this fascinating volume written by a local newspaper reporter.

The Diaries of Samuel Pepys (HarperPaperbacks/US, 1995): These personal, often titillating journals were written between 1660 and 1669 by the most famous (some might say infamous) personality of his era. They offer a unique look at life in the capital during the tempestuous period following the Restoration, including such momentous events as the Great Plague and the Great Fire, although the reader is also told about Pepys's hangovers, parties, and flirtations. A fun browse.

Dickens' Journalism: Volumes 1 and 2, edited by Michael Slater (Dent, 1996): Most people know Charles Dickens as a great novelist, but he was also a crusading newspaper reporter, publishing vivid, sharply critical, and sometimes heartbreaking accounts of life in Victorian London, many of which are collected in this volume.

The Great Plague of London, by Walter George Bell (Bracken Books, 1994): This fascinating look at the medical disaster that hit the capital in 1665 also examines the lifestyle of Londoners during the Commonwealth and Restoration.

The Inns of Court, by Jill Allibone and David Evans (Black Dog, 1996): The mysteries of London's legal enclave are explored in great detail in these essays, illustrated by many evocative black-and-white images by architectural photographer Helene Binet.

Lights Out for the Territory, by Iain Sinclair (Granta, 1996): By walking around the city, observing and eavesdropping on Londoners in their daily lives, Sinclair has produced an interesting book of odd vignettes and offbeat quotes.

London—A Companion to Its History and Archaeology, by Malcolm Billings (Kyle Cathie Ltd, 1994): The capital's history is revealed through its archeological finds, including the Roman Wall, the Temple of Mithras, and Celtic war artifacts.

London: A Guide to Recent Architecture, by Samantha Hardingham (Ellipsis, 1995): This excellent, pocket-size guide contains pictures and descriptions of 100 modern building projects, from shops and bars to the megadevelopments in Docklands.

London as It Might Have Been, by Felix Barker and Ralph Hyde (John Murray, 1982): What if **Sir Christopher Wren**'s original plans to re-create London after the Great Fire of 1666 had not been rejected? Barker and Hyde speculate on what the city would have looked like if this building plan, along with several others that were proposed and rejected throughout the years, had been carried out. The text is supplemented by drawings of the bridges, parks, monuments, and streets that never came to be.

London's Statues and Monuments, by Margaret Baker (Shire Publications, 1995): Believe it or not, you can explore London's lengthy history without setting foot in a single museum. This book, organized into 20 districts (with clear maps), examines every statue and monument within the city limits, explaining the history behind each one in a light, readable style.

The Oxford Book of London, edited by Paul Bailey (Oxford University Press, 1995): The London-born editor has collected off-the-beaten-track descriptions of the capital that run the gamut from 12th-century monks' chronicles to current novels, interspersed with a variety of interesting quotes.

The Queen: A Biography of Elizabeth II, by Ben Pimlott (HarperCollins, 1996): The many recent difficulties of the royal family add poignancy to this well-written, well-assessed portrait of the monarch, written by a history professor.

A Spy's London, by Roy Berkely (Leo Cooper, 1994): The author, a police officer originally from Vermont, describes some 21 walks through the streets of London, revealing the places where famous spies lived, rendezvoused, and sometimes were killed.

Walking London, by Andrew Duncan (New Holland Publishers Ltd, 1991): The 30 walks described in these pages are a delight for visitors who enjoy exploring hidden corners of such well-known neighborhoods as **Kensington**, **Soho**, and **Bloomsbury**. The maps are excellent, the directions detailed, and the anecdotes enlightening.

and a much talked-about monkfish cooked with tandoori spices and served with black rice. The desserts are regarded as a highlight and include a trio of sorbets including black currant and tamarillo and a variety of crème brûlées, which are scented with fennel. ♦ M–Sa, dinner until 2AM (last orders 11PM). 9 Conduit St. 0870/777.4488. Tube: Piccadilly Circus, Oxford St

26 RIGBY & PELLER

Mrs. Rigby and Mrs. Peller were two ladies who cared about foundations. Not architectural, but sartorial. In 1939 they set up their corsetière on South Molton Street. And today, with the addition of HM the Queen's own Royal Warrant in 1960, it is still going strong on Conduit Street. Their expert lady fitters don't even need to use tape measures—they just fix you with a beady stare and announce your dimensions. They say that 85 percent of the women who walk through their shop are wearing the wrong-size bra. They make bespoke bras and corsets, for underwear or outerwear. And they are gorgeous. Even their off-the-shelf lingerie is beautiful. ♦ M–Sa. 22(a) Conduit St (between Mill and New Bond Sts). 491.2200. Tube: Oxford St

27 LE MÉRIDIEN GROSVENOR HOUSE HOTEL

$$$ This grand old hotel has been a London institution since 1927. It boasts (it says) some of the largest bedrooms in the city. There are around 448 of them, most with panoramic views over Hyde Park, ranging from standard to Royal Club suites. All rooms have everything you could hope for, including marble bathrooms, nonallergic linen, and both UK and US plug sockets, but the **Royal Club** occupies floors 5–7 of the building, and its rooms have private check-in facilities and a private lounge where breakfast, morning coffee, and traditional afternoon tea are served to club residents only. The Grosvenor also has 137 luxury apartments. The ultimate luxury in a city is, of course, space, and these apartments range from 800 to 1,600 square feet. The hotel's Great Room is the largest ballroom in London, so bring your longest-wearing dancing shoes. ♦ 90 Park La. 499.6363, 800/225.5843; fax 493.3341. Tube: Bond Street, Marble Arch

Within the hotel:

THE PARK ROOM

Now refurbished and much larger than before, the Park Room offers a wide range of dining, from sandwiches (including a hot steak sandwich, of which they are particularly proud) to salads (including a warm Mediterranean vegetable salad) to antipasti platters and bruschetta. There is a pasta of the day. Though the food is good, there is no necessity to eat—the coffee is also recommended. ♦ Daily, breakfast through late dinner

28 CONNAUGHT

$$$$ At the time of writing, the Connaught is undergoing an extensive refurbishment, and it should be open again by the time you are reading this. So you will know better than I whether it comes up to scratch! ♦ Carlos Pl (at Mount St). 499.7070. Tube: Bond St. www.theconnaught.co.uk

29 VIVIENNE WESTWOOD

This most influential of British designers is unstoppable, still grabbing the headlines with her collections for men and women. Her couture clothes (Gold Label) are at this little shop. ♦ M–Sa. 6 Davies St (near Mont Row). 629.3757. Tube: Bond St. The Man Collection and the less expensive range (Red Label) are at 40 Conduit St (between New Bond St and Savile Row). 439.1109. Tube: Bond St, Oxford Circus. The affordable, street-style range with the young in mind is at 430 Kings Rd (between Park Walk and Limerston St). 352.6551. Tube: South Kensington

30 SAVILE ROW

Many of the tailors on this street, rightly famed the world over for their expertise, have been in this location for at least 200 years. It is benefiting from the resurgence of interest in British fashion, attracting young, flashy tailor-designers to open shops next to the traditional establishments. ♦ Between Vigo and Conduit Sts. Tube: Oxford Circus, Piccadilly Circus

On Savile Row:

GIEVES & HAWKES

Founded in 1785, this is the oldest tailor on the street. Its representatives once followed the British fleet around the world, dressing such illustrious figures as Admiral Horatio Nelson, the Duke of Wellington, David Livingstone, and Henry Stanley, not to mention the infamous Captain Bligh of the *Bounty*. ♦ M–Sa. No. 1 (at Vigo St). 434.2001

OZWALD BOATENG

One of the flamboyant new breed of tailors, Boateng is also a designer of men's suits and shirts. At 30, he was the youngest person to open his own shop here in 1996. ♦ M–Sa. 9 Vigo St (at Savile Row). 734.6868

Restaurants/Clubs: Red | Hotels: Purple | Shops: Orange | Outdoors/Parks: Green | Sights/Culture: Blue

DEGE

Four top tailors (including one who makes women's clothing) work under one roof at this shop, whose name is pronounced *Deej*. Customers for their suits and sports clothes include heads of state. ♦ M–F; Sa, 9:30AM–12:30PM. No. 10 (between Vigo and New Burlington Sts). 287.2941

HENRY POOLE & CO.

This establishment has tailored gentlemen's clothes for 170 years; in Victoria's day, it dressed the French aristocracy (or what was left of it), including Baron de Rothschild and Prince Louis Napoleon. ♦ M–F. No. 15 (between Vigo and New Burlington Sts). 734.5985

RICHARD JAMES

This tailor is very much in the forefront of the fashion scene. His many clients in the creative professions appreciate the sharp cut and bold-colored fabrics of his made-to-measure and ready-to-wear men's suits, as well as his coordinated shirts. Famous shoppers here include Elton John and Christian Lacroix. ♦ M–Sa. 31 Savile Row (between Burlington Gardens and Clifford St). 434.0605

ANDERSON & SHEPPARD

The tailor here, Arthur Mortenson, is renowned for his ability to sew a Sholte shoulder, which is softer and deeper than the traditional English cut. One of the most discreet tailoring establishments in London, it considers merely being listed in shopping guides as vulgar advertising. Ironically, the now over-the-top fashion genius Alexander McQueen, who presently heads Givenchy in Paris, started here and even made suits for Prince Charles. ♦ M–F. No. 30 (at Clifford St). 734.1420

31 CAFÉ ROYAL

The famed multiple rooms of the Café Royal, founded in 1865 by a French wine merchant, Daniel Nicholas Thévenon, and long known as an elegant hangout for London painters and literati, from Max Beerbohm and George Bernard Shaw to Dylan Thomas, are now mostly venues for private functions. ♦ M–Sa. 68 Regent St (at Air St). 437.9090. Tube: Piccadilly Circus

32 PICCADILLY THEATRE

This large, comfortable theater has air conditioning, which is fortunate, given that it seats 1,213. It's a good venue for the less-hyped musicals. ♦ Denman St (at Sherwood St). 369.1734. Tube: Piccadilly Circus

33 RAINFOREST CAFÉ

★★$$$ This is Europe's first branch of the American-themed restaurant chain. For the uninitiated, expect regular thunderstorms and a cacophony of wildlife noises. Food is American Caribbean with a jungle twist: treetop tenderloin, chicken monsoon, and Amazon flatbread are featured. ♦ American Caribbean ♦ Daily, lunch and dinner. 20 Shaftesbury Ave (at Great Windmill St). 434.3111. Tube: Piccadilly Circus

34 BERKELEY SQUARE

Like Grosvenor Square, this Georgian square is associated with the rich and famous. In the late 1890s, Waldorf Astor lived at **No. 54**, followed by department store tycoon Gordon Selfridge, whose legacy stands in Oxford Street. More recently, in the early 1970s, the elusive Lord Lucan played poker at the **Clermont Club** (**No. 44**). Accused of murder, he disappeared but is regularly "spotted" in some country or other. At **No. 45**, Lord Clive, better known as Clive of India, committed suicide in 1774. The Clermont Club, built by **William Kent**, is said to be the finest remaining example of a Georgian terraced house in central London. Centuries-old plane trees shade the west side of the square, where privileged young men and women sip Champagne at the annual Berkeley Square Ball. ♦ At Bruton and Hill Sts and at Berkeley and Davies Sts. Tube: Green Park, Bond St

35 BROWN'S HOTEL

$$$$ Brown's Hotel celebrated its 170th birthday in 2007 with a £24 million facelift. No Hollywood A-Lister ever tucked up better. The hotel has also joined The Rocco Forte Collection. Brown's is made up of 11 Georgian townhouses, which have been creatively rearranged to offer 117 bedrooms including 29 suites. As with the rest of The Collection, design is by Olga Polizzi, and she does have a way of making you feel that when you lay your hat here (as the song says), it's your home. Each room has its own mini library of books and selection of original paintings. There is also broadband connection, flat-screen TV, and all the other little luxuries of modern life. ♦ 30–34 Albemarle St. 493.6020

Within Brown's Hotel:

THE GRILL AT BROWN'S HOTEL

★★★$$$ British classics with a modern twist are what you will get here—although Brown's famous lunchtime carvery trolley is pretty traditional, and none the worse for it! Off the menu rather than the trolley you can enjoy excellent oysters, marvelous Morecambe Bay shrimps, or baked razor clams, followed by all manner of hot pots and braises, topnotch grills, and superb game (wild duck with Cox's apple mash, celeriac, and cèpes, anyone?). Lee Streeton is the man in the kitchen, and very, very good he is, too. ♦ Daily, breakfast, lunch, and dinner. 493.6020

36 BURLINGTON ARCADE

This Regency promenade of exclusive shops, designed and completed in 1819 by **Samuel Ware**, might be considered a forerunner to modern shopping malls, even though they bear little resemblance to it. Inspired by Continental models and built in the years after Waterloo for Lord George Cavendish, the arcade provided the gentry with a shopping precinct free of the mud splashed by carriages and carts on Piccadilly, and it prevented the locals from flinging their garbage into his back garden. The three cheerful top-hatted beadles who patrol the arcade today are the smallest police force in the world. Originally they were installed to protect prosperous shoppers from pickpockets and beggars. Now they will ask you not to whistle or run, and they lock the gates at 6PM Monday through Saturday. Though the promenade was badly damaged in the Blitz, it was rebuilt and today exudes an atmosphere of intimate but conceivable elegance, lined with shops abounding in luxury goods. Admire the glass roof as well as the iridescent green paintwork comple-mented by gold lettering on the delicately detailed shop fronts. The ostentatious façades were added in 1911. ♦ Between Piccadilly and Burlington Gardens. Tube: Green Park, Piccadilly Circus

Within Burlington Arcade:

IRISH LINEN COMPANY

Linen napkins that could sail a small ship, sheets that assume you use a professional laundry service, and special cloths for drying the Waterford crystal wineglasses that grace fine linen tablecloths can be found in this shop. ♦ M-Sa. Nos. 35-36. 493.8949

N. PEAL

Wise Englishwomen would rather be draped in cashmere than diamonds, and they stroll through the arcade on weekdays wearing the clothes to prove it. The two N. Peal shops in the arcade have the best cashmere in London—from the addictive knee socks for women to the handsome capes. Remember when you enter these shops that you get what you pay for. ♦ M-Sa. Women's shops: Nos. 37-40. 493.9220; men's shop: No. 71. 493.0912

ST. PETERSBURG COLLECTION

Living up to his illustrious name, Carl Fabergé's grandson, Theo, continues the family tradition of creating exquisite objets d'art and jewelry. The gallery also shows decorative antiques, Russian lacquer boxes, fine porcelain, and paintings. Surprisingly for such small premises, there are three stories to browse in. ♦ M-Sa. No. 42. 495.2883

RICHARD OGDEN

Come here for antique jewelry, including museum-quality pieces of Art Nouveau. ♦ M-Sa. Nos. 28-29. 493.9136

MAP WORLD

All sorts of antique maps—including such oddities as "A New Mappe of the Romane Empire" by John Speed, created around 1626—are available for all sorts of prices. ♦ M-Sa. No. 25. 495.5377

MICHAEL ROSE

Mr. Rose calls his shop "the source of the unusual." It specializes in handmade period and modern engagement and wedding rings ("the largest collection in Europe"), as well as all types of antique jewelry, including Fabergé. ♦ M-Sa. No. 3. 493.0714

THE VINTAGE WATCH COMPANY

This is the place to come if you are after a vintage Rolex—that is all they sell. Over the last 8 years they have been dedicated to creating Vintage Rolex as a brand and they now have over 400 in their collection, from 1915 to 1960. ♦ 27 Burlington Arcade. 499.2023. www.vintagewatchcompany.com

CARR'S SILVER

This specialist silversmith has outlets in 60 countries. The company is based in Sheffield, where there is a tradition in the art of silversmithing going back more than 300 years. Carr's features both traditional and modern designs. ♦ 22/23 Burlington Arcade. 449.8223. www.carrs-silverware.co.uk

MILLEPERLE

Two showrooms dedicated to pearls—Japanese Akoya, Australian, South Sea, Tahitian, black, and Indonesian gold pearls are just some of the many gorgeous varieties on display here. As well as selling you the necklaces, earrings, collars, and brooches, milleperle will maintain your pearls, whether they need cleaning, oiling, or restringing. ♦ 50 Burlington Arcade. 499.3535; 70 Burlington Arcade. 499.3434. www.milleperle.co.uk

SANDRA CRONAN LTD

SANDRA CRONAN

High-quality antique jewelry, especially from the Art Nouveau and Art Deco eras, is among the interesting wares on display. The staff are very knowledgeable about vintage jewelry, and the shop stages periodic themed exhibitions on such subjects as cufflinks through the ages or the changing look of paste jewelry. ♦ M–F. No. 18. 491.4851

BEATRIX ONG

Trained under the great Jimmy Choo himself, Ong has been named as one of the world's top 10 shoe designers. Till now she has been drawing discerning shoe lovers to Primrose Hill, but she has come down to town. The shop is gorgeous—a spiral staircase, a chandelier, and tea and cakes for private clients! ♦ M-Sa. 4 Burlington Arcade. 499.4089

LADURÉE

This is the Tiffany of teacake shops, the Sears of sweet thing purveyors. It's from Paris, as if you might not guess as soon as you see the perfection in patisserie that floats behind this shop front. The original was opened in 1862. This is their latest shop. Their world-famous macaroons are made fresh each morning in Ladurée's "laboratory." Each new season, Ladurée pays tribute to its most famous creation and creates a new flavor. I warn you: these things are so delectable that if you take one mouthful, chances are, you will cry. And the presentation boxes are almost as gorgeous as the macaroons. ♦ M-Sa. 71-72 Burlington Arcade. 491.9155. www.laduree.fr

BI ZU

A lovely little place specializing in coral and turquoise jewelery. The pieces are bespoke and handmade in Italy, and they can be made to your personal request. ♦ M-Sa. 5 Burlington Arcade. 495.6162

37 DORCHESTER

$$$$ Wow! That is the only word for the Dorchester. Forget egalitarianism. The

Dorchester is always busy, and that can only be because all men are *not* equal . . . some are simply rich. It opened in 1931, welcoming the cream of international society, and it is welcoming you still. It has just undergone a multimillion-pound refurbishment that it calls "The New Flowering," and its 195 king, queen, and twin rooms (no pokey singles here) and 53 suites are breathtaking. The four roof garden suites are very close to heaven, literally and metaphorically. No two rooms are alike, and all have bespoke furniture in walnut, mahogany, and fruitwoods; soft furnishings in damask, cashmere, and silk; plasma-screen TV; personally controlled air conditioning; and bathrooms completely rebuilt in '30s-style Italian marble, etched glass, and chrome. There are stunning displays of the most perfect of fresh flowers in every room. There is even a specially designed chair—the Alice Chair—that is specifically for watching television from and is exclusive to the Dorchester. There is a ratio of three staff members to each bedroom, and if that isn't enough, logging on to your personal Internet link will find you your e-butler. Talking of technology, the in-room communication and Internet facilities are stellar. Every special request you make is entered into the Dorchester's computerized guest history for your return visit. The hotel has a barber and ladies' hairdresser, the **Dorchester Spa**, a limousine service, and specially equipped rooms for guests with disabilities. Should you be arriving en famille, or with entourage, rooms can be connected to form suites of any size. Let's face it, this is the hotel that completely converted one of its luxury bathrooms into a kitchen for Pavarotti when he came to stay—the Dorchester can do anything. Staff members are utterly charming from the moment you arrive at the door. If you want the luxury end of London, this would be where to come. But beware—luxury at this level is addictive. You will want to return. One of the many marvelous things about the Dorchester is that you can, should you not be able to stay here, enjoy the "Dorchester experience" by spending time dining or drinking in one of the hotel's wonderful restaurants and bars. The welcome at the door is no less warm and you are made to feel no less special because you don't have a room key. ♦ Park Lane. 629.8888, 800/727.9820; fax 409.0114. Tube: Hyde Park Corner, Marble Arch. www.dorchesterhotel.com

Within the Dorchester:

THE KRUG ROOM

★★★★$$$$ Underneath the hotel and within the kitchen itself is a glass-fronted

"London—the smoky nest fated to be my favourite residence."

—Mendelssohn

private dining room that seats 12. The privacy of creamy opaque glass can be turned into a close-up and personal view of Henry Brosi, executive chef of the hotel, as he cooks exclusively for you, at the flick of a switch. Menus give diners the chance to taste some of the renowned chef's signature dishes, and each course is accompanied by a complementary Krug Champagne. For somewhere so far underground, it is very close to heaven.

CHINA TANG

★★★★$$$$ David Tang, founder of China Clubs in Hong Kong, Shanghai, and Singapore, and creator of the Shanghai Tang lifestyle empire, has brought the full weight of his creativity to bear on the downstairs restaurant at The Dorchester. It is outrageously kitsch in décor and outrageously delicious in cuisine. Art Deco meets Tokyo Joe is what it conjures to the eye: there is black lacquer and silver chopsticks, your sake or rice wine comes in cut-glass decanters, and the walls are decorated with original painted silks. The food is predominantly dim sum, but China Tang does dim sum the way Tiffany does diamonds. The place has instantly become one of the most talked-about restaurants in town. Seafood dumplings and stir-fried minced pigeon wrapped in cunningly sculpted lettuce leaves plus the (critics say) best barbecued pork in London are on the menu. The Peking duck is the talk of the town and comes served by a white-gloved waiter. The restaurant never uses MSG. ◆ Daily, lunch and dinner. 629.9988 Tube: Marble Arch

THE PROMENADE

★★★$$$ Even if you have no appetite, the Promenade is worth a visit. Seemingly endless yards of sofas, twinkling lights, and marble columns create the perfect setting for a coffee and a sandwich, some freshly made pastries, or yet another of the Dorchester's special offerings—the Champagne Afternoon Tea. ◆ Daily, till midnight

THE BAR

Unlike The Grill, which has emerged from the recent refurbishments as a garish nightmare, The Bar has emerged as a cocktail lover's dream—all rich colors and mirrored glass, lacquered mahogany, and abstract red glass shards. The cocktails are classic and the wines and spirits classy. The bar food is pretty good too—especially if you like caviar. And if you fancy a Champagne-based afternoon tea, this is a great place to come. ◆ Daily

38 ENGLISH-SPEAKING UNION (ESU)

US Ambassador Charles Price II called the ESU "without doubt the most effective and vigorous private group linking the United Kingdom, the United States, and many other nations in a worldwide effort to improve mutual understanding." Its headquarters—draped with both the Union Jack and the Stars and Stripes—has been located in **Dartmouth House** since 1927. The house dates to 1757, and a number of British aristocrats, including the Earl of Dartmouth, have lived here. Today, in addition to providing an assortment of educational opportunities and exchanges, the building hosts cultural activities—concerts, readings, lectures, and dramatic events. ◆ M–F. 37 Charles St (between Hay's Mews and Chesterfield Hill). 493.3328. Tube: Green Park

39 ZEN CENTRAL

★★$$$ This chic noshing hole serves nouvelle Chinese dishes in designer surroundings. Entrées include sea bass with black bean sauce and rice wine-marinated chicken. The people watching is as good as the food. Zen Central is part of a chain of Zen Garden restaurants, all of which have *Zen* in the name. ◆ Chinese ◆ Daily, lunch and dinner. 20 Queen St (between Curzon and Charles Sts). 629.8089. Tube: Green Park. Also at 85 Sloane Ave (between Petyward and Ixworth Pl). 589.1781. Tube: Sloane Square, South Kensington

40 RADISSON EDWARDIAN MAYFAIR

$$$$ The hotel was originally opened in 1927 by the then King George V. Now it is part of Radisson's empire. It does look fantastic—not very Edwardian, it must be said, but very chic. There are 407 bedrooms and suites with deep, handmade wool carpets and leather beds and bedside tables by the Italian design kings Cattelan. Phillipe Hurel has designed their occasional furniture, and every room has a Bang &

Olufsen TV (plasma screens in the suites), triple-glazed windows, and a Sicilian marble bathroom. Deluxe rooms have designer chaise longues in a separate sitting area and walk-in wardrobes with floor-to-ceiling mirrors. There is a state-of-the-art business center open to guests 24 hours a day and the fabulous luxury Mayfair Spa, which offers The Cleopatra Bathing Experience, Hammam relaxation beds, and aromatic steam rooms. ◆ Stratton St (at Berkeley St). Reservations (toll free US) 800/333.3333, (toll free UK) 0800/37 4411; 629.7777. Tube: Green Park www.radissonedwardian.com

Within the Radisson Edwardian Mayfair:

The Amba Restaurant and Bar

★★★$$$$ This is a very chic eatery with granite floors, leather upholstery, and rich amber wall coverings. The open kitchen means that if conversation palls at your table, you always have something to divert you! The menu is described as "seasonally British" and includes cottage pie (made with Aberdeen Angus beef), Cornish crab cakes, and London cured salmon. There is traditional English trifle as a dessert, and the house specialty is a bread-and-butter pudding ice cream. The bar serves terrific cocktails and the wine list is good, if not inspired. ◆ Daily, breakfast, lunch, and dinner. Bar open till 2AM. 915.3892. amba@radisson.com

Mayfair Bar

The upholstery is in lilac, which isn't nearly as alarming as it sounds! There is a lovely open fire, and the whole room is designed with the focus on the impressive, glass-columned bar. Cocktails here are very much the thing, and they are terrific: lots of fresh fruit concoctions, one of the best collections of vintage rums in London, and the Mayfair mojito is the thing to try! ◆ Daily, noon-11PM

CHEZ GÉRARD

41 Chez Gérard

★★$$$ Here you will find good food and wine at unpretentious prices, served efficiently in smart surroundings. Brasserie classics are on the menu: *moules marinières*, onion soup, chicken liver pâté, Chateaubriand, and the best *frites* in London. A bottle of Côtes du Rhône will enhance the meal, and either the excellent cheese board or a chocolate concoction from the dessert menu will bring it to a satisfying conclusion. ◆French ◆M-F, lunch and dinner; Sa, Su, dinner.

Reservations recommended. 31 Dover St (between Piccadilly and Hay Hill). 499.8171. Tube: Green Park. Also at 8 Charlotte St (between Percy and Windmill Sts). 636.4975. Tube: Goodge St, Tottenham Court Rd; first floor Opera Terrace, Covent Garden Central Market (facing Russell St). 379.0666. Tube: Covent Garden; 119 Chancery La (between the Strand and Carey St). 504.0290. Tube: Temple

ROYAL ACADEMY OF ARTS

42 Royal Academy of Arts, Burlington House

The house on this site has undergone many changes since its construction in 1707. In 1717, the building was acquired by Richard Boyle, third Earl of Burlington, and he immediately commissioned architect **Colen Campbell** to remodel it. Campbell redesigned the rather unprepossessing structure in classical Palladian style, and it became a textbook example of the genre. The present staircase and other decorative features were added by **Samuel Ware** in 1815, when the house was purchased by Lord George Cavendish. In 1854, the government bought the building and made it the permanent home of the Royal Academy of Arts, which had been sited in various locations since its founding in 1768. **R.R. Banks** and **E.M. Barry** were hired to add new wings and side buildings, and later, in 1872, **Sydney Smirke** added a second story (spoiling the structure's classical Palladian look) and a number of exhibition galleries. **Sir Norman Foster** added the **Arthur Sackler Galleries** on the top floor in 1991. The complex's imposing grandeur is lightened by banners heralding the exhibitions inside.

In the courtyard stands *Sir Joshua Reynolds*, a statue of the first president of the academy. In the rooms along the quadrangle, learned societies have their headquarters: the Geological Society, the Royal Society of Chemistry, the Society of Antiquaries, and the Royal Astronomical Society.

The Royal Academy marked the recognition of the importance of art and artists in this country and, for better or worse, made artists members of the Establishment. Artistic temperament being what it is, many painters refused to exhibit at this "Official Marketplace for Art": George Romney, William Blake, Dante Gabriel

Rossetti, and James Abbott McNeill Whistler declined, whereas Thomas Gainsborough exhibited for a few years but stopped because he was dissatisfied with the way his works were displayed. The division hasn't really healed with time—you can be certain that Francis Bacon was not part of the academy, yet David Hockney is. The initials *RA* after artists' names (meaning they are among the 80-odd Academicians) may add to the price of their works in the salesrooms but do not significantly affect their reputations in the art world.

In the center of the entrance hall are ceiling paintings by Benjamin West: *The Graces Unveiling Nature* and *The Four Elements*. There are two paintings by Angelica Kaufmann at each end: *Genius and Painting*, near the door to the **Friends Room** on the east, and *Composition and Design*, on the west. Above the central staircase is a circular painting by **William Kent**: *The Glorification of Inigo Jones*. The first floor includes the **Saloon**, the only surviving part of **Campbell**'s Burlington House, with a ceiling by William Kent.

Exhibitions of paintings, sculpture, and architectural drawings and models take place in the rooms on the first and second floors. The Summer Exhibition is the big event of the year at the academy and one of London's more important social occasions. Some 14,000 works by 4,000 artists are submitted, with 1,300 finally selected. The gala opening in June looks like a royal garden party with pictures. The academy's reputation now rests on its international art exhibitions. Parts of the permanent collection are on view in the **Private Rooms** on the first floor. Splendid pictures by Sir Joshua Reynolds, John Constable, Sir Henry Raeburn, Sir Alfred Munnings, and Walter Sickert may be seen, whereas sculptures by Sir Eduardo Paolozzi and Dame Elizabeth Frink are displayed around the building.

The second floor houses the award-winning **Sackler Galleries**, which are reached by a glass elevator. Here is the spacious sculpture gallery where the academy's most prized possession, Michelangelo's *Madonna and Child with the Infant St. John*, carved in 1505, is on permanent display. It is one of only four major sculptures by the artist outside Italy. ♦ Admission. Private Rooms: free tours Tu–F, 1PM. Free public gallery talks Tu,

George Bernard Shaw offered Winston Churchill tickets for the first night of *St. Joan* for himself and a friend, "if you have one." Churchill replied that he was sorry he would not be able to attend and asked for tickets for the second night, "if there is one."

2:30PM. Daily. Piccadilly (between Albany Ct Yd and Burlington Arcade). 439.7438. Tube: Green Park, Piccadilly Circus

Within the Royal Academy of Arts, Burlington House:

ROYAL ACADEMY SHOP

Jam-packed with wonderful items, this store offers easels, brushes, paints, a framing service, jigsaw puzzles of paintings, a large collection of art books, catalogs from exhibitions abroad, original items by academy artists and silk scarves designed by them, plus the obligatory canvas museum bags. ♦ Daily. 439.7438

ROYAL ACADEMY RESTAURANT

★★$ Big and cafeteria-like, this eatery provides a welcome refuge from the nonstop glamour of Piccadilly. Women in tweed suits and sensible shoes, in town for the day, sit in the attractive paneled room, tranquilly sipping tea and indulging in cakes. Hot and cold meals are served at lunchtime, and there's a decent salad bar. ♦ International ♦ Daily, lunch and afternoon tea. 439.7438

43 ALBANY

Sir William Chambers built this residence for Viscount Melbourne in 1774. It looks like an English Palladian version of a Parisian *hôtel particulier* (mansion). Henry Holland converted its garden to chambers for bachelor gentlemen in 1803. This building has been the home of Lord Byron, Thomas B. Macaulay, Lord Gladstone, and, more recently, J.B. Priestley, Graham Greene, and 1960s British film star Terence Stamp (featured prominently in the campy 1994 film *The Adventures of Priscilla, Queen of the Desert*). ♦ Albany Ct Yd (off Piccadilly). Tube: Green Park, Piccadilly Circus

44 SACKVILLE STREET

Take a quick look at this almost purely Georgian street, which radiates a confident modesty. ♦ Between Piccadilly and Vigo St. Tube: Green Park, Piccadilly Circus

On Sackville St:

HENRY SOTHERAN LTD.

Row on row of glorious antique leather-bound books greet you here, glistening like chestnuts. ♦ M–Sa. No. 2. 439.6151

FOLIO SOCIETY

This bookshop in the basement of **Henry Sotheran Ltd.** makes handsome editions of all the favorite English works. A beautifully bound and printed set of Jane Austen novels is a timeless treasure. ♦ M–Sa. No. 2. 629.6517

45 CORDINGS

If London weren't a Dickensian tangle of ground leases, this shop would have been abolished and the grandeur of Le Méridien Piccadilly extended. Only the web of property laws enabled the ceremonial designs of **John Nash** to be destroyed and this little store to remain. Located here since 1839, it has kept its character in an ever-changing world. You can get terrific raincoats, waterproof boots, country woolens, and tweeds, all high quality. ♦ M–Sa. 19 Piccadilly (at Air St). 734.0830. Tube: Piccadilly Circus

46 VIRGIN MEGASTORE

Almost a whole block to itself, this store is filled with DVDs, videos, CDs, games, computer and hi-fi accessories, clothes, books, and odd little gifts. The staff are young and reasonably knowledgeable, and there are good sections for classic movies, jazz, blues, spoken word, and stage and film soundtracks. Whether we are talking album releases or UMD for PSP, this store generally has whatever is newest and hottest, as well as the classics. ♦ M–Sa, 9AM–midnight; Su, noon–6PM. 1 Piccadilly Circus (at Regent St). 439.2500. www.virgin.com

47 EROS

The city's best-loved statue, depicting the God of Love, symbolizes London itself to people all over the world. It is a memorial to the virtuous Lord Shaftesbury, a tireless reformer and educator who lived from 1801 to 1885. The sculptor, Alfred Gilbert, was no less idealistic; he believed Shaftesbury deserved a monument that would represent both generosity of spirit and love of humankind, and would symbolize, according to the sculptor, "the work of Lord Shaftes-bury, the blindfolded Love sending forth indiscriminately, yet with purpose, his missile of kindness, always with the swiftness the bird has from its wings, never ceasing to breathe or reflect critically, but ever soaring onwards, regardless of its own perils and dangers." (According to legend,

Gilbert also intended Eros's bow and arrow to be a pun on Lord Shaftesbury's name.) Gilbert created his statue in aluminum, marking the first time the material had been used for such a sculpture. As a result, the 8-foot figure is so light that it sways in the wind. Gilbert was paid £3,000 for his work, even though it had cost him £7,000 to make it. His eventual and inevitable bankruptcy left him with little alternative but to leave the country, living first in Belgium and then in Italy. Lord Shaftesbury himself died lamenting, "I cannot bear to leave this world with all the misery in it." He would presumably have been sadder still to know how much misery had afflicted the artist who tried to honor him. Although the creator of Eros was rejected, the statue has an enduring place in the hearts of Londoners. ♦ In the center of Piccadilly Circus. Tube: Piccadilly Circus

48 REGENT STREET

Signs of the grand designs of **John Nash** are apparent here, with Regent Street running southward to Waterloo Place and the Mall, and northward to Oxford Street and Regent's Park. Unfortunately, what you see now is not what Nash created. Nash planned Piccadilly Circus as an elegant square with a long arcade, very much like the rue de Rivoli running alongside the Tuileries in Paris. The Quadrant, an even larger version of the crescent at Regent's Park, was the essence of the scheme—so crucial that Nash financed its construction out of his own pocket, persuading his builders to accept leases instead of payment when his money ran out.

Completed in 1819, the Quadrant must have been very handsome indeed. Its destruction began in 1848, and it was completely obliterated by 1905. Since then, planners have tried with monotonous regularity to restore and re-create Piccadilly Circus. The latest attempt is the 1986 effort visible today: a precinct that one hopes won't succumb to the shabbiness to which the area is prone.

Sightseers should go to Regent Street when the shops are closed; it is at its most attractive when deserted. Remember to look up: A lot of fine detail can be found at the tops of the buildings. For shopping, the street is somewhat deficient; considering its central location and length, it has more than its share of airline offices and ordinary chain stores. However, there are some notable exceptions. Start with **Aquascutum** (reputed to be Lady Margaret Thatcher's outfitter) at the Piccadilly Circus end, followed by **Garrard** (the queen's jewelers), and then walk purposefully up to **Mappin & Webb**, another high-class jewelry store. If you feel the urge to buy china, wait until you've seen the extraordinary department store **Liberty** (see page 76), which is much loved by the English gentry. Don't forget to look in **Hamleys** toy shop (see page 76), but be prepared to stay a long time if you bring your children—they'll never want to leave.

To the right of Regent Street (the bottom end) is Waterloo Place, presided over by the **Duke of York Column**, created in 1834 by **Benjamin Dean Wyatt**. This street was meant to mark the southern end of Nash's triumphal way from Carlton House Terrace to **Regent's Park**. In the distance you can see the **Victoria Tower** of the **Houses of Parliament**. Over the past few years, Regent Street has been more hoarding and scaffolding than shop front, but it is sorting itself out now. ◆ Between Piccadilly and Oxford Circuses. Tube: Piccadilly Circus, Oxford Circus

49 CRITERION THEATRE

Tawdry signs have long buried the French-château façade of this elaborately refurbished theater, designed in 1870 by **Thomas Verity**. Seating 598, it is London's only underground theater in the physical sense of the word: Patrons go down a series of steps, even for the upper circle. The lobby is decorated with Victorian tiles. ◆ Piccadilly Circus (at Piccadilly). 369.1747. Tube: Piccadilly Circus

49 FRANKIE'S AT THE CRITERION

★★$$ The chef is still Marco Pierre White, but now in collaboration with jockey Frankie Dettori (unlikely as that might sound). They serve pizza, pasta, and a little bit more. Very family friendly. The food is good and reliable, the wine list generous, the staff well trained and charming, and the whole dining experience is made surreal—if gorgeous—by the fact that the Criterion Brasserie (which the room once was) has one of the most opulently, glitteringly ornate and beautiful ceilings in London—quite literally "over the top." ◆ Daily. 224 Piccadilly (at Piccadilly Circus). 934.0488. Tube: Piccadilly Circus

50 DOVER ST. MARKET

It might not look very pretty, but this place is one of *the* favorite hangouts of the London fashion set. Here you are in with the most modishly dressed in-crowd, shopping at a collection of stalls selling serious sartorial sophistication from the most haute of catwalk creations to simple suits and shirts. There are great accessories and other designs too. This place has quasi-iconic status amongst the fashionistas. The more you know your fashion stuff, the more you'll get out of it. ◆ M-Sa. 17-18 Dover St (at Piccadilly). 518.0680. Tube: Green Park. www.doverstreetmarket.com

51 PICCADILLY ARCADE

Thrale Jell built this extension of the **Burlington Arcade** a century later, in 1910. Today, its charming, casual row of shops connects Piccadilly to Jermyn Street. ◆ Between Jermyn St and Piccadilly. Tube: Green Park, Piccadilly Circus

Within Piccadilly Arcade:

ST. JAMES'S ART

Originally an art bookshop, now one of the most charming little galleries in London, this establishment is well worth a visit for its collection of graphics from the School of Paris. Names to conjure with include Chagall, Matisse, and Picasso. They also have an impressive raft of Soviet Impressionists and inexpensive oils. Word has it that this kind of thing is becoming increasingly collectible, so this could be your big chance—buy now! ◆ 15 Piccadilly Arcade. M-Sa, 10AM-6PM. 495.6487; fax 495.6490. Tube: Piccadilly Circus, Green Park. www.artstjames.com

WATERFORD WEDGWOOD

These china specialists have a complete and tempting collection of Wedgwood and Spode. All the price lists include the import cost and the amount in dollars. ◆ M-Sa. No. 173 Piccadilly (at the arcade entrance). 629.2614

FAVOURBROOK

Sumptuous materials are used in fashioning waistcoats and Nehru-collar jackets for women only. ◆ M-Sa. Nos. 9-21. 491.2337. Menswear only is sold at 55 Jermyn St (between Duke and St. James's Sts). 493.5060. Tube: Green Park

NEW AND LINGWOOD LTD.

On the Jermyn Street side is one of the best and least-known shops in the arcade. It started as the London branch of the **Eton** shop, which has been outfitting Etonians for decades. The branch here has splendid, ready-made shirts and a small but choice selection of sweaters. The cotton shirts and lambs'-wool sweaters from this shop are worth every pound and pence. Shirts are also made to order. Upstairs is **Poulsen and Skone**, makers of fine footwear; a custom-made pair requires another serious investment, but the shoemakers share the burden, providing lifelong care and

---

Regent Street Shopping

OXFORD STREET

clothing **United Colors of Benetton**
clothing **French Connection**

Tezenis *underwear/pajamas*
Coast *womenswear*
Principles *clothing*
Mamas & Papas *maternitywear*
Accessorize *accessories*
National Westminster Bank

PRINCES STREET

womenswear **Karen Millen**
limited edition clothing **Ted Baker**
Apple Mac computerware **The Apple Store**
sportswear **Lacoste**
street/surfwear **Quicksolver**

LITTLE ARGYLL STREET

Armani Exchange *seasonal fashions*
Nokia *phones*
Banana Republic *casualwear*

HANOVER STREET

toiletries/fragrances **Molton Brown**
Café Nero
opticians **Dolland & Aitchison**

GREAT MARLBOROUGH STREET

Cos *mens-/womenswear*
Disigual *Spanish design*
Gap & Baby Gap *American casualwear*

MADDOX STREET

building society **Pravins**
womenswear **Hobbs**
handmade men's shoes **Barker**
womenswear **Hoss Intropia**
clothing **Scottishwear**
bags **Kipling**
shoes **Clark's**

CONDUIT STREET

men's shoes **Church's**
pens **The Pen Shop**
clothing **Racing Green**
womenswear **Gerry Weber**
hi-fi **Bose**

FOUBERT'S PLACE

Jaeger *clothing*

Kurt Geiger *shoes*

Hamley's *toys*

NEW BURLINGTON PLACE

womenswear **Viyella**
shirtmakers **Hawes & Curtis**
shirts **TM Lewin**
bureau de change **The Exchange Group**
travel accessories **Samsonite**
cashmere **Regents**

REGENT STREET

Hugo Boss *menswear*

Esprit *clothing/accessories*
Levi Strauss & Co. *clothing*
Reiss *clothing*

NEW BURLINGTON STREET

clothing **Burberrys**
shirts/ties **Duchamp**
jewelry/accessories **Frey Willie**

TENNISON COURT

Calvin Klein Jeans *clothing*
Next *clothing*
Wedgwood *china/glassware*
Massimo Dutti *clothing/shoes/accessories*

NEW BURLINGTON MEWS

toiletries/fragrances **Crabtree & Evelyn**
toiletries **l'Occitane**

BEAK STREET

Brooks Brothers *casual-/businesswear*
Timberland *outdoorwear/boots*
Tommy Hilfiger *casualwear*
Mappin & Webb *jewelry/watches*

HEDDON STREET

menswear **Hacket**
tartan outfitters **Oxford's**
chocolates **Godiva**
crystal **Swarovski**
bank **HSBC**

HEDDON STREET

home furnishings **Zara Home**
perfume **Penhaligons**
contemporary home furnishings **Habitat**
jewelry **Secrets Shh**
clothing **Talbots**

REGENT PLACE

Russell & Bromley *fashion*
Littila *Scandinavian-designed homeware*
Folli Follie *jewelry/accessories*
The Body Shop *toiletries/beauty supplies*
Zara *Spanish designerwear*
Mango *womenswear*

Map continues on next page

Regent Street Shopping, cont.

VIGO STREET

womenswear **Austin Reed**
shoes **Clarks**
fabrics/tailoring **London Textile Co.**

SWALLOW STREET

café **Caffe Concerto**
menswear (incuding Barbour) **The Highlands**
porcelain/crockery **Royal China Shop**

optician **Paris Miki**
hair salon **Tony & Guy**
tea/coffee **Whittard**

GLASSHOUSE STREET

Aquascutum *clothing*
Chemistry Branded *menswear*
Moss Bros. *menswear*
Uniglo *clothing*

Lush *handmade toiletries/fragrances*
Folli Follie *jewelry/accessories*
Pole Position *motorsport merchandise*
Starbucks *coffee*
McDonalds *fast food*

REGENT STREET

AIR STREET

ties/scarves/accessories **Andrew's Ties**
textiles/clothing **Excellence of London**
shirts/ties **Café Coton**
beauty products **Virgin Cosmetics**
records/DVDs/CDs/games **Virgin Megastore**

Cheers *ersatz American bar*
Hawes & Curtis *classic shirtmakers*
Café Royal *conference and banqueting suite*
Bukhara *womenswear*
Estridge of Piccadilly *menswear*
Washin Optical *optician*
Global Luggage *luggage*

PICCADILLY CIRCUS

service. The ready-made shoes are quite wonderful too. ♦ M–Sa. No. 53. 493.9621

FORTNUM & MASON

52 FORTNUM & MASON

Inside one of the world's most magnificent groceries and oldest carryout stores, crystal chandeliers reflect off polished mahogany, highlighting temptations of caviar, truffles, marrons glacés, hand-dipped chocolates, Stilton cheeses, teas, honeys, Champagnes, and foie gras. On the hour, two mechanical figures emerge from the store clock's miniature doors: Dressed in the livery of 18th-century servants, Mr. Fortnum and Mr. Mason turn and nod to each other while the bells chime sweetly. The clock was placed here in 1964, making it a relatively recent addition to this treasure house, which has been serving the privileged since 1707.

Those luxurious hampers filled with gourmet foods, always seen at Ascot and Glyndebourne, began in 1788 as packed lunches (known as "concentrated lunches") for hunting and shooting parties as well as for members of Parliament who were detained in chambers. The fortunate recipients would dine on game pies, boned chickens, lobster, and prawns. During the Napoleonic wars, officers in the Duke of Wellington's army ordered hams and cheeses. Baskets were sent to Florence Nightingale in the Crimea, to Henry Stanley while he was looking for David Livingstone, and to suffragettes confined in London's Holloway Prison, who shared their hampers with fellow prisoners. You order the hamper the day before you want it and choose among the cold delicacies, which include Parma ham and melon, smoked salmon cornets, fresh-roasted poussin, ox tongue, salad, profiteroles, cheeses, Champagne, and chocolate truffles.

Over the past couple of years the old girl has been getting herself a face-lift from internationally acclaimed "designer to the sophisticated classes" David Collins. And most people agree that it has been £24 million well spent. All the departments are here: the cookshop and the glassware, the silverware and the leather and luggage, the accessories and the toiletries, the fragrances and the candles, each and every department a beautiful display of classic desirables. Now there is a wonderful beauty department with all manner of treatments and treats to be had for the booking. But it is still the Food Hall that takes your breath away. It is uniquely, Britishly, top-drawer stuff. And one of the wonderful things about F&M is the extent to which its own brands and "curiosities" dominate its shelves, from the Damson gin they have infused exclusively for Fortnums in

---

Restaurants/Clubs: Red | Hotels: Purple | Shops: Orange | Outdoors/Parks: Green | Sights/Culture: Blue

TE LONDON HAUNTS

As you might expect from a city with such a long and distinguished history, London has a goodly number of spectral residents. Here are some of the most popular ghost stories floating around town:

Like many of their living counterparts, the dearly departed seem to enjoy hanging around pubs. For example, at the **Grenadier** (18 Wilton Row, off Old Barrack Yd), there's the spirit of a young military officer who was caught cheating at cards in the pub and subsequently beaten to death. He seems to favor the month of September, as that is when most of the alleged sightings have occurred. And the ghost of a Tudor maiden who was supposedly murdered and dumped in the **Thames** makes appearances at the **Silver Cross** (33 Whitehall, between Great Scotland Yd and Craig's Ct), a pub near **Trafalgar Square**. (Her portrait hangs over the fireplace, so you'll know her if you see her.)

The theatrical world has produced its share of spectral presences, the most famous of which is probably the Man in Grey. Wearing a three-cornered hat, a powdered wig, and a gray riding cloak, he favors the **Theatre Royal Drury Lane** (Catherine St, between Tavistock and Russell Sts); he has been seen walking along the back of the upper circle of seats. Rumor has it that he's the ghost of a man whose skeleton—with a dagger embedded between the ribs—was found in a hollow section of this wall during the 19th century. His appearances are usually welcomed because over the years they've been associated with successful plays. According to the legend, he was sighted during the London premieres of the hit musicals Oklahoma!, South Pacific, and The King and I.

At the **Theatre Royal, Haymarket** (Haymarket, between Suffolk Pl and Orange St), where Ibsen's Ghosts was performed in 1914, another ghost lingers, that of John Buckstone, who was the manager here between 1853 and 1878. Dressed in a black frock coat, he is usually sighted in the Royal Box occupying the chair he used when royal visitors attended a performance. And one of the dressing rooms at the

Adelphi Theatre (Strand, between Southampton and Bedford Sts) is said to be spooked by Victorian actor William Terriss. He apparently had a part to die for—a rival actor stabbed him to death there.

Somerset House (Lancaster Pl, at Strand), where the **Courtauld Galleries** are now, housed the Admiralty for a time after it was built in 1776, and it has a famous specter of its own. Admiral Horatio Nelson, with an empty sleeve where his arm is missing, has been seen walking across the old cobbled quadrangle here. Ghost busters would find quite a few apparitions slipping through their fingers at the **Tower of London** (Tower Hill, at Tower Bridge Approach). Anne Boleyn appears on **Tower Green** near the scaffold where she was executed in 1536, as well as in the **Chapel Royal** inside the **White Tower**. (As an old song has it, "With her head tucked underneath her arm, she walks the bloody tower . . . at the midnight hour.") Henry VI has been seen in the chamber where he was stabbed to death just before midnight on 21 May 1471. According to legend, the sight of St. Thomas à Becket's ghost in the building over **Traitor's Gate** inspired Henry III to include a small chapel here (it was his grandfather, Henry II, who had caused Becket's murder in 1170 at **Canterbury Cathedral**). And Sir Walter Raleigh's ghost still takes his exercise along **Raleigh's Walk**, a stretch of wall beside the **Bloody Tower**. (The pitiful ghosts of two Little Princes who were brutally murdered to further their uncle Richard III's ambitions and who used to haunt the **Bloody Tower** disappeared after their bones were moved to **Westminster Abbey** in 1485.)

The spirits of two of Henry VIII's wives still linger at **Hampton Court Palace**. Jane Seymour, who died in childbirth a year after becoming queen, wafts through what is now called **Haunted Gallery**, clad in white and holding a candle. And Catherine Howard, executed for her adultery with the dashing Thomas Culpepper, is heard rather than seen: Her cries echo through the galleries, and her fists pound on the chapel door, just as they probably did when she pleaded with the king to spare her life.

the Lake District through the rose petal jelly made each year with petals from a single garden in Oxfordshire, Fortnum's own Gentleman's Relish, Sir Nigel's Vintage Marmalade No. 1 (originally made to order for a famous actor in the 1920s), to the range of Tercentenery products brought out to celebrate 300 years of deliciousness (the Tercentenery Beluga pot holds 200g and costs £1,000!). The fresh food counters offer prime meats and fish, charcuterie and cheeses, and everything in season from vegetables to truffles. You can have smoked salmon from any part of the British Isles and honey from everywhere from Jamaica and Vietnam to Newmarket!

As for cakes . . . how about a Gamekeeper's fruitcake fortified with sloe gin? It's still the world's fanciest grocer after 300 years! ♦ M-Sa, 10AM-8PM; Su, noon-6PM. 181 Piccadilly. 734.8040. Tube: Piccadilly Circus. www.fortnumandmason.com

Within Fortnum & Mason:

1707

★★★$$$ London is very much the better for the opening of Fortnum & Mason's new wine bar, named for the founding year of the store. It is situated right in the middle of the Food Hall, so the scenery is great! You can order any bottle you like from F&M's extensive wine department for a small corkage fee, and the menu (by the wonderful Shaun Hill) sets the standard for all good wine bars everywhere. Choose from fresh oysters, cold partridge with lentil salad, caviar, and pork pie with Montgomery cheddar and chutney. Try them all. Or don't. Even if you are not hungry, come in and have a cocktail, because you really shouldn't leave London without trying the Fortnum & Mason 75 (mmm!) or the Rose Garden (Fortnum's own rose petal jelly shaken with U'luvka vodka topped with Fortnum's own Champagne). ♦ M-Sa, noon-11PM; Su, noon-5PM

St. James's Restaurant

★★★★$$ A traditional British lunch menu is served here, using all that is best from the Food Hall. Imagine starting with black pudding with poached rare-breed egg and devil'd sauce, going on to fillet of sea bream and new potato fondant with cauliflower purée and shallot jus, then finishing with William pear crumble and clotted cream. But the main draw of this restaurant up on the fourth floor of Fortnum's is the famous afternoon tea, which, in my opinion, is the most fabulous mix of truly imaginative savories and tempting sweets available on a London afternoon. Although The Ritz is on the same street, it just isn't in the same league. ♦ M-Sa, noon-7PM; Su, noon-5PM

The Fountain

★★★$$ One of the best breakfasts in London kicks off the day here (how often are you offered duck eggs with your toast soldiers?), after which The Fountain is open all day for lunch and pre- or post-theater dinner. The much-vaunted Fortnum's Welsh rarebit is a specialty, offered alongside such temptations as leek and truffle tart with dandelion and endive salad and burnt honey and buttermilk pudding with cardamom baked figs. All can be washed down with your choice of wine from the wine department, or your choice of Fortnum's incredible range of rare and interesting teas. ♦ M-Sa, 7:30AM-11PM; Su, noon-6PM

Parlour Restaurant

★★★$$ This is the way it goes here . . . vanilla bean and strawberry-and-cream ice creams with raspberries, pineapple, raspberry coulis, whipped cream, and candy sugar. That is a Fortnum's knickerbocker glory. And that, along with other ice creams and sorbets, sundaes and shakes, delicious cakes and pastries, and extraordinary hot chocolate, is what you get up here on the first floor. ♦ M-Sa, 10AM-7PM; Su, noon-5PM

The Gallery

★★★$$$ The "Tastes of the Food Hall" menu is constantly changing, inspired as it is by what is best on the ground floor. It might be saffron risotto with baby zucchini, exotic mushroom and Parma ham lasagna, or smoked eel with celeriac remoulade. Of course there are desserts (Muscat crème caramel with prunes in Armagnac, anyone?) and great cheeses. Yet another great restaurant by F&M! ♦ M-Sa, 10AM-6PM; Su, noon-5:30PM

53 Princes Arcade

Right next to **Hatchards** (below) is an arcade of genteel, smart shops that tends to get overshadowed by the more famous **Burlington Arcade** just down the road. But the stores here are just as noteworthy, including **Jones the Bootmakers**, **Jeremy and Guy Steel** for jewelry, **Richard Caplan** for cameras, **Prestat** for chocolates, and **N. Peal** for exquisite woolens. ♦ M-Sa. 192 Piccadilly (between Church Pl and Duke St). 437.0106. Tube: Green Park, Piccadilly Circus

53 Hatchards

When this bookseller opened in the 18th century, it fostered a clublike atmosphere by laying out daily newspapers by the fireplace and putting benches outside for the customers' servants. The shop (now affiliated with the **Dillons** chain of bookstores) still has the rambling charm of that age, but it has made the transition to the paperback era with intelligence and style. One of the best-known bookstores in England, it currently holds three Royal Warrants. It proudly displays a copy of a telegram from Queen Victoria ordering a Portuguese dictionary. (She probably wanted to be able to say "We are not amused" in as many countries as possible.) Hatchards is a veritable book emporium, with an excellent selection of children's books (third floor), art books (second floor), and reference volumes (first floor), including dictionaries, Bibles, and the Oxford companions to music and literature. You can find the complete works of your favorite British writers here, as well as secondhand and rare books. As you enter, have a look at the latest hardcover fiction releases or browse through the extensive biography department with its special royalty section. The literature department stocks a wide selection of leather-bound volumes. The charming shop assistants can trace any book you care to name, if it's still in print, and will ship it to you anywhere in the world. If books are your passion, this is paradise. ♦ Daily. 187 Piccadilly (between Church Pl and Duke St). 439.9921. Tube: Green Park, Piccadilly Circus

54 MIDLAND BANK

Built by **Sir Edwin Lutyens** in 1922, this charming neighbor of **St. James's, Piccadilly** (below) is worth a glance. The architect kindly deferred to **St. James's** by creating a bank on a domestic scale in brick and Portland stone. ♦ 196A Piccadilly (between Church Pl and Duke St). Tube: Green Park, Piccadilly Circus

54 ST. JAMES'S, PICCADILLY

Sir Christopher Wren, the man who gave London **St. Paul's Cathedral** and some 50 other churches, completed this place of worship in 1684. From the outside, the newly pointed brick, the replaced and restored spire, and the Piccadilly Market in the courtyard give no clue of the miracle within. But when visitors walk inside, they are typically awestruck by the wide-open space, the barrel-vaulted roof, the rows of two-tiered windows, the Corinthian columns, the brass, the gilt, and the paint. This has always been a fashionable church, specially designed for large weddings. The organ was built for James II. In 1757, William Blake was christened at the wonderful white-marble font, whose figures of Adam and Eve and the Tree of Life were carved by **Grinling Gibbons**. Of this, his favorite church, Wren said, "There are no walls of a second order, nor lanterns, nor buttresses, but the whole rests upon pillars, as do also the galleries, and I think it may be found beautiful and convenient; it is the cheapest form of any I could invent." The church is also a moving tribute to its congregation. Almost completely destroyed in the bombing of 1940, it was restored through determination and dedication. The spire was completed in 1968 by **Sir Albert Richardson**. This is an active church today, offering lunchtime concerts on Wednesday and Friday and running lectures on various aspects of faith most evenings. ♦ Daily. Services: Su, 8:30AM, 11AM, 5:45PM. 197 Piccadilly (at Church Pl).734.4511; concert box office 437.5053. Tube: Green Park, Piccadilly Circus

Within St. James's Yard:

THE WREN AT ST. JAMES'S

★$ Come to this cheerful place for home-made vegetable soups (served with thick slices of whole-grain bread), herbal teas, and fresh salads, as well as cakes, fruit tarts, and coffee. ♦ Vegetarian ♦ M-Sa, breakfast, lunch, and dinner; Su, breakfast, lunch, and afternoon tea. No credit cards accepted. 35 Jermyn St (at Church Pl). 437.9419

ST. JAMES'S CRAFT MARKET

This lively crafts market with some 30 stalls always attracts large crowds for its good and modestly priced assortment of pottery, hand-knit sweaters, carved wooden toys, and enameled jewelry. ♦ Antiques: Tu. Crafts: W-Sa

55 SHEPHERD MARKET

The best way to reach this tiny square, filled with small white houses, boutiques, restaurants, and pubs, is from Curzon Street, through the covered passage at **No. 47**. This is the site of the infamous **May Fair**, begun by Lord St. Albans in 1686 and described on a local shop wall as "that most pestilent nursery of impiety and vice." In 1735, Edward Shepherd obtained a grant from George II for a marketplace to be located on the former grounds of the revelry. Although the market sent most of the bawdiness elsewhere, upscale ladies of ill repute are still occasionally seen flitting from doorway to doorway like beautiful ghosts. ♦ Between White Horse and Trebeck Sts. Tube: Green Park, Hyde Park Corner

On Shepherd Market:

L'ARTISTE MUSCLÉ

★★$$ Nicknamed "the Muscley Artist" by the students and weary businesspeople who come here to regroup, this bistro feels like a Left Bank wine bar, complete with sullen French waitresses. Sit in the tiny upstairs dining room or at a bare wooden table in the wonderfully bohemian cellar; both areas fill quickly after 8PM. *Boeuf bourguignon* and duck breast are good choices, and there's tarte tatin for dessert. Wine is available at decent prices, but the service is annoyingly slow. ♦ French ♦ Daily, lunch and dinner. 1 Shepherd Market (at White Horse St). 493.6150

AL HAMRA

★★★$$ Many patrons think this eatery has the best Lebanese food this side of Beirut. The tabbouleh, hummus, and *ful medames* (broad beans sprinkled with parsley, olive oil, lemon juice, and garlic) are as well presented as they are tasty, and the lamb minced with pine nuts and onions cooked inside double layers of cracked wheat is delicious. The atmosphere is noisy and informal, with taped Lebanese music in the background. ♦ Lebanese ♦ Daily, noon-11:30PM. Reservations recommended. 31-33 Shepherd Market (at Trebeck St). 493.1954

56 HALF MOON STREET

Poke around for a few minutes—this street is haunted by some very distinguished ghosts.

Author and reluctant lawyer James Boswell resided here, recording his walks with Samuel Johnson and trying endless remedies for his gonorrhea, which he described graphically in his London journal. Novelist Fanny Burney also called the street home for a time, as did the essayist Hazlitt and the poet Shelley. Inside the world of fiction, this street was the address of P.G. Wodehouse's Bertie Wooster and his faithful valet Jeeves. ♦ Between Piccadilly and Curzon St. Tube: Green Park

57 RITZ

$$$$ A more evocative word is hard to imagine. Such is its power that the name can be spelled in lightbulbs and still look glamorous. The hotel, named for César Ritz, the Swiss hotelier who founded the **Savoy**, was built in the style of a Beaux Arts château with a Parisian arcade from the designs of **Mewes and Davis** in 1906. For ordinary, aspiring folk, this is an aristocratic world of elegance, beauty, and perfection that is rooted in the past, even if the Champagne era has little in common with the Perrier age. Applying gallantry to 21st-century service, the 133-room property is dedicated to the memory of that bygone age when men and women once danced cheek to cheek while orchestras played, when waiters were anonymous and moved like members of a corps de ballet, and when hotels were an art, one of the civilizing forces in any capital city. Even today there is a staff-to-guest ratio of 2:1, a pillow menu as long as your bed, and a Ritz Rolls-Royce Phantom for the use of you, the guest. Afternoon tea in the Palm Court is still an experience much sought after, so if you fancy the ultimate in afternoon delight, make sure you pack jackets and ties for the gents and something smart for the ladies, and book 4 months in advance (the hotel says). ♦ 150 Piccadilly (between Arlington St and Queen's Walk). 493.8181, 877/748.9536; fax 493.2687. Tube: Green Park. www.theritzlondon.com

57 THE WOLSELEY

★★★★$$$ From the partnership that originally brought you The Ivy, this restaurant is absolutely adorable. It richly deserves its 41st place on *Restaurant Magazine*'s list of the World's Top 100 Restaurants. A former car showroom, it features huge vaulted ceilings held up by great, thick pillars and is hung with massive Gothic-meets-Art Nouveau chandeliers. Everything about the place is great: staff are genuinely friendly, the food is terrific, the wines are well selected and not overpriced, and the bar has a man who really understands cocktails. The restaurant is open for breakfast, which is fabulous, with everything from the fullest of full English through superb eggs Benedict to healthy-but-lovely options. If you really want to breakfast like a king, they do a great caviar omelette! From then until late, it is possible to order anything you want from the extensive and enticing menu, any time you want it. The seafood is impeccably fresh, the salads are inventive, and the grills are good. There is everything from nursery food or seared foie gras and duck egg on toasted brioche to a fabulous choucroute garni. The wine list is intelligent and reasonable, and the bar mixes excellent cocktails from premium spirits. ♦ 160 Piccadilly. 499.6996. Daily (from 7AM weekdays, 9AM Saturdays, and noon Sundays). www.thewolseley.com

58 LE CAPRICE

★★★$$$$ Because the restaurant takes orders at midnight, London's chic set nibbles and chatters the night away, amid white walls, a black-tiled floor, and David Bailey's black-and-white photographs, while glancing around to see who else is here. The menu is always eclectic, with such appetizers as sesame oil–infused crispy duck salad and old favorites like haddock and chips with peas, or liver and bacon with colcannon (potatoes and cabbage). *The* place to go, it is located just behind the Ritz. ♦ Brasserie ♦ Daily, lunch and dinner. Reservations required. Arlington House, Arlington St (off Piccadilly). 629.2239. Tube: Green Park

59 STATUE OF ACHILLES

Behind **Apsley House** in **Hyde Park** is a memorial to the Duke of Wellington financed by the Ladies of England. The statue was cast by Sir Richard Westmacott in 1822 from French cannons captured at Salamanca, Vitoria, and Waterloo. At one time Achilles' flagrant nudity was a shock (a fig leaf was even added to protect Victorian sensibilities). ♦ SE corner of Hyde Park (near Park La). Tube: Hyde Park Corner

60 INTERCONTINENTAL PARK LANE

$$$ A cool $150 million has been spent on the refurbishment of this once "too dull to be in the Access Guide" hotel. Now it is the flagship of the Intercontinental brand, and it's a terrific place for many reasons—primarily, for me, the staff. From the moment you come through the door they have a sense of humor, and they are friendly,

---

Restaurants/Clubs: **Red** | Hotels: **Purple** | Shops: **Orange** | Outdoors/Parks: **Green** | Sights/Culture: **Blue**

93

helpful, personal, and knowledgeable. It's hard to believe you are in England! The foyer is quite retro, with lots of cascading chandeliers, but the Foyer Bar is a joy: big leather wing chairs, a polished wood bar, the finest of premium spirits, and some of the most delicious cocktails in London. The staff is absolutely charming and, frankly, you won't want to go up to your room. The hotel now boasts 447 guest rooms, including suites. The standard rooms are fine. You won't be whipping out your camera to show the folks back home, but they have everything you might need—telephone and Internet, cable and movies, bar and coffeemaker, shoeshine and babysitting services, air conditioning and fluffy bathrobe. There are 60 new designer suites, including four jawdroppingly impressive Signature Suites designed by Khuan Chew. The Royal Suite has views over Hyde Park, vast living/dining/entertaining space, and a canopied bed that sleeps 10; the London Suite has views of Buckingham Palace, a floating staircase to its upstairs level, a walk-in shower with eight body jets, and a bathtub with a view over the whole of London; the Wellington Suite is all dark wood and gorgeous leather, with a fabulous stone-walled bathroom; and the Cinema Suite has its own six-seater screening room. Guests of all suites have access to the exclusive **Club InterContinental** for breakfast, coffee, drinks, canapés, relaxation, business, and anything else you could order from its dedicated team of expert butlers. As well as all the business facilities you might need, there is a terrific spa. And all right on Hyde Park Corner. ♦ 1 Hamilton Place (at Old Park La) 409.3131; fax 493.3476. Tube: Hyde Park Corner. www.ichotelsgroup.com

Within The InterContinental Park Lane:

COOKBOOK CAFÉ

★★★$$ A fun concept done really rather well. The Cookbook Café is open for breakfast, lunch, and dinner every day and does a spectacular Sunday brunch with a cold table featuring choices like North Sea crayfish cocktail with spicy tomato dressing, as well as a hot table offering goat's cheese ravioli with nuts, pesto and arugula alongside traditional English roast beef and Champagne and limitless Bloody Marys. Of course, if you'd rather just have cereal and toast, you can do that too! Lunch and dinner menus change every day, and each menu is inspired by the cookbook being featured that day. You have to hope they will repeat their Sunday brunch with the **Jewish Princess Cookbook**! The café hosts cheese and wine master classes, cocktail master classes, and chocolate workshops. As

hotel restaurants go, this is so much fun you may never leave the hotel! ♦ Daily, breakfast, lunch, tea, and dinner. 318.8563. www.cookbookcafe.co.uk

THEO RANDALL

★★★★$$$$ Most foodies have heard of the great River Café in Hammersmith. Well, Theo Randall was the man behind the menu there from the day it opened. He is charming, passionate, lovely to his staff (who all obviously love working for him), and a gloriously great chef. This is the spirit of Italy living in a London five-star hotel. Simon King is Theo's front of house manager, and you will never be better or more caringly "managed" than by Simon and his team. The food is stunningly good. *Punterelle alla Romana* is not something you often see outside Rome itself, but here the crunchy salad curls with their anchovy dressing are served perfectly. Rack of lamb with wood-roasted vegetables is unimprov-able, and the veal chop with salsa verde, chard, and fennel was so huge and so delicious the wonderful Simon had to make us a "doggie bag" to take home what we couldn't manage. The desserts are fabulous, the expertly kept cheeses come served with wet walnuts and muscatel raisins on the vine, and Theo himself spent a weekend tasting more than 300 wines to choose his list. It is a masterpiece of good taste and good value. This place may have the look of high-end impersonality, but it has a heart of gold and the soul of an Italian gentleman. ♦ M-F, lunch and dinner; Sa, dinner; Su, lunch. 318.8747. www.theorandall.com

THE ATHENÆUM HOTEL

61 ATHENAEUM HOTEL AND APARTMENTS

$$$$ Smaller than its modern neighbors, this property boasts 111 rooms and 12 suites and 33 apartments. Every room is luxuriously decorated, with a two-tone marble bath, hand-printed wall coverings, mahogany furnishings, a CD player, and a DVD player. But the icing on the cake is the friendly staff, some of whom have worked here for more than 20 years. There's also a health spa with a gym, pool, steam room, and sauna, and a stylish dining room. The hotel is a favorite stop on the international celebrity circuit, drawing such guests as Richard Dreyfuss, Charles Dance, Val Kilmer, and Patrick Bergin. ♦ 116 Piccadilly (at Down St). 499.3464, 800/335.3300; fax 493.1860. Tube: Hyde Park Corner, Green Park

62 PARK LANE HOTEL

$$$$ Old, lovely, and full of character, this property isn't actually on Park Lane but rather on Piccadilly, overlooking **Green Park**. It is now part of the Sheraton Group. The 307 rooms are individually furnished, the 42 suites have their original 1920s décor and dreamy Art Deco bathrooms, and the clientele is fiercely loyal. The hotel's ballroom—a monument to the Art Deco period—regularly hosts debutante and charity balls. ♦ Piccadilly (between Brick and Down Sts). 499.6321; fax 499.1965. Tube: Hyde Park Corner, Green Park

63 GREEN PARK

Greener than emeralds from Asprey, these 60 acres of sable-soft grass offer the kind of luxury money can't buy in a city. The land was first enclosed by Henry VIII as a hunting ground, then made royal by Charles II, who established the **Snow House** in the center (now marked only by a mound) for cooling the royal wines. There are no flower beds in the park. Instead, ancient beech, lime, and plane trees spread their limbs like maps of the world. In spring, a tapestry of daffodils and crocuses is woven. Renting one of the sloping canvas chairs costs a few pence; the chair collector will give you a little sticker as proof that you have paid. Near the gates by The Mall is a strikingly unusual fountain-cum-monument erected in 1994 to the one million Canadians who fought with Britain in both world wars. Maple leaf silhouettes are embedded onto a slab lapped by constantly flowing water; somehow the effect is of falling leaves. ♦ Bounded by Queen's Walk and Duke of Wellington Pl, and Constitution Hill and Piccadilly. Tube: Green Park

64 QUEEN ELIZABETH GATE

The name refers not to the present sovereign but to her mother, affectionately known as the Queen Mum. The frilly wrought-iron gates, designed by **Giuseppe Lund**, were erected in 1993, along with a sculpture by David Wynne. The installation has provoked controversy, but the queen mother herself seemed pleased. ♦ S Carriage Dr (at Serpentine Rd). Tube: Hyde Park Corner

65 FOUR SEASONS HOTEL

$$$$ This really stunning hotel, in the heart of Mayfair and virtually on the verge of Hyde Park, has 219 rooms, including 26 suites, all with city or park views. Superior rooms have a separate sitting room, Deluxe rooms have full-length sliding windows overlooking Hyde Park, and Conservatory rooms have conservatories overlooking Old Park Lane. And suites have it all! Exercise equipment is available in the bedroom should you wish it alongside all the other modern conveniences you know are going to be there. You can book the hotel's massage services to have in your room afterward if you like: aromatherapy, shiatsu, and deep tissue massages are all available. You even get a complimentary newspaper with breakfast. If you are traveling with small people, cribs and rollaway beds can be provided; books, games, and DVDs are available on request, as are coloring books, crayons, balloons, candy, and chocolates. There are also complimentary cotton balls, talc, and assorted baby products. Children's bathrobes hang in the bathroom, and there are children's menus in the restaurants. The Conservatory Fitness Club on the second floor has all the cardio, cross-training, and running and cycling machines you could want, plus TVs to watch and complimentary fitness videos to give you ideas. ♦ Hamilton Pl (between Piccadilly and Park La). 499.0888, 800/332.3442; fax 493.1895. Tube: Hyde Park Corner

Within the Four Seasons:

LANES

★★★$$$$ Lanes was awarded the Silver Sausage Award by *Business Traveller Magazine* for serving the Best Business Breakfast! The 90-seater restaurant is gorgeous—wood paneled, with stained glass and marbling in deep jewel colors. The central buffet is of glass and marble, topped by an 81-element glass sculpture. Lanes serves lunch and dinner as well as that award-winning breakfast, offering what they describe as "contemporary, cosmopolitan" cuisine. Chef Bernhard Mayer conjures up some impressively inventive dishes, such as red snapper tempura with Thai green papaya salad, or seared diver scallops with marinated pineapple and sweet chili. His meat is carefully sourced, and the Welsh lamb is a specialty. Even his game dishes have an inventive twist—like his venison loin, which is served with braised red cabbage and a bittersweet chocolate sauce. ♦ International ♦ Daily, breakfast, lunch, and dinner. Reservations recommended; jacket and tie required for dinner. 499.0888

66 HARD ROCK CAFE

★★$$ For almost three decades, people have been willing to wait in line, undeterred by rain, sleet, or snow, to eat here. There is even a line at the souvenir shop at the side.

Restaurants/Clubs: Red | Hotels: Purple | Shops: Orange | Outdoors/Parks: Green | Sights/Culture: Blue

---

THE BEST

Matthew Saunders
Architectural Historian

Sir John Soane's Museum—an intense and idiosyncratic house-museum, created by England's most influential neoclassical architect.

Highgate Cemetery—Victorian bombast with Egyptian catacombs and Baroque tombs of the 19th century, set amid trees and foxes. Includes the grave of Karl Marx.

Bloomsbury—set-piece 18th-century townscape around the **British Musem**—the Georgian terrace was England's greatest gift to European architecture alongside Perpendicular Gothic.

St. Bartholomew's the Great—glorious internally begrimed Romanesque—so unexpected in the **City**. Founded 1123.

Spencer House (open on Sundays except in August)—London's most spectacular reclaimed 18th-century interior.

For Americans, a meal here is a nostalgic trip home to the 1960s: Budweiser beer, Chicago Bears, hamburgers the size of a catcher's mitt, waitresses with names like Dixie and Cookie, and hot fudge sundaes. The best time to go is late afternoon, when the music isn't brain-damagingly loud and you may not have to wait. Leave time to visit the rock museum in the basement!
♦ American ♦ Daily, lunch and dinner. 150 Old Park La (at Piccadilly). 629.0382. Tube: Hyde Park Corner

67 PICCADILLY

Once the "Magic Mile" was simply a western route out of London, but when a 17th-century tailor named Robert Baker came on the scene, the street's name and image changed forever. Baker made his fortune selling the picadil, a stiff, ruffled collar, to slaves of fashion at court. The mansion he built was called **Piccadilly Hall**, and the name stuck. Now Piccadilly (not to be confused with Piccadilly Circus) is lined with sights, some appealing, some overbearing.
♦ Between Piccadilly Circus and Hyde Park Corner. Tube: Hyde Park Corner, Green Park, Piccadilly Circus

68 APSLEY HOUSE (WELLINGTON MUSEUM)

Although the austere façade of this building makes it appear permanently closed, and its location on a traffic island means it can

be reached only via a maze of pedestrian tunnels, the effort is well worth it—especially after its £6 million restoration completed in 1996. Originally built in 1771-1778 by Robert Adam for Henry Bathurst, Baron Apsley, the honey-colored stone house was enlarged and remodeled in 1828-1830 by **Benjamin Dean Wyatt**. This was the home of Arthur Wellesley, the Duke of Wellington, sometimes known as the Iron Duke and forever remembered as the man who finally defeated Napoléon. The Marquess of Douro, the heir to the present duke, lives on the top floor of the house, and the duke himself has an apartment on the ground floor.

The structure is a mix of flawless proportions and appended grandeur made possible by a gift of £200,000 to the duke from a grateful Parliament. Inside the house, Napoléon looms considerably larger than he did in life: A statue by Canova expands the French emperor to an idealized 11 feet and covers him not in medals but with a fig leaf. Napoléon commissioned the statue, then rejected it for failing to express his calm dignity—and because it depicts the winged figure of Victory turning away from him. It stayed packed away in the basement of the Louvre until 1816, when it was bought by the British government and presented by George IV to the Duke of Wellington, to whom Victory had eventually turned.

The museum contains an idiosyncratic collection of victors' loot, along with glorious batons, swords, and daggers. The grateful emperors and kings of the time presented the duke with magnificent dinner services of Sèvres, Meissen, and Berlin porcelain, plus silver and gold plate on display (including the ultimate extravagance: a silver-plated dinner service). The focal point of the china collection is the Sèvres service that Napoléon commissioned as a divorce present for Josephine (she refused to accept it). Together in a museum as they would never have been in life are the Duke of Wellington's sword and Napoléon's court sword (taken from his carriage after the Battle of Waterloo), along with flags, medals, and snuffboxes.

> "Royalty is a government in which the attention of the nation is concentrated on one person doing interesting actions. A Republic is a government in which that attention is divided between many, who are all doing uninteresting actions. Accordingly, so long as the human heart is strong and the human reason weak, Royalty will be strong because it appeals to diffused feeling, and Republics weak because they appeal to the understanding."
> —Walter Bagehot

The **Waterloo Gallery**, designed by Wyatt in 1828, is the showpiece of Apsley House. A banquet was held in this vast 90-foot corridor each year on the anniversary of the great victory over the French at Waterloo. The room was designed to showcase the magnificent art collection, particularly the Spanish pictures presented to the duke by King Ferdinand VIII of Spain in gratitude for the defeat of Napoléon.

The collection includes works by Rubens, Murillo (the beautiful *Isaac Blessing Jacob*), Correggio (*The Agony in the Garden*, which was the duke's favorite), and four outstanding pictures by Velázquez, including the early *Water Seller of Seville*. One of the two notable Van Dycks in the room is *St. Rosalie Crowned with Roses by Two Angels*. At the far end of the gallery is Goya's *Equestrian Portrait of Wellington*. But X rays show the picture was originally of Joseph Bonaparte, Napoléon's brother. Last-minute political alterations called for the head to be replaced with the duke's; Wellington never liked the painting and kept it in storage in his country house at Stratfield Saye, Berkshire. But another portrait of the duke may be more familiar (at least to Britons): Painted by Sir Thomas Lawrence, this likeness of the duke appeared on the back of every £5 note until mid-1990, when it was replaced with a portrait of George Stephenson, inventor of the steam locomotive. The windows, which are fitted with sliding mirrors that at night evoke Louis XIV's Galerie des Glaces at Versailles, are almost as fascinating as the pictures. ♦ Admission. Tu–Su. 149 Piccadilly (at Park La). 499.5676. Tube: Hyde Park Corner

69 HYDE PARK CORNER

"It is doubtless a signal proof of being a London-lover *quand même* that one should undertake an apology for so bungled an attempt at a great public place as Hyde Park Corner." That, at least, was Henry James's opinion, written at the turn of the 19th century. Many decades, improvements, and embellishments later, this triangular patch remains lost in confusion and now suffers the ultimate indignity: It has become a traffic island (albeit a grand one). To reach it, you must go into a warren of underpasses, where you can probably find your way by following the forlorn sounds of an equally forlorn harmonica player.

On top of the arch is the beautiful and dramatic *Goddess of Peace*, depicted reining in the Horses of War. Placed on the corner in 1912 after the Boer War, the statue presents an almost identical profile from either side. Looking at her, you almost forget that 200 cars a minute are circling the corner. The sculptor was Adrian Jones, a captain who had spent 23 years as a cavalry officer. The chariot is a quadriga: it is pulled by four horses abreast. Sadly, World War I broke out 2 years after this monument to peace was placed here, and the memorials that surround the statue today are for the many thousands who died in the worldwide stampede of the Horses of War.

Few arches have been pushed around as much as the one here, which was designed by **Decimus Burton**. It was originally built as a northern gate to the grounds of **Buckingham Palace** and crowned with a statue of the Duke of Wellington; then it was aligned along the same axis as the neighboring Ionic Hyde Park Screen, which Burton also designed in 1825. The arch was placed here in 1828. In 1883, however, it was repositioned along the axis of Constitution Hill, and now it leads nowhere. It has been called **Wellington Arch** and **Green Park Arch**, but it's now usually referred to as **Constitution Arch**.

A statue of David, with his back to the motorized world, commemorates the Machine Gun Corps. Designed by sculptor Francis Derwent Wood in 1925, it proclaims that "Saul hath slain his thousands but David his tens of thousands." Facing the **Lanesborough Hotel** is the massive, splendid **Royal Artillery Monument**, designed by **C.S. Jaeger** in 1920. It bears the simple, sad inscription: "Here was a royal fellowship of death." Four bronze figures surround a huge gun aimed at the Somme, a battlefield in France where so many men of the Royal Artillery died during World War I. Finally, the statue facing **Apsley House** was created by Sir J.E. Boehm in 1888. It shows the Duke of Wellington on his beloved horse, Copenhagen, who bore his master nobly for 16 hours at the Battle of Waterloo. (When Copenhagen died in 1836, he was buried with full military honors.) ♦ Between Piccadilly and Knightsbridge. Tube: Hyde Park Corner

---

Restaurants/Clubs: Red | Hotels: Purple | Shops: Orange | Outdoors/Parks: Green | Sights/Culture: Blue

KING'S ROAD/CHELSEA

Avant-garde King's Road, once synonymous with the swinging London of the 1960s, runs the entire length of the affluent riverside village known as Chelsea. A highway created by Charles II as his royal route to **Hampton Court Palace**, the street is now a stage set for an assortment of marginal, hip Londoners, in sharp contrast to the surrounding cosmopolitan village of upscale town houses (there are relatively few apartments in this area) inhabited by privileged professionals. Chelsea dwellers live on tree-lined streets in domestic tranquility and endure the anarchy and decadence of King's Road with humor. In fact, they're more preoccupied

with changes in their lifestyle (boutiques and antiques markets have replaced the local fishmonger, greengrocer, and baker) than they are with the eclectic parade of denizens along the borough's main route.

Cozying up to the **River Thames** southwest of **Westminster** and south of **Hyde Park**, this section of London is one of the most intimate in the city. The human-scale streets and architecture provide a counterpoint for the imposing public buildings and monuments of other areas that dwarf pedestrians. Some Londoners consider **Christopher Wren**'s magnificent **Royal Hospital** here one of the most beautiful buildings in the city. Aesthetics aside, the building still functions as a hospital and residence for war veterans (mostly alumni of World War II), whose distinguished scarlet-and-blue uniforms are part of the iconography of Chelsea life.

It is here, in Chelsea, in houses that appear grand even by today's standards, that writers Oscar Wilde, Thomas Carlyle, and George Eliot and painters James Whistler, John Singer Sargent, and J.M.W. Turner lived. Novelist Henry James and painters Augustus John and Dante Gabriel Rossetti were among the illustrious intellectuals, artists, and bohemians who resided in the neighborhood at one time or another. It doesn't take a vivid imagination to picture them walking these streets, which have changed so little since their tenure here.

Chelsea is known for its vitality, but also for trendsetting and juxtaposing styles. Until 1985, Lady Margaret Thatcher's private London address was here; but this is also where Mary Quant launched miniskirts, where the Rolling Stones lived once they'd gotten some satisfaction, and where punk began (and lingered long past its demise in less colorful quarters). The village is also home to the **Designers Guild**, a fabric, furniture, and interior-design shop where the latest trends are being set; and to **Sloane Square**, a small plaza that has become synonymous with a type of upper-class, inbred Londoner known familiarly as Sloane Rangers. Sloanes are preppy to the extreme: The women have a marked preference for pearls (even with sweatshirts), ruffles, and floral prints, especially in the country-style interiors of their homes. They favor phrases that brand them as Sloanes, and they have a distinctive accent.

The ideal day to visit Chelsea is Saturday, when King's Road is in full bloom, complete with archetypes, poseurs, newlyweds on their way to **Chelsea Town Hall** for the final formalities, Sloane Rangers, and tourists. To get a feel for the yin and the yang of the quarter, make sure you spend some time exploring side streets as well as King's Road. *Note:* The only underground station that serves Chelsea is **Sloane Square Station**, via the **District** and **Circle Lines**, though **South Kensington Station** is closer to the shops on the far end of King's Road. Also, to get to the far end of King's Road from Sloane Square, take bus numbers **11, 22,** or **211.**

City code 0207 unless otherwise noted.

1 ADMIRAL CODRINGTON

★★$$ A haunt for both yuppies and Sloanes, **The Cod**, as it's affectionately known, welcomes children in the restaurant and conservatory in back but not in the pub. Even if it's raining, the Plexiglas roof allows you to sit in a bright, cheery room, surrounded by hanging plants. When it is not raining (honestly, it does sometimes stop!), the roof retracts, allowing for delightful alfresco dining. The menu is definitely more gastro than pub—even the cod is recommended in the Michelin Guide. Caesar salad comes with crispy pancetta and poached egg, starters include foie gras and Armagnac and chicken liver parfait with toasted brioche and main courses are of the ilk of baked sea bass with sautéed gnocchi and pesto dressing. The wine list is supplied by Berry Brothers and Rudd, which is about as good a recommendation as you can get. ◆ Pub: M-Sa; Su, noon-10:30PM. Restaurant: M-Th, lunch and dinner; F-Su, lunch. 17 Mossop St (between Draycott Ave and Lever St). 581.0005

2 TOM AIKENS RESTAURANT

★★★★$$$$ Tom Aikens is an extraordinarily, mouth-wateringly, lip-smackingly good chef. He richly deserved the second Michelin star he won in the 2008 Guide, and all the many awards he has picked up since opening here in 2003. The room seems intimate, and the colors are browns and creams. The staff is as charming as it is efficient. Award-winning sommelier Gearoid Devaney is such a joy to have around at dinner, you will be hard pressed to stop yourself insisting he pull up a chair and join you. Take all the advice he gives you; he knows his stuff without being in the least stuffy. His wine list is terrific. The food is a thrill. The eight-course Classic Menu is as much a work of art as anything you will see hanging in The National Gallery, and an eight-course Tasting Menu changes to showcase the best of what Tom is cooking. But it is all good. Starting with chilled cocoa bean soup with poached chicken, Sauternes, and chicken jelly will give you an idea of what you are in for. Roasted partridge with truffle apple purée, sauerkraut, and caramelized pear is a masterpiece, and roasted John Dory with papardelle, glazed veal shin, and pumpkin purée is a thing approaching genius. Desserts are very grown-up, but leave room for the petit fours—they are fabulous. The set lunch is no low-rent alternative, but the same exquisite cooking for what would seem to be a giveaway price. ◆M-F, lunch and dinner. 43 Elystan St (at Petyward). 584.2003

3 TOM'S PLACE

★★★$$ Fish and chips is, of course, a great British working-class gastronomic tradition and, when done well, is a great treat. What is happening at Tom's Place is a little like de Beers diverging into rhinestones. Michelin-starred Tom Aikens (see above) has hired accomplished chef Yves Girard (not British working-class—the clue is in his name), whose batter was the crispest he could find, to make the most chic fish'n'chips in the world of deep-fat frying (here they fry in beef dripping . . . *sooo* much more delicious than it sounds). All fish is sustainable, so instead of cod and halibut you will get Cornish gurnard, pollack, and megrim. The potatoes are organic, the plates and cutlery are compostable, and a huge TV screen plays a film made by Aikens himself about the dangers of overfishing. You can eat in or take out. ◆ Daily, lunch until 11PM. 1 Cale St (between Markham St and Jubilee Pl). 351.1806

4 THE CHELSEA RAM

★★★$ Something of an institution, this gastropub gains brownie points in restaurant guides for its unpretentious décor and ambience and its comfy bar (with newspapers to browse). You can just hang out and enjoy a pint of something warm and quintessentially English (by which I mean beer, of course), explore the excellent and very generously priced wine list, or eat. The menu has, over the years, gone more and more "gastro," but it has done it well. Smoked salmon and oyster tartare comes on toasted crostini and grilled loin of roe deer with roast potatoes, bacon, red cabbage, and mulled wine. Of course, you could opt for bangers and mash followed by chocolate banana pudding with butterscotch sauce. If you are in the area, and feel like a convivial foodie or drinkie moment, it's definitely worth popping in. ♦ Daily. 32 Burnaby St. 351.4008; fax 349.0885. Tube: Fulham Broadway

4 FURNITURE CAVE

One of London's largest places to buy antique furniture, this market contains 17 dealers selling antiques from all over the world. If you are even remotely interested in antiques, this place is definitely worth a visit. ♦ Daily. 533 King's Rd (at Lots Rd). 352.5748

4 CHRISTOPHER WRAY'S LIGHTING EMPORIUM

Actor-turned-shopkeeper (and later millionaire) Christopher Wray gave up the lure of the bright lights to make bright lights himself, restoring antique lamps, shades, and bulbs (and later manufacturing his own reproductions) to be snapped up by the style-conscious middle class. His once-tiny shop is now the largest center of its kind in Europe, selling restored antique and reproduction Georgian, Victorian, Art Deco, and Tiffany lamps and light fittings. For the Tiffanys, he imports handmade opalescent glass from America. The shops themselves are Victoriana personified, with old-fashioned cast iron–and–glass awnings. ♦ M-Sa. 600 King's Rd (near Lots Rd). 751.8650

5 ROCOCO CHOCOLATES

Good taste and imagination are the two prime ingredients in the most eccentric chocolate shop in the world. This art gallery for chocoholics indulges both the eye and

the palate with its displays of Baroque and contemporary-style Belgian chocolates, ranging from sardine-shaped chocolates to Nipples of Venus (mounds of white chocolate topped with coffee beans), the delicacies that Salieri offers to Mozart's wife in the film *Amadeus*. ♦ Daily. 321 King's Rd (at Beaufort St). 352.5857

6 BLUEBIRD

Sir Terence Conran, London's self-appointed style and gourmet food guru for the last four decades, has cast his eye on this end of King's Road and transformed the 1920s garage building on this site to another of his Gastrodome complexes. (There is one beside Tower Bridge on the south bank.) In fact, this locale is particularly significant for Conran, who in 1956 opened one of his first restaurants just a couple of hundred yards away. In any new Conran enterprise, an important consideration is that the location be in an architecturally significant building. The former garage here is a rare survivor of an unusual building type, with the upper floor having a navelike appearance enhanced by a skylight running through its entire length. The tiled frontage boasts floor-to-ceiling windows, and it has all been carefully restored. Thanks to Conran's development, this tired-looking end of King's Road should benefit from a welcome injection of style as other shops spring up to bask in its inevitable fashionability. ♦ Daily. 350 King's Rd (between The Vale and Beaufort St). 559.1000

Within Bluebird:

BLUEBIRD CAFÉ

★★★$ This place is light, airy, and friendly, with great food and a smart drinks list. In the summer it opens out onto the courtyard, and the only problem apart from finding a table is dragging yourself away. Summer, too, brings the legendary Bluebird barbecue, the aromas from which all but stop the traffic on the Kings Road. The café does a lovely breakfast, terrific cakes and pastries, great salads, marvelous seafood, and an ever-changing menu of imaginative main courses. There is a good selection of beers, wines, and cocktails. ♦ Daily

BLUEBIRD RESTAURANT

★★★$$ The restaurant has been given a new look for its 10th birthday. Executive chef Mark Broadbent is a smart man, and his menu is a lesson in New British—which basically means British with some stuff nicked from the rest of the world. He sources his ingredients

---

Restaurants/Clubs: **Red** | Hotels: **Purple** | Shops: **Orange** | Outdoors/Parks: **Green** | Sights/Culture: **Blue**

impeccably and has a wonderful, understated way with them. His chicken and mushroom pie, for example, boasts maize-fed chickens, and porcini mushrooms. His creations frequently pack a little surprise: Cornish crab is served on tiny, warm potato-drop scones with young sorrel, and venison shank comes with parsnips, pancetta, and bitter chocolate. And his food looks beautiful. The scarlet crème brûlée is a veritable Julia Roberts of a dessert. The wine list is, of course, exemplary. This is also a terrific place for Sunday lunch. Mr. Broadbent's traditional Sunday roast is a thing to be savored. ♦ Daily, lunch and dinner

BLUEBIRD EPICERIE

Mark Broadbent is also responsible for the fabulous Epicerie downstairs. Foodie heaven. With angel choirs. Broadbent, leading wine buyer Bill Baker, and the legendary Francophile and restaurateur Max Renzland have sourced and selected the finest produce and stocked this wonderful deli/takeout/grocery. ♦ Daily. 559.1140

7 NEW CULTURAL REVOLUTION

★★$ This good, basic dumpling and noodle bar has fast, charming service, plain but smart surroundings, and noodles and dumplings every way—fried, in soup, with meat, with seafood, or vegetarian. There are also some nice salads. Everything is freshly prepared and portions are pleasingly generous. There is a limited but perfectly acceptable wine and beer list, and the green tea is very refreshing. ♦ Daily, lunch and dinner. 43 Pkwy. 267.2700

7 ARROGANT CAT

A smart, sexy shop selling smart, sexy clothes in three ranges—Arrogant Cat for ladies, Arrogant Kitten for the younger credit card bearer (and children), and Vintage Cat for the lady who purrs for retro. They call the clever designs "objects of desire," and that is just what they are. The store itself is pretty desirable. Just out is a glorious new line of knitwear for grown-up cats and loveliness in denim for those "kittens." Worth trekking this far down the Kings Road for! ♦ M-F, 9:30AM-7PM; Sa, Su, 11AM-6PM. 311 Kings Rd. 349.9070. www.arrogantcat.com

OSBORNE & LITTLE
FABRICS & WALLPAPERS

8 OSBORNE & LITTLE

The location is conveniently across the street from the **Designers Guild** (see below); if you like one shop, you will probably like the other. The wallpaper and fabric in florals, and clever trompe l'oeil marbles and stipples, are all in excellent taste. The shop has a range of Italian 15th century-style wallpaper in subtle autumnal shades, complete with golden stars like those in Juliet's house in Verona. ♦ M-Sa. 304 King's Rd (between Old Church St and The Vale). 352.1456

9 OLD CHURCH STREET

A spate of early 19th-century terraced houses surround this rambling stretch of pavement to the west of Carlyle Square. **No. 127** was home to potter-novelist William de Morgan, whereas **No. 141A** was the last London address of writer Katherine Mansfield. A small plaque on the wall of Bolton Lodge, at **No. 143**, announces the address of the elusive and exclusive **Chelsea Arts Club**, founded in 1891. Inside its comfortably shabby surroundings, modern creators strive to follow in the footsteps of early members such as James Whistler, W.R. Sickert, and Wilson Steer. ♦ Between King's Rd and Fulham Rd

MANOLO BLAHNIK®

10 MANOLO BLAHNIK

Many a Sloane Ranger can be seen wearing Blahnik heels. Glamorous women in London have long sported this designer's beautiful footwear. The impeccably made shoes arrive from Italy in very limited numbers (12 to 15 pairs of each design) and are worth every pound of the considerable price you will pay for them. ♦ M-Sa. 49 Old Church St (between Paultons St and King's Rd). 352.3863

11 DESIGNERS GUILD

Sofas, rugs, and fabrics that are modern, timeless, and country-house comfortable all at the same time are the specialty of Tricia Guild's boutique. She designs and produces exquisite fabrics, which look like brilliant Impressionist watercolors of English gardens. Other patterns, based on African and Italian art, will appeal to those who shun florals; and the stunning accessories, especially the pottery, baskets, and lamps, will make you want to move into a bigger home. If you're at a loss as to how to coordinate the fabrics, there's an interior design service. ♦ M-Sa. 267–271 and 277 King's Rd (between Bramerton and Old Church Sts). 351.5775

potato skins, nachos, hamburgers, hot dogs, chili, pecan pie, cheesecake, ice cream, brownies, and ice-cold American beer. The huge garden out back makes this a sunny-day favorite on King's Road, and there is a marquee (tent) in winter. ♦ American ♦ Daily, lunch and dinner. 195–197 King's Rd (between Chelsea Manor and Oakley Sts). 352.9255

13 CHELSEA FARMER'S MARKET

This collection of small food shops, open-air cafés, delicatessens, and restaurants, some of which stay open all night, is a popular stop for Chelsea residents, who drop in for a cappuccino before zipping into the **Chelsea Gardener** (352.5656) to replenish their window boxes and the greenery on their tiny patios. Other stores here include **Neal's Yard Remedies** (351.6380), a homeopathic apothecary; **Non-Stop Party Shop** (937.7200), selling balloons, party supplies, and gifts; and the **Monkey Bar** wine merchants (823.3878). The **Market Place Restaurant** offers an interesting menu, with items including crumbed jalapeño peppers stuffed with cream cheese and smoked salmon carpaccio with dill sauce on mixed leaf for starters, followed with Thai spiced fish cakes and char-grilled chicken Caesar salad. The restaurant is one of the growing band that, admirably, guarantee that their food is free of genetically modified ingredients. ♦ Daily. 125 Sydney St (at King's Rd). 352.5600

11 GREEN AND STONE

Here's one of the original shops on King's Road that hasn't gone trendy or upscale. It recently celebrated its 75th birthday. These dealers in art supplies carry beautiful sketchbooks and a prismatic selection of oils and watercolors. A tempting assortment of old and new silver and leather frames, and a very good framing service, are available for those who have a masterpiece to hang. The shop also stocks materials for creating your own decorative wall finishes, as well as for gilding and frame restoration. ♦ Daily. 259 King's Rd (between Bramerton and Old Church Sts). 352.0837

11 NORTHCOTE GALLERY

This very smart, intelligently programmed modern art gallery features good contemporary British painting, sculpture, and glass over three nicely laid-out floors. An interesting find! ♦ M-Sa, 11AM-6PM; Su, 1PM-4PM. 253 Kings Rd. 351.0830

12 HENRY J. BEAN'S BAR AND GRILL

★$ Fifties freaks, trendies, and the occasional punk join tourists and nuclear families in this Chelsea branch of yet another chain that combines American-style fast food and retro ambience. Here is an English pub converted into an American saloon, with 1950s and 1960s rock 'n' roll as aural background. The all-star cast includes

14 STEINBERG & TOLKIEN

A little gem of a shop specializing in period costume jewelry and vintage and designer clothing. Quite fabulous and very dangerous to your credit card. Their special period is 1890–1990, so everything from Art Deco through Flower Power to New Romantic is covered. Be prepared to wrestle over the racks with *Vogue* editors, models, and designers. This is serious fashionista territory. Pucci, Westwood, and Ossie Clark are all in there somewhere. ♦M-Sa, 11AM-7PM; Su, noon–6PM. 193 King's Rd. 376.3660; fax 376.3630. Tube: Sloane Sq

15 HEAL'S

Opened in 1997, this small branch of a major furniture and home furnishings store in the West End makes for cozier browsing than its main outlet. Still a family business, the firm has been known for good design since it was founded in 1810, particularly because it was

---

involved in the Arts and Crafts movement of the early 20th century. The gift department features stylish glassware, including vases and candleholders. ♦ Daily. 234 King's Rd (at Sydney St). 349.8411. Also at 196 Tottenham Court Rd (between Alfred Mews and Torrington Pl). 636.1666. Tube: Goodge St

15 CHELSEA TOWN HALL

On Saturday, busy shoppers trek in for the antiques fairs and jumble sales that are regularly held here. A stream of wedding parties—brides in long white gowns with their grooms and retinue—wends in and out of the **Chelsea Registry Office** throughout the day. Formal wedding photographs are usually taken on the steps outside the hall, slowing traffic to a standstill. ♦ King's Rd (between Chelsea Manor and Oakley Sts)

16 DAISY AND TOM

"Growing up should be a magical voyage of discovery," says the mission statement of this marvelous shop. Well, here it is: clothes, toys, accessories, lovely handknitted cuddly things—in other words, a glorious shop of favorite childhood memories. Prices range from the affordable for the pocket-money spender to those that necessitate an indulgent auntie's credit card. A lovely place to look around, however big a kid you are. ♦ M, Tu, Th, F, 9:30AM-6PM; W, Sa, 10AM-7PM; Su, 1PM-5PM. 181 Kings Rd. 349.5800

17 HABITAT

Sir Terence Conran began his career in style by founding the first Habitat stores for home furnishings. He is no longer involved in the company, but it continues to cater to young Londoners who want affordable yet handsome furniture and accessories. There's also a large selection of gift items and knickknacks for souvenirs. ♦ M-Sa; Su, noon-6PM. 208 King's Rd (between Burnsall and Chelsea Manor Sts). 0844/499.1144. Also at several locations throughout the city Within Habitat:

MUNCH CAFÉ

★★$ A smart "modern" international menu is pulling in the smart Chelsea set to this chic, spacious café. Even if you are not shopping, this is a good place to stop and eat. ♦ Daily, lunch and snacks. 351.6645

18 ANTIQUARIUS

This is one of the earliest and best-known antiques hypermarkets, and still one of the best. You'll get agreeably lost in the maze of over 120 stalls, but you can find wonderful Georgian, Victorian, Edwardian, and Art Nouveau jewelry, antique lace, superb antique clocks, pictures, prints, and tiles; and if you shop carefully, you can expect to pay less than in an antiques shop. One of the longtime dealers, Trevor Allen, has irresistible antique jewelry and a good selection of Georgian and Victorian rings and earrings to offer. When your energy's flagging, slide into a seat in the café. ♦ M-Sa. 135-141 King's Rd (between Shawfield and Flood Sts). 351.5353

19 ROYAL AVENUE

Originally intended to be a triumphal route connecting the **Royal Hospital** with **Kensington Palace**, this ambitious avenue, conceived by **Sir Christopher Wren** for William III, never got beyond King's Road. But the four rows of majestic plane trees, with 19th-century houses as a backdrop, make a magnificent impression. The avenue is also James Bond's London address. Bram Stoker, writer of *Dracula*, lived at **No. 18 St. Leonard's Terrace** (just around the corner) between 1896 and 1906. To the south lies **Burton's Court**, a large playing field with an 18th-century gate that was the original entrance to the **Royal Hospital**. Open-air art exhibitions are held here some Saturdays in the summer. ♦ Between St. Leonard's Terr and King's Rd

20 CHELSEA KITCHEN

★$ Cheap and honest, this eatery is an offshoot of the **Stockpot** chain of restaurants; after three decades, it has become a King's Road institution. Everything is fresh and homemade, including the breads, scones, and pastries. The menu changes twice daily, and regulars play "name that cuisine," trying to identify whether the dish they order is Italian, Spanish, French, or English. This place is also good for English and continental breakfasts. ♦ International ♦ Daily, breakfast, lunch, and dinner. 98 King's Rd (between Lincoln and Anderson Sts). 589.1330

21 HOBBS

Comfortable shoes with great style and a look definitely the company's own are the stock in trade. The additional good news is that the footwear coordinates beautifully with the linen-mix suits, dresses, and cashmere-blend coats that appeal to young career women. ♦ M-Sa; Su, noon-6PM. 84 King's Rd (between Lincoln and Anderson Sts). 581.2914. Also at numerous locations throughout the city

22 John Sandoe Books

Just off King's Road, this is one of the best literary bookshops in London, beloved by readers and writers alike. The staff has a knowledge of books that would put many an Oxford don to shame. The shop, which allows writers to buy books on credit, has a devoted clientele of literate aristocrats and will send your books to you anywhere in the world. The man himself died 27 December 2007, but his shop will live on. ◆ M–Sa. 10 Blacklands Terr (between King's Rd and Bray Pl). 589.9473.

23 Duke of York's Headquarters

Behind the iron railings lie what was the barracks of several London regiments of the Territorial Army. The handsome Georgian brick building with its central Tuscan portico (best viewed from Cheltenham Terrace) was originally built in 1801 by **John Saunders**, a pupil of **Sir John Soane**, as a school for the orphans of soldiers. Called the **Royal Military Asylum**, the school split into separate girls' and boys' academies, moving to Southampton and Dover, respectively. The place has—in the way of the modern world—been transformed into a posh shopping mall. In the pleasant open, blond-paved spaces of the new mall you will find ways to apply your credit card to yourself from toe (with smart fashion shoes at **Kate Kuba** and **Pied à Terre** and classics at **LK Bennett**) to top (with gorgeous natural cosmetics at **Fushi Eternal Living,** where you can also pamper your inner self with organic juices, smoothies, and teas). There is designer fashion from **Ted Baker, Agnès B,** and **Joseph,** terrific skiwear for buying or hiring at 47 Degrees, and sexy underwear from **Myla**. **Secrets Shhh** offers delightful designs in diamonds and other jewelry, and the **Ringmaker** will create for you a bespoke designed ring. Should all this spending have worked up an appetite, the fabulous pastries and cakes in **Patisserie Valerie** will kill any diet stone dead (you deserve it . . . you've probably walked right up the King's Road!); **Manicomo Café and Deli** does great panini, snacks, and light meals with good Italian coffee; and the **Manicomo Restaurant** is gaining an enviable reputation for good Italian cuisine. ◆ King's Rd (between Sloane Sq and Cheltenham Terr)

24 Peter Jones Department Store

This landmark department store, happy hunting ground to Sloane Rangers and Chelsea Girls for generations, has emerged from £107 million of renovation looking fabulous. It is open and airy and, frankly, a joy to shop in. All the original departments are there—fashion and fabrics, furnishings and gifts, rugs and ceramics, perfumery and lingerie and all the rest. But now Peter Jones offers personal shoppers, fashion advisors, and even nursery advice—should you need help buying for the smallest holiday-maker in your family. There is "Haby Heaven," a new haberdashery department boasting a choice of 3,000 buttons; a fabulous flower shop; a made-to-measure linen department (so if you have a heart-shaped bed and nothing to put on it, this is where to come); a made-to-measure menswear department; a personalized stationery corner; gift-wrapping service; and a specialized bra-fitting center. The store now has a fabulous Clarins Spa with five treatment rooms (for men as well as women!) and "Footopia," a unique foot clinic. On the fifth floor is Peter Jones's best-kept secret—they have been well respected antique dealers (specializing in furniture, mirrors, and glassware) since 1915. The serious shopaholic, or anyone in need of a little intensive retail therapy, can buy the Peter Jones Experience—a whole day in the store with a custom-created schedule of personal shoppers, spa moments, and refreshments. Peter Jones has excellent disabled access, and anything and everything you purchase can be shipped home, so as not to interfere with your baggage restrictions on the flight back! ◆ Sloane Sq at Kings Rd. M–Sa, 9:30AM–7PM; Su, 11AM–5PM. 730.3434. www.peterjones.co.uk

Within Peter Jones:

2nd Floor Café Bar

A great place to relax with a light meal, salad, or snack from what they describe as an "eclectic" menu. The wine list is pleasing and the staff sweet. ◆ 901.8070

Top Floor Restaurant

★★$$$ A wonderful place to breakfast, not so much for the food—which is everything you would expect and nicely made—but for the 360-degree panorama, particularly lovely in the morning light. The sixth-floor airy, open-plan restaurant, with a modern, eclectic, ever-changing menu, serves lunch and dinner as well as breakfast. For the reopening it commissioned "the Chelsea Salad," created for them by the wife of celebrity chef Gordon Ramsay. ◆ M–Sa, lunch and dinner; Su, lunch

---

Restaurants/Clubs: Red | Hotels: Purple | Shops: Orange | Outdoors/Parks: Green | Sights/Culture: Blue

THE GENERAL TRADING COMPANY

25 GENERAL TRADING COMPANY (GTC)

This huge store epitomizes everything Sloane—and if you still aren't sure what that means, go in and look around. Once, nice young girls (pronounced *gels* in Sloane-speak) worked in florist shops in the hope that they might meet their prince. Now that the royal life has been found lacking, the gels work in estate agencies or the GTC, waiting for lords rather than princes to whisk them off their feet. The store resembles a Sloane-size country house, with charming knickknacks that fit into English country life with a touch of London style. Check out the china department, the antiques, the garden department, and the children's toy department. There's also a good selection of souvenirs and gifts. The café at the back serves Sloanish foods like lasagna and salad, lemon syllabub, and chocolate cake. Although you can expect long lines at lunchtime, this is an excellent place to observe Sloanedom in general.
♦ M-Sa. 2 Symons St. 730.0411

26 HOLY TRINITY

Despite the destruction of the vault over the nave by German bombs in World War II, this church, built between 1888 and 1890 by **J.S. Sedding**, remains a Gothic Revival homage to the 19th-century Arts and Crafts movement. Among the pre-Raphaelite treasures are the stunning east window, designed by **Sir Edward Coley Burne-Jones** and made by William Morris, and the grill behind the altar. ♦ Services: M-F, 9:30AM, 5:30PM; Sa, 10:30AM, 4:30PM; Su, 8:45AM, 11AM. Sloane St (between Sloane Sq and Sloane Terr). 730.7270

27 DAVID MELLOR

Outstanding contemporary designs for the kitchen and dining room are the hallmark of this inimitable store, whose offerings include handmade wooden salad bowls, pottery bowls, and glassware—the best from British craftspeople, along with a superb selection from France, Poland, and Spain. The specialty is the cutlery designed by Mellor. There are also lots of interesting deli-style food products in jars and bottles, especially the flavorful olives. ♦ M-Sa. 4 Sloane Sq (between Eaton Terr and Sedding St). 730.4259

28 SLOANE SQUARE

$$ A huge improvement on the Moat House, the hotel has now been taken over by the private partnership responsible for Cliveden House Hotel in Berkshire. It seems they have considered everything, from special rooms for taller guests with longer beds and bigger baths to international newspapers available and free chauffeured rides into London each morning. There are 102 rooms, all beautifully designed, from singles to family rooms, many with upholstered window seats and views over Sloane Square, all with Philippe Starke ergonomically designed basins. The hotel's **Chelsea Brasserie** has the former head chef of Racine in the kitchen, so guests are assured of a treat every time they call room service. Breakfast is served here each morning and is very much worth getting up for. ♦ Sloane Sq. 896.9988. Tube: Sloan Sq. www.sloanesquarehotel.co.uk

28 ORIEL

★$$ This French café has most of the usual advantages of the genre: hot coffee and croissants served early in the morning, good wine by the glass, and attractive cane chairs pulled up to marble-top tables. This is the best place in the area for observing Sloanes and Chelsea poseurs. The menu offers a selection of salads and seafood (including *moules marinières*), grills, pastas, and a regular "sausage of the day" served with herb mash. Very popular, so often very crowded. ♦ French ♦ Daily, breakfast, lunch, and dinner. 50-51 Sloane Sq (at Cliveden Pl). 730.4275

29 SLOANE STREET

At the upper end of the street you'll find designer shops, enhanced by the prestige of being located next to **Harvey Nichols**. The lower half is residential until **Sloane Square** with its array of chic stores. ♦ Between Sloane Sq and Knightsbridge

30 ROYAL COURT THEATRE

Look Back in Anger, an explosive 1950s drama by John Osborne whose kitchen-sink realism was unlike anything the class-conscious English theater had ever seen before, put this venue on the map. But it wasn't the first time the theater had shocked audiences: It had also produced the provocative early plays of George Bernard Shaw. The structure was originally designed by **Walter Emden** and **W.R. Crewe** in 1887-1888 and was rebuilt once and remodeled twice. The theater has recently reopened after a multimillion-pound refurbishment that has transformed it. It still has its main house—**The Jerwood**—and the smaller, upstairs theater—**The Jerwood Theatre Upstairs**—and now has a spacious downstairs bar and restaurant offering great food with a Mediterranean twist and serving both main meals and bar snacks. There is also a small bookshop downstairs. ♦ Sloane Sq (between Holbein Pl and Bourne St). Information: 565.5000

31 BASIA ZARZYCKA

Custom-made clothes for fancy occasions are the specialty of this pretty shop. Bridal gowns and other formal wear are the mainstay of the business, but there are also fabulous one-of-a-kind accessories such as hats, shoes, and antique handbags and jewelry. Her newest collection is an English summer garden in pale lilacs and vivid blues. There are butterflies on bracelets and hair ornaments that are diamanté twigs and porcelain flowers. Chokers are a necklet of pansies, and instead of feathers in a boa, there are white organza petals. Unbelievably feminine. Fabulous. The clients include foreign royalty and celebrities such as the Rolling Stones, Bob Geldof, Tom Cruise, and opera singer Jane Anderson. The staff is used to dealing with rush orders by telephone and shipping items to the US. ♦ M-Sa. 52 Sloane Sq. 730.1660; fax 730.0065. www.basias.com

31 SLOANE SQUARE

Chelsea begins here, under a tent of young plane trees. A running soundtrack of cars and taxis in the background drowns out the watery music of Gilbert Ledward's Venus fountain, presented to Chelsea by the **Royal Academy** in 1953. Nothing grows in the square save trees, but color is provided by the flower sellers who purvey fluorescent blooms here. The square was named after one of Chelsea's most distinguished residents, Sir Hans Sloane, a wealthy physician at the beginning of the 18th century who was also president of the Royal Society, an organization founded more than 300 years ago to further scientific knowledge. Sloane, who at one time owned practically all of the village of Chelsea, lived in Henry VIII's former manor house. His vast collection of plant specimens, fossils, rocks, minerals, and books, amassed over a lifetime, formed the foundation of the **British Museum**. ♦ At Cliveden Pl and King's Rd and at Lower Sloane and Sloane Sts

32 W.H. SMITH

This chain bookseller is a good place to acquire maps, guidebooks, writing paper, pens, magazines, newspapers, and paperbacks. There is also a large selection of international periodicals. ♦ Main shop: M-Sa. Newsstand: M-F. Sloane Sq

(between Sloane Gardens and Lower Sloane St). 730.0351; fax 259.0242. Also at numerous locations in the city, including many British Rail stations

33 L'ARTISAN DU CHOCOLAT

For my money (and it frequently is), the chocolates are even more delicious here than at Rococo. And the range of flavors and fillings is unbelievable. The lapsang souchong–flavored chocolate is quite a Zen-like experience, but my favorites are the liquid salted caramels. This is where they were created, although now they are much copied. ♦ M-Sa. 89 Lower Sloane St (near Pimlico Rd). 824.8365. Tube: Sloane Sq

34 EBURY WINE BAR

★★$$$ One of the first wine bars to open in London in the 1970s, it is still one of the best. The bar in front leads to two dining areas; head for the back room, where murals line the dark green walls and lots of dark wooden furniture adds to the cozy air. English chef Trevor John produces good food with flavors of the Pacific and the Mediterranean plus such British basics as black pudding with potato cake. There is an excellent range of moderately priced wine. The place is humming weekdays. ♦International ♦Wine bar: daily. Restaurant: M-Sa, lunch; dinner daily. 139 Ebury St (at Elizabeth St). 730.5447

34 LIME TREE HOTEL

$$ David and Marilyn Davies run this 26-room, superior bed-and-breakfast establishment. The cheerful rooms, most with bath or shower, have ivory walls set off with pastel spreads and floral curtains. They're comfortable, well maintained, and, amazingly for such a posh district, very reasonably priced. A full English breakfast is served in a pleasant room overlooking the handsome street, which is on the fringe of Chelsea and a useful link to Victoria, with its bus, train, and tube stations. ♦ 135-137 Ebury St (between Elizabeth and Eccleston Sts). 730.8191; fax 730.7865. Tube: Victoria

35 L'INCONTRO

★★★$$$$ A serious restaurant, even by London standards, L'Incontro specializes in Venetian cuisine and boasts Venetian-born Simone Rettore in the kitchen to make sure it gets done just right. And it does. Pasta is made on the premises and comes as spaghetti with lobster, or as that most Venetian of dishes, *bigoli in salsa* (fat spaghetti in a tangy sauce made from anchovy, onion, and garlic). Cuttlefish is sauced with its own ink and served (as befits northern Italian cooking) with polenta. Sea bass is served in a balsamic sauce and, should you prefer meat, L'Incontro can rustle up a superb wild boar with pear and chestnut. The wine list is top end and top quality. The surroundings are opulent but comfortable, the staff faultless and even friendly. A truly classy dining experience, which you can have for a much more reasonable amount by going for lunch (a trick that will let you try some of London's most exuberantly priced eating places for much more bang for your buck). ♦ Italian ♦ M-Sa, lunch and dinner; Su, dinner. Reservations required. 87 Pimlico Rd. 730.3663. Tube: Sloane Sq

35 PLUS ONE GALLERY

This is an approachable and impressive gallery. The space is light and airy, and the artwork (by a forty-strong international collection of painters, photographers, and sculptors) is all passerby-stopping stuff. The works on display in the minimalist-chic pair of galleries on the ground floor and the delightful lower-level exhibition space unfailingly have a sort of sharp focus about them that is very attractive in an art world where all too often one is left wondering whether one is looking at a modern masterpiece or the after-effects of a hot dog. The only danger here is that, yes, the gallery *can* ship the canvases and sculptures home for you, so your vacation could become just a *little* more expensive than you had planned. But then scale models of the Houses of Parliament and photos of you with a man in a busby are *so* not what the smart traveler is taking home with him this year. ♦ M-F, 10AM-6:30PM; Sa, 10AM-3PM. 91 Pimlico Rd. Tel 730.7656. Tube: Sloane Sq, Victoria. www.plusonegallery.com

36 CHELSEA HARBOUR

The western end of Cheyne Walk, where it becomes Lots Road, is now the site of this fashionable condominium development with some of the most expensive apartments in London. A much-sought-after place to live, it has attracted British television, pop, and sports personalities with its luxurious surroundings and terrific views. Houses, offices, shops, restaurants, gardens, and the **Conrad London** hotel are all crushed into this tiny area set around a 75-berth yacht marina. Hoppa buses (the small red buses that supplement the regular bus system) from Earl's Court and Kensington High Street serve the area regularly. ♦ Lots Rd (off Cheyne Walk)

Within Chelsea Harbour:

WYNDHAM GRAND LONDON CHELSEA HARBOUR

$$$$ London's only five-star, all-suite hotel has 154 suites and 6 penthouses, each with hallway, lounge, bedroom, and bathroom. Guests have access to a dedicated chauffeur, a regular shuttle service from the hotel to Harrods, and a luxurious spa, and can even bring their pets to stay (up to, the hotel says, a weight limit of 20 pounds). For those who can't face the trip to Harrods, there are several stores within the hotel. The hotel restaurant, **Aquasia**, offers a Mediterranean menu and is on the waterfront, with floor-to-ceiling windows that open in the summer onto a lovely terrace. More interesting, it offers unlimited Theophile Roederer Champagne with your Sunday brunch! The hotel bar is quite a local watering spot for the chic and well-heeled. ♦ Chelsea Harbour. 823.3000. Tube: Fulham Broadway. www.wyndham.com

37 LINDSEY HOUSE

Remarkable for its beauty and its survival against all odds, this large country house is the only one of its date (circa 1640–1674) and size in Chelsea. The vast residence was built on the site of a farmhouse by Theodore Mayerne, the Swiss physician to James I and Charles I. In the 1660s, it was sold to Robert, third Earl of Lindsey, who substantially rebuilt it. In subsequent years, the building was divided into several connected houses with separate ad-dresses. The remarkable cast of residents in the 1770s included painter John Martin; engineer Sir Marc Brunel, who built the first tunnel under the Thames; and Brunel's son **Isambard Kingdom Brunel**, another engineer, who built many of England's suspension and railway bridges and lived at **No. 98**. (**Brunel House**, 105 Cheyne Walk, is named after the father and son.) James Whistler lived at **No. 96** between 1866 and 1878 (one of his nine Chelsea addresses). It was here that he painted the famous portrait of his mother. Elizabeth Gaskell, the novelist, was born here. The gardens connected to **Nos. 99** and **100** were designed by **Sir Edwin Lutyens**. ♦ 96-100 Cheyne Walk (between Beaufort and Milman's Sts)

37 TURNER'S HOUSE

England's greatest painter, J.M.W. Turner, lived in this tall, narrow house during his last years. To remain anonymous, he adopted his landlady's surname—he was known locally as Admiral Booth. Turner died here in 1851, uttering his last words, "God is Light." ♦ 119 Cheyne Walk (between Beaufort and Milman's Sts)

38 BEAUFORT STREET

One of the busiest crossroads in Chelsea that connects the King's Road to Battersea Bridge, this street cuts across the site of Sir Thomas More's country house. The residence was demolished when Sir Hans Sloane acquired the estate in the 1740s. ♦ Between Cheyne Walk and King's Rd

39 CROSBY HALL

Three hundred years after Sir Thomas More was executed, this splendid mansion he once owned was transported, stone by stone, from Bishopsgate in the City to Chelsea. Originally built in 1466, the hall was then made into a royal palace by Richard III and finally purchased in 1516 by More himself. For a time it was the dining room of the British Federation of University Women. Now privately owned, this building is no longer open to the public, which is unfortunate because the superb hammer beam roof, the stunning oriel window, the long Jacobean table (a gift from Nancy Astor), and the Holbein painting of the More family are all worth seeing. ♦ Cheyne Walk (between Danvers and Beaufort Sts).

40 JUSTICE WALK

This narrow footpath is a relic of the days when Chelsea was a real village rather than a trendy enclave of London. Note the pub sign, "The Courthouse," which remains over the advertising business at **No. 9**. Both the street and the sign here recall the memory of John Gregory, a justice of the peace who once lived here. ♦ Between Lawrence and Old Church Sts

41 ROPER GARDENS

This garden, created in the 1960s on the site of part of Sir Thomas More's estate, is named after Margaret Roper, More's beloved eldest daughter. It replaced a garden destroyed by German bombs. Note the stone relief of a woman walking against the wind by Jacob Epstein. ♦ Cheyne Walk (at Old Church St)

42 CHELSEA OLD CHURCH

Also known as **All Saints**, this church was founded in the middle of the 12th century. In spite of the heartless traffic that passes it daily and the German bombs that flattened it in 1941, this lovely old church is spiritually intact, a glorious monument to its former parishioner, Sir Thomas More. Hans Holbein the Younger, a friend of More's, contributed to the restoration and redesign of the chapel in 1528. The atmosphere resonates with the deep sadness of the gentle, pious man whose conscience would allow him neither to recognize his friend Henry VIII as head of the Church of England nor to sanction the king's divorce. More, who wrote his own epitaph (against the south wall to the right of the altar) 2 years before his death in 1535, paid for his conscience with his life. The remains of the saint are believed to be buried at Canterbury, but a Chelsea legend holds that More's daughter, Margaret Roper, made her way back here with her father's head and placed it in the Gothic tomb inside the church.

The ornate tomb with the urn in the chapel is the burial place of Chelsea's next best known citizen, Sir Hans Sloane. The half dozen chained books (before books were mass-produced, hand-inscribed manuscripts were chained to desks to avoid theft) include the 1717 edition of the Vinegar Bible, which contains a printer's error that converted the parable of the vineyard into the parable of the "vinegar." These volumes are the only such books still found in a London church. The square tower, which has since been carefully rebuilt, was the casualty of a German air raid. Off to the left side is the **Lawrence Chapel**, where Henry VIII is supposed to have secretly married Jane Seymour a few days before their official wedding in 1536, a year after Sir Thomas More had ceased to be a conscience to the king. Today, the church is still the setting for weddings, and each July a sermon written by More is read from the pulpit. A memorial stone commemorates American writer Henry James, who lived in Chelsea and died near here in 1916. ♦ M-F. Guided tours: Su, 1:30–5:30PM. Old Church St (at Cheyne Walk). 352.5627

43 CARLYLE'S HOUSE

It's a short walk up Cheyne Row to **No. 5**, now known as **No. 24**. One of the most fascinating homes in Chelsea, it is in the care of the National Trust. Set in a terrace of redbrick houses begun in 1703, this was the residence of the writer Thomas Carlyle and his wife, Jane. The rooms are almost exactly as they were 150 years ago when *The French Revolution* made its author famous, and Charles Dickens, Robert Browning, Charles Darwin, Alfred Lord Tennyson, and Frédéric Chopin were visitors. Most of the furniture, pictures, and books seen here today belonged to the Carlyles—his hat is still on the hat stand by the door. Go down into the kitchen and see the pump, the stone trough, and the wide grate where kettles boiled. Tennyson and Carlyle used to escape to the kitchen when they wanted to smoke without provoking Mrs. C. Examine the rooms upstairs, with their four-poster beds, piles of books, mahogany cupboards, and dark Victorian wallpaper (which covers 18th-century pine paneling). Look at the double-walled attic study, carefully (if unsuccessfully) designed to keep out the noises of the house and the street. The 19th-century painting *A Chelsea Interior* hangs in the ground-floor sitting room and shows how little the house has changed.

The tombstone in the small garden behind the house marks where Mrs. Carlyle's dog Nero lies buried. Carlyle was a famous Chelsea figure: the "sage of Chelsea" took solitary walks along these streets throughout his life. A bronze statue of Carlyle (by Boehm and erected in 1883) in the **Embankment Gardens** of Cheyne Walk is said to look very much like him. Here the essayist and historian sits surrounded by a pile of books and gazes sadly at the river through an invasion of Mack trucks. ♦ Admission. W–Su, Apr–Oct. 24 Cheyne Row (between Cheyne Walk and Upper Cheyne Row). 352.7087

44 ALBERT BRIDGE

Lovers propose here and tired commuters refresh themselves looking at this bridge, the one Londoners love the most. Although it was strengthened in 1973, the bridge still has a weight limit, which means that red London buses and lorries never darken its tarmac. There is even a notice telling foot soldiers to break step when crossing. The latticework suspension bridge, built by **R.M. Ordish** in 1873, is painted in ice-cream pastels—pistachio and cream—and at night is illuminated with strings of lights. The best time to view the bridge is at dusk from **Chelsea Bridge** (downriver), when the sun sets behind it and the bridge takes on a fairy-tale quality. At night, see it from **Battersea Bridge** (upriver); the red lights of Chelsea Bridge glow behind it to lovely effect. ♦ Between Parkgate Rd and Chelsea Embankment

45 CADOGAN PIER

Every July, this pier is the finishing point of one of England's oldest contests, the Doggett's Coat and Badge Race. The race began in 1715 to celebrate the accession of George I to the throne and was sponsored by Thomas Doggett, actor-manager of the **Drury Lane Theatre**, who awarded a coat and badge to the winner. A moving ceremony reenacting the final journey of Sir Thomas More from his home here on the river to the **Tower of London**, where he was imprisoned and executed, also takes place at the pier in July. ♦ Chelsea Embankment (just east of Albert Bridge)

46 CHEYNE WALK

Where Royal Hospital Road and **Chelsea Embankment** converge, this elegant street begins. The embankment (somewhat) protects the single row of houses from traffic, and the

lucky residents have a view of the Thames through a row of trees. Some of the happy few who have lived in these priceless Georgian brick houses include Rolling Stones guitarist Keith Richards and the beknighted, sadly reclusive J. Paul Getty Jr. But residents from the more distant past haunt the high windows as well. George Eliot lived at **No. 4** for 19 days after her late-in-life wedding to John Cross; she was 61 at the time and died only a few months later. Pre-Raphaelite painter and poet Dante Gabriel Rossetti lived at **No. 16**, then known as **Tudor House**, the finest residence on the street. He led an eccentric *vie de bohème* here while mourning the loss of his wife, Elizabeth Siddal (the model for Sir John Everett Millais's painting of the dying Ophelia and the deadly beauty in *Beata Beatrix* by Rossetti—both in the **Tate Gallery**). Rossetti's Chelsea menagerie included a kangaroo, peacocks, armadillos, a marmot, and a zebu, and he received frequent visits from fellow pre-Raphaelites William Morris and his wife, Janey, who inspired great passion in Rossetti. Today, **No. 16** is known as **Queen's House** because of the initials *RC* on the top of the iron gateway. Long assumed to stand for *(Regina) Catherine of Braganza*, Charles II's wife, the initials in fact stand for *Richard Chapman*, who built the house in 1717.

Opposite the house in the **Embankment Gardens** is the **Rossetti Fountain**, a memorial to the artist from his friends, including Millais and G.F. Watts, unveiled in 1887 by William Holman Hunt. The fountain is by J.P. Seddon, and the bust of Rossetti is by Ford Madox Brown. Unfortunately, the original bronze bust was stolen, so it was replaced by this fiberglass copy. The plaque on **No. 23** commemorates the site of Henry VIII's **Manor House**, which stood where **Nos. 19** to **26** are now. Henry VIII became fond of the Chelsea riverside during his many visits to his friend Sir Thomas More, and the year after More's death, he built a palace along the embankment. Before Henry died, he gave the house to Catherine Parr, his last wife. One hundred years later, the house was purchased by Lady Jane Cheyne—the Cheynes were lords of Chelsea Manor between 1660 and 1712 (in 1737, Sir Hans Sloane bought the manor). More's house was demolished a few years later. The gateway by **Inigo Jones** was given to the Earl of Burlington, who erected it in the gardens of **Chiswick House**, where it still stands. ♦ Between Royal Hospital Rd and Old Church St

47 CHELSEA EMBANKMENT

This unbeatably beautiful strip of land along the river, part of **Sir Joseph Bazalgette**'s dual sewage–roadway system, suffers from the noise of the relentless traffic it was built to support. Still, it's worth making an effort to transcend the motorized roar to see this miraculously unchanged patch of London. The embankment begins at **Chelsea Bridge**. Built in 1934 by **G. Topham Forrest** and **E.P. Wheeler**, this graceful suspension bridge edges up to the massive and dramatic **Battersea Power Station**. The station's four chimneys are part of London's industrial archeology. So far, the power station has been protected officially from demolition, even after the chimneys were retired. (In fact, only two ever functioned: The front pair were added purely for aesthetic reasons, to provide a sense of balance.) The power station currently stands empty after an abortive attempt to transform it into a leisure center. However, the plan is revived regularly by business investors and may yet succeed. ♦ Between Chelsea Bridge and Cheyne Walk

48 CHELSEA PHYSIC GARDEN

Swan Walk, with its row of 18th-century houses, is edged on one side with a brick wall containing handsome iron gates. Behind them is the second-oldest surviving botanical garden in England. Founded by the Worshipful Society of Apothecaries in 1673 (100 years before **Kew Gardens**), the garden occupies 4 acres of land belonging to Charles Cheyne (pronounced *Chain-ee*). In 1722, Sir Hans Sloane, apothecary and physician to George II and Lord of the Manor, granted a continuous lease, requiring the apothecaries to present 50 plant species a year to the Royal Society (an organization founded in 1660 to further scientific knowledge) until some 2,000 had been acquired. Sloane was a member and eventually succeeded Isaac Newton as president of the Royal Society. After the invention of the Wardian case, a container for carrying plants that prevented them from perishing, the staff members here became instrumental in distributing the world's staple crops. In 1722, the first cotton seeds were exported from the South Seas to a garden in the US state of Georgia. Robert Fortune, a curator of the garden, carried tea to India from China, and Malaya got its rubber from South America. The garden opened its doors to the public in 1983 for the first time in 300 years. Now, under the watchful eye of Sir Hans Sloane himself (depicted in a statue by Michael Rysbrack), you can examine some of the 7,000 specimens of plants that still grow here. The magnificent trees include the pomegranate and the exotic cork oak. Plants and seeds are for sale. ♦ Admission by appointment. 66 Royal Hospital Rd (between Chelsea Embankment and Swan Walk). 352.5646

49 GORDON RAMSAY

★★★$$$$ This was Ramsay's first solo venture (opened in 1998), after his leap to fame at **Aubergine**. The premises were formerly La Tante Claire, another of London's landmark restaurants. The good news is that the food *is* everything you would expect from a three-starred Michelin establishment and one just declared No. 5 in *Restaurant Magazine*'s list of The World's Top 100 Restaurants. The room is really quite intimate, just 14 tables giving a feeling of genuine exclusivity. The décor features Ramsay's signature purple with cappuccino and beige leather seating. Sculptural *objets* in Murano glass complete the opulent look. The bad news is that there is more of a relaxed, feel-good atmosphere in The Vatican. This is very much the Temple of Gordon, and you come here to worship. The staff are incredibly efficient and starchily formal. The food is an art form and comes as a three-course à la carte menu, a relatively reasonable set lunch, or a "Prestige" Menu. Expect dishes such as *bouillon de poule* with black truffle, roasted foie gras with caramelized endive, carrot purée and Sauternes *jus*, or a risotto of globe artichoke with sautéed veal sweetbreads and wild mushrooms. The wine list is heavily French biased to match the cooking and has over 1,000 bins. Jacket preferred, and booking essential! ♦ French ♦ M-F, lunch and dinner. 68 Royal Hospital Rd (between Paradise and Swan Walks). 352.4441

50 FOXTROT OSCAR

★$$ "Hooray Henrys" (London's glitterati) and Sloanes alike were distraught at the closure of a restaurant that had become quasi-iconic in the area. Owned by a delightful Old Etonian, it was the ultimate triumph of atmosphere over cuisine (albeit the cuisine was perfectly okay). The place had real character. Though Foxtrot Oscar has reopened, it is a little like finding out that the Chelsea Hotel had been closed and reopened as a Sheraton. The man responsible is none other than Gordon Ramsay, who has corporatized the menu, synthesized the music, and generally done a dreadful thing to a wonderful place. ♦ Corporate Brasserie ♦ Daily. 79 Royal Hospital Rd (between Tite St and Paradise Walk). 352.7179

51 TITE STREET

The favored haunt of artists and writers in the late 19th century, this street sheltered a number of celebrated people. The brilliant and eccentric Oscar Wilde lived at **No. 34**

Restaurants/Clubs: Red | Hotels: Purple | Shops: Orange | Outdoors/Parks: Green | Sights/Culture: Blue

CHRISTMAS IN THE CAPITAL

London is a fun place to be during the holidays. There are always several pantomimes and seasonal shows from which to choose. **The Old Vic**'s pantos are becoming the stuff of legend since Kevin Spacey took over as Artistic Director. (0870/060.6628. Tube: Waterloo. www.oldvictheatre.com)

The **Frost Fair** on Bankside on the south side of the Thames is becoming a regular Christmas highlight with husky-drawn sleigh rides, ice sculptures, boat races, and more than 70 stalls laden with food, drink, and last-minute gift ideas. (Mid-December. Tube: Southwark. www.visitsouthwark.com)

Covent Garden Christmas Deluxe is exactly what it sounds! The Twelve Days of Christmas Food Market will leave you stuffed like a Thanksgiving turkey. There are also spectacular evening aerial and theatrical shows. And all in the fabulous Covent Garden Piazza. My Christmas Fair Lady, you might say. (December. Covent Garden Piazza 12–23. Tube: Covent Garden/Leicester Sq. www.christmas-deluxe.com)

Even **The London Eye** goes festive, with **Mistletoe Cupids Capsules**, complete with chocolate truffles and Champagne, in case nibbling each other under the mistletoe isn't enough. (South Bank. 0870/5000.600. Tube: Westminster. www.londoneye.com)

At this time of year, no matter the weather, London develops a whole Ice Age of its own. Open-air ice rinks spring up everywhere, some of the most spectacular being in the courtyard of the stunningly beautiful **Somerset House** (0844/847.1520. Tube: Embankment. www.somersethouse.org.uk), in front of the awe-inspiring **Natural History Museum** (0844/847.1576. Tube: South Kensington. www.nhm.ac.uk), and within the famous **Kew Gardens.** (0870/4000.797. Tube: Kew Gardens. www.kewgardensicerink.com)

The **Trafalgar Square Christmas Tree** (a present from Norway each year) is always worth a visit, especially on the evening the 500 lights go on. There is caroling here too, by a variety of well-bundled choirs. (Tube: Leicester Sq, Charing Cross. www.london.gov.uk/trafalgarsquare)

And, of course, there are carols to be sung, most famously at the Candlelight Carol Service at the **Royal Albert Hall.** (589.8212. Tube: South Kensington. www.royalalberthall.com)

---

with his wife between 1884 and 1895. The study where he wrote *Lady Windemere's Fan*, *An Ideal Husband*, and *The Importance of Being Earnest* was painted buttercup-yellow with red lacquer accents. The dining room, in shades of ivory and pearl, exuded tranquillity, the one quality that permanently and fatally eluded Wilde. Convicted of sodomy and other "homosexual offences," the author was imprisoned between 1895 and 1897; while he was in Reading Jail, he was declared bankrupt and the house at No. 34 was sold. When he was released, he moved to France, where he died in 1900. A plaque was placed on Wilde's former house in 1954, on the centenary of his birth, by Sir Compton MacKenzie, before an audience of Chelsea artists and writers.

American artist John Singer Sargent lived at **No. 31** in a studio house that is pure Chelsea. Here he painted his portraits of the rich, famous, and often beautiful, including actress Ellen Terry, who lived nearby on King's Road, and the American writer who lived around the corner on Cheyne Walk, Henry James. Sargent died here in 1925.

The bohemian portrait painter Augustus John had his studio at **No. 33**, and **No. 13** is the former home of one of America's greatest painters, James Abbott McNeill Whistler. A libel suit he brought against critic John Ruskin left Whistler with huge

and unpayable legal costs, and he was declared bankrupt in 1879. No. 13 was his first permanent address after the lawsuit, but the disgruntled artist lived at a total of nine Chelsea addresses before he died in Cheyne Walk in 1903. ♦ Between Chelsea Embankment and Tedworth Sq

52 NATIONAL ARMY MUSEUM

The **Royal Hospital** doesn't feel like a hospital, and it doesn't exude military history, though many of the pensioners are war heroes. Just next door, however, is this museum, which covers British Army history from the 15th century to the present, including the Falklands War of 1982. The museum's galleries have exhibits on the Peninsular War, the Victorian soldier, and World Wars I and II (with sections devoted to the Far Eastern campaign and the history of women in the army). There are lots of models and dioramas of battles, and the skeleton of Napoléon's horse, Marengo. The museum owns Hitler's telephone switchboard, which was captured in Berlin in 1945. On the board are direct lines to infamous people like Goebbels and Himmler. There is also a permanent exhibit of the Battle of Waterloo, which includes a 400-square-foot model of the battle itself, as well as a gallery with works by Sir Joshua Reynolds, George

Romney, Sir Thomas Lawrence, and Thomas Gainsborough. A new permanent display is called *The Rise of the Redcoat: the British Army from Henry V to George III.* ♦ Free. Daily. Royal Hospital Rd (between West Rd and Tite St). 730.0717

53 ROYAL HOSPITAL

Guidebooks perpetuate the myth that Nell Gwyn, mistress of Charles II, was so moved when a wounded soldier begged for alms that she persuaded the king to build this hospital. It's more likely, however, that Charles, impressed and inspired by reports of Louis XIV's Hôtel des Invalides, decided to emulate him. In 1682, diarist Sir John Evelyn and army paymaster General Sir Stephen Fox drew up plans for a hospital and residence for army pensioners, and Charles II commissioned **Sir Christopher Wren**, who chose the magnificent river site, to build it. This building, finished in 1686, is considered one of Wren's masterpieces, second only to **St. Paul's**. The glorious elders' home still provides shelter to 400 war veterans known as the Chelsea Pensioners, and there's a waiting list to get in.

In early June each year, the pensioners celebrate Oak Apple Day, commemorating Charles II's escape from Cromwell's troops (he hid in an oak tree after the Battle of Worcester) by placing a wreath of oak leaves around the neck of the bronze statue of the king in the **Figure Court**. The statue was cast in 1676 by Grinling Gibbons. On Oak Apple Day, the pensioners change from their blue winter uniforms, designed in the time of the Duke of Marlborough, to their scarlet summer tunics. This colorful ceremony is not open to the public, but throughout the year you can see the pensioners proudly walking the streets of Chelsea resplendent in their red or navy blue uniforms. Some can be spotted watching the Changing of the Guard ceremony at **Buckingham Palace**, where they often pose for photos with tourists.

The hospital consists of a central block, which houses the chapel and the main mall, connected by an octagonal vestibule. The pensioners live in the twin galleries, or wings, which run at right angles to the river. The small museum in the **Secretary's Office Block** on the east side of the hospital, designed in 1816 by **Sir John Soane**, contains prints, uniforms, medals, and photographs associated with the hospital and its history, including two large paintings in **Wellington Hall**: the *Battle of Waterloo* by George Jones and Haydon's *Wellington Describing the Field of Waterloo to George IV.* The pensioners have their meals in the **Great Hall** under the *Triumph of Charles II*,

a huge painting by Antonio Verrio of the king on horseback crushing serpents, with the Royal Hospital in the background. Around the hall are portraits of British kings and queens, from Charles II to Victoria. When Wellington was laid in state here in 1852, two mourners were trampled to death by the crowds.

The chapel is pure Wren, with his signature black-and-white marble floor, fine carved paneling by Gibbons, and Sebastiano Ricci's *Resurrection* over the altar. The glass case beside the altar contains a prayer book, placed there in 1690, opened to a prayer of thanksgiving for the Restoration (the reestablishment of the monarchy under Charles II in 1660), without which there would be no Royal Hospital. Visitors are welcome to attend services on Sunday. Although one of the pensioners can be booked to show a group around, individual visitors should invest in the compact, inexpensive guidebook (available in the chapel).

In the 18th century, the vast **Ranelagh Gardens** of the hospital had a gilt rotunda and a site for eating, drinking, music, masquerades, fireworks, and balloon flights. Canaletto painted them, Mozart played in them, the royal family enjoyed them, and all levels of London society took pleasure in them—until 1803, when they closed their doors. Now the gardens and some of the Royal Hospital grounds are the site of **Chelsea Flower Show**, and for 4 days in May some of the exuberance and pleasure of those early times is rekindled. The gardens are open to the public. ♦ Free. Grounds, chapel, and Great Hall: M–Sa, 10AM–noon, 2–4PM. Museum: Su, 2–4PM. Services: Su, 8:30AM, 11AM, and noon. Royal Hospital Rd (between Chelsea Bridge and West Rds). 730.0161

54 JAPANESE PEACE PAGODA

If you walk down the streets off Royal Hospital Road (such as Tite Street or Swan Walk) to the Chelsea Embankment, you can see this pagoda across the Thames in **Battersea Park**, the latest addition to the London riverside. The 100-foot bronze and gold-leaf Buddha, staring out over the river, was inaugurated in May 1985. This temple of peace was built in 11 months by 50 monks and nuns, mainly from Japan. Much to the amazement of locals, the pagoda is tended by several Buddhist monks who actually live in a small wooded area nearby. It is the last great work of the Most Venerable Nichidatsu Fujii, the Buddhist leader who died at the age of 100, 1 month before his noble and majestic temple was completed. ♦ Daily, 7:30AM–dusk. Terrace Walk (off Carriage Dr N). 0181/871.7530

Restaurants/Clubs: **Red** | Hotels: **Purple** | Shops: **Orange** | Outdoors/Parks: **Green** | Sights/Culture: **Blue**

KENSINGTON/ KNIGHTSBRIDGE

Cromwell and **Brompton Roads** gently embrace in front of the flamboyant Baroque **Brompton Oratory**, the first important Roman Catholic church built in London after the Reformation, uniting at an almost imperceptible angle: two roads, two villages (Kensington and Knightsbridge), and two worlds. Victorian, high-minded **South Kensington**, with its nexus of museums, is evidence of the high regard that one man—Prince Albert—had for the educational and moral value of art, whereas luxurious and high-spirited Knightsbridge is the province of the chic, sophisticated, and fashionable. It seems an improbable union, but the two adjoining neighborhoods bring out the best in each other, and a day spent in the company of both is unimaginably satisfying.

Together, these areas encompass everything from exhibits of dinosaurs and their living descendants to a quarter of a million butterflies, a launch pad and the *Apollo 10* space capsule, an enormous bed for weary travelers that was mentioned in *Twelfth Night*, 15 acres of fabulous furniture and other highly desirable goods (which you can buy if you like), and 10 acres of the greatest collection of antique furniture and decorative art in the world (which you can't).

Begin at the **Natural History Museum**, a grandly Victorian building that looks more like an ecclesiastical railway station than a museum. As you continue along **Exhibition Road**, you'll see several monuments to the purposeful Prince Albert, including the **Science Museum**, the **Victoria and Albert Museum**, and the **Royal Albert Hall**, presided over by the **Albert Memorial**. Then again, there are those two shrines to consumerism that sum up the area: **Harrods**, whose motto is

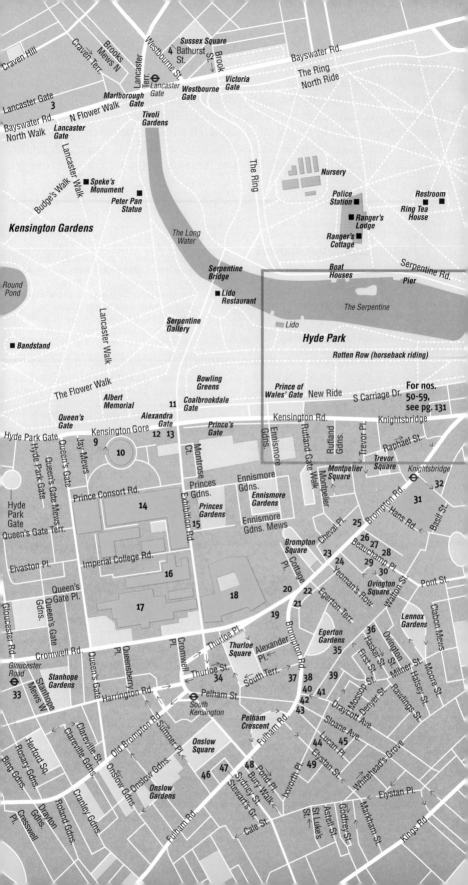

Craven Hill

Craven Terr.

Brooks Mews N

Westbourne St.

Lancaster Terr.

Sussex Square

Bathurst St.

4

Brook St.

Bayswater Rd.

The Ring North Ride

Lancaster Gate

Lancaster Gate

Lancaster Gate

Westbourne Gate

Victoria Gate

Bayswater Rd.

3

Marlborough Gate

N Flower Walk

Tivoli Gardens

Bayswater Rd. North Walk

Lancaster Gate

Lancaster Walk

Budge's Walk

Speke's Monument

Peter Pan Statue

The Ring

Nursery

Police Station

Restroom

Ring Tea House

Ranger's Lodge

Ranger's Cottage

Kensington Gardens

The Long Water

Serpentine Bridge

Boat Houses

Serpentine Rd.

Pier

Round Pond

Lancaster Walk

Lido Restaurant

The Serpentine

Serpentine Gallery

Lido

Hyde Park

■ Bandstand

Rotten Row (horseback riding)

The Flower Walk

Bowling Greens

Prince of Wales' Gate

New Ride

S Carriage Dr.

For nos. 50–59, see pg. 131

Albert Memorial

Coalbrookdale Gate

11

Kensington Rd.

Knightsbridge

Queen's Gate

Alexandra Gate

Kensington Gore

12 13

Prince's Gate

Ennismore Gdns.

Rutland Gate Walk

Rutland Gdns.

Trevor Pl.

Raphael St.

Hyde Park Gate

Jay Mews

9

10

Montrose Ct.

Montpelier Square

Trevor Square

Knightsbridge

Queen's Gate Mews

Prince Consort Rd.

14

Princes Gdns.

Exhibition Rd.

Princes Gardens

15

Ennismore Gdns.

Ennismore Gardens

Ennismore Gdns. Mews

Montpelier Walk

Montpelier

Cheval Pl.

25

Brompton Rd.

Hans Rd.

Basil St.

32

31

Hyde Park Gate

Queen's Gate Terr.

Imperial College Rd.

16

18

Brompton Square

Cottage Pl.

23

24

26

27 28

Beauchamp Pl.

29

30

Ovington Square

Pont St.

Elvaston Pl.

Queen's Gate Pl.

17

20 22

21

Egerton Terr.

Yeoman's Row

Walton St.

Lennox Gardens

Clabon Mews

Gloucester Rd.

Queen's Gate Gdns.

Cromwell Rd.

Queensberry Pl.

Cromwell Pl.

Thurloe Pl.

19

Brompton Rd.

Egerton Gardens

35

36

Hasker St.

First St.

Ovington St.

Milner St.

Moore St.

Halsey St.

Rawlings St.

Gloucester Road

Stanhope Gardens

Harrington Rd.

Thurloe Square

Thurloe St.

34

Alexander Pl.

South Terr.

37

38

39

Mossop St.

Denyer St.

Draycott Ave.

33

Stanhope Mews W

Pelham St.

South Kensington

40 41

42

43

Sloane Ave.

Lucan Pl.

44 45

Elystan St.

Whitehead's Grove

Herford Sq.

Clareville St.

Clareville Gdns.

Old Brompton Rd.

Summer Pl.

Onslow Gdns.

Pelham Crescent

Fulham Rd.

Ixworth Pl.

49

Astell St.

Markham St.

Godfrey St.

Elystan Pl.

Rosary Gdns.

Bina Gdns.

Onslow Square

46 47

48

Pond Pl.

Bury Walk

Sydney St.

St Luke's St.

Kings Rd.

Cranley Gdns.

Drayton Gdns.

Roland Gdns.

Cresswell Gdns.

Onslow Gardens

Fulham Rd.

Stewart's Gr.

Cale St.

"*Omnia, Omnibus, Ubique* [All Things, for All People, Everywhere]," and **Harvey Nichols**, the fashion designer department store.

If a morning of museum-going has filled your mind with things cultural but left you craving the outdoors, you can enjoy the refreshing greenery of **Hyde Park** and **Kensington Gardens**. In the morning you might also see the queen's horse-drawn carriages travel down **Serpentine Road**; in May or June, you can watch soldiers practicing with their horses on **Rotten Row** for the Trooping the Colour ceremony.

City code 0207 unless otherwise noted.

1 PORTOBELLO ROAD MARKET

A mile-long stretch of this street erupts with about 1,500 dealers on Saturday, creating one of the largest open-air markets in London. It bills itself as the world's largest antiques market, and it's easy to see why. Between 6AM and late afternoon, thousands of tourists and bargain and antiques hunters congregate in search of unique souvenirs or a silver teapot. There's loads of junk and kitsch, but then, the fun is in the search. With some dedicated rummaging, it is possible to find desirable items at reasonable prices, particularly in the surrounding shops and arcades. An information booth, open 9AM to 2PM, offers guides to the specialist dealers. If you can't get there on Saturday, go during the week; the shops are generally open, and there are plenty of places to eat and drink and just watch the scene. Portobello Road is the main shopping street, but there are dealers in adjoining streets too. Down toward the Golborne Road end of the market are stalls selling fruits and vegetables, artisanal breads, bargain groceries, and all manner of street food. You'll find shops for other goods, such as the excellent **Portobello China and Woolens** at **No. 89** (727.3857), a factory outlet for quality Scottish cashmere and knitwear; it also carries the big names in china. ♦ Market: Sa; shops: M-Sa. Between Chepstow Villas and Golborne Rd. 229.8354. Tube: Notting Hill Gate, Ladbroke Grove. www.portobelloroad.co.uk

On Portobello Road:

THE ELECTRIC CINEMA

Remember what cinema-going was like when it was special? The Electric is a fully refurbished picture palace. The seats are leather, there are footstools and tables for your drinks, and there's more leg room than Goliath would need. There are even two-seater leather sofas for those who are looking for a more "friendly" viewing experience. The bar opens a half hour before the screening, selling great cocktails, wines, beers, and delicious snacks. The program is intelligent and eclectic. For a real treat, try a Sunday matinee, where the choice can come from the wilder shores of cinema and the price is just £10. ♦ Daily. 191 Portobello Rd. 908.9696. www.electriccinema.co.uk

1 EARL OF LONSDALE

★$$ After a morning spent fighting the hordes on Portobello Road, rest your legs in the shade of this pub's ailanthus tree (which has white blossoms in springtime) or enjoy a pint inside the pretty conservatory. Standard pub fare accompanies the brews. ♦ Pub ♦ M-Sa, lunch and dinner; Su, lunch. 277 Westbourne Grove (at Portobello Rd). 727.6335. Tube: Notting Hill Gate, Ladbroke Grove

2 GEALES

★★$$ This fish-and-chips spot has been here for almost 60 years, and its cottage dining room and rustic furniture remain loved by all who come here. The fish is fresh from Billingsgate and Grimsby, and the batter that coats it is made with beer. Try the fish soup with croutons, rouille, and cheese before tucking into a large cod and chips, then finish with the apple crumble for dessert. Beer, wine, and Champagne are available, but, oddly, you must pay your waitress immediately for alcoholic drinks, which is a bit inconvenient. Some say service can be rather slow. ♦ Fish and chips ♦ M-Sa, lunch and dinner. 2 Farmer St (between Hillgate Pl and Notting Hill Gate). 727.7528. Tube: Notting Hill Gate

"The passion for crowds is nowhere feasted so full as in London. The man must have a rare recipe for melancholy who can be dull in Fleet Street."
—Charles Lamb, 1802

3 THISTLE HYDE PARK

$$$ The most impressive thing about this place is the exterior and the location, overlooking Hyde Park and Kensington Gardens. The hotel has all modern conveniences and the "safety factor" of being part of a huge and more-or-less reputable chain. It has just 54 bedrooms, which is nice, and offers a base close enough to the center to make all your sightseeing a breeze, as well as close enough to some more interesting areas to make them within easy exploring distance. ♦ 90–92 Lancaster Gate (between Bayswater Rd and Leinster Terr). 0870/333.9110; fax 0870/333.9210. Tube: Lancaster Gate, Queensway. www.thistlehotels.com

4 ANGELUS

★★★★**$$$** When I first visited Angelus when it opened in 2007, I proposed marriage to the chef, Olivier Durret. You may well do the same (even you guys—same-sex partnerships are official here!). Yes, it *is* that good. Thierry Tomasin is the owner, and it is he who will look after you front of house. He was sommelier at Le Gavroche, and I expect they are still weeping at their loss. Now Thierry is the boss, and his restaurant is practically perfect. In a converted 19th-century pub, the room is all rich colors and fabrics, leather, and stained glass. The welcome is warm. If you are lucky, Thierry will talk you through the wine list—you will get goose bumps. And that is before you even taste the wine. The food will stop all conversation. The signature starter is a foie gras crème brûlée with toasted bread, quite possibly the best thing on a plate in London. Shoulder of lamb confit with Moroccan spices and crispy dried fruit polenta is thrillingly good, and the chef's rabbit pie is fast becoming the stuff of legend. Desserts are no less exciting. Roasted figs with gingerbread and cinnamon ice cream is rich but not heavy. You can manage a portion; you know you can. Angelus's lovely lounge bar serves light meals and snacks. It is simply not possible to recommend this place too highly. The only bad thing about it is that, eventually, you have to leave. ♦ French ♦ Tu-Su, lunch and dinner. 4 Bathurst St. 402.0083. www.angelusrestaurant.co.uk

5 KENSINGTON PALACE

If this building looks more like a grand English country house than a palace, it's because that is exactly what it once was. Known in royal circles as KP, it is very much a living palace. The late Princess of Wales occupied the largest apartment, with three floors on the north side. Current residents include Prince and Princess Michael of Kent; and the Duke and Duchess of Gloucester and their three children, with 35 rooms at their disposal. The Prince of Wales used to live here, but now he resides at **Clarence House**. The queen decides who lives in the palace, and the residents don't pay rent, though they are responsible for alterations and decorating and pay their own electricity, telephone, and heating bills.

The palace's historical claims are quite considerable, dating back to 1689, when William III commissioned **Sir Christopher Wren** to build a palace out of the existing **Nottingham House**, away from the damp conditions of **Whitehall Palace**, which aggravated his asthma. Past residents include six monarchs: William and Mary, Anne, George I, George II, and William IV. This nonpalatial palace, formerly known as **Kensington House**, was Queen Victoria's birthplace, and it was here that she was awakened with the news that she was queen. In 1899, on Queen Victoria's 80th birthday, the **State Rooms** were opened to the public; in 1975, more rooms followed. Tours start in the more intimate rooms, finishing with the grand ones. The **Queen's Staircase** leads to the Queen's Apartments, which look much as they did when Wren decorated them for William and Mary. Next door to the **Queen's Gallery**, with fine carvings by Grinling Gibbons, is the **Queen's Closet**, which is anything but a closet. It was here that Queen Anne and her lady-in-waiting, the Duchess of Marlborough, had the angry quarrel that ended their long-standing friendship.

After you pass the **Queen's Bedchamber** with its tempting four-poster bed, the rooms become grander. The **Privy Chamber** has Mortlake tapestries by William Kent on the ceiling and overlooks the state apartments of the late Princess Margaret; beyond are the **Presence Chamber** and the **King's Staircase**. One of the most stunning rooms—looking even more splendid after its refurbishment—is **King William's Gallery**, designed by Wren, with wood carvings by Gibbons and an Etruscan ceiling painted by Kent. This room leads into the Duchess of Kent's drawing room and its anteroom, which contains Queen Victoria's Georgian dollhouse and her toys. But perhaps the favorite room is **Queen Victoria's Bedroom**, where the young princess received the news of her accession. It is now filled with mementos of the long-reigning queen, including the curtained cradle where her babies, and those of Queens Alexandra and Mary, slept. A collection of dresses worn at court is displayed in the costume gallery.

The trim palace garden and the **Orangery**, where lunch and tea are served, reflect the taste of Queen Anne, who relied on both **Nicholas Hawksmoor** and **Sir John Vanbrugh** to help her change the previous formal Dutch-style layout to a more natural appearance. The queen spent much of her time here and eventually died here from an attack of apoplexy due to overeating. ♦ Admission. Daily, 10AM–6PM except Christmas Eve, Christmas Day, and Boxing Day. Palace Ave (off Kensington Rd). 937.9561; evening activities and private tours: 376.2452. Tube: High St, Kensington

6 LINLEY SAMBOURNE HOUSE

This Victorian house and its contents—even the letters in desk drawers—have been left intact since the owner, Sir Linley Sambourne, a cartoonist for the satiric magazine *Punch*, lived there between 1874 and 1910. A visit here is a perfect, personal way to step into the Victorian era. ♦ Admission. Guided tours of no more than 12, Sa, Su, at 10AM, 11:15AM, 1PM, 2:15PM, and 3:30PM. 18 Stafford Terr (between Argyll Rd and Phillimore Gardens). 602.3316. Tube: High St, Kensington

6 LEIGHTON HOUSE

A flamboyant home and studio built in 1866 by **George Aitchison** for the classicist artist Lord Leighton (1830–1896), it is a wonderful extravaganza of high Victorian art. All the intricately decorated rooms reflect Leighton's opulent vision of living in a private palace devoted to art. Displays include his own paintings as well as those of Edward Burne-Jones and John Everett Millais. The centerpiece is the **Arab Hall**, designed to display his Islamic tiles and Walter Crane's gilt mosaic frieze. ♦ Free. Daily, except Tu. 12 Holland Park Rd (between Melbury and Addison Rds). 602.3316. Tube: High St, Kensington

7 KENSINGTON HIGH STREET

Ken' High Street, as it is known, has always been a bit of a magnet for shoppers for fashion. It isn't, I'm afraid, the place it was. There is really nothing fashion-wise that you can get here that you can't get elsewhere, but it has most of the higher-end High Street chains for clothes and accessories. And it is a much nicer experience shopping here than on Oxford Street!

On Kensington High Street:

BYRON

★★★$ Very smart, very impressive "hamburger chic." The space is very light and white, with line-drawn murals of your hamburger when it was still on the hoof. The beef comes from fully traceable, grass-fed Scottish Aberdeen Angus herds, hung for a minimum of 21 days. The buns come from a fourth-generation East End family baker and all the garnishes, salads, coleslaws, and pickles are top notch. There is a short, smart wine list and half a dozen well-chosen bottled beers. The service manages to be welcoming, warm, and efficient. ♦ Daily, lunch and dinner. 222 Kensington High St. 361.1717. www.byronhamburgers.com

STICKY FINGERS

★★$ Great for kids, Rolling Stones fans, and anyone who likes the Hard Rock Café or Planet Hollywood but wants to get out of the red-hot center of London and pay a little less for the same kind of food done quite a lot better. Sticky Fingers is the creation of Bill Wyman, and runs the gamut of finger-sticking food from wings and ribs to burgers and brownies, all to the accompaniment of pounding rock music. If you can't bear to be offline even while you eat, you will be glad to know Sticky Fingers is Wi-Fi-enabled. There is, of course, merchandising on the menu, but even that is, I think, cooler, better, and much less of a rip-off than anything Hard Rock or Planet Hollywood will wave at your wallet. ♦ Daily, lunch and dinner. 1 Phillimore Gardens. 395.5805. www.stickyfingers.co.uk

TROTTERS

A lovely little store for little people. Kids' clothes, accessories, toys, and books are all set out in a wonderfully fun, friendly interior. Trotters' staff members are all specialist-trained and truly kiddie friendly. The shoe department offers not only a great variety, but a proper fitting service. Trotters' little secret is a children's hair salon with specialist hairdressers snipping and brushing in front of sparkly mirrors and a wall-sized aquarium. First haircuts are free and come with a Certificate of Bravery to take away! ♦ M-Sa, 9AM–6PM. 127 Kensington High St. 937.9373. www.trotters.co.uk

BARKERS ARCADE

This is something of a Grand Old Lady of Kensington who fell on hard times. Now some of the ground floor of what was one huge department store houses the Arcade—amika, Hobbs, Monsoon, Jigsaw, Karen Millen, and Warehouse—basically a little fashion High Street in a circle around a café selling rather good coffee. ♦ M-Sa, 9AM-6PM. 63-97 Kensington High St

WHOLE FOODS

This is to "real" food what the Louvre is to art, offering three vast floors, 13 dining venues, 640 varieties of fruit and vegetables, and 10,989 grocery items. It is, quite literally, awesome. All the food is either Fair Traded, ethically sourced, free range, organic, or artisanal, or comes with the approval of one of the burgeoning number of bodies who purport to police the social and environmental acceptabilities of our consumables. Were I to nitpick, while I absolutely loved my wander through the huge expanse of the fresh fruit and vegetable hall, they could probably buy their own farm if they cashed in the air miles they must have amassed flying in the huge green papayas, fresh black pepper-corn, and rainbow of exotic fruit you can buy all neatly prepared in chunks or even juiced. The fresh meat and wet fish counters are unbelievably impressive, with top-quality meat and fish expertly prepared. And the staff not only is charming but oozes expertise. The breads are perfect, the deli counters are so many square yards of fresh foodie paradise, the cheese section (including a proper cheese room) would reform any vegan, the aisles of chocolate—in rows sorted by country, percentage, spicing, and flavoring—will destroy any diet, and the pie counter is un-walkpastable. There are natural beauty products, organic cotton clothing and bedding, gifts, toys, books, and CDs. There are machines for making your own nut butters and huge piles of eggs of all sorts available to buy loose. Upstairs there is a light, airy space where you can sit and enjoy tapas, sushi, organic pizza or pasta, or fabulous ice creams, perch at the Oyster Bar, or custom squeeze an organic juice. The best thing to come over here from America since *The David Letterman Show!* ♦ M-Sa, 8AM-10PM; Su, noon-6PM. 63-97 Kensington High St. 368.4500.www.wholefoodsmarket.com

ST. MARY ABBOTTS CHURCH

At the corner of Kensington Church Street and Kensington High Street is a bit of a gem. Although the current building is only a 130-year-old baby, there has been a place of community worship here for over a millennium. The present building (built 1872) was designed by **Sir George Gilbert Scott** and is a perfect example of Victorian Gothic. But don't just look at the outside. If you have any sort of a thing for churches, you will love this one. Inside it is like a cathedral—179 feet long, 109 feet wide, and soaring to a roof height of 72 feet. It is a glorious feast of marbles and mosaics, artwork, and a lovely Florentine crucifix. St. Mary Abbotts has the tallest spire in London, a team of highly regarded campanologists (no, nothing to do with stage musicals, it's bellringers), and some of the loveliest examples of stained glass in London, most notable being the famous "Healing Window," funded by the Royal College of Surgeons. St. Mary Abbotts' celebrity worshippers over the centuries have included William Wilberforce, Sir Isaac Newton, and Beatrix Potter. ♦ Kensington High Street/Kensington Church St. www.stmaryabbottschurch.org

The Milestone Hotel and Apartments

8 THE MILESTONE HOTEL AND APARTMENTS

$$$$ A uniquely idiosyncratic hotel, one of Mrs. Bea Tollman's Red Carnation Group. What you get here is the personal touch. The group president herself has chosen every pattern (and there are a lot of patterns) on every wall, drape, and cushion and every knickknack and ornament (and there are a *lot* of knickknacks and ornaments) in your room. The hotel has 45 deluxe rooms and 12 suites, and when it says deluxe it means deluxe. These rooms are gorgeous, and come with absolutely every modern convenience you can imagine and some you can't—like your own personal local business cards printed ready for your arrival! The suites have even more goodies attached: four-poster beds, split-level rooms, 24-hour butler service, a platter of canapés delivered to your room each evening, and use of the hotel's Bentley to take you to and from the airport. There are also, next door, six self-contained apartments that have all the facilities of the hotel suites. The hotel's **Stable Bar** is snug and welcoming, the **Park Lounge**

(which does indeed overlook the park) does a glorious afternoon tea, the **Conservatory** offers great lunches and light meals, and the **Chenstone Restaurant** has a very accomplished chef offering an international menu. If you feel the need to work off what you have just devoured, the hotel has a perfectly appointed little gym and a resistance pool. This hotel should be a tourist attraction itself. It has won several awards (quite rightly), most recently the 2007 Condé Nast Readers' Choice Award for British Hotels. ◆ 1 Kensington Court, Knightsbridge. 917.1000; fax 917.1010. Tube: High St, Kensington. www.milestonehotel.com

9 ROYAL COLLEGE OF ORGANISTS

This eccentric four-story building was designed in 1875 by **H.H. Cole**, a soldier in the Royal Engineers who preferred engineers and artists over architects. The building delights passersby with its euphoria of decoration and colors and its frieze of musicians. What's missing from this picture? Well, there is neither an organist nor an organ. In fact, the building is completely empty, and there are no plans for filling it in the immediate future. ◆ Kensington Gore (at Jay Mews). Tube: South Kensington

10 ROYAL ALBERT HALL

This stupendous piece of Victoriana is a memorial to Prince Albert, ordained and encouraged by Queen Victoria. Oddly enough, it was designed not by architects but by

Albert Memorial

two engineers: Captain Francis Fowke and Major-General H.Y. Darracott Scott, who used Roman amphitheaters as their inspiration. The redbrick elliptical hall with its 135-foot glass-and-iron dome can hold about 7,000 people, and its acoustics are superb. Apparently the prince approved of the design (although he had wanted this site for another **National Gallery**), and it is a fitting climax to the cultural complex honoring the education of the mind and spirit in which he so strongly believed.

Still operating under a Royal Charter, the hall is the venue for sporting events, beauty contests, pop concerts, military exercises, and most famous of all, the annual Henry Wood Promenade Concerts, performed daily between mid-July and mid-September. Known as the Proms, these performances of classical and popular pieces have an informal atmosphere and are packed with true music lovers. Most of the seats are sold well in advance, but there are always inexpensive standing-room tickets available on the day of the performance (sales begin at 6:30PM). The last night of the Proms is famously emotional, and tickets are so much in demand that they are sold by lottery. Recently introduced, and wildly successful, is a wide-screen showing of the last night to delighted spectators in adjacent **Hyde Park**. ◆ Kensington Gore (between Exhibition Rd and Jay Mews). 589.3203, box office 589.8212. Tube: South Kensington

11 KENSINGTON GARDENS AND HYDE PARK

The difference between the two parks and just where they merge is a mystery to many. But true lovers of London earth and sky can define perfectly the area that begins at **Kensington Palace** and extends to **Alexandra Gate** on the south and **Victoria Gate** on the north, with the connecting Ring as the boundary.

The gardens, which were in large part laid out by Queen Anne, were originally the private property of Kensington Palace, and they still have a regal air, enhanced by the presence of the royal home. They were opened by George III to the public in the 19th century—"for respectably dressed people" on Saturday only—and Queen Victoria opened them fully in 1841, after which they became a fashionable venue for promenades. Many English writers, among them Thackeray and Matthew Arnold, have praised their "sublime sylvan solitude," as Disraeli put it. The **Round Pond**, constructed in the 18th century, was originally octagonal, and the **Broad Walk** was once lined with magnificent elm trees. Today, there are occasional skateboarders and roll-erskaters, whereas the Round Pond plays host to young skippers.

Neighboring Hyde Park's 390 acres are, by contrast, an informal swath of green. Once yet another hunting ground for Henry VIII, it was given to the public by James I. Rotten Row, which runs along the south side, is thought to be a corruption of *Route du Roi* (French for "Road of the King"). ♦ Bounded by Park La and Palace Ave and by Knightsbridge, Kensington Rd, and Bayswater Rd. Tube: South Kensington, Marble Arch, Hyde Park Corner, Knightsbridge, Lancaster Gate, High St Kensington, Queensway

Within Kensington Gardens and Hyde Park:

ALBERT MEMORIAL

Slightly west of the **Crystal Palace** (which housed the Great Exhibition of 1851) is the Albert Memorial, the famous statue of Prince Albert, now dazzling after having undergone a £14 million restoration. Fifty thousand pounds alone were spent on a double layer of 23-carat gold leaf.

The monument portrays Prince Albert holding the catalog of the Great Exhibition of 1851 and gazing down on the museums, colleges, and institutions that his vision, energy, and endeavor inspired. (Profits from the Great Exhibition funded most of the museums in this area.) The memorial earned its creator, George Gilbert Scott, a knighthood. Albert's throne, crowned by a spire of gilt and enameled metal that ends in a cross rising 180 feet, is an imposing piece of Victorian art made lovable by its sheer excess. The monument was commissioned by the prince's mournful widow, Queen Victoria, and unveiled by her in 1876. Below the bronze statue of the prince consort are marble statues of animals representing the four continents; allegorical figures representing Agriculture, Commerce, Manufacture, and Engineering stand at the four angles. Nearest the top of the 175-foot-high monument rest figures of Faith, Hope, Charity, and Humility. On the pedestal is a magnificent procession of reliefs of the greatest artists, writers, and philosophers of the Victorian era. The **Albert Memorial Visitor Centre**, located beside the statue, contains displays that reveal the extent and scope of the renovation, as well as a 6-foot-high model of the memorial, exhibits about the life of Prince Albert, and a gift shop.

Strangely, for many years the monument was denounced as an example of the worst of Victorian sentimentality and ugly excess. But a new appreciation of Victorian architecture has brought the memorial into deserved veneration, along with the prince it honors. ♦ 2PM and 3PM, first Su of every month Mar-Dec. 495.0916

THE DIANA MEMORIAL FOUNTAIN

Seven years after Princess Diana's death, Queen Elizabeth unveiled £3.6 million worth of memorial fountain. US architect Kathryn Gustavson's design was chosen, by Diana's close friend Rosa Monkton, from over 1,000 submissions. Since its unveiling, the fountain has required numerous repairs, and at the time of writing, the popular opinion is that it should be demolished. If you are a Diana fan, come and check, but be forewarned . . . www.royalparks.gov.uk

SERPENTINE GALLERY

Once the **Kensington Gardens Tea House**, the beautiful building is now the ideal art gallery, ambitiously providing a setting for monthly exhibitions of contemporary art. Gallery talks are given on alternative Saturdays and Sundays at 3PM. ♦ Free. Daily. 402.6075

SERPENTINE

This 41-acre artificial lake was formed in 1730 by damming the Westbourne, a stream that no longer exists. The resulting riverlike lake (the name comes from its winding shape) is home to a vast range of waterfowl. In 1816, Harriet Westbrook, the first wife of the poet Percy Bysshe Shelley, committed suicide by drowning herself in this lake. The swimming hole, the **Lido**, has been closed because of pollution (although members of the Polar Bear Club take a dip in the water here every New Year's Day). There is a small paddling pool for kids in summer. Nearby is the **Boathouse**, where rowboats may be hired by the hour for a perfect afternoon, as depicted by Renoir. Along the **Long Water**, that part of the lake that is located within **Kensington Gardens**, stands Sir George Frampton's **Peter Pan**, the most enchanting figure in the park. The statue, erected overnight in 1912, has been rubbed nearly smooth by adoring little hands. Just beyond him are the **Tivoli Gardens**, four ornate shimmering fountains bedecked with flowers that are more characteristic of Italy or France than of London.

12 ALBERT HALL MANSIONS

The warm brick mansions, built between 1879 and 1886 by **Norman Shaw**, were one of the earliest blocks of flats in London. If they weren't so utterly English—the style is Queen Anne Revival with oriels, gables, dormers, and arches—they would seem almost European in their scale and grandeur.

Restaurants/Clubs: Red | Hotels: Purple | Shops: Orange | Outdoors/Parks: Green | Sights/Culture: Blue

The flats are extremely desirable because of their superb location and palatial rooms. They are occupied by an appreciative elite: The late English designer Jean Muir decorated her flat entirely in white. ♦ Kensington Gore (between Exhibition Rd and Jay Mews). Tube: South Kensington

13 ROYAL GEOGRAPHICAL SOCIETY

Gables and chimneys are features of the former **Lowther Lodge**, which became the home of the Royal Geographical Society in 1913. The building was designed by **Norman Shaw** between 1873 and 1875, and the statues outside are of two notable explorers: Sir Ernest Shackleton, who commanded three expeditions to the Antarctic and discovered the location of the south magnetic pole in 1909, and David Livingstone, who discovered the Zambezi River, Victoria Falls, and was attempting to find the source of the Nile when he was famously rescued by the journalist H.M. Stanley. Inside is the outstanding Map Room, with a collection of more than 900,000 maps, an extensive library, a photographic collection, and the **Expedition Advisory Centre**, which offers information, training, and advice to expeditions conducting geographical research overseas. Only the Map Room is open to the public (professional researchers preferred). Viewings of the library, the picture library, and the archives are by appointment. There is a small charge for nonmembers. The society's official name now includes "with the Institute of British Geographers" to show its recent link-up with that organization. ♦ M-F. 1 Kensington Gore (at Exhibition Rd). 591.3000. Tube: South Kensington

14 ROYAL COLLEGE OF MUSIC

Inside this elaborate building, designed by **Sir Arthur Blomfield** in 1894, is a remarkable collection of more than 500 musical instruments, ranging from the earliest known stringed keyboard instruments to some wonderfully bizarre creations of the 19th and 20th centuries. Here, Handel's spinet rests amiably with Haydn's clavichord. There's also a collection of portraits (seen by appointment only) in various media, including more than 100 paintings and several thousand engravings and photographs. ♦ Admission. Music collection: W only, 2PM-4PM. Closed Jan. Portrait collection: M-F, by appointment only. Prince Consort Rd (between Exhibition and Callendar Rds). Museum: 591.4346; Department of Portraits: 591.4340. Tube: South Kensington

15 OGNISKO POLSKIE

★★$$ This popular Polish hangout, whose name translates to "Polish Hearth," is the supposedly secret haunt of many South Kensington bohemians and intellectuals. The high-ceilinged room housing the bar and restaurant is set off with chandeliers, patterned rugs, gilt chairs, and portraits on the paneled walls. The menu has evolved over the years. Starters now range from herring with sour cream to fabulous blinis with smoked salmon, Sevruga caviar, and cream to grilled goat cheese with sultana and balsamic vinegar. Mains range from veal *escalope* served with fresh figs to traditional pork knuckle and pierogi to corn-fed guinea fowl with apples and Calvados. You *must* have the pancake with sweet cheese in orange sauce to finish. You won't forgive yourself if you don't. Wash it down with one of the lethal Polish vodkas. ♦ Polish ♦ Daily, lunch and dinner. 55 Exhibition Rd (at Watts Way). 589.4635. Tube: South Kensington

16 SCIENCE MUSEUM

The Science Museum has more or less been in existence since 1851. Then, the basis of the collection formed part of the Great Exhibition held in a huge glass building in Hyde Park. It proved so popular that it made a profit, which patron Prince Albert suggested should be spent creating a permanent home for the exhibits. A museum was opened in 1857 on the site of what is now the **V&A**. It was an iron-framed structure covered in sheets of corrugated iron, and its sheer ugliness and industrial brutality earned it the nickname the "Brompton Boilers." (Hmmm, so that's where they got the idea for the Pompidou Centre!) Work on the current building began in 1913, was interrupted by World War I, and was completed in 1928.

This inspired tribute to science couldn't be more appropriately located than in the nation that gave the world Newton, Darwin, Davy, Huxley, Thomson, Rutherford, and Fleming. A visit here leaves you with the inevitable realization of just how many fundamental scientific discoveries have been British. The museum is especially enjoyable for the young, who can push, pull, and operate the countless knobs, buttons, and gadgets on display. Just like scientific theories, exhibitions change regularly, so check at the information desk to see what's currently being displayed and for the events of the day. The free map will help!

The basement area, divided into three spaces, is heaven for curious toddlers, filled with such items as a burglar alarm to test and a periscope for spying on the floor above. The space called The Garden has a giant kaleidoscope at the end of a "noisy, feely tunnel"; The Secret Life of the Home is loaded with ingenious gizmos and gadgets; and Things shows how everyday objects work. There are also "explainers"—museum staff in green shirts—to help the kids enjoy the exhibits.

The Launch Pad section dominates the basement. This hands-on gallery is where kids between 6 and 60 can test the scientific principles behind the modern technology used every day.

The emphasis on the ground floor is on power, transport, and exploration, with the **Foucault Pendulum** demonstrating the rotation of the earth on its own axis. Also on display are Puffing Billy, which, dating from 1813, is the oldest locomotive in the world; the Boulton and Watt pumping engine, designed in 1777; a full-scale model of a moon lander; and, most popular of all, the actual *Apollo 10* capsule.

Here there is also the SlimEx Simulator ride—it's supposed to be for kids, but it is awesome for ex-kids as well! You can "experience" explosions in space, dinosaur breath . . . just choose your simulation and strap yourself in.

On the first floor are the Science of Materials (including the Atomic Disco, which is great fun), the whole story of telecommunication, a great exploration of farming (drive a combine harvester, anyone?), a weather and meteorology section, and a really fascinating display called "Who Am I"—you *will* find out.

The second floor has Shipping and Diving, Mathematics and Computing. To say nothing of a real Spitfire!

The third floor starts to get medical and historical and, in the new Wellcome Wing, also offers a super-duper Motionride Simulator. (Eat after you ride.)

The next two floors deal with medical and veterinary history, incorporating items collected between 1896 and 1936 by Sir Henry Wellcome, and now called the **Wellcome Museum of the History of Medicine**. It shows objects from important (if now primitive-looking) developments in medical history: trepanning (cutting out a circular core of the skull) in neolithic times and open-heart surgery in the 1980s. Clever, often spine-chilling displays cover tribal, Oriental, classical Greek, Roman, medieval, and Renaissance medicine. The

vast collection of curiosities includes Florence Nightingale's moccasins, Dr. Livingstone's medicine chest, and Napoléon's beautiful silver toothbrush. Don't miss the **King George III Collection**, otherwise known as "Science in the 18th Century," which shows just how many advances in knowledge were made during the sovereign's reign.

The **Wellcome Wing** offers exhibits on the very latest in scientific news, information on genetics, and digital technology. This wing also houses an IMAX cinema showing two-dimensional and three-dimensional films on a screen the height of four double-decker buses. Breathtaking! ♦ Admission: free. Daily, 10AM–8PM. Exhibition Rd (between Cromwell and Imperial College Rds). 0870/870.4868. Cinema: 0807/870.4771. Tube: South Kensington. www.sciencemuseum.org.uk

Within the Science Museum:

REVOLUTION CAFÉ

★$ This snackery is in the Energy Hall and offers soups, sandwiches, salads, and a small selection of hot meals. Or just coffee and a piece of cake.

DEEP BLUE

★$ Deep Blue is a fun family restaurant on the ground floor, offering views of the new Wellcome Wing. There's pizza and pasta (and other healthier stuff!) and good desserts. If the food is not enough to keep everyone entertained, there are Activity Boxes for the younger kids.

SCIENCE MUSEUM STORE

A terrific store full of gizmos and fun stuff, clever gadgets and perfect gifts! www.sciencemuseumstore.com

WATERSTONES BOOKSHOP

This shop offers a good range of books for all ages on all things scientific.

THE
NATURAL
HISTORY
MUSEUM

17 NATURAL HISTORY MUSEUM

I have never really been one to get excited by museums, but this is different. From the

Restaurants/Clubs: **Red** | Hotels: **Purple** | Shops: **Orange** | Outdoors/Parks: **Green** | Sights/Culture: **Blue**

123

outside, it is like a fabulous, fairy-tale castle. You cannot but want to go inside. And when you do . . . wow! I realize that is not a very scientific reaction, but it is the only one. Even if you only make it to the entrance hall, you will get a thrill. Writer H.V. Morton described the museum as "a gothic building that gives the visitor the impression that the zoo has escaped from Regents Park and taken refuge in a cathedral." He is not wrong. And the place is not just a feast for the eyes and an education but, according to the charming press officer, a nasal voyage of discovery as well! The Zoology Department smells of alcohol, the Dermestarium of rotting flesh, and the Botany Department is still perfumed with a preservative they stopped using a decade ago but still lingers.

The museum is home to over 70 million specimens, many collected and pressed by Charles Darwin himself. It began with the private collection of Sir Hans Sloane (1660–1753), which was bequeathed to the nation and originally formed the basis of the British Museum in 1759. In the 1870s Richard Owen, a philanthropist (and, fascinatingly, the man who named dinosaurs, the name being Greek for "terrible lizard"), wanted to move the Natural History sections of the museum to a building of their own, or in his words, to separate "the works of God from the works of man." And when Alfred Waterhouse's stunning building was opened on Easter Monday 1881, there was a mile of wall space and four acres of flooring for those works. Even God must have been pleased. Owen wanted the building to reflect its contents, and so Waterhouse's façade is covered with an outrageous menagerie of creatures, and topped with statues of animals and plants both living and extinct. The interior is cleverly accessorized with monkeys scampering up arches and columns that look like fossilized trees. ◆ Admission weekends. Free weekdays. Daily, 10AM–5:50PM. Cromwell Rd (between Exhibition Rd and Queen's Gate). 942.5000. Tube: South Kensington. www.nhm.ac.uk

The whole Paddington area has undergone massive changes over the past few years, especially the area now known as Paddington Basin. There is a series of guided walks that explore the area—where Fleming discovered penicillin, where Brunel built his great station (now looking very perky after its own renovation), and where that Bear from Darkest Peru got his name. A good one starts at 1PM each Thursday at Starbucks, 15 Sheldon Square (313.1011), and explores the waterside. Others have names like Ducks and Duchesses or Quirky Shopping, and there is even one that claims to be guided by Brunel himself! www.paddingtonwaterside.co.uk

Within the Natural History Museum:

THE CENTRAL HALL

The Natural History Museum has just been voted one of the "Seven Wonders of London" by *Time Out magazine*, and entering this hall you can see why. The main exhibit has been here for 100 years! "Dippy" (short for Diplodocus) is a full-size (26 meters long) replica of the 150-million-year-old skeleton in the Carnegie Museum of Natural History.

THE BLUE ZONE

This encompasses galleries dedicated to dinosaurs, fish, amphibians and reptiles, marine invertebrates (23 million of them!), sea mammals (with a 30-meter-long model of the blue whale), land mammals, and even human biology (starting with a single cell and going right up to many interactive exhibits where you yourself become part of the exhibition).

THE GREEN ZONE

Here are the Bird Gallery, the Creepy Crawlies, Minerals Gallery (which is almost exactly as it was when the museum opened in 1881), Meteorites (including one that is 3.5 tons!), Plants (with the famous 5-meter-wide slice of a 1,300-year-old Sequoia tree), Primates, and, yes, more about Us.

THE RED ZONE

This is really all the Earth galleries. It is pretty awesome stuff. The Earth Hall is three stories high and is dominated by a vast metallic globe with an escalator running through it, which takes you through the molten heart of a volcano. The Restless Surface hall looks at the awesome power of water and wind. Here you can even see the *complete* history of the universe along one long, dramatic gallery. Some of the fossils are more than 3,500 million years old. Here also, for lovers of sparkle, is an entire gallery devoted to precious gems . . . diamonds, sapphires, emeralds, and rubies, some of them the very ones dug out of South Africa.

THE WILDLIFE GARDEN

Created between 1993 and 1995, this is a lovely spread of different British habitats: meadow, chalk downland, pond and wetland, and hedgerow. Recently they added an orchard and an "urban" area.

THE DARWIN CENTRE

The museum's new Darwin Centre was designed with three aims: to maintain and expand the museum's collection of specimens, to provide state-of-the-art scientific research facilities, and to create better opportunities for public understanding of nature by bringing people closer to scientists' research and giving them access to one of the world's finest collections of natural history specimens. The first part of the center was opened in 2002 to house the Spirit Collection—22 million specimens from microscopic plankton to komodo dragons, armadillos, and Archie the 8.62-meter-long giant squid, collected over 200 years and preserved, yup, in spirit—and its attendant 100 scientists. Phase Two is due to open in 2009. There are touch-screen terminals and interpretative graphics, photography, and exquisite illustrations from the collection. The building itself is gorgeous, huge, and airy, with an "intelligent skin" that changes daily according to weather conditions and the time of day.

NATURAL HISTORY MUSEUM SHOPS

A wonderful selection of terrific items from the educational (books and toys, kits and posters) to the decorative (some lovely jewelry, glasswork, and scarves) to the downright odd (notepaper and journals made from dried elephant dung!). ♦ Daily. 942.5000

NATURAL HISTORY MUSEUM DINING

All the food served in the museum dining outlet is prepared on the premises. The café behind the Central Hall does good coffee and delicious cakes, the café in the Earth Hall does soups and baguettes, and the family restaurant does a good choice of hot main courses and light meals. All the coffee served is certified Rainforest Alliance, the tea is Down To Earth organic, and the kids' lunch boxes are all organic.

18 VICTORIA AND ALBERT MUSEUM

If you have a curious mind and a receptive heart, and if you like *stuff*, this fascinating institution will become one of your favorite places on earth. It is one of the most addictive and rewarding museums in the world, covering 12 acres with items of enchantment and delight. The museum is the prodigious offspring of the **Great Exhibition of 1851**, opening a year later as the **Museum of Manufactures**, with a collection of objects purchased from the exhibition. The initial intent was to display manufactured art, but when great works of art were bequeathed to the museum (including the permanent loan of the **Raphael Cartoons** and the largest collection of Constable drawings in the world), the scope expanded and the intention and name were changed to the **Museum of Ornamental Art**. In her last major engagement, Queen Victoria laid the foundation stone for the buildings that face Cromwell Road in 1899, and at her request the museum was renamed once again. The Victoria and Albert Museum, affectionately known as the **V&A**, is eclectic, idiosyncratic, and immense, yet accessible and gracious, a museum that is truly worthy of the vision and energy of its founders.

If there is such a thing as the "South Kensington Style," the V&A structure is its finest example. The massive building is a construction of redbrick, terra-cotta, and mosaic, with assertions of Victorian confidence towering beside equally Victorian gloom. Sir Henry Cole, the museum's first director, preferred engineers and artists to architects. The resulting cast-iron and glass structure with corrugated-iron facings—built by **William Cubitt** in 1855—looked like a decorated factory and quickly became known as the "Brompton Boilers." It was moved eastward in 1867 to form the **Bethnal Green Museum of Childhood**. The buildings that make up the main quadrangle of the museum began in 1857 with Captain F. Fowke's **Sheepshanks Gallery** along the east side, followed by the **Vernon and Turner Galleries** in 1858 and the **North**, **South**, and **East Courts** between 1861 and 1873.

A succession of craftspeople were responsible for further additions, among them **Godfrey Sykes**, **James Gamble**, **Frank Moody**, and **Reuben Townroe**. **Sir Aston Webb**'s Cromwell Road façade, begun in 1891 and completed in 1909, evokes the Victorian ethos of pomp and imperial importance. It is flanked by statues of Queen Victoria and Prince Albert by Alfred Drury, and Edward VII and Queen Alexandra by W. Goscombe John. On top of the great central tower is the figure of Fame resting on a lantern shaped like an imperial crown.

Restaurants/Clubs: Red | Hotels: Purple | Shops: Orange | Outdoors/Parks: Green | Sights/Culture: Blue

Entering the museum is like embarking on a great, extravagant, and wonderful expedition. There are seven miles of galleries: the **Art & Design Galleries** contain masterpieces grouped around a style, nationality, or period, whereas **Materials & Techniques** galleries revolve around a type of object, like glass or ceramics. The enormous collection is constantly being added to and new permanent exhibitions created, such as the **Silver Galleries**, which show the national collection of English silver between 1300 and 1800. And don't miss the **Frank Lloyd Wright Gallery** (level B, **Henry Cole Wing**), which displays a re-creation of the 1936 office of Edgar J. Kaufmann's Pennsylvanian department store—it is the only complete interior of Wright's exhibited in Europe.

You will get lost in the more than 150 rooms, but don't despair. The V&A is the best place in town to be lost: Every cul-de-sac is a treasure trove of discovery. And the museum tries to help visitors by displaying color-coded banners to indicate directions. It also publishes a guide that gives museum-goers a taste of its displays by introducing 100 of the most significant and spectacular things to see. The collections are vast, so be warned: You shouldn't attempt to see everything in one visit.

You may want to take advantage of the free, hour-long guided tours that leave from the main (Cromwell Road) entrance, or special tours announced daily to specific areas of the collection. There are also free gallery lectures that often focus on one particular topic, such as furniture or 18th-century British landscape artists. It is pleasant to visit on Wednesday evenings 6:30–9:30: Selected galleries are open; there are gallery talks and live music, plus a special menu in the restaurant. ◆ Admission: free. Daily, 10AM–5:45PM, open till 10PM W and last F of each month. Guided tours: M, 12:15, 2, and 3PM; Tu–Sa, 11AM, noon, 2PM, and 3PM. Special tours: M, 1:30PM; Tu–Su, 11:30AM, 1:30PM. Gallery lectures: daily, 2:30PM. Exhibition and Cromwell Rds. 938.8441. Tube: South Kensington

Within the Victoria and Albert Museum:

GREAT BED OF WARE

This huge Elizabethan bed, circa 1590, was said to have been occupied by 26 butchers and their wives on 13 February 1689. In the 1830s, Charles Dickens tried to purchase the bed from the innkeeper who owned it, but he was outbid. This is easily the most famous bed in the world, mentioned by Shakespeare in *Twelfth Night* and by countless other writers and historians. It is nearly 9 feet high, 11 feet long, and 10.5 feet wide, a size that sometimes distracts from the beauty of the carved, painted, and inlaid decoration. ◆ Room 54

RAPHAEL CARTOONS

This gallery's treasures have been restored recently. The cartoons, works of art in their own right, were drawn with chalk on paper and colored with distemper by Raphael and his scholars in 1516 as designs for tapestry work for Pope Leo X. The tapestries are still at the Vatican. Three of the cartoons are lost; the others are here because Rubens advised Charles I to buy them for the newly opened tapestry factory at Mortlake. One of the tapestries made here is part of the display now. After Charles's death, Cromwell bought the cartoons for £300, and they remained at **Whitehall Palace** until William III moved them to **Hampton Court**. They have been on permanent loan to the V&A since 1865. ◆ Room 48A

GLASS GALLERY

The national collection of 7,000 glass objects tells the story of glass from ancient Egypt to the present day. The range includes commemorative pieces as well as tableware. ◆ Room 131

MORRIS, GAMBLE, AND POYNTER ROOMS

The museum's original tearoom, café, and restaurant occupied this space until 1939, and once again it houses the museum's restaurant; the rooms almost knock you sideways with longing for those aesthetically elaborate and civilized days. The **Green Dining Room**, decorated for the museum by William Morris and Philip Webb, features Burne-Jones stained glass and painted panels representing the months of the year. The wallpaper and furniture are by Morris. The chimney piece in the **Gamble Room** came from **Dorchester House** on Park Lane. It is surrounded by pillared and mirrored ceramic work and a ceiling of enameled iron plates that incorporates a quotation from Ecclesiastes. The dazzling materials were chosen not so much for their beauty but because they are fire resistant and easy to clean! The **Grill Room**, designed by Sir Edward Poynter, still has the original grill, set in Minton blue-and-white tiles representing the seasons and the months. The three rooms present a first-class example of Victorian design. ◆ Level A

DRESS COLLECTION

This room houses a collection of fashion dating from around 1580 to the present and draws more crowds than any other exhibition in the V&A. The English and Continental male and female fashions, with outfits from the 1960s and early 1970s, are strangely exotic and, some say, still eminently fashionable. ♦ Room 40

FAKES AND FORGERIES

Even the floor of this gallery has criminal undertones; it was laid by the women inmates of Woking Prison. The best fakes of their kind are housed here from the hands of master forger Giovanni Bastianini, whose work is displayed among a host of other bogus objects purporting to be something they are not. ♦ Room 46

BRITISH GALLERIES

Huge sealed glass rooms were built to house the objects that trace British design from the Arts and Crafts movement, started by William Morris in the 19th century, to the functionalism of the 20th. These galleries were expanded and redisplayed and show decorative and fine art by such artists as Grinling Gibbons, Robert Adam, and Thomas Chippendale. ♦ 20th-Century Exhibition Gallery

ORIENTAL ROOMS

Turn right from the Cromwell Road information desk and you will find a series of galleries showcasing art from the east. The **T.T. Tsui Gallery of Chinese Art** houses objects from 3000 BC to the present, the **Toshiba Gallery of Japanese Art** has the best collection of lacquer outside Japan, and the **Samsung Gallery of Korean Art** explores the much-underexposed art of that country. The **Cast Courts** hold full-size plaster casts of European architecture and sculpture, including Michel-angelo's *David* and Trajan's column.

PHOTOGRAPHY GALLERY

The new Photography Gallery highlights works from the V&A's world-renowned photography collection, begun in 1852 and now containing 300,000 images from photographers such as Cindy Sherman, William Henry Fox Talbot, Julia Margaret Cameron, Paul Strand, Willi Brandt, and Irving Penn. Further information on the exhibition will be available in a special information technology area.

PAINTINGS GALLERY

The museum's remarkable collections of watercolors and oils, including works by Turner, Constable, Botticelli, and Degas, is returning to the elegant galleries originally built during the 1850s to house them. Having them together again will provide viewers with the chance to appreciate the extraordinary range of the collection. One suite of rooms will focus on the landscape with Turner, Constable's oil sketches (such as *Brighton Beach with Colliers*), and Gainsborough's glass transparencies. A further gallery will house the magnificent bequest of Old Master and 19th-century paintings made by Constantine Ionides in 1900. This will be complemented by items of sculpture, furniture, and decorative art evocative of the Aesthetic Movement. Here you can see a fabulous grand piano designed by William Morris. The final gallery will celebrate the richness of British paintings with works by Blake, Landseer, and Millais.

V&A CAFÉ

★★$ Pretty good as museum eating goes. The café is on the ground floor in the museum's original refreshment area, the Morris, Gamble, and Poynter Rooms. These three rooms formed the first museum restaurant in the world. All the food is freshly prepared each day on the premises and there is always a good and interesting choice of hot dishes, salads, sandwiches, and delicious desserts. The café is licensed. On the last Friday of each month you can enjoy live music, a late bar, and guest DJs. ♦ M-Th, Sa, Su, 10AM-5:15PM; F, 10AM-9:30PM. 581.2159

V&A SHOP

Located to the left of the entrance is the main shop, run as a separate entity, but the profits are all poured back into the museum. There is also a small shop near the restaurant. On sale are replicas of individual works of art displayed in the V&A, including the *Statue of Shakespeare* in terra-cotta and the ceramic alphabet tiles from the **Gamble Room**, known as the *Kensington Alphabet*; in addition, there is an impressive array of stationery, diaries, and William Morris needlepoint cushions. The postcards, books, and other publications are outstanding, as are the ornaments at Christmastime. Just inside is the **Crafts Council Shop**, a showcase for British craftspeople, with original jewelry and objects in pottery, silver, gold, and glass—future treasures for the museum itself. ♦ Daily. 938.8434

19 REMBRANDT HOTEL

$$ The hotel was originally commissioned as luxury apartments for Harrods, and many of

---

Restaurants/Clubs: Red | Hotels: Purple | Shops: Orange | Outdoors/Parks: Green | Sights/Culture: Blue

the original Edwardian features are still there, although the hotel's 2007 refurbishment has added a chic and classy contemporary gloss. There are 194 rooms in three classes with Jacuzzi baths, Wi-Fi, air conditioning, and all modern conveniences. The hotel's fitness center, **The Aquila**, is top-of-the-range and has a gorgeous swimming pool along with a well-equipped gym. The **1606 Lounge Bar** is a comfortably sophisticated delight offering premium drinks, good snacks, and gorgeous sofas. The more formal **Palette Restaurant** has a good, dependable, seasonal menu and classy service. ♦ 11 Thurloe Pl (between Brompton Rd and Thurloe Sq). 208/819.9606. Tube: South Kensington. www.splendia.com

19 M.P. LEVENE LTD.

This much-respected silver shop is a favorite with the diplomatic community in London. It carries an impressive choice of old Sheffield plates and a beautiful selection of objects that are the epitome of the English country house. If you ask, the salespeople will patiently explain the markings on the English silver. ♦ M–Sa. 5 Thurloe Pl (between Brompton Rd and Thurloe Sq). 589.3755. Tube: South Kensington. www.mplevene.co.uk

20 BROMPTON ORATORY (LONDON ORATORY OF ST. PHILIP NERI)

Built between 1880 and 1893 by **Herbert Gribble** and officially named the **London Oratory of St. Philip Neri**, this was the first important Roman Catholic church to be constructed in London after the Reformation. Of the few beautiful Catholic churches in London, this one is sensational. The smell of incense greets you on entering the High Roman oratory, with domes and vaults, a domed nave, and Italian ornaments and statues. Included are Carrara marble statues of the apostles carved by Giuseppe Mazzuoli, a disciple of Bernini, which stood for 200 years in Siena Cathedral, and the altar in the **Lady Chapel**, constructed in 1693 by Francis Corbarelli and his sons Dominic and Antony, which came from Brescia, Italy. In ecclesiastical and liturgical terms, an oratory is a congregation of secular priests living together without vows. The fathers of the oratory are not monks and thus are not bound together by the three religious vows but by the internal bond of charity and the external bond of a common life and rule. St. Philip founded the Institute of the Oratory in Rome in 1575.

The Oratorian movement in England came about as the result of John Henry Newman, a Victorian whose conversion to Catholicism shook the Anglican establishment. It was Father Faber who bought the site for this building in 1853, despite protests from his fellows of its being in "a neighborhood of second-rate gentry and second-rate shops." Don't miss the triptych paintings of saints Thomas More and John Fisher (and their execution at Tyburn Gallows) by Rex Whistler in **St. Wilfred's Chapel**, and the dome, designed by G. Sherrin, with wooden ribs faced with 60 tons of lead. At 11AM on Sunday, the church is packed with nearly 2,000 people, both parishioners and visitors, for Latin High Mass with a full choir after the Italian manner. (Family Mass is at 10AM.) It also holds concerts. ♦ Daily. Mass: M–Sa, 7AM, 12:30PM (Latin Mass), 10AM, 6PM. Benediction: Tu, Th, 6:30PM. Family Mass: Su, 10AM. Latin High Mass: Su, 11AM. Brompton Rd (at Cottage Pl). 808.0900. Tube: South Kensington

21 BRASSERIE ST. QUENTIN

★★$$ Don't expect to find nouvelle cuisine; at this dining spot, classic food is in. The décor is traditional brasserie, with a long zinc bar, mirrors, brass, chandeliers, glass, and wait staff who dress and occasionally act the part. So it is not that the staff hates you; it's just part of the place's Gallic charm. The best value is the two-course set menu (available for lunch and early dinner) that offers such tasty items as fish soup, rump steak with horseradish sauce, and fillet of mackerel. ♦ French ♦ Daily, lunch and dinner. 243 Brompton Rd (at Egerton Gardens). 589.8005. Tube: South Kensington

22 JAMES HARDY AND CO.

Ring the bell first and you will be warmly welcomed by these silversmiths, whose company has been here since 1853 and still has the original storefront to prove it. The shop carries silver frames, jewelry, antiques, and silverware. They specialize in Georgian silverwork and design, and buy and sell all manner of lovely things. ♦ M–Sa. 235 Brompton Rd (between Egerton Terr and Egerton Gardens). 589.5050. Tube: South Kensington

23 CRANE KALMAN GALLERY

This gallery sells the works of established 20th-century British and European artists such as Calder, Léger, Degas, Dufy, Nicholson, Moore, and Sutherland, to name a distinguished few. Even if you're not planning to buy, stopping in here is like visiting a small museum. ♦ M–Sa. 178 Brompton Rd (between Montpelier St and Cheval Pl). 584.7566. Tube: Knightsbridge

FREE FOR ALL IN LONDON

London, one of the most exhilarating cities to visit, is also one of the most expensive. Pricey temptations abound, from queenly lodgings and luxurious restaurants to exquisite antiques and trendy boutiques. Still, there are plenty of great things to do in this city that don't cost a king's ransom. In fact, the following activities are free to royals and commoners alike.

- **Watch** the traditional spectacles of the Changing of the Guard at **Buckingham Palace** (in the morning) and the Ceremony of the Keys at the **Tower of London** (at night).

- **Listen** to the rabble rousers and soapbox pontificators who address crowds at **Speakers' Corner** in the northeastern corner of **Hyde Park** on Sunday mornings. It's a great bit of real-life theater.

- **Browse** one of the great museums in London, including the **British Museum**, the **National Gallery**, the **National Portrait Gallery**, **Sir John Soane's Museum**, the **Wallace Collection**, and the **Tate Gallery**. And several smaller museums also admit visitors gratis, such as the **Bank of England Museum**, the **National Postal Museum**, and the **Guildhall Clock Museum**.

- **Sit** in the public galleries at the **Houses of Parliament** and witness the intricate machinations of British politics.

- **Stroll** through the lovely small oasis of **St. James's Park**, with its peaceful, tree-bordered lake, flowers, ducks, geese, and even pelicans. From the footbridge spanning the lake, there's a fine view of **Buckingham Palace**.

- **Check out** original artworks and handicrafts (and meet their creators) on Sunday in front of the railings on **Bayswater Road**, near **Speaker's Corner**.

- **Attend** the peaceful 8AM communion service at **Westminster Abbey** and get a sense of this beautiful church sans crowds of tourists.

- **Listen** to sublime chamber or choral music at **St.-Martin-in-the-Fields** at lunchtime concerts held Mondays, Tuesdays, and Fridays at 1:05PM. (Call 0171/839.8362 to reserve seats.) Also, some of the small churches in the **City of London** present lunchtime concerts during the week. (For details, call or visit the **City of London Information Centre**, St. Paul's Churchyard, 0171/332.1456.)

- **Inspect** the usually valuable and frequently artistic possessions of other people by attending the pre-auction displays at **Bonham's**, **Christie's**, **Phillips**, and **Sotheby's**. It's like visiting a museum, art gallery, and antiques shop in one go.

- **Picnic** in **Hampstead Heath** on the verdant lawn of historic **Kenwood House**, which slopes down to a splendid ornamental lake. On most summer weekends, strains of symphonic works can be heard wafting from the concert bowl on the site. And before or after your alfresco meal, see the paintings of Gainsborough and Vermeer in the **Robert Adam**-designed 18th-century house.

24 BUNCH OF GRAPES

★$$ Once upon a time, glass partitions separated the six bars in this authentic Victorian pub, which has kept some of the screens, etched glass, and wood carving. Homemade pub grub, such as fish and chips and steak-and-Stilton pie, is served at lunch, and as snacks until 9:45PM, all accompanied by real ale. ♦ Pub ♦ Daily, lunch and snacks. 207 Brompton Rd (at Yeoman's Row). 589.4944. Tube: Knightsbridge

25 BONHAM'S

Founded in 1793, but not as internationally famous as Sotheby's or Christie's, this auction house is nevertheless well worth checking out for its oil paintings, watercolors, carpets, clocks, porcelain, furniture, wine, silver, and jewelry. The firm, which has a sixth-generation

Bonham on staff, normally has set days for certain items, so call ahead for sale details. When special events are held in London, such as the Chelsea Flower Show or the National Cat Show, the house usually holds a paintings auction to match. ♦ M, 9AM-7:30PM; Tu-F, 9AM-5PM; Su, 11AM-3PM. Montpelier St (between Brompton Rd and Cheval Pl). 393.3900. Tube: Knightsbridge

26 EMPORIO ARMANI

This Italian designer's store operates on the grand scale, with sections for every kind of clothing—men's, women's, and *bambini*, together with every accessory they'll need to go with the suits and sportswear. Should you not be worried about being able to fit into Giorgio's designs, you can tuck into caramelized scallops, crispy prosciutto and *mizuna* vine tomatoes, lobster raviolo,

Restaurants/Clubs: Red | Hotels: Purple | Shops: Orange | Outdoors/Parks: Green | Sights/Culture: Blue

wilted sorrel and crab butter, or a champagne risotto with asparagus and white truffle oil in the **Emporio's Café**. Finish with *crostata de mele* (honey fritters) if you dare! The café is licensed, and Italian beers and the decent short selection of wines are inviting. The place can get really hopping: The coffee machine makes up to 400 cups an hour! ♦ M–Sa. 191 Brompton Rd (between Beaufort Gardens and Beauchamp Pl). 823.8818. Tube: Knightsbridge. Also at 112a New Bond St (at Brook St). 491.8080. Tube: Bond St

Reject China Shops

26 REJECT CHINA SHOPS

The name is from the 1960s, when bargain hunters snapped up the seconds it stocked then. Now high-quality china is carried, as well as the best crystal. But with a policy of offering special promotions, the shops keep prices lower than comparable stores. You can still pick up some reasonably priced seconds, as well as oddly shaped novelty teapots and mugs that might make amusing souvenirs. ♦ M–Sa; Su, noon–6PM. 183 Brompton Rd (at Beauchamp Pl). Tube: Knightsbridge

27 BEAUCHAMP PLACE

Temptations are many on this Regency street (pronounced *Beech-um*), where you can easily spend a whole day or a whole week browsing in the boutiques and smart shops. You will find the best of British designer clothes, old maps and prints, antique silver, made-to-measure shoes, and lingerie fit for royalty. While struggling to resist the many covetables on the street (or not), you can eat delectable food in restaurants that are equally stylish and fun. ♦ Between Walton St and Brompton Rd. Tube: Knightsbridge

Beauchamp Place Shopping

BROMPTON ROAD

Left side	Right side
Italian menswear **Pellini Uomoi**	**Reject China Shops** *china*
	Simply Food *groceries*
hairdresser **Naim**	
womenswear **Ocelot**	**Rotana Lounge** *Lebanese restaurant*
jewelry **Dower & Hall**	**The Aga Shop** *kitchens*
hair/beauty **Joseph**	
	Piero Zuliani *Italian shirts/ties*
designerwear **Caroline Charles**	**Patara** *Thai restaurant*
womenswear **AND**	**The Caspian** *Persian restaurant*
maps **The Map House**	
	HB *beauty*
womenswear **Gallery 53**	**Laura B** *bridal/eveningwear*
jewelry/silverware **Hamilton & Inches**	
	Nozomi *Japanese restaurant*
womenswear **Ana Lucy**	**L'Adrene** *womenswear*
beauty **Groom**	
menswear/tailoring **Santarelli Santoria**	**Paddy Campbell** *designerwear*
Russian restaurant **Borscht'n'Tears**	
	Magaschoni *womenswear*
pub **The Beauchamp**	**San Lorenzo** *Italian restaurant*
pearl jewelry **Coleman Douglas Pearls**	
womenswear **Also**	**Maison Panache** *fashion/accessories*
Portuguese restaurant **Carabela**	**Junior Green** *hair/beauty*
Lebanese restaurant **Maroush**	**Jangminsook** *contemporary jewelry*
home accessories **Venetia Studium**	**Bruce Oldfield** *designerwear*
optician **36 Optician**	
womenswear **Kruszynska**	**McKenna & Co** *contemporary jewelry*
	Suzanne Neville *bridal/eveningwear*
Danish clothing **Haute Couture**	
restaurant/bar **Town House**	

(BEAUCHAMP PLACE runs down the center)

WALTON STREET

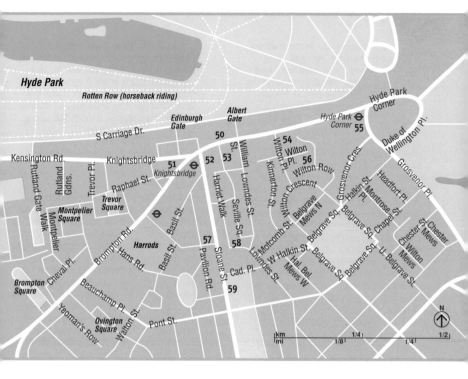

Hyde Park

Rotten Row (horseback riding)

28 SAN LORENZO

★$$$$ It is more photographed than Liz Taylor, and just as timeless. The rich, the famous, the noble, and those fans with the wherewithal to pay big prices for small portions are who tend to eat here. Acceptable modern Italian food is served up beautifully in exclusive surroundings. Go if you like to drop the name and remember the clientele long, long after you have forgiven the food and the feeling of being a second-class customer. ♦ Italian ♦ M–Sa, lunch and dinner. Reservations recommended. 22 Beauchamp Pl (between Walton St and Brompton Rd). 584.1074. Tube: Knightsbridge

29 MAP HOUSE

Antique, rare, and decorative maps, botanical prints, lithographs, and aquatints line every inch of this tiny town house and at honest prices. ♦ M–Sa. 54 Beauchamp Pl (between Walton St and Brompton Rd). 589.4325. Tube: Knightsbridge. www.themaphouse.com

29 CAROLINE CHARLES

This top English designer sells only the finest silks and linens. Charles's style is very English, but it's flavored with her own brand of sophisticated elegance. She creates

clothes that you will want to wear for a lifetime. ♦ M–Sa. 56–57 Beauchamp Pl (between Walton St and Brompton Rd). 589.5850. Tube: Knightsbridge.

30 ALSO

Designer **Eileen Coyne**'s work used to be on sale at **Harvey Nichols**, but now her semiprecious jewelry is available here, in her own shop. There is also designer womenswear (formal and daywear) from names like Kaneko, Carter Smith, and Zanda Ellis. A lovely little shop. ♦ M–Sa, 10AM–6PM. Beauchamp Pl. 584.0231. Tube: Knightbridge

31 HARRODS

In the past, the desire for greatness led to the creation of cathedrals and palaces. Today, it leads to department stores, and this one is Notre Dame, the Taj Mahal, and Blenheim Palace, all rolled into one. Even as the silk-scarfed ladies of England vow that it has gone downhill, the fact remains that this cathedral of consumerism is hard to beat.

Behind the solid and elegant Edwardian façade built between 1901 and 1905 by Stevens and Munt, 4,000 employees in 230 departments stand ready to fulfill almost every request. You can book a trip around the world, reserve theater and concert tickets, and get your lighter repaired, your

---

Restaurants/Clubs: Red | Hotels: Purple | Shops: Orange | Outdoors/Parks: Green | Sights/Culture: Blue

clothes dry-cleaned, your financial affairs expertly advised upon, your golf swing improved, and your nails polished. There's even a special long-hair department in the beauty salon. Two bagpipers in Harrods tartan play in the store almost every day.

Above all, don't miss the **Food Halls**, with their stunning mosaic friezes and fabulous displays of food. (The wet-fish display is a masterpiece!) Harrods began as a grocer's shop, and even now their food hampers are musts at posh picnic events like the Henley regatta and Wimbledon, and as Christmas presents (when 300,000 of them are sold). If you're afraid this palace of temptation will make you forget the limitations of your bank balance, plan to visit London just after New Year's Day, when Harrods' month-long January sale begins. The most famous shopping event of the year, it is a true test of consumer stamina, but those who are tenacious and strong will be rewarded with real bargains.

The store does have some quirks. Its dress code states that doormen will not admit customers "who wear ripped jeans, cropped tops, high-cut athletic shorts, or dirty and unkempt clothes. Men are not allowed to wear cycling shorts and footwear must be worn at all times." ♦ 87-135 Brompton Rd (between Hans Crescent and Hans Rd). 730.1234; theater tickets, 255.6666. Tube: Knightsbridge

Within Harrods:

Okay, hold onto your calorie counters, because there are no fewer than 25 dining options within Harrods—and not one of them is less than worth a visit.

On the **Lower Ground Floor** is the Green Man Pub and an excellent tapas bar. On the **Ground Floor** you will find the Pizzeria (with a traditional wood-fired oven and the offer of a Neapolitan breakfast), a Krispy Kreme dough-nuts franchise, Morelli's Gelato traditional ice cream (who will make your own bespoke flavor in 24 hours dead), and the Rotisserie. If your tastes are a little more genteel, you might try the Ladurée tearoom (complete with their world-famous macaroons), the Sushi Bar, the Sea Grill (choose your fish from the fish counter and have it cooked to order!), the Bar Charcuterie, Café Espresso, and (of course) the Champagne and Oyster Bar.

The First Floor offers the Dress Circle Restaurant (with a menu of fresh salads and baked potatoes) and the Bagel Factory.

The Second Floor houses Harrods Chocolate Bar (you'll feel like Charlie in the Chocolate Factory), The Harry Morgan Deli, and Ishbilia, a terrific mezze place where all the meat is special.

On the **Third Floor** is the Harrods Creperie and Café Punch (decorated accordingly!).

The **Fourth Floor** is where you'll find Mo's Diner (good burgers and shakes) and Planet Harrods (perfect for families with the very youngest shoppers in tow. It even does baby food.). For real grownups, there is also the Terrace Bar (great for breakfast and afternoon tea) and The Georgian, Harrods fine dining restaurant. And it is very fine.

Finally, the **Fifth Floor** has the East Dulwich Deli and the Illy Espresso Bar.

32 L'HÔTEL

$$$ This small, friendly hotel is really a small country inn—the kind you never seem to find anymore. There are only 11 rooms, so you have to book well in advance to enjoy the Frette linen and Nina Campbell décor, all at reasonable prices. For the lone traveler, this is one of the best places to feel at home. For non-loners, there is a babysitting service available. A continental breakfast is included in the price. The hotel's basement bar/restaurant—**Le Metro**—does a decent British menu. ♦ 28 Basil St (between Hans Crescent and Hooper's Ct). 589.6286; fax 823.7826. Tube: Knightsbridge

32 CAPITAL HOTEL

$$$$ Scotsman David Levin is a first-class hotelier, and when he decided to open his own establishment, he went about creating the very best. He opened the Capital 35 years ago, and it is still family run. There are 49 rooms including 8 suites, 7 deluxe doubles, and a newly refurbished twin bedroom suite. All have handmade mattresses, Egyptian linen sheets, marble bathrooms, power showers, gorgeous Molton Brown toiletries, and even an umbrella for use during your stay (well, you are in England now). The hotel is Wi-Fi–enabled and has a laundry and pressing service, a babysitting service, personal shoppers in Harrods and Harvey Nichols, a DVD library, and 24-hour room service. ♦ 22 Basil St (between Hans Crescent and Hooper's Ct). 589.5171. Tube: Knightsbridge. www.capitalhotel.co.uk

Within the Capital Hotel:

CAPITAL RESTAURANT

★★★$$$ This two-Michelin-star restaurant is something of a foodie legend in its own lunchtime. The regularly changing menu is the creation of Eric Chavot, himself something of a legend. He offers a stunningly good-value, two-course special lunch menu. On that, the dinner menu, or the degustation menu, you might start with foie gras and passion fruit or home-cured treacle salmon with deep-fried soft-shell crab and finish with cumin and Ivoire jelly, crunchy yogurt and mango sorbet, peanut and salt caramel Moelleux, or Jivara mousse with banana and passion fruit sorbet. I know. Mmmm! Should you be in Knightsbridge on an afternoon, there are many, many worse things to do than to fetch up at the Capital, settle in the lounge, and indulge in a really good English afternoon tea. Okay, a glass of Champagne is an optional extra. Talking of which, the wine list draws oenophiles from near and far, and none has ever regretted being drawn. The Capital even has its own vineyard in the Loire Valley! ♦ Modern French ♦ Daily, lunch and dinner. Reservations recommended. 589.5171

33 TEXAS LONE STAR

★★$ It's loud and raucous, but the ribs are cooked right and the accompanying cocktails are authentic and cheap (for London, anyway). If you get a hankering for enchiladas and chimichangas along with live country-and-western music, this is your place. ♦ Tex-Mex ♦ Daily, lunch and dinner. 154 Gloucester Rd (between Courtfield Rd and Harrington Gardens). 370.5625. Tube: Gloucester Road

34 DAQUISE

★$$ Regular visitors to the **V&A** often stop by this Polish café for lemon tea and apple strudel. The quality of the food varies and the surroundings are dingy, but the atmosphere's the thing. Nothing has changed since World War II: not the look of the Polish waitresses, nor the menu of *golabki* (stuffed cabbage), *kasza* (boiled buckwheat), and *zrazy* (beef rolls stuffed with cucumber, bacon, and mushrooms). Polish émigrés meet here for morning coffee, lunch, afternoon tea, or dinner. ♦ Polish ♦ Daily, lunch and dinner. 20 Thurloe St (between Thurloe Sq and Cromwell Pl). 589.6117. Tube: South Kensington

35 MONOGRAMMED LINEN SHOP

This is where the cognoscenti come to buy monogrammed Irish linen sheets, duvet covers, dressing gowns, and handkerchiefs. If you like, all the items can be tastefully embroidered with your initials. ♦ M-Sa. 168 Walton St (between Glynde Mews and Draycott Ave). 589.4033. Tube: South Kensington

36 DRAGONS

This enchanting shop is for grownups who want to give their youngsters the childhood they never had. The exquisite, hand-painted children's furniture is made for royal children and other fortunate little ones; there are children's fabrics, tiny seats, and even some toys (to keep the kiddies amused while their

parents browse). ♦ M-Sa. 23 Walton St (at Hasker St). 589.3795. Tube: South Kensington

36 TAPISSERIE

This well-established shop sells hand-painted canvases (for making tapestries), all designed exclusively for sale here. You can also commission or even design your own clutch or tote bag. ♦ M-Sa. 54 Walton St (between Glynde Mews and Ovington Square). 581.2715. Tube: South Kensington

37 LA BRASSERIE

★★$$ A permanent London fixture, this restaurant has been here for 25 years and looks just like the type of brasserie you'd expect to find in Paris, right down to the imported wait staff. In addition to the substantial main menu, there is a weekly changing regional menu. It's a great place for noshing and watching London's glamorous residents gird their loins for an onslaught on **Harrods** and **Beauchamp Place**. The service is efficient even when the place gets busy. ♦ French ♦ Daily, breakfast, lunch, and dinner. 272 Brompton Rd (between Pelham St and South Terr). 581.3089. Tube: South Kensington

38 BETTY JACKSON

For 2 decades, this British designer has been producing understated, stylish, yet classic clothes that suit women who like to feel comfortable. Her clothes include dresses, coats, separates, and knitwear at midrange prices. ♦ M-Sa. 311 Brompton Rd (between Draycott Ave and Egerton Crescent). 589.7884. Tube: South Kensington

39 ALASTAIR LOCKHART

Fans of luxurious writing paper love this special boutique that stocks Crane's 100% cotton paper in a wide spectrum of colors. The paper can be imprinted to your specifications, as can visiting cards, invitations, and announcements. ♦ M-Sa. 97 Walton St (between Draycott Ave and First St). 581.8289. Tube: South Kensington

---

Restaurants/Clubs: Red | **Hotels: Purple** | **Shops: Orange** | **Outdoors/Parks: Green** | Sights/Culture: Blue

40 JOE'S

★★$$$ Owned by Joseph Ettedgui (of **Joseph** shops fame), this remains a style-conscious restaurant following a major renovation from minimalist black and white to trendy beige and brown. Try the smoked goat cheese–and–apple tart with fruit relish and the blackened cod with prawn and chili sticky rice. ♦ Modern British ♦ M–F, lunch and dinner; Sa, late breakfast, lunch, and dinner; Su, late breakfast and brunch. 126 Draycott Ave (at Walton St). 225.2217. Tube: South Kensington

41 WALTON STREET

Only the elegant window displays on the rather bare façades of the buildings at the lower end of the street reveal the array of goods inside. Restaurants such as **Ma Cuisine** and **San Martino** have loyal followings, and the **Enterprise**, once a pub and now a trendy restaurant, is a **Walton Street** landmark. New shops spring up along the street to join the old favorites. As you wander toward Beauchamp Place, the street's domestic side becomes apparent. The shops are less frequent, turning into noble, neatly formed town houses guarded by iron gates at the more affluent end of the street. ♦ Between Draycott Ave and Beauchamp Pl. Tube: South Kensington

41 VAN PETERSON

A bijou shop on a bijou street, it sells charming, elegant jewelry, created by a husband-and-wife team. It is all of fine quality and not overly expensive. ♦ M–Sa, 10AM–6PM; Su, noon–5PM. 194–196 Walton St (between Draycott Ave and First St). 584.1101. Tube: South Kensington

42 JOSEPH

Joseph Ettedgui's two-floor department store contains a selection of everything that is designer chic in clothing: It sells his own collection and those of other designers for women. ♦ M–Sa, Su, 1PM–6PM. 77 Fulham Rd (at Sloane Ave). 823.9500. Tube: South Kensington. A smaller boutique on the same stretch of road sells more exclusive Joseph clothes: 16 Sloane St. 235.7541. Tube: Knightsbridge. Also at 23 Old Bond St (between Piccadilly and Burlington Gardens). 629.3713. Tube: Piccadilly Circus. His new menswear store is at 74 Sloane Ave. 591.0808. Tube: South Kensington

43 BIBENDUM

★★$$$ This restaurant is set in a spectacular Art Deco building once owned by the Michelin Tire Company, whose unlikely mascot is Bibendum, a bespectacled chap made entirely of white tires. The image of "the Michelin Man" can be seen everywhere you look in the large dining room—etched into the glasses and plates, on two large stained-glass windows, and in prints and posters on the walls. It was opened in 1987 by Sir Terence Conran, Paul Hamlyn, and founding chef Simon Hopkinson and opened up a whole new smart world of fine dining, Modern British–style. Now the Modern British has developed into a more European thing with *escargots de Bourgogne* and grilled onglet with baby turnips and Bordelaise sauce on offer. Although you could still tuck into deep-fried haddock with chips and English strawberries with Jersey cream. The wine list is a prize-winner, so take your reading glasses if you need them—there's lots of small print. ♦ Modern European ♦ Restaurant: daily, lunch and dinner. Oyster bar: daily, lunch and dinner. Reservations required in the restaurant. Michelin House, 81 Fulham Rd (at Sloane Ave). 581.5817. Tube: South Kensington

Within Bibendum:

BIBENDUM OYSTER BAR

★★$$ On the ground floor of the building, in a lovely Art Deco tiled room, is the Oyster Bar. There are always several types of oysters to choose from (natives in season, of course), platters of crab and prawns, langoustines and mussels, and towering altars of *plateaux de fruits de mer* (seafood platter). The wine list is excellent. ♦ Daily, noon–11PM. 589.1480

BIBENDUM COFFEE BAR

The coffee bar is in the forecourt of the building and is a great place to drink very good coffee, eat very good pastries, and watch the Kensington world go by. It is quite a smart place to be seen! The café also does decent hot salt beef sandwiches, panini, and salads. ♦ Daily, 8:30AM–6PM. 590.1189

CRUSTACEA VAN

This shop features top-quality crustaceans and caviar—everything from freshly picked white crabmeat through scallops, shrimp, whelks, and, of course, oysters. They also have a good range of smoked fish, and every Saturday morning there is a lobster sale! ♦ Tu–F, 9AM–5PM. 589.0864

43 THE CONRAN SHOP

Above ground and to the side of **Bibendum** is this emporium, Sir Terence Conran's personal apotheosis. A legend in his lifetime, Conran has been bringing style to London since the 1960s. This is his flagship and his original store, opened in 1987. You can buy everything here, from leather-encased pencil sharpeners to bedspreads and furniture.

♦ Daily. 81 Fulham Rd (at Sloane Ave). 589.7401. Tube: South Kensington

44 PELLICANO

★★$$ Interesting and healthy Italian food in nicely relaxing surroundings. There's always a risotto of the day, and the unusual *culurgiones con Pecorino, patate, e menta* is a Sardinian kind of ravioli with Pecorino cheese, potatoes, and mint. Mains include wild sea bass with artichokes and a roasted spiced baby chicken. ♦ Daily, lunch and dinner. 19-21 Elystan St. 589.3718. Tube: South Kensington

45 OZEN

★★$$$ This Japanese restaurant situated in the heart of Chelsea offers authentic cuisine at a reasonable price. The main dining area is spacious, and there is also a comfortable sushi bar serving all the best-loved sushis plus less usual sushis like flying fish roe. Lunch menus are reasonable and offer a choice of set meals (which come with soup, rice, salad, and fruit). The à la carte menu offers pot dishes such as *shabu shabu* (thin slices of beef presented like a Japanese fondue with assorted vegetables prepared at your table) and sukiyaki. There is also salmon grilled with miso paste and the renowned black cod grilled with teriyaki sauce. There is an interesting selection of vinegar relish salads (including an assorted seaweed salad and a salad of sliced eel with seaweed and cucumber). ♦ M, dinner; Tu-Su, lunch and dinner. Chelsea Cloisters. 85 Sloane Ave (between Makins St and Ixworth Pl). 589.1781. Tube: South Kensington

46 NUMBER 16

$$ Even though the Victorians did everything in the grand manner, when four Victorian houses are smacked together it doesn't neces-sarily mean that the resulting hotel is large or spacious. This elegant but somewhat cramped 42-room property is a case in point. But nostalgia buffs will forgive the occasional tiny guest room because, from the pretty morning room onward, all are beautifully decorated in fresh, contemporary English style and have the kind of modern conveniences that would put many major hotels to shame. The hotel has valet service, 24-hour room service, and a gorgeous conservatory and garden. It offers much more of a wonderful London experience than many of its bigger brethren. ♦ 16 Sumner Pl (between Fulham Rd and Onslow Sq). 589.5232; fax 584.8615. Tube: South Kensington. www.firmdale.com

47 BUTLER & WILSON

The late Princess Diana sometimes used to nip into this shop for a little bauble to match a designer ensemble. It sells fake antique and gemstone jewelry to, well, everyone, *dahling* (everyone who counts, that is). The range of costume jewelry is also sold at **Harrods**. ♦ M-Sa, Su, noon–6PM. 189 Fulham Rd (between Stewart's Grove and Sydney St). 352.3045. Tube: South Kensington. Also at 20 S Molton St (between Brook and Davies Sts). 409.2955. Tube: Bond St

48 THEO FENNELL

The owner is both a silversmith and a jeweler who enjoys fashioning novelty souvenir miniatures such as a London phone booth or mailbox. Well known as the unstuffy alternative to the likes of Cartier and Garrard, he works from his new five-story flagship store. He also will custom-design a piece of jewelry to your specifications. Some of his designs are for sale at **Harrods**. ♦ M-Sa. 169 Fulham Rd (between Bury Walk and Pond Pl). 591.5000. Tube: South Kensington

49 TOM AIKENS

★★★★$$$$ A little like Gordon Ramsay before he became the celebrity chef he always denies he is, Tom Aikens has such passion, such intensity in his cooking, and you can taste it in every mouthful you eat. This is a great place to dine. It manages to be both perfectly chic and wonderfully welcoming. The staff are delightfully friendly, the sommelier is your instant and genuine new best friend, and there is not a more obliging Michelin-starred chef cooking today. Everything from the warm breads to the gorgeous petit fours is just perfect. The tasting menu here must make God glad he thought to add taste buds when he was designing man. Broad-bean gazpacho comes with ricotta gnocchi and broad-bean shoots; the tenderest, tastiest piglet is in a lasagna of pork; pigeon is accompanied by red pepper, honey-roasted eggplant, and spiced couscous; and roasted sea bass has cucumber ravioli on the side. And Tom's roasted pineapple with sesame is the most fabulous serving suggestion for that fruit since Carmen Miranda. ♦ French ♦ M-F, lunch and dinner. 43 Elystan St. 584.2003. Tube: Sloane Square. www.tomaikens.co.uk

50 MANDARIN ORIENTAL HYDE PARK HOTEL

$$$$ All five of the stars this place has are twinkling like diamonds. There is nothing understated or low-key about the luxury here. The splendor is Edwardian: marble entrance hall, gilded and molded ceilings, and Persian carpets the size of cricket fields.

Restaurants/Clubs: Red | Hotels: Purple | Shops: Orange | Outdoors/Parks: Green | Sights/Culture: Blue

Guests have included Winston Churchill and Mohandas Gandhi, for whom a goat was milked each day. The hotel keeps adding luxury refurbishments with no expense spared. There are 200 rooms with queen- or king-size beds, and prices (and to some extent, size) change depending on whether your room has a view over the inner courtyard, Knightsbridge, or Hyde Park. There is Frette cotton and Irish linen, aromatherapy bath products, a fully stocked minibar, personalized wake-up calls, and much more. The 29 Junior Suites generally have views over Knightsbridge, and the 25 full suites—which come in several stages of fabulous, from Superior through Deluxe, Grand, Executive, and Presidential to Royal—mainly have Hyde Park outside the windows. The hotel's renowned spa, which has just been voted Condé Nast's Favorite Hotel Spa, boasts a state-of-the-art gymnasium and offers shiatsu, ayurveda, reflexology, and Thai massage. There are also several ESPA treatments exclusive to the Mandarin Oriental. Madonna has stayed here. So have the three famous operatic tenors: Pavarotti, Domingo, and Carreras. ♦ 66 Knightsbridge (between Albert and Edinburgh Gates). 235.2000, 800/526.6566 in the US; fax 201.3619. Tube: Knightsbridge

Within the Mandarin Oriental Hyde Park Hotel:

THE SPA

Multi-award–winning and reckoned to be one of the finest spa facilities in the country, it has eight treatment rooms, a massive menu of treatments to aid both health and beauty, the Amethyst Crystal Steam Room, the Zen Colour Therapy Relaxation Room, and the Vitality Pool. You could spend a week there! ♦ Daily, 7AM-10PM. 838.9888

FOLIAGE

★★★$$$ This restaurant is everything you dream of—if you happen to dream about five-star hotel restaurants. The interior was designed by Adam Tihany with butterscotch leather upholstery, rosewood paneling, and giant glass wall double panels pressing 24,000 white silk leaves between them, which are lit different colors in different seasons. Every morning one of the waiting staff picks leaves from the park and places them under the restaurant's specially commissioned glass plates. When Tihany redesigned the restaurant, he also raised the restaurant floor so that every diner would have a view of the park. Chef Chris Staines is no slouch either—he serves Dover sole with burnt butter, cockles, and dried grapes; beef with smoked onion, oxtail, and foie gras cream; and desserts that always have a delicious twist

like coffee syrup or sea salt caramel. The wine list is worth saving up for! ♦ Continental ♦ Daily, lunch and dinner. 235.2000

THE PARK

★★$$ The hotel's other restaurant also has views over Hyde Park, Italian linen, and bespoke English china, and everything including the furniture is again designed by New Yorker Adam Tihany. Chef Chris Tombling's menu has lots of oriental influences and offers healthy and veggie options. His Dover sole is wok-fried with Thai asparagus, shiitake mushrooms, bok choi, and black bean sauce, and the black Alaskan cod is marinated in miso, sake, and mirin with Japanese ginger, lemon, and miso sauce. ♦ Daily, 7AM-11PM. 235.2000

THE MANDARIN BAR

Surrounded by the hotel's not-unimpressive wine celler in temperature-controlled glass-walled racks, this is a buzzy, busy bar frequented by Knightsbridge locals. You can choose from 23 vodkas, 42 whiskeys, and accomplished, but annihilating, cocktails. The superb range of martinis can be tried in a little three-glass taster rack—the Boca Raton features mint and black currant and the Vong hits you with mango and lychee liqueur with blue curaçao. The bar serves some of the tastiest bar nibbles in the city and has great live jazz. ♦ M–Sa; Su, noon–10:30PM

51 MR. CHOW

★★★$$$ The restaurant's popularity dates back to 1968, when owner Michael Chow decided to combine the style and exuberance of an Italian restaurant with the finest Chinese cooking. The décor is chrome and dimmed glass, and the inventive menu is explained in down-to-earth language. Try the velvet chicken or specialty noodles. ♦ Chinese ♦ Daily, lunch and dinner. Reservations recommended. 151 Knightsbridge (between Brompton Rd and Knightsbridge Green). 589.7347. Tube: Knightsbridge

52 HARVEY NICHOLS

This iconic temple to all things fashionable—from lipsticks to handbags to evening gowns to furniture to food—now has branches in Edinburgh, Manchester, Birmingham, Leeds, and Dublin. But the big mama store is still where it has been since the 1880s. It's eight floors of fabulous. If it's in *Vogue*—or even if it is just in vogue—it will be in Harvey Nicks. The store's own label fashions, food, and homeware are terrific. And make great gifts for those who like a label. Even the Food Hall is currently announcing its new Daylesford Organic (the ultra-chicest of organic merchandising for the sophisticated discerning diner) concession as if it were the new Armani collection. ♦ M-Sa, 10AM-8PM; Su, noon-6PM. 109 Knightsbridge (at Sloane St). 235.5000.Tube: Knightsbridge. www.harveynichols.com

Within Harvey Nichols:

FIFTH FLOOR BAR

The new interior is—get this!—"an ode to the early 20th Century Constructivist Art Movement." Big, bold, sharp-angled murals are paired with leather banquettes, and the layout is very much as before. One new addition is the Toasting Room, a red pod that holds eight people who want to indulge in that great Russian pastime of vodka toasting. The new drinks menu has been created by Nick Strangeway and features new ways with old classic cocktails, as well as the Fifth Floor's Champagne menu and a new range of infused Stolichnaya vodkas. There is also a decent bar food menu (daily, noon-4PM) and the usual nibbles. A great place to take the weight off your carrier bags! ♦ M, Tu, 11AM-11PM; W-Sa, 11AM-1PM; Su, noon-6PM. 235.5250

5TH FLOOR CAFÉ

★$$ Designed by Wickham and Associates, the café is marvelously airy, being walled in glass and opening onto a terrace that, when the weather allows, seats 40 lucky diners. The menu, offered from an open servery, is overseen by executive chef Helena Puolakka, and there is a very popular dinner set menu. ♦ 823.1839

5TH FLOOR RESTAURANT

★★$$ The restaurant has not only a new, relaxed blue color scheme but also a new executive chef in Jonas Karlsson. He offers a lunch menu, a dinner menu, a market menu, and a tasting menu (with each dish partnered by a wine chosen by the sommelier). The food is stout stuff! Lunch can start with sweet corn soup with golden raisin and sweetcorn parcels, and dinner with caramelized veal sweetbreads. The smaller market menu offers slow-cooked pork cheeks with basmati and hazelnut rice and truffle sauce. The wine list is a thing of great intelligence, and the house wines are a very good value. ♦ Modern British ♦ M-Sa, lunch and dinner; Su, lunch. Reservations recommended. 235.5250

53 SHERATON PARK TOWER

$$$$ You get what you pay for here, and you get a lot. All guest rooms are equipped with high-speed Internet—both wired and wireless. There is duck down bedding and marble bathrooms, bathrobes, slippers, and fresh flowers, personalized wake-up calls, and a fully stocked minibar. The hotel even offers spa and beauty treatments in your room as well as in its own great spa/gymnasium. Avail yourself of one of the new butler rooms and you get your own dedicated staff member as well. Views are over the city or over the park—all pretty mind-blowing, and the higher up you go, the blowier it gets! ♦ 101 Knightsbridge (at William St). 235.8050, 800/334.8484; fax 235.8231. Tube: Knightsbridge

Within the Sheraton Park Tower:

RESTAURANT 101

★★$$$ The 101 has won Harden's London's Best Fish Restaurant award for the last five years, so it must be doing something right. Its glorious views and conservatory-like ceiling help, as does the cooking of Breton chef Pascal Proyart. He offers signature dishes like sea bass baked in Brittany sea salt and zingy specials like king crab with sweet ginger chili and spiced cuttlefish tagliatelle. ♦ Continental ♦ Daily, breakfast, lunch, and dinner. 235.6067

THE TERRACE

★★$$ Open May through September, this is a gorgeous place for light meals and snacks. ♦ Daily

54 BERKELEY

$$$$ The hotel is situated on what was once the parade ground of the **Barracks of the First Regiment of Foot Guards**, later renamed the Grenadiers. Distinguished architect **Brian O'Rourke** designed the new hotel—moved from its original location in Berkeley Street—and it opened in 1972. No two of the 214 rooms and 65 suites are alike—except that they all have two direct-dial phone lines, US plugs, Internet modems, Floris toiletries and luxury bathrobes and slippers, twice-daily maid service, baby-sitting on request, an optional Japanese breakfast on room service, children's books and games on request, and even picnics made up for you should you fancy a day in the park. Kosher menus are available. A whole swatch of designers, such as John Stefanides, Tessa Kennedy, and Alexandra Champalimaud, have created the different looks. There is also a rooftop swimming pool (with retractable roof—this is England) and a marvelous health club and spa offering LaStone and Crystal Point therapies. Jogging maps will guide your sneakers, shopping maps will guide your credit card, and if you really have no sense of direction, the hotel will provide you with a chauffeur-driven limo. ♦ Wilton Place (between Wilton Crescent and Knightsbridge). 235.6000; fax 235.4330. www.savoygroup.com

Within the Berkeley:

THE CARAMEL ROOM

Created by New York designer Alexandra Champalimaud with chocolate-colored walls and faux crocodile fabrics and situated in the former lobby lounge, the room offers a morning menu incorporating a range of Illy gourmet coffees and an entire menu of miniature doughnuts with fillings from red fruit to Valrhona chocolate. ♦ Daily.

THE BLUE BAR

A lovely little bar designed by the renowned David Collins. Cherubic friezes look down on faux ostrich-leather stools and a black crocodile-print floor. Favorite cocktails are the Berkeley Champagne Cocktail, the Ginger Cosmopolitan, and the Lutyens Gimlet. For those who don't like to mix, there is a choice of over 50 premium whiskeys. There is also a bar menu of savory and sweet tapas-style dishes. ♦ Daily

PETRUS

★★★★$$$ Two Michelin stars and a yearly clutch of awards keep this place at the top of the "most wanted" tables in London. The design is by David Collins and the menu by Marcus Waring. And what a menu! Native Scottish lobster comes poached with pickled vegetables, tomato, and black pepper jelly, pigeon is poached and roasted with walnut gnocchi, kohlrabi, and apple, and one taste of the buffalo ricotta tortellini with confit egg yolk, creamed spinach, and truffle butter could turn you vegetarian! The wine list—as you might expect from the name of the restaurant—is fabulous. ♦ Daily. 235.1200

GORDON RAMSAY'S BOXWOOD CAFÉ

★★$$ Having spent time in New York researching café dining, Ramsay opened his most relaxed restaurant yet. Like most Ramsay restaurants now, it has his name above the door but not the man in the kitchen. That man here is Stuart Gilles. What the restaurant offers is not *quite* New York dining and definitely not New York ambience or service.

"You ask, what was that song they sang at the opening—that's 'God Save the King.' You thought it was 'Sweet Land of Liberty'? So it is. You Yankees took it from us and put new words to it. As a matter of fact we took it from the Ancient Britons—they had it, England-may-go-to-hell—and the English liked it so much they took it over and made it 'God Save the King.'"
—Stephen Leacock,
Welcome to a Visiting American

Starters include fried oysters with fennel and lemon, chilled melon soup with Parma ham and basil oil, and salad with spider crab, squid, and borlotti beans. There is an already-famous lobster roll with Thousand Island dressing and a luxury veal and foie gras burger. Be aware that Gordon's kitchen takes it upon itself to salt your fries before serving them, thus taking away that pesky "choice" thing you get in most restaurants as to whether you want salt or not. Desserts include sugared doughnuts cooked to order and served with yogurt ice cream and a poppyseed knickerbocker glory. Good news for light or solo drinkers is that there is a genuinely good choice of wines by the glass. ♦ Daily, breakfast, lunch, and dinner. 235.1010

55 LANESBOROUGH

$$$$ Overlooking the hurly-burly traffic chaos of **Hyde Park Corner**, this property was originally a hospital built in the classical/Greek Revival style of Portland stone in 1829. Now it's a welcoming, self-indulgent place to stay where every detail has been thoughtfully considered. When billionaire Texan Caroline Rose Hunt acquired the property, she flew in the face of prudence by spending a reputed $1.7 million on each of the 49 guest rooms and 46 suites—for a total of $161.5 million—despite the recession at the time. Well, the *Times* heralded the result as "a sumptuous temple of luxury," and a stunning landmark was transformed. Now the Lanesborough is a St. Regis Hotel. Inside are polished marble floors and neo-Georgian furnishings; even the windows are triple-glazed against traffic noise. There is 24-hour butler service for all rooms on a complimentary basis, so you don't even have to unpack yourself (or iron the wrinkles from your clothes). You'll find fresh fruit, confectionary, and mineral water on your arrival, and these are replenished each day. The Lanesborough even offers complimentary tea of coffee with your wake-up call. The hotel has a 24-hour business center at guests' disposal and an excellent gym and spa. ♦ Hyde Park Corner (at Knightsbridge). 259.5599, 800/999.1828; fax 259.5606. Tube: Hyde Park Corner

Within the Lanesborough:

CONSERVATORY

★★$$$ The setting is perfect for hot summer nights, with a high glass roof, giant potted palms, candlelight, and piano music setting a serene mood as you enjoy your meal. Chef Paul Gaylor's imaginative dishes include turbot roasted on the bone with rosemary *jus* or spice-roasted duckling with ginger and star anise. Good vegetarian choices include basil gnocchi with seasonal green vegetables. There is live music Monday through Thursday and jazz at Sunday lunch; on Friday and Saturday, a full band provides the sound for dancing. The Conservatory is a winner of the Top London Afternoon Tea Award, so if you fancy trying this particularly English of dining experiences, this is a lovely place to do it. Even (or maybe especially) when all is gray and rain-lashed outside, it is a wonderful place to eat. ♦ International ♦ Daily, breakfast, lunch, afternoon tea, and dinner. Jacket required at dinner. 259.5599

The Library Bar and Withdrawing Room

These are lovely places to sit and drink—even if it is only coffee, which here is served impressively strong and flavorful. If you are after something even more powerful, the Library Bar has an enviable range of the finest premium spirits and a vast wine list. Many bins are available by the glass, including Champagnes. The Library has, sadly, bidden farewell to the legendary Salvatore Calabrese, but many of his team are still there and the cocktails on the generous list are still expertly mixed. The nibbles served with the drinks are top notch. The Withdrawing Room is all Georgian upholstery, dark wood furniture, and an open fire. The Library itself is like something out of a Sherlock Holmes movie—hugely atmospheric, and one of the nicest hotel bars in the city.

56 Grenadier

★★★$$$ The atmosphere of this pub is as old and military as in the days when it was the officers' mess for the Duke of Wellington's soldiers, complete with a ghost of an officer who was beaten to death for cheating at cards. Service in either the à la carte restaurant or, more simply, in the bar provides pub fare in the finest British tradition. But if at the end of a long day spent in South Kensington and Knightsbridge all you want is a bitter, you can count on the best. ♦ British ♦ Daily, lunch and dinner. Reservations recommended. 18 Wilton Row (off Old Barrack Yd). 235.3074. Tube: Hyde Park Corner

57 Millennium Hotel

$$ This four-star hotel is part of a small chain of four Millennium Hotels in London. They are chic, modern, sophisticated hotels, perfect if you don't mind a bit of high-end, efficient 21st-century international blandness. There are 222 rooms, each with all that comes with four stars. There is a same-day laundry and dry cleaning service, and car rentals; theater bookings will be taken care of, room service is 24 hours, and the hotel has its own bureau de change. Knightsbridge Tube Station, Harrods, and Harvey Nichols are all just five minutes away. ♦ 17-25 Sloane St. 235.4377. Tube: Knightsbridge

Within the Millennium Hotel:

Mju Bar

This very chic, very contemporary bar serves rather good cocktails. ♦ M-Sa, 3PM-11PM

Mju Restaurant

Serves Pacific Rim cuisine, including a nicely varied buffet breakfast. ♦ Breakfast, 7AM-10:30AM; lunch, noon-2:30PM; dinner, 6PM-10:30PM

Pavilion Lounge

Open for light meals and drinks. ♦ Breakfast, 8AM-11AM; open all day

58 Zafferano

★★★$$$ Give body and soul a treat and take them to Italy for the evening—in Chelsea. This much-awarded restaurant no longer has the legendary Giorgio Locatelli in the kitchen, but it is still a wonderful place to eat. Seared tuna is served in a salad with blood orange, fennel, and mint; the restaurant's famous *malfatti di patate* (big ravioli made with potato) come with morel mushrooms; roast duck is accompanied by *mostarda di frutta*, and panna cotta has rhubarb and basil sugar sharing its plate. Cheeses are a tribute to their makers in Italy, and the wine list is lush and long. Surroundings are conducive to long lunches and lazy dinners. The cellar vault was recently turned into a venue for private dining (up to 20 guests), but, better still, on weekends it is transformed into a children's room with cartoons, movies, pizza, and just about anything that goes toward making kiddie heaven. So mom and dad can have grown-up heaven upstairs! Give yourself a treat. ♦ Daily, lunch and dinner. 15 Lowndes St. 235.5800. Tube: Knightsbridge. www.zafferanorestaurant.com

59 Lulu Guinness

Yes, of *the* Guinnesses. They don't make just beer, you know. Lulu is a designer with exquisite, feminine flair. She makes fabulously quirky handbags, designed with a sense of humor . . . tubs of flowers are very in this season. The shop displays the bags in technicolor spotlights. The famous arms from which her bags regularly hang include those of Madonna, Liz Hurley, and Jerry Hall. ♦ M-Sa, 10AM-6PM. 3 Ellis St SW1. 823.4828. Tube: Knightsbridge. www.luluguinness.com

---

Restaurants/Clubs: Red | Hotels: Purple | Shops: Orange | Outdoors/Parks: Green | Sights/Culture: Blue

MARYLEBONE/CAMDEN TOWN

Putting Marylebone and Camden together is a little like putting Julie Andrews and Courtney Love on the same album. Margaret Harley, daughter of Edward Harley, the Earl of Oxford, originally inherited the land currently known as Marylebone, which has frequently been owned by and passed on to women. J.M.W. Turner and Allan Ramsay were just two of the artists who exercised their talents on **Harley Street**, and Elizabeth Barrett scribbled in secret while waiting for her true love, Robert Browning, to whisk her away from nearby **Wimpole Street**. Today, enigmatic Marylebone displays a doppelgänger personality. On the one hand, it's cultured and

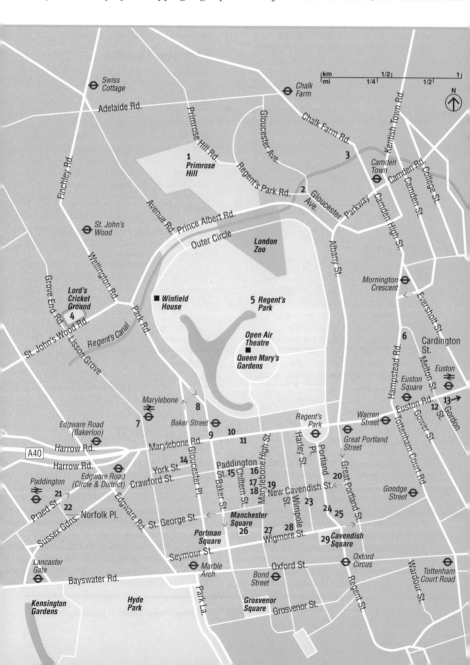

refined: You can stroll through the royal lawns at **Regent's Park**, take in Shakespeare at the **Open Air Theatre**, or visit the **Wallace Collection**, a mansion containing a number of artistic treasures, including an astounding array of 18th-century French furniture and Old Master paintings. On the other hand, the neighborhood is playful and whimsical: There's the **London Zoo**, **Madame Tussaud's**, **Lord's Cricket Ground**, and **Baker Street**, home to the most famous detective (either real or make-believe) ever to have sleuthed through London: Sherlock Holmes.

Northeast of Marylebone (a shortened version of the church name, **St. Mary by the Bourne**—*Bourne* being an alias for the **Tyburn River**) lies Camden Town, which also originally belonged to a woman—in this instance, the wife of the first Earl of Camden. Once pastures and coal wharfs, Camden Town is now a going-on-grungy bohemian neighborhood, its cottages furnished to overflowing with antiques and cellular phones. When not converting Victoriana, the occupants, who range from novelists to spiritual seekers, wander down to **Camden Market**, one of London's most interesting street markets, and to the burgeoning artists' and crafters' colony of **Camden Lock**.

City code 0207 unless otherwise noted.

1 PRIMROSE HILL

Sixty-two acres seem inconsequential in comparison to **Regent's Park**, its larger neighbor to the south, yet this green space is beloved and well used by nearby residents for everything from kite flying to druidical ceremonies (seriously!). The grounds were once owned by **Eton College**, but in 1841, the site was made public, given in return for royal land closer to the school in Windsor. On a clear day, you can get a fantastic view from the top of the park—the summit measures around 219 feet—both of Regent's Park and of the whole vista of central London. No wonder Alan Bennett, V.S. Pritchett, and other celebrated literati have moved into the area.
♦ Bounded by Regent's Park, Prince Albert, and Primrose Hill Rds. Tube: Chalk Farm

2 CECIL SHARP HOUSE

This is the headquarters of the **English Folk Dance and Song Society** and England's **National Folk Centre**. It was built in 1929 by **H.M. Fletcher** in honor of Sharp, who pioneered techniques of collecting and preserving folk songs. Inside, the **Vaughan Williams Memorial Library** houses more than 11,000 books on folklore, folk songs, and related interests, and more than 3,000 recordings. The center is busy, with dance and music sessions of all types taking place every day. If you'd like to learn morris dancing or clogging or want to take part in a Celtic singers' night, you've come to the right place. A cafeteria and a bar are open during events. ♦ Library: M–F and alternate Sa.

2 Regent's Park Rd (at Gloucester Ave). 485.2206. Tube: Camden Town

3 CAMDEN MARKETS

Camden Town markets just keep spreading and now cover several adjoining sites. The famous one is **Camden Market**, a huge weekend affair beginning in the northern reaches of Camden High Street, where stallholders gather to sell fashion clothes and jewelry, as well as all sorts of artistic items. At Camden Lock Place is the **Camden Lock Market**, an area that is a crafts aficionado's paradise, with shops occupied by working artists who sell handmade furniture, rugs, pottery, baskets, and an abundance of high-quality gift items. On the weekends, it changes its face, and the stallholders invade to lure tourists with everything from secondhand clothing to New Age crystals. Don't worry if you get lost; that's half the fun of experiencing Camden, because as long as you keep walking, you're bound to stumble onto something you simply can't resist purchasing. Be warned: It gets very crowded.
♦ Camden Market: Th–Su. Camden High St and surroundings. Tube: Camden Town. Camden Lock Market: Sa, Su; indoor stalls and shops: Tu–Su. Camden Lock Pl (off Chalk Farm Rd). 284.2084. Tube: Camden Town

Within Camden Lock Market:

JONGLEURS

The comedy-cabaret show held in this nightclub inside **Ted's Bar** has spawned a wealth of famed British performers. Lenny

---

Restaurants/Clubs: **Red** | Hotels: **Purple** | Shops: **Orange** | Outdoors/Parks: **Green** | Sights/Culture: **Blue**

Henry, Ben Elton, Ruby Wax, Stephen Fry, and Hugh Laurie (to name just a few) have all walked the boards here, and the club prides itself on providing the "Best of British Comedy." It is generally well worth the admission charge, which includes temporary membership, reserved seating, a drink from the bar, dinner, and entrance to the on-premises disco. The club is usually open only on Friday and Saturday, but it sometimes operates during the week as well; call ahead. ◆ Admission. F, Sa, 7:30PM–2:30AM. 0207/564.2500 (central booking line). Also at 49 Lavender Gardens (between Clapham Common North Side and Lavender Hill) and Bow Wharf E3

4 LORD'S CRICKET GROUND

The gentle pop of a leather ball being hit by a willow cricket bat characterizes a game that remains a mystery to many Americans (and quite a few Brits as well). In England, if not around the world, this field beats at the very heart of the cricket scene, particularly once a year, when English teams attempt to overthrow the regular cricket dominance of Australia, Pakistan, and New Zealand. The current site was established in 1814, following a move by founder Thomas Lord from the Dorset Square area. You'll find the entrance to this hallowed ground farther along St. John's Wood Road, where the **W.G. Grace Memorial Gates** open onto the **Marylebone Cricket Club (MCC)**, the owners of this field, officially called **Lord's**. Guided tours of the grounds, including a museum of memorabilia dedicated to the sport, are now available daily year-round, except during matches. ◆ Admission for tours. Tours: 1 Apr–30 Sept, 10AM, noon, 2PM; 1 Oct–31 Mar, noon, 2PM. St. John's Wood Rd (between Wellington and Grove End Rds). 432.1033. Tube: St. John's Wood

5 REGENT'S PARK

London is a city of parks and squares, and nowhere do nature and people coexist more gloriously than in this green space. The essence of **John Nash**'s original plan of 1811 to turn almost 500 acres of farmland into a park survived 8 years of government commissions. His spectacular terraces, iced with stucco and lined with columns, surround the park, making it look like a gigantic wedding cake; the terraces are named after the titles of some of George III's children. **Cumberland Terrace** is the most splendid, with its magnificent pediment and 276-yard façade lined with Ionic columns; **Chester Terrace** is the longest, stretching 313 yards with 52 Corinthian columns. The elegant **Clarence Terrace**, designed by **Decimus Burton** in 1823, is the smallest. The neo-Georgian **Winfield House**, now the residence of the US ambassador, is located on the site of **St. Dunstan's Lodge**, designed in 1825 by

Burton; the house was donated by F.W. Woolworth heiress Barbara Hutton and now forms one of the few private areas of the park. The curiously shaped boating lake, reaching out in every direction and surrounded by ash groves, is undeniably romantic, as is the exquisite **Queen Mary's Garden**, which contains 40,000 rose bushes laid out in large beds, each with a different variety. **Regent's Canal** skirts the northern boundary of the park and runs for 8 miles from Paddington to Limehouse, past the animals at the **London Zoo**. ◆ Daily. Bounded by Outer Cir. Tube: Regent's Park

Within Regent's Park:

LONDON ZOO

LONDON ZOO

As the oldest zoo in the world, created in 1826, the gardens of the **Zoological Society of London** (the first society to shorten its name to *zoo*) now spread over 36 enchanting acres of Regent's Park. Rather than being cooped up in depressing iron cages, most of the 12,000 animals from 500 different species roam in settings similar to their natural habitats—separated from the public by moats. A large aquarium and a children's zoo were designed to make the animals more accessible, and the **Mappin Terraces** have been redesigned to house Asian mammals such as sloth bears. Ask on arrival about the schedule for feeding the lions, sea lions, and penguins, as well as washing the elephants. On Friday, see the snakes feeding on whole dead animals (ugh!). The brand-new **Gorilla Kingdom** is home-away-from-home to a colony of Western Lowland gorillas and is as close as you'll get to the African rainforest in the heart of London. The **Clore Rainforest Lookout** brings the South American rainforest to the zoo, too. Here you will find marmosets, tamarins, birds, and invertebrates. You walk across the rainforest canopy before descending to the forest floor. For the brave, there is the possibility of a close encounter with a Komodo dragon, the world's largest lizard. The zoo's focus is now on captive breeding of endangered species. It recently won the Best New London Experience Award in the Visit London Awards, as well as the Best for Kids Award. And it is pretty good for ex-kids as well. ◆ Admission: £12 adult, £9 child, £10.20 concessionary entry fee for elderly. Daily,

10AM–5:30PM; last entry at 4:30PM. 722.3333. Tube: Camden Town. www.zsl.org

OPEN AIR THEATRE

From May through early September, this delightful outdoor amphitheater, which seats 1,187, presents a season of Shakespeare works, as well as the occasional musical. For refreshments, there's a barbecue, café, and salad bar, or you could opt to bring along a hamper from **Harrods** or **Fortnum & Mason**. That old adage "The show must go on" is taken as gospel here—it always does, despite rain, roaring jets, and hay fever. ◆ Daily, June–Sept. 486.2431

6 THISTLE EUSTON

$$ Conveniently close to Euston Station, this is a modern property—not the place to stay if you're looking for traditional English ambience. Although **Regent's Park** and **Madame Tussaud's** are nearby, the hotel also provides easy access to most of central London. All 362 rooms are equipped with hair dryers and tea- and coffee-making facilities. The **Palate Bar and Grill** has an international menu and a decent carvery lunch on Sundays. The **Westminster Bar and Grill** offers snacks like hamburgers and a soup of the day. Both are open for breakfast. ◆ 43 Cardington St (between Drummond St and Hampstead Rd). 0870/333.9107, 800/847.4358. Tube: Euston

7 SEA-SHELL

★$$ The wooden booths of this famous fish-and-chips restaurant are always full despite the fact that the prices are a little higher than at most other eateries of this kind. The menu is very much more than a standard "chippie," as they are known here. Yes, you can enjoy haddock, cod fillet, or skate and chips, but the menu also encompasses excellent tarragon chicken (a char-grilled breast marinated in lemon and tarragon), excellent salads (including one with goat cheese served on a bed of arugula and grilled tomatoes), and desserts such as apple pie, treacle sponge puddings, and fresh strawberries with cream. The wine list is pretty good . . . you can even wash your chips (french fries) down with Champagne! ◆ Fish and chips ◆ M–Sa, lunch and dinner. 49–51 Lisson Grove (at Shroton St). 224 9000. Tube: Marylebone

8 SHERLOCK HOLMES MUSEUM

It's now possible to visit the fictional detective's "home"—at a fictional address, of course—in this fine Victorian house devoted to the supposed memorabilia of Holmes and Watson. The rooms are crammed with mementos—particularly the study, where you'll find souvenirs of the cases solved and letters written by the duo, along with Holmes's opium pipe and deerstalker hat. Kitschy details include the costumed "maid" who helps visitors take photos of the rooms. The basement shop sells mugs, ceramic figures, playing cards, and many other trinkets. ◆ Admission. Free entry to the shop only. Daily. 221b Baker St (between Melcombe St and Park Rd). 935.8866. Tube: Baker St

9 BAKER STREET

The street is named after William Baker, who built it in 1790, but everyone knows it as the home of the fictional sleuth Sherlock Holmes and his colleague, Dr. Watson, who lived at **No. 221b**. Their house also was a fiction, but the Abbey National Building Society at **No. 215** is approximately at the right site, and it employs someone to answer letters still written to the great detective! ◆ Between Orchard St and Park Rd. Tube: Baker St

9 SHERLOCK HOLMES MEMORABILIA COMPANY

Badges, chess sets, deerstalker hats, refrigerator magnets, key rings, pens, sweatshirts —whatever Sherlockiana you can imagine is for sale at this upscale shop. The shop has a worldwide mail-order service with over 100 collectible items. ◆ M–Sa. 230 Baker St (between Marylebone Rd and Allsop Pl). 486.1426. Tube: Baker St. www.sh-memorabilia.co.uk

10 MADAME TUSSAUD'S

The queues are long here, but everyone thinks it's worth the wait. Forget whatever reservations you may have about waxworks—there is nothing ordinary about this place. A British institution since 1802, it continues to be extensively refurbished and keeps up to date with current world personalities.

Mme. T learned her trade making death masks in Paris during the French Revolution, and those of Louis XVI and Marie Antoinette are displayed on spikes beside the actual blade that beheaded them. The oldest

Restaurants/Clubs: Red | **Hotels: Purple** | **Shops: Orange** | **Outdoors/Parks: Green** | **Sights/Culture: Blue**

143

surviving likeness, dating from 1765, is that of Mme. du Barry, also known as "the Sleeping Beauty." A mechanism hidden in the bodice of her dress allows the figure to "breathe." King Henry VIII is shown surrounded by all six of his wives, and there is a full re-creation of the royal family. The wax likenesses are most often modeled from life and are never displayed behind glass. They stand in small tableaux, grouped as figures from history, politics, literature, sports, and entertainment, and new figures are added regularly, such as Pierce Brosnan after his first James Bond film.

One room is devoted to Contemporary Heroes, where Arnold Schwarzenegger and Bill Clinton share space with Oprah Winfrey, Elizabeth Taylor (this is her third model), magician David Copperfield, and Joanna Lumley (who plays Patsy in the hit BBC sitcom *Absolutely Fabulous*). Culture buffs can admire figures ranging from highbrow (Luciano Pavarotti) to down-to-earth (Dudley Moore). Superstars and Legends includes Elvis Presley and Marilyn Monroe.

The Chamber of Horrors has been completely revamped to create realistic sets and spine-tingling sound effects. Displays include Visions of Hell with Vlad the Impaler and torture wheels with suspended victims. There is also Joan of Arc at the stake, a drowning pirate at his execution, and Newgate prisoners from the Victorian era. Serial killers start with Jack the Ripper. Elsewhere you can see James Dean and Humphrey Bogart on a Hollywood set.

The £11 million ride Spirit of London has visitors traveling in cars representing London taxis (the same firm builds both) through a dark tunnel. The city's heritage is brought to life by modern technology, as animated wax figures take you through London's great events. One of the most impressive is the figure of William Shakespeare, quill in hand, writing plays.

Even the café has entertaining things to do, thanks to its traditional amusement arcade machines. And the shop is furnished to represent different eras of shopping in London.

Also on the grounds is the **London Planetarium**, which has had a £4.5 million relaunch of its shows and keeps adding new ones like **Planetary Quest**, which uses state-of-the-art three-dimesional computer and video effects to take you into the solar system as if you were a space traveler. You see Neptune's hurricane storms, the rings and moons of Saturn, whirling star fields, footsteps on the moon, and a sky glow from Earth, and you even zoom through London. To avoid waiting in line for the museum, either visit the planetarium first and buy a combined ticket or book by credit card 24 hours in advance. ♦ Separate admissions to Madame Tussaud's and the planetarium (combined tickets also available). Daily. Marylebone Rd (between York Gate and Allsop Pl). 935.6861. Tube: Baker St

11 ST. MARYLEBONE PARISH CHURCH

Built by **Thomas Hardwick** between 1813 and 1817, this church is splendidly ornate on the outside, with gold caryatids on the steeple. Halfway through its construction, plans shifted, turning what had begun as a chapel into a parish church. The resulting interior was therefore quite dramatic—much more like a theater than a church—but today its simplicity gives the place a tranquil atmosphere. Elizabeth Barrett and Robert Browning were married here. These days, the building doubles as an active holistic healing center. ♦ M–Sa. Marylebone Rd (between Marylebone High St and Nottingham Pl). 935.7315. Tube: Baker St

12 THE WELLCOME COLLECTION

A fascinating place. Be warned: if you have any tendency toward hypochondria, you may never leave. This building, purpose built in 1932 to the specifications of Sir Henry Wellcome, houses his collection—the world's foremost—relating to medicine and health through the ages. There are three exhibitions; the world-famous **Wellcome Library**, with over 2 million items to browse; a bookshop; a café, and a members' club. Among more than 1,500 exhibits, spanning six centuries, you will find an ancient mummy, Napoléon's toothbrush, King George III's hair, Darwin's walking stick, a DNA-sequencing robot, and a Marc Quinn sculpture. You can view everything from a giant jelly baby to the guillotine blade used to execute Jean-Baptiste Carrier (a Jacobin extremist who reportedly committed atrocities during the French Revolution).

Two of the exhibitions—*Medicine Man* and *Medicine Now*—are permanent; the other changes. And every week there is something new happening in the Events department here, usually linked to the current exhibition. There has been a symposium on The Broken Heart, a "Travelling Apothecary" with old-style stalls selling cures for everything modern, and even a chance to witness live open-heart surgery.

The café is smart, its wares tasty, and the bookshop is just as smart, although its wares are tasty in a different way. If you are interested in yourself at all, you will be fascinated by this place. And forever grateful to Sir Henry. ♦ Free. Tu–Su. 183 Euston Rd (at Gordon St). 611.2222. Tube: Euston, Euston Square, Warren St. www.wellcomecollection.org

13 BRITISH LIBRARY

The move from its location within the **British Museum** to a newly built £500 million home at St. Pancras is finally complete. In addition to this great library's 12 million volumes, a

host of treasures—illuminated historical, musical, and literary manuscripts and maps—are on display in three galleries, including the large, firm signature of Elizabeth I on the order sentencing Robert Devereux, Earl of Essex, to death by beheading; two of the four surviving copies of the *Magna Carta* issued in 1215 by King John; the *Lindisfarne Gospels*, written and illuminated in 698; a Gutenberg Bible; the 15th-century *Canterbury Tales*; and a *First Folio* of Shakespeare's works. There are also a bookshop and a restaurant. On Tuesday evenings at 7PM, the library has an extensive program of talks and concerts.
♦ Free. Daily. 96 Euston Rd (between Midland Rd and Ossulston St). 412.7332. Tube: King's Cross, St. Pancras. www.bl.uk

13 St. Pancras International

At Grand Central Station, they may well be sitting down and weeping, because there is now another station to rival it. Yes, after an £800 million makeover, this gorgeous, dilapidated, ignored, sad old station has been reborn, and wow! The old girl has certainly brushed up beautifully.

The original Gothic gorgeousness was designed by **Sir George Gilbert Scott** and built by engineer Sir William Henry Barlow. "My own belief is that it is possibly too good for its purpose," he said. Completed in 1877, although the station lasted, the hotel closed in the 1930s and was converted into offices. In the 1960s the whole place barely escaped demolition. The roof timbers had rotted, and the building's detractors insisted it was unsafe. But Scott had built his floors in concrete and iron and, while the building was looking a little sad, unsafe it was not! However, it has lain empty since. But now St. Pancras is the London home of Eurostar—and you can take eight Eurostar trains every hour. Two hours fifteen minutes away, you are in Paris, which rather qualifies it for inclusion in the Day Trips section at the end of this book. However, there is an excellent Access Guide to Paris available, so should you plan on taking the trip, perhaps you should consult that! The hotel is being restored to its full former glory—and glorious it is. Scott's **Midland Grand Hotel** will open in 2009 and feature luxury apartments by Manhattan Loft Company on the top floor and a palatial five-star Marriott Hotel below. Two tunnels that bring the Eurostar to St. Pancras run under 2,600 properties, 7 miles of surface rail lines, and 600 gas, water, and sewage pipelines. Sixty million bricks were used in the original building and the renovation used 1.6 million more for the hotel extension. The bricks were specially made to match the originals. The enormous amount of work on

such a long-disused area disturbed, of course, some of St. Pancras's "informal residents." Engineers had to rehouse a colony of hazel dormice and build 78 bat roosts, eight ponds, and several badger setts, to say nothing of the remains of two French bishops who had sought refuge in London during the French Revolution.

The new station was opened in November 2007 by HM the Queen, who pronounced it "magnificent" and said she hoped it would become "not just a station, but a destination." The original station was raised 18 feet above street level by engineer William Barlow, in order to make the trains' arrival smoother and safer. The undercroft, with its famous vaulting ceilings, was used to store beer—28 million pints' capacity, to be precise. Slightly less excitingly, it now holds the new Eurostar ticketing offices, passport control desks, and a lovely shopping mall. It is still a beautiful place. English Heritage gave the architects permission to remove four sections of the undercroft roof, so the mall is lit naturally. Most of St. Pancras's planned 44 retail outlets will be here.

At platform level, you can relax and enjoy a little light refreshment at Europe's longest Champagne bar (more than 90 meters), or have something less glamorous but totally delicious at the **Betjeman Arms** (the cakes are great, and in winter the mulled wine really hits the spot on a cold platform). There is a plan to have regular farmers' markets at the station. And *no* plans, so far, for a McDonald's!

At the front of the Eurostar platforms is a stunning, 9-meter-high bronze statue by Paul Day depicting a couple locked in a passionate embrace, entitled *The Meeting Place*, reminiscent of the famous French photograph. Sir John Betjeman, poet, Englishman, and the man who spearheaded the campaign to save St. Pancras in the 1960s, also gets a statue; his is by Martin Jennings. And the famous St. Pancras clock has been reconstructed by its original makers, Dents, and once more hangs high at the apex of Barlow's arch. ♦ Closed Christmas Day. St. Pancras International Euston Rd. 843. 4250. Tube: Kings Cross, St. Pancras. www.stpancras.com.

14 22 York Place

$$ If you want the London townhouse hotel feel without paying Hazlitt's prices, then 22 York Street is the place for you. It is, strictly speaking, a B&B as opposed to a hotel, but it is charming: two Georgian town houses with a few lovely bedrooms up a sweeping stone staircase, immaculately kept with wooden floors and period details. Your breakfast is served at an antique dining table in the traditional kitchen. This is a really lovely

Restaurants/Clubs: **Red** | Hotels: **Purple** | Shops: **Orange** | Outdoors/Parks: **Green** | Sights/Culture: **Blue**

also a lovely "real" place—to base
London. ◆ 22 York St. 224.2990.
r St. www.22yorkstreet.co.uk

15 A&D GALLERY

When this place opened, its owners and curators had two primary objectives for their new gallery. They wanted a platform for contemporary artists with talent who did not fit into the ethos of many West End galleries. They also wanted to provide a gallery atmosphere that demystified the concept of art collecting, so as to encourage first-time buyers to have the courage of their own taste and judgment. It has been described in the press as "the friendliest gallery in London" (not much competition there, of course . . .), and its exhibits have ranged from Chinese art to working phone sculptures to commissioned editions by 100 artists for a Valentine's Day exhibition. The widest selection of their works is available online, but a visit to the gallery is always worthwhile. ◆ M–Sa, 10AM–7PM. 51 Chiltern St. 486.0532. Tube: Baker Street. www.a-and-d.co.uk

16 THE CONRAN SHOP

Before he was one of London's highest-profile restaurateurs, **Terence Conran** (now Sir Terence) was a designer. And it shows in his shops. This one is in a beautifully converted stable and offers some truly elegant modern furniture, an excellent display of smart glassware and ceramics, and the choice of clean-line homeware that is what we now expect from Conran. ◆ M–W, 10AM–6PM; Th, 10AM–7PM; F, 10AM–6PM; Sa, 10:30AM–6:30PM; Su, noon–6PM. 55 Marylebone High St. 723.2223; fax 535.3205. Tube: Baker St. There are also Conran Shops at 12 Conduit St (at Regent St), 399.0710; Michelin House, 81 Fulham Rd (at Brompton Rd), 589.7401; and in Manhattan and Paris.

Above the Conran Shop:

ORRERY

★★★$$$ An orrery is an intricate cosmological model—a model of the skies and all they contain. The restaurant is paradigm Conran: elegant, clean lines, and kitted out with total attention to detail. The new head chef came to the kitchens from the Michelin-starred Hare Restaurant. He serves terrine of foie gras with apple and marinated beetroot, roast saddle of venison with pickled pear purée, veal cheek with crayfish, orange, and turnip purée, and a rich Valrhona chocolate fondant with praline ice cream. It is accomplished stuff. Robert Giorgione is the sommelier, and he has created a terrific wine list characterized by Conran's one-glass-drinker-friendly selection. The views over Marylebone are beautiful, and there is a lovely roof terrace just in case England gets a day's sunshine. ◆ Restaurant: daily; terrace: summer, from noon (weather permitting). 616.8000

ORRERY EPICERIE

Next door to the restaurant you will find the Epicerie, where you can buy bread, olive oil, coffee, pastries, antipasti, and confectionary. And if you don't trust yourself to get your takeout home, you can eat it there—breakfast and light meals are all prepared in the Orrery kitchens upstairs. ◆ Daily. 616.8036

17 DAUNT

Tall and effete, James Daunt was a Cambridge graduate turned New York City banker before he started this travel bookshop, a place that makes it seem unnecessary to travel anywhere else. The shop takes you back in time to a turn-of-the-century galleried Bloomsbury studio, where books are arranged by nation rather than by genre, with fiction, poetry, and nonfiction grouped together. ◆ M–Sa. 83 Marylebone High St (between Moxon and Paddington Sts). 224.2295. Tube: Baker St

17 FISHWORKS

★★★$$$ This restaurant (part of a small exclusive chain) has just been given a Best Fish Restaurant award. The unique feature of the Fishworks is that each restaurant has, at its entrance, a very fine fresh fish shop, so you can eat and shop knowing that the fish is the finest and freshest. And these people really know how to work with it. You could start with a plate of salted Cantabrian anchovies and then have baked sea bream with roasted garlic, rosemary, chili, and olive oil, or enjoy their renowned *zuppa del pescatore*. Excellent native lobsters are available in season. The wine list is almost exclusively European but very well chosen. ◆ Seafood ◆ Daily, lunch and dinner. 89 Marylebone High St. 935.9796. Tube: Baker St

18 PATISSERIE VALERIE AT MAISON SAGNE

★★★$ This link in the popular chain of London tearooms has become a Marylebone institution. It is a gathering place of great cachet—everyone is someone at **Valerie's** on Saturday morning. Chef Ray Hall creates butterfly-light croissants and French cakes and pastries, and light salads and sandwiches are served for lunch. ◆ Café ◆ Daily, breakfast, lunch, and afternoon tea. 105 Marylebone High St (between St. Vincent and Moxon Sts). 935.6240. Tube: Baker St, Bond St.

19 MARYLEBONE LANE AND MARYLEBONE HIGH STREET

An old village at heart, this area is full of expensive specialty food shops and boutiques that cater to the wealthy (and healthy) relatives of the ill who pay court to the good doctors of nearby Harley Street. Charles Dickens, who lived all over London, wrote 11 books when he resided here. ♦ Marylebone La (between Oxford and Thayer Sts); Marylebone High St (between Thayer St and Marylebone Rd). Tube: Baker St, Bond St

On Marylebone High Street:

The street has become one of London's greatest paradises for shopaholics and foodies. There are so many interesting, independent little stores here, so much nicer than the chain of chains that is Oxford Street.

The tiny **Paul** (No. 115) sells some of the finest breads and patisserie around. At the opposite end of the foodie scale, the new giant **Waitrose** (No. 99/100) also sells some pretty decent bread and much, much more besides. Up at No. 78 you will find the **Natural Kitchen** (daily, 486.8065), which sells organic, wild, and artisan food from hand-picked sources in biodegradeable wrapping. They have a nice café and a good bookshop, and their foodie events are always worth checking out.

Brora (No. 81; 736.9944) sells a terrific selection of the finest Scottish cashmere in designs for all the family. The **White Company** (No. 12; 935.7879) is a marvelous concept: soft furnishings and accessories for the home, all elegantly designed in white. They also have the most wonderful range of deliciously scented candles and toiletries—their hand creams are well worth stocking up on. **Rococo Chocolates** (No. 45; 935.7780) have an incredibly inventive and truly mouthwatering range of high-quality handmade chocolates. They are also very proud of their equally inventive "jellyfish" chandelier. Should a visit to Rococo make you feel peckish but you want to remain virtuous, there is **Eat and Two Veg** (daily, breakfast, lunch, and dinner; 258.8595), a terrific vegetarian restaurant.

Now revived, popping into **Cath Kidston** (No. 51; 935.6555) is never a bad idea—her signature quirky, kitschy fabrics and accessories are distinctive and desirable. At No. 26 (but you will smell it long before you get there) is the beautiful **Terre d'Oc**, a shop filled with the perfumes of Provence—in candles, diffusers, and room scents. On a Saturday morning you will find a fabulous farmers' market imaginatively titled **Cabbages and Frocks** outside the church. It is tremendously good fun.

Lady shoppers who can't find what they want to wear on Marylebone High Street can try **Chiltern Street**, which runs parallel and is renowned as home to a great number of ladies' fashion stores.

20 VILLANDRY

Now in a new location, this shop may have high white ceilings and automatic glass doors, but what it lacks in charm and character, when compared to the original, it more than makes up for with a greater choice of goods—and there is an even larger restaurant attached. Delicacies, collected by foodie-owner Jean Charles Carrarini, include a variety of breads—such as French, Italian, and Parisian sourdough—as well as jams and olive oils, original salads, picnic baskets, and special pastries baked on the premises. The shop also offers gourmet cheeses and chocolates, some made in Britain and others imported from the Continent. Neighborhood residents, dressed in their best tweeds, gather here every Wednesday when fresh produce arrives from Paris. ♦ M-Sa. 170 Great Portland St (at Weymouth St). 631.3131. Tube: Great Portland St

Within Villandry:

VILLANDRY DINING ROOM

★★$$ Deceptively plain-looking, with a warehouse-like floor, pale walls, and high ceilings, this restaurant offers some first-rate fare, on a menu that changes every month. In season you will get Cornish crab with avocado salad, ham hock terrine with baby leeks and hazelnut dressing, or linguine with queen scallops, wild garlic, and fresh herbs. Of course, the tarts and patisserie are fabulous. ♦ French ♦ M-Sa, lunch and dinner; Su, brunch. 631.3131

VILLANDRY BAR

★★$$A great bar with a good range of premium spirits and a nice way with a classic cocktail—including a regular cocktail of the week. It also does great coffee. And there is free wireless Internet access while you sip. If you want a really nice breakfast in this part of town, Villandry Bar offers some delicious options, from free-range boiled eggs with sausages to French toast with maple syrup. You can lunch on a Villandry burger with dill pickle or enjoy an early-evening platter of charcuterie from the deli. Every Saturday, Giu Risi & the Villandry Allstars play chilled-out jazz, which you can enjoy with a special three-course menu. ♦ M-Sa, breakfast, lunch, and dinner

21 PADDINGTON HILTON INTERNATIONAL

$$$ If it is ease you want, a London visit doesn't get much easier than staying at the Paddington Hilton International. Your journey would go something like this: Arrive at Heathrow, get off plane, get on Paddington Express, spend 15 minutes enjoying the scenery (well . . . reading your Access Guide), arrive at Paddington, get off train, walk across footbridge, get into hotel. And it is a nice hotel, with everything you would

---

Restaurants/Clubs: Red | **Hotels: Purple** | **Shops: Orange** | **Outdoors/Parks: Green** | **Sights/Culture: Blue**

expect from a Hilton. The rooms have marble bathrooms and wireless Internet, Executive Rooms come with access to the Executive Lounge for free continental breakfast or morning coffee, suites have balconies with quite a view, and the hotel has its own casino with bar, fitness room with sauna, and a couple of decent eating places (if you don't want to use the 24-hour room service). The all-day breakfast in the Steam Bar is pretty reliable if you need to fuel up for a day in the city. As with all hotel chains, check for deals and discounts; rack rates are for the very rich or the very silly. ♦ 146 Praed St (near Norfolk Pl). 850.0500; fax 850.0600. Tube: Paddington. www.hilton.co.uk.

22 THE FRONTLINE CLUB

★★★$$ Here's a unique chance to do good for the world by eating and drinking some very exceptional food and wine. The **Frontline Restaurant** is part of the Frontline Media Club, which holds a weekly program of cutting-edge documentaries and discussions on current affairs, crises, and causes. It works to keep important topics and debates going after they have slipped from the headlines. It's intelligent, politicized, and just occasionally ever-so-slightly smug, but a fascinating place to be and a terrific place to eat. Profits from the restaurant go toward helping the work of the Frontline Forum. Food is seasonal and British, all sustainably, ethically sourced. They will respect your allergies, cook gluten free, keep your carbs low, and even serve halal if you wish. Start with smoked eel with beetroot and St. Tolas goat's cheese, and you will be very happy. The saddle of Welsh mountain lamb is served with plum and pistachio-stuffed belly. Queen Mab's pudding is served with raspberries and shortbread and is as quintessentially English as the excellent Sunday roast (although not quite as filling). The wine list is probably unique in London. It is the lovechild of Malcolm Gluck, celebrated and much-awarded wine writer and expert. "In sourcing the Frontline winelist I was aiming to create something I have been searching for in 30 years of eating out in London and never found: a restaurant with an extraordinary range of delicious wines, many of them unusual and out-of-the-way, all affordable at non rip-off prices," he says. How can you not go? ♦ Daily, breakfast, lunch, and dinner. 13 Norfolk Pl (between Sussex Gdns and Praed St). 479.8960. Tube: Paddington. www.frontlineclub.com

23 HARLEY STREET

This area is one gracious band of stately Georgian houses, all designed with the eye for proportion and attention to detail that this era left as its architectural legacy. Artists such as J.M.W. Turner and Allan Ramsay lived here first;

then, beginning in the 1840s, private doctors took it over, and today it is wall to wall with specialists catering to the ills of the wealthy. ♦ Between Cavendish Sq and Marylebone Rd. Tube: Regent's Park, Oxford Circus

24 PORTLAND PLACE

When **Robert Adam** laid out this thoroughfare between 1776 and 1780, it was considered one of the finest London streets in an architectural sense—that was part of the reason **John Nash** came here to bring Regent Street to its southern end. ♦ Between Langham Pl and Park Crescent. Tube: Regent's Park, Oxford Circus

24 BROADCASTING HOUSE

On Portland Place, at the curve of Langham Street, stands the BBC's Broadcasting House, built by **George Val Myers** and **F.J. Watson-Hart** in 1931. Sculpture by Eric Gill decorates the outside, including the Shakespearean figures of Prospero and Ariel from *The Tempest*; this was Gill's way of showing Ariel, who has become the symbol of broadcasting, being sent out into the world. ♦ Portland Pl (between Langham and Duchess Sts). 580.4468. Tube: Regent's Park, Oxford Circus

25 ALL SOULS CHURCH

John Nash designed this church (his only one in London) as an architectural landmark for the end of Regent Street and to mark the bend of the road westward that links up with Portland Place. Built in 1822–1824, the church was much criticized then because it looked so unusual. Nash had given it a round portico, and the whole edifice was topped by a very sharp spire encircled with another round colonnade of pillars. Although his stagy mix of architectural styles was ingenious, Nash was publicly lampooned. A cartoon showed the architect impaled on the metal spike atop his steeple. Nash's reply was that criticism exalted him. The church is now the venue for musical events and some broadcasts for the nearby BBC. ♦ M–F, Su. Langham Pl (at Riding House St). 580.3522. Tube: Oxford Circus

26 WALLACE COLLECTION

This off-the-beaten-path museum houses one of the finest collections of French furniture and porcelain, Old Master paintings, and objets d'art in the world. It is arguably one of London's major museums—and it's also one of its best-kept secrets. But visiting this grand town house, built between 1776 and 1788, and seeing its owner's private art collection is a much more intimate experience than going to a museum. The rich and varied collection of 5,470 objects was acquired by successive marquesses of Hertford during the 18th and 19th centuries. The first marquess (1719–1794) was partial to Canalettos; the second, who lived between 1743 and 1823, added Gainsborough's *Mrs. Robinson* and Reynolds's *Nelly O'Brien*. He acquired the lease on **Hertford House** (the name of the present building) in 1797. The third marquess (1777–1842) was a close friend of the Prince of Wales (later George IV) and collected French furniture and porcelain and 17th-century Dutch paintings. The fourth marquess (1800–1870), an eccentric who lived most of his life in seclusion in Paris, collected a large number of 18th-century French paintings by Watteau, Boucher, Fragonard, and Greuze, as well as works by several Old Masters (including master-pieces by Rembrandt, Rubens, Poussin, and Velázquez). He also made lavish purchases of 18th-century French furniture by Boulle, Crescent, and Riesener, including the chest of drawers made for Louis XV's bedroom at Versailles and various pieces made for Marie Antoinette, not to mention what is now the world's richest public collection of Sèvres porcelain. Don't miss the exquisite gold boxes or the wrought-iron and gilt-bronze staircase balustrade, which was made in about 1720 for Louis XV's Palais Mazarin (now the Bibliothèque Nationale). It was sold around 1870 as scrap iron but rescued by Sir Richard Wallace, the fourth marquess's illegitimate son, who inherited the collection and brought it to Hertford House, adding the European arms and armor and medieval and Renaissance works of art.

Just after Wallace's death in 1890, his widow bequeathed the collection to the nation, and it opened to the public in 1900. In recent years the museum has become a real "destination," and its program of evening talks and activities is more popular with every passing month. The evening "Salon with Marie Antoinette" features Champagne and a recital on the queen's own piano. There are weekend art classes for aspiring painters led by professional artists and sculptors. And the museum's shop is a treasure trove. ♦ Free. Daily, 10AM-5PM. Manchester Sq (between Spanish Pl and Manchester St). 563.9500. Tube: Bond St. www.thewallacecollection.org

Within the Wallace Collection:

THE WALLACE RESTAURANT

★★★$$ Even if you are left cold by the Collection, the Wallace Restaurant is worth coming here for. Another from the larder of Oliver Peyton, this one is garnished with a beautiful courtyard spotted with camellia trees and silken parasols. The food is top-of-the-range French brasserie stuff: there is a fabulous seafood display to choose from, a whole menu of pâtés and terrines, and a wonderful and well-kept selection of cheeses. And all that is available all day. Come mealtime, steak tartare is served with a truffle vinaigrette, sea bream is cooked in fig leaves and served with roast figs and lemon confit, and there is a whole roasted black leg chicken stuffed with foie gras for two to share. Tarte tatin after that? You'd be a fool to refuse. It is gorgeous. The Parisien Afternoon Tea comes with croque monsieur and the Wallace Afternoon Tea with foie gras and brioche; Champagne is optional. Going around the Collection might have to wait for another day! This restaurant has had more great reviews than Meryl Streep, and it has deserved them all. ♦ Daily, lunch, tea, and dinner. Reservations recommended for dinner. ♦ 563.9505

27 BUTTON QUEEN

This tiny, old-fashioned shop really lives up to its name: It is stocked with every kind of button you can imagine—from ordinary modern styles to antique military ones. The buttons are made of materials ranging from plastic and metal to leather and animal horn. ♦ M-Sa, 10AM-5PM. 19 Marylebone La (between Wigmore and Hinde Sts). 935.1505. Tube: Bond St

28 WIGMORE HALL

Friedrich Beckstein built this concert hall in 1901 as an afterthought to his spacious piano showrooms. Its near-perfect acoustics make it a regular venue for classical concerts, particularly those performed by chamber orchestras. Performances take place daily, including Sunday morning. ♦ Box office: daily. 36 Wigmore St (between Wimpole and Welbeck Sts). 935.2141. Tube: Bond St

29 CAVENDISH SQUARE

It's always so cold and windy in this stately square that it's almost possible to feel the tears of Mrs. Horatio Nelson (who lived here in 1791) at being continually abandoned by her admiral husband. John Prince laid the square out in 1717, but it wasn't until 1761, when George II's daughter Amelia came to live at **No. 16**, that it really came into its own. You can see Jacob Epstein's sculpture *Madonna and Child* standing among the trees. ♦ At Cavendish Pl and Wigmore St and at Holles and Harley Sts. Tube: Oxford Circus

BLOOMSBURY/HOLBORN

Bloomsbury is the **Oxford** of London, a sheltered kingdom of scholars that is ruled both by the past, in the form of the **British Museum**, and by the future, which is constantly being shaped in the halls of the **University of London**. Between these institutions lie spacious squares filled with shade trees and rose bushes. Illustrious ghosts haunt the streets where Clive Bell struggled with literary criticism, W.B. Yeats struggled with poetic philosophy, and Virginia and Leonard Woolf struggled with themselves and each other—and with T.S. Eliot whenever he came to tea. Though a bookish air pervades the neighborhood, Bloomsbury is not devoid of everyday pleasures. Modern minds swap theories over a pint in the **Plough** and budding novelists buy pullovers in **Westaway & Westaway**.

In striking contrast, Holborn is decidedly Dickensian, almost as if the author himself still resided at **Dickens House**. His footsteps are easy to follow, through the ancient legal byways of two **Inns of Court**; into **Bleeding Heart Yard**, which is portrayed

in *Little Dorrit;* and finally to the **Old Bailey** and the largest meat market in the world, **Smithfield**, with their grim atmospheres of crime and slaughter. Because this area covers so many miles of terrain, you should pick and choose your stops in keeping with your interests.

City code 0207 unless otherwise noted.

1 THOMAS CORAM FOUNDATION FOR CHILDREN

Also known as the **Foundling Hospital**, this museum owes its existence to sea captain Thomas Coram, who lived between 1668 and 1751 and made his name by helping to colonize America. Returning to London, Coram was shocked at the number of abandoned infants. He enlisted 21 noblewomen, 11 earls, and 6 dukes to petition George II for assistance in establishing a home for the foundlings.

William Hogarth was one of the original governors; he and his wife served as foster parents to the children. A major Hogarth work, the *March to Finchley* (1746), and the superb portrait of a robust *Captain Coram* (1740) are two of the treasures in the museum's picture collection, which includes works by Gainsborough and Reynolds. The composer Handel was

also an early benefactor. He not only donated a pipe organ and gave performances to raise money for the children but also bequeathed his own copy of the manuscript for his *Messiah*. An unforgettable collection is found in the lovingly preserved 18th-century **Courtroom**. Mothers often left mementos in the baskets of their abandoned infants, and many of these are displayed here: coral beads, locks of hair, a section of a map of England, earrings, watch seals, coins, a crystal locket, a single lace glove, and the letter *A* cut in metal. These tokens were the foundlings' only clues to their personal histories. ♦ Admission: £9.50. Currently under refurbishment; will open spring 2004. 40 Brunswick Sq (off Hunter St). 841.3600; fax 837.8084. Tube: Russell Sq

2 DICKENS HOUSE

The sheer quantity of Dickensiana crammed into this row house is all the more amazing because the structure is one of four Dickens houses open to the public. (The others are outside London, although he did live and work at other city addresses.) The author lived here between 1837 and 1839, writing the last part of *The Pickwick Papers*, most of *Oliver Twist* and *Nicholas Nickleby*, and the beginning of *Barnaby Rudge*. He also penned some 550 letters here. In the sitting room, Dickens's 17-year-old sister-in-law, Mary, died in his arms, a blow from which he never recovered. Visitors can see the writer's desk, the china monkey he kept on it for good luck, and the family Bible, as well as portraits, illustrations, autographed letters, and other personal relics. The first-floor drawing room has been reconstructed to appear as it did in Dickens's time, as have the study and basement. ♦ Admission. M-Sa. 48 Doughty St (between Roger and Guilford Sts). 405.2127. Tube: Russell Sq

3 MORO

★★★$$$ Run by a husband-and-wife team called Sam Clark and Sam Clark, this was London's first A-list Spanish-Moorish restaurant. The big room is loud, friendly, and full of some of the sexiest smells in London. The Clarks have a wood-burning oven that they use not only for meat and bread but for some fish as well. The tagines are full flavored and exciting and the salads are zingy; the Clarks do things with chicken that that Sanders man can only dream of— and cheeses are a delicious adventure. Why not start with one of their extensive sherry selections as an aperitif, enjoy the music, and get a little spicy! ♦ Spanish-Moorish ♦ M-F, 12:30PM-2:30PM, 7PM-10:30PM, bar 12:30PM-11PM; Sa, 7PM-10:30PM. 34-36 Exmouth Market EC1. 833.8336. Tube: Farringdon

the Quality Chop House

4 QUALITY CHOP HOUSE

★★$$ With the opening of the **Quality Fish Bar** next door, the menu (which is the same in both restaurants) has been extended to include fish in a big way. There's everything from jellied eels to Sevruga caviar. Gaslight enhances the historical ambience. ♦ M-F, Su, lunch and dinner; Sa, dinner. Reservations recommended. 94 Farringdon Rd (at Exmouth Market). 837.5093. Tube: Farringdon

5 THE EAGLE

★★★$$ London's first gastropub and still one of the very best. The cooking at the open-plan kitchen is heavily Mediterranean and changes twice a day, 6 days a week. What you will get is what is best in the markets, cooked with skill and served with a smile. There are always soups and big salads, the char grill never cools, and the only dish that never comes off the menu is the famous steak sandwich. There is a famously impressive wine list, and beers include Cambrinus, Leffe, and the aptly named Eagle. ♦ Mediterranean ♦ M-Sa, noon-11PM; Su, noon-5PM. 159 Farringdon Rd. 837.1353. Tube: Farringdon

6 ZETTER HOTEL

$$$$ This is one of London's newest and chicest hotels, housed in a former warehouse, now all fashionably retro-styled. The bedrooms are elegantly designed in cream and gray, and the rooftop suites have wooden decks for good-weather relaxing. The hotel is

Courtesy of Charles Dickens House, London

notable not just for its trendiness, but for its ecological awareness—when you open a window, the air conditioning automatically switches off; all the hotel's water comes from its own well; and there are smart vending machines in the corridors offering everything from cappuccino to Champagne instead of individual minibars in the rooms. The Zetter also offers disabled-adapted rooms.
♦ 86-88 Clerkenwell Rd. 324.4444. Tube: Holburn. www.thezetter.com

7 UNIVERSITY OF LONDON

In 1826, a group of enlightened sponsors decided to establish a center of higher learning that would not be tied to the Anglican Church and would offer a more liberal and wide-ranging curriculum than those of other universities. Opponents said it wouldn't last. But over the next 170 years, the "godless college in Gower Street" built a formidable reputation, and today it comprises 50 colleges. Currently, its full-time student body exceeds 75,000.

Although the university received its charter relatively late, it has made up for lost time, scoring a string of firsts over the years. Medical research in its facilities led in 1846 to the first use of ether and in 1867 to the first antiseptic surgery. In 1878, it became the first British university to admit women. Today, Princess Anne is its chancellor.

Many university buildings are in the area around Gower and Malet Streets. The best-known is **Senate House**, which was designed by **Charles Holden** in 1932. The huge Portland stone structure contains the university's massive library, with its specialist collections of Elizabethan books and music.
♦ Bounded by Bedford Way and Gower St and by Montague and Gower Pls. Tube: Russell Sq, Goodge St

Within the University of London:

GORDON SQUARE

Considered the birthplace of the Bloomsbury Group, this was the home of Virginia Woolf and her sister, Vanessa Bell, before they were married. Later Vanessa occupied the house with her husband, Clive Bell, until 1916, when John Maynard Keynes, the economist and another member of the group, took up residence. Now owned by the University of London, it's not open to the public. However, the garden at **Gordon Square** is, looking much as it did when Virginia Woolf described it in her memoir *Old Bloomsbury*: "It was astonishing to stand at the drawing room window and look into all those trees; the tree which shoots its branches up into the air and lets them

fall in a shower; the tree which glistens after rain like the body of a seal." ♦ East side of the square (near Endsleigh Pl)

8 HOTEL RUSSELL

$ This rambling Bloomsbury institution (now managed by Principal Hotels) looks and feels as if it should be attached to the Great Western Railway. Built by **Charles Fitzroy Doll** in 1898, it tempers the Victorian appetite for size with modesty. The stairway is grand, and, after a £20 million refurbishment, the 373 rooms are too. The best rooms are on the seventh floor. Talking of which, the beautiful mosaic floor in the lobby was first laid when the hotel was originally built. The owners were smart enough to spend part of the £20 million fund on putting to rights the war damage that had kept the mosaic under wraps for decades. This is a really wonderful old hotel at a surprisingly low rate. **Benjamin's Bar** is friendly, and great if you like watching sports, and the **Kings Bar** is rather chic, does good cocktails, and offers an okay afternoon tea. ♦ Russell Sq (between Guilford and Bernard Sts). 837.6470; fax 837.2857. Tube: Russell Sq. www.londonrussellhotel.co.uk (special rates for online booking)

9 RUSSELL SQUARE

The west side of London's second-largest square is lined with huge plane trees and houses once favored by lawyers and merchants. Readers of Thackeray's *Vanity Fair* may recognize this as the turf of the Sedleys and Osbornes. The square was laid out between 1800 and 1814 by **Humphrey Repton** and named after the Russells, Dukes of Bedford, who owned the land. The elaborate statue of Francis Russell, fifth Duke of Bedford, created in 1809 by Sir Richard Westmacott, portrays him leaning on a plow. Some of the original houses by **James Burton**

Restaurants/Clubs: **Red** | Hotels: **Purple** | Shops: Orange | Outdoors/Parks: **Green** | Sights/Culture: **Blue** remain, including **Nos. 25** to **29**, which now contain two branches of the **University of London**: the **Institute of Commonwealth Studies** and the **Institute of Germanic Studies**. The great law reformer Sir Samuel Romilly lived (and died by his own hand) at **No. 2**. Sir Thomas Lawrence had his studio at **No. 67** from 1805 until his death in 1830 (the building was later demolished). Here he painted his portrait series of princes, generals, and statesmen who helped bring about Napoléon's downfall; these works were painted for the **Waterloo Chamber** at **Windsor Castle**. Stop at the wooden coffee booth on the square's northern tip for a frothy cappuccino and enjoy it at one of the outdoor tables. ♦ At Guilford St and Montague Pl and at Southampton Row and Woburn Pl. Tube: Russell Sq

10 THE MONTAGUE ON THE GARDENS

$$$ A stone's throw from the **British Museum**, this elegant addition to London's hotel scene boasts 88 deluxe rooms and 11 suites over four floors. There are garden-view rooms, smoking rooms, and now Bloomsbury Rooms— 42 individually decorated rooms with luxury fabrics, handcrafted furnishings, marble bathrooms, and features like private balconies. The suites all have Jacuzzis, and many of them are split-level. The doormen are dressed in top hat and tails, the sitting room is lit by a crystal chandelier, and the conservatory has a lovely view over the Duke of Bedford's gardens. Group CEO Bea Tollman's unmistakable touch is evident everywhere in this Red Carnation Hotel. The group has just been named the Small Hotel Group of the Year. Deservedly so. Amenities include the **Terrace Bar** and the **Blue Door Bistro**. ♦ 15 Montague St (between Great Russell St and Russell Sq). 637.1001; fax 637.2516. Tube: Russell Sq, Holborn

11 ST. MARGARET'S HOTEL

$$ Friendly and quiet (for central London, anyway), this establishment is part of a Bloomsbury estate owned by the Duke of Bedford and has been managed by the same Italian family for 52 years. Although some of the 64 rooms are small, all are sparkling clean and have TVs and phones. There are also large triple rooms, which are good for families. St. Margaret's describes itself as a bed-and-breakfast hotel, and full English

breakfast there certainly is. If you want a private bath or shower, book well in advance, as not all the rooms have them. There are also two lounges for guests to use. If you're flying into **Heathrow**, you can take the **Piccadilly** line straight to the nearby underground stop (although those with heavy bags may need a taxi; it's a 6-minute walk from either **Russell Square** or **Holborn** tube station). ♦ 26 Bedford Pl (between Great Russell St and Russell Sq). 636.4277; fax 323.3066. Tube: Russell Sq, Holborn. www.stmargaretshotel.co.uk

12 GRAY'S INN

In the 14th century, the manor house of Sir Reginald le Grey, Chief Justice of Chester, was located here. By 1370, the grounds had developed into a hostel for law students, which was expanded during the Tudor period. Unfortunately, the inn was badly damaged during World War II; despite much restoration, it lacks the authentic feeling of **Lincoln's Inn**, its neighbor to the south. But be sure to walk through the passage in the southwest corner of the 17th-century **Gray's Inn Square** (off Gray's Inn Rd). Laid out by Sir Francis Bacon in 1606 and known affectionately as "The Walks," these sloping, tree-filled lawns delighted Samuel Pepys, who noted "fine ladies" promenading there, whereas Charles Lamb called them the "best gardens of the Inns of Court." The square and the chapel here are the only parts of the inn open to the public. In addition to the main entrance, there is a narrow passageway into the inn off High Holborn (between Gray's Inn Rd and Fulwood Pl). ♦ Gray's Inn Square: daily, noon–2:30PM, May–Sept. Chapel: M–F. Gray's Inn Rd (between High Holborn and Theobald's Rd). Tube: Chancery La

13 LEATHER LANE MARKET

You can reach this lunchtime street market via a passage down the east side of the **Prudential Assurance Building**. Shop for new clothes at bargain prices—shoes, jeans, and lamb's wool sweaters. Some plants, fruit, vegetables, and glassware are also sold. However, the only leather that can be found is at a stall that sometimes offers genuine chamois. ♦ M–F, 10:30AM–2PM. Between Greville St and Clerkenwell Rd. Tube: Chancery La, Farringdon

14 HATTON GARDEN

Named for Elizabeth I's chancellor, Sir Christopher Hatton, the center of the diamond trade isn't what it used to be. Office blocks have descended and ascended, and most of the shops look so vulgar or so impenetrable that you'd have to be an expert shopper to take them on. Behind the walls of the impressive building that houses the London

Diamond Club at **No. 87** (which is not open to the public), dealers buy and sell the precious gems to jewelry shops on a commission basis. ♦ Between Holborn Circus and Clerkenwell Rd. Tube: Chancery La, Farringdon

14 ST. JOHN

★★★★$$$ The wonderful Fergus Henderson has championed what he calls "nose-to-tail eating" in Britain. His restaurant is in a high-ceilinged, white-painted former smokehouse near Smithfield meat market and is a revelation. It is also No. 10 on *Restaurant Magazine's* list of the World's Top 100 Restaurants. Everything on any plate is the highest quality produce to be sourced. The menu is difficult to choose from because you'll want everything on it. Oxtail with beetroot and pickled walnut is a stunning starter, as is classic smoked eel and horseradish. Henderson's most famous appetizer is his roast marrow bone and parsley salad. Main courses might include chitterlings with dandelion, pheasant and trotter pie, or a more simple rack of lamb. And you can finish with chocolate cake and milk toffee ice cream. Very English. Very, very good. The wine list is exemplary and not overpriced. And the bread is so good you'll want to take some home. Luckily, at St John, you can. ♦ M-F, lunch and dinner; Sa, dinner. 26 St. John St. 251.0848. Tube: Farringdon

Bleeding Heart

15 BLEEDING HEART YARD

The yard is said to take its name from the 17th-century murder of Lady Elizabeth Hatton, which took place there. Lady Elizabeth was young, rich, and beautiful—and, having been widowed, much sought after. Her Annual Winter Ball on 26 January 1626 was as popular an event as the Oscars are today. The story says that the doors to the ballroom were flung open at one point in the evening and the saturnine, claw-handed European ambassador swept in and danced the lady around the floor and out into the courtyard. The next morning her lifeless body

was found there, torn limb from limb, her heart still pumping blood over the cobblestones. Hardly far-fetched at all! Charles Dickens, who wrote about the yard in his novels, told of another legend—that of a young woman imprisoned there by her cruel father for remaining true to her love, a young man not approved of by Daddy. ♦ Off Greville St (between Saffron Hill and Hatton Garden). Tube: Farringdon

Within Bleeding Heart Yard:

BLEEDING HEART RESTAURANT

★★★$$$ This place recently won awards for Best Restaurant for Business Lunches or Dinners, Best Service in London, Best in Britain for Private Dining, and Most Romantic Restaurant in London. So it seems fair to let you know about it. How can you resist a place that offers truffled parsley soup with poached egg? Or warm salad of smoked eel with marinated new potatoes, watercress, and horseradish cream and mustard beignets? Sea bass comes with crab and ginger, and roast broadside farm suckling pig with *choux farci* (stuffed cabbage), parsnip-potato purée, and mustard sauce. The menu is French, so there must be soufflé . . . and here it is pistachio! Pascal Evan is the man in the kitchen. The wine list has been described as one of the best in the world and offers more than 450 bins to choose from, including some from the Bleeding Heart's own vineyard in Hawkes Bay, New Zealand. ♦ French ♦ Daily, lunch and dinner. Reservations recommended for lunch. Bleeding Heart Yard, off Greville St (between Saffron Hill and Hatton Garden). 242.8238. Tube: Farringdon. www.bleedingheart.co.uk

BLEEDING HEART BISTRO

★★$$ Buzzy and fun, this place is less formal than the restaurant but just as French. There's coq au vin and steak frites; artichoke vinaigrette comes with an herb salad, and crème brûlée with peanut brittle. There's that same award-winning wine list and the chance to try at least a dozen bins by the glass. ♦ M-F, lunch and dinner. 242.2065

BLEEDING HEART TAVERN

★★$ The tavern has been here since 1746, at which time the proprietors boasted that the clientele could get "drunk for a penny and dead drunk for two pence." It's slightly more expensive nowadays, but the atmosphere is still friendly and the beer good (and properly English!). Downstairs

---

Restaurants/Clubs: **Red** | Hotels: **Purple** | Shops: **Orange** | Outdoors/Parks: **Green** | Sights/Culture: **Blue**

there is an open rotisserie and grill, where all the meat is free-range and British. The breakfast here is terrific (especially the full English). ♦ M-F, from 7:30AM. 242.2056

16 ST. JOHN STREET

An off-the-beaten-path in place for high-flying City workers, this street is attracting innovative chefs to open stylish restaurants. It is part of **Clerkenwell**, an interesting area that is fun to explore. ♦ Between Charter-house St and Clerkenwell Rd

17 SIR LOIN

★$ This is the only other Smithfield Market venue besides the **Fox and Anchor** (see below) for hearty English breakfasts, sometimes downed with Champagne. Lunch dishes include leek-and-potato soup, roast pork loin, and lamb cutlets. The restaurant is a no-nonsense, oak-paneled room above the rather basic **Hope Pub**, which offers hefty sandwiches at lunch. ♦ English ♦ M-F, breakfast, 7AM-9:30AM; lunch. Reserva-tions required. 94 Cowcross St (between Charterhouse St and Farringdon Rd). 253.8525. Tube: Barbican, Farringdon

18 FOX AND ANCHOR

★★$ Bleary-eyed medical students, young doctors and nurses, and butchers from **Smithfield Market** come here in the morning to enjoy huge platters of eggs, bacon, sausages, black pudding, baked beans, and fried bread (but you can get a vegetarian breakfast if you prefer). The special early-morning market license that allows alcohol to be served between 6 and 9AM to market workers now applies to all diners. The façade is Art Nouveau, and the interior has been refurbished to match, but the ambience and the food are the real attractions—best appreciated after working up a hearty appetite. The pub is popular with office work-ers, so it is essential to book on weekdays. ♦ Pub ♦ M-F, breakfast, lunch, and dinner, 7AM-9PM. Reservations required for early breakfast and lunch. 115 Charterhouse St (between Charterhouse Sq and St. John St). 253.5075. Tube: Barbican, Farringdon

19 COMPTOIR GASCON

One of the great things about London is that there are so many little doors that you can step through and go to another land altogether. Step through the door of this wonderful shop in London's **Smithfield Market** and you are transported to Gascony in southwest France. Owned and run by the same people who have the heavily awarded **Club Gascon** restaurant across the road, the shelves and cabinets are groaning with French regional specialties, like their many ways with foie gras, their charcuterie, and their specialist French caviar from the waters around Aquitaine. Their patisserie counter serves delicious pastries and a great range of homemade breads, including the traditional naturally fermented bread (sourdough to you!). They offer a wide range of Gascon artisanal cheeses, some pasteurized and others not. Be aware that if you don't go in with a lot of willpower, you'll come out with a lot of bags! ♦ M-F, 8AM-8:30PM; Sa, 10AM-5PM. 61-63 Charterhouse Street EC1, 608.0851. Tube: Farringdon, Barbican

20 SMITHFIELD MARKET

At midnight, the vans start arriving at the oldest and largest "dead meat" market in Europe. Covering 10 acres and 2 miles of shop frontages, this wholesale market is still on its original medieval site. Unloading, weighing, cutting, marking, and displaying all take place before selling begins at 5AM. Starting the day at dawn amid the orderly bustle of City life makes you feel like both an honorary and an ordinary citizen, no matter where you come from. When you stroll through the market, surrounded by white-coated butchers and bummarees (porters) effortlessly conveying pink, red, purple, and brown carcasses, you may feel like a background figure in a surreal painting; you'll see calves by Georgia O'Keeffe, piglets by Mother Goose, rib cages by Francis Bacon. Feathered chickens, geese, and turkeys hang alongside furry rabbits. A pervasive sense of the history of this trade allows guilt and nausea to recede: Life depends on markets, markets depend on death.

Signs announcing beef from Australia, New Zealand, and Scotland hang between the shining hooks. The arches, pillars, ornaments, and swirls of ironwork that adorn the trading halls are worthy of a City church. Though the animated atmosphere is pure Gothic, the long iron-and-glass building, modeled on **Sir Joseph Paxton**'s **Crystal Palace**, is mid-Victorian; designed by **Horace Jones**, it opened in 1868 with a meaty banquet for 1,200 people. With typical Victorian high-mindedness, a small park was built in the center of **Smithfield** where the bummarees could rest, but they choose now, as they chose then, the pubs in the area, which have special licenses to serve liquor in the early morning (but only to market workers).

The site has far more sinister associations than the slaughter of animals for consump-tion. Originally, it was a grassy "smooth field," or level, just outside the City walls for citizens' entertainment and exercise (hence the name, a corruption of "Smoothfield"). Executions were held here as early as 1305, when Scottish patriot William Wallace (whose life is depicted in Mel Gibson's 1995 film *Braveheart*) was put to death on St. Bartholomew's Day. Roger Mortimer, who murdered Edward II and loved his queen, was executed here on the orders of Edward III, and it was here, in 1381, that the confrontation over a poll tax took place between Wat Tyler with his band of revolutionaries and the 14-year-old Richard II. The young king calmed the angry mob and promised them mercy and justice. The crowd took him at his word and peacefully dispersed, but Richard II delivered neither justice nor mercy, and Tyler, stabbed by Sir William Walworth during the confrontation, died a few hundred yards away at **St. Bartholomew's Hospital**. From the 15th century onward, Smithfield was the execution place for all who were convicted of heresy, including the Catholics set ablaze by Henry VIII and most of the 277 Protestant martyrs who also were burned alive for their faith during the reign of Mary I. Smithfield's history is not entirely grim, however. The great St. Bartholomew's Fair was held here every August, from Henry II's time until 1855. The 3-day event was the most important cloth fair in England, expanding as the export of wool and fabric grew. The Royal Smithfield Show (now held at Earl's Court) began here in 1799, and as far back as medieval times there was a large horse-and-cattle market; live animals were herded across the streets of London to reach it. The days of great fairs have passed, but the area has been kept vital by the remarkable and ironic juxtaposition of its two principal institutions: the meat market and the hospital. Both are under threat, however. The former may be moved elsewhere, whereas the latter is struggling against government cutbacks and privatization of medical services. ♦ M–F, 5–10:30AM. Bounded by Lindsey St and Farringdon Rd and by W Smithfield and Charterhouse St. Tube: Barbican, Farringdon

Within Smithfield Market:

BUBBS

★★$$$ Tucked on the outskirts of Smithfield Market, this bistro is a series of connecting rooms packed with City ladies and gents. The fish specials change daily, but meat lovers should stick with the entrecôte Béarnaise. And if you're still hungry, there are several delicious desserts to choose from, like chocolate truffle mousse and ice-cream nougat served with raspberry sauce. ♦ French ♦ M–F, lunch; Tu–Th, lunch and dinner. 329 Central Market (between W Poultry Ave and Farringdon Rd). 236.2435

20 SMITHS OF SMITHFIELD

★★★$$$ This four-story Grade II–listed building was originally a warehouse but lay empty for 40 years before John Torode, the exciting young chef whose passionate cooking made dining at Terence Conran's

now defunct Mezzo restaurant such a joy, restored it and created Smiths of Smithfield.

The **Ground Floor** is a casual bar/diner and opens at 7AM for one of the best breakfasts in London. You can have just porridge with honey or sugar, or maybe English muffins and honey, or you can choose from one of five all-day breakfasts that will keep you going all day. The ground floor does a great brunch (terrific eggs Benedict), interesting composed salads, burgers, and sandwiches, and its juice bar also does smoothies and shakes. If you are in the area and want something quick, casual, and delicious, you could do a great deal worse than this.

The **First Floor** is all tricked out in warm reds and is a rather good cocktail bar, offering an intelligent and innovative list accompanied by "Nibbles," such as Thai-spiced fish cakes or fried salt-and-pepper squid.

Floor Two is the dining room—all exposed brick and wooden tables. The food here is simple but very good. A spinach and watercress salad comes with soft-boiled egg, and the pumpkin ravioli with mascarpone and sage. There is a good selection of grills, finely done, and a much better-than-average choice of vegetarian options. Each day there is a Lunch Market Special. Wednesday is Meatloaf Day!

The **Third Floor** is a private dining room, bookable should you have a large number of friends in London with whom you wish to dine.

The crowning glory, as it were, of Smiths is the rooftop restaurant on the **Fourth Floor**. It has a terrace for dining in good weather, with a superlative view over the City of London. This floor is dedicated to the best of British and rare-breed meats. As throughout the restaurant, all the meat is organic and additive free. As well as grills, you could opt for a foie gras terrine with baby artichokes, a rare-breed raviolo with parsnip purée and foie gras sauce, or a terrific venison Wellington. The wine lists throughout the place are well put together and very reasonable. ♦ Ground Floor, daily from 7AM; cocktail bar, daily till late; 2nd Floor, daily, lunch and dinner; 4th Floor, daily, lunch and dinner; Su, brunch. 67-77 Charterhouse St. 251.7950. Tube: Farringdon. www.smithsofsmithfield.co.uk

21 CLOTH FAIR

This street in the heart of old London retains the style that the whole City of London had before it was destroyed by money, the Great Fire of 1666, and World War II. **No. 41** is the only house in the City built before the fire. Sir John Betjeman, a beloved poet laureate, once resided at **No. 43**. Now the short terrace of the 18th-century houses is owned by the **Landmark Trust**, a charity that rescues minor buildings in distress before

---

Restaurants/Clubs: **Red** | Hotels: **Purple** | Shops: **Orange** | Outdoors/Parks: **Green** | Sights/Culture: **Blue**

they are knocked down by vandals or developers. **Nos. 43** and **45A** are available for short holiday rentals; to book, contact the Landmark Trust (Shottesbrooke, Maidenhead, Berkshire, SL6 3SW; 0162/882.5925) a year in advance. ♦ Between King St and Little Britain. Tube: Barbican

22 ST. BARTHOLOMEW'S HOSPITAL

When Wat Tyler was stabbed by Sir William Walworth during the 1331 peasants' confrontation with Edward II, he was brought to **Bart's**, as this institution is commonly called, and died in the "emergency room." Though still treating patients and considered part of the **University of London**, it faces closure owing to the government's recent privatization of health care—despite the fact that it's the oldest hospital in London and the only one of London's medieval foundations to remain on its original site. Like **St. Bartholomew the Great** (see below), the hospital was founded in 1123 by Thomas Rahere, although Henry VIII is regarded as a kind of second founder after he dissolved the adjacent priory during the Reformation and granted a royal charter refounding the hospital in 1546. The gateway, built in 1702 by Edward Strong the Younger, is topped by a statue of Henry VIII by Francis Bird. The collegiate-style buildings inside the great quadrangle were added by **James Gibbs** between 1730 and 1770. There are weekly guided tours of the hospital's historic sights, including The Pool of Bethesda and The Good Samaritan, two large murals painted in 1737 by William Hogarth, a governor of the hospital. They line the staircase that leads to the **Great Hall**. The **Medical School**, which is a vital part of the hospital, is the oldest in London, founded in 1662. A small museum opened in May 1997. ♦ Free. Hospital: guided tours on Friday, 2PM. Museum: Tu–F. W Smithfield (between Little Britain and Giltspur Sts). Guided tours, 837.0546; museum, 601.8152. Tube: Barbican, Farringdon, St. Paul's

Within St. Bartholomew's Hospital:

ST. BARTHOLOMEW THE LESS

This octagonal chapel is the parish church of St. Bartholomew's Hospital and was founded in the 12th century, rebuilt 300 years later (two 15th-century arches survive under the tower), rebuilt again in 1789 and 1823, and restored in 1951 following damage suffered during World War II. The register dates back to 1547 and indicates that **Inigo Jones** was baptized here in 1573. ♦ Open to tourists daily for services and prayers. Open 24 hours for friends and families of hospital patients. 601.8888 (ask for the church)

22 ST. BARTHOLOMEW THE GREAT

For lovers of antiquity and lovers of London, this church is a shrine. It's the oldest parish church in London (only **St. John's Chapel** in the **Tower of London** exceeds it in age) and the City's only surviving Norman church. Thomas Rahere, a favorite courtier of Henry I, built it as a priory in 1123, along with **St. Bartholomew's Hospital**, as an act of gratitude after he had a vision during a fever in which St. Bartholomew saved him from a monster. The building's simple majesty and ancient beauty quicken the hearts of all who enter: An inexplicable power comes from the stones, the strong pillars, the pointed windows, the tomb of Rahere, and the miracle of survival to which the church is witness. Today's visitors do not see it quite as Rahere, first canon and first prior, saw it. The massive nave was the choir of the original church; the original nave is now part of the courtyard; and the 13th-century entrance gate was originally the west entrance to the south aisle. But the choir and vaulted ambulatories, crossing, chancel with apse, two transepts, and at least one bay of the nave have changed little since Rahere's time. The music sung during the choral service on Sunday seems to reach back in time, forming a heavenly connection among stones, centuries, saints, and angels.

The restored **Lady Chapel** dates from the 14th century and contains the only medieval font in the City; William Hogarth was baptized here in 1697. The five pre-Reformation bells in the tower peal before Evensong on Sunday. The crypt and cloister have been restored, and the large chamber is dedicated to the City of London squadron of the Royal Air Force, which holds a memorial service here each year.

During the Reformation, the church was sold and fell on hard times. The cloisters became a stable, the crypt was used for storing coal and wine, and the Lady Chapel became a printer's office where a young Benjamin Franklin worked in 1725. There was a blacksmith's forge in the north transept.

In the 1860s, architect **Sir Aston Webb** began the Parliament-funded restoration of the church. With the assistance of his colleague, **F.L. Dove**, Webb saved both the reality and the spirit of the structure. The gateway has been restored in memory of the two architects—notice their coats of arms. The wooden figure of Rahere was carved from a beam taken from the church and placed here in memory of Webb's son, Phillip, who was killed in action in France during World War I.

Film buffs might like to know that it was the location for the wedding that didn't happen in the movie Four Weddings and a Funeral. ♦ M–F, Su; Sa, 10:30AM–1PM; closed Monday in August. Services: Su, 9AM, 11AM, 6:30PM. W Smithfield (at Little Britain). 606.5171. Tube: Barbican

23 BISHOP'S FINGER

★★$ This pub used to be called the **Rutland**, but Bishop's Finger is the name of one of the beers made by the brewery Shepherd Neame, to which the pub is tied, and the name stuck. Meat carriers from the market, doctors and medical students from **Bart's**, lawyers and reporters from the **Old Bailey**, and moneymakers from the City all drink in the two bars, which spill over into the park opposite on sunny days. The place serves traditional pub grub at lunch and sandwiches and meat pies at dinner. ♦ Pub ♦ M–F, lunch and dinner. 9–10 W Smithfield (at Hosier La). 248.2341. Tube: Barbican, St. Paul's

24 ST. BARTHOLOMEW'S HOSPITAL ARCHIVES AND MUSEUM HISTORY TRAIL

This little guided walk is a meander through some wonderfully atmospheric parts of London. Knowing what all the places are makes it more interesting . . . but just the walk itself is picturesque and very Olde London!

25 BRITISH MUSEUM

"Ennui," wrote the lyricist of an old song, "was the day when the British Museum lost its charm." For those still excited by history, this institution is as charming as ever; the only problem is managing to see the exhibitions through the crowds.

When physician and naturalist Sir Hans Sloane died in 1753, his will allowed the nation to buy his vast collection of art, antiquities, and natural history for £20,000—less than half of what it cost to assemble. With the additions of Robert Cotton's library and antiquities and the manuscripts of Robert Harley, Earl of Oxford, the collection grew, and when George II's 12,000-volume library was dedicated in 1823, it filled **Montagu House**, where it had been on display since 1759. A decision was then made to build new quarters for the burgeoning national collection. **Sir Robert Smirke** designed a large quadrangle with an open courtyard behind Montagu House, then surrounded it with a fine neoclassical façade. In 1847, he added an Ionic colonnade and a pediment decorated with Sir Richard Westmacott's figures representing the progress of civilization. The architect's brother, **Sydney Smirke**, began the courtyard's conversion into the beautiful, blue-domed **Reading Room** in 1852 according to a plan by Sir Anthony Panizzi, the principal librarian. Space problems were alleviated in the 1880s, when the natural history exhibitions moved to the **Natural History Museum**, and in 1970, when the ethnographic exhibitions were moved to the **Museum of Mankind**.

Start with the **Egyptian Sculpture Gallery** (**Room 25**) on the ground floor. The massive granite figures can be seen over the heads of any number of people. To the left of the door is the **Rosetta Stone**, not so much fascinating in itself (it is an irregularly shaped, tightly inscribed piece of black basalt) as in the way it changed our understanding of history. Written in Greek and in two forms of ancient Egyptian script, the stone's Greek translation provided the key to hieroglyphics undeciphered for 1,400 years and finally made sense of all the previously mysterious symbols found on so many monuments. In the rest of the gallery, enormous sculptures, intricate pieces of jewelry, and carvings give an overwhelming introduction to the ancient Egyptians. There is a haughty bronze cat from 600 BC, sacred to Bastet (an Egyptian deity); a large reclining granite ram with a tiny figure of King Taharqa tucked beneath his chin; and from the Temple of Mut in Thebes, carved in about 1400 BC, are four huge granite representations of the goddess Sakhmet, with the body of a woman and the head of a lion. The rest of the Egyptian exhibitions are on the upper floors (**Rooms 60** through 66). The Etruscans, the Italian civilization that reached its peak of power in the seventh and sixth centuries BC, were fine metalworkers and potters. Here their achievements in jewelry and ornamentation are revealed; some of the pieces are so intricately wrought that modern jewelers cannot copy them (**Room 71**). Before climbing the stairs, visit **Rooms 1** through **15**, which hold the museum's collection of Greek and Roman antiquities, including the hotly contested **Elgin Marbles** (**Room 8**), sculptures from the Parthenon and the Erechtheum that Lord Elgin brought to England in 1816 and that the government of Greece is seeking to have returned. Mostly fragments, they are described in the diary of an attendant, John Conrath, who helped move them into the museum and was assigned to the gallery where they were displayed. This diary can be seen in the **British Library Galleries**. "Northside," he wrote, describing the frieze that had been inside the great colonnade, "a young man almost naked, putting a Crown on his head, another ready to mount, attended by his grooms, around the west corner a single person, a magistrate or director, two Chariots . . . South frieze, Seven more Bulls, a man Crowning himself." Although the eroded and broken state of the marbles disappointed some early visitors, they also attracted such illustrious fans as the Grand Duke Nicholas, later Czar Nicholas I of Russia, who spent 2 days looking at the marbles in 1817. At the head of the stairs in **Room 37**, the well-preserved body of Celtic Lindow

Man (discovered in a Cheshire bog) lies in an airtight chamber; even the brutality of his death as a religious sacrifice cannot detract from the gleaming artistry of the golden torques in the rest of the Celtic collection. The upper floors also hold "Medieval and Later Antiquities from Europe" (**Rooms 41** through **48**), with lethal bronze weapons and the extraordinary **Lycurgus Cup**, a Roman goblet carved from a single block of green glass that shows the tortured face of the Thracian king Lycurgus, imprisoned by the tendrils of a vine. The rooms also contain remarkable displays of jewelry. The **Gallery of Clocks and Watches** (**Room 44**) exhibits a range of timepieces from the Middle Ages to the beginning of this century.

With the move of the **British Library** to its new St. Pancras headquarters complete, renovation and roofing on **Smirke's Great Court** has been completed, opening up the museum's inner court for the first time in 150 years. Visitors once again have access to the famed **British Library Reading Room**, with its domed ceiling, which has been used by readers as diverse as Marx, Lenin, Gandhi, George Bernard Shaw, and Thomas Carlyle. The reading room will become a study center, surrounded by the **Great Court**, redeveloped to provide visitor facilities including bigger shops and restaurants.

The British Museum occupies the site of the first Duke of Montagu's house. Needing to replenish a fortune ravaged by the extravagances of building this mansion, he set out to win the hand of the extremely rich (and quite mad) second Duchess of Albemarle. The duchess, who insisted that she would marry only a crowned head of state, happily offered her hand when the duke convinced her that he was the emperor of China. The ghost of the erstwhile empress is probably roaming contentedly through the collection of Oriental antiquities, in **Room 33** on the ground floor and **Rooms 91** through **94** on the upper floor.

There is a useful selection of tours available. They are limited to 25 people, so booking is advisable. The Highlights Tour takes you around the classic "must see" exhibits. It lasts 90 minutes and sets off at 10:30AM, 1PM, and 3PM. Tickets cost £8/£5 concession. 323.8299 or e-mail visitorinformation@thebritishmuseum.ac.uk. There are also the "Eye Openers"—10 different free tours concentrating on one gallery each. These last 50 minutes and kick off regularly. www.museum-mile. org. ♦ Free. Su–W, 9AM–6PM; Th–Sa, 9AM–11PM. Great Court opening times: M–W, 9AM–9PM; Th–Sa, 9AM–11PM; Su, 9AM–6PM. Great Russell St (between Montague and Bloomsbury Sts). General information, 636.1555; recorded information 580.1788. Tube: Russell Sq, Holborn, Tottenham Court Rd

Within the British Museum:

THE COURT RESTAURANT

★$$ Under the famous Norman Foster roof, this restaurant serves an international cuisine, from mozzarella with poached figs and artichoke salad to caramelized scallops and tuna rolls with lime and wasabi dressing and sweet soy sauce. Even desserts run the international gamut from American cheesecake to blackberry crepes. Afternoons teas can be traditional English, Chinese, Viennese, or Champagne. To get a table overlooking the lovely 19th-century Reading Room, you need to book well in advance. ♦International ♦Sa–W morning, coffee, lunch, and afternoon tea; Th, F, also dinner. 323.8990

THE COURT CAFÉ

★$ Freshly made sandwiches and snacks, salads and cakes. ♦ Su–W, 9AM–5PM; Th–Sa, 9AM–9PM

GALLERY CAFÉ

The most family friendly of the museum's eating places, the Gallery Café serves hot dishes like pasta and soups, salads, sandwiches, desserts, and cakes. ♦ Daily, 10AM–5PM

BOOKSHOP

A good, generous selection of coffee-table art and history books, with a reasonably but not overly informed staff. Go for an older staff member, who will know more. Sa–W, 9:30AM–6PM; Th, F, 9:30AM–8PM

CHILDREN'S SHOP

Lots of small items, available for only pocket money, to delight the younger shopper. A great idea for kids. M–Sa, 9:30AM–6PM; Su, 10AM–6PM

SOUVENIRS SHOP

Guides and postcards, films and disposable cameras, stationery and inexpensive gifts . . . all with the ubiquitous museum logo, just to show you were there! Sa–W, 9:30AM–6PM; Th, F, 9:30AM–8PM

GRENVILLE SHOP

Replica sculpture, jewelry, silk scarves, and ties—if you want a souvenir that is more than an eraser with a logo, then this is the shop for you. Some of the stuff is even really nice! ♦ Sa–W, 10AM–6PM; Th, F, 10AM–8PM

26 WESTAWAY & WESTAWAY

London's most reliable and most affordable dealer in woolens carries scarves, blankets, hats, and socks—everything for keeping

ON THE TRAIL OF LONDON'S LITERATI

The streets of London have long echoed with the footsteps of the many British novelists, essayists, and poets who lived there at least part of the time and drew inspiration for their immortal works. Happily, it is still possible to soak up the literary atmosphere by visiting the haunts of such leading lights as Virginia Woolf, Samuel Johnson, and Charles Dickens, among others (see Shakespeare's Globe Comes Full Circle, on page 196).

Bloomsbury conjures up the eponymous group of writers and artists centered on Virginia Woolf and Lytton Strachey during the early 1900s. It was here that the friends, many opposed to Victorian restrictions, wrote and painted; conducted their passionate affairs; discussed art, literature, and society; and deeply influenced the British avant-garde. In this lovely tree-shaded neighborhood of pleasant Georgian squares, behind the **British Museum**, you'll find **Gordon Square**, with its clutch of houses displaying blue plaques to show where members of the circle lived until World War II.

Their central meeting place was **No. 46**, the home of Virginia and her sister, Vanessa. Nearby (in a building that no longer exists), Virginia and Leonard Woolf ran Hogarth Press between 1925 and 1939 and published several of her works, including the classic feminist essay A Room of One's Own and the acclaimed novel The Waves. Bloomsbury aficionados won't want to miss the **Bloomsbury Workshop**, a little gallery and shop that stocks many first editions of the Bloomsbury writers. Another London literary denizen was Dr. Samuel Johnson, whose traces remain in **Westminster Abbey** (a bust of the essayist, poet, and scholar is near his grave in **Poets' Corner**), and **St. Paul's Cathedral**, where his statue stands beneath the dome. There's also a statue behind his parish church, **St. Clement Danes**, in the **Strand**: With book in hand, his figure gazes toward the **Fleet Street** he found so convivial and stimulating. In fact, Johnson lived mostly around Fleet Street in at least 13 addresses, but the one place open to visitors is **Dr.**

Johnson's House (17 Gough Sq, at Pemberton Row, 0171/353.3745), where he resided between 1748 and 1759 and compiled his famous Dictionary. Nearby was, and still is, **Ye Olde Cheshire Cheese**, his favorite watering hole, where he met with local wits who called themselves the Literary Club; his favorite armchair still sits in the **Chop Room**. There's now a large **Johnson Bar** on the first floor, where a display case holds a huge seventh edition of his dictionary. Johnson's acerbic humor is evident in such entries as "Oats—a grain, which in England is generally given to horses but in Scotland supports the people."

And then there's Charles Dickens, a literary great whose spirit totally pervades London. In fact, this author, possessed of feverish energy, seems to pop up everywhere: in the same **Ye Olde Cheshire Cheese**, mentioned in A Tale of Two Cities; in **The George**, near **Southwark Cathedral**, cited in Little Dorrit; in the **George & Vulture** on **Cornhill**, where he wrote part of The Pickwick Papers. However, the best place to immerse yourself in Dickensiana is at the much-visited **Dickens House** (48 Doughty St, between Roger and Guilford Sts, 0171/405.2127), a charming 18th-century building on a lovely Georgian street. During the 2 years Dickens lived there (1837–1839) he was remarkably prolific, working on The Pickwick Papers, Oliver Twist, and Nicholas Nickleby; he also composed over 500 letters and even began Barnaby Rudge. It was here too that tragedy struck the household when the author's cherished sister-in-law, Mary, died in 1837 at age 17.

The house is chockablock with memorabilia, and the restored study and first-floor drawing room vividly evoke the author's presence. Among the house's treasures are the author's desk, his good-luck china monkey and other personal relics, first editions, autographed letters, and portraits and illustrations. In fact, you will come across Dickens's well-recorded footsteps throughout the pages of this guide: He was the ultimate chronicler of London.

warm. The variety of Scottish cashmeres, woven in Scotland from the wool of cashmere goats in China, gives you a better selection here than in Scotland. ♦ Daily. 62-65 Great Russell St (at Bury Pl). 405.4479. Tube: Holborn, Tottenham Court Rd. Also at 92–93 Great Russell St (at Bloomsbury St). 636.1718. Tube: Tottenham Court Rd; 26 Henrietta St (between Southampton and Bedford Sts). 497.5060. Tube: Covent Garden

27 L. CORNELISSEN

This is an old-fashioned shop with old-fashioned and very special art supplies—its own brand of violin varnish (with the imaginative name of Dragon's Blood), cobalt blues, British and French gold leaf, pure squirrel-mop brushes, and quill brushes. Every kind of ink is available, along with pencils, paper, and objects related to aesthetic writing. ♦ M–Sa. 105 Great Russell St (between

Restaurants/Clubs: Red | Hotels: Purple | Shops: Orange | Outdoors/Parks: Green | Sights/Culture: Blue

Bloomsbury St and Adeline Pl). 636.1045. Tube: Tottenham Court Rd

28 PLOUGH

★$ The feel of Bloomsbury lingers in this literary pub, perhaps because it has remained popular with publishers and writers for so long. They appreciate its coziness in winter and the outdoor tables in summer, as well as the bar lunch menu and wide selection of ales. ♦ Pub ♦ Daily, lunch and dinner. 27 Museum St (at Little Russell St). 636.7964. Tube: Holborn, Tottenham Court Rd

29 MUSEUM STREET

This narrow, friendly street is lined with some of the best antique-print dealers and bookshops in London. ♦ Between Bloomsbury Way and Great Russell St. Tube: Holborn, Tottenham Court Rd

30 RENAISSANCE CHANCERY COURT HOTEL

$$$ It's a Marriott, so don't expect much in the way of individualism or quaint eccentricity. Having said that, it was voted one of *Condé Nast Traveller*'s top five business hotels in the UK. It is all impressively historical frontage and vaulting lobby when you arrive and everything a big five-star hotel usually is—all very smart and efficient, with decent-sized rooms (there are 357 over 7 floors, including Club Rooms and Suites) with Internet, choice of foam or down pillows and comforters, bathrobes to swan around your marble bathroom in, minibar and coffeemaker, 24-hour room service, air conditioning, and the whole nine yards. The location is right in the heart of everything, so from reading about a theater show in your daily-delivered newspaper to walking up to the theater itself will take about 15 minutes, unless you opt for the hotel's limousine service, when it will take about 3 hours in London traffic. The hotel also has an award-winning day spa. One fun deal on offer here is the Babymoon Break, for expectant couples! You get breakfast in bed (could be the last time for a while), a copy of the *Yummy Mummy's Survival Guide*, a Musical Energy Balancing Treatment (for two) in the spa, and a goody bag with stuff like cupcakes and nibbles in it, just for those late-night munchy moments. The **CC Bar** is elegant and impressive, and does good cocktails. **The Lounge** is open for breakfast, lunch, dinner, and afternoon tea, and offers one of those five-star international menus I am sure you could recite in your sleep. ♦ 252 High Holborn (near Procter St). 829.9888/829.7076. Tube: Holborn. www.marriott.co.uk

Within the Renaissance Chancery Court:

PEARL

★★★$$$$ This place went from a standing start in 2004 to receiving cascades of accolades. And talking of cascades, before you put *amuse-gueule* to taste bud, the décor here will have you drooling. It occupies the former banking halls of the Pearl Assurance Company and is the work of the same design team who brought the glitterati Nobu, Le Cercle, and the Metropolitan. Tables in the bar are inlaid with mother-of-pearl, and trails of hand-strung pearls cascade all over the main room, which is otherwise done out in marble, polished walnut, and pearlescent leather. Jun Tanaka, the chef, is quite a guy. At 19, he asked his father which restaurants were the best and then applied to each of them for work. He started at Le Gavroche and worked his way through seven Michelin-starred kitchens before getting his own. He offers ever-changing lunch and dinner menus as well as tasting and vegetarian menus. Sea bass comes at lunch with zucchini pesto and black olive oil; caramelized scallops come at dinner with herb-crusted frogs' legs, parsley purée, and garlic foam. Vegetarians can enjoy the absolutely gorgeous warm salad of winter vegetables with watercress, walnut paste, and horseradish dressing, and "tasters" get to try little bits of everything accompanied by the sommelier's suggestion of wine (or sometimes beer). The wine list is 200 bottles thick, and the beer menu a lesson for high-end restaurants everywhere. ♦ M-F, lunch and dinner; Sa, dinner. 829.7000. www.pearl-restaurant.com

31 CITTIE OF YORKE

★★★$ One of the largest pubs (with the largest bar) in London, this 17th-century establishment must have served most of Holborn in bygone days. A capacious three-sided fireplace and little cubicles keep the place warm and intimate. The bar food is excellent, and the real ales are much appreciated by the legal clientele. ♦ Pub ♦ M-Sa, lunch and dinner. 22–23 High Holborn (between Gray's Inn Rd and Warwick Ct). 242.7670. Tube: Chancery La

32 STAPLE INN BUILDINGS

A pure, domestic remnant of Elizabethan London, this pair of houses dates from 1586 and displays black-and-white timber and plaster, gables, overhangs, and oriels. Badly damaged by a bomb in 1944 and then carefully restored, the inn now comprises offices and Old World shops, including the **Institute of Actuaries**, which is one of the **Inns of Chancery** affiliated

with **Gray's Inn**. Dr. Samuel Johnson moved into **No. 2** in 1759, following his wife's death and his departure from Gough Square. The silver griffin on the stone obelisk in front marks the boundary of the City of London. ♦ Off Holborn (between Furnival St and Southampton Bldgs). Tube: Chancery La

33 PRUDENTIAL ASSURANCE BUILDING

This is an example of what the late Sir John Betjeman, poet laureate and longtime resident of the neighborhood, admired, defended, and fought to save: high Victorian architecture. Also known as "The Pru," the Gothic redbrick immensity, built by **Alfred Waterhouse** between 1879 and 1906, no doubt infuses passersby with confidence in this large insurance company. It stands on the site of **Furnival's Inn**, where Charles Dickens lived and wrote part of *The Pickwick Papers*. Only the structure's façade remains. The building is closed to the public. ♦ 142 Holborn (between Leather La and Brooke St). Tube: Chancery La

34 ELY PLACE

A watchman in a small gatehouse still guards this charming cul-de-sac of 18th-century houses. As the land belongs to Ely Cathedral in Cambridgeshire, the street remains legally under the jurisdiction of the bishops of Ely, meaning London police cannot automatically enter—perhaps a more useful edict now that the lovely doorways by the **Adam** brothers lead to lawyers' and accountants' offices rather than to private houses. Sadly, as with many other parts of historic London, the developer's ax threatens to fall here. ♦ Off Charterhouse St (between Farringdon Rd and Holborn Circus). Tube: Chancery La, Farringdon

On Ely Place:

ST. ETHELDREDA (ELY CHAPEL)

This church, once the chapel to **Ely Palace**, is all that is left of the building, which belonged to the bishops of Ely. When it was built in 1290, it was, of course, Catholic, and like all churches in England during the Reformation, it became Protestant. In 1874, the Roman Catholics bought it back and named it St. Etheldreda, making it the first pre-Reformation church to return to the fold. This masterpiece of the 13th-century Early Decorated style has a mood of great antiquity and quotidian warmth thanks to **Sir Giles Gilbert Scott**'s sensitive restoration in 1935. The windows at the east and west ends are noted for their superb tracery; the west window, which dates from around 1300, is one of the largest in London. Modern stained-glass windows by Charles and May Blakeman depict English martyrs. Very much a living church, it is active in the community and in such organizations as Amnesty International.

THE CRYPT

★★$$$ The Crypt is 600 years old and was the venue for King Henry VIII's wedding feast. Still available for hire as a venue for celebrations, it can seat up to 130 people for dinner and offers the same menu as the Bleeding Heart Restaurant (see page 155). ♦ Daily (for private hire). 242.2056

35 YE OLDE MITRE TAVERN

★★$ Just to the south of the church, down a little passageway, is this atmospheric pub built in 1546 for the Bishop of Ely's servants. In the corner of the front bar is an unusual relic: A five-foot section of trunk from the cherry tree around which Elizabeth I once danced is on view in a glass display case. Pub food includes sausages and sandwiches, pork pies, and Scotch eggs. ♦ Pub ♦ M-F, lunch and dinner. Ely Ct (between Ely Pl and Hatton Garden). 405.4751. Tube: Chancery La, Farringdon

36 STATUE OF PRINCE ALBERT

The almost whimsical statue of Prince Albert on a horse in the middle of a traffic island is unworthy of the man who worked tirelessly for his adopted country, left a legacy of great museums, and introduced the Christmas tree to Britain. The monument was created by Charles Bacon in 1874 and heralds the beginning of **Holborn Viaduct**. ♦ Holborn Circus (at Holborn Viaduct and Holborn and at St. Andrew St and Hatton Garden). Tube: Chancery La, Farringdon

37 ST. ANDREW HOLBORN

Sir Christopher Wren built his largest parish church in 1690, on the remains of a church founded in the 13th century. In 1704, he refaced the medieval tower of the original church, which miraculously survived the five bombs that destroyed its interior during World War II. In the 1960s, the furnishings

---

Restaurants/Clubs: **Red** | Hotels: **Purple** | Shops: **Orange** | Outdoors/Parks: **Green** | Sights/Culture: **Blue**

were replaced with treasures from the **Foundling Hospital Chapel** in Bloomsbury, including the gilded 18th-century organ that Handel gave to the hospital and the 18th-century font and altar rails. The church records show the 1770 burial of Thomas Chatterton, the poet who committed suicide by poison at the age of 18 after despairing over his poverty and lack of recognition (he later became a symbol of the Romantic movement). Essayist William Hazlitt was married here in 1808, with Charles Lamb as his best man and Mary Lamb as a bridesmaid. The Jewish-born prime minister Benjamin Disraeli was baptized here in 1817 at the age of 12. And the tomb of Captain Coram, founder of the **Foundling Hospital**, withstood the bombing of World War II; a weeping cherub watches over the good man.
♦ Holborn Circus (at St. Andrew St). Tube: Chancery La, Farringdon

38 HOLBORN VIADUCT

The world's first overpass, 1,400 feet long and 80 feet wide, was constructed between 1863 and 1869 by William Haywood to bridge the valley of the River Fleet and to connect Holborn with Newgate Street. The cost was 4,000 dwellings and £2.5 million. Its elaborate cast-iron work is best seen from Farringdon Street. Four bronze statues representing Agriculture, Commerce, Science, and Fine Art grace the north and south sides of the bridge section, and at the corners are four City heroes: Henry FitzAilwin, first lord mayor of London; Sir Thomas Gresham, founder of the Royal Exchange; Sir Hugh Myddelton, who brought fresh water to London; and finally antihero Sir William Walworth, who fatally stabbed rebellion leader Wat Tyler. Before the viaduct was built, the steep banks of this part of the river were very difficult to negotiate. Steps lead down to Farringdon Street and **City Thameslink Station**, a small railway depot that serves commuters to the southern counties.
♦ Between Giltspur St and Holborn Circus. Tube: Farringdon, St. Paul's

39 HOLY SEPULCHRE

Often referred to as **St. Sepulchre's**, the spacious church was originally dedicated in 1137 to King Edmund (who ruled East Anglia in AD 841–870). It was rebuilt in the 15th century, restored after the Great Fire (possibly by **Sir Christopher Wren**), heavily Victorianized in 1878, and sensitively repaired after World War II. Known as the Musicians' Church, it has a long tradition of memorial services for composers and singers, a **Musicians' Chapel** with windows dedicated to opera singer Dame Nellie Melba and composer John Ireland, and exquisite

kneelers with names of great musicians, bars of music, and musical instruments in fine needlepoint. Sir Henry Wood, the founder of the Promenade Concerts, was baptized here, became assistant organist when he was 12, and is remembered in Gerald Smith's central window of the north chapel, which is also dedicated to St. Cecilia, the patron saint of music. American associations with the church inspired the south aisle's stained-glass window of Captain John Smith, who led the expedition to Virginia that began in 1606. Taken prisoner by Native Americans, he was saved by the chief's daughter, Pocahontas, just as he was about to be killed. The English captain became governor of Virginia, and his savior married another settler, John Rolfe, who brought her to England. Sadly, Pocahontas's health declined quickly, and she died a year later. Smith is buried here, but the resting place of his rescuer is at the appropriately named town of Gravesend in Kent.

To the right of the altar, a small glass case encloses a hand bell that was tolled outside the cell of a condemned man at midnight on the eve of his hanging. The bellman recited the following verses: "All you that in the condemned hole do lie; Prepare you, for tomorrow you shall die; Watch all and pray; The hour is drawing near; That you before the Almighty must appear; Examine well yourselves; in time repent; That you may not to eternal flames be sent; And when St. Sepulchre's Bell in the morning tolls, Lord have mercy on your souls." All this, including the ringing of the great bell of St. Sepulchre on the morning of the execution, was arranged and paid for by an endowment of £50 made by parishioner Robert Dowe in 1605. ♦ M–F. Holborn Viaduct (at Giltspur St). 248.3110. Tube: St. Paul's

40 VIADUCT TAVERN

★★$ A fascinating pub, this one, built in 1869 over the debtors' cells of the old **Newgate Prison**, was named for **Holborn Viaduct**. It's a Victorian extravaganza, the interior lavished with gold mirrors and large paintings. The proprietor arranges tours of the cells now and then. ♦ Pub ♦ Daily, lunch. 126 Newgate St (between King Edward and Giltspur Sts). 600.1863. Tube: St. Paul's

41 MAGPIE AND STUMP

★★$ The original pub faced the gallows of Newgate jail and rented out its upper floors for all-night parties before an execution. Today's incarnation, built after the recent redevelopment of this corner, is modern, complete with air conditioning and an elevator. ♦ Pub/pizza ♦ M–F, lunch and dinner. 218 Old Bailey (at Bishop's Ct). 248.5985. Tube: St. Paul's

42 OLD BAILEY (CENTRAL CRIMINAL COURT)

The figure of Justice, holding scales but neither blind nor blindfolded, stands atop the dome, a bronze-gilded prelude to countless TV and film thrillers. The carved inscription over the main entrance, "Defend the Children of the Poor and Punish the Wrongdoer," proves as difficult a combination today as it was when Fagin went to the gallows on this very site in Chapter 52 of *Oliver Twist*. Old Bailey is the more familiar name for the Central Criminal Court, which serves Greater London and parts of Surrey, Kent, and Essex; it's where the most serious, dramatic, and celebrated criminal cases are heard. A medieval gatehouse where murderers and thieves were imprisoned originally stood on this site. It was part of **Newgate Prison**, which for centuries played an important and dreadful role in London life, especially during the late 18th and 19th centuries, when it was the city's chief penitentiary. Methods of execution were particularly horrible, including death by pressing. The conditions, despite numerous extensions and the installation of a windmill on the roof to improve ventilation, were just as notoriously barbaric. In 1750, a plague of "gaol fever"—actually a nasty strain of typhoid—swept through the prison, killing more than 60 people, including the lord mayor, jury members, and three judges. This was the origin of a tradition still honored today whereby judges carry nosegays on the first day of each session to protect against vile smells and diseases.

The first Old Bailey (or **Sessions House**) was built in 1539 for trials of the accused. Those tried here include the men who condemned Charles I in 1660; Oscar Wilde (for "homosexual offences") in 1895; and famous 20th-century murderers Dr. Crippen, J.R. Christie, and Peter Sutcliffe (the Yorkshire Ripper). In 1973, a terrorist bomb went off in the building during a trial of members of the Irish Republican Army, which led to fortresslike security during IRA trials. Public executions were held outside this building between 1783 and 1868, replacing **Tyburn Gallows**. The road was widened to accommodate the large number of spectators.

The present building with an elaborate Edwardian frontage (built in 1907) and its extension (built in 1972) accommodate 19 courts. Ten of them are in the old building, entered on Newgate Street, which has a very unassuming door with the words "Ring bell hard" written above the doorbell; the other nine courts are in the newer building. Visitors watch trials from the public gallery; few experiences are more fascinating than seeing the English judiciary at work, with the judge and barristers in their traditional white wigs and the accused in the dock. Major trials held in courts 1 through 4 attract large numbers, so you may have to wait in line. ♦ Free. M–F (court opening times vary). No children under 14, cameras, tape recorders, large carryalls, or bags allowed. Old Bailey (at Newgate St). 248.3277. Tube: St. Paul's

43 GREAT QUEEN STREET

This once-fashionable thoroughfare, named in honor of Henrietta Maria, the devoted wife of Charles I, is now lined with restaurants along one side. Though similar in feel to the **Covent Garden** area, of which it is an extension, this neighborhood has lost some of its cozy charm because of the presence of a conference center and the **Freemason's Hall**. ♦ Between Drury La and Kingsway. Tube: Holborn, Covent Garden

44 SIR JOHN SOANE'S MUSEUM

Go out of your way to visit this museum. **Sir John Soane**, the official architect of the **Bank of England** for 45 years, chose the largest square in central London for the site of his house, which was actually three domestic residences. He required an appropriate setting for his enormous collection of international antiquities and art, and the result is a fascinating dwelling that is unique in London. Moving through rooms of unusual proportions, built on varying levels with cantilevered staircases and hundreds of mirrors, you will feel that time has been suspended and that you are experiencing the mind of a brilliant and eccentric master builder. Incorporated within the house are a sculpture gallery, a crypt, and a mock ruin of a medieval cloister. The colored glass in the skylights (which was bombed out during World War II) was replaced, re-creating the ingenious lighting effects so beloved by Soane. In the **Picture Room**, you can see William Hogarth's two famous series: *The Rake's Progress* and *The Election*; the latter is cleverly mounted so that the first paintings pull away from the wall to reveal hidden panels with subsequent paintings. Other "secret" panels hold Soane's architectural drawings for this house. A well-known highlight of the collection, found in the **Sepulchral Chamber**, is the magnificent **Sarcophagus of Seti I**. Discovered at Thebes in 1815, it dates from 1300 BC—Soane snapped it up when it was passed over by the **British Museum**. The collection contains unpredictable juxtapositions of fragments salvaged from various buildings (such as the original **House of Lords**) destroyed during Soane's lifetime. Glancing through a window into the court known as the **Monk's Yard**, it is possible to glimpse a huge melancholy tomb inscribed "Alas, Poor Fanny"—a monument to Soane's favorite dog.

The **Shakespeare Recess** features a bust of the playwright and several paintings by Henry Howard depicting some of his most famous characters. The new **Soane Gallery**, designed by **Eva Jiricna**, stages two exhibitions annually and features works from the museum's 30,000 architectural and decorative drawings.

Guided tours are given Saturday at 2:30PM; 22 tickets are distributed on request from 2PM, so go early to avoid disappointment. Even more atmospheric, on the first Tuesday of every month there is a candlelit evening. Really quite special. ♦ Free. Parties of more than six must book in advance, and a donation is requested. Tu-Sa, 10AM–5PM; first Tu of month, 6PM–9PM. Tickets £5 (tickets go on sale at 10:30AM the same day). 13 Lincoln's Inn Fields (north side, between Newman's Row and Gate St). 405.2107; recorded information, 405.2107. Tube: Holborn

45 LINCOLN'S INN FIELDS

When property developer William Newton won the right to build here in 1620, angry lawyers appealed to the **House of Commons**. They won, and the space was left open. Adjacent to **Lincoln's Inn**, the largest rectangular square in central London is surrounded by tennis courts, flower beds, and a bandstand, and is graced by many distinguished houses, including stately **Lindsey House** (**Nos. 59–60**), which may have been based on plans by **Inigo Jones**, and its imitative younger neighbor (**Nos. 57–58**) by **Henry Joynes**. The queen's solicitors are at **No. 66**. **Canada Walk** commemorates the Royal Canadian Air Force, which was based here during World War II. ♦ At New Sq and Sardinia St and at Portsmouth and Gate Sts. Tube: Holborn

46 LONDON SILVER VAULTS

English silver, marked with the emblem of the British lion, deserves its rich reputation: the silver content is the highest in the world,

and the tradition of design has been consistently strong. Unless you're familiar with hallmarks, makers, and dealers, however, buying silver is bound to be an unnerving experience, and coming to this subterranean site in **Chancery House**, with 35 silver vaults and shops containing the greatest concentration of silver dealers in London, certainly won't set you at ease. You have to make your way through a lot of junk, and once you come on desirable silver, you'll find it hard to interact with the taciturn dealers. If you persevere, though, and have a clear idea of what you want, you will eventually find prices lower here than elsewhere. Study a simple hallmark card, the guide to hallmarks (on sale here), or the hallmark plaques on the wall before making a major purchase. ♦ M-F; Sa, 9AM–1PM. 53-64 Chancery La (at Southampton Bldgs). 242.3844. Tube: Chancery La

47 LINCOLN'S INN

Of the four great **Inns of Court** (**Lincoln's Inn**, **Inner Temple**, **Middle Temple**, and **Gray's Inn**), this is the most unspoiled and the only one to have escaped World War II without major damage. The inns were formed in the Middle Ages to provide lodgings for solicitors, barristers, and law students. They now belong to barristers' societies, which control the admission of students to the bar, finance, law reform, legal education, and the maintenance of professional standards for lawyers.

This inn was established on the site of the Knights Templar's tilting ground after the dissolution of the order in the early 14th century. Reflecting the times when a great majority of highly educated people became lawyers, the rolls of the inn contain famous names: Sir Thomas More, John Donne, Oliver Cromwell, William Penn, Horace Walpole, William Pitt, Benjamin Disraeli, William Gladstone. The brick-and-stone buildings, arranged in a collegiate plan, date from the 15th century.

There is a sentry box and an entrance in the southeast corner of **Lincoln's Inn Fields**, or you can enter through the gatehouse, facing Chancery Lane, which dates from 1518

THE BEST

Mark Rylance

Actor and Artistic Director of Shakespeare's Globe

Swimming in **Brockwell Lido** on Sunday morning before breakfast.

Riding my bicycle anywhere late at night.

Walking from **Poets' Corner** via the **Temple** to **Shakespeare's Globe** with a book of sonnets.

Sitting in the **Temple** church after walking around the **Temple**.

Looking at the river.

Smelling the smell of fresh-carved oak and new thatch at the **Globe**.

Looking at the birds in **St. James's Park** at night.

Standing on **Parliament Hill**.

Wandering aimlessly in the **West End**.

Having a bagel late at night on **Brick Lane**.

And talking with angels and lunatics impersonating Londoners.

---

and bears the arms of Lincoln's Inn: a lion rampant. The Tudor redbrick **Old Buildings** date from the early 16th century, and the **Old Hall**, built around 1491 and approached through the archway and small courtyard, contains a superb wooden roof, linen-fold paneling, and William Hogarth's painting *St. Paul Before Felix*, completed in 1748. The hall was the **Court of Chancery** from 1737 to 1883; the fictional case of Jarndyce vs. Jarndyce in Charles Dickens's *Bleak House* took place here. **Henry Serle**'s 1697 **New Square**, which faces toward Lincoln's Inn Fields, is a tranquil and pretty courtyard of solicitors' offices; this is where the 14-year-old Dickens was once employed as a clerk. Built in the 1840s, **Philip Hardwick**'s redbrick **New Hall** contains a vast mural by G.F. Watts, *Justice, a Hemicycle of Lawgivers*. With nearly 100,000 volumes, Hardwick's library is the oldest and most complete law library in England. The rebuilding of the Gothic chapel was finished in 1623. John Donne laid the foundation stone and gave the first sermon. The buildings themselves are closed to the public, but the chapel and gardens may be visited. ♦ Chapel and gardens: M-F, 12:30–2:30PM. Chancery La (between Bishop's Ct and High Holborn). 405.1393. Tube: Chancery La

48 BARNARD'S INN

On the south side of Holborn lies the City of London's oldest surviving secular building, which incorporates the remains of the **Inn of Chancery**, where Pip and Herbert Pocket shared rooms in *Great Expectations*. The 14th-century hall has 16th-century paneling and fine heraldic glass. From 1894 to 1958, this was the hall of **Mercer's School**. ♦ Off Norwich St (between Fetter La and Furnival St); the passage to the hall is beside Nos. 20–23 Holborn (between Fetter La and Furnival St). Tube: Chancery La

49 BHATTI

★★$$ Highly recommended by the Curry Club of Great Britain, an organization for fans of Indian cooking, this restaurant occupies a 17th-century "listed building" that retains its original paneling, stenciling, and fireplaces. (Because listed buildings have been deemed important to England's heritage, they cannot be knocked down and the structure of the interiors cannot be altered.) Try the lamb *pasanda* (lamb fillet sliced thinly, marinated in spices and yogurt, and cooked with herbs) or the chicken *jalfrezi* (boneless chicken pieces cooked with tomatoes, onions, peppers, and a blend of spices, including ginger). Also a fine value is the vegetarian *bhojan*—that's simply the Gujarati word for "meal." The set lunch and the popular pre-theater menu are good bargains. ♦ Indian ♦ Daily, lunch and dinner. Reservations recommended. 37 Great Queen St (between Drury La and Newton St). 831.0817. Tube: Holborn, Covent Garden

50 FREEMASON'S HALL

The imposing headquarters of the United Grand Lodge of England, built by **H.V. Ashley** and **F. Winton Smith** in 1933, boasts a central tower rising 200 feet above the street. The Art Deco building was conceived as a memorial to Masons who died in World War I. Today, it houses an exhibition on the history of English Freemasonry, which may help to dispel the suspicion surrounding the "funny handshake brigade." This is the largest collection of Masonic regalia, medals, art, and glassware in the world, though few of the sect's secrets are divulged. Look for angels and pyramids, both Masonic symbols. Guided tours are given several times a day (visitors on Saturday are admitted only on the tours). ♦ Free. M-F, 10AM–5PM. 60 Great Queen St (at Wild St). 831.9811. Tube: Holborn, Covent Garden

---

Restaurants/Clubs: Red | Hotels: Purple | Shops: Orange | Outdoors/Parks: Green | Sights/Culture: Blue

SOHO/COVENT GARDEN

The whole of Covent Garden revolves around the **Piazza**, an open square with a covered arcade modeled on Italian lines by **Inigo Jones**.

But of the 1631 original, only **St. Paul's, Covent Garden**—the church that Jones built between 1631 and 1633—survives. By 1830, it was fashionable for the rich to mingle in the square alongside farmers and flower girls, and this is where George Bernard Shaw got his inspiration for *Pygmalion*. Walk along these streets, once haunted by the poor, and you will tread in the footsteps of kings and actors. Nowadays, designers, ad execs, and PR people make their living in this area, and they are the clientele that so many excellent restaurants here strive to impress (all the better for visitors to London, who are typically drawn to the warren of boutiques, colorful street stalls, and sidewalk entertainment in Covent Garden). Fashion buffs shop in **Floral Street, Neal Street,** and **Long Acre.**

West of Covent Garden is Soho, a neighborhood that began as a royal park but gradually deteriorated into squalor, slums, and sex shops. (Incidentally, the neighborhood's name comes from the ancient hunting cry of "So-ho!" that rang out in this area when it was a game preserve for Henry VIII.) Now Soho is one of the busiest and buzziest parts of London. Restaurants, bars, great delis, a street market, the campery of London's "Pink Town," and the tastes and smells of London's Chinatown are all in this area.

City code 0207 unless otherwise noted.

1 OXFORD STREET (EAST)

The continuation of Oxford Street from Oxford Circus to Tottenham Court Road is peppered with more small shops and eateries. Having said that, London's biggest young fashion store—**Topshop**—is at Nos. 216-212. Kate Moss has her designer line there, which is great if you are 21 and size 1. Along this side of the street you will also find **H&M**, a Scandinavian-based company selling terrific-value, great casual fashion (daily, 174–176 Oxford St, 612.1821) and **Uniqlo**, who also specialize in well-made, good-value casual fashion (daily, 172 Oxford St, 290.7701). Mobile-phone shops and fast-changing discount outlets characterize much of Oxford Street now, and on weekends the crowds are almost unbearable.

Down at the Tottenham Court Road end you will find **Red** (No. 42), which offers smart, up-to-the-minute designs in ladies' boots and shoes. At the east end at Nos. 14–16, **Zavvi**—apparently the world's largest entertainment store (music, video, posters, clothing)—has taken over from Virgin Megastore. There is also a clutch of new snack outlets, some of them very good. **Inn Noodle** (No. 25) and **Wok in a Box** (Nos. 29–31) are good, basic takeout noodle joints. Tube: Oxford Circus, Tottenhan Court Rd

Other snack places on Oxford St:

WASABI

This shop offers sushi and bento to go—all freshly prepared and set out in cellophane-wrapped rows and very reasonably priced. Hot food is also available. ♦ Daily. No. 58

PRET A MANGER

This is now a huge chain, but a very good one. Everything is freshly made and ethically sourced. I love the hummus salad sandwich, the soups are always great, and the Danish pastries are warm and wonderful. ♦ Daily. Nos. 54–56. Also at other locations around town

BEARD PAPA

The oddest and tastiest addition to Oxford Street snacking does amazingly moreish deep-fried puffy things that come with all manner of stuffings, from crème to jam. It's the sort of snack that makes you feel positively wanton as you lick your lips. ♦ No. 143

Also on Oxford St:

100 CLUB

Smoky and slightly seedy, this underground nightclub is famed not for its décor (plastic tables and hard chairs) but for its musicians—Charlie Parker, Earl Hines, and George Lewis have played here. The club emphasizes jazz, swing, blues, and rhythm and blues, and rock 'n' roll bands perform here too—including the Rolling Stones and the Sex Pistols. There's live music every night, and the atmosphere is especially lively on Fridays and Saturdays, when there's dancing. ♦ Cover charge. M-Th, Su, 7:30PM–midnight; F, 7:30PM–3AM; Sa, 7:30PM–1AM. 100 Oxford St (between Newman and Berners Sts). 636.0933. Tube: Tottenham Court Rd

SWAROVSKI

At the end of the 19th century, Daniel Swarovski, born in Bohemia, invented an automatic machine for cutting gemstones to an unsurpassable level of precision, and a whole new sparkly world was created. Optical instruments and road safety benefited from the cut of Swarovski's tools, but he is best known for making crystal the ordinary girl's best friend. In 1975, the company created the Hot Fix method, which allowed crystals to be ironed onto clothing; in 1977 they produced their first jewelry collection; and in 2006 Swarovski reinvented the Three Graces as the embodiments of his beautiful creations, standing as they do for radiance, joy, and abundance. So if you fancy sparkling like a Grace yourself, this Swarovski outlet can

help. The jewelry, ornaments, and bags all glitter and dazzle. Lovely stuff! ♦ Daily. 147 Oxford St. 287.5780

2 SOHO SQUARE

Begun in 1677 in honor of Charles II—that's his statue in the center—this was one of the first squares laid out in London. The Elizabethan hut in the middle is actually a folly tool shed built in 1870. Stargazers should keep their eyes open: Sir Paul McCartney, knighted in 1996, occasionally visits his offices here. ♦ At Sutton Row and Carlisle St and at Greek and Soho Sts. Tube: Tottenham Court Rd

3 MILROYS

A truly amazing place—nirvana for whiskey drinkers. The shop on the ground floor has over 700 whiskeys for sale, around 600 of which are Scottish, and they range from youngsters to 60-year-olds. There are all strengths, regions, countries, and depths of flavor. The staff members know everything you could ever want to ask. This shop is an education as well as an entertainment and a place to make friends. Just don't bring your car. And if you don't like whiskey, they have a very intelligent selection of wines. Downstairs is an atmospheric cellar where Milroys will be delighted to host a tasting for you. Although the cellar can hold a score or more tasters, you can book for half a dozen like-minded chums and enjoy a themed flight of whiskeys, a bottle of excellent wine or Champagne, and a tasty, well-thought-out buffet of farmhouse cheeses, charcuterie, pâtés, and artisan breads. It really is a tremendous way to spend an evening in London. Milroys also run a number of tutored tastings throughout the year. Check at the shop or on their web site to find out what is happening. ♦ M-Tu, 11AM-7PM; W-Sa, 11AM-11PM; Cellar: M-F, 6 PM-10PM. 3 Greek Street (at Soho Square). 437.0893. Cellar bookings: 235.3138. Tube: Tottenham Court Rd. www.milroys.co.uk

3 JAZZ AFTER DARK

This excellent jazz venue offers decent blues and Latin music. There is an ever-changing program, with some serious musicians lining up to play. To go with your jazz, the club offers a tapas menu and a wide-ranging cocktail list. ♦ M-Th, 5PM-2AM; F, Sa, till 3AM. 9 Greek St. 734.0545. Tube: Tottenham Court Rd

4 GAY HUSSAR

★★$$$$ A favorite with Londoners since 1953. Famous for its old-fashioned, discreet service, this eatery is a bastion of Hungarian food; try the Transylvanian stuffed cabbage, veal goulash, or the chicken paprikash. Well-known politicians dive in here to gossip in private. ♦ Hungarian ♦ M-Sa, lunch and dinner. Reservations required. 2 Greek St

(between Manette St and Soho Sq). 437.0973. Tube: Tottenham Court Rd

5 FOYLES

Walt Disney and George Bernard Shaw were just two of the illustrious customers of this British institution. It's chaotic and crammed from floor to ceiling with books, and a particular title can be as hard to find as a knowledgeable assistant. Don't knock it, though, as the British defend this oddity to the hilt. ♦ M-Sa. 119 Charing Cross Rd (between Manette St and Goslett Yd). 437.5660. Tube: Tottenham Court Rd

5 WATERSTONES

This chain store is eminently refined and sensible—in other words, it's packed with all the latest books, and they're easy to find. ♦ Daily. 121-129 Charing Cross Rd (between Manette St and Goslett Yd). 434.4291. Tube: Tottenham Court Rd. Also at locations throughout the city.

6 MONMOUTH STREET

A great little street packed with interesting little shops. This part begins at the top end of Shaftesbury Avenue and runs to Seven Dials. Right at the Shaftesbury Avenue end is a useful little shop that will find you theater tickets, a wonderful emporium of the paranormal called **Mysteries** (Nos. 9–11), and cosmetics from the Dead Sea at **Ahava** (No. 39; 240.7589).

At the other end of the street, past Seven Dials, you will find a clutch of über-fashionable little boutiques: **Fifi Wilson** (No. 38; 240.2121) does women's fashions; **Laura Lee Jewellery** (No. 42; 379.9050) will undertake personal commissions or let you pick from the beautiful wedding and engagement rings she makes, the **West Village** (No. 44) has gorgeous new and vintage fashions; and at No. 46, **Arrogant Cat**'s idiosyncratic sophisticated designs are fast gaining an international reputation. Across the road, **Poste Mistress** is heaven on heels for any budding Imelda Marcos who wants to expand her shoe collection, and **Koh Samui** (Nos. 65–67; 240.4280) is internationally renowned for its clever, classy collections of designer fashion and accessories.

On Monmouth Street:

SEVEN DIALS HOTEL

$ A decent little family-run hotel. All rooms have phone, television, and coffee-making facilities. ♦ 7 Monmouth St. 681.0791

MON PLAISIR

★★★$$ An authentic bistro and pre-theater stalwart, this eatery presents good food and service to match. Garlic-laden escargots and coq au vin star on the French classics menu, along with vegetarian options. There's also a

convenient prix-fixe pre-theater menu.
♦ French ♦ M–F, lunch and dinner; Sa, dinner.
21 Monmouth St (between Seven Dials and
Neal's Yard). 836.7243. Tube: Covent Garden

Coco de Mer

Sam Roddick, daughter of the late great Anita
Roddick of Body Shop fame, has opened her
own sort of "body shop" here. Exclusive,
expensive, luxurious, beautiful, and, frankly,
erotic things are what is sold here. There is a
definite "olde worlde" feel to the place.
Lingerie, oils, candles, books, objets d'art,
and toys are tempting to buy and at least
lovely to look at. Saucy was never more
sophisticated. ♦ Daily. 23 Monmouth St

Monmouth Coffee Co

The company was founded in the late 18th
century and their shop here first ground a
bean 25 years ago. They have a terrific range
of single-farm and single-estate coffees
from South and Central America, East Africa,
the Caribbean, and Asia. They also have
water-process decaffeinated coffees—so
much healthier than the more usual stuff. At
a small tasting room at the back of the shop,
you can taste and try before you buy. ♦
M-Sa, 8:30AM-6:30PM. 27 Monmouth St
(between Seven Dials and Neal's Yard).
379.3516. Tube: Covent Garden

The Covent Garden Hotel

$$$$ This most trendy of central London hotels
is the regular lodging of many famous names
from theater and film. It is small, discreet, and
very luxurious. There are 58 air-conditioned
rooms and suites, each pretty distinctive. The
most impressive room is the 4 Poster Room—
boasting an 8 X8-foot four-poster bed modeled
on the Great Bed of Ware! This room has a
granite and mahogany bathroom and Philippe
Starke fixtures, as well as all the modern
conveniences you could dream of. The two loft
suites have 15-foot ceilings and are designed
on two levels, with king-size beds and state-of-
the-art entertainment systems. The hotel has a
drawing room and library for relaxing in or
meeting friends and colleagues. There is a
state-of-the-art gymnasium, and beauty rooms
should you feel that a little extra pampering is in
order. The hotel's Brasserie Max, under chef
Paul Shields, has a terrific modern menu and
also serves as a bar offering good cocktails, a
nice wine list, and a range of Champagnes.
♦ 10 Monmouth St. 806.1000.
covent@twindale.com. Tube: Leicester Sq

The Loft

If you have an eye for fashion, it will water
here. There are second-hand and nearly new

fashions from Prada, Gucci, Versace, and the
rest of the big boys. Beautiful bargains are
what this place offers. ♦ Daily. 35
Monmouth St. 240.3807

Seven Dials

A tall column stood in the center of this
junction of seven streets, and each of the
column's seven faces contained a sundial—
hence the name. The area was once a
notorious thieves' quarter—Dickens described
it in Sketches by Boz, published in 1834—
and when word got out that the column was
built by Thomas Neale, Master of the Mint
(where British coins are struck), a legend
grew that treasure was buried at the bottom
of the column. It was actually dug up in 1773,
but nothing was there. The pillar was sent to
Weybridge in Surrey at the time, and it wasn't
until 1989 that some locals banded together
to pay for a replacement. ♦ At Monmouth
and Mercer Sts. Tube: Covent Garden

Dress Circle

About as close as London gets to Broadway,
this is a fabulous specialist shop full of the
magic of the musicals in sound and in
pictures. There are posters, books, and a
truly wonderful, dedicated, and comprehen-
sively knowledgeable staff. It's a lovely,
welcoming place to browse and listen to
something tuneful. ♦ Daily. 57–59
Monmouth St. 240.2227

Gili Gulu

★★$ This place offers incredibly good value
for a Japanese kaiten restaurant—the one
where little plates of sushi go around on a
conveyer belt. Sashimi and noodles are also
available. The quality and variety are good,
and amazing for the price in central London.
♦ Daily. Monmouth St (at the corner of Tower
Street). 379.6888

7 Kite Store

Drop in here for kites, Frisbees, boomerangs,
and anything else that flies. ♦ M-Sa. 48
Neal St (at Shorts Gardens). 836.1666.
Tube: Covent Garden

7 Morrison Craft Shop

The high quality and reasonable prices of the
leather bags sold at this tiny, eccentric store
mean there's usually a line to get in. ♦ M-Sa.
50 Neal St (between Shorts Gardens and
Monmouth St). 836.0928. Tube: Covent Garden

7 Hat Shop

As you might expect, the specialty here is
headgear—everything that's in fashion.

THE DOCKLANDS: VIBRANT REVIVAL

The Docklands area is bursting with energy and regeneration, and its spirit will rub off on visitors who elect to spend an afternoon or evening here. It's a wonderful place to walk, feast, sightsee, relax, shop, and enjoy an unparalleled look at the luminous **Thames** from a Docklands pub or restaurant.

Once a bustling crossroads of merchant ships trading goods from around the world, the area declined when the shipping trade dried up. By the 1960s the docks had become a riverside wasteland. Then the government and private developers teamed up to revitalize the area. High-tech industries and newspaper offices began moving in. Restaurants, shops, and pubs sprang up. Old warehouses were converted to smart residences, and the small brick dwellings were restored and now stand proudly alongside some of the most innovative architecture in London.

The 8.5-square-mile patch of Docklands, which lies just east of **Tower Bridge**, is divided into four areas: **Wapping and Limehouse**, the **Isle of Dogs**, the **Royal Docks** (awaiting development), and the **Surrey Docks** (south of the Thames and stretching well into the heart of London, with such attractions across from the **Tower of London** as the **Design Museum**, the **Bramah Tea and Coffee Museum**, **HMS *Belfast***, and the **London Dungeon**—for more information, see "The City/The Thames").

The **Docklands Light Railway** (DLR; 363.9700) runs a frequent service to the Docklands (except the **Surrey Docks**) starting at **Tower Gateway**, a minute's walk east from the **Tower Hill** tube station, and ending at **Lewisham**. Part of the Underground system (see a tube map for stops), the DLR accepts tube tickets and Travelcards. The trains are automated, but at certain times guides are aboard to present a running commentary about sites along the route. Trains with guides leave on the hour 11AM to 4PM between Easter and October and 10AM to 2PM between November and Easter. You can also buy a "Sail and Rail" ticket allowing you to travel to **Island Gardens** on the DLR and to return by riverboat to **Westminster Pier**.

First-time visitors should head for the **London Docklands Visitor Centre** (3 Limeharbour, just north of the **Crossharbour DLR** station, 0171/512.1111); it's open daily. Ask questions, get free maps and leaflets directing you to the best sights, and watch a video dramatizing how this area was transformed from a virtual ruin to a vibrant urban space.

On the Isle of Dogs, Docklands' proud centerpiece is also Britain's tallest building—the 50-story **One Canada Square**, also called the **Canary Wharf Tower** (at Churchill Pl). Designed by American architect **Cesar Pelli**, the distinctive pyramid-topped dome dominates London's eastern skyline. The building, part of **Canary Wharf**, the commercial heart of the Docklands, has offices on the upper floors and a shopping mall on the two lower floors. You'll also find such pubs as the **Corney & Barrow** (9 Cabot Square, at West India

Avenue, 0171/512.0397), an ultraslick watering hole with tiled walls and chrome tables, attracting a stylish crowd; and the fun **Cat and Canary** (14 Wren Landing, between Cabot Square and Fishermans Walk, 0171/512.0397) with its mock-Victorian décor, including furnishings from former churches.

The DLR's **Island Gardens** stop, a small, grassy park by the Thames, affords the best view of the palatial skyline of **Greenwich**, scarcely changed since Canaletto painted it in 1775. From here, it is only a 10-minute walk to Greenwich via the **Greenwich Foot Tunnel**, beneath the Thames. Lined with 200,000 tiles, the 9-foot-high tunnel (with two elevators) was built in 1902.

You may also wish to stroll along the Thames on the Docklands side. "Thames Path," a free leaflet available at the visitors' center, shows the route. The path goes through Limehouse and Wapping, taking in some atmospheric pubs. You can enjoy great fish and chips at **The Grapes** (76 Narrow Street, at Duke Shore Stairs, Limehouse, 0171/987.4396), with its creaky wooden veranda overhanging the river. The cozy Victorian pub the **Town of Ramsgate** (63 Wapping High Street, 0171/488.2685) is sited beside the eerie-looking **Wapping Old Stairs**, which condemned pirates descended, to be chained to a post in the river and drowned as the tide rose. Also in Wapping is the beautiful riverside **Prospect of Whitby** (57 Wapping Wall, between Glamis Road and Garnet Street, Wapping, 0171/481.1095), which began as the **Devil's Tavern** in about 1520 when it was a haunt of thieves and smugglers. A lovely finish to a Docklands visit would be a meal at the Prospect's famous restaurant, from which you'll enjoy the same views over the Thames that inspired the paintings of Whistler and Turner.

Canary Wharf

Customers often have to wait in line to enter this tiny shop. ♦ M-Sa. 58 Neal St (between Shorts Gardens and Monmouth St). 836.6718. Tube: Covent Garden

8 DIANA'S DINER

★$ Here's a great place for cheap and good (if unimaginative) British/Italian café grub. The hearty food will weigh you down, so complete the day's sightseeing before you come here. If you're into British food, feast on the liver and bacon with chips followed by one of the filling desserts; otherwise, opt for spaghetti carbonara, lasagna al forno (baked lasagna), or cannelloni. You'll have to adjust your waistband, but your wallet will remain relatively unscathed. ♦ British/Italian ♦ M-Sa, breakfast, lunch, and dinner; Su, breakfast, lunch, and afternoon tea. 39 Endell St (between Shelton St and Shorts Gardens). 240.0272. Tube: Covent Garden

9 NEAL'S YARD

This quaint little courtyard is jammed with tiny shops specializing in top-quality food popular with the health conscious. ♦ Between Shorts Gardens and Monmouth St. Tube: Covent Garden

Within Neal's Yard:

NEAL'S YARD DAIRY

Give your nostrils the thrill of their life! If you think all things cheesy peaked with Monterey Jack, think again! Everything is British here, from the blue sheeps' cheeses to the little round goat cheeses and the well-matured cheddars. It's like walking into an edible map of England: Caerphilly, red Leicester, sage Derby . . . all with their own names and from those parts of the country that provided them. Ask to taste any or indeed all of them. Move over, France—the British cheesemakers are here. ♦ M-Sa 645.3550

NEAL'S YARD BAKERY AND TEAROOM

★$ Soups, pizza, and salads can be eaten in the upstairs tearoom, whereas the shop sells organic vegetable juice and Indian vegetarian curries to take away. ♦ Vegetarian ♦ M-Sa, early lunch and early dinner. 836.5199

"I have often amused myself with thinking about how different a place London is to different people."

—James Boswell

THE WALK-IN BACKRUB

A lifesaver! This little corner space, smelling sweetly of essential herbs, is a mobile-free zone where New Age music tinkles relaxingly and fully trained therapists offer back rubs and massages in 10-minute, 20-minute, 30-minute, and 1-hour lengths. By the time you get this far into Covent Garden, you'll probably need it! It also sells massage toys, aromatherapy oils, and something (with which you apparently massage your scalp) called the Orgasmatron! ♦ M-F, 11:30AM-7PM; Sa, 11:30AM-6PM; Su, 1PM-6PM. 836.9111. www.walkinbackrub.co.uk. Also at 11 Charlotte Pl (near Oxford St). 436.9876; 4th floor Selfridges, Oxford St

NEAL'S YARD REMEDIES

Catering to New Age health enthusiasts, this apothecary sells herbal medicines packaged in old-fashioned blue-glass jars and bottles. ♦ Daily. 379.7222

10 OCTAVE

London's newest jazz and cocktail bar offers, alongside some very cool jazz each evening, a list of 70 cocktails, canapé platters to share, and a main menu (for lunch or dinner) that is described as "international" and, indeed, runs from seafood chowder, through pan-fried foie gras with a krupnik and honey *jus* or Moldavian eggplant with green peppers and pine nuts, to blackened salmon with mango and spicy onion and lime salsa. A great addition to the Covent Garden scene. ♦ M-W, 5PM-11PM; Th-Sa, 5PM-1AM. 836.4616. 27-29 Endell St. Tube: Tottenham Court Rd

11 FOOD FOR THOUGHT

★$ This tiny restaurant describes itself as being for "gourmets on a budget." There's often a line to get in, especially at lunch (it also has take-out food), but if you don't mind being hurried and eating practically in someone else's lap, try the carrot, orange, and ginger soup, cauliflower quiche, or penne pasta Milano. The menu changes each day, but it always features soup, three types of salad, and either a stir-fry, a casserole, or a hot bake (a baked dish with some kind of meat or fish). And try the

---

Restaurants/Clubs: Red | Hotels: Purple | Shops: Orange | Outdoors/Parks: Green | Sights/Culture: Blue

scrunch, a legendary dessert with a thick oat base topped with fruit, yogurt, cream, and/or honey. No alcohol is sold, but you can bring your own wine for evening meals. ◆ Vegetarian ◆ M-Sa, breakfast, lunch, and dinner; Su, lunch. 31 Neal St (between Earlham St and Shorts Gardens). 836.9072. Tube: Covent Garden

12 SPACE NK APOTHECARY

Known as the coolest beauty shop in London, this place pioneered the nonintimidating, help-yourself school of selling cosmetics. Beauty labels such as Stila (makeup-artist cosmetics) and Philosophy are the stock in trade. ◆ Short Gardens (between Neal and Monmouth Sts); additional entrance on Earlham St (between Neal and Monmouth Sts). 379.7030. Tube: Covent Garden. Also at 307 Kings Rd (between Old Church St and The Vale). 351.7209. Tube: South Kensington; 307 Brompton Rd (between Draycott Ave and Egerton Crescent). 589.8250. Tube: South Kensington

13 BELGO CENTRAAL

★★$ This is the best place for *moules* this side of Brussels, so if you can't make it to the Continent, come here. The restaurant is large and boisterous, but people flock here for the mind-bogglingly huge selection of Belgian beer and mind-bending schnapps. Dishes include great roast chicken, wild boar sausages with *stoemp* (mashed potatoes), and mussels every which way. ◆ Belgian ◆ Daily, lunch and dinner. Reservations required. 50 Earlham St (at Neal St). 813.2233. Tube: Covent Garden. Also at 72 Chalk Farm Rd (between Ferdinand and Belmont Sts). 267.0718. Tube: Chalk Farm; and various locations around the city

14 LONDON PALLADIUM

On Sunday nights during the 1950s and 1960s, most people in Britain tuned in to the TV show *Sunday Night at the London Palladium*, broadcast from this luxurious 1910 music hall. With a seating capacity of 2,286, it remains the home of great variety shows such as the *Royal Variety Performance*, which is presented especially for the queen, as well as the occasional musical. ◆ Argyll St (between Great Marlborough St and Oxford Circus). 494.5020. Tube: Oxford Circus

15 LEON

★★$ The first of a terrific new mini-chain of café/takeouts serving tasty, healthy, frequently organic snacks and hot meals. Their breakfasts—from a choice of accesorized porridges to traditional bacon wraps—are not just tasty, but healthier than a run around Central Park. Their muffins and cakes are almost too delicious to be

believably good for you. Great soups, terrific salads, friendly staff. Not particularly cheap, but worth it! ◆ Daily. 35 Great Marlborough St (at top of Carnaby St). 437.5280. Tube: Oxford Circus. Also at 275 Regent St (closed Su). Tube: Piccadilly Circus; 3 Crispin Pl (daily). Tube: Liverpool St; 33 Villiers St (closed Sun). Tube: Embankment

16 BERWICK STREET MARKET

Lots of cheap fruits and vegetables are on sale in this traditional London street market. Its lower end leads into Rupert Street, where there are stalls with clothes, records, and miscellanea. There's been a market here since the 1700s. ◆ M-Sa, 9AM-3:30PM. Between Peter and Broadwick Sts. Tube: Piccadilly Circus

17 SOHO HOTEL

$$$$ Another smart, chic place to stay, thanks to the expertise of Kit Kemp, who is also responsible for the **Covent Garden Hotel**. It opened in 2004 to much excitement among the chattering classes. The property was an NCP car park and has, of course, been almost completely rebuilt. The hotel now has a warehousey feel: the rooms are spacious, the public areas even more so, and the lobby is the kind of place that makes you feel like a mover and a shaker just by sitting there. You will certainly be able to eavesdrop on any number of "media meetings" while you sip a coffee. All rooms have all the modern conveniences. There is a fully equipped gymnasium, a beauty salon, two screening rooms, and one of the hippest bars in Soho. ◆ 4 Richmond Mews. 559.3000. Tube: Tottenham Ct Rd, Oxford Circus. www.sohohotel.com

18 RED FORT

★★★$$$ The restaurant was named after the red sandstone fort built by Emperor Shah Jahan, and its cooking is definitely fit for a Mogul king. The chefs will tandoori anything, and the ambience is swank and elegant, with patterned tapestries and rugs, cream-colored walls, and soft Indian music playing in the background. There are regular food festivals highlighting regional Indian food and entertainment. ◆ Indian ◆ Daily, lunch and dinner. 77 Dean St (between Meard St and Richmond Bldgs). 437.2525. Tube: Piccadilly Circus, Leicester Sq

19 L'ESCARGOT

★★$$$ London's ad land comes to this Soho institution to gossip in public and be overheard. You can order snails or succulent duck confit in the brasserie downstairs, and a different but equally French selection in the more expensive, opulent dining room upstairs. ◆ French ◆ Restaurant: Tu-F, lunch and dinner; Sa, dinner. Brasserie: M-F, lunch; Sa, dinner. Reservations recommended. 48 Greek St (between Old Compton and Bateman Sts). 437.2679. Tube: Tottenham Court Rd

20 GOPAL'S SOHO

★★$$ Chef N.P. Pittal (nicknamed Gopal) worked at the best Indian restaurants before opening his own place here in the late 1980s. Try the curry, the fish in coconut curry, the chicken *jalfrezi* (boneless chicken), or the delectable king prawns with spring onions. The selections on the wine list are good. ◆ Indian ◆ Daily, lunch and dinner. 12 Bateman St (between Frith and Dean Sts). 434.1621. Tube: Leicester Sq, Tottenham Court Rd

21 FRITH STREET

Mozart and his papa lived at **No. 20** from 1764 to 1765. Later, in 1926, John Logie Baird brought the street into the 20th century when he gave the first public demonstration of television at **No. 22**; the original equipment is now on display in the **Science Museum**. ◆ Between Shaftesbury Ave and Soho Sq. Tube: Leicester Sq, Tottenham Court Rd

On Frith Street:

RONNIE SCOTT'S

This club is one of the best-known jazz venues in the world. Sarah Vaughan, George Melly, and Maynard Ferguson are just some of the names who have played here, not to mention the late legend Ronnie Scott himself. It's a good place to kick back, relax, and enjoy the rhythm. There's even a menu of steaks, burgers, pasta dishes, and salads, though you don't have to eat here (but you must book a table in advance). ◆ Admission. Shows: 8:30PM–3AM (starting times vary, so call ahead). Reservations required. 47 Frith St (between Old Compton and Bateman Sts). 439.0747

ALASTAIR LITTLE

★★★$$$$ Another haunt of London foodies, here is a restaurant where people go for serious eating—now nothing to do with the eponymous Alastair title, after a semiamicable split, but still worthwhile visiting. The décor is stark and minimalist, but there's an ever-changing menu of modern Continental dishes, featuring such entrées as grilled tuna with tomato sauce and risotto with morels. There's also a fixed-price menu. ◆ Continental ◆ M–F, lunch and dinner; Sa, dinner. 49 Frith St (between Old Compton and Bateman Sts). 734.5183

GARLIC AND SHOTS

★★$$ London's one and only garlic restaurant. Absolutely everything comes flavored with the stuff—even the ice cream! And it is actually delicious, albeit it doesn't make you many friends once you go outside. The restaurant also offers a selection of 101 flavored vodkas—just to live up to the second part of its name. ◆ Daily, 6PM–midnight. 734.9505

OMYGOD

This amazingly twinkly little jewelry and accessory shop has everything you could dream of in diamante, including smart designs in fabulous colors by St. Martin's School of Fashion graduate Steven Sin. In addition to necklaces, bracelets, collars, and earrings, there are belts and masks, sunglasses and hair accessories. All very reasonably priced for designer stuff! ◆ M-W, noon-8PM; Th-Sa, noon-9PM; Su, 2PM-7PM. 38 Frith St. 287.2662. Also at 178(a) Kings Rd

ARBUTUS

★★★★$$$ Arbutus opened in 2006 and has had nothing but well-deserved rave reviews ever since. If you love good food and appreciate really good wines, then you should come here. A.A. Gill, *The Sunday Times*'s velociraptor of a restaurant critic, described the menu as "an ode to joy." He was not wrong. The menus change weekly, sometimes daily. Only what is great gets a place. But if you see the smoked eel with beetroot and horseradish cream, take it . . . or the squid and mackerel burger that Gill described as "damn near perfect." Entrées can range from salt beef *pot au feu* to sea bass with risotto of curly kale. Don't even think about turning down a dessert—the warm chocolate soup with caramelized milk ice cream is a life-enhancing experience. The brilliantly constructed wine list is made almost unimprovable by the fact that the wines are all offered not just by the bottle, but by the carafe. ◆ Daily. 63–64 Frith St. 734.4545. www.arbutusrestaurant.co.uk

BAR ITALIA

Right beside Little Italy—and owned by the same family—is the legendary Bar Italia, on Frith Street for 55 years and still going as strong as the espresso it serves all day every day. The coffee is the thing, but the panini are also good, as are the pastries in the morning. And if you are interested, there is generally Italian TV on in the back of the room. Service is marvelously Italian. ◆ M-Sa, open 24 hours; Su, 7AM-4AM. 22 Frith St. 437.4520

22 PATISSERIE VALERIE

★$ It's fabulous, fattening, and full of artsy Soho wannabes and cussing regulars

SMALL WONDERS

The most famous museums in London—the **British Museum**, the **National Gallery**, the **Tate**, the **National Portrait Gallery**, and the **Victoria and Albert Museum**—are far too large to be fully appreciated in a single visit. At these grand behemoths, the most you can hope to do is get a sense of all the riches they contain. But London also boasts a number of small, special museums that are far less daunting. Most of them focus on one particular theme, and they can be easily seen in an hour or so. Here are some of the best.

Bank of England Museum   Although the fortresslike bank that houses the nation's gold supply is off-limits to visitors, the on-site museum tells the history of its monetary maneuvers and offers money-minded gawkers vicarious satisfactions with its display of gold bars and coins and even surprisingly good forged notes. ♦ Free. M–F. Bartholomew La (between Threadneedle St and Lothbury). 0171/601.5792.

Carlyle's House   The 18th-century house in **Chelsea** where the writer and historian lived with his wife, Jane, for 47 years has been faithfully preserved in Victorian splendor, including the authentic furnishings, books, portraits of the Carlyles, oil lamps—even Carlyle's hat, still hanging on the hat stand by the door. ♦ Admission. W–Su, Apr–Oct. 24 Cheyne Row (between Cheyne Walk and Upper Cheyne Row). 0171/352.7087.

Florence Nightingale Museum   Appropriately located in **St. Thomas's Hospital**, at which the renowned nurse inspired Britain's first nursing school in 1860, this museum documents the life and career of the "lady with the lamp." Among the items displayed here are Nightingale's prescription book, medicine chest, and the famous lamp she carried during the Crimean War. ♦ Admission. Tu–Su. 2 Lambeth Palace Rd (at Westminster Bridge Rd). 0171/620.0374.

Freud Museum   Set in the house in **Hampstead** where the Viennese father of psychoanalysis lived from 1938 until his death in 1939, the museum contains antiques and Freud-related books, but the main attraction is the actual couch on which his patients reclined while he delved into their psyches. ♦ Admission. W–Su, noon–5PM. 20 Maresfield Gardens (between Fitzjohn's Ave and Nutley Terr). 0171/435.3471.

Keats House   John Keats, author of such evocative poems as "Ode on a Grecian Urn" and "The Eve of St. Agnes," lived in this Regency house between 1818 and 1820. He wrote "Ode to a Nightingale" while sitting under a plum tree in the garden. On display in the house are letters, manuscripts, books, and other memorabilia of the tragically short-lived romantic English poet. ♦ Free. Apr–Oct: M–F, 10AM–1PM and 2–6PM; Sa, 10AM–1PM; Su, 2–5PM. Nov–Mar: M–F, 1–5PM; Sa, 10AM–1PM and 2–5PM; Su, 2–5PM. Keats Grove (between South End Rd and Downshire Hill). 0171/435.2062.

Museum of Garden History   A special treat for visitors who share the English passion for gardening, this museum, located in the deconsecrated 14th-century church of **St. Mary's-at-Lambeth**, explores the subject at length, with display panels showing how gardening evolved from monastic herb cultivation to country cottage profusion. There's even a little garden of plants that are labeled to show when they were introduced to England, such as the then-exotic irises (1373), geraniums (1375), lungworts (1525), and lilies (1634). ♦ Free. M–F, Su, Mar–Dec. Lambeth Palace Rd (at Lambeth Rd). 0171/401.8865.

National Postal Museum   The history of Britain's postal service is lovingly chronicled here. Among the exhibits are stamps, postal documents, drawings, letter boxes, and a bit of rock 'n' roll memorabilia—the postal album belonging to the late Freddie Mercury, philatelist and lead singer of the band Queen. ♦ Free. M–F. King Edward St (between Newgate St and Little Britain). 0171/239.5420.

St. Bride's Church   In this grand church designed by **Sir Christopher Wren**, the crypt contains a museum dedicated to the history of the printing process and **Fleet Street** journalism. Displays include examples of 18th- and 19th-century pamphlets and newspapers, as well as photographs showing Fleet Street in its heyday. ♦ Free. Daily. Bride La (off Fleet St). 0171/353.1301.

Thomas Coram Foundation   Accessible only by appointment, this museum, founded by sea captain and philanthropist Thomas Coram, displays several paintings by Hogarth, Gainsborough, and Reynolds. Another precious item here is Handel's original manuscript of the *Messiah*. ♦ Admission. By appointment only. 40 Brunswick Sq (off Hunter St). 0171/278.2424.

squashed for space—they all come for the cakes. Try the chocolate-truffle cake, but be prepared: There is never a time, day or night, when this café/pastry shop isn't packed. Like the other members of this chain, it also serves good, light salads and sandwiches for lunch. ♦ Café ♦ Daily, breakfast, lunch, and afternoon tea. 44 Old Compton St (between Frith and Dean Sts). 437.3466. Tube: Piccadilly Circus, Tottenham Court Rd. Also at 215 Brompton Rd (between Yeoman's Row and Egerton Terr). 823.9971. Tube:

Knightsbridge; 105 Marylebone High St (between St. Vincent and Moxon Sts). 935.6240. Tube: Baker St

23 KETTNERS

★$$ Once Oscar Wilde's favorite club, it then became Frank Sinatra's. The dining rooms and piano bar are beautifully decorated, but the fare is fairly standard: pizzas, hamburgers, and salads. Young, glittery advertising types froth and flutter in the Champagne bar here, swallowing copious quantities of Champagne cocktails. This room gets unbearably noisy and crowded at lunchtime and between 6:30 and 7:30PM. ◆ Pizzeria ◆ Daily, 11AM-1AM. 29 Romilly St, corner of Frith St. 734.6112. Tube: Leicester Sq, Tottenham Court Rd

24 MAISON BERTAUX

Don't be fooled by the spartan surroundings: This bakery has produced the lightest croissants in town since 1871—even during a 5-year period when the ovens weren't working well. Only fresh butter and cream are used, so cholesterol counters should avoid the scrumptious French cream cakes and meringues. Try to stop in when the owners dress up to celebrate Bastille Day on 14 July. ◆ Daily. 28 Greek St (between Romilly and Old Compton Sts). 437.6007. Tube: Leicester Sq, Tottenham Court Rd

24 COACH & HORSES

Most of Soho's pubs are hot and cozy but have nothing much to distinguish them from one another. This one, however, has cartoons all over the walls and lots of drunken journalists. It's a well-known atmospheric Soho drinking place—in fact, it no longer serves food. The pub was immortalized in the West End because it was the setting for the play *Jeffrey Bernard Is Unwell*. ◆ Daily. 29 Greek St (at Romilly St). 437.5920. Tube: Leicester Sq, Tottenham Court Rd

25 NO. 84 CHARING CROSS ROAD

This address (which no longer exists) used to be the site of the **Marks & Co.** bookshop. In 1945, American bibliophile Helene Hanff began writing letters to the shopkeeper. The two corresponded for years and developed a close, long-distance friendship, although they never actually met in person. In 1987, the story was made into a film starring Anne Bancroft and Anthony Hopkins, but by then, the bookshop no longer existed. ◆ At Cambridge Circus. Tube: Tottenham Court Rd

26 ST. MARTIN'S

Agatha Christie's *The Mousetrap*, the world's longest-running play (as listed in the *Guinness Book of World Records*), transferred to this 550-seat venue from the nearby **Ambassador** in 1974. The play premiered in 1952 and, because everyone who sees it is sworn to secrecy, the whodunit factor has remained an attractive draw. A popular show with families, it is well worth the cost (discount tickets are unobtainable). ◆ West St (between Litchfield St and Cambridge Circus). 836.1443. Tube: Leicester Sq

27 THE BEAD SHOP

A glorious little place that will make you long to get creative. It sells books on jewelry-making; tools, clips, and other twiddly bits; and looms, but most of all it sells beads—absolutely every size, shape, color, and sheen of bead you can imagine, all laid out in yards of little open boxes. You get a tiny basket and wander off to pick your treasures. Talking of which, there are beads made from semiprecious stones and even Swarovski crystal beads here. ◆ M-Sa. 21(a) Tower St (at corner of Monmouth St). 240.0931. Tube: Leicester Sq

28 TEA HOUSE

If you like London police officers, you can buy a ceramic one here that will pour your tea forever. The shop is packed with eccentric and absurd teapots and a vast array of teas, from decaffeinated and jasmine blends to spiced Christmas teas. ◆ M-Sa; Su, noon-6PM. 15 Neal St (between Long Acre and Shelton St). 240.7539. Tube: Covent Garden

28 NATURAL SHOE STORE

It seems like this shop has been here forever, selling well-made traditional English shoes for men and women. They also do "Jesus boots": healthy shoes with thick soles and straps for people who believe that comfort comes before looks. ◆ M-Sa; Su, noon-5:30PM. 21 Neal St (between Long Acre and Shelton St). 836.5254. Tube: Covent Garden. Also at 325 King's Rd (at Beaufort St). 351.3721

29 FIELDING

$$ This is a rare hotel in London: small, relatively inexpensive, quiet, and recently refurbished. It attracts performers from the **Royal Opera House**, a stone's throw away, and media and arts clientele, who are drawn by the discreet charm and perfect location. The 24 rooms are modest and small—all have

showers instead of baths—and there's no restaurant, but the pedestrians-only street outside spares you from the sounds of cars at night. The hotel is named after Henry Fielding, the author of *Tom Jones*. He was also a magistrate at Bow Street Court nearby. ◆ 4 Broad Ct (at Crown Ct). 836.8305; fax 497.0064. Tube: Covent Garden

30 CAFÉ DES AMIS DU VIN

★★$$ This elegant, popular restaurant with a distinctive apricot interior features French cuisine with Italian, British, and Thai influences. Start with boiled quail's eggs on prosciutto or scallop *boudin* with crab coleslaw. Then move on to corn-fed chicken with wild mushroom polenta or traditional sirloin steak and french fries. For dessert, try the iced Calvados parfait with glazed apples and cinnamon sauce. There's a pre- and post-theater menu. ◆ French ◆ M-Sa, lunch and dinner. Reservations recommended. 11–14 Hanover Pl (between Floral St and Long Acre). 379.3444. Tube: Covent Garden

31 ROYAL OPERA HOUSE

Three theaters have stood on this site since 1732. The great dome you see today is **E.M. Barry's** 1858 design, capable of seating 2,096. The frieze under the portico, *Tragedy and Comedy* by Flaxman, was salvaged in 1855 from a fire at the theater. In 1946, **Covent Garden** became the home of the **Royal Opera**. Recently the Opera House has been transformed by a 2-year £214 million refurbishment by architects **Dixon Jones BDP**. Architecturally, the building now completes the **Piazza** of Covent Garden with a colonnaded walk of shops along the southeast side. The building is now home to the **Royal Ballet** as well as the Royal Opera and boasts three state-of-the-art auditoria. The main auditorium is, to the naked eye, completely unchanged. It has, however, been completely refurbished; sightlines have been improved, air conditioning has been put in, and extra seating has been added. Backstage, there is now an entire acre of storage space, with 39 elevators carrying up to 10 working stage sets at any time. Two studio theaters have been added—the **Linbury** (400 seats) and the **Clore** (200 seats). Facilities for the inner opera-goer or balletomane are now as glorious as the music and dance onstage. The Opera House opens an hour and a half before the performance, and all the restaurants open at that time. The lovely **Amphitheatre Restaurant** (212.9254) serves a chic modern menu, and you can enjoy a starter and main course before the show and retire to your table in the interval for dessert. How civilized is that? The **Amphitheatre Bar** is elegant and very grown-up. It has a loggia that allows you to sip your drink while gazing out over Covent Garden Piazza. ◆ Opera House: M-Sa, 10AM–4PM. Bow St (at Floral St). Box office: M-Sa, 10AM–8PM. 48 Floral St (between Hanover Pl and James St). 304.4000. Tube: Covent Garden. www.royaloperahouse.org.uk

Within the Royal Opera House:

THE CRUSH ROOM

★★★$$$ This place lives up to all that the words *royal* and *opera* conjure up. Huge and sumptuous, with vast chandeliers and walls decorated with huge portraits and gold overlay, the Crush Room is part of the original opera house. Here you are served by butlers from a selection of cold foods, from open sandwiches to lobster, with main courses such as organic salmon with coriander-scented cauliflower cream and caviar dressing, and desserts from tarte tatin to Neal's Yard cheeses. The restaurant also does a very fine afternoon tea. The combination of the food, the service, and the surroundings is a theatrical experience in itself. ◆ Matinee and evening performances. Both table and food must be booked in advance. 212.9254. searcys@roh.org.uk

THE BALCONIES RESTAURANT

★★$$$ Again, your surroundings are spectacular, and the set menu the Balconies offers is pretty good too. There are six or seven choices for each course, such as Covent Garden gravlax to start, followed by grilled free-range pork cutlet with Parmesan mash and Calvados & thyme jus, and—during intermission—dark chocolate brownie with caramelized pear and vanilla ice cream. The Balconies have the buzz and visual spectacle of the bars below, and the famous domed glass roof above. The sense of space is headier than a double brandy from the Balconies' excellent list! ◆ Matinee and evening performances. Booking essential. 212.9254

PAUL HAMLYN HALL

Awesome! Come down the escalator from the Amphitheatre Bar and you will know how Aïda feels coming in to *The Grand March*. This is the most spectacular bar space in London. It incorporates the Perrier-Jouët Champagne Bar and also serves light snacks, platters of crudités, Pata Negra ham with pickles, smoked salmon sandwiches, and more.

32 BOW STREET

This street really is shaped like a bow. **Covent Garden**'s café society reads like a who's who of English history and literature. Some of it happened in the long-departed **Will's Coffee House** on Bow, where you could expect to meet Pepys, Dryden, Pope, Swift, Johnson, Boswell, Sheridan, and Henry Fielding—though not all at the same time. This area was poor and dangerous in the late 18th century, and eventually things got so unruly that Fielding, who was a local magistrate, established the forerunners of today's police force to catch thieves; they were called the Bow Street Runners. There is still a **Bow Street Magistrates' Court**. ♦ Between Russell St and Long Acre. Tube: Covent Garden

33 CARNABY STREET

During the 1960s, this street was a center of modern fashion. Its shops full of flared jeans and psychedelic patterns attracted scores of hippies and some celebrated personalities such as the Beatles and Mary Quant. Having spent many years wallowing in the retail doldrums, Carnaby Street is now enjoying something of a renaissance. Especially if casual fashion and sportswear are what you are after, Carnaby Street will offer you much of the best of what is around. ♦ Between Beak and Great Marlborough Sts. Tube: Oxford Circus

On Carnaby Street:

B NEVER TOO BUSY TO BE BEAUTIFUL

A gorgeous shop full of oils and powders and all the things that make you smell delicious and look even tastier! Many of the oils, perfumes, and potions can be had in lovely recycled ornamental bottles and bejeweled pots from Morocco and India. Nothing is tested on animals, all ingredients are scrupulously ethically sourced, and many of the cosmetics are vegan! Perfumes have fabulous names like "Two Hearts Beating as One." Lovely, natural, different, feel-good products. ♦ Daily. 39 Carnaby St. 287.5492

34 CONTEMPORARY CERAMICS

This stunning gallery and shop in **William Blake House** has been doing a brisk trade in Soho since 1960, selling the pottery and ceramics created by members of the Craft Potters Association. Throw out your ideas of quaint pottery; what's on sale here is exquisite and infinitely collectible. ♦ M–Sa. 7 Marshall St (at Broadwick St). 437.7605. Tube: Oxford Circus

35 JOHN SNOW

In 1854, Londoners were dropping like flies from cholera until Dr. John Snow figured out that the bacteria were carried by water. The water pump he turned off, thereby saving countless lives, was near the site of this pub. There's a model of a steam train named after the doctor and all sorts of memorabilia in the rather shabby pub. ♦ M–Sa, 11AM–

11PM; Su, 11AM-10:30PM. 39 Broadwick St (between Lexington and Marshall Sts). 437.1344. Tube: Oxford Circus

36 ANDREW EDMUNDS

★★★$$ This award-winning wine bar-restaurant is a romantic, candlelit little place with a friendly staff serving a daily changing menu of lovingly sourced, well-thought-out food. Foie gras, seared tuna, and interesting warm salads appear frequently. The wine list is the love child of the eponymous Mr. Edmunds, and many of the reds particularly come into their own with one of his fabulous cheese selections. Beware—it's hard to get a seat at lunch (reserve well in advance). ♦ British ♦ Daily, lunch and dinner. Reservations required for lunch. 46 Lexington St (between Brewer and Beak Sts). 437.5708. Tube: Piccadilly Circus

37 FRATELLI CAMISA/LINA STORES

Soho's Italian delis go on forever, selling delicious fresh pasta, hundreds of cheeses, and panettone. Salamis hang from the ceilings; breads are stacked in baskets on the floor. ♦ M–Sa (both stores). Fratelli Camisa: 61 Old Compton St. 437.7610. Lina Stores: 18 Brewer St (between Wardour and Rupert Sts). 437.6482. Tube: Piccadilly Circus

38 FRENCH HOUSE

★$ Originally called the **York Minster**, this pub picked up the affectionate nickname the **French House** because of M. Gaston, its French owner. After Gaston gave up the property, the new owners changed the name officially. It was the official headquarters of the Free French in World War II. There are still signed photos of famous French people on the walls. The place has the best Bloody Marys and among the most interesting and delicious bar food of any pub in London. Mobile phones are banned, and if you want to sit in comfort, go to another pub, because this one tends to be standing room only. ♦ M–Sa, lunch and dinner. 49 Dean St (between Romilly and Old Compton Sts). 437.2799. Tube: Piccadilly Circus, Tottenham Court Rd

Within the French House:

FRENCH HOUSE RESTAURANT

★★★$$ Situated over the pub, the dining room is small . . . small enough to feel special. And it is. Chef Andy Campbell offers starters including seared king scallops with gazpacho dressing, jasmine tea–smoked brown trout, and roast beetroot horseradish and crème fraiche. Main courses include quails, figs and grapes with white wine, and couscous salad.

Restaurants/Clubs: **Red** | Hotels: **Purple** | Shops: **Orange** | Outdoors/Parks: **Green** | Sights/Culture: **Blue**

Neal's Yard supplies a daily selection of top British cheeses, and there is a daily dessert board. ♦ M–Sa, lunch and dinner

39 RICHARD CORRIGAN AT THE LINDSAY HOUSE

★★★$$$ Some of the most delicious and atmospheric dining you will do in London. The restaurant is in an actual Soho townhouse and is spread around several little rooms with more nooks and crannies than you can imagine. The service is absolutely charming and the food stunningly good. Corrigan is Irish and is so talented a chef that he could make a soufflé out of the Blarney Stone itself. His cooking is famously intense—big flavors, deep and delicious. He loves to use offal, black pudding, and cheap cuts of meat and does so with such accomplishment they impress the *Michelin Guide*. The menu changes constantly, as you would expect from a chef who takes such pains over his ingredients, but you might get lucky and try his cured foie gras rolled in gingerbread or butter-poached haddock with parsnip cream. If you want a taste to remember, forgo dessert and opt for Stinking Bishop (cheese) and brioche. The wine list is seriously intelligent and wide-ranging. If you are really looking to give tummy and tastebuds a treat, go for the six-course tasting menu. ♦ M-F, lunch and dinner; Sa, dinner only. 21 Romilly St. 439.0450. Tube: Leicester Sq, Tottenham Court Rd

40 SHAFTESBURY AVENUE

Named after the beloved seventh Earl of Shaftesbury, whose **Eros** memorial stands in Piccadilly Circus, this avenue opened up in 1886. Almost immediately, a host of London theaters sprang up, and many of them are still here. For a British playwright to get a play "in the West End" is considered the pinnacle of success. ♦ Between Piccadilly Circus and New Oxford St. Tube: Leicester Sq, Tottenham Court Rd, Piccadilly Circus

40 PALACE THEATRE

This theater is as grand as its name, which is understandable because it was designed by Collcutt and Holloway in 1891 as the home of the **Royal English Opera**. This is where Sarah Bernhardt played the title role in *Cleopatra* and where Pavlova made her London debut in 1910. In recent years, the 1,400-seat venue has hosted megahits such as *Les Misérables*. The theater is now owned by Andrew Lloyd Webber. ♦ Shaftesbury Ave (at Cambridge Circus). 434.0909. Tube: Leicester Sq

41 IVY

★★★$$ "Luvvies' Paradise," as it is known, is probably more famous for the famous faces who eat there than it is for its food. Which is a shame, because the food is very, very good— everything from a perfectly executed sashimi to a seared foie gras with duck egg (and talking of eggs, this is one of the few places where you can treat yourself to a boiled gull's egg in season!). You can get a perfect Champagne risotto, a grilled Barnsley chop, or a whole *poulet de Bresse* with a truffle jus (for two, unless you are very greedy). Desserts are a delight, from a regular fruit crumble to frozen Scandinavian berries with cream or a proper selection of cheeses. The wine list is intelligent, wide-ranging, and fairly priced, with much available by the glass. The Ivy's tiny bar does some truly masterful cocktails and, I would contend, serves the best Negroni in London. One more thing that makes The Ivy well worth the effort to book is the absolutely charming staff. They are a delight—and might help to reassure you that not all service in England is bad. ♦ Modern British ♦ Daily, lunch and dinner. Reservations required at least 1 month in advance. 1 West St (at Litchfield St). 836.4751. Tube: Leicester Sq

42 SHIPLEY SPECIALIST ART BOOKSELLERS

Ian Shipley opened his shop here 25 years ago. The open fireplace and floor-to-ceiling shelves to browse makes this one of the coziest bookshops on the street. He stocks old books, new books, rare books, and out-of-print books. Photography, fashion, and graphic books are at No. 70, and the rest—including politics, literature, and history—are at No. 72. The catalog is available online, and you can ask for particular books to be sourced for you. ♦ M-Sa. 70 Charing Cross Rd (between Great Newport and Litchfield Sts). 836.4872. Tube: Leicester Sq. www.artbook.co.uk

42 ZWEMMER ARTS BOOKSHOP

Picasso, Mondrian, Warhol, Gainsborough . . . this art historians' mecca sells fabulous, opulent books on art and architecture. It's the leading shop of its type in Britain—possibly in Europe. There's a second branch a few yards away that concentrates on photography, design, film, and graphic arts books. ♦ M-Sa, 10AM-6PM. 80 Charing Cross Rd (at Litchfield St). 240.4157. Also at 72 Charing Cross Rd (between Litchfield and Great Newport Sts). 240.1559. Tube (for both): Leicester Sq

42 G SMITH & SON

In these days, when even connoisseurs of the finest Havana cigars have been stripped of the right to appreciate them indoors, a shop like this is quite a thrill. There is actually a "condition of lease" stating that the site can only ever house a tobacconist. G Smith has been here since 1869, and the shop hasn't changed a great deal since then. The finest cigars and loose tobaccos are in perfectly conditioned cases and jars. Pipes and their cleaners, cigars and their cutters, and even a choice of snuff are available here. It could make a out-and-proud cigar smoker out of anyone, I reckon! ♦ M-Sa. 74 Charing Cross Rd. 836.7422. Tube: Leicester Sq

43 LONG ACRE

Once the medieval market garden for Westminster Abbey (where monks grew crops such as potatoes or apples for sale), this street became the center of both coach and furniture making by the middle of the 18th century. It's easy to imagine Thomas Chippendale walking to his workshop here from his home in St. Martin's Lane. ♦ Between Bow St and St. Martin's La. Tube: Covent Garden

44 FLORAL STREET

This tiny, unassuming street running parallel to Long Acre is a real treasure trove if you are shopping for clothes. **Paul Smith** has a whole row of shops here selling his internationally adored range of men's clothes in distinctive stripes and prints, his women's fashions, and a very wantable selection of accessories and jewelry (No. 40-44; 379.7133, daily). Then there is **Joseph** for men and women (240.1199), **Nigel Hall** for men (379.3600), **Sandro** womenswear and accessories (836.4970), **Nicole Farhi** for men and women (497.8713), and **Ted Baker** for women. **Agnès B**'s chic French designs cater to the whole family (379.1992). Tube: Convent Garden

Also on Floral Street:

THE SANCTUARY

Just to help the ladies get into those fashions, Floral Street offers one of London's premier day spas. You have probably seen the place in a movie . . . it is like a tropical lagoon paradise inside, with a whirlpool, therapy rooms, masseuses, and a steamroom and sauna. Shampoo, conditioner, towels, soap, body lotion, and cologne are all free. The Sanctuary's range of beauty treatments will make your face look as fabulous as your

Nicole Farhi! ♦ Daily. Women only. ♦ 12 Floral Street. 0870/063.0300

44 TINTIN SHOP

The Belgian cartoon character is emblazoned on every item in the store, including mugs and T-shirts. The books featuring the character are also sold here. ♦ M-Sa. 34 Floral St (between Banbury and Conduit Cts). 836.1131. Tube: Covent Garden

45 THEATRE ROYAL DRURY LANE

The present theater is the fourth on the site since 1663; two were destroyed by fire and one was demolished. "What, sir," said owner Sheridan, as his life's work went up in flames, "may a man not warm his hands at his own fireside?" Few London theaters have so illustrious or lengthy a past as this one. Nell Gwyn made her debut in *Indian Queen* in 1665, with King Charles II, her future lover, in the audience. King George II was shot at in the theater in 1716, as was his grandson George III in 1800. One of Gainsborough's favorite models, Mary Robinson, was discovered here by the Prince of Wales while she was playing Perdita in *A Winter's Tale* in 1779, and this is where the Duke of Clarence, later William IV, first saw Dorothea Jordan, the Irish actress who became his mistress and mother of 10 of his children. The theater was also the scene of riots over admission prices and impromptu duels that spilled over from the pit onto the stage.

Today, it is the safer home of musicals. **Benjamin Dean Wyatt** modeled the present theater, which seats 2,237 people, after the great theater at Bordeaux in 1811. The portico was added in 1820, and the pillars came from **John Nash**'s quadrant on Regent Street. The interior was reconstructed in 1921. ♦ Catherine St (between Tavistock and Russell Sts). 494.5060. Tube: Covent Garden

46 LE CAFÉ DU JARDIN

★★★$$ Although the ground floor is on the smallish side and feels like a foyer, the basement is spacious and has its own bar and pianist. The menu is eclectic and features dishes such as warm salad of spicy sausage, black pudding, spinach, bacon, and mushrooms; and as an entrée, roast leg of

---

Restaurants/Clubs: Red | Hotels: Purple | Shops: Orange | Outdoors/Parks: Green | Sights/Culture: Blue

rabbit stuffed with chorizo on a pearl-barley risotto. There is a pre- and post-theater prix-fixe menu. ♦ Modern European ♦ Daily, lunch and dinner. Reservations advised for lunch. 28 Wellington St (at Tavistock St). 836.8769. Tube: Covent Garden

47 London Transport Museum

Housed in a former flower market hall, this fun museum has lots of hands-on exhibits, videos, and touch-screen displays. It was recently refurbished to the tune of a £22 million grant from the Heritage Lottery Fund. A "time-travel" elevator takes you to the top floor and the 18th century, where the first thing you see is an original sedan chair (a mode of transport that probably moved just slightly *faster* than today's black cabs in the London traffic). You can get into one of the original horse-drawn omnibuses of 1829 (and learn, among other facts, that 1,000 tons of horse dung were being deposited on London streets each day by the end of the 19th century), and see the first electric trams and the first steam-driven underground trains. If you are remotely claustrophobic, you might want to pass on the chance to experience the windowless, padded carriage of the first electric underground train. Londoners will add (with tongue firmly in cheek) that some of the exhibits are still in use on the Northern Line. There is a corner where kids can play in their own taxis, buses, and trains, and another where big kids can try driving a London Underground train simulator. Take tissues to the area where you can relive the delight that was the old London Routemaster bus, precursor to the ghastly monstrosity that is the Bendy Bus (so called because they drive Londoners around the bend!). The shop has great souvenirs for kids and a wide choice of charmingly nostalgic transportation posters. A café called The Upper Deck serves drinks, snacks, and lunches, and there are plans for it to open in the evenings as a bar. ♦ Admission. Daily. 39 Wellington St (between Tavistock and Russell Sts). 565.7299. Tube: Covent Garden. www.ltmuseum.co.uk

PENHALIGON'S

47 Penhaligon's

Straight from the world of *Brideshead Revisited*, this shop is filled with silver mirrors and dressing-table treasures. The bottles are exclusive and as exquisite as the scents; you won't find them elsewhere. Bluebell, in particular, is divine. ♦ M–Sa; Su, noon–5:30PM. 41 Wellington St (between Tavistock and Russell Sts). 836.2150. Tube: Covent Garden

48 Christopher's

★★★$$$ Owner Christopher Gilmore once lived in Chicago, where he fell in love with American cuisine (i.e., clam chowder, Maine lobster, and New York strip steak). So here you can sample Maryland crab cakes and grilled rib eye steak, and vegetables such as red cabbage with apple or mashed potatoes with nutmeg. The wine list includes a good American selection, and the desserts are a sure cure for homesickness. Sunday brunch is a good value. ♦ American ♦ M–F, lunch and dinner; Sa, brunch and dinner; Su, brunch. Reservations required. 18 Wellington St (at Exeter St). 240.4222. Tube: Covent Garden

49 Melati

★$ Cheap and cheerful (and popular with people who are long on fine food but short on cash), this restaurant offers Indonesian cuisine. Try the *ayam percik* (grilled chicken in spicy coconut sauce) or the excellent *tahu goreng* (fried bean curd and vegetables covered in peanut sauce). You can book a table, but you'll probably still wait (especially on weekends). ♦ Indonesian ♦ Daily, lunch and dinner. 21 Great Windmill St (between Archer and Brewer Sts). 437.2745. Tube: Piccadilly Circus

50 Dean Street

In 1763, Mozart's father wanted to publicize the child prodigy's sight-reading ability, so the 7-year-old Wolfgang and his 4-year-old sister gave a performance on Dean Street at **Caldwell's Assembly Rooms, No. 21**. Karl Marx lived at **No. 28**. ♦ Between Shaftesbury Ave and Oxford St. Tube: Tottenham Court Rd, Piccadilly Circus

51 Chinatown

London's first Chinatown was actually in Limehouse, around the Docklands area, as Chinese sailors arriving there began to stay. By the beginning of the 20th century it was quite well established. The area was demolished in 1934 and most of the Chinese community moved. After the Second World War, Britain developed a taste for Chinese food and that, coupled with an influx of immigrants from Hong Kong, led to the opening of a cluster of restaurants along Gerrard Street. This area came to be known as Chinatown, although today it is home to Japanese, Singaporeans, and Koreans as well as Chinese.

Along **Gerrard Street**—which is only two blocks long—there are now more than 25 Chinese restaurants of various kinds. The **Luxuriance** is Pekinese; the **Golden Dragon,** the **Harbour City** (chef Marco Pierre White brings his kids here on a Sunday—you don't get a higher recommendation than that!), and the **New Loon Fung** do terrific dim sum, and if you have a taste for it, the Golden Dragon does karaoke as well!. **Ikkyusan** offers Japanese and Thai; the **Four Seasons** is a "roast duck specialist"; the **Far East** has a wonderful bakery in the front, and the **Wonderful Patisserie** is just that. Along the way there is also the **Loon Fung**—a supermarket that really is super—and **Everwell**, an herbalist that has treatment rooms upstairs where you can get a truly expert and relaxing massage. Parallel to Gerrard Street runs **Lisle Street**, where there are a dozen or so more restaurants—and not really a bad one among them. Some are smaller and dingier, but all serve really decent food at pretty decent prices. In the smaller restaurants, the composite dishes—where noodles or rice are included—are among London's few remaining bargains. Walking the length of the street will take you all of five minutes. So do that, look in all the windows, and decide which one tempts you most. On Lisle Street, the **See Woo Supermarket** is another revelation to the eyes and nose. One piece of advice is to curb your natural American tendency toward friendliness. Take your cue from the waiters here: a stony face and a fair-to-mid-curt ordering style is what will do the trick. Never apologize, but be sure you really know what you are doing if you complain. And you will eat really well! Chinese New Year—in February—is as noisy and colorful here as it is in New York's Chinatown. ◆ Tube: Leicester Sq, Piccadilly Circus

52 MR. KONG

★★$$ A foodie's Chinese restaurant crushed into three little floors, this dining spot offers innovative combinations and attracts many Western customers who enjoy dishes like sautéed chicken with fresh mango and asparagus. ◆ Chinese ◆ Daily, lunch and dinner. 21 Lisle St (between Newport Pl and Wardour St). 437.7341. Tube: Leicester Sq

53 QUINTO AND FRANCIS EDWARDS BOOKSHOP

Look at the glorious leather-bound first editions and antiquarian books here or study the impressive collection of old military maps and prints. There are secondhand books too. ◆ Daily. 48a Charing Cross Rd (at Great Newport St). 379.7669. Tube: Leicester Sq

54 ANY AMOUNT OF BOOKS

Here you'll find just what it says—this bookstore catches the overflow from nearby **Charing Cross Road Books**. ◆ Daily. 62 Charing Cross Rd. 836.3697. Tube: Leicester Sq. www.anyamountofbooks.com

54 PHOTOGRAPHER'S GALLERY

This is probably the best gallery for photographic art in London, usually running three exhibitions by international photographers at a time. It is split into two venues a couple of doors apart, with a café at **No. 5**. There are free gallery tours as well as admission-only lectures; times vary. ◆ Free. Admission for lectures. Daily. 5, 8 Great Newport St (between Upper St. Martin's La and Charing Cross Rd). 831.1772. Tube: Leicester Sq

55 EDWARD STANFORD

The largest collection of maps, guides, charts, atlases, and travel books in the world is located in this Edwardian shop, built in 1901. David Livingstone had his maps drawn here. ◆ M-Sa. 12-14 Long Acre (between Slingsby Pl and Upper St. Martin La). 836.1321. Tube: Leicester Sq

56 ST. MARTIN'S LANE

Furniture builder Thomas Chippendale once lived here, but that didn't stop the city from knocking down the buildings to make way for **Trafalgar Square**. Unfortunately, they didn't renumber the street, so it starts at No. 29! ◆ Between William IV and Litchfield Sts. Tube: Leicester Sq

57 LAMB & FLAG

★★$ The cobbled courtyard of this lovely 1627 pub is always full of office workers, who love its ancient charm. But it wasn't always nice: It used to be nicknamed the Bucket of Blood because local fighters drank here. In 1679, the poet John Dryden was beaten up just outside for writing nasty things about the Duchess of Portsmouth, Charles II's mistress. ◆ Pub ◆ Daily, lunch and dinner. 33 Rose St (at Garrick St). 497.9504. Tube: Covent Garden, Leicester Sq

58 CALABASH

★$$ African food is served in a laid-back, slightly seedy dining room in the **Africa Center**, a change from the hectic tourism of Covent Garden. Masks, headdresses, and batik cloths decorate the walls and tables. Choose from Ghanaian ground-nut stew, Tanzanian beef stew with green bananas and

---

Restaurants/Clubs: Red | **Hotels: Purple** | **Shops: Orange** | **Outdoors/Parks: Green** | **Sights/Culture: Blue**

coconut cream, vegetarian couscous, and excellent Zimbabwean and Algerian wines. It's been going strong since the 1960s. ♦ African ♦ M-F, lunch and dinner; Sa, dinner. 38 King St (between Covent Garden Market and Garrick St). 836.1976. Tube: Covent Garden, Leicester Sq

59 ST. PAUL'S, COVENT GARDEN

When the thrifty fourth Earl of Bedford was developing **Covent Garden**, he asked **Inigo Jones** to design an economical church not much bigger than a barn. Jones complied, creating what he called the handsomest barn in Europe. The redbrick church features a pitched roof, overhanging eaves, and a famous Tuscan portico; the interior is now frequented by artists and actors; the portico serves as a backdrop for many of the street performers who play here, especially during summer. Gutted by fire in 1795, the church was carefully restored by **Philip Hardwick**. Today, it is known as the Actors' Church because of its close association with the theater; numerous plaques inside commemorate actors and playwrights. ♦ The Piazza (between Henrietta and King Sts). Tube: Covent Garden

60 COVENT GARDEN MARKET

Covent Garden once produced fruits and vegetables for a 13th-century abbey in Westminster, and a market was established here in the 1700s. Immortalized by the first scene of George Bernard Shaw's *Pygmalion*, in which Cockney flower girl Eliza Doolittle sold violets to rich operagoers leaving the nearby **Royal Opera House**, the market today has more in common with the luxurious tastes of Henry Higgins. It is nonetheless a brilliant example of urban survival: The restored central market is a picturesque structure of iron-and-glass roofs covering a large square, which was designed in 1831 by **Charles Fowler**. The market's revitalization has dramatically altered this part of London, providing shops, restaurants, cafés, and pubs. At the same time, it has freed the area of the wholesale fruit and flower market that, for all its sentimental charm, clogged the surrounding streets. Although the shops in the **Piazza** are mainly boutique-size branches of existing chain stores, the surrounding stores often sell one-offs (merchandise that is sold in one shop only, for a limited period). There is an antiques market within the Piazza on Monday, a crafts market Tuesday through Saturday, and occasional fairground amusements. ♦ At Russell and Henrietta Sts and at Southampton and James Sts. Tube: Covent Garden

Within Covent Garden Market:

CHEZ GÉRARD

★★$$ Facing the **Piazza** from the second level of the market, this glorious glass restaurant (formerly **Opera Terrace**) provides a lovely escape from the crowds in spring and summer. A branch of the steak-and-*frites* minichain of restaurants, it features crudités as a light starter or *moules marinières* (marinated mussels), followed by grilled meat dishes served with *pommes frites* (french fries). A bottle of Côtes du Rhône enhances the food, and either the excellent cheese board or a chocolate concoction from the dessert menu rounds out the meal. ♦ French ♦ Daily, lunch and dinner. 45 E Terr. 379.0666

CULPEPER

Mrs. C.F. Leyel founded this herbal remedies firm in 1927, naming it after Nicholas Culpeper, an herbalist from 1616 to 1652. The products, which include lotions, soaps, and the like, are made of natural ingredients and are not tested on animals. ♦ Daily. Unit 8. 379.6698. Also at 21 Bruton St (between New Bond St and Berkeley Sq). 629.4559. Tube: Green Park, Bond St

BENJAMIN POLLOCK'S TOY SHOP

Traditional toys, including hand-stitched teddy bears like the one you had as a child, can be found in this gem of a shop, as can miniature, paper-cut model theaters. ♦ Daily. Unit 44. 379.7866

61 JUBILEE MARKET

Pay a fraction of the price you would in a regular shop for homemade silk lingerie, hand-knit sweaters, pottery, hand-carved wooden salad bowls, and other items. It takes time and patience to poke around the 180 stalls, but the merchandise here is worth it. The prices seem particularly good after shopping at the smart boutiques in the area. There are even a few fruit and vegetable stalls for old time's sake. There's also an antiques section, offering small items such as glassware, knickknacks, china, pottery, jewelry, and clothing. ♦ Tu-F, general market; Sa, Su, arts and crafts. Tavistock St (between Wellington and Southampton Sts). Tube: Covent Garden

"The Victorian middle classes thought the theatre was only one step removed from the brothel. . . . Audiences at the ordinary theatres were too rough for the queen . . . so command performances were arranged for the court at Buckingham Palace, Windsor, and even Balmoral."

—Graham Norton, *Victorian London*

62 ORSO

★★$$$ Much beloved by those in the know, this flourishing first-class trattoria (run by the same group that owns **Joe Allen**) is a haven for good food and attentive service. As well as good pasta, interesting dishes featured here include fried *courgette* (zucchini) flowers filled with wild mushrooms, ricotta, and basil, and grilled scallops with artichokes and new potatoes. Some excellent Italian wines add to the pleasant dining experience. ◆ Italian ◆ Daily, lunch and dinner. Reservations required. 27 Wellington St (between Exeter and Tavistock Sts). 240.5269. Tube: Covent Garden

63 JOE ALLEN

★★$$ This is one of London's favorite American restaurants, known for its big burgers and salads, good cocktails, and an extensive blackboard of unchanging favorites, including chili. It has become a London institution and is particularly popular with the theater crowd, so you should book ahead. Be aware that the service can be so slow that new species of mammals can evolve while you are waiting for your Caesar salad. ◆ American ◆ Daily, lunch and dinner. Reservations recommended. 13 Exeter St (between Wellington and Burleigh Sts). 836.0651. Tube: Covent Garden

64 GLOBAL CAFÉ

★$ For Internet users, this café is one of the roomiest and most modern. Located opposite the London ad agency Saatchi and Saatchi, it attracts smooth-talking executives as well as mere fanatics. The décor is fashionable with art on the walls and music in the background for those who just want to tuck into smoked salmon open sandwiches or a salad and a glass of wine. ◆ Continental ◆ M-Sa, lunch, snacks, and dinner. 14 Golden Sq (between Lower James and Lower John Sts). 287.2242. Tube: Piccadilly Circus

65 CHUEN CHENG-KU

★★$$ Though it seats 400, this restaurant still gets crowded. Opt for dim sum at lunch, or try the lemon-sauced roast duck in the evening. ◆ Chinese ◆ Daily, lunch and dinner. 17 Wardour St (between Coventry and Lisle Sts). 437.1398. Tube: Piccadilly Circus, Leicester Sq

66 POON'S

★★$$$ This is the posh version of its cheaper sibling around the corner. Here, the look is elegant and contemporary, with white tablecloths and napkins and attractive wood furniture; the less chic version has wind-dried ducks, sausages, and bacon hanging from the window. Typical main courses include fried bean curd with mincemeat and chili. ◆ Chinese ◆ Daily, lunch and dinner. No credit cards accepted. 4 Leicester St (between Leicester Sq and Lisle St). 437.1528. Tube: Leicester Sq. Also at 27 Lisle St (between Newport Pl and Wardour St). 437.4549. Tube: Leicester Sq

67 CORK & BOTTLE

★★$ The location—Central London's slightly sleazy Leicester Square area—hasn't stopped lots of locals from frequenting this basement haunt since 1971. It still gets very crowded. The food is simple, good, and plentiful. But the real reason to come here is the extraordinary, eclectic, award-winning but unbelievably reasonably priced wine, served by staff members who really know their Chablis from their Zinfandel. Try a wedge of the ham-and-cheese pie with a glass of New World or French wine. ◆ Wine bar ◆ Daily, lunch and dinner. Reservations recommended. 44–46 Cranbourn St (between Charing Cross Rd and Bear St). 734.7807. Tube: Leicester Sq

68 DAVID DRUMMOND AT PLEASURES OF PAST TIMES

Showtime is captured forever in the books sold here—plays, star biographies, and other theatrical books. You also can buy printed Victoriana—the greeting cards are a real find. ◆ M-F, 11AM-2:30PM and 3:30-5:45PM. On the first Sa of the month, open 11AM–2:15PM. 11 Cecil Ct (between St. Martin's La and Charing Cross Rd). 836.1142. Tube: Leicester Sq

68 BELL, BOOK AND RADMALL

This shop is reserved for the dedicated bibliophile only. Expensive first editions reside in locked glass cabinets tended by a knowledgeable staff. ◆ M-Sa. 4 Cecil Ct (between St. Martin's La and Charing Cross Rd). 240.2161. Tube: Leicester Sq

69 J SHEEKEYS

★★★★$$$ Started in 1896, this is among London's oldest and best-loved seafood restaurants, tucked away on St. Martin's Court alongside two theaters—**Wyndham's** and **Albery**. It is now under the same expert management as the Ivy. Arranged as a series of rooms, the restaurant has a traditional and somewhat formal atmosphere, with mahogany-paneled walls, antique reproductions, and lots of photos of actors, directors, and other theater people who have eaten

---

Restaurants/Clubs: Red | Hotels: Purple | Shops: Orange | Outdoors/Parks: Green | Sights/Culture: Blue

THE GAME'S AFOOT

For legions of visitors, a trip to London means a chance to steep themselves in the mystique of Sherlock Holmes, whereas Sir Arthur Conan Doyle is relegated to second place behind his creation. With societies devoted to the fictional hawk-eyed sleuth and fans continuing to write him, it's not surprising that the upper part of **Baker Street** (around the Baker Street tube) has become an enclave of Holmes enterprises. There's now the **Sherlock Holmes Museum**, kitted out with kitsch—deerstalker hat, cloak, fan letters—it's all there in a fine old house. The Victorian bobby standing guard outside completes the scene. (The address is faked—the "real" site of the fictional address was down the road at **No. 215**, home of the Abbey National Building Society.) If you're looking for better-quality souvenirs than the schlock Sherlock baubles at the museum, cross the street to the **Sherlock Holmes Memorabilia Company**, where you'll find everything from tweed hats and T-shirts to playing cards and postcards.

For researchers and scholars, a small room at **Marylebone Library** (Marylebone Rd, at Upper Montagu St, 0171/798.1206) is devoted to a collection of books on both Holmes and Conan Doyle. The custodian, Catherine Cooke, is the person to contact for an appointment to view the collection.

Thirsty Sherlockians will want to quaff an ale at the **Sherlock Holmes Pub** (10 Northumberland Ave, at Craven Passage, 0171/930.2644), near **Trafalgar Square**. Located on the site of the Northumberland Hotel, where Sir Henry Baskerville (*The Hound of the Baskervilles*) lived, the pub, like the museum mentioned above, is crammed with memorabilia about the great detective. Upstairs you'll see a replication of Sherlock's Baker Street sitting room, overflowing with mementos representing his famous cases—from footprint casts to handcuffs to a pistol. You can almost hear his violin and smell his pipe tobacco.

Recently, Sir Arthur Conan Doyle started to get some recognition in his own right. Near Baker Street, at **7 Upper Wimpole Street** (between Weymouth and Devonshire Streets), is a plaque put up by the **City of Westminster** and the Arthur Conan Doyle Society that reads: "Arthur Conan Doyle, Author, 1859–1930, worked and wrote here in 1891." (Note that a block away, at **2 Devonshire Place**, corner of **Devonshire Street**, is a building called **Conan Doyle House**; the resident dentist who named it was hoping that the commemorative plaque would grace *his* building. Nice try, but your motives, dear dentist, were elementary.)

here over the years (including Laurence Olivier, Maggie Smith, Vanessa Redgrave, and Christopher Plummer). Immaculate lobster, potted shrimps, flambéed scallops, Dover sole—you name it, they serve it. Even the humble fish cake tastes dreamlike here. Have a dozen oysters with a bottle of house wine or a full meal at the long oyster bar. Pre-theater dinners and set lunches offer the best value. While you're here, take a look at a genuine Van Gogh—the artist's painting *The Indian Maiden* is displayed prominently on one wall. ♦ Seafood ♦ Daily, lunch and dinner. Reservations recommended on Sa. 28–32 St. Martin's Ct (between St. Martin's La and Charing Cross Rd). 240.2565. Tube: Leicester Sq

70 GIOVANNI'S

★★$$$ Pictures of the West End stars who pop across after they're finished for the night fill this good old-fashioned Italian restaurant that offers about 60 traditional dishes on its menu. It seems like Giovanni's has been here forever. A bonus is its location, a gem of a passageway lined with charming 17th-century houses. ♦ Italian ♦ M-F, lunch and dinner; Sa, dinner. 10 Goodwin's Ct (at Bedfordbury). 240.2877. Tube: Leicester Sq

71 PORTERS

★★$$ Owned by Richard, the seventh Earl of Bradford, this restaurant serves English fare: pies, sausages, and delicious nursery puddings like apple and blackberry crumble, bread-and-butter pudding, spotted dick (a sponge cake baked with currants or raisins), and sherry trifle. The prices are honest, and it's fun for babies and toddlers too. ♦ British ♦ Daily, lunch and dinner. 17 Henrietta St (between Southampton and Bedford Sts). 836.6466. Tube: Covent Garden, Charing Cross

72 RULES

★★★$$$ Founded in 1798, London's oldest restaurant has always been a museum of London's literary and theatrical beau monde, and it still is today. The Prince of Wales (later Edward VII) and his mistress Lillie Langtry drank Champagne behind a special door on the first floor, and Dickens had a regular table across the room. The cuisine has changed very little since then! You can start with brown Windsor soup with Welsh rarebit (which is brown and soupy, with what is glorified toasted cheese on top. But it is *very* British), and follow with steak kidney and oyster pudding or, in season, any wild game dish your heart could desire, and some it might not have heard of. Desserts are as dreamed of on the playing fields of Eton, and the selection of cheeses includes Stinking Bishop, which is *sooooo* much more delicious than it sounds! The wine list is potentially ruinous to liver and wallet. But fabulous. Rules breaks its Britishness once a year by offering an American Thanksgiving Dinner. ♦ British ♦ Daily, lunch and dinner. Reservations required. 35 Maiden La (between Southampton and Bedford Sts). 836.5314. Tube: Covent Garden. www.rules.co.uk

73 COMEDY STORE

The pioneer of the avant-garde comedy scene in London, this club for improvisational and stand-up comedy was founded by Don Ward in 1978. At the time, it was such a new concept that *Time Out* magazine did not have a category for it; today, there are more than 50 similar clubs throughout the city. This venue, however, is still the top spot for seeing stand-up comedians, revues, improvisational comedy, and open-mike sessions. Although you may never have heard of any of them before, the performers are bright, energetic, talented, and above all, funny. (That's particularly true of the **Comedy Store Players**, who are well established as individual performers; they play here on Wednesday and Sunday.) Many performers have gone on to work for the **BBC** and **Channel 4**, and a couple have appeared in movies as well (such as Mike Myers in the *Wayne's World* and *Austin Powers* movies). The lines of people waiting to get in can be formidable, but some tickets are available in advance through **Ticketmaster**. However, if you do wait in line, you'll find it great for people watching; this corner of Leicester Square has attracted such theme restaurants as **Planet Hollywood** and **Fashion Cafe**, which draw the occasional celebrity. ♦ Tu–Su. Haymarket House, Oxendon St (at Coventry St). For information, 344.0234; bookings, 344.4444. Tube: Piccadilly Circus

74 BROWNS

★★$$ This brasserie, one of a chain that began in Oxford and Cambridge, is housed in a grand building formerly occupied by local magistrates' courts. Where once crimes and sentences were duly considered by judges and lawyers, now reasonably priced meals are served in a handsome, spacious room with enormous mirrors, brown leather banquettes along beige walls, black lacquer-topped tables, and lots of plants. English and French dishes are featured, such as country chicken pie or *gigot* of lamb. ♦ English/French ♦ Daily, lunch and dinner. 82–84 St. Martin's La (between St. Martin's Pl and Cecil Ct). 497.5050. Tube: Leicester Sq. Also at 47 Maddox St (between St. George and New Bond Sts). 491.4565. Tube: Oxford Circus; 114 Draycott Ave (between Donne Pl and Walton St). 584.5359. Tube: South Kensington

75 DROOPY & BROWNS

This designer of dreamy wedding gowns, party dresses, and ball gowns set up shop here with opera- and ballet-goers in mind. As you leave the **Coliseum** opposite, next week's opening-night outfit beckons from window displays. Lace, velvet, satin, and silk—all are available at a price. ♦ M–Sa. 99 St. Martin's La (between St. Cecil Ct and St. Martin's Pl). 379.4514. Tube: Leicester Sq

76 COLISEUM

This 2,356-seat theater is the home of the **English National Opera**, which sings only in English. It has a very splendid interior, complete with chariots, granite columns, and 20 boxes. The globe on top was designed to revolve, but an obscure 1904 legal ordinance prevented this; the flashing lights on the globe are the next best thing. ♦ St. Martin's La (between Brydges Pl and Mays Ct). 632.8300. Tube: Leicester Sq

77 ELECTRIC BIRDCAGE

★★$$ An extraordinary and flamboyant newcomer to Haymarket, this is essentially a great cocktail bar and a decent Pan-Asian restaurant wrapped in a sort of outrageous 1970s fantasy setting, with a white leather-fronted bar, stained-glass windows, a fluorescent pink ceiling, and a couple of huge ebony stallions! Of course, there are giant white birdcages, as well as 14-foot turquoise log standard lamps and giant turquoise hands that turn out to be chairs. The cocktail menu is impressive—especially the Electric Birdcage itself, mixed for parties of eight and based on a bottle of Champagne. Staff are dressed, for some reason, as 1950s air stewards and stewardesses! There is a huge selection of dim sum and lots of stir-fries and curries. On the main menu, salads such as chicken, mango, and papaya are available alongside char-grilled sirloin steak with fresh chilies, lemon, and lime juice on a bed of cucumber and noodles. Oriental teas are available for nondrinkers. ♦ Food, M–F, noon-10PM; Sa, 5PM-late, bar till 3AM. 11 Haymarket (at Orange St). 839.2424. Tube: Piccadilly Circus. www.electricbirdcage.com

---

Restaurants/Clubs: **Red** | Hotels: **Purple** | Shops: **Orange** | Outdoors/Parks: **Green** | Sights/Culture: **Blue**

THE STRAND/FLEET STREET

For the curious, the city lover, the history-minded, and the Dickensian-spirited, the treasures of the Strand and Fleet Street are many. This seamless thoroughfare that runs parallel to the **River Thames** has connected the center of government (the **City of Westminster**) to the center of finance (the **City of London**) for more than a thousand years and through 16 reigns.

Fleet Street also served as London's journalistic hub for more than 250 years. William Caxton's printing press was set up here, and England's first daily newspaper, *The Daily Consort*, was issued from **Ludgate Circus** around 1702. Today, however, all of the major British press organizations have moved from their Fleet Street locations. Veteran journalists sometimes return to their old watering holes and gaze at the buildings they once occupied, now more likely to be home to financiers and stockbrokers.

Long gone, however, are the days when the mansions of wealthy bishops, surrounded by gardens that led down to the river's edge, lined the Strand. Gone too are the days of elegance, when magnificent hotels, sophisticated restaurants, and glamorous theaters reflected in the glory of the newly opened **Charing Cross Station**. Although the Strand survived the Reformation, when aristocrats, not bishops, lived in the great houses, it failed to triumph over another type of reformation: the building in 1867 of the **Victoria Embankment**, which reclaimed land from the Thames (and removed its stench) but resulted in the isolation of the Strand from the river. Happily, the revitalization of **Covent Garden** to the north and a thriving theater scene kept the many massive office towers from dehumanizing this well-used thoroughfare.

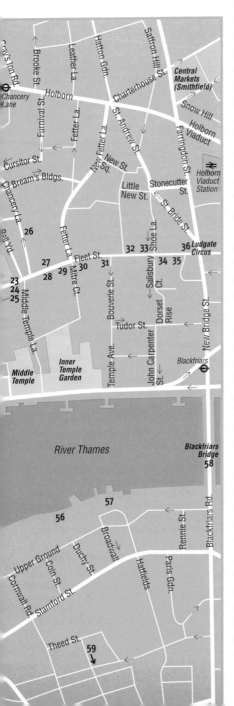

Those who stroll down the Strand and Fleet Street follow in the footsteps of an impressive list of walkers and talkers: Sir Walter Raleigh, William Congreve, Richard Sheridan, Samuel Johnson, James Boswell, Samuel Coleridge, Charles Lamb, Henry Fielding, William Thackeray, Mark Twain, and the omnipresent Charles Dickens.

Along the way, stop for a port in London's oldest wine bar (**Gordon's**); have lunch in a 17th-century pub (**Ye Olde Cheshire Cheese**); peek in on the **Law Courts**; examine the building in which the first English dictionary was written (**Dr. Johnson's House**); buy tea from the shop that supplies the queen (**Twinings**); visit the best Impressionist collection this side of Paris (at the newly refurbished **Courtauld Gallery**); catch a show at the venue that helped make Gilbert and Sullivan famous (the faithfully restored **Savoy Theatre**); or attend a concert, play, or movie just across the river at Western Europe's largest arts complex (South Bank Centre), which also offers one of the best vantage points to gaze at the stretch of London that Henry James called "a tremendous chapter of accidents." Indeed, all the best views of London are from the south side of the river, whether from its walkways or the increasing number of attractions and restaurants, particularly the wonderful new Oxo Tower Wharf, a £20 billion riverside project combining residential and business development with designer workshops and restaurants.

City code 0207 unless otherwise noted.

1 CRAVEN STREET

The street forms the western border of Charing Cross Station, with Villiers Street on the east, and reaches down to the Embankment. Its greatest claim to fame is that Benjamin Franklin lived at No. 36 between 1757 and 1762 and then again between 1764 and 1772; a recent effort to create a Franklin museum failed. Today, the street is a row of dilapidated buildings with officially protected façades waiting to be developed. ♦ Between Northumberland Ave and Strand. Tube: Charing Cross

2 CHARING CROSS STATION

With the arrival of the railway at this huge station in 1863, the Strand became the busiest street in Europe, lined with enormous hotels, restaurants, and theaters built in the euphoria of the age. British Rail has reconstructed the cobbled driveway to the station and rebuilt the exterior walls as they were originally, adorned with 21 cast-iron lanterns. In the station yard stands what is known as an Eleanor Cross (see Charing Cross Monument below). ♦ Strand (between Villiers and Craven Sts). Tube: Charing Cross

2 CHARING CROSS MONUMENT

In 1290, a bereaved King Edward I placed 12 Eleanor Crosses along the route of the funeral cortege of his beloved consort, Queen Eleanor, from the north of England near Lincoln to Westminster Abbey. The final stopping place was a few yards from here, where the statue of Charles I now stands looking down Whitehall. But the octagonal Charing Cross placed here was torn down by Puritans in 1647; today, a replica stands in this spot, surrounded by eight statues of Eleanor. The cross you see in the forecourt of Charing Cross Station was designed by E.M. Barry in 1865; it is a memorial, not a replica of the original Charing Cross. ♦ Strand (between Villiers and Craven Sts). Tube: Charing Cross

2 THISTLE CHARING CROSS HOTEL

$$$ The hotel, designed by E.M. Barry and built between 1863 and 1864, sits over the train tracks of Charing Cross Station and houses its waiting room. Railway hotels have a certain mystique, appealing to writers with vagabond souls and melancholy hearts. An extensive redevelopment has completely revamped the interior. The 239 rooms, many of them spacious, have been redecorated; deep red and blue predominate in the curtains, bedspreads, and wallpaper, and they have satellite TV and tea- and coffee-making equipment. The refurbishment of the Strand Bar and the Strand Terrace Restaurant has also been completed, with an international cuisine emphasizing seasonal ingredients featuring dishes such as Thai curries and salmon en croute, as well as steaks and grills, and there is a new Buckingham Wing, where guests enjoy a 24-hour butler service—the butlers, dressed in tails, oversee room service, laundry, shoe cleaning, and the purchasing of theater tickets. The air-conditioned rooms with double-glazed windows have the latest electronic facilities. Breakfast is served in the elaborately renovated Betjeman Room. ♦ Strand (between Villiers and Craven Sts). 0870/333.9105; fax 0870/333.9205. Tube: Charing Cross

3 COUTTS BANK

The bank of the royal family, established in 1692, has occupied this block of John Nash–designed buildings since 1904. In a daring and skillful act of restoration in 1979, Sir Frederick Gibberd & Partners created an ultramodern interior behind Nash's neoclassical stucco façade and pepper-pot corner cupolas. ♦ 440 Strand (between Agar and Adelaide Sts). Tube: Charing Cross

4 THE NELL GWYNNE TAVERN

★★$ If you walk along the Strand from the direction of Charing Cross toward the Adelphi Theatre, just before you reach the theater turn into Bull Inn Court, and you'll find one of the friendliest pubs in London. It was squeezed into the narrow passageway back in 1623. Every tourist's picture of an old London pub, it is warmly lit and richly Victorian. It's also very small so there is no room for a kitchen, but sandwiches are brought in from a nearby Italian restaurant. ♦ Pub ♦ M–Sa, lunch and dinner. 2 Bull Inn Ct (off the Strand). 240.5579. Tube: Charing Cross

5 ADELPHI THEATRE

Paternal devotion created this theater. In 1806, local tradesman John Scott built it to help launch his daughter's acting career. From 1837 to 1845, many of Charles Dickens's novels were adapted into plays and performed here. But a real drama took place out front in 1897, when actor William Terris was shot by a lunatic. The theater's simple interior, with its straight lines and angles and deep-orange paneling, dates from the extensive remodeling job by **Ernest Schaufelberg** in 1930. Today the 1,478-seat venue is the home of popular musicals. ♦ Strand (between Southampton and Bedford Sts). 0870/403.0303. Tube: Charing Cross

6 VAUDEVILLE THEATRE

Opened in 1870, this structure was completely refurbished in 1969 and is now one of the most delightful theaters in the city, with an elegant gold-and-cream décor, plum-covered seats, and a beautiful chandelier in the foyer. Built by **C.J. Phipps**, the 1,067-seat theater has many long runs to its credit, including the first performances of Ibsen's *Hedda Gabler*, Barrie's *Quality Street*, and Julian Slade's *Salad Days* (which ran from 1954 to 1960—a London record at the time). ♦ Strand (between Southampton and Bedford Sts). 836.9987. Tickets: 0870/890.0511. Tube: Charing Cross

6 STANLEY GIBBONS INTERNATIONAL

Since Stanley Gibbons opened this place in 1874, it has become the largest stamp shop in the world and, quite naturally, *the* source of British and Commonwealth stamps. Two huge floors are filled with stamps, albums, hinges, magnifying glasses, and stamp catalogs. Stamp auctions are held regularly. ♦ M–Sa. 399 Strand (between Southampton and Bedford Sts). 836.8444. Tube: Charing Cross

7 SHELL-MEX HOUSE

Beyond Adam Street, the vista is changed dramatically by the cold, white bulk of this structure. The immense building, designed by the **Messrs. Joseph** architectural firm in 1931, stretches from the Strand all the way to the **Embankment**. The frontage of redbrick and stone is all that remains of the

19th-century, 800-room **Hotel Cecil**, once the largest property in Europe, which was demolished in 1930 to make way for this Deco-style office block. The front is best seen from the other side of the river on the South Bank, a favorite view for theatergoers during intermissions at the **National Theatre**, thanks to its clock, which is larger than **Big Ben**. ♦ Strand (between Carting La and Adam St). Tube: Charing Cross

8 SAVOY THEATRE

Londoners feared this revered venue would never open its doors again after it was destroyed by fire in 1990. Built in 1881 by **Richard D'Oyly Carte**, it was the first public building in the world to be lit by electricity, providing audiences with opulence and comfort. The theater also became famous for staging Gilbert and Sullivan's wonderful comic operas. Happily, the 1,158-seat theater has arisen from the ashes, with a re-creation of its 1929 Art Deco interior by **Basil Ionides**: Chinese lacquerwork, a five-shade color scheme, and aluminum-leaf fluted walls. The theater will remain open during the refurbishment of the **Savoy Hotel**. Note that Savoy Court is the only road in Britain where driving must keep to the right, as allowed by a special Act of Parliament to provide easier access for carriages delivering their passengers to the theater. ♦ Savoy Ct (at Strand). 0870/164.8787. Tube: Charing Cross, Covent Garden

9 SIMPSON'S-IN-THE-STRAND

★★★$$$$ Only a meal at **Eton** or **Harrow** could be more English than this at lunchtime during the week, with a sea of dark-suited men watching as joints of beef and lamb are wheeled to their tables on elaborate silver-domed trolleys and carved to their specifications. Roast beef served with cabbage and roasted potatoes and saddle of lamb are classic British meals, and the waiters who bring them to your table have all the welcoming friendliness of Captain von Trapp before he met Julie Andrews. The daily consumption averages 25 loins of beef and 23 saddles of lamb. Approach a meal here as an authentic English experience, and finish it off with Stilton cheese, treacle tart, and house claret. The ground-floor restaurant has added hearty, full breakfasts to its repertoire. Simpson's has two bars, the **Grand Divan** on the ground floor and the **Knight's Bar** on the first floor, which is more of a cocktail bar. ♦ British ♦ M–F, breakfast (7:15AM–10:30AM), lunch, and dinner; Sa, Su, lunch and dinner. Smart dress required. 100 Strand (between Savoy St and Savoy Ct). 836.9112. Tube: Charing Cross, Covent Garden

---

Restaurants/Clubs: Red | Hotels: Purple | Shops: Orange | Outdoors/Parks: Green | Sights/Culture: Blue

9 SMOLLENSKY'S ON THE STRAND

★★$$$ Michael Gottlieb must have designed this with his tongue firmly in cheek—its exterior is exactly the same as **Simpson's-in-the-Strand** just up the street. Although it's actually located underground, the eatery is on the side of a steep hill with a view of the delightful **Queen's Chapel of the Savoy**, which is sometimes lit up at night. This large Prohibition-era Deco-themed restaurant offers hearty American-style food, burgers, steaks, and corn-fed chicken, with informal, friendly service. Finish off with a peanut butter cheesecake or chocolate mousse, and, on Saturday evenings, you can dance off all the added calories on the spot to live jazz; a pianist plays on the other nights. ♦ American ♦ Daily, lunch and dinner. 105 Strand (between Savoy St and Savoy Ct). 497.2101. Tube: Charing Cross, Covent Garden. During Saturday brunch, kids love the party atmosphere—clowns, Punch and Judy shows, face painting, magicians, and bedlam.

10 LYCEUM TAVERN

★★★$ The taproom downstairs pours real ale; the ground floor serves good salads, terrines, and tarts; and the bar upstairs has views over the Strand. ♦ British ♦ Daily, lunch and dinner. 354 Strand (at Wellington St). 836.7155. Tube: Charing Cross, Covent Garden

10 LYCEUM THEATRE

Splendidly renovated for £14.5 million to the ornate look of its Victorian heyday, when Henry Irving and Ellen Terry appeared most frequently in elaborate dramas, this 2,000-seat theater was reopened in late 1996 and became home to a revival of the Andrew Lloyd Webber musical *Jesus Christ Superstar*. It now is home to *The Lion King*. ♦ Wellington St (at the Strand). 420.8114. Tube: Charing Cross, Covent Garden

11 ALDWYCH

The crescent, identified mainly by the name on the street wall, sweeps around an immense stone fortress occupied by **Australia House**, **India House**, and **Bush House**, the latter decorated with symbolic figures of England and the United States. The street is named after the Danish word meaning "an outlying farm." Its familiarity is enhanced by also being the name of a theater, the **Aldwych**. ♦ Off the Strand. Tube: Covent Garden, Temple

12 DUCHESS THEATRE

This 475-seat theater, though one of the smallest in the West End, is one of the best designed in London, with excellent views from every seat. ♦ Catherine St (between Aldwych and Tavistock St). 0870/890.1103. Tube: Covent Garden

13 NOVELLO THEATRE

Another venue to be recently refurbished to the tune of £3.25 million, this theater (formerly the **Strand Theatre**) is the "twin" of the Aldwych Theatre on the opposite side of the mighty **Waldorf Hilton**. Built as a pair, both are quite magnificent. The proscenium above the arch in the 1,067-seat Novello depicts Apollo in his horse-drawn chariot, with goddesses and cupids, and the whole is so ornately decorated that it's almost wanton to ignore it and rush out for that intermission drink. ♦ Aldwych (at Catherine St). Box office: 0870/950.0925. Tube: Covent Garden

14 THE WALDORF HILTON

$$$$ Following a change in ownership and £26 million worth of refurbishment, the Waldorf Hilton created a spectacular space that combines modern and classic ideas of luxury. Built by **A. Marshall McKenzie** in 1907, this is a truly imposing building. Rooms come as Hilton, deluxe, executive rooms, and suites. All boast wall-mounted plasma screens, the latest high-tech showers, and what the hotel mysteriously describes as "the ultimate sleeping experience." (From the look of the rooms, they mean a bed.) Tea in the **Grand Salon** (which is also a grill room and modern European restaurant featuring classic European dishes such as wild mushroom velouté, baked goat's cheese and seared duck breast, lamb shanks, tiramisù, and a fantastic *tarte au citron*) is to the accompaniment of the Waldorf's resident piano player, the Homage Bar is a great place for a classy pre- or post-theater drink (it also offers one-plate meals), and the Homage Patisserie offers pastries, teas, and coffees throughout the day. ♦ Aldwych (between Catherine St and Drury La). 836.2400; fax 836.7244. Tube: Covent Garden. www.hilton.co.uk/waldorf

15 ALDWYCH THEATRE

Slums between Drury Lane and **Lincoln's Inn** were razed to make room for Aldwych and Kingsway Roads, and in 1905, this theater, along with the **Strand**, was among the first to take up residence. Designed by **W.G.R. Sprague** for Charles Frohmant, the 1,180-seat Georgian structure is handsome and ornate, uncomfortable yet wonderful. This was the home of the **Royal Shakespeare Company** from 1960 until the troupe moved to the **Barbican** in 1982. ♦ M-Sa, 10AM-10PM. Aldwych (at Drury La). Inquiries: 0207/379.3367; bookings: 0870/400.0805; 24 hrs. Tube: Covent Garden

16 BUSH HOUSE

Namesake American Irving T. Bush wanted to erect a trade center with shops and marbled corridors, but it didn't work out that way. Since 1940, the **BBC World Service**, one of the most important broadcasting institutions in the Western World, has used the building for its transmissions. "To the Friendship of English Speaking Peoples" is carved into the stonework of this vital building erected in 1935 by **Harvey W. Corbett**. The entrance for both office workers and shoppers is opposite **St. Mary-le-Strand**. Inside is **Penfriend** (836.9809), a rather splendid pen shop offering the kind of personal service you just don't get in department stores. Access is to the shopping arcade only. ♦ Aldwych. Tube: Temple

17 St. Mary-le-Strand

St. Mary-le-"Stranded" is the sadder, more apt name for this jewel of a church once half surrounded by houses on the north side of the Strand but, since 1910, isolated by the widening of roads. Built between 1714 and 1717, this is the first major work of Scottish architect **James Gibbs**. It is essentially a Baroque church with its half-domed porch and numerous vertical pediments. As though in self-fulfilling prophecy, the upper order contains the windows, whereas the lower order is solid to keep out the noise from the street. The entire structure was restored a few years ago, and the splendid five-stage steeple, weakened by wartime bombing, pollution, traffic vibration, and rusting iron clamps that bind the Portland stone, was dismantled stone by stone and then rebuilt. The barrel-vaulted building has ornate plasterwork and a coffered ceiling. Thomas à Becket was lay rector of the medieval church that originally stood on the site, and the parents of Charles Dickens were married here. Poet laureate Sir John Betjeman made it his life's work to save this beautiful church from demolition. Who can blame him? ♦ M-F, 11AM-4PM; Su, 10AM-3PM; times may vary. Check their web site, www.stmarylestrand.org, for current opening and service times. There are sometimes lunchtime concerts. Strand (between Aldwych and Montreal Pl). 836.3126. Tube: Temple

18 King's College

Founded in 1829 by the Duke of Wellington, several archbishops, and 30 bishops of the Church of England, this college adjoins the east wing of **Somerset House** and has formed part of the **University of London** since 1898. Contained within the College is **King's College Chapel**, designed by **George Gilbert Scott** in 1860 and renovated in 2000. ♦ Strand (at Surrey St). Tube: Temple

19 Roman Bath

Tucked away down Strand Lane along the east side of **Somerset House** under a dark archway, this 15-foot enigma is considered by many to be Roman; others say it is possibly Tudor, but more likely 17th century. Built over a tributary of the River Fleet, a small underground stream that flows into the Thames, it fills each day with 2,000 gallons of icy water that drain into a pipe and down into the Thames. David Copperfield used to take cold plunges here, but now the bath belongs to the **National Trust** and must be seen by appointment (book a week in advance). However, it's mostly visible from the pathway through a specially arranged window that has a light switch that illuminates the whole bath. ♦ Admission. W, 2-5PM by appointment only. 5 Strand La (off Temple Pl). 641.5264. Tube: Temple

20 Statue of W.E. Gladstone

The statue designed by Sir Hamo Thornycroft in 1905 looks out bravely onto the sea of uncaring traffic from the middle of the roadway where the Strand is rejoined by the Aldwych. Gladstone, a liberal statesman, was prime minister four times. He introduced educational reform in 1870 and the secret ballot in 1872 and succeeded in carrying out the Reform Act of 1884. But he failed to gain support for home rule in Ireland, which would no doubt have made the history of the 20th century in these islands more tranquil. This statue shows him robed as Chancellor of the Exchequer, with Brotherhood, Education, Aspiration, and Courage represented at the base. ♦ Strand (at Aldwych). Tube: Temple

21 St. Clement Danes

Now the official church of the Royal Air Force (RAF), **Sir Christopher Wren**'s oranges-and-lemons church (so called because the church's bells play the tune from the nursery rhyme "Oranges and Lemons") was built between 1680 and 1682, blitzed during World War II, and skillfully rebuilt by **W.A.S. Lloyd** in 1955. (The steeple, added in 1720, was designed by **James Gibbs**.) The floor is inlaid with slabs of Welsh slate carved with the 735 units of the RAF, and the rolls of honors contain the 125,000 men and women of the RAF who died in either World War I or II. The original pulpit by Grinling Gibbons was shattered in the bombing and painstakingly pieced together from the fragments. The organ was a gift from members of the US Air Force, and there is a shrine to the USAF

Restaurants/Clubs: Red | Hotels: Purple | Shops: Orange | Outdoors/Parks: Green | Sights/Culture: Blue

THE BEST

William Forrester
Registered Guide

Upper Crust Baguettes—available at most rail stations. Brits suffer a culinary inferiority complex with the French—here is beautiful French bread with sandwich fillings and proof that a rail-station snack really can be edible.

The **Reading Room** at the **British Library**—one of the world's great spaces. It'll soon be much more accessible to the general public when it becomes part of the **British Museum**.

Coffee at the **Cloister** of **Westminster Abbey**—American friends are annoyed that (sometimes) the Brits can do good coffee.

Evensong at **Westminster Abbey** or **St. Paul's Cathedral**—an opportunity to hear one of the world's greatest choirs with one of the world's greatest acoustics *for free*. Ask to sit in the choir area.

Summertime band concerts in the parks—or on Thursday, summer lunchtimes in **Westminster Abbey**'s private gardens.

Sir John Soane's Museum—an eclectic collection given to the nation by this great architect and unaltered ever since. A real window into the mind of a 19th-century collector. Trust me and just see it!

Pret a Manger's crème (without the brûlée)—one branch under the Impressionists at the café in the **National Gallery**—just the thing to recover from cultural exhaustion.

---

under the west gallery. Each March, oranges and lemons are distributed to the children of the parish in a special service. Samuel Johnson worshiped here and is now depicted in bronze behind the church, where he gazes nostalgically down the street he believed to be unequaled: Fleet Street.
♦ Strand (between Bell Yd and Clement's Inn). Tube: Temple

Michael Storrings

22 ROYAL COURTS OF JUSTICE

Better known as the **Law Courts**, this dramatic Gothic ramble of buildings (see above), with a 514-foot frontage along the Strand, was built in a period of Victorian reorganization of the legal system and opened by Queen Victoria in 1882, with the power and glory of the law architecturally proclaimed. The main entrance is flanked by twin towers and slate roofs. Solomon holds his temple

above the entrance on the left, and on the right is the founder of English law, Alfred the Great. The lofty **Great Hall** (238 feet long and 80 feet high) contains a monument to the original architect, **G.E. Street**, who, in the Victorian tradition of tutelage, was a pupil of **Sir George Gilbert Scott** and teacher of **Philip Webb** and **William Morris**.

The buildings house 64 courts spread over 7 miles of corridors and 1,000 rooms. They are reached by way of the hall, and when the courts sit, the public is admitted to the back two rows of the courtrooms. Take time out for a visit if you're at all interested in seeing the English justice system at work, visually enhanced by the wigged presence of judges and barristers and undisguised solicitors. Read the *Daily Lists* in the central hall to decide what appeals to you in the still faintly Dickensian world of probate, bankruptcy, and divorce. These days, there are many libel cases. You're free to enter any court except those marked "court in camera" or "chambers." (Note that criminal cases are tried in the **Old Bailey**.) ♦ M-F. Strand (between Bell Yd and Clement's Inn). 947.6000. Tube: Temple

23 FLEET STREET

This lively, congested street has a glorious and eclectic mix of styles and levels and a tremendous skyline defined by the tower and pinnacles of the **Law Courts**, the tower of **St. Dunstan-in-the-West**, and the dome of **St. Paul's Cathedral**, best seen from the north side of the street. Sadly, the editorial offices of the nation's newspapers last left Fleet Street in 1989. ♦ Between Ludgate Circus and Middle Temple La. Tube: Temple, Blackfriars

23 TEMPLE BAR MONUMENT

This spiky dragon (which is definitely *not* a griffin), created in 1880 by Horace Jones, stands on the site of **Sir Christopher Wren**'s three-arched gateway, which was here between 1672 and 1878. (The gate was dismantled because it obstructed traffic and was moved to Theobald's Park in Hertfordshire.) The dragon is a mythical beast famous for its voracious appetite, and appropriately, it marks the boundary between the City of Westminster, impelled by restraint, and the City of London, inspired by acquisition. The dragon here also marks the end of the broad, dozy Strand and the beginning of Fleet Street. The figures on either side of the dragon are Queen Victoria and Edward VIII, Prince of Wales. ♦ Fleet St (at Strand). Tube: Temple

24 ROYAL BANK OF SCOTLAND

Founded in 1671, this is the oldest bank in London, and it was the inspiration for Tellson's Bank in Dickens's *A Tale of Two Cities*. The nonfictional list of customers includes Charles II, the Duke of Marlborough, Nell Gwyn, Samuel Pepys, Oliver Cromwell, and John Dryden. ♦ 1 Fleet St (between Middle Temple La and Devereux Ct). Tube: Temple

25 TWININGS

Chinese Mandarins guard the Georgian entrance to London's narrowest shop and oldest business still to stand on its original site. (The store has been paying taxes longer than any other business in Westminster.) Thomas Twining opened the shop in 1706 as **Tom's Coffee House**, and it has been selling tea ever since it became the national drink. Alas, you can't drink a cup of tea here; you can only buy it unbrewed or find out about it in the small museum in the back. ♦ Free. M-F. 216 Strand (between Middle Temple La and Devereux Ct). 353.3511. Tube: Temple

26 PUBLIC RECORD OFFICE (PRO)

Once a favored haunt of genealogists for the records that were stored here, this building is now a business office and is not open to the public. The **PRO** has moved to a huge modern complex at Kew Gardens. ♦ Chancery La (between Fleet St and Bream's Bldgs). Tube: Chancery La

27 ST. DUNSTAN-IN-THE-WEST

This architectural gem—London's Romanian Orthodox patriarchal church—is beautifully situated on the north side at the curve in Fleet Street. Designed by **John Shaw**, the Victorian church, with its octagonal tower, openwork lantern, and pinnacles, was built in 1831 at the beginning of the Gothic Revival movement on the site of an earlier church whose great treasures were saved when it was demolished to widen Fleet Street.

The church is unusually placed, with the tower and entrance on the south and the brick octagon of the sanctuary and altar on the north. Treasures from the original church include the communion rail carved by Grinling Gibbons and the old wooden clock dating from 1671, with two wooden giants that strike each hour. In 1830, the Marquis of Hertford bought the clock for his house in **Regent's Park**. Viscount Rothermere, a British newspaper proprietor, later purchased the clock and returned it to the church in 1935 to commemorate King George V's Silver Jubilee. The statue of Elizabeth I over the door (believed to be the oldest outdoor statue in London) and the statues of King Lud and his sons came from the Ludgate when it was torn down in 1760. The bronze bust of Lord Northcliffe, who lived from 1865 to 1922 and was newspaper proprietor and founder of the *Daily Mail*, was sculpted by Lady Scott in 1930. ♦ Fleet St (between Fetter and Chancery Las). Tube: Temple, Chancery La, Blackfriars

28 PRINCE HENRY'S ROOM

Located above the archway leading to the **Temple**, the timbered house containing **Prince Henry's Room** was built in 1610 as a tavern with a projecting upper story. The great treasure inside is the Jacobean ceiling, one of the finest remaining enriched plaster ceilings of its time in London, with an equally enriched set of stories to go with it. The most persistent tale claims that the initials P.H. and the **Prince of Wales's Feathers**, which decorate the ceiling, commemorate the 1610 investiture of Henry, eldest son of James I. The prince died 2 years later, and the title passed to his younger brother, who would become the luckless King Charles I. The room also contains mementos of diarist Samuel Pepys, who was born in 1633 in nearby Salisbury Court, Fleet Street, was baptized in nearby **St. Bride's Church**, and lived most of his life close by Tower Hill. His remarkable shorthand diary, recording the period between 1660 and 1669, fills many volumes and is the liveliest and fullest account of London life ever written, including such events as the Plague of 1665 and the Great Fire of 1666. The wide oriel windows overlooking Fleet Street and across to Chancery Lane manage to frame London's

---

Restaurants/Clubs: **Red** | Hotels: **Purple** | Shops: **Orange** | Outdoors/Parks: **Green** | Sights/Culture: **Blue**

SHAKESPEARE'S GLOBE COMES FULL CIRCLE

Shakespeare buffs, rejoice! After 400 years, the "Wooden O" is back! The famous thatch-roofed, half-timbered, open-air **Globe Theatre** has been authentically reconstructed about 200 yards from the original spot in **Southwark**, on the south bank of the **Thames**. Since its grand opening in 1997 (with productions of *Henry V* and *The Winter's Tale*), aficionados have been flocking to see the Bard's plays performed very much as they were in his day: A thousand spectators sit in three galleries of the amphitheater while 500 "groundlings" stand in front of the open arena in front of the stage. (Elizabethan theatergoers who watched performances from the pit were called groundlings because they had only the ground for a floor.)

The history of the original Globe was set in motion in 1576 when the actor James Burbage built an amphitheater to stage plays in the **Shoreditch** area of London. Before then, actors had been traveling players performing in courtyards of inns like the **George** or in great halls such as the one at **Middle Temple**. Burbage simply called his new structure **The Theatre**; there wasn't any other. When the Shoreditch building was torn down, the timber frames were used in the building of the Globe in 1599. There Shakespeare presented and acted in many of his plays. Performances took place in natural light and sometimes in the rain. The groundlings had a boisterous time. They walked around, talked loudly, ate fruit—and threw some of it at the actors during performances. Theater people had to put up with a lot in those days; it was a risky business in which all the members of a company were shareholders. Not only was there no guarantee that a new play would ever see more than one performance but also periodic outbreaks of plague meant that large gatherings were forbidden.

Southwark was where Shakespeare played as well as worked. The red-light district of its day, it was full of bear-baiting pits, brothels, taverns—in fact, it welcomed all the entertainment the City merchants banned in their own neighborhood, though they didn't mind crossing London Bridge to enjoy the delights on offer. Shakespeare and his cronies drank at the first incarnation of the **Anchor**. He worshiped at **Southwark Cathedral**, which now holds a marble effigy of him, looking thoughtful. Above the statue, a stained-glass window depicts many of his characters.

Shakespeare and his players did cross the Thames for special performances. In the gorgeous **Middle Temple Hall** (Middle Temple Lane, between Victoria Embankment and Crown Office Row), where lawyers still dine today, they performed *Twelfth Night* in 1602. The gardens outside were immortalized in *Henry VI, Part I* in connection with the plot that began the War of the Roses. Lord Suffolk says, "Within the Temple Hall we were too loud/The garden here is more convenient." Then the characters pluck first a white and then a red rose to indicate which side they back. Visitors can still admire the garden from the park benches in **Fountain Court** outside the hall.

The *Globe* burned down in 1613: A spark from a stage cannon that was fired to announce the entrance of King Henry VIII ignited the thatch roof. The same fire also caused the original Anchor to go up in smoke. And Shakespeare died three years later. It's interesting to note that his favorite pub was rebuilt twice—the atmospheric, creaky-boarded Anchor of today dates from 1760—but the rebirth of his theater had to wait 400 years, and then it was American actor-director Sam Wanamaker who sparked its revival. When Wanamaker came to London in the 1950s, he was dismayed to find nothing of the Globe remaining; the only reference was a dusty plaque on a disused warehouse in a derelict street. Wanamaker's disbelief that the world's greatest playwright had no suitable tribute in the city in which he wrote his plays led him to embark on a 40-year crusade to re-create the original theater. Finally, in 1970 he established the **Globe Playhouse Trust**, and the Southwark Council offered the trust a 1.2-acre site near the original theater. Unfortunately, Sam Wanamaker died in 1993 before the new theater was completed. It is appropriate that a memorial to him adjoins the one to Shakespeare in Southwark Cathedral.

Costing $47 million, the re-created theater is the first thatch building to be erected in London since the Great Fire of 1666. Its materials include green oak, willow, and sand mixed with lime and goat's hair to create plaster for the walls. In fact, it's the Wooden O Shakespeare would recognize—except that this one has a sprinkler system hidden within the thatch.

timelessness the way one longs to see it. ♦ Free. M-F, 11AM–2PM. 17 Fleet St (at Inner Temple La). Tube: Temple. Closed for refurbishment. No date given for reopening. Call City of London information line on 7332/1456 for further information

28 YE OLDE COCK TAVERN

★★$$ Another illustrious roll call of former regulars—Nell Gwyn, Pepys, Goldsmith,

Sheridan, and Garrick—once drank in this small tavern when it was located across the road. It was moved here in 1887 with many of the original building's fittings. Unfortunately, a fire in 1990 destroyed a number of the details, but the building has been re-created as completely as possible. The Olde Cock is hoping to refurbish again to restore more of its olde world charm. It still offers traditional ambience, an excellent bar lunch, and delicious roasts and desserts. The modern clientele is a civilized mix of journalists and barristers. ◆ Pub ◆ M-F, 6AM-11:30PM, breakfast, lunch, and dinner; Sa, noon-6PM. Reservations recommended for the restaurant. 22 Fleet St (between Mitre Ct and Inner Temple La). 353.8570. Tube: Temple

28 HOARE'S BANK

The only private bank left in London is still as old-fashioned, discreet, and attractive as when it was founded in 1672. It's well worth a peek inside. ◆ 37 Fleet St (between Mitre Ct and Inner Temple La). Tube: Temple

29 THE TEMPLE

An oasis of calm between the traffic of the **Embankment** and the bustle of Fleet Street, this structure was originally the headquarters of the Knights Templar, a monastic order founded in 1119 during the Crusades to regain Palestine from the Saracens for Christianity. They settled here in 1160 but were suppressed by the pope, and all that remains of their monastery is the **Temple Church** and the **Buttery**. Since the 14th century, the buildings have been leased to lawyers. Today, they house two of England's four **Inns of Court** (**Inner Temple** and **Middle Temple**), the voluntary legal society that has the exclusive privilege of calling candidates to the bar. Visitors are free to stroll through the warren of lanes, courtyards, and gardens and to admire the buildings, each composed like an **Oxford** or **Cambridge** college, with chambers built around steep stairways, communal dining halls, libraries, common rooms, and chapels. The tranquility of the setting is disrupted by the speed with which the lawyers—either wearing their gowns or carrying them over their arms, and loaded down with books and papers—race between their chambers and the **Law Courts**, the vast Gothic world that stretches from **Temple Bar** to the Adlwych.

The Temple Church, located within the precincts of the **Inner Temple**, was badly damaged during the Blitz but has been skillfully repaired. The beautiful round nave, completed in 1185, is modeled after the Church of the Holy Sepulchre in Jerusalem. It's the only circular nave in London, and one of the only five in England, all connected with the Knights Templar. The chancel was added in 1240, and the rib vaulting within the Gothic porch is original.

The **Middle Temple Hall**, also painstakingly restored after the Blitz, is a handsome Elizabethan building with a splendid double-hammer beam roof and carved-oak screen. Here, aspiring barristers are called to the bar on passing their examinations. Daily, lunch and dinner are served in the hall, and though residence at the inns has become vestigial,

the students must eat three dinners during each term here. Shakespeare's *Twelfth Night* was performed in the hall in 1602, and the round pond amid the mulberry trees outside the **Fountain Court** was featured in Dickens's novel *Martin Chuzzlewit*. The **Inner Temple Gateway**, leading back to the Strand, is a half-timbered three-story house that looks suspiciously like a stage set, but it is genuinely 17th-century, with **Prince Henry's Room** (see page 195) on the top floor. ◆ Bounded by Victoria Embankment and Strand and by Mitre Ct and Essex St. Tube: Temple

30 DR. JOHNSON'S HOUSE

This great English city is full of the houses of famous English men and women. Many of these historic homes have been lovingly bought and preserved, restored, rearranged, and revitalized in the spirit of the departed. They usually possess an orderliness that the former inhabitants would find astonishing, especially if they were writers. Among the most tempting for the London lover is the house of Samuel Johnson, one of his London residences and the place where he produced the first complete dictionary of the English language, published in 1755. Until he moved to Gough Square, Johnson had lived in miserable lodgings, taking whatever literary hackwork he could find. But with the advance he was given to write the Dictionary, he leased this house in 1748. On the day he signed the contract to write the Dictionary, he composed the following prayer: "Oh God, who hast hitherto supported me, enable me to proceed in this labour, and in the whole task of my present state; that when I shall render up, at the last day, an account of the talent committed to me, I may receive pardon. For the sake of Jesus Christ, amen." Johnson installed his assistants in the huge attic, and for the next 9 years, they worked at their task. In 1752, his beloved wife, Tetty, 15 years his senior, died. Seven years later, in 1759, melancholy and impoverished, Dr. Johnson went to live in one of the **Staple Inn Buildings**. ◆ M-Sa, 11AM-5PM, Oct-Apr; 11AM-5:30PM, May-Sept. Admission: £4.50 adults; £3.50 group; £1.50 children; under 5 free; £10 family ticket; private viewings available for additional fee. Guided tours are provided free to groups (min. 10). 17 Gough Sq (at Pemberton Row). 353.3745. Tube: Blackfriars. www.drjohnsonshouse.org

31 EL VINO'S

★$ Whoever said *"in vino veritas"* didn't hang out at this historic wine bar opened in 1879. A lot of history (some truthful, some apocryphal) was written over bottles of wine here when this place was the haunt of boozy journalists. What started as a piece of gossip, idle speculation, or a mischievous rumor would become an item in the *Standard Diary* or an article in *Private Eye*, sometimes progressing to "something worth checking out" by more serious writers. Throughout most of its life, the bar has been a masculine institution (women weren't allowed to drink here until 1982). These days, it is packed daily with lawyers and City businesspeople. The wine list is long, as you might expect, and the menu in the small basement restaurant consists of simple British foods such as Scottish salmon and steak-and-kidney pie. Sandwiches are served at the bar. No jeans, leggings, track suits, or shorts are allowed. The bar also operates as a wine merchant and delivers orders to its customers all over Britain. ♦ Wine bar ♦ Bar: M, 8:30AM-9PM; Tu-F, 8:30AM-11PM; lunch, noon-3PM. Closed weekends. Limited number of tables outside during summer. 47 Fleet St (between Bouverie St and Mitre Ct). 0207/353.5384. Tube: Temple, Blackfriars. www.elvino.co.uk

32 YE OLDE CHESHIRE CHEESE

★★★$$ This 17th-century hostelry is probably the most profitable institution on Fleet Street and one of the few remaining of its kind in London. "The House," as it's also known, has witnessed 16 reigns and hardly changed since it was rebuilt after the Great Fire of 1666. The 14th-century crypt from **Whitefriars** monastery is beneath the cellar bar and is available for private parties. The sawdust on the floor, changed daily, and the oak tables in "boxes" with benches on either side enchant foreigners, who long to visit an England frozen in time. Considering the unrivaled popularity of the place (which can sometimes cause culinary neglect), the food is pretty good, although the famous pudding of steak, kidney, mushrooms, and game, which celebrated its bicentenary in 1972, no longer feeds 90 people nor requires 16 hours to cook. Nor does it contain oysters and lark, as it once did, but it's still sustaining and flavorful. The biggest pies now serve up to 35 people with steak, kidney, venison, and game packed under a delicious pie crust. Rich game puddings are served in autumn and winter. Follow the pudding with Stilton cheese or lemon pancakes and relish the Englishness of it all. ♦ British ♦ Bar: M-Sa, 11AM-11PM; Su, noon-3PM. Restaurant: M-Sa, noon-11:30PM; Su, noon-2:30PM. Reservations recommended. 145 Fleet St (between Shoe La and Hind Ct). 353.6170. Tube: Blackfriars

32 DAILY TELEGRAPH BUILDING

This massive, modernish neo-Greek structure, designed in 1928 by **Elcock, Sutcliffe, and Tait**, once housed London's most sensible conservative paper. The *Telegraph* was the capital's first daily penny paper, founded in 1855. The paper moved to Docklands, but the building's façade remains. The building is now occupied by offices. ♦ 135 Fleet St (between Shoe La and Hind Ct). Tube: Blackfriars

33 DAILY EXPRESS BUILDING

Nicknamed the **Black Lubyanka** because of the glossy appearance of its façade, this building's black-glass tiles and chrome represent one of the finest examples—inside and out—of Art Deco in London. It was designed by **Ellis Clarke and Atkinson**, with **Sir Owen Williams**, and built in 1932. The *Daily Express* departed for a building on Blackfriars Bridge in 1989, and the building now houses offices. ♦ 121-128 Fleet St (at Poppins Ct). Tube: Blackfriars

34 REUTER'S

Although its news department now works elsewhere, this famous international news agency is still headquartered in these two 1939 buildings, which are another example of the genius of **Sir Edwin Lutyens**. Lutyens's last commercial buildings in London, they are next door to **Christopher Wren**'s beautiful **St. Bride's Church**; the Edwardian architect was wisely inspired by and respectful of the wedding cake–style structure, conceiving his L-shaped plan as a backdrop. One of the buildings is linked to the church by a high vaulted passage. The buildings are closed to visitors. ♦ 85 Fleet St (between Ludgate Circus and Bride La). Tube: Blackfriars

35 ST. BRIDE'S CHURCH

Wedged between the ponderous buildings that used to house newspaper offices is **Sir Christopher Wren**'s "madrigal in stone," one of his grander creations, with the tallest of his steeples (226 feet) resting on a plain, squarish nave—the origin and inspiration of the traditional wedding cake. Damaged in the Blitz, the church was beautifully restored in the 1950s. Optimistic journalists still marry and attend memorial services for fellow journalists here. The crypt—established in memory of Lord Beaverbrook—is now a museum about the history of Fleet Street and printing. ♦ Free. M-F, 8AM-6:30PM; Sa, 11AM-4PM; Su, open for services at 11AM and 6:30PM. Recitals on Tu and F, 1:15PM-1:45PM. Bride La (off Fleet St). 0207/427.0133. Tube: Blackfriars. www.stbrides.com

36 OLD BELL TAVERN

★★$ **Sir Christopher Wren** built this intimate, warm pub in 1678 to house and serve the workmen rebuilding **St. Bride's** nearby after it was destroyed in the Great Fire. Sandwiches, sausages, and other traditional pub fare are served. They're best known for their wide selection of cask ales and traditional fish and chips. Like other

CHILD'S PLAY

Although London may seem like a grand, serious, even forbidding city at first (especially to children), there are lots of fun things for families to see and do. These 10 suggestions are just the beginning.

● **Feed** the ducks, geese, and pelicans in **St. James's Park**.

● **Create** the perfect toothbrush on the computer at the **Design Museum**.

● **Explore** the HMS *Belfast*, a real World War II battleship, from stem to stern.

● **Read** the news or do an interview—and then watch yourself on TV—at the **Museum of the Moving Image**.

● **Get** some hands-on knowledge of starfish and other sea creatures at the **London Aquarium**.

● **Operate** the automated wood and metal sculptures at the **Cabaret Mechanical Theatre**.

● **Play** the stock market on the computer at the **Bank of England Museum**—and afterward, take a look at some real gold bricks.

● **Fly** an airplane (well, a simulated one, anyway) at the **Science Museum**.

● **Whiz** through 2,000 years of history at the **Tower Hill Pageant** ride—and then visit the **Tower of London** next door for a look at where a lot of that history was made.

● **Ride** the old-fashioned merry-go-round and set mechanical toys in motion at the **London Toy and Model Museum**.

Fleet Street pubs that catered to journalists in the newspapers' heyday, it's now crowded with lawyers and bankers. ◆ Pub ◆ M-F, 11AM–11PM; Sa, noon–6PM. 95 Fleet St (between St. Bride La and Salisbury Ct). 0207/583.0216. Tube: Blackfriars

36 THE PUNCH TAVERN

★★$ This splendidly Victorian pub is closely associated with the humor magazine *Punch*, which was founded in 1841. (After having ceased publication for a few years, the magazine started up again in 1996.) This was the watering hole for the staff of the first *Punch* and for decades of journalists afterward. Major refurbishment in 1997 has enhanced its historic features, including a display of original cartoons and caricatures from early copies of the magazine. Refurbishment has brightened and restored the interior to bring out the older Victorian detail, and along with a recent change in management they have turned their lunch menu into a buffet to include unlimited roast pork, applesauce, sautéed potatoes, and veggies galore. The new owners have also found artifacts related to Punch and Judy, the traditional English puppet show characters—it was the irascible Punch puppet who inspired the magazine's title. ◆ Pub ◆ Daily, lunch. Drinks: M-F, 11AM–11PM; Sa, Su, noon–3PM, 7PM–10:30PM. 99 Fleet St (at Bride La). 353.6658. Tube: Blackfriars

37 ROYAL SOCIETY OF ARTS (RSA)

This is easily the most interesting building in the maze of streets that once comprised the

Adelphi. Completed by **Robert Adam** in 1754, it has all the noble tranquillity, purity, and order that epitomize **Adam** architecture, complete with a Venetian window with a scalloped stone arch and acanthus-leaf capitals. The society was founded in 1754 with the aim of encouraging art, science, and manufacturing, and it employed talented artists and craftspeople of the day. The fine hall is decorated with 10 vast paintings by **James Barry** depicting the progress of civilization. Barry is regarded by some art critics as the first Impressionist and a source of inspiration for Turner. The pictures have recently been cleaned as part of a £1.3 million program to restore the building to its full Georgian splendor. To see them, apply to the society librarian after 9:30AM. ◆ Free. 8 John Adam St (between Adam and Durham House Sts). 451.6874. Tube: Charing Cross, Embankment. www.rsa.org.uk

38 THE ADELPHI

Parallel with the Strand is John Adam Street, the site of the late, lamented **Adelphi**, a stunning architectural and engineering achievement and London's first grand speculative housing development. It was built between 1768 and 1774 by the **Adam** brothers, **William, James**, and **Robert**, with John as economic adviser. With brilliant vision and dreamy optimism, the brothers leased the land between the Strand and the Thames and built a quay above the river, with four stories of arched brick vaults for warehousing. On top of this structure they created four streets—Adelphi Terrace, John

---

Restaurants/Clubs: Red | **Hotels: Purple** | **Shops: Orange** | **Outdoors/Parks: Green** | **Sights/Culture: Blue**

Adam Street, Robert Street, and Adam Street—and a terrace of 11 four-story brick houses that faced the river, inspired by the fourth-century Palace of Diocletian on the Adriatic coast, as well as by Pompeii and Athens.

The scheme was a testament to fraternal genius (and was named accordingly—*adelphos* is the Greek word for "brother"), but it proved a financial disaster. The project almost ruined the Adam brothers, and the houses were eventually occupied by a £50-per-ticket lottery sponsored by Parliament in 1773. In the 19th century, the Adelphi was popular with artists and writers, and it became home for such literary celebrities as Thomas Rowlandson, Charles Dickens, John Galsworthy, Thomas Hardy, Sir James Barrie, H.G. Wells, and George Bernard Shaw. Richard D'Oyly Carte lived at **4 Adelphi Terrace** while producing the comic operas of Gilbert and Sullivan. In 1936, most of the development was demolished, a wanton act still lamented by architects and lovers of fine buildings. The legacy of the visionary speculation consists of the streets that the Adam brothers named after themselves, as well as a few fragments: **1–3 Robert Street**, with the honeysuckle pilasters that were the trademark of the Adelphi; **7 Adam Street**, which is pure Adam in style; and **4–6 John Adam Street**, which still contains features of the original scheme. Undaunted, the Adam brothers went on to design and build Portland Place, north of Oxford Street.
♦ John Adam St (between Robert and Adam Sts). Tube: Charing Cross, Embankment

The Savoy

39 Savoy Hotel

In December 2007, The Savoy Hotel closed its doors for the first time in over 100 years. It is currently undergoing a £100 million refurbishment, and is due to reopen sometime in 2009.

40 Queen's Chapel of the Savoy

This haven of tranquillity belongs to the Duke of Lancaster, who is in fact the queen (the reigning monarch—whether male or female—keeps this title, which goes back to Henry IV, who was Duke of Lancaster before he usurped the throne from Richard II). Erected in 1505 in the late perpendicular style on the grounds of the **Savoy Palace**, the chapel has been used by royalty since the reign of Henry VII. The present building is almost entirely Victorian, rebuilt by **Sir Robert Smirke** in 1820 and restored by his brother **Sydney Smirke** after a fire in 1864. The origi-

nal chapel was once part of the Order of St. John (1510–1516), and since 1937, it has been part of the chapel of the Royal Victorian Order, one of the orders of chivalry. The heraldic plaque in the vestibule is made of gilded marrow seeds crushed into the seductive forms of the leopards of England. The stained-glass window commemorates Richard D'Oyly Carte (1844–1901), and another window is in memory of Queen Mary, who died in 1953. The window with heraldic designs of the Royal Victorian Order was designed in part by King George VI. ♦ Tu-F, 11:30AM-3:30PM, Oct-July. Savoy St (at Savoy Row). Tube: Embankment, Temple

41 Courtauld Gallery/ Somerset House

Architect **Sir William Chambers** designed this Georgian stronghold between 1776 and 1786 to replace the 16th-century Renaissance palace that occupied the site. As one of London's premier neoclassical buildings, it stands facing the Thames east of Waterloo Bridge and is one of the few Georgian buildings still gracing the riverside. Like the old **Adelphi, Chambers's Somerset House** rose out of the Thames before the construction of the **Embankment**. The great palace of the Protector Somerset (1547–1572), with its magnificent chapel by **Inigo Jones** and riverside gallery by **John Webb**, originally stood on this site and was lived in by Elizabeth I when she was a princess, as well as by the queens of James I, Charles I, and Charles II.

The present building had suffered a less-than-illustrious existence, housing administrative offices and institutions and the Registry of Births, Deaths, and Marriages (which have moved to Islington, north London, as the Family Records Centre, 0181/392.5300). Since 1990, the building has been home to the **Courtauld Institute of Art** and the recently reopened Courtauld Gallery. The restoration work focused on the **Fine Rooms** and the **Great Room**, designed between 1776 and 1780 by Chambers and among the most important 18th-century interiors in London. The original inhabitants of this block were the Royal Society, the Royal Academy of Arts, and the Society of Antiquaries, who finally left in 1850 and were replaced by the Registrar General until the 1970s. The rooms then remained empty for 20 years.

The Courtauld is one of the galleries that most people mean to visit but don't quite get around to, yet it has the best Impressionist and post-Impressionist collection in Britain, not to mention a fabulous classical collection. The major collections were assembled by Samuel Courtauld and Viscount Lee of Fareham (the British counterpart of the Guggenheims), who founded the institute in 1931.

Resist all temptations to use the elevator and take the magnificent spiral staircase instead, dubbed the "Rowlandson" after a painting by Thomas Rowlandson, showing revelers falling down it at a party. The works to see include the **Prince's Gate Collection** of Italian Renaissance and Dutch art from the 15th and 16th centuries that were given to the institute in 1978 by Count Antoine Seilern. The range of art is extraordinary, from Palma Vecchio's lush *Venus in a Landscape* and Van Dyck's *Portrait of a Man in an Armchair* to Botticelli's *Holy Trinity* and Albertinelli's *Creation*. There is also Rubens's spectacular Baroque work *Descent from the Cross*, which was the model for the altarpiece in Antwerp Cathedral. Other works are from the Rubens school, including *The Bounty of James I Triumphing Over Avarice*, a *modello* for the ceiling corners at **Banqueting House**, Whitehall. The haunting *Landscape by Moonlight*, at one time owned by Sir Joshua Reynolds, inspired both Sir Thomas Gainsborough and John Constable.

The Impressionist works are so familiar and frequently reproduced that they seem almost like icons of a world religion called 19th-century art. The surprise is that all the major Impressionist and post-Impressionist artists are here, beginning with Boudin, Daumier, Manet, Monet, Degas, Renoir, Pissarro, Sisley, Cézanne, Gauguin, van Gogh, Seurat, Bonnard, Vuillard, and Modigliani.

Exhibitions change regularly, but don't miss the following:

Cézanne's *Mont Ste-Victoire*. Cézanne was the artist who inspired Braque and Picasso during their Cubist periods. In this painting, the green, gold, and blue of the landscape form a geometric pattern so exquisite that you feel you could step into the frame and walk away.

Renoir's *La Loge*, with a man staring at the stage through opera glasses while the viewer stares with equal intensity at his voluptuous companion, her neck wound around with crystal beads and her boldly striped opera cloak falling open to reveal a rose tucked between her breasts.

Manet's *A Bar at the Folies-Bergère*. Manet was an inspiration to the Impressionists, and this is his last major work. His blond barmaid is instantly recognizable, and after you look at this work, no tawdry barroom can ever be quite the same again.

Van Gogh's *Peach Blossom in the Crau* and *Self-Portrait of the Artist with a Bandaged Ear*, which together sum up van Gogh at his happiest and his most despairing. Van Gogh left Paris for Arles in 1888, and almost immediately the orchards of Provence became a foaming cascade of blossom. Here, he spent the happiest eight months of his brief life. Nearby is the tragic self-portrait, painted

a few months earlier when he was recovering from a fit during which he had attacked Gauguin, then cut off his own ear.

Gauguin's *Nevermore*. Paa'ura was Gauguin's 14-year-old mistress, and this naked South Sea beauty somehow sums up his reaction against Impressionism. This painting and his *Te Rerioa (The Dream)*, also here, will make you want to cut loose and fly to the islands.

Monet's *Vase of Flowers*, full of pink and mauve mellows and so evocative of summer light that it cuts through the grayest London day.

Modigliani's *Female Nude*, which even thousands of reproductions have failed to spoil.

There is also Gainsborough's portrait of his wife, as well as paintings by Allan Ramsay, George Romney, Roger Fry, and the Omega Workshop's collection, along with Oscar Kokoschka's huge *Prometheus Triptych*. The 19th- and 20th-century works include such artists as Walter Sickert and Ben Nicholson.

The gold treasures from the Italian and Netherlands collections of the 14th, 15th, and 16th centuries are tiny, gold-ground panel paintings such as the *Madonna* by Fra Angelico's workshop and the *Master of Flemalle Deposition*, an exquisite triptych by Bernardo Daddi from 1338.

The Courtauld Collection also contains magnificent Old Master drawings by Michelangelo, Rubens, and Rembrandt on the ground floor. You must make arrangements in advance to view some of the 25,000 Old Master prints. ♦ Courtauld Institute, 848.2526; Somerset House, Strand, 845.4600. Tube: Temple

There are weekly guided walks on Saturday afternoons around highlights of Somerset House and of the **Gilbert Collection**. Call 845.4600 to book.

There are also weekly talks each Tuesday, focusing on a particular work or theme in the collection. For up-to-date information on topics, go to www.courtauld.ac.uk.

The Courtauld Institute of Art also runs nonresidential summer schools and study

Michael Storrings

Restaurants/Clubs: Red | **Hotels: Purple** | **Shops: Orange** | **Outdoors/Parks: Green** | **Sights/Culture: Blue**

201

trips on a wide variety of fascinating subjects. For information, visit the web site above.

Each winter the courtyard of Somerset House becomes a beautiful ice rink open daily from 10AM till 10PM, with occasional late-night events organized.

42 STATUE OF ISAMBARD KINGDOM BRUNEL

Son of the equally famous Marc Isambard Brunel, he was the brilliant engineer who designed the **Great Western Railway** and built the *Great Eastern*, the first steamship to make regular voyages between Britain and America. His statue by Baron Marochetti dates from 1871. ♦ Victoria Embankment and Temple Pl. Tube: Temple

43 SHERLOCK HOLMES PUB

★★$$ Stuffed to the gills with memorabilia from the Sherlock Holmes Society, including a re-creation of the great detective's study, this flower-bedecked pub is where Holmes supposedly met his adversaries from the underworld. Although the place seems to cater to tourists, its eccentricity also attracts local office workers. There's a small restaurant serving British fare upstairs, and bar meals are available in the pub. The restaurant keeps up the theme by naming all its dishes after Sherlock Holmes stories and characters. For example, Hound of the Baskervilles is traditional toad (sausages) in the hole (Yorkshire pudding) served with buttered mashed potatoes, gravy, and vegetables! In Arthur Conan Doyle's day, this was the site of the **Northumberland Hotel**, which appears in *The Hound of the Basker-villes*. Holmes and Watson used the Turkish bath next door (colorful tiles from the bathhouse can be seen on the side wall of **Barclays Bank**, now on the site). ♦ Pub/British ♦ Daily, lunch and dinner. Reservations recommended for the restaurant. 10 Northumberland St (at Northumberland Ave). 930.2644. Tube: Charing Cross, Embankment

44 PLAYERS' THEATRE

This was once the site of Craven Passage, immortalized in the Flanagan and Allen song

"Underneath the Arches" and in George Orwell's *Down and Out in Paris and London*. The 275-seat Players' Theatre was built in its place as part of the massive rebuilding program at Charing Cross. It has recently undergone a huge refurbishment, while keeping its charms and its very user-friendly auditorium. It offers a truly interesting program and is one of the new generation of what might almost be termed "Off West End" theaters. The Players' has a new air-conditioned lounge, with an upstairs VIP area, which is open every day, even if there is no performance in the theater. After 11PM there is live music every night. Above the station complex is **Embankment Place**, a giant and appropriately tunnel-like glass and concrete landmark occupied by offices and shops. ♦ Admission M-Sa, open till 2:30AM. Meals served noon-2AM. The Arches, Villiers St (between Hungerford La and Strand). 930.5868. Tube: Charing Cross, Embankment

45 BUCKINGHAM STREET

The street runs parallel to Villiers Street and is named after the same Duke of Bucking-ham whose mansion was built here in 1626 on land formerly occupied by the Bishops of Norwich and York. One of the street's most famous residents, philosopher Francis Bacon, was evicted by Buckingham during his expansionist building program. Yet many other well-known people have stayed here, among them Samuel Pepys, Henry Fielding, Jean-Jacques Rousseau, and Samuel Taylor Coleridge. In place of the duke's mansion stands **Canova House**, an 1860s Italian-Gothic structure with redbrick arches built by **Nicholas Barbon**. ♦ Between Watergate Walk and John Adam St. Tube: Charing Cross, Embankment

46 GORDON'S WINE VAULTS

★★★$ Even though this wine bar looks every day of its 300 years, it feels very 1940s, like a film set of wartime London, with dim vaults stretching back beneath the street. The bottles are stored behind a locked grill; the tables and chairs don't match; and the food is basic but good, laid out the way it must always have been, as a buffet, with freshly made terrines, smoked hams, roasts, casseroles, fish dishes, and a large choice of fresh salads, as well as first-class English and foreign cheeses. Sherries, ports, and Madeiras poured by the glass straight from the cask are impressive, as are the house wines chosen from the best districts and producers. ♦ British ♦ Daily, lunch and dinner. 47 Villiers St (at Watergate Walk). Tube: Charing Cross, Embankment. www.gordonswinebar.com

In 1840 the "penny post" was introduced to replace the old system under which the recipient of a letter had to pay heavily for its delivery. Under the new rule, a letter could be delivered anywhere in the British Isles for a penny; the "penny black" was the world's first adhesive stamp.

"Christopher Wren went to dine with some men. 'If anyone calls, say I'm designing St. Paul's.'"

—Anonymous

47 VILLIERS STREET

The road was named for George Villiers, Duke of Buckingham, whose immense **York House** was built in 1626 on a piece of land occupying both this site and Buckingham Street. It has a feeling of the past, with flower, fruit, and newspaper sellers, as well as two special attractions: the **Players' Theatre** and **Gordon's Wine Vaults** (see above for both). Villiers was a clever opportunist, but not quite clever enough. A favorite of James I and his son Charles I, the duke progressed in less than 10 years from being plain George Villiers to viscount, marquis, and, finally, Duke of Buckingham. His ruthless behavior led to his assassination in 1628 and probably set the stage for Charles I's estrangement from Parliament, the Civil War, and the king's own execution. ♦ Between Embankment Pl and Strand. Tube: Embankment, Charing Cross

48 VICTORIA EMBANKMENT GARDENS

During summertime, office workers and tired tourists relax in deck chairs, children sprint along the grassy slopes, and bands play in this secluded riverside garden with a café. This is excellent picnic territory, with a population of 19th-century statues among the dolphin lamp standards and camel and sphinx benches. One of the best statues is of Arthur Sullivan, Gilbert's writing partner. The statue's inscription "Is life a boon?" is from their opera *Yeoman of the Guard*. Another favorite is the World War I memorial to the Imperial Camel Corps, complete with a fine miniature camel and rider. ♦ Victoria Embankment (between Golden Jubilee Bridges and Savoy Pl). Tube: Embankment

Within Victoria Embankment Gardens:

YORK WATER GATE

Located in the western corner of the garden, this is a fairly ironic monument to George Villiers, the corrupt Duke of Buckingham. Built in 1626 in the Italian style with the duke's motto in Latin, *Fidei Coticula Crux* (which means "The cross is the touchstone of faith"), and his coronet, the gate stands at the point where the Thames reached before the Embankment was built. It also marks the Duke of Buckingham's entrance to his gardens from the Thames at the bottom of the street.

EMBANKMENT UNDERGROUND STATION

For the best route to **Golden Jubilee Bridges**, walk into the station from Villiers Street and out the other side, turn right, and go up the flight of stairs to the bridge. ♦ Villiers St (at Embankment Pl)

49 CLEOPATRA'S NEEDLE

Rising 68 feet high and weighing 180 tons, this pink-granite obelisk is one of a pair created around 1500 BC by Thothmes III in Egypt on the edge of the Nile. Cleopatra had nothing to do with the obelisk, but some say it was named after her when it was moved to Alexandria (her royal city) in 12 BC, during the Greek dynasty. Others claim it was named after the barge that transported it to Britain in 1819 after it was given to the country by the viceroy of Egypt. The obelisk was placed here by the river in 1878, and its companion is now in New York City's Central Park. ♦ Victoria Embankment (between Golden Jubilee and Waterloo Bridges). Tube: Embankment

50 WATERLOO BRIDGE

Designed by **Sir Giles Gilbert Scott** and completed by 1942 (but not opened until 1945 because of the war), this bridge replaced a Regency river crossing that opened on the second anniversary of the Battle of Waterloo. The original design was supposed to have been more elegant than **Scott**'s cantilevered concrete construction. But no one can deny the splendor of both City and Westminster views from the bridge itself. On the right of the bridge is the only floating police station in London, manned by the Thames Division, which patrols the 54-mile precinct of river in police-duty boats 24 hours a day. ♦ Between Waterloo Rd and Victoria Embankment. Tube: Waterloo, Temple

51 CABMAN'S SHELTER

This Victorian green wooden hut, with a gingerbread-style roof still lined with its original shingles, is a café for drivers of the officially licensed black cabs only. It is one of 13 such structures dotted around London, the only ones left from the original 64. Built by such philanthropists as Lord Shaftesbury (whose memorial is the famous **Eros** statue), the shelters were designed to offer the cabbies (who were reputed to be heavy drinkers) cheap meals and hot, nonalcoholic drinks. These little buildings are now maintained by the English Heritage, a preservation organization. ♦ Northumberland Ave (at Craven St). Tube: Embankment

52 THE PLAYHOUSE THEATRE

On the north side of **Golden Jubilee Bridges** is this late Victorian 800-seat theater. George Bernard Shaw had his first West End production, *Arms and the Man*, at this theater. It was successful enough to allow him to drop his music criticism in favor of playwriting. Since then, the beautiful Playhouse has hosted the likes of W.S. Gilbert, legendary actress-manager Gladys Cooper, the BBC, the Almeida Theatre Company, the Peter Hall Company, and Janet McTeer. It underwent major renovation in the 1980s, and is one of the few West End theaters to have its stalls at ground level, making it particularly good for access. Box office: 0870/060.6631. Tube: Embankment

53 SIR JOSEPH BAZALGETTE STATUE

It's sad that a man who had such a profound effect on London and its people should be so totally forgotten, but such is the fate of this chief engineer, depicted in this statue by George Simonds. It was under Bazalgette that the solid granite **Albert, Victoria**, and **Chelsea Embankments** were built between 1868 and 1874. The project reclaimed 32 acres of mud and cost a cool £1.55 million, but unlike most new developments, it was welcomed. Bazalgette had an even more important role, however: He built London's original sewer system between 1858 and 1875, saving the citizens from utterly disgusting conditions, including an overpowering stench, regular sewage floods, and cholera epidemics. ♦ Embankment Pl (at Northumberland Ave). Tube: Embankment

54 GOLDEN JUBILEE BRIDGES

Two stunning footbridges opened up the heart of the river at its most historic location, linking the south bank with the West End. The Golden Jubilee Bridges were officially opened in summer 2003 and became a great new landmark for London. The elegance and tranquility they offer in one of London's most breathtaking locations, with the **Palace of Westminster** on the north bank facing BA's **London Eye** on the south bank, have made the footbridges an attraction in their own right. The footbridges traverse the river as its busiest point and are pivotal to the continued regeneration of the south side of the river. The original structure was designed by internationally renown architectural practice Lifschutz Davidson, responsible for much of the other stunning architecture along the south bank. The practice's design was chosen after an international competition with judges praising its bolds lines combined with historical relevance. At night the award-winning lighting, created by Speirs and Major, creates an iridescent effect which adds an entire new dimension to central London. The footbridges replace the old Hungerford footbridge, a narrow single link

which ran across the Thames at this point. ♦ Between Belvedere Rd and Victoria Embankment. Tube: Embankment

55 SOUTH BANK CENTRE

At the eastern end of **Golden Jubilee Bridges** sits the largest arts center in Western Europe. The center's massive structures have been described by Prince Charles as a "concrete bunker." ♦ For all enquiries relating to performances or exhibitions in any of the venues, call either the switchboard (0871/663.2501) or the ticket office (0871/663.2500). Tube: Embankment, Waterloo

Within South Bank Centre:

ROYAL FESTIVAL HALL

Recently reopened after a £90 million refurbishment, the first building you'll encounter is the **Royal Festival Hall**, which, in addition to hosting performances by visiting musicians, singers, and the like, is the permanent home of the **London Philharmonic Orchestra**. Jazz, rock, pop, and folk music are also performed here. Inside the hall is a **Foyles** bookstore with thousands of titles, sheet music, and gifts (440.3213); and a selection of restaurants and cafés where you can eat lunch or have a drink to the strains of free music in the foyer.

Within the Royal Festival Hall:

SKYLON BAR AND GRILL

★★$$ The newly opened Skylon Bar and Grill offers all-day dining including afternoon tea. Taking its name from the original iconic structure of the 1951 Festival of Britain, it has been redesigned to echo the style of the refurbished Royal Festival Hall with contemporary touches added, such as uniquely designed chandeliers and surfaces of bronze, walnut, and slate. Skylon is centered around a raised cocktail bar serving a range of classic and contemporary cocktails and an extensive wine list. The restaurant features a stylish modern British menu created by executive chef Helena Puolakka. If the eggs Skylon, a delicious variation on eggs Benedict with fresh crabmeat and spinach, are on the menu, have them, with perhaps the caramelized shoulder of lamb, pan-fried fillet and kidneys with gratin of Swiss chard and Parmesan, and griotte marmalade to follow, rounded off with crepes Suzette. ♦ Bar: Su-W, noon-midnight; Th-Sa, noon-1AM. Grill: Su-W, noon-10:45PM (last booking 10:30PM, last orders 10:45), Th-Sa, noon-11:30PM (last booking 11:15PM, last orders 11:30). Restaurant: lunch, noon-2:30PM; dinner, 5:30PM-10:45PM. Call 0207/654.7800, or book your table reservations online at www.skylonrestaurant.co.uk

COMEDY

Should you want a really good laugh while in London, you could try one of the capital's many comedy clubs. Now please don't start thinking Caroline's—most of these are just rooms above or behind or even below pubs. The only real purpose-built comedy clubs are **The Comedy Store** (1A Oxenden St, 08700 612.630, www.thecomedystore.co.uk, tube: Piccadilly Circus), which was London's first and still offers the biggest names on a regular basis; **Jongleurs** (Battersea Bar Risa, 49 Lavender Gardens, 0870787.0707, www.jongleurs.com, rail: Clapham Junction), which also has branches in Camden and in Bow (in the East End); and **The Comedy Café** in Shoreditch, a terrific club with good quality control, decent food, a good bar, and a friendly atmosphere. The owner, Noel Faulkener, had a huge hit with his own show at the Edinburgh Festival last year, so he knows what he is doing! (66-68 Rivington St, 739.5706, www.comedycafe.co.uk, tube: Old St) Other fairly reliably good clubs are **Bound and Gagged**, which has lots of fairly big names on a regular basis (The Fox, 413 Green Lanes, Palmers Green, 450.4100, www.boundandgaggedcomedy.com, bus: 329, W2, W6), and **Ha Bloody Ha**, which hosts its own annual Ealing Comedy Festival each July. If you are a film buff, the added interest is that it is held in the old Ealing Studios (Ealing Studios, Ealing Green, St. Mary's Rd, 0208/566.4067, www.headlinerscomedy.biz, tube: Ealing Broadway).

POETRY LIBRARY

This is Britain's largest public collection of 20th-century poetry and poetic ephemera. Browse though 60,000 books, magazines, tapes, and videos, including ones for kids. Next door is the **Queen Elizabeth Hall** and the **Purcell Room**. ◆ Daily. Belvedere Road (between Golden Jubilee Bridges and Waterloo Road). 921.0809; box office, 960.4242

HAYWARD GALLERY

The separate concrete structure that houses the art gallery is one of the largest and most versatile art exhibition spaces in Britain. The gallery focuses on retrospectives of individual artists' work, historical themes and artistic movements, and contemporary artists exploring new directions. To coincide with exhibitions, there are workshops, tours, lectures, and special publications. Also within is a permanent café and an art bookshop. The Hayward Gallery re-opened in October 2003 following a £1.8 million foyer extension. The project was a collaboration between American artist **Dan Graham** and **Graham Haworth** of British architects **Haworth Tompkins**. New facilities at the Hayward include Dan Graham's pavilion, a new café, education and corporate entertainment spaces, and better access, including elevators and automated doors. ◆ Daily, during exhibitions. Belvedere Rd (at Waterloo Rd). 0207/921.0813; recorded information, 261.0127. Tube: Embankment, Waterloo. www.hayward.org.uk

ROYAL NATIONAL THEATRE

The world-famous **National Theatre Company** was created in 1962 under Sir Laurence Olivier and opened with Peter O'Toole starring in *Hamlet* at the **Old Vic**. In 1971, construction of a new concrete cultural headquarters for the company, designed by **Sir Denys Lasdun**, was started on the South Bank, and the curtain was finally raised in 1976, with Sir Peter Hall as artistic director and Olivier as proud papa of the company. Under one vast roof are three theaters, eight bars, the **Mezzanine** restaurant (928.3531), the **Terrace Café** (401.8361), a bookshop, modern workshops, paint rooms, wardrobes, rehearsal rooms, and advanced technical facilities. The theaters differ in design, but all have first-class acoustics and good seats, and the tickets are reasonably priced, with the added bonus of magnificent views from their foyers of the Thames, the **Houses of Parliament**, and **St. Paul's**. The **Olivier** seats 1,160 people in its fan-shaped auditorium. The dark-walled, rectangular **Cottesloe** (named after Lord Cottesloe, the chairman of the South Bank Board and Council) is the smallest and most flexible, with removable seating for 400. Experimental plays and fringe theater are performed here. The 890-seat **Lyttelton** is a proscenium theater, with roughly finished, shuttered concrete walls for better acoustics.

Insightful tours of the three theaters and the backstage area can be arranged for a nominal fee at the information desk in the Lyttelton. Tickets for plays can be purchased in advance either at the main box office or by

---

Restaurants/Clubs: Red | Hotels: Purple | Shops: Orange | Outdoors/Parks: Green | Sights/Culture: Blue

phone. In addition, if you join the mailing list (either by mail, phone, or in person at the box office), you can reserve seats from anywhere in the world—usually before tickets are sold to the general public (if writing, include international reply coupons and a self-addressed envelope: Mailing List, Royal National Theatre, South Bank, London SE1 9PX). The theater also offers tickets for same-day sale. Forty cheap "day" seats (20 on press nights) are available for the Olivier and Lyttelton—the line forms by 8:30AM (the box office opens at 10AM); only two tickets per person. Friday and Saturday nights are usually sold out, but inexpensive standby seats are often available for the rest of the week. These go on sale two hours before performances at the Olivier and Lyttelton, 45 minutes before performances at the Cottesloe. Live music, including folk and jazz, is presented free in the foyers of the Olivier and Lyttelton before evening performances, usually between 6 and 8PM, and before Saturday matinees, between about 1 and 3PM. *Platforms* is a program of talks, dialogues, interviews, readings, debates, and panel discussion by playwrights, directors, and actors, as well as poets and authors, that are held in all three theaters. Some discussions focus on the plays currently being shown. Events usually start at 6PM, and reasonably priced tickets can be purchased at the box office or by phone. ◆ M-Sa. Upper Ground (at Waterloo Rd). Tube: Waterloo. Box office: 452.3000. Backstage tours: 452.3400. Tube: Waterloo. www.nationaltheatre.org.uk

Within the Royal National Theatre:

MEZZANINE BRASSERIE

★$$ This restaurant offers an international menu and a decent wine list—simple stuff but reasonably well done and incredibly handy if you're theater-going. With an emphasis on fresh fish, the seasonal menu also includes shared dishes for two, such as tiger prawn and monkfish curry. There are set-price menus of two and three courses at lunchtime. ◆ Daily, noon-2PM (matinee days only); 5:30PM-11PM. 452.3600. Between ground floor and Olivier Cloakroom level.

TERRACE BAR AND FOOD

Recently refurbished, Terrace Bar and Food provides an informal and comfortable environment for a drink, snack, or more substantial meal before the theater. Small plates of mezze-style food are complemented by a short menu of main courses and rounded off with delicious desserts, including the legendary RNT ice-cream sundae. Tables for pre-theater eating can still be reserved by phone or online, and food can also be ordered at the bar, which has informal seating, without reservations.

◆ Level 2 (on the Lyttelton side of the building). 0207/452.3555

NATIONAL FILM THEATRE

More than 2,000 screenings and events a year take place in three cinemas. ◆ Daily. Off Upper Ground (at Waterloo Rd). Box office: 928.3232

BFI LONDON IMAX CINEMA

A second IMAX cinema for London, opened in June 1999, is the biggest screen in Europe—10 stories high. It shows IMAX two- and three-dimensional films every hour. There are also a shop and café in the foyer area. ◆ Daily, 11:30AM-10PM. South Bank (by Waterloo Station). 0870/787.2525. Tube: Waterloo

56 GABRIEL'S WHARF

Here is a tiny shopping enclave a short stroll from the **South Bank Centre** arts complex with designer clothing stores, jewelers, restaurants, and crafts shops. Its location right on the Thames offers terrific views of the river and the city. The restaurants with views are **Gourmet Pizza** (928.3188) and the **Riviera Restaurant** (0207/401.7314). Other eateries include **House of Crepes** (401.9816), **Studio Six** (928.6243), and **Sarnis Sandwich Bar** (928.6654). ◆ Shops: Tu-Su. Restaurants: daily, lunch and dinner. 56 Upper Ground (between Bargehouse St and Waterloo Rd). 401.3610. Tube: Embankment

57 OXO TOWER WHARF

A £20 billion development program has transformed a derelict eight-story building, the **Oxo Tower**, into a stylish shopping and eating venue with fabulous views over the Thames. Situated on its own wharf, the Art Deco building was once used as a cold storage warehouse for the Oxo bouillon-cube company, but it was always a distinctive landmark because the letters *OXO* are etched in dark brick on the building's tower. Also containing offices and apartments, the building is generating excitement because of its designer workshops—there are no mass-produced items here. Shoppers can talk to the designers as they work and also commission items. Offered here are etchings, collages, and handmade cards; hand-tufted rugs and wall hangings; scarves, wraps, and jewelry; and sculptures, lamps, and furniture. **Harvey Nichols**, the fashion department store of Knightsbridge, caused a stir by opening a stylish restaurant on the top floor with sweeping views of London's skyline across the Thames, as well as a free viewing gallery for the public. The renovation of this wharf was an initiative by the Coin Street Community Builders, a group that set out to revive this riverside and has succeeded

IN THE FOOTSTEPS OF JANE AUSTEN

In such classic novels as *Persuasion, Pride and Prejudice, Sense and Sensibility*, and *Emma*—all of which have recently been adapted into successful and acclaimed movies or TV series—Jane Austen (1775–1817) demonstrated a sharp, satirical wit, keen powers of observation, and an innate understanding of human nature. Her specialty was the comedy of manners, and she delighted in pointing out the ironies and hypocrisies of upper-class society. Although she spent most of her short life in the county of Hampshire, she has several links to London, **Bath**, and **Winchester**.

IN LONDON

Start your Austen tour by viewing the tributes to the author that reside in London's major institutions. For example, the only known likeness of Jane, a tiny portrait in pencil and watercolor by her sister, Cassandra, is displayed in the **National Portrait Gallery**. An Austen work called *A History of England by a partial, ignorant, and prejudiced historian*, which she wrote when she was 15, can be seen in the **British Museum**. And **Poets' Corner** at **Westminster Abbey** holds a memorial plaque that simply reads "Jane Austen 1775–1817."

Other Austen associations around the city are a bit harder to find. On the building at **23 Hans Place** (between Pont Street and Walton Place) in **Knightsbridge** is a plaque stating that Austen lived with her brother Henry "in a house on this site." She and her brother also lived at **10 Henrietta Street** (between Southampton and Bedford Streets), **Covent Garden**, but there's no plaque to mark it; the fine Georgian house has been converted into a men's shop called **Rohan**.

Although her novels appeared anonymously, most members of the literary community of the time knew that Austen was the author. Sir Walter Scott praised her work in the *Quarterly Review* in 1815. Even the prince regent (who later became George IV) kept a set of her novels in each of his residences, and in 1815, he invited her to visit his London palace, **Carlton House**. He was so impressed that he asked her to dedicate her next work to him—which turned out to be *Emma*. The palace, alas, was demolished in the mid-19th century; it was replaced by **Carlton House Terrace**, a long row of grand buildings opposite **St. James's Park**.

IN BATH

Austen and her family lived in Bath for five years after her father retired from his Hampshire vicarage in 1801. She made good use of the time, focusing on the manners and mores of Bath's high society; her insightful observations are reflected in *Persuasion* and *Northanger Abbey*. The Austens lived in several different residences, including **No. 1 The Paragon** (at Lansdown Road) and **4 Sydney Place** (between Beckford and Sydney Roads), which lies on the other side of the River Avon and is reached by crossing the charming, shop-lined **Pulteney Bridge**.

Austen set many scenes of her novels in various locations around Bath, including the **Abbey Church Yard** (next to Bath Abbey), where her characters would promenade in their fashionable attire to see and be seen; and the **Assembly Rooms** (Bennett Street, between Oxford Row and Circus Place, 01225/46.1111), the venue for grand balls; the rooms are now the site of the **Costume Museum**. It is believed that Austen also visited the **Pump Room** (above the Roman Baths, Abbey Churchyard, at York Street, 01225/ 44.4477), where today's visitors may still lunch, take tea, or try the spa water; the Georgian **Theatre Royal** (Saw Close, at Barton Street, 01225/44.8844), the major playhouse in the area; and **No. 1 Royal Crescent**, an elegant town house that is decorated and furnished as it was during Austen's era. Her letters described how much she enjoyed her rambles in the leafy hills that cradle the city.

IN WINCHESTER

On 18 July 1817, Jane Austen died of Addison's disease in Winchester. She had spent the last few months of her life in a house at **8 College Street** (between College Walk and Kingsgate Street) so she could be near her doctor; today, a plaque on the side of the building honors her memory. The **City Museum** (The Square, at Symonds Street, 01962/863064) displays several of her manuscripts, as well as some of her personal possessions, including two pretty little purses. And she is buried inside the 11th-century **Winchester Cathedral**. The gravestone mentions "the sweetness of her temper and the extraordinary endowments of her mind" but nothing about her books. When Emma Thompson won an Academy Award in 1995 for her screenplay adaptation of *Sense and Sensibility*, she spoke of coming here to visit Austen's grave and referred to the incomplete inscription: "I went to pay my respects . . . and to tell her about the royalties."

Restaurants/Clubs: Red | Hotels: Purple | Shops: Orange | Outdoors/Parks: Green | Sights/Culture: Blue

BEAUTY OR BLIGHT: THE MODERN FACE OF LONDON

The classical look is what appeals to British architecture's most famous outspoken critic, Prince Charles, who firmly stated, "There's no doubt in my mind that something like a spire or a dome, something which gives an inspired finish to the top of the building, has the effect of raising one's spirit in a remarkable way."

These days, informed critics disagree, disdaining buildings that they see as a pastiche of an earlier era. They speak out for architects to forge a truly modern look. Increasingly, most people concur, especially in recent years when they have been offered bold new buildings like the copper-clad **Ark** office block in west London (Talgarth Road, between North End and Fulham Palace Roads). Designed jointly by **Lennart Bergstrom Architects** and **Rock Townsend Architects**, it is indeed ark shaped and presents a distinctive silhouette.

When **Docklands** was redeveloped in the 1980s (see "The Docklands: Vibrant Revival," on page 172), it set the tone for this new spirit of adventurous building. The policy there was to save and refurbish small-scale housing, restore old warehouses, and create new buildings of glass and steel. The rest of London now reflects this approach. Perfect Georgian streets are conserved gems to come across in any stroll, but so are modern buildings erected with flourish and dynamism.

It was primarily the stark look of buildings erected in the 1960s and 1970s that set many people against what they saw as architecture that didn't belong in London and that even entailed the demolition of Victorian and Georgian buildings. Prince Charles publicly singled out the **Royal National Theatre** (South Bank Centre, Upper Ground, at Waterloo Road), by **Sir Denys Lasdun**, saying it looked like "a concrete bunker." He further deplored a proposed **Sainsbury Wing** extension to the **National Gallery**, maintaining that it would be "like a carbuncle on the face of a much loved and elegant friend." His opinions carried some weight. Plans were scrapped, and the Philadelphia firm **Venturi, Scott Brown & Associates** designed a new building faced with Portland stone to blend with the neoclassical original gallery. The result is considered a modern architectural success. Prince Charles himself laid the foundation stone in 1988.

The structures below exemplify the new spirit of building in London today:

Lloyd's of London Building (1 Lime St, at Leadenhall Street) is the capital's most famous piece of modern architecture—and possibly one of its most controversial. Designed in 1979 by **Sir Richard Rogers** (creator of the Pompidou Center in Paris), the building shows all of its structural details, such as service pipes, metal flooring, and glass. Once maligned, it is now regarded as a striking landmark.

The **Broadgate** complex (bounded by Liverpool Street rail station and Wilson Street and by Eldon and Sun Streets) is chockablock with contemporary buildings, the most striking of which is **Broadgate Arena**. The circular, open-air structure, designed by **Arup Associates**, is made of granite and glass and boasts several tiers of terraces bedecked with greenery, slanted glass windows, and modern sculptures.

The design of **Minster Court** (Mark Lane, at Great Tower Street) echoes the look of a Gothic cathedral, complete with mock buttresses, vestige towers, and granite panels, some of which are a story high. Built in 1991 by the **GMW Partnership**, the building contains the offices of several London insurance companies, as well as shops and restaurants.

One building designed so that its look meshes perfectly with its function is **Vauxhall Cross**, the headquarters of the **Secret Service's MI6**. Situated beside Vauxhall Bridge facing the **Tate Gallery**, the **Terry Farrell**-designed structure has a fortresslike façade lined with green concrete slabs and features low-rise bunkers topped with menacing spikes.

The **Millennium Dome** in **Greenwich** by architect **Sir Richard Rogers** is the largest domed structure in the world—encompassing the equivalent of 13 **Albert Halls**. Made of a translucent material, it is used as a projection screen for spectacular evening lighting displays. Other changes in the skyline came from the erection of the **Millennium Wheel**, a giant silver-and-white Ferris wheel on the south bank; a new bridge over the **Thames**; and a new **Tate Gallery of Modern Art** designed by Swiss architects **Herzog and de Meuron** in a former power station in Southwark. Ironically, the gallery is a neighbor of the new **Globe Theatre**, rebuilt as a replica of the original, using 16th-century techniques.

brilliantly. It also runs a summerlong events program, the Coin Street Festival, between June and September. ♦ Shops: Tu–Su. Bargehouse St (off Upper Ground). 401.3610. Tube: Blackfriars, Waterloo

Within the Oxo Tower:

OXO TOWER RESTAURANT AND BAR

★★★$$$$ This restaurant offers dishes such as wild sea bass, root vegetables, scallops in Pinot Noir sauce, and mallard with gingerbread, foie gras, and orange sauce, and offers you the rather lovely idea of ordering a dish to share—such as leg of Pyrenean milk-fed lamb, Vacherin, purple potatoes, and sprouting broccoli. The wine list is smart and not necessarily too damaging to the wallet. The restaurant is a lovely, airy room with fabulous views over the Thames and the City. However, the climb up the ghastly eponymous tower block in which it is situated is depressing, to say the least.

♦ Continental ♦ Daily, lunch and dinner. 0871/961.2085

OXO Tower Brasserie

★★★$$$ Linked to the more formal restaurant by a terrace, the Brasserie offers an eclectic menu featuring dishes such as char-grilled quail, soba noodles, crunchy watercress salad, and peanut-lime sauce or rare beef, fried Pedron peppers, Manchego cheese emulsion, and paprika oil. There is a very decent fixed-price, three-course pre-theater menu on offer. ♦ Mediterranean ♦ Daily, lunch and dinner. Reservations required. 0871/223.8004

58 Blackfriars Bridge

Built in 1869 by **Joseph Cubitt** and **H. Carr**, this bridge, carrying cars and pedestrians, has five handsome wrought-iron arches and, on its north side, a statue of Queen Victoria, who officially opened the bridge. A smaller, railway-only bridge constructed in 1886 by **John Wolfe-Barry** and **H.M. Brunel** stands to the east. Between the two bridges is a curious architectural sight—a series of red cast-iron columns with water lapping around them but supporting nothing. And the massive pylons of the partly demolished bridge still stand on either bank. It seems that Cubitt and **F.T. Turner**, who had built it for the **London, Chatham and Dover Railway** in 1864, did their job so well that their old bridge couldn't be completely demolished to make way for Barry and Brunel's bridge without making the riverbed unstable, so there the old pylons remain. This oddity is described by some imaginative tour guides as looking like a Victorian Stonehenge. ♦ Between Upper Ground and Victoria Embankment. Tube: Blackfriars

59 Meson Don Felipe

★★$ Perch on stools at the high wooden bar or squeeze around one of the closely packed tables, but arrive early to be sure of a seat of some kind. Popular with businesspeople at lunchtime and theatergoers in the evening, the bar serves a wide assortment of delicious, traditionally cooked tapas, ranging from Spanish omelettes to peppers stuffed with chicken and herbs in a cream sauce. The *pan Catalán* (a do-it-yourself toasted bread with garlic, tomatoes, and olive oil) is highly recommended. To experience true Spanish style, don't miss the *fino* or *oloroso*

sherry, served chilled, as it should be. final flourish is a flamenco guitarist who plays nightly starting at 8:30PM. ♦ Spanish ♦ M–Sa, lunch and dinner. 53 The Cut (at Short St). 928.3237. Tube: Waterloo

59 Livebait

★★$$ Dark green-and-white-tiled walls are the background of this simply decorated fish restaurant with booth seating. The seafood tastes as fabulous as its showy display would imply. Main dishes include roast hake with warm beetroot salad, cornichons, capers, and wild mushrooms. ♦ Seafood ♦ M–Sa, lunch and dinner. 41–43 The Cut (between Blackfriars Rd and Short St). 928.7211. Tube: Waterloo. Also at 21 Wellington Street, Covent Garden. 836.7161

59 Old Vic

Between 1962 and 1976, this venue was the temporary home of the **National Theatre Company**, under the direction of Sir Laurence Olivier. Though the foundation stone, taken from the demolished **Savoy Palace**, dates from the theater's opening in 1818, the rest of the structure has changed interiors and owners many times, most recently in 1982, when Canadian entrepreneur Ed Mirvish took over and gave it a £2.5 million face-lift. His son, David, appointed Sir Peter Hall artistic director. Founder of the **Royal Shakespeare Company** in 1960 and later director of the **Royal National Theatre** for 15 years, Hall presented in repertory five classic dramas and five new plays. Now the theater has been given a new lease on life and an injection of Hollywood glamour by Kevin Spacey, its new artistic director. He has brought a much-needed burst of energy, passion, and A-list stars to the old place. ♦ Waterloo Rd (at The Cut). 928.7616. Tube: Waterloo

59 The Young Vic

Established in 1970, on The Cut just down the road from the Old Vic, the Young Vic has established a powerful reputation at home and abroad. Having re-opened in 2006 after a two year refurbishment, their renewed auditorium has added two smaller, flexible spaces, welcoming public areas, including a terrace bar, and a ground floor cafe and restaurant which serves core classics and inspired specials, fish and chips, steak bearnaise, and a variety of salads are among the dishes on offer. Box Office: 922.2922.

Restaurants/Clubs: Red | Hotels: Purple | Shops: Orange | Outdoors/Parks: Green | Sights/Culture: Blue

HE THAMES

between England's capital and its main waterway dates back more
than ... years, when the origins of what is now the City of London took root
on the banks of the river. The small area that now includes the site of the **Lloyd's of London Building**, the **National Westminster Tower**, and other skyscrapers is often
referred to as the Square Mile, or as just "the City."

Commerce gave birth to the city, and that commerce was possible mainly because of the Thames. What the Roman conquerors called "Londinium" in AD 43 had been a hub of trade between Britain and the Continent since the Bronze Age. Everything from spices and jewels to silks and tea arrived on the wharves of the river, brought to Britain by explorers and captains who forged a seafaring tradition for their island nation.

Amid this incessant trade governed by a powerful merchant class, the river fulfilled another function: It was the highway of sovereigns, as well as of those who served or displeased them. Barges plowed slowly through the dark waters, ferrying monarch to castle, bishop to church, and prisoner to the execution block. They also ferried actors to theaters, for on the south bank the likes of William Shakespeare and Richard Burbage were shaping the history of English-language drama in **Southwark**.

Today, the Thames is basking in a new appreciation by Londoners. More attractions are opening, especially on the south bank, where theater is flourishing again in Southwark, thanks to the rebuilding of **Shakespeare's Globe**. Next door a huge, windowless former power station has been converted to the **Tate Modern**. The river is spanned by the **Millennium Bridge**–also known as the **Blade of Light**–and the skyline is dominated by the **British Airways London Eye**. Finance still rules the City, though computers in the **Stock Exchange** now clinch deals once made with handshakes in coffeehouses or on the docks. The **Docklands** area is still a center of commerce, but it no longer handles crates of tea. Instead, offices and tourist attractions are its mainstay. Finally, the merchant class's struggle for dominance (it jousted with the crown and the church for centuries) is still evident in the buildings of the **Bank of England**, the **Guildhall**, and the **Tower of London**, a prison for traitors in medieval times. In the midst of it all stands stately and solemn **St. Paul's Cathedral**, London's epicenter. **Sir Christopher Wren**'s splendid cathedral has weathered countless changes but has always managed to keep its soul intact, just as London itself has.

City code 0207 unless otherwise noted.

1 BARBICAN CENTRE

When Queen Elizabeth II opened this cultural center in 1982, she called it one of the wonders of the modern world, and, as usual, she was not exaggerating. Designed by the architectural firm **Chamberlin, Powell and Bon** on a site that was heavily bombed during the Blitz, this walled city within the City covers 20 acres, rises 10 levels, descends 17 feet below sea level, and caps it all with the largest unsupported dome roof in Europe.

The concert hall (on levels 5 and 6) is the permanent home of the **London Symphony Orchestra**, and visiting orchestras also present here. In the foyers, the live music runs from chamber to folk. The art gallery (on level 3) stages major exhibitions, whereas the foyers mount more offbeat shows. The theater (levels 3 to 6) is the London home of **BITE (Barbican International Theatre Events)** and hosts visiting productions from internationally recognized companies from all over the world. There are usually some seats still available on the day of the performance. The theater has 1,166 seats, with raked stalls and three circles projecting toward the stage, putting every member of the audience within 65 feet of the action. The 109-foot, double-height fly-tower above the stage, used for scenery storage, is believed to be the tallest in the world. A remarkable stainless steel safety curtain descends during intermissions. Smaller-scale productions including dance pieces are performed in the **Pit**, which is a rehearsal space that was redesigned as a flexible auditorium seating 200 people. The Barbican complex also includes a library, cinema, and bookshop. There are coffee stalls and a cafeteria, and **Searcey's** brasserie (level 2; 588.3008), should you fancy something substantial. This restaurant offers a British menu with tempting combinations such as sloe gin–cured salmon, pickled cucumbers and Irish soda bread, and braised oxtail, mash, and winter vegetables. The area around the Barbican is slowly acquiring restaurants and cafés, but it's still pretty much a windy wasteland at night. ◆ Daily. Silk St (at Whitecross St). 638.8891. Tube: Barbican, Moorgate. www.barbican.org.uk

2 MUSEUM OF LONDON

Two thousand years of London's history have been immortalized on this site, along the line of the old City wall. The Romans took up residence in AD 43 and built a wall that was 3.25 miles long with six main gates; this wall was demolished during the 18th century, although bits of it still survive. The explanation of how London came to be as it is today can be found here, starting with a splendid Roman gallery and ending with the newest gallery, **London Now**, which depicts how London has changed more in the last 50 years than in the previous 100.

A museum showpiece is the spectacular **Lord Mayor's Coach**, which is wheeled out on state occasions. There are four main themes. **Prehistoric and Roman** includes sculpture and artifacts from the **Temple of Mithras** (see page 218). **Medieval** spans a thousand years, from the 5th-century Dark Ages to the 15th century. **Tudor and Stuart** contrasts those glittering eras against the Great Plague of 1665 and contains a re-creation of the Great Fire of 1666, which destroyed 80% of London, and, in turn, allowed **Sir Christopher Wren** his prolific church-building career. The **Modern** galleries cover the Georgian and Victorian periods and the 20th century. A painted line called the Catwalk leads visitors to computer screens for information and to display points where objects can be handled. It gets its name from the museum's logo, which shows Dick Whittington, a 15th-century lord mayor of London, followed by his cat. An outdoor attraction is the tiny **Nursery Garden**, which traces the development of the English garden from the Middle Ages to today by devoting each section to a particular nurseryperson and displaying the plants he or she introduced. Please note that the lower galleries are currently undergoing refurbishment and expect to reopen in 2009. ♦ Free. Tu-Sa; Su, noon–6PM. 150 London Wall (at Aldersgate St). 0870/444.3852. Tube: St. Paul's, Barbican. www.museumoflondon.org.uk

Within the Museum of London:

Museum Café

★$ In summer, do as the locals do and enjoy a bite to eat at one of the outdoor tables here—arrive by 12:30PM to get a spot. The sandwiches and salads are imaginatively done. The homemade cakes are delicious, and the sun and fresh air are definite pluses. ♦ Daily, lunch, afternoon tea, and early dinner. 600.3699

3 Broadgate

Within this modern office complex, built during the 1990s, is the notable **Broadgate Square** with an amphitheater at its center. Containing shops and trendy wine bars and restaurants at ground level, the amphitheater surrounds an open-air arena that in winter becomes an ice rink, one of a growing number in London. Skates are available for rent; note that opening times vary, so call for

information. In summer, the arena is given over to musical events and other entertainment. Free leaflets describing the events are on display throughout the area. ♦ Shops and restaurants: M-Sa. Ice rink: daily, Oct-Mar (call for times). Bounded by Liverpool St rail station and Wilson St and by Eldon and Sun Sts. 505.4000. Tube: Liverpool St

4 Spitalfields

Famous for its weekend markets, this raffish district has always been home to immigrants, but the Huguenot churches have now become Bengali mosques. On Sunday morning, the **Petticoat Lane Market** is noisy and cheerful, full of stalls purveying cheap clothes and snack bars selling salt beef (corned beef) sandwiches and bagels with smoked salmon. Also on Sunday morning, the nearby **Brick Lane Market** offers a mishmash of junk and cheap goods of all sorts. And then there is Spitalfields market itself. You really should try to get down to this fun, eclectic market in the old Spitalfields Market building with its soaring, vaulted roof and iron pillars. It has undergone a renovation process—narrowly escaping being "redeveloped" (thank you if you signed the petition)—and has lost some of its dilapidated charm, but there is now even more to browse through than before! The market itself sells practically everything—from handmade jewelry and idiosyncratic designer clothing and accessories through gloriously hand-dyed sheepskins to aromatherapy products, CDs, and movie posters. It is a marvelous place to wander. The food court sells deliciousness from all over the world, as well as local artisanal breads and cheeses. The smell is fabulous. When you can't hold off any longer there is the now-famous **Square Pie Company** to feed you, or if you want the best ribs in London, there is the legendary **Bubba's Arkansas Café** (★★★$). The man is a genius with a homemade barbecue pit and a terrific host whose way with duck, chicken, brisket, and pork is just as expert as his way with ribs (M-F, noon-2:30PM; Su, noon-4PM; dinner by appointment. 377.6999). All around the outside of the market are fascinating, highly individual little shops selling second-hand books and cool vintage furniture. ♦ Commercial St (between Lamb and Brushfield Sts). 247.8556. Market week: M-Tu: all shops and no stalls; W: records and books (first and third of the month in Spitalfields Traders Market); Th: antiques and vintage; F: fashion and art; Sa: all shops and no stalls; Su: busiest day—all shops and stalls. Market stalls: M-F, 10AM-4PM; Su, 9AM-5PM. Restaurants: M-F,

---

Restaurants/Clubs: Red | Hotels: Purple | Shops: Orange | Outdoors/Parks: Green | Sights/Culture: Blue

11AM-11PM; Su, 9AM-5PM. Shops: Times vary, but in general M-Su, 11AM-7PM. Brick Lane Market: Su, 9AM–2PM; Spitalfields Market: Sa, Su; Petticoat Lane Market: Su. Bounded by Brick Lane and Bishop's Gate and by Middlesex, Whitechapel High, and Quaker Sts. Tube: Aldgate East

Within the new part of Spitalifelds:

CANTEEN

★★★$$ Voted UK Restaurant of the Year by *The Observer Food Monthly* in 2007, this minimalist box offers all-day dining using the finest British ingredients, with a rapidly changing menu reflecting the best ingredients available. The breakfast menu is served throughout the day. At mealtimes enjoy traditional pies, fresh fish, rib-eye steaks, and daily roasts. Desserts are complemented by a daily selection of freshly baked cakes and biscuits. ♦ Meals served M-F, 8AM-11PM; Sa, 9AM-11PM; Su, 9AM-10:30PM. 0845/686.1122

Around Spitalfields:

CHRIST CHURCH SPITALFIELDS

This stunning example (one of the finest) of a **Nicholas Hawksmoor** church was closed for years while being lovingly restored. Recently reopened, it has definitely been worth the wait. Built in 1711 under an Act of Parliament that decreed 50 new churches had to be built each year, it has a beautifully austere rectangular nave and an impressive three-stage tower with a Gothic steeple. The restoration has reversed the changes made in 1866 by Ewan Christian, the architect of the **National Portrait Gallery**, who removed the interior galleries and pews and enlarged the windows. The church is now as it was around 1750, and the full splendor of Hawksmoor's interior can be enjoyed. ♦ Su, 1PM-4PM; Tu, 11AM-4PM. Commercial Street (opposite market). www.christchurchspitalfields.org

ST. JOHN BREAD AND WINE

★★★$$ This is an offshoot of Fergus Henderson's multi-award-winning restaurant, **St. John**, which is not far away (page 155). The mouthwatering possibilities, posted on a blackboard, are a mix of Henderson's famous "nose-to-tail eating" (so you get everything from ox cheek to pig's trotters) and good French country fare, so the breads alone are worth the trip, the cheeses fabulous, the charcuterie superb. You really cannot eat badly here, and the atmosphere is terrific. The place is open all day, and the menu sort of segues from morning coffee (with fabulous pastries) through lunch, afternoon, and early evening nibbles to dinner. Very relaxed. Very foodie. Very un-British, in fact. You will never want to leave! ♦ Daily, 94-96 Commercial St. 251.0848

5 POSTMAN'S PARK

The City of London is long on big buildings and short on green spaces, so this tiny emerald enclave behind **St. Botolph's** churchyard is all the more welcome. The park is named for its proximity to the London Chief Post Office building across from King Edward Street, which served as the **National Postal Museum** from 1965 to 1998 (the collections can now be seen at the **Post Office Archives**; see "Small Wonders" on page 176); though the museum is gone, the name is unchanged. A long wall was dedicated in 1900 as a monument to those who died while rescuing others. Some of the plaques' inscriptions may bring tears to your eyes, such as this one, dated 12 July 1886: "William Fisher aged 9 lost his life on Rodney Road, Walworth, while trying to save his little brother from being run over." ♦ King Edward St (between Angel St and Little Britain). Tube: St. Paul's, Barbican

6 ST. BOTOLPH'S WITHOUT ALDERSGATE

One of four churches in London built in the 10th century for the spiritual comfort of travelers, this one is dedicated to St. Botolph, a 7th-century Saxon abbot who is the patron saint of travelers. It has been rebuilt twice, the last time by **Nathaniel Wright** in 1788-1791. Despite its dull exterior, it is quite lovely inside because of its preserved 18th-century architecture, with big plaster rosettes covering the ceiling, three wooden galleries, barrel-vaulted roof, and exquisite stained-glass windows (including the *Agony in the Garden*). Methodists will love this church because, close by in Little Britain, John and Charles Wesley were converted back in 1736, a fact that is commemorated outside the church and on a big bronze scroll outside the nearby **Museum of London**. ♦ M-F. Services: Tu, Th, 10:30AM. Aldersgate St and Little Britain. 606.0684. Tube: St. Paul's, Barbican

7 GUILDHALL

The city's first lord mayor, Henry FitzAilwin, was installed here in 1192. The Gothic porch, which is still the entrance to the hall from Guildhall Yard, was finished in 1430; the main structure was finished in 1439. The most extensive medieval crypt in London today still exists beneath the hall, and it has one of the finest vaulted ceilings in the city. London's second-largest hall (after Westminster Hall), the building was once used for treason trials, such as that of Lady Jane Grey. Nowadays, it is used for state occasions. It survived the Great Fire but was bombed out in World War II; it was repaired by **Sir Giles Gilbert Scott**, who also worked on the **Houses of Parliament**. The newer buildings east of the Guildhall, designed by **Sir Giles Scott, Son & Partners**, seem to put a 1960s twist on the Gothic classical look of the original structure. Before you visit, call ahead to check whether a state occasion is scheduled. In late 1998, a newly built **Guildhall Art Gallery** opened to show the City of London's many artworks. ♦ Free. Daily, May–Sept; M–Sa, Oct–Apr (except during state occasions). Basinghall St (between Gresham St and Aldermanbury Sq). 606.3030. Tube: St. Paul's

Within the Guildhall:

GUILDHALL LIBRARY

Dick Whittington, thrice lord mayor of London, left enough money to start this library in 1423. The entire contents were pilfered by the Duke of Somerset in 1549 and recovered in 1824. The library is the greatest source of information on England's capital, with genealogical histories, parish registers, and heraldic histories of important Londoners. ♦ M–Sa. 332.1868

CLOCK MUSEUM

This museum in the library's precincts contains clocks from many centuries, as well as books dating back to 1814. There are 700 exhibits under one roof (including a pocket watch said to have belonged to Mary, Queen of Scots), making it one of the foremost horological museums in the country. ♦ Free. M–F

8 ST. LAWRENCE JEWRY

On the wall of this church is one of the few remaining blue police phone boxes in London. The building suffered great damage during World War II, losing its **Christopher Wren** features; nevertheless, it was restored and is pleasant enough for the lord mayor and corporation to worship here. ♦Gresham and King Sts (at Guildhall Yard). 600.9478. Tube: St. Paul's

9 BANK OF ENGLAND MUSEUM

During a session of the **House of Commons** in 1797, Richard Brinsley Sheridan referred to this bank as "an elderly lady in the city of great credit and long standing," and it's still called the Old Lady of Threadneedle Street to this day. The institution looks after the nation's gold and the National Debt, issues banknotes, and acts as the government's and bankers' bank (it also handles a very small number of private accounts). A figure of a woman holding a model of the building on her knee rests above the portico.

The Old Lady is the bank itself, according to those who work there. Established in 1694, it moved to Threadneedle Street 40 years later, where architect **Sir John Soane** rebuilt it between 1788 and 1808. The bank itself cannot be visited, but on the premises is a small museum that holds gold bars, coins, interactive videos, and even Roman mosaics, found beneath the site. There are fun interactive displays, such as the chance to see if you can pick up a real gold bar with one hand! There is also a re-creation of a Victorian banking hall. ♦ Free. M–F. Bartholomew La (between Threadneedle St and Lothbury). 601.5545. Tube: Bank. www.bankofengland.co.uk

10 TOWER 42

Formerly the headquarters of NatWest Bank, and built in the shape of the bank's logo, this building now houses a mixture of office and restaurant spaces. On the ground floor there is a Wagamama noodle bar and a café, but the fun begins when you start to ascend. However, due to security restrictions, there are no public viewing platforms, and all restaurant and bar bookings must be made in advance. Not the place for an impulse drink, or lunch, but the views are astonishing. ♦ 25 Old Broad Street. Tube: Liverpool St, Bank

Within Tower 42:

RHODES 24

★★$$$ On the 24th floor is a very popular restaurant from TV chef Gary Rhodes, Rhodes 24, with superb views over St. Paul's. Start with the guinea fowl sausage with button onions, mushrooms, bacon, and a red wine sauce, or the lobster thermidor omelette; follow with the rabbit with pearl barley risotto or one of the many fish dishes, and finish with a classic bread-and-butter pudding (Gary's signature dish) or the ginger baba with spicy poached pears. The wine list is extensive, with a heavy bias toward France, though there are some interesting New World examples; the prices do tend to rise rather steeply, perhaps reflecting the predominantly business clientele. Booking is essential. ♦ M–F. 877.7703

VERTIGO 42

The jewel in this particular high-rise crown is Vertigo 42. On the 42nd floor, an astonishing 590 feet above the ground, sits this unique Champagne bar. Wrapped around the top floor of the building, with a jaw-dropping

---

Restaurants/Clubs: **Red** | Hotels: **Purple** | Shops: **Orange** | Outdoors/Parks: **Green** | Sights/Culture: **Blue**

panoramic view over London, this is a bar unlike any other. Practically every major landmark in London is visible from a perspective an eagle would envy. On a clear day you can see nine counties, and at night the view is breathtaking. Enjoy smoked salmon, or foie gras terrine with a spicy raisin dressing, or a plate of charcuterie with a glass or two of Champagne, the only drink sold here (many are available by the glass), and take in the view. Not for the faint-hearted, but not to be missed either. Booking is essential. ♦ 877.7842.

11 St. Paul's Cathedral

The glimpses you'll have of this cathedral while walking up Ludgate Hill are inspiring, reassuring, and awesome. But when you're within a few yards, the building grows smaller, the road veers too close, and a statue of Queen Anne seems dumpy and distracting. It's worth stepping back a moment when you reach **Sir Christopher Wren**'s greatest masterpiece to try and see what the architect himself intended: the slight curve of the road; the scale, monumental in the context of the medieval perspective; the magnificent dome, second only in Christendom to St. Peter's in Rome; and the skyline, uncluttered and harmonious. Even as late as 1939, before the Germans chose St. Paul's as a primary bombing target, the cathedral stood in a tapestry of streets, courts, squares, and alleys, and medieval London was still recognizable.

Five churches have stood on this site. The first, founded by King Ethelbert of Kent for Bishop Mellitus in AD 604, was destroyed by fire and then rebuilt between 675 and 685 by Bishop Erkenwald. This church, in turn, was destroyed by a ninth-century Viking raid but was rebuilt in 962. In 1087, this Saxon structure also burned, but rebuilding began almost immediately, at the behest of William Rufus, son of William the Conqueror. It was this great stone cathedral, unfinished until 1240, that became known as **Old St. Paul's**. But the magnificent cathedral, with one of the tallest spires in Europe, fell into desperate decay, and after the Great Fire of 1666, it lay in ruins. Six days after the fire, Wren, then 33, submitted his plan for rebuilding the City and the cathedral. It was rejected, but the architect remained undaunted. In May 1675, his design for the cathedral was approved, though his layout for the City never was. His master mason laid the first stone on 21 June 1675, and the last was set by Wren's son, 33 years later.

In his proposal, the architect managed to win an important concession that gave him the freedom to make "ornamental rather than essential" changes during construction. He took full advantage of the clause, modifying his design considerably—including deleting a tall spire—during the three decades he spent

building the church. When it was complete, Wren, who was retired and living in **Hampton Court**, would still come and sit under the dome of his monument: "If I glory, it is in the singular mercy of God, who has enabled me to finish a great work so conformable to the ancient model."

The structure's splendidly Baroque style was enhanced by an exterior of Portland stone, and when it was cleaned in the 1960s, Londoners were astonished to discover a dazzling, honey-colored building. In front of the cathedral stands the statue of Queen Anne looking down Ludgate Hill. The original statue, carved in 1712 by Francis Bird, suffered from decay and occasional attacks—she lost her nose, orb, and scepter—and was removed to the grounds of a girls' school in East Sussex in 1884. The statue and the forecourt were originally inside a railing, which was sold at auction in 1874. At the same time, the road was expanded, bringing St. Paul's closer to the hellish stream of traffic en route to the City.

The spacious 78,000-square-foot interior accommodates tourist groups more readily than **Westminster Abbey** and, in spite of its three centuries and large population of statues and monuments, there is a lack of clutter, unique in cathedral design. The focal point is the huge dome space at the crossing. The dome rises 218 feet above the floor and is supported by eight massive double piers with Corinthian capitals. There are actually three domes: a lead outer dome, a wooden one for support, and a painted inner one of brick and plaster. The spandrels under the **Whispering Gallery** contain 19th-century mosaics executed by Antonio Salviati, depicting the four evangelists (Matthew, Mark, Luke, and John) and the four prophets (Isaiah, Jeremiah, Ezekiel, and Daniel). The surface of the dome is decorated with eight large monochrome frescoes by Sir James Thornhill, depicting scenes from the life of St. Paul. The epitaph for Wren, who is buried in the crypt, is written in Latin on the pavement under the dome, and a plaque in honor of Winston Churchill is also set into the floor here.

If you are sound of lung and limb, it is well worth inspecting the dome more closely. For a small fee, you can climb the 259 steps to the Whispering Gallery, thus named because if you stand at the entrance you can hear what is being said in a normal voice on the other side 107 feet away. The gallery offers spectacular views of the concourse, choir, arches, clerestory, and the interior of the dome. If you're still feeling fit, climb the steeper spiral to the **Stone Gallery**, which surrounds the little dome outside. From here you can see all of London. For the heartiest, the **Golden Gallery** at the top of the dome takes you to the lantern and the golden ball.

The best place to start a tour of the cathedral is at the west entrance in the small

Chapel of All Souls, a 1925 memorial to Field Marshall Lord Kitchener, who died in 1916, and "all others who fell in 1914–18." Behind the splendid ornamented wooden screen—carved by Jonathan Maine, one of Wren's greatest craftsmen, in 1698—is **St. Dunstan's Chapel**, reserved for private prayer. Beyond the chapel in the main aisle are various monuments (though Wren himself did not want memorials in the cathedral). Most impressive is the monument to the Duke of Wellington, which fills the central bay. Painter and sculptor Alfred Stevens spent the last 20 years of his life creating it, and it wasn't completed until 1912, nearly 40 years after Stevens's death. The equestrian statue on top was made by John Tweed. The third bay in the aisle contains an eerie Victorian monument to Lord Melbourne, Queen Victoria's first prime minister, who died in 1848. The inscription above the double doors guarded by two angels reads: "Through the Gate of Death we pass to our Joyful Resurrection."

The **North Transept Chapel**, also called the **Middlesex Chapel**, is reserved for private prayer and contains a large marble font carved by Francis Bird in 1726–1727. Beyond the crossing is the **North Chancel**, with a memorial screen that lists the names of former St. Paul's choristers who died in the two world wars. The carved paneling on the right is the work of Grinling Gibbons. The aisle ends in the **Altar of the Modern Martyrs**, where the names of all known Anglican martyrs since 1850 are recorded in a book kept in a glass-topped casket. Pass through the fine ironwork gate by Jean Tijou into the **American Memorial Chapel**, paid for entirely by contributions of the British people as a tribute to the 28,000 members of the American forces who lost their lives in Britain or in active service from Britain during World War II. The names fill 500 pages of illuminated manuscript, bound in a red-leather volume and presented to St. Paul's by General Dwight Eisenhower on 4 July 1951.

The choir is enclosed by a low screen made from the original altar rail by Jean Tijou and contains the exquisite carved choir woodwork made in the 1690s by Grinling Gibbons. The carved oak baldachino (canopy) above the high altar was inspired from some of Wren's unused drawings by Godfrey Allen and Stephan Dykes Bower. It replaced the reredos damaged in 1941. The high altar serves as Britain's memorial to the more than 324,000 men and women of the Commonwealth who died in the two world wars.

The **Lady Chapel**, in the eastern end of the south choir aisle, contains the cathedral's original high altar. Nearby is a statue of John Donne, the poet who became one of the finest Anglican preachers ever and the most famous dean of St. Paul's, serving from 1621 to 1631. When Donne believed he was about to die, he called for sculptor Nicholas Stone the Elder to come and draw him in his shroud, and the artist used his sketch as the basis for the statue. It is the only effigy that survived the Great Fire intact.

On the second pillar in the south aisle hangs William Holman Hunt's most famous painting, *The Light of the World*, depicting a pre-Raphaelite Christ knocking at a humble door overgrown with weeds. The door has no handle and can be opened only from the inside; this is the door of the heart. Nearly life-size, it is the third and largest version of the painting Hunt produced and was presented to the cathedral by wealthy shipowner Charles Booth in 1908. It looks even more striking now after conservation work.

The **Chapel of the Order of St. Michael and St. George**, with its beautiful woodwork by Jonathan Maine and colorful banners, can be entered only via a 1.5-hour Supertour (which begins at the **Friends' Table** near the west door). The order is awarded to British and Commonwealth subjects for overseas service. The chapel was dedicated in 1906 by Bishop Henry Montgomery, with the stirring words: "You who represent the best of the Anglo-Saxon race at work beyond the seas are now made the guardians of the west door of the cathedral." As you leave the chapel and continue westward along the aisle, you will reach the **Geometrical Staircase** (accessible only on a Supertour), designed by Wren and built with a railing by Jean Tijou. Each stone step is set into the wall only a few inches, the weight at each level carried by the step below.

The crypt, entered from the **South Transept** and covering the whole length of the cathedral, is probably the largest in Europe. Many famous people are buried here, including Nelson in the elegant black tomb Cardinal Wolsey had built for himself before he fell out of royal favor, as well as Wellington, and Wren and his family. The artists' corner commemorates Van Dyck, Blake, Turner, Reynolds, Constable, and many others. Especially noteworthy are the memorials to John Singer Sargent, designed by the artist himself, and Sir George Frampton, which includes a small replica of the statue of Peter Pan he sculpted for **Kensington Gardens**. A welcome recent development is the new café-shop in a section of the crypt that can also be reached by a separate entrance next to the tombs. Here you'll find a warm, sheltering area containing a coffee stall; a huge shop selling postcards, slides, scarves, books, and other items related to the cathedral; and rest rooms. Visitors may now rent audio guides, which are excellent for helping them pick out the highlights at the cathedral. Also, concerts and organ recitals are often given. ◆ Admission. Daily. Tours: 11AM, 11:30AM, 1:30PM, 2PM. St. Paul's Churchyard (at Ludgate Hill). 246.8357. Tube: St. Paul's, Blackfriars

Within St. Paul's:

St. Paul's Refectory Restaurant

★★$$ As part of the recent extensive renovation of St. Paul's, this has reopened as a self-service restaurant—well, they do say "God helps those who help themselves!" It offers a selection of hot and cold food, with homemade soups and quiches, as well as imaginative salads, and a changing hot dish of the day. Don't miss the opportunity to try the homemade cakes and biscuits. ◆ Daily, lunch and afternoon tea.

Crypt Café

★★$ Interesting and tempting sandwiches include avocado and roast pepper arugula salad on focaccia, and tuna and sweet red onion and black olives with mixed leaves on granary bread. There are also quiches (always one vegetarian), salads, scones, and home bakery items. An exceptional find! ◆ Daily

12 St. Mary-le-Bow

It's said that every true Cockney is born "within the sound of Bow Bells." The church, which has stood on this spot since 1091, has a very bloody history: The tower collapsed sometime in the 12th century, killing 20, and people seeking sanctuary here got short shrift—and usually death, too. **Sir Christopher Wren** rebuilt it in 1670, and the exterior is rather stunning. In the garden, note the splendid statue of Captain James Smith, who settled Jamestown, Virginia. ◆ M-F (services offered several times daily). Cheapside (at Bow La). 248.5139. Tube: St. Paul's, Mansion House. www.stmarylebow.co.uk

Within St. Mary-le-Bow:

13 Bow Lane and Watling Street

This is one of the oldest parts of London. **Watling Street** was first mentioned in 1230, but it is believed to have been part of the main Roman road between Dover and St. Albans, built nearly 1,000 years earlier. The tiny streets here show graphically just how chaotic the City is, lacking any formal plan. After the Great Fire of 1666 (which destroyed 80% of London's buildings), Londoners were desperate to get back to work and to make money. **Sir Christopher Wren**, among many others, drew up spectacular plans for a

beautiful city. But changing the street plan would have taken a long time and cost a lot of money, so the medieval plan remains to this day. The only difference is that the buildings are made of stone, not wood. Today, **Bow Lane** is quaint and kitschy. Still, ancient pubs like **Ye Olde Watling** (built from ships' timbers by Wren in 1668) and **Williamson's Tavern and Library Bar** (an old lord mayor's house dating back to the 17th century) are still intact, as are the **Bow Wine Vaults**, the haunt of City businesspeople. ◆ Tube: St. Paul's, Mansion House

14 Temple of Mithras

This is an archeological showpiece of Roman London, with the remains of the brick walls neatly reconstructed to show the layout of a pagan temple that was built around AD 200. The temple was dedicated to Mithras, a sun god who appealed to Roman soldiers because he symbolized bravery, virility, strength, and action. It looks rather small and out of place next to a large office complex, but it was the construction of the complex in 1954 that led to the discovery of the temple. The statues, tiles, and artifacts that were excavated are now displayed in the **Museum of London**. A plaque explains the site's layout. ◆ Queen Victoria St (at Garlick Hill). Tube: Mansion House, Bank

15 Mansion House

Lord mayors in London serve just one year in office, so they have a mere 365 days to live and work in the splendor of this Palladian mansion, constructed between 1739 and 1753 by George Dance the Elder. There are a series of superb state rooms leading to an Egyptian banqueting hall with giant columns along each side on the first floor and the ballroom on the second. Note the pediment frieze depicting London defeating Envy and bringing in Plenty. ◆ Open by appointment only. T, W, Th, 11AM and 2PM; minimum 15 people, maximum 40. Write to Diary office: Mansion House, London, Ecy N8BH. Free. Mansion House St (at Walbrook). 626.2500. Tube: Bank

16 St. Stephen Walbrook

Behind the **Mansion House** is this gem of a church. Built in 1679, it has one of **Sir Christopher Wren**'s most celebrated interiors, although it is exceedingly plain on the outside except for an ornate tower. Inside, a marvelous spatial harmony is created by intricate crosses, squares, and arches leading up to a dome. There are services Th, 12:45PM, and organ recitals, F, 12:30PM. ◆ Open M-F, 9AM–4PM. Walbrook (between Bond Ct and St. Stephen's Row). Tube: Bank

17 ROYAL EXCHANGE

A building where merchants can meet and conduct business has been on this site since 1566 and received royal approval from both Queen Elizabeth I and, later, Queen Victoria. This classical building, designed in 1844 by **Sir William Tite**, is the third to stand here; the other two were destroyed by fire. It is now a luxury shopping arcade, where British companies **Lulu Guinness**, **Paul Smith**, and **Penhaligon's** rub shoulders with international brands such as **Chanel**, **Cartier**, **Hermès**, and **Tiffany's**. In the middle of this inspiring building sits the **Royal Exchange Grand Cafe and Bar** (681.2470), open for breakfast, lunch, and dinner. You can dine down here surrounded by the shops and vaulting arches, or go to the mezzanine level, which houses two chic bars. Choose your location and then from a menu that includes English asparagus with truffle vinaigrette, *plateau de fruits de mer* (seafood platter), 28-day–aged sirloin steak, hand-cut chips and foie gras butter, and for dessert perhaps the warm chocolate fondant, the English berries, or the elderflower sorbet. On the Threadneedle Street side, note the statues of Henry FitzAilwin, the city's first lord mayor, and of Dick Whittington, the famous City merchant who was elected lord mayor three times. The outside steps are traditionally used to proclaim a new sovereign.
♦ Threadneedle St and Cornhill. Tube: Bank

At the Royal Exchange:

GEORGE PEABODY STATUE

William Wetmore Story's bronze statue of American philanthropist George Peabody was erected in 1869. Peabody spent most of his life in Britain building 5,000 homes for the poor, which still stand today, and he was the only American ever to be buried in **Westminster Abbey**. (His remains are now reburied in Massachusetts, his native state.)

18 CORNHILL

Once a grain market, this is the highest hill in the City. Today, it is packed with office workers, bankers, and stockbrokers; a century ago, these streets were traversed by authors like Elizabeth Gaskell, Thackeray, and the Brontës. ♦ Between Gracechurch and Lombard Sts. Tube: Bank

19 ST. MICHAEL'S ALLEY

Here is one of the few places in London that make you draw in your breath, for it is Dickensian London as you will rarely see it anywhere else. There's no need to rush along this alley, though—it ends within eyeshot and

becomes modern London again. Just two buildings, the **Jamaica Wine House** and the **George & Vulture**, face each other across the street, sharing experiences of days gone by. ♦ Off Cornhill, between Gracechurch St and Birchin La. Tube: Bank

Within St. Michael's Alley:

JAMAICA WINE HOUSE

★★$$ This popular pub got its name from customers back in the 1670s who were trading in Jamaica. When it opened in the mid-17th century, it was the first coffeehouse in London. At one time, it served Jamaican rum; today, the brews on tap include beer and real ale. The inn prides itself on its Doorstep Sandwiches filled with roast beef and mustard or roast lamb with mint jelly. Diners unable to cope with them could opt for a summer salad (spinach, carrot, and walnut served with hummus and flatbread). ♦ Pub ♦ M–F, lunch. 929.6972

GEORGE & VULTURE

★★$$ This is a restaurant, not a pub, and it's very popular, so make reservations the day before—at least. A live, caged vulture used to serve as the establishment's sign. Charles Dickens used the place as a setting in *The Pickwick Papers*. The brass plate outside is worn thin from its daily cleaning; inside, the place is just as pristine. There is rack of roast lamb, Stilton cheese, and port at the end of your classic English meal. The restaurant is full of stockbrokers, bankers, and insurance magnates, and the wine list reflects its international clientele. ♦ British ♦ M–F, lunch. Reservations required. 3 Castle Ct (at St. Michael's Alley). 626.9710

20 LEADENHALL MARKET

A very pretty area crisscrossed with glass-roofed alleys, this market was built in 1881 by **Sir Horace Jones**. Intricately decorated iron-and-glass façades cover what was one of the few places in the City where Londoners could buy fresh food. Nowadays it is more of a small shopping arcade, with clothes shops, bars, and restaurants. It has retained a lot of its original charm, and Hollywood noticed the charms of Leadenhall in 2001 when it was used as Diagon Alley in *Harry Potter and the Sorcerer's Stone*. ♦ M–F. Gracechurch St (between Fenchurch and Leadenhall Sts). Tube: Bank, Monument

21 LLOYD'S OF LONDON BUILDING

If you liked his Pompidou Center in Paris, this building by **Sir Richard Rogers** will also amuse, as it is a much smaller version squashed into a confined space. Erected in

---

Restaurants/Clubs: Red | Hotels: Purple | Shops: Orange | Outdoors/Parks: Green | Sights/Culture: Blue

1986 around a central atrium and bedecked with oversize pipework, metal flooring, and glass, this zoo-style design allows the public to look inside and watch the office workers busying about their day. (The building is otherwise closed to visitors.) That such a traditional insurance company as Lloyd's should be housed in this flamboyant structure is a surprise in itself. Although the building was controversial when it was completed, it is now seen as a bold landmark in a city packed with building blocks. ♦ 1 Lime St (at Leadenhall St). Tube: Bank, Aldgate

22 Mary Janes

This is an extraordinary place. It's worth popping in just to gasp at the audacity of the décor. The only possible explanation is that the interior designer suffered from multiple personality disorder and all of his personalities came out to design this bar. Darkwood spaces sparkle with glitzy glass chandeliers, columns are covered in assorted framed pictures, exposed brick glitters with mirrors, velvet swags across doorways, a glass balcony hangs above a dance floor, a whole wall of drink bottles is lit up in scarlet—and that's before I talk you through the huge tropical aquarium. The cocktail list is creative, and the Champage Club is a magnet for aficionados of fizz. There is a happy hour from 5 to 7PM; when not even the terrible dollar exchange rate will stop you from enjoying some bubbles or a Champagne-based cocktail. The Mary Jane has rose Champagne over Sputnik rose petal vodka with a dash of watermelon. If you have a sweet tooth, you will love the Sweet Shop Shooters—candy-inspired shots such as Toblerone, After Eight, and Jam Donut! Food is of the burgers'n'salads'n'sundaes variety and the snacks are tasty—scooped potato skins and duck rolls go surprisingly well with a glass of Champagne. Tube: Aldgate. www.maryjanes.co.uk

23 The Monument

These days, it has become more difficult to see things from the top of this block of Portland stone, because it is now surrounded by taller structures; nevertheless, you can still get a pretty good view of neighboring churches, the **Docklands** area, and **St. Paul's**. Built by **Sir Christopher Wren** and city surveyor **Robert Hooke** between 1671 and 1677, the monument was commissioned by Charles II to "preserve the memory of this dreadful visitation" (i.e., the Great Fire). If the 202-foot column were laid down, it would touch the exact spot where the Great Fire began on 2 September 1666, in a baker's oven in Pudding Lane. Unfortunately, The Monument is currently being renovated and there is no specific date

for reopening. ♦ Monument St (between Pudding La and Fish St Hill). 626.2717. Tube: Monument

24 Minster Court

In contrast to **Lloyd's**, this modern building echoes the monumentality of a Gothic cathedral but translated into a modern silhouette with mock buttresses and faux towers. Completed in 1992, it houses the London Underwriting Centre and a mall-like hall with shops and eating places. ♦ M–F. Mark La (at Great Tower St). Tube: Tower Hill

25 All-Hallows-by-the-Tower

William Penn was baptized in this church in 1644, and John Quincy Adams was married here in 1797. Although the first church on the site was Saxon, there are Roman tiles and a tessellated pavement in the crypt. Samuel Pepys watched the Great Fire of London from the church's spire. After many centuries of rebuilding, it was extensively renovated in 1950 because of war bomb damage. ♦ M–F, 8:30AM–6PM; Sa, 10AM–5PM; Su, 1PM–5PM. Services throughout the day every day. Donations welcome. Byward St (between Tower Hill and Lower Thames St). 481.2928. Tube: Tower Hill

26 Tower of London

Though the crowds can be as thick and forbidding as the grayish brown stone, this medieval monument, with its displays of armor and exquisite **Crown Jewels**, must be seen at least once in a lifetime. Nine hundred years of fascinating, though brutal, history are embraced within these walls, and even though the tower's violent years are long past, an atmosphere of impending doom still lingers. The tower has been used as a royal palace, fortress, armory, treasury, and menagerie, but it is best known as a merciless prison. Being locked up here, especially in Tudor times, was tantamount to certain death. Anne Boleyn, Catherine Howard, Lady Jane Grey, Sir Thomas More, and Sir Walter Raleigh are but a few who spent their final days, and in some cases, years, in the tower.

The buildings of **Her Majesty's Palace and Fortress of the Tower of London**, as it is officially known, reflect almost every style of English architecture, as well as the different roles the tower has played. William the Conqueror started the **White Tower** in 1078, and it was completed 20 years later by his son, William Rufus (William II). Richard the Lionhearted strengthened the fortress in the 12th century by building a curtain wall with towers, of which only the **Bell Tower** remains. Henry III and his son Edward I completed the transformation into the medieval castle that stands today.

The 120-foot-wide moat, now covered with grass, was kept flooded with water by a series of sluice gates until 1843; today, it serves as the village green for the 50 or so families who live on the tower grounds. Prisoners and provisions were brought in through the **Traitors Gate** when the Thames was still London's main highway. A gate in the **Bloody Tower** leads to the inner precincts. This tower acquired its unpleasant name after the Little Princes mysteriously disappeared from it in 1483. Controversy still rages over whether Richard III, their uncle and protector, had them murdered so he could secure the throne. Sir Walter Raleigh wrote *A History of the World* during his imprisonment in the Bloody Tower between 1603 and 1616. Almost every stone in **Beauchamp Tower** is covered with desperately scratched messages from prisoners—pathetic reminders of those who perished. Nearby is the **Chapel Royal of St. Peter ad Vincula**, built in the 12th century and restored by Henry VIII in 1520 after a fire in 1512. The chapel is the burial place of the Duke of Somerset, the Duke of Northumberland, Anne Boleyn, Catherine Howard (two of Henry VIII's six wives), and Lady Jane Grey, all of whom were beheaded.

Glittering amid the historical doom and gloom are the Crown Jewels, the tower's most popular attraction. Dazzling and brilliant, the spectacular collection far exceeds its reputation. The jewels were housed in **Martin Tower** until 1671, when the audacious Colonel Blood came very close to making off with them. They are now displayed in the ground-floor strongroom of **Waterloo Barracks**, known as the **Jewel House**. Here, robes, swords, scepters, and crowns adorned with some of the most precious stones in the world are shown to about 20,000 people every day. Most of the royal regalia was sold or melted down after the execution of Charles I in 1649. Only two pieces escaped: the **Anointing Spoon**, probably first used in the coronation of King Henry IV in 1399, and the 14th-century **Ampulla**. The rest of the collection dates from the restoration of Charles II in 1660. **St. Edward's Crown** was made for Charles II and has been used by nearly all of his successors, including Queen Elizabeth II. It weighs almost 5 pounds and is adorned with more than 400 precious stones. The priceless **Imperial State Crown**, originally made for Queen Victoria, contains some of the most famous stones in the world, including the 317-carat **Second Star of Africa**, the **Stuart Sapphire**, and the Black Prince's balas ruby. Monarchs have worn this crown when leaving **Westminster Abbey** after coronation ceremonies, at the State Opening of Parliament, and at other state occasions. The exquisite **Koh-i-noor** diamond adorns the **Queen Mother's Crown**, made especially for her to wear at the coronation of George VI in 1936 (she also wore it for Queen Elizabeth II's coronation in 1953). But even grander is the 530-carat **Star of Africa**, believed to be the largest cut diamond in the world, which is on the **Sovereign's Sceptre**. Most spectacular of the many swords is the **State Sword**, decorated with diamonds, emeralds, and rubies that form the national emblems of England, Scotland, and Ireland.

The imposing Kentish and Caen stone walls of the **White Tower** dominate the complex. Started in 1078 for William the Conqueror by a Norman monk, the walls are 15 feet thick at the base, 11 feet thick at the top, and 90 feet above ground level. In 1241, Henry III added a great hall and royal apartments and had the exterior whitewashed, hence the name. The **Royal Armory** was housed here until recently, when the collection was moved to Leeds. However, some armor is still on display, mostly pieces that belonged to Henry VIII, who established a fine armor-making foundry here.

St. John's Chapel, on the second floor of the White Tower, is one of the finest examples of early Norman architecture, with simple columns, roundheaded arches, and beautiful tunnel vaulting. It was here in 1503 that the body of Elizabeth of York, wife of Henry VII, lay in state surrounded by 500 candles, and here that Lady Jane Grey prayed before her execution in 1554.

The tower's great sense of history and tradition lives on through ceremonies that have been performed virtually unchanged for centuries. The most famous one is the Ceremony of the Keys, perhaps the oldest military ceremony in the world. Every evening at precisely 10 minutes to 10PM, the chief yeoman warder, wearing a large scarlet coat and accompanied by four soldiers, secures the main gates of the tower. As the clock strikes 10, a bugler sounds the Last Post. To attend the Ceremony of the Keys, write at least 6 weeks in advance to the Resident Governor, Operations Department, Waterloo Barracks, HM Tower of London, London EC3N 4AB. Enclose a self-addressed envelope with two international reply coupons. Only 70 people are allowed to watch each night, so make your request as far in advance as possible (and suggest alternative dates).

On 21 May of each year, representatives from **Eton College** and **King's College, Cambridge**, place lilies and white roses in the oratory of **Wakefield Tower**, where Henry VI, the founder of the two schools, was murdered on the orders of Edward IV in 1471. The ceremony is closed to the public. Wakefield Tower serves as one of the settings for a re-creation of the medieval palace that used to occupy this area. Costumed players representing courtiers, knights, and servants tell visitors about the details of daily life at the royal court. The re-creation takes place several times daily.

Another long-standing tradition is the daily feeding of the ravens who live within the tower walls. Since Charles II decreed there should always be at least six ravens at the tower, there have always been six with two reserves. In 1989, the tower managed to breed the birds successfully for the first time. Their wings are clipped to keep them here because legend has it that if they leave, the tower will fall and the monarchy with it. Watch out: Ravens are much bigger than crows and sometimes peck at the ankles of unsuspecting tourists.

Contained within the tower are several cafés and the new **Armouries**, a spacious restaurant serving homemade food all day, every day. It's an ideal refreshment stop for coffee and cake or for lunch, which includes homemade soups, sandwiches, and salads. ♦ Admission. Daily. Tower Hill (at Tower Bridge Approach). Tickets: 0844/482.7799. Information: 0844/482.7777. Tube: Tower Hill. www.hrp.org.uk

27 ST. KATHARINE'S DOCK

For about 300 years, beginning in the 16th century, London's **Docklands** had a proud heritage as working dockyards, but in Victorian times the area became poor, and crime rampant. During World War II, the Docklands area was devastated by bombs and remained largely unrepaired until the mid-1980s, when attempts at revitalization began (see "The Docklands: Vibrant Revival" on page 172).

This dock was the pioneer of the entire redevelopment plan. Designed by **Thomas Telford** in 1828, the dock offers lovely views of small ships and boats in the marina, as well as several shops, pubs, and restaurants. Because its warehouses were built close to the water, thieving was minimal. Eventually, the dock closed because it was unable to accommodate large ships. Today, however, it's a thriving marina, playing host to the big oceangoing yachts of the wealthy, and several upscale jewelry and fashion boutiques flourish on the waterside. It is next to the **Docklands Light Railway**, whose trains travel deeper into the Docklands. ♦ St. Katharine's Way (off E Smithfield). Tube: Tower Hill

At St. Katharine's Dock:

DICKENS INN

★$$ This rambling pub looks like a Walt Disney World creation, but it's a genuine 18th-century spice house that has been overhauled and converted to the style of a 19th-century balconied inn. Inside, it's all wood tables and beams, and the most pleasant place for a drink in the whole of St. Katharine's Dock; the locals use it (always a good sign), and it fills up on a Friday night. Upstairs, two restaurants offer fish dishes, but the ground-floor **Tavern Bar** is really the main attraction here. ♦ Pub ♦ Daily, lunch and dinner. 488.2208

TOWER THISTLE HOTEL

$$$ Sandwiched between the Thames and St. Katharine's Dock with its colorful yachts and shops, this vast, ziggurat-like property offers guests four-star accommodations in 803 plush, refurbished rooms right around the corner from that "other" tower. The hotel seems designed for the business executive, but plenty of tourists stay too. Hotel dining offers a choice of the **Carvery**, where a traditional British roast is always served, including Scottish forerib of beef and Norfolk bronze turkey; **Xi Bar**, which offers stunning views across the Thames; and **The Gallery at The Tower**, offering hot drinks, snacks, light meals, and a full bar all day (until 2AM on Friday and Saturday); it's also the place for full traditional English afternoon tea, served all day, every day. ♦ 0870/333.9106; fax 0870/333.9206. www.thistlehotels.com/tower

28 MILLENNIUM BRIDGE

London's newest bridge—the Blade of Light—connects Bankside with the City. It truly is beautiful, fragile, and elegant to look at. Designed by **Arup/Foster & Partners** along with the sculptor **Sir Anthony Caro**, the bridge was six months late in opening and was promptly closed after it was decided that it was too "wobbly" to be safe. All is now well, although there is a certain amount of movement to be felt. Take seasickness pills and go. ♦ Embankment. Tube: Blackfriars. www.arup.com/millenniumbridge

29 TATE MODERN

The £134.5 million conversion (by architects **Herzog and De Muron**) of the old **Bankside Power Station** into the new **Tate Modern** made, in its first year, this gallery the most popular modern art gallery in the world: 5.25 million people came into the vast **Turbine Hall** to where the **Tate** now houses its international modern collection. At the risk of sounding smug, that is five times the number of visitors to New York's Museum of Modern Art in the same period.

Spread over seven floors, the Tate Modern exhibits at any one time over 600 works of art from the collection. All the favorites are here . . . Rodin's *The Kiss*, the Mark Rothko room, an assortment of Andy Warhols, Henri Matisse's *L'Escargot*, a whole palette of Picassos, and those bricks!

Floors 3 and **5** house the permanent collection, with each floor being divided into four suites. **Floor 4** is reserved for temporary collections, and the fabulously huge **Turbine Hall** (on **Floor 1**) itself is home to the **Unilever Series** of exhibitions, which are ever changing. **Floor 6** is exclusively reserved for members, and **Floors 2** and **7** offer succor to the inner gallery-goer.

The gallery has several auditoria that are used for lectures in their education program. There is also a variety of audio guides available, including one specifically for children.

There are excellent facilities for the disabled, with ramps and elevators everywhere. Parking spaces and wheelchairs can be booked. ♦ Su-Th, 10AM-6PM; F, Sa, 10AM-10PM. Free. Bankside. 887.8888 or 887.8008 for recorded information. Tube: Blackfriars. www.tate.org.uk/modern

Within the Tate Modern:

2ND FLOOR CAFÉ
A spacious and airy café serving truly delicious modern British food—wonderful homemade soups, great open sandwiches, delicious salads, and very nice pasta. There are also great beers and a selection of fruit juices, good coffee, and many, many teas. Staff members are young and helpful. You'll never believe this is a gallery café.

7TH FLOOR RESTAURANT
★$$$ The view alone is worth the price of a meal up here. Head chef Chris MacLean has created a menu that showcases quality ingredients, often sourced locally, but also taking the best from other countries, particularly Spain and Italy. The menu changes seasonally; on the current winter menu, choose from venison carpaccio with celeriac remoulade, duck leg confit with polenta and cipollini onions, and toasted ciabatta with seasonal mushrooms and poached duck egg. For traditionalists, the finest Cornish haddock and chips is a favorite. The views up on the skyline are of practically the whole of London. If you think you'd get seasick on the London Eye, this would be the place to go instead. The restaurant welcomes bookings for lunch Monday through Friday, and for dinner on Friday and Saturday evenings. ♦ 887.8888

TATE MODERN BOOKSHOP
Everything you've ever wanted to know about modern art but were afraid to ask, as Woody Allen might put it. Yards high and wide of books, gifts, wrapping papers, postcards, posters, and knickknacks. Set aside time for a browse. ♦ Su-Th, 10AM-6PM; F, Sa, 10AM-10PM. 401.5167. www.tate.org.uk/modern

30 SHAKESPEARE'S GLOBE
Shakespeare lovers who have longed to see the Bard's plays performed as they were in the 16th century can now do just that. The new **Globe Theatre**—a thatch-roofed, half-timbered replica of the original open-air theater that premiered some of Shakespeare's plays—opened in June 1997 with Mark Rylance as artistic director, now succeeded by Dominic Dromgoole. (See "Shakespeare's Globe Comes Full Circle" on page 196.) Between June and September, four plays are performed in repertory during the day and early evening in the open arena, including those of such other Elizabethan dramatists as Thomas Middleton and Beaumont and Fletcher. As of old, the actors enjoy a great rapport with the audience, especially the "groundlings" who stand in the yard around the stage. (In Elizabethan theater, those who watched performances from the pit had only the ground for a floor.) The rest of the spectators are seated in the three galleries of the amphitheater.

Part of an education charity project, the new Globe was born of American actor-director Sam Wanamaker's 40-year-plus struggle to re-create the theater near the original site. (Unfortunately, he died before construction began.) The Globe complex also includes an exhibition center with displays about the theater's history, the building's restoration, and Shakespeare's works (including videos and slides). Guided tours of the center explain the rise of Elizabethan theater, the playwright's links to this area, and the construction techniques of the time. There are also 40-minute guided walking tours starting at the exhibition and finishing at the site of the original theater. ♦ Admission to the exhibition. Additional fee for tours. Performances: daily, June-Sept. Tours: daily; call for times. Walking tours: F-Su, every hour on the half hour, 11:30AM-4:30PM, Apr-June; daily, June-Nov. New Globe Walk (at Bankside). 928.6406; box office, 401.9919; tours, 902.1500. Tube: Blackfriars, Waterloo, London Bridge

31 ANCHOR
★★★$$ Dr. Johnson drank here, and Shakespeare imbibed as well, in an earlier version of this watering hole. The fine old pub

with creaking floorboards galore also has a minstrels' gallery, a riverside terrace with tables that enjoy a fantastic view of **St. Paul's**, plus good bar snacks and a restaurant serving such English fare as lamb hot pot and steak-and-ale pie. The place gets very crowded. ◆ Pub ◆ Daily, lunch and dinner. 34 Park St (at Bank End). 407.1577. Tube: London Bridge

32 VINOPOLIS: CITY OF WINE

An £18 million, 2.25-acre multimedia exhibition celebrating wine. The **Wine Odyssey** takes you through the history of wine and winemaking and through all the major wine-producing regions of the world. New World, Old World—even China, Japan, and India get a look in. You can meander through the complex on a variety of self-guided tours depending on how much time and money you want to spend. The basic "original" tour offers you the exhibition; five wine-tasting vouchers; a free Bombay Sapphire cocktail in the Bombay Sapphire Experience section of the tour, created by Vinopolis's expert mixologists; a tasting notebook; and an audio guide recorded by Oz Clarke to fill in the blanks in your knowledge. Other tours offer, in addition, guided and premium wine tastings, whiskey tastings in The Still Room (which doesn't stay still after a few tots!), Champagne tastings in the new Ruinart Champagne Bar (dangerous, you won't want to leave), beer tastings, and even absinthe tastings. If you really want to learn, Vinopolis also offers guided tours that last one hour, and there are regular tasting events throughout the year. This is an absolutely fascinating way to spend an afternoon. At the end of it all there is, of course, a chance to buy your preferred tipples to take home. There is also a gift and bookshop to further stress your credit card. ◆ Admission. M, Th, F, noon-10PM; Sa, 11AM-9PM; Su, noon-6PM. 1 Bank End SE1 (on Bankside between London Bridge and Shakespeare's Globe). 940.8300. Booking almost essential. Tube: London Bridge. www.vinopolis.co.uk

Within Vinopolis:

WINE WHARF BAR

Spartan in décor, but a great place to try out your newfound knowledge of wines, the Wine Wharf has more than 100 wines by the glass. Jazz Mondays are fun, with good live music to help mellow each sip! ◆ Daily. 940.8335. www.winewharf.com

BREW WHARF BAR

If beer is your thing you'll appreciate this place, which has its own microbrewery attached. Great space, too—high vaulting ceilings, exposed brickwork, and white tiled floor, with that brewery chugging away down one side. It also does good, hearty pub grub. ◆ Daily. 378.6601. www.brewwharf.com

CANTINA VINOPOLIS

★★$$ Good Mediterranean cuisine in a lovely old space. The food is really quite classic, with starters such as goat's cheese oven-roasted beetroot and onion salad with balsamic dressing or pan-fried scallops with a delicious herb salad. Rib of beef is for two to share (and it is still a biggie!), monkfish comes spice baked, and venison is served with butternut squash mash and baby onions. Desserts have something to please just about everyone, from New York cheesecake with poached strawberries to fig and almond tart with bitter fig syrup. Best of all, every single dish on the menu is carefully matched with a wine, a beer, or a port by the sommelier. And yes, you can enjoy just that glass with just that course and not be forced into buying a bottle! A truly excellent idea. And wonderful to find it extended right across the menu. The suggested wines, by the way, are a thrill to read through. I found myself ordering those scallops just because of the fabulous '05 Gruner Veltliner that was partnered with them! ◆ Daily, lunch and dinner. 940.8333. www.cantinavinopolis.com

THE WHISKY EXCHANGE

Oh joy, oh happiness! What a great place for whiskey lovers! Actually, even if you are not a whiskey lover when you go in, you will be when you come out. They offer expert, enthusiastic advice and a stunning selection of whiskeys from Scotland, Wales, Ireland, Japan, and elsewhere. There is bourbon, and there is even something labeled Kentucky Moonshine. Casks stand in one corner, and you can have your bottle drawn straight from the wood if it takes your fancy. I would make the journey here even if I wasn't visiting the other 2.24 acres of the place. ◆ Daily. 403.8688. www.thewhiskyexchange.com

33 CLINK EXHIBITION

"In the clink" became a common expression to describe a jail term, thanks to the original jail in this alley. It now has display boards about the area's history, the brothels, the bull- and bear-baiting pits, and the theaters of its medieval and Tudor heyday. Ironically, the area was owned by the Bishop of Winchester, whose palace ruin is on this street. ◆Admission. Daily. 1 Clink St (at Stoney St). 0207/403.0900. Tube: London Bridge. www.clink.co.uk

34 GOLDEN HINDE

This galleon is an exact reproduction of the ship Sir Francis Drake sailed when he circumnavigated the globe in 1577–1580. Now moored permanently, this little vessel, only 20 feet wide and 120 feet long, has also sailed Drake's route. Visitors can see the re-created living quarters, armory, and captain's cabin, but it's hard to imagine how the crew of 60, as well as 20 officers and gentlemen, lived in such a tight space. Kids can have a pirate party onboard, play pirate games, and go on a treasure hunt. There are also 4-hour workshops for kids in which they can learn to raise the anchor and, slightly more worrisome, load cannon! Families can even stay overnight. Dressed in period clothes, you will play the part of crew members (scurvy optional). Meals are all in Tudor style (so if you are gluten intolerant, hard luck), and the visit lasts from 5PM on one day till 10AM the next. ♦ General admission: £12 family, £6 adult, £4.50 child. Special event admission (e.g., Pirate Fun Day): £15 family, £7 adult, £5 child. St. Mary Overie Dock (at Clink St). 0870/011.8700; fax 0207/407.5908. Tube: London Bridge. www.goldenhinde.co.uk

35 LONDON BRIDGE

Imagination is required here, because "London Bridge has fallen down" time and time again. Twenty yards or so downstream was the site of the first wooden bridge to cross the Thames, built during the first century at the behest of Roman emperor Claudius. A succession of wooden bridges followed until 1176, when Peter de Colechurch constructed a 10-arch stone bridge for Henry II; it was embellished with ramshackle wooden houses, and a few traitors' heads were spiked on for good measure. The heads were eventually removed, but the bridge remained until John Rennie erected a new one, 20 yards upstream, in 1831. This one was moved to Lake Havasu City, Arizona, in 1971, when the current cantilevered affair was constructed. ♦ Between Borough High St and King William St. Tube: London Bridge, Monument

36 WRIGHT BROTHERS OYSTER AND PORTER HOUSE

★★★$$ Don't you just love it when a restaurant lives up to its name? This lofty-ceilinged, exposed-brick-and-dark-wood place offers eight kinds of oysters and nine porters and stouts. Obviously that's not all, but it is a delicious start! Oysters are both rock and native (and you can get a mixed plate of 12), and there is always an Oyster of the Day. The day I was there it was the Cornish Fisherman's Creek. There are also Oyster Specials such as New Orleans (deep-fried with tartar sauce) or Japanese (with soy, wasabi, and ginger). The oyster rarebit is a little culinary masterpiece. I have the recipe, but I'm not telling you! You could choose a beef Guinness and oyster pie, or various daily specials involving excellent fish and shellfish well cooked. The kitchen is open, and you can make your meal even more interesting by bagging a seat at the bar and watching the chefs at work. The wine list is small but perfectly formed and the house Champagne is excellent, either on its own or in the Black Velvet that appears on the list of porters and stouts, although the wines are, to my mind, slightly ambitiously priced. Cheeses are as you would expect from a place around the corner from Neal's Yard. This is a great place for lunch if you are in the area, and a fabulous idea for a mid-afternoon oyster pick-me-up. ♦ M-Sa, noon-10:30PM (3PM-6PM, cold crustaceans and shellfish only). ♦ 11 Stoney St. 403.9554. Tube: London Bridge. www.wrightbros.eu.com

37 SOUTHWARK CATHEDRAL

The fourth church on this site and the earliest Gothic church in London, this charming cathedral is not to be missed. The oldest oak effigy, dating from 1275, is of a knight, ankles crossed, one hand on his sword, and even the ravages of time can't erase the eerie feeling that he's just fallen asleep. John Harvard, founder of Harvard University, was born in Southwark in 1607 and baptized here. The reconstruction in 1907 of the Harvard chapel was paid for by the university. Among those buried here is John Gower, known as the "first English poet" because he wrote in English, not French or Latin. The **South Aisle** features a **Shakespeare Memorial**, and every year on 23 April, a service is held here in the Bard's honor. Touchingly, now beside the Bard is a memorial to the late Sam Wanamaker, the American actor-director whose dream of re-creating Shakespeare's theater has come true upriver.

Behind the cathedral, redevelopment hasn't entirely overtaken the ancient Georgian warehouses of **Borough Market**, where lorries laden with fruit and vegetables still draw up before dawn. This is how **Covent Garden** once looked. Four hundred years ago, this area was the haunt of Shakespeare, Marlowe, and other Elizabethan playwrights, as well as their audiences. ♦ Daily; call ahead for times of services. Montague Close (at London Bridge).

367.6700. Tube: London Bridge.
www.southwark.anglican.org

38 LONDON DUNGEON

Opposite the more refined pleasures of **Hay's Galleria** stand the gruesome delights of the world's first medieval horror museum—founded, as it happens, by a Chelsea housewife! Within its gloomy vaults beneath **London Bridge**, you can learn the finer points of hanging, drawing and quartering, boiling, and pressing people to death. Relive the Great Fire of 1666 and wander through the Jack the Ripper Experience exhibit. The Dungeon has recently added a *Bubonic Plague* exhibit. Nice! This rivals the **Chamber of Horrors** at the pricier **Madame Tussaud's**, especially because of the atmospheric setting in the arches under the railway. But be forewarned: It's not for the fainthearted—people have passed out in here. ♦ Admission. Daily. 28–34 Tooley St (between Stainer and Joiner Sts). 403.7221. Tube: London Bridge

39 HAY'S GALLERIA

A yellow brick–built dock, now under a glass atrium, it's close enough to the City to be crowded during the day with bustling workers rushing to the delis, sandwich bars, and pretty shops. In summer, they eat outside, so get here early if you want to do the same. The fine **Horniman's** pub has a re-created Victorian interior and great waterfront views. Although the structure's design is hardworking Georgian warehouse architecture, its renovation has added charm. Watch out for David Kemp's *The Navigators*, a 60-foot-tall bronze moving sculpture with water jets and fountains. ♦ Tooley St (at Battle Bridge La). Tube: London Bridge

40 HMS *BELFAST*

This World War II cruiser is now a floating museum with seven decks to explore. Visit the **Captain's Bridge**, the mess decks, the sick bay, and even the boiler room to get a feel for how the sailors lived. ♦ Admission. Daily. Morgan's La (off Tooley St). 940.6300. Tube: London Bridge. www.hmsbelfast.iwm.org.uk

41 CITY HALL

City Hall is the home for the mayor of London, the London Assembly, and the Greater London Authority (GLA). It was built for the job and designed (after beating the incredibly hot competition) by **Fosters and Partners**, one of Britain's leading architects and the designers of the **Millennium Bridge** and the **British Museum**'s new **Great Court**. The company was also involved in the restoration of the Reichstag in Berlin. Amazingly, it was built in just 30 months, coming in on time and on budget. This makes it something of a modern miracle in London. Each of the glazing panels is unique in shape and size and was laser-cut using data from the designers' computer model. It is a modified sphere, leaning slightly backward to present less surface area to the sun, thus requiring less air conditioning to cool the offices inside. It stands nearly 45 meters high, but—again because of the backward tilt—doesn't cast a huge shadow over the riverside walkway alongside which it stands. It uses only about a quarter of the energy of a standard office building, and recycled materials are used in many of its fittings and furnishings. Just how politically correct can a building get? Members of the public are welcome to visit and to attend many of the meetings held there. To find out in advance what meetings are being held, visit the GLA web site, at www.london.gov.uk, and look for "public meetings," at www.london.gov.uk/gla/city-hall-publicaccess.jsp. ♦ City Hall, the Queen's Walk. Public Liaison Unit, 983.4100. Tube: London Bridge

42 TOWER BRIDGE

London's most famous bridge has been a museum since 1982. The original hydraulic machinery that operated the bridge until 1976 is on display, along with exhibitions that explain the Victorian genius behind the design. Built in 1894 by **Sir Horace Jones** and **John Wolfe-Barry**, the Gothic towered bridge represents Victorian architecture and engineering at its best. The twin towers of steel encased in stone support the 1,000-ton weight of the bascules that were raised and lowered by hydraulic machinery located in piers at the base of the towers. At the peak of London's river traffic, and before steam replaced tall masts, the bascules rose as many as 50 times a day. Now they are operated by electricity and open only a few times a week. The glass-enclosed walkway, stretching across the London sky 145 feet above the Thames, offers splendid views in every direction. From here you can step back and see the architectural variety of the city, from the Portland stone office buildings on Tower Hill to the brick and concrete of the postwar rebuilding to the glass and steel of the last 20 years. The **Tower Bridge Experience**, located inside the bridge, offers a high-tech exhibition recounting the history and function of the bridge. ♦ Admission. Daily. Between Tower Bridge Rd and Tower Bridge Approach. 403.3761. Tube: Tower Hill

43 BUTLERS WHARF

Here, among the streets and alleyways, is the best place to capture the mood of the old **Docklands**. The spices that were once shipped in from the Orient are still sold here. Dickens had Bill Sykes from *Oliver Twist* meet his end on Shad Thames, which is now the home of restaurants. ♦ Shad Thames (off Tooley St). Tube: Tower Hill, London Bridge

Within Butlers Wharf:

Le Pont de la Tour

★★★★$$$$ In Xanadu did Kubla Khan a stately pleasure dome decree . . . in Butlers Wharf did Terence Conran create Le Pont de la Tour; albeit it is now part of the D&D group. Tony Blair entertained Bill Clinton here, and here Ken Livingstone bought Rudy Giuliani dinner. The views are stunning, the space is as impressively designed as it was in the days of Conran. Head chef Lee Bennett's menu is rooted in French tradition. Time-honored French recipes have been given a lighter feel, creating unfussy and appetizing dishes such as smoked eel, poached egg, pancetta, beetroot and mustard, spiced ceviche of hand-dived Scottish scallops, smoked salmon, *crêpe parmentier*, and crème fraiche. And that's just the starters. Main courses include poached Cornish brill with apples, cider, and crème fraiche, whole grilled Dover sole, roast partridge with quince purée and *choux farcie* (stuffed cabbage), and whole roast grouse, bread sauce, and game chips. And to finish? Why not try the warm chocolate fondant with pistachio ice cream, or the Madagascan vanilla crème brûlée. All of which can be washed down with a sensational selection of wines and Champagnes. ♦ Su–F, noon–3PM; M–Sa, 6–11:30PM; Su, 6–11PM. 403.8403

Le Pont de la Tour Bar and Grill

Specializing in seafood and crustaceans at top quality, this less formal dining space also offers salads and grills. Expect dishes such as sea bass with lemon and oil, classic fish pie, and a staggering *plateau de fruits de mer* (seafood platter). Champagne is something of a specialty. And a pianist adds a little atmosphere in the evenings and at lunchtime on Sundays. ♦ M–Sa, 11:30AM–11:30PM; Su, noon–11PM. 403.8403; fax 403.0267

Le Pont de la Tour Food Store

The most luxurious corner deli imaginable, this place also sells fantastic sandwiches and a great range of wines. ♦ M–F, 8:30AM–7:30PM; Sa, Su, 10AM–6PM. 940.1830

The Wine Merchant

Taste buds still reeling from the fabulous wine you enjoyed in the restaurant? Take a bottle home from this most upmarket of off-licenses. Staff members are nicely knowledgeable. ♦ M–Sa, noon–8:30PM; Su, noon–6PM. 940.1840

The Butlers Wharf Chop House

★★★$$$ Don't let the basic sound of the name put you off. There's a lot more than chops on offer here. Chef Sylvain Le Gleud has put together an impressive menu encompassing many marvelous traditional olde English dishes . . . such as the game terrine with greengage chutney, which heads the list of starters on his menu. Main courses include steak and kidney pudding, charcoal-grilled marinated rabbit legs, Swiss chard and lentils, roast Suffolk pork loin, watercress mash and Bramley apple sauce, and an impressive roast rib of beef.

The Chop House Bar

This establishment offers top-quality steaks, oysters, smoked salmon, and lobster, and a dessert list that has the pride of English puddingry—steamed treacle pudding—on it. Have some. Consider the calories later. There is also an excellent weekend brunch. ♦ Chop house: M–Su, noon–3PM; M–Sa, 6–11PM. Bar: M–Sa, noon–11PM; Su, noon–4PM. 403.3403. www.chophouse.co.uk

Cantina del Ponte

★★★$$ You're in Italy on Thames in this part of the Conran empire. Chef Brian Fantoni has fitted his menu to the huge mural of an Italian market that runs the length of the dining space. There are pizzas, of course, but the menu also offers roast pepper and tomato soup with creamed goat's cheese; grilled baby octopus with a white bean salad; beef carpaccio with artichoke, arugula, and Parmesan; homemade *trofie* with eggplant, zucchini, and basil pesto; fillet of sea bass with fennel mash, tomato, and fresh basil; and fillet of beef with marinated Portobello mushrooms and Chianti sauce. The wine list is sunny and delightful. ♦ M–Su, noon–3PM; M–Sa, 6–11PM; Su, 6–10PM

Design Museum

The pet project of Sir Terence Conran, this trendy museum draws fashionable folks sporting designer gear, designer spouses, and, of course, designer children. But

---

Restaurants/Clubs: Red | Hotels: Purple | Shops: Orange | Outdoors/Parks: Green | Sights/Culture: Blue

...ople watching, the museum ...n its own right. The **Review** ...es international design, ... the **Collection** shows design in its historical context. ♦ Admission. M-F; Sa, Su, noon-6PM. 0870/833.9955. www.designmuseum.org

Within the Design Museum:

Blue Print Café

★★★$$ This smart little restaurant, with its fabulous river view, has stark white walls hung with colorful prints and red or blue vinyl-topped tables displaying blue vases, each with a single fresh flower. It's a charming backdrop for the flamboyant creations of chef Jeremy Lee. Expect such dishes as grilled pork livers with sage and bacon and whole grilled bream, cucumber, and dill salad. ♦ Modern British ♦ M-Sa, lunch and dinner; Su, lunch. 378.7031

44 Paul Smith

It's like finding Posh Spice at a backyard barbecue! Yup, *the* Paul Smith has a tiny shop on Park Street, selling casualwear, accessories, perfumes, and a strange assortment of "curiosities," as the charming assistant manageress told us. ♦ M-F, 10AM-6PM; Sa, 9:30AM-6PM. 13 Park St. Tube: London Bridge

45 Neal's Yard Dairy

A bigger, airier, and, yes, more awesome version of the Covent Garden original. This Dairy has two big, cool, cheese-scented rooms full of some of the finest things that can happen to milk. It is a cheese education and adventure. And don't ever worry that you haven't heard of any of these lactic masterpieces; you can always taste. You are *encouraged* to taste. There is always a cheese of the month, there are frequent tutored tastings, and everything can be bought mail order. This shop sells fantastic breads and crackers, too. ♦ Daily. 6 Park St. 645.3554. Tube: London Bridge. www.nealsyarddairy.co.uk

45 Shipps Tearooms

★★$ S*ooo*o sweet it had to go in. This is a real English tearoom, but with a cutesy modern feel. An endearingly and cleverly eclectic mix of crockery means you are always sneaking a look at the teapot next door. It makes for a great conversation starter. All manner of teas and tisanes are offered, of course, but you can have coffee if you prefer, or one of a delicious-sounding selection of old traditional soft drinks. Sandwiches and cakes are the order of the day, and those cakes are straight from the days of croquet on the lawn, genteel "gels,"

and the *Women's Rural Institute Cookbook*: Victoria sponge, lemon drizzle cake, and toasted muffins. And if that doesn't entice, there is the offer of what Shipps calls "decadent cakes"! ♦ M-F, 10AM-7PM; Sa, 9AM-5PM; Su, 11AM-4PM. 4 Park St. Tube: London Bridge

46 Borough Market

London's first and still greatest farmers' market is found in the old fruit market on Southwark Street, near London Bridge. If food is what turns you on, then this is your red light district! No longer strictly a farmers' market, Borough Market has goodies from all over the world. **Brindisa** holds everything good to eat that comes from Spain (and has opened a café on the corner of the market where you can make a lunch of it!), a stall showcasing the wares of the **Antica Farmacia dei Monaci Canaldolesi** has jam made by nuns and honey made by monks, and **Le Marché du Quartier** is a tasty little slice of France (fresh foie gras and vacuum-packed confit duck . . . mmm!). The fabulous **Cool Chile Company** has one of its few outlets here. There is even an absolutely adorable little German deli just across the road on Park Street, where the pretzels are hot, fresh, and *wunderbar*. But best of all for visitors to London, a trip to Borough Market is like a tour of the gastronomic hot spots of the whole British Isles. From the original Boston in Lincolnshire come **Mountain's Boston Sausages**, made to a traditional family recipe by a company established in 1852 and sold to you by the fourth generation of that same company. Made from shoulder of free-range pork and very little else, their sausages are superb. And they are made at 2:00 each morning before being driven down to London! They also make delicious haslet—another great Lincolnshire delicacy rarely seen these days (Th-Sa; 0120/536.2167. www.bostonsausage.co.uk). From the wide-open spaces of the Devon hills comes **Wild Beef**, from local breeds left to roam the hills, then killed locally and hung for three to four weeks. Beef for connoisseurs (F, Sa; 0781/046.3187). From Wales comes a real treat: a tiny stall (open Friday and Saturday) dedicated to just one thing—Caerphilly cheese. **Gorwydd Caerphilly** is a king among cheeses. It is utterly delicious. Great rounds of it are driven here direct from the dairy, through the early morning of each Friday. Congratulations! You have found a British treasure. **The New Forest** is well known for literary children and wild ponies, but in Borough Market it is known for its excellent New Forest cider. The Burley cider farm is a family forest holding with registered Commoners Rights. But the cider is uncommonly good (Th-Sa; 0142/540.3589. www.newforestcider.co.uk). From Cumbria comes **Farmer Sharp Ltd**, with a stall full of reasons to let a lamb grow up a bit before sending it to the table. The team of experts behind the counter here are an entertainment in themselves. Have you heard the one about castrating rams early? (W-Sa; 0122/958.8299. www.farmersharp.co.uk) Also from Cumbria, one of the most regularly impressive stalls in the market is **Furness Fish, Poultry, and Game Supplies**. Free-range meat and wild game in season, along with puddings black and white and marvelous sausages, are here for amazingly reasonable prices. The most English of meats are here . . . hare and pheasant, venison and woodcock. Sometimes still in fur and feather! The fish side of matters is stunning: fish and crustaceans from all around the British coastline, and all shiny-eyed fresh. The great English delicacy of potted **Morecambe Bay** shrimps is a specialty (Th-Sa; 0153/955.9544. www.morecambebayshrimps.com). **The Borough Cheese Company** (open Thursday through Saturday) is lactic heaven. **Borough Wines** have a beautiful, intelligent selection including wines from their own vineyards, and offer daily tastings and charming and delightful gentlemen to guide you. Local London bread experts **Flourpowercity Bakery** have a small mountain of the very best of carbohydrate for you each week. The variety and creativity of their breads is a thrill. However, it is their almond croissants and the mere scent of their double-chocolate brownies that make me weak at the knees (Th-Sa; 208/691.2244). Should you want a healthy boost, the market's **Totally Organic Juice Bar** is here to give it—fresh juices and shots, hot chais and herbal teas, fantastic salads and soups. This place could give health a good name!

Be aware that if you are into food and drink at all, a visit here is going to take up at least a morning. But it will be a glorious morning. And you will spend more money than you really intended to, but it will be money well spent. Borough Market was voted London's Best Shopping Experience of 2007. You'll soon see why. ♦ Th, 11AM-5PM; F, noon-6PM; Sa, 9AM-4PM (although on Thursdays and Fridays many of the stalls are open earlier!) Southwark St SE1. 407.1002. Tube: London Bridge. www.boroughmarket.org.uk

Within Borough Market:

ROAST

★★★$$$ New, trendy, and very highly thought of, the space itself is worth a visit. Floor-to-ceiling windows make the experience of sitting perched right above the market a real entertainment. The view of Southwark Cathedral is also so much better than you get from down below. Roast is exactly what it says and a little bit more. Terrific produce from the market—beef and pork, lamb and fish—is simply and well cooked. There is a chance to try some traditional British specialties like potted salt beef with celeriac, horseradish, and shallots before tucking into a range of roasts that runs from belly of pork to rib of beef. Come along in season and you can choose from a selection of game, feathered or furred. Roast also does a fabulous breakfast. Breakfast with a capital B. If you don't even have time for their quickie 1-Hour Lunch, then right outside there is Roast To Go (take wet wipes!). ♦ Daily. Breakfast till late. 940.1300

47 BRAMAH TEA AND COFFEE MUSEUM

Next door to the **Design Museum** is a former warehouse chock-full of displays that tell you everything you ever wanted to know about tea and coffee. The teapots, drinking cups, and tea- and coffee-making machinery have been collected by Edward Bramah, a former tea merchant who is delighted to answer questions. There's also a café in which to sample the beverages. ♦ Admission: adults, £4; concession, £3.50. Daily, 10AM-6PM. 40 Southwark St. 403.5650, Tube: London Bridge. www.teaandcoffeemuseum.co.uk

48 THE GEORGE INN

★★$ This pub is a must-see for great atmosphere. Dwight Eisenhower and Winston Churchill are just two of the famous patrons who drank beer here. And as a child, Charles Dickens walked here every Sunday from Camden Town to visit his father in nearby **Marshalsea Prison**; you'll even find the inn mentioned in *Little Dorrit*. Rebuilt in 1676, this is an extraordinary survivor of bygone days—the last timbered, galleried inn in London. Before theaters like the **Globe** and the **Swan** were built, plays were presented in these inns, with "groundlings" standing in the courtyard and wealthy patrons seated on the balconies. The bar food is tasty, and there's a fine range of beers. The upstairs restaurant serves more expensive food: steak-and-mushroom pie, stuffed chicken breast, and apple crumble with custard. ♦ Pub/English ♦ Daily, lunch and dinner. 77 Borough High St (near Southwark St). 407.2056. Tube: London Bridge

DAY TRIPS

For all its myriad green spaces and riverbanks, London remains a city, with as much chaos and traffic as (if not more than) downtown Manhattan. And although most visitors agree that every British experience has to include the City, few ever make it beyond central London, let alone into the historic towns and villages that lie within striking distance. Just 1 or 2 hours' traveling out of London by car, bus, or train can take you to the spires of ancient **Oxford University**, to the quieter but no less impressive college town of **Cambridge**, to the Roman ruins of **Bath**, or the glorious cathedral at **Canterbury**. Faded Edwardian elegance resides on **Brighton**'s south coast, whereas the mystery of **Stonehenge** remains unsolved on **Salisbury Plain** to the southwest. Closer to home, one can stroll about bohemian **Hampstead** or trace part of Britain's lengthy maritime history at **Greenwich**. And those yearning for the full royal treatment may sail up the **Thames** to **Hampton Court Palace**, home to kings and queens from Henry VIII to Georgian times. If you have time during your visit to London, allow a day or two for a jaunt into the stunningly verdant countryside—the charms of rural England await.

One other trip around London that will stay in your memory forever is a balloon ride over the city. There is no more elegant way to see the capital (Adventure Balloons, 01252/844222, www.adventureballoons.co.uk).

City code 0208 unless otherwise noted.

1 CAMBRIDGE

Established in the 13th century and a few decades younger than **Oxford**, it is architecturally more cohesive, more beautiful, and less interrupted by the City itself. The university is located in a part of England called East Anglia, on the edge of the River Cam, and the backs of the colleges face the river (hence the term *Backs*). The most interesting of the 31 schools are **St. John's Trinity,** founded by Henry VIII; **Clare; King's,** where the chapel has exquisite stained-glass windows, fan vaulting, and lofty spires; **Corpus Christi,** where the **Old Court** is worth a visit; **Queen's; Peterhouse;** and **Jesus**.

If you are really looking to find out about this lovely old town, you could do worse than take a **Cambridge Walking Tour.** Two hours in the company of some like-minded people and a charming, encyclopedically informed guide will make sure you get what they call "the classic Cambridge experience." Those less inclined to activity can enjoy a 45-minute chauffered punt trip that takes in **Kings' College Chapel,** the **Wren Library,** and the **Bridge of Sighs** (for information/booking both, call 0871/226.8006).

Also, be sure to visit the **Fitzwilliam Museum** (Trumpington St, between the Fen Caliseway and Silver St, 01223/332900), one of the oldest public museums in the country. Founded in 1816, the institution boasts paintings by Delacroix, Renoir, Stubbs, Titian, and Tintoretto; prints and drawings; Islamic and Far Eastern crafts and artifacts; music scores by Handel, Bach, Chopin, Britten, and Elgar; European and Oriental fans; and West Asiatic, Egyptian, Greek, and Roman antiquities. ♦ Free. Tu–Su. The ideal time to visit is May Week (which is held in June), a 10-day period when graduating seniors receive their degrees. Festivities take place throughout the city, including a rowing competition on the Cam. Plan your day to include Evensong at King's College Chapel, if you are at all musically or religiously inclined.

If you are interested in more earthly joys, you might want to visit Cambridge's only vineyard, at **Chilford Hall** (Balsham Road, Linton; www.chilfordhall.co.uk). Just outside Cambridge itself, the vineyard was first planted across 18 acres in 1972, since which time Chilford Hall's wines have been winning awards and gaining customers. The vineyard is open Friday through Sunday from 1 March to 1 December. Winery tours leave at 11:30AM/2PM/3:30PM and last 90 minutes. No booking required. You can also check out the gorgeous statues and marble work at **Marble Traditions,** also at Chilford Hall–though sadly, the "one piece of carry-on baggage" rule probably means you can't take anything home! Also just outside Cambridge is the only remaining working watermill on the River Ouse. It is lovely, and maintained by the National Trust (Houghton. 0148/030.1494 www.nationaltrust.org.uk).

The **Cambridge Tourist Information Centre** (Wheeler St, at Peas Hill, 01223/322640) is open Monday through Saturday; it's also open Sunday between April and September. However, I have found that the web site www.visitcambridge.org is very helpful–and always available! ♦ Cambridge, 54 miles from London, can be reached by train direct from **King's Cross Station** in 55 minutes, from **Liverpool Street Station** in 80 minutes, by bus from **Victoria Station** in a little less than 2 hours, or by car on the **M11** in 90 minutes.

Fans of cathedral architecture might consider continuing their journey to **Ely**, 16 miles north of Cambridge. The crowning glory of this charming market town is the medieval **Ely Cathedral** (the Gallery, at Steeple Row), whose lantern tower can be seen for miles around. There is a stained-glass museum inside. ♦ Admission. Daily

Oliver Cromwell, who was born in Cambridgeshire, had a family home in Ely. Called **Oliver Cromwell's House** (29 St. Mary's St, next door to **St. Mary's** church, 01353/662062), it has been beautifully restored in 17th-century style to house both the **Tourist Information Centre** and a Cromwell exhibition. ♦ Free. Daily, Apr–Sept; M–Sa, Oct–Mar. Ely is 70 miles from London. The Cambridge-bound trains continue to Ely (add another 20 minutes to the journey time). If you're driving, continue on the A10 from Cambridge.

2 THE COTSWOLDS

New York has the Hamptons, and London has the Cotswolds. RVs packed with the rich and the posh flock from London to the Cotswolds for the weekend like desert wanderers rushing to the solace of a cooling oasis.

The Cotswolds covers more or less the area between the M5 and the M40. The countryside

Restaurants/Clubs: Red | Hotels: Purple | Shops: Orange | Outdoors/Parks: Green | Sights/Culture: Blue

is lovely and the whole area, dotted with picturesque little villages, is about as English as stiff upper lips and damp weather.

It is perfectly possible to visit your chosen part of the Cotswolds as a day trip, but it would be a pity, because sunrise and sunset are two of the loveliest times in the area. Whether you are looking for history, scenery, gastronomy, or oddity, you will find it here. To get to Cotswalds: Trains from **Paddington Station** take about 90 minutes. Head for Bath, Cheltenham, Stratford-upon-Avon, Moreton-in-Marsh, Oxford, Kingham, Kemble, or Chippenham. Car rental is available in all these places. Driving from London: Take the **M4** or **M40** and follow the unusually helpful signs for whichever town or village you are heading.

One other way to get "the Cotswolds experience" is to rent a cottage for the weekend. This is a real experience. I discovered these places recently, and staying there almost feels like being in a movie, so perfect are they. Book at www.bruern-holiday-cottage.co.uk

3 OXFORD

The university here has existed since the 1200s, making it the oldest institution of learning in England. The center of the city is dominated by the Gothic turrets, towers, and spires of the famed university's 30 colleges, all of which have unique charm. **St. Edmund Hall**, **Merton**, and **Balliol**, built in the 13th century, are the oldest colleges; **Christ Church**, whose august alumni include John Locke, W.H. Auden, and Lewis Carroll, and the academically distinguished **All Souls** probably are the best known. Bill Clinton attended **University College** as a Rhodes scholar. **Magdalen** (pronounced Maud-lin), whose 15th-century tower was used by Charles I as an observation post during his attack on the city in the civil war, has educated such notable students as Cardinal Thomas Wolsey and Oscar Wilde. Today, this is the central point of the May Morning festivities, a medieval celebration. A visit during the academic year (between mid-October and mid-May) is most interesting; during summer holidays, the colleges are deserted or filled with American students. Visiting times vary greatly: some of the colleges can be visited only in the afternoon during the school year.

Besides all of its other distinctions, this university also contains Britain's (and possibly Europe's) first public museum—the **Ashmolean Museum of Art and Archaeology** (Beaumont St, between St. Giles and St. Johns Sts, 01865/278000). Opened in 1863, it features an eclectic collection of art and antiquities, including Guy Fawkes's lantern; Powhatan's mantle; bronze works from China, India, Greece, and the Italian Renaissance; ceramic pieces from Asia, England, and Europe; and paintings by Dutch, Flemish, English, French, and Italian artists. There's truly something here for everyone. ◆ Free. Tu–Sa; Su, 2–4PM

(schedule varies during the Easter and Christmas holidays, so call ahead).

The **Oxford Tourist Information Centre** (The Old School, Gloucester Garden, at the bus bays, 01865/7268711) is open Monday through Saturday. It's also open on Sunday between April and September. ◆ Oxford is 56 miles from London and can be reached by train from **Paddington Station** in an hour (trains leave hourly), or by bus from **Victoria Coach Station** in 1 hour and 45 minutes. If you're driving, take the **M40**, then the **A40** (the journey takes 1 hour).

4 BATH

Elegantly laid out and proportioned, this ancient city is as perfect as a novel by Jane Austen—and why not, because the writer walked along the streets here, sipped the water in the **Pump Room**, and captured its grace, elegance, and usefulness in *Northanger Abbey* and *Persuasion*. This city of terraces, crescents, and squares is the most famous spa in England (and the only one with hot springs); it's worth a visit for its Roman ruins, glorious architecture, and gentle Austenesque atmosphere.

The Georgian perfection seen here today is largely the work of two 18th-century architects—a father and son, both named **John Wood**—but Bath existed long before that. The Romans, nostalgic for the warm waters of home, founded the city in AD 43 and stayed for four centuries. Bath declined rapidly after the Romans departed, and it wouldn't become fashionable again until the 18th century, when luminaries such as Gainsborough and Lord Nelson were regular visitors. The **Roman Baths** (Abbey Church Yd, at York St, 01225/444477), among the most striking ruins in Europe, are still the major attraction here. Excavations nearby have unearthed relics ranging from coins to a sacrificial altar. You can sample water from the fountain in the **Pump Room** above the baths, which Charles Dickens said tastes like warm flatirons—he was right! ◆ Admission. Baths: daily. Pump Room: daily

As for the modern architecture—well, just close your eyes and pretend it isn't there. After its heyday in the 18th century, the city went downhill. But the last two decades have brought new life to Bath. Today, Londoners come here for the city's cultural life the way they used to for the waters. If you're interested in art and antiquities, don't miss the **Holburne Museum** (Great Pulteney St, at Sydney Rd, 01225/466669), which houses one of the largest collections of silver in the country, along with porcelain and paintings by major British artists. ◆ Admission. Daily; Su, from 2:30PM, Feb–Dec

The most elegant street is the famous **Royal Crescent** with its curved sweep of Georgian houses. To get an idea of life in a grand town house of this era, visit **No.1**, which has been restored using materials available in the 1700s. ♦ Admission. Tu–Su. 1 Royal Crescent (at Brock St). 01225/428126

One of Bath's greatest achievements is the renovation of the **Theatre Royal** (Saw Close, at Barton St, 01225/448844), which hosts some of the country's top productions before they move on to London.

In a mansion on a hilltop a few miles outside Bath is the **American Museum in Britain** (Claverton Manor, A36. 01225/460503), the first museum of Americana outside the US. Its rooms are furnished to show domestic life in America from colonial times to the end of the 19th century. Opened in 1961, the museum was founded by Dallas Pratt and John Judkyn, two Americans with a deep appreciation of American arts who wanted to foster mutual understanding between Britain and the US. ♦ Admission £5. Tu–Su, 2–5PM. Take bus No. 18 or 25 at the bus station at Newark and Dorchester Sts

The **Bath Tourist Information Centre** (Abbey Chambers, Abbey Church Yd, at York St, 01225/477101) is open daily. ♦ Located 116 miles from London, Bath can be reached by high-speed train from **Paddington Station** in 70 minutes, by bus from **Victoria Station** in 3 hours, or by car, from the **M4** to Junction 18 to the **A46** and the **A4**, in 2 hours.

5 WINDSOR

Home to a magnificent park, a famous boys' school, and **Windsor Castle**, which has been the residence of kings and queens for more than 900 years (and is the largest castle in the world still occupied by royalty), this town lies on a pretty bend of the Thames. The construction of Windsor Castle (01753/868286, ext 2235) started in 1078, when William the Conqueror built a round keep made of timber here; over the centuries, successive monarchs have enlarged the castle and added new buildings. In the 1820s, Edward IV began **St. George's Chapel**, a fine example of Perpendicular architecture, with its elaborately carved stone vaulting. Henry VIII, his third wife, Jane Seymour, Charles I, and other monarchs are buried in the choir. Windsor's ultimate accolade came in 1917, when George V declared that henceforth, his family and descendants would take the surname Windsor. The **State Apartments**, used by the royal family when in residence, are decorated with paintings by Van Dyck and Rubens. Within the complex is Queen Mary's **Dolls' House**, designed by **Sir Edwin Lutyens** in 1921–1924. Everything is a magical one-twelfth of life-size, with 1-inch books by Kipling in the library.

In 1992, while Queen Elizabeth looked on in sorrow as Windsor, her favorite castle, went up in flames, her son Prince Andrew became a vital link in a human chain that saved almost all the priceless paintings and art treasures. Only the structure of the **Great Hall** was badly damaged. The following year, as part of the effort to raise funds for the restoration, the queen opened part of **Buckingham Palace** to the public for the first time, allowing visitors to tour 18 of the rooms (including the **State Rooms**, the **State Dining Rooms**, and the **Throne Room**) for two months during the summer. On one side of the castle is the **Great Park**, which is equally fascinating, with 4,800 acres of lawns, trees, lakes, herds of deer, ruins, and Prince Charles—when he is playing polo on **Smith's Lawn**. ♦ Admission. Castle: daily. St. George's Chapel: M–Sa; Su, 2–4:45PM

The newest Windsor attraction, **Legoland** (Winkfield Rd/B3022, 2 miles from the center of Windsor, 0870/562.6375), is a theme park with 150 acres that spell fun, especially for the kids. Outdoor activities include adventure playground areas, rides, and plastic Lego cars that children can drive. Everyone can enjoy the costumed performers who put on street shows throughout the area. Indoor activities include theater spaces with circus acts and the chance for kids to join in or to try face painting or magic tricks. There are also workshops with millions of bricks for the kids to build models. The site offers eateries as well as a lakeside picnic area. ♦ Admission. Daily, Mar–Sept; Sa, Su, Oct

Another noteworthy attraction in Windsor is the **Household Cavalry Museum** (Combermere Barracks, St. Leonard's Rd, between Bolton and Osborne Rds, 01753/868222 ext. 5203), which houses equipment and other items dating from the reign of Charles II to the present. The swords and uniforms are particularly interesting. ♦ Free. M–F

Across the cast-iron footbridge from Windsor, in the adjacent small town of **Eton**, is **Eton College** (01753/671177), the best-known public school in Britain, founded in 1440 by Henry VI. It is best to visit the school and its museum during term time (September through Christmas, January through Easter, and April through June), when you can see the 1,200 students in their wing collars and tails. Etonians exude an air of confidence that is unrivaled, and it is no surprise that 20 British prime ministers are among the alumni. ♦ Admission. Term time: daily, 2–5PM; school holidays: daily

The **Windsor Tourist Information Centre** (24 High St, between Sheet and Peascod Sts, 01753/852010) is open daily.

♦ Just 21 miles west of London, Windsor is 27 minutes by train from **Paddington** (change at **Slough**) or 50 minutes direct from **Waterloo**. Green Line buses (**Nos. 700 and 702**) leave from **Hyde Park Corner** or **Victoria Coach Station** (90 minutes). Driving takes 1 hour; take the **M4** to the **A332**.

Restaurants/Clubs: Red | Hotels: Purple | Shops: Orange | Outdoors/Parks: Green | Sights/Culture: Blue

Near Windsor:

BRAY

Just a couple of miles upstream from Windsor is Bray, an extraordinary place that has grown from being a lovely little village in rural Berkshire with an interesting history to a unique gastronomic mini-paradise. There are more Michelin stars here than in any other place outside London. And Bray is only a tiny village.

It does appear to have existed in some form from Roman times. In 1293 the old Saxon church was pulled down and the entire village rebuilt, as decided upon and paid for by all of the villagers. There is a Sheela-Na-Gig (the Celtic mother-goddess, depicted as a small large-breasted figure with legs akimbo) in the rafters of St. Michael's—the present church that is said to have come from that older church—as is the dog (some say it's a horse!) built into the outer wall of the **Chantry Chapel of Our Lady**. The church is fascinating and well worth a visit. Under the center of the nave you will (allegedly) find the most famous inhabitant of the village, the 17th-century singing Vicar of Bray, who in an ever-changing political climate caroled "whatsoever King may reign, I'll be the Vicar of Bray." One of the other citizens of Bray who is commemorated there is William Goddard, who founded the Jesus Hospital in the village in 1609 to house 34 of the aged poor of Bray. The hospital is still here and also worth a look.

The newest attraction in Bray is the latest restaurant from Giancarlo and Katie Caldesi (see what I mean about gastronomic mini-paradise?). **Caldesi in Campagna** is a delight—as one would expect from these most loved of Italian restaurateurs in England. The menu is regional Italian (mainly Sicily, Tuscany, and Liguria) and as authentic as you can get two miles upstream from Windsor. The Sunday lunch is awesome, and the wonderful Caldesis aren't even the Michelin star holders! ♦ Daily. 01628/788500. www.campagna.caldesi.com

To get to Bray, take **M4** from London to J8/9, then **A308**, then **B3028** to Bray. Or take the train from London **Paddington** to **Maidenhead**. The restaurants are a 5-minute taxi ride from the station.

THE FAT DUCK AT BRAY

★★★★ $$$$ This restaurant is a phenomenon. Voted Best Restaurant in the World 2005 by *Restaurant Magazine*, it scored an almost unprecedented 19/20 in the *Gault Millau Guide*, was Michelin's Restaurant of the Year in 2001, and has three Michelin stars. Heston Blumenthal, chef, proprietor, and philosopher-in-chief, was recently awarded an Honorary Doctorate of Science by Reading University for his pioneering work in food science. You absolutely must book, and bookings are taken two months in advance for Blumenthal's world-famous "molecular gastronomy." The Fat Duck offers an á la carte menu and a tasting menu. Both thrill with dishes such as Blumenthal's signature snail porridge with Joselito ham, mango and Douglas fir purée, nitro-scrambled egg and bacon ice cream, and scallop tartare with white chocolate and caviar. The wine list will thrill you almost as much as Blumenthal's menu and, frankly, there is no higher praise for a wine list. ♦ Tu-Sa, lunch and dinner. 0162/858.0333. www.fatduck.co.uk

THE WATERSIDE INN AT BRAY

★★★ $$$$ A gorgeous restaurant exactly where it says it is, with the added bonus that it has rooms as well, so if you feel you really can't move after several courses of classic French cuisine, you can simply stay where you are. The inn was opened by Michel Roux, brother of Albert (with whom he opened Le Gavroche in London), and the current chef-patron is Alain, Michel's son. The food is as impressive under the one as the other. Starters might include pan-fried escalope of foie gras served on a thin slice of homemade gingerbread with pickled damsons and cranberries. To follow, you might try the Challandais duck glazed with spices and served with confit kumquats, horseradish gnocchi, and a Cabernet Sauvignon. The golden plum soufflé is worth the trip out of London all on its own. The wine list is, predictably, heavily French biased and classy reading. ♦ Feb-Dec, W-Su, lunch and dinner (plus Tu dinner, June-Aug). Ferry Road, Bray, Berkshire. 0162/862.0691. www.waterside-inn.co.uk

6 HAMPSTEAD

All the centuries of London's history converge in this little village—a must-see for architecture buffs—as houses and cottages of all shapes, styles, and periods ramble up and down the hills. This is one of the prettiest of London's villages, and the residents are wealthy enough to keep it that way. ♦ The best tube stations for Hampstead are Hampstead and Belsize Park. If driving, take the **S21** north from central London as far as Swiss Cottage, then the **B511** north from there to Hampstead.

7 HAMPTON COURT PALACE

Not really out of town but 15 miles down the road from London (and better still, up the river), this special palace is a must as far as day trips go. The structure was begun in 1514 by Cardinal Thomas Wolsey, minister to Henry VIII. However, Wolsey's elaborately designed mansion and lavish lifestyle made him fear the envy of his king (and its possible deadly consequences)—so when the construction was almost complete in 1525, he presented the palace to Henry VIII in return for **Richmond Palace**. Henry VIII added a moat, a drawbridge, and a tennis court, plus new royal lodgings, galleries, and chambers. His third queen, Jane Seymour, was married, gave birth, and died at the palace, and Henry lived there for a number of years with his sixth and last queen, Catherine Parr. Elizabeth I loved the palace, and Charles I lived in it both as king and as a prisoner of Cromwell.

When William and Mary came to the throne in 1689, they revamped the palace, with **Sir Christopher Wren** and **Grinling Gibbons** in charge. The south front was severely damaged in a fire in 1986, but luckily, most of the paintings and art treasures were saved, and it has now been fully restored. Signs will help you find the **Renaissance Picture Gallery**, with works by Titian and Brueghel; the aromatic and evocative **Tudor Kitchen**; the **Great Hall**, site of Henry VIII's banquets and performances of Shakespeare's plays by the Bard's company; and the lower **Orangery**, featuring *The Triumphs of Julius Caesar*, a series of nine tempera paintings created between 1485 and 1492 by Andrea Mantegna. The 50 acres of landscaped gardens are beautiful, and the maze is irresistible but challenging—so leave plenty of time to explore it.

The **Tiltyard Café** is situated in what was once Henry VIII's jousting space. Jousting is discouraged nowadays. The food is all good English home cooking and changes seasonally. There is also a coffee bar in the same area should you simply require caffeine and carbohydrate (daily, 10AM-6PM; 10AM-4:30PM from 28 Oct to 29 March). Right in the heart of the palace is the **Privy Kitchen,** which was once part of Elizabeth I's private kitchen. Liz's place offers hot and cold drinks, pastries, cakes, sandwiches, and light lunches (10AM-5PM; 10AM-4PM from 28 Oct to 29 March).

If you really enjoy the royal atmosphere here, you can choose to stay in one of two self-catering apartments at the palace. Each flat sleeps six to eight people and features a full kitchen and living room. Guests also have access to the rest of the palace during its normal operating hours. The price is actually quite reasonable for families or large groups. For more information about the flats, contact the **Landmark Trust** (Shottesbrooke, Maidenhead, Berkshire SL6 3SW, England, 01628/825925). ♦ Admission. Daily. Off **A308**, Hampton. 781.9500. In summer, boats leave regularly from **Westminster Pier** to **Hampton Court**; call 0171/930.4721 for more information. The train from **Waterloo Station** takes 32 minutes. You can also hop a **Green Line bus—Nos. 415** or **718**; allow 1 hour. 668.7261

8 KEW GARDENS (ROYAL BOTANIC GARDENS)

What began as a hobby for Princess Augusta (mother of George III) back in 1759 has blos-somed into the most famous collection of flowers and plants in the world.

Having said that, there has been important stuff going on down here for much longer than that! Two thousand years ago Julius Caesar crossed the Thames river here to claim Britain as his own. In the early 14th century, Edward III created the first Royal Palace near here and later Henry VII built Richmond Palace, also nearby. The area came to be favored by royals for hunting in winter and "getting away from it all" in summer. There have been gardens here since the early 17th century. While he was still a prince, King George II and his wife, Caroline, developed and landscaped the park next to the river, and in the 1730s their son bought Kew House and leased the lands beside his parents.' These two estates make up the basis of what is Kew today, which is why it is called Kew Gardens (plural). Queen Caroline hired Charles Bridgeman and William Kent (considered the fathers of the English Landscape Movement) to turn her gardens into the latest fashion: groves of trees, water features, follies, and a riverside walk known as The Terrace. Prince Frederick went one better, creating a lake and planting hundreds of interesting trees. He died before his plans for the gardens were completed, and his widow, Princess Augusta, carried them on to create a botanical garden on nine acres of land. Today the Royal Botanic Gardens cover 300 acres and include an extensive arboretum, herbaceous borders, water features, a rock garden, a conservation area, and some of the world's largest greenhouses. In 2003, the Gardens were awarded World Heritage Site status by UNESCO.

This garden is a botanical paradise of more than 40,000 varieties, set along the east side of the Thames. It was given to the nation by the royal family in 1841 and is, for all its pleasure-giving, a scientific institution where plants are studied, classified, and cultivated. It offers a constantly changing display of flowers, as well as rock gardens and lakes with aquatic birds; stunning paths down to the river afford a sublime view of **Syon House**, the stately home of the Duke of Northumberland, across the Thames. Amid the greenery are 18th-century garden follies designed by **Sir William Chambers** for Princess Augusta: classical temples, ruins of a Roman arch, a fanciful 10-story pagoda, and an orangery, now containing a shop and a restaurant.

The **Palm House**, with its sweeping curves of glass and iron, was built in 1844 by **Decimus Burton** and houses tropical plants from both hemispheres. All the greenhouses are masterpieces, as are the grand entrance gates on the corner of **Kew Green**, also built by Burton. Be sure to see **Queen Charlotte's Cottage**, the **Chinese Pagoda**, and, if you come in springtime, the **Rhododendron Dell**. The **Evolution House** opened in 1994 and the **Princess of Wales Conservatory** in 1987. The lovely **Davies Alpine House** opened in 2006. Kew has also taken over **Wakehurst Place** in Sussex (a National Trust property) and used the land and that next door to found the Millennium Seed Bank in 2000. The **Kew Gardens Gallery** (332.5618) has exhibitions year-round. ◆ Separate admissions for Queen Charlotte's Cottage and the Kew Gardens complex. Gardens: daily. Queen Charlotte's Cottage: Sa, Su, Apr-Sept

The best way to get to Kew Gardens is either by riverboat (in summer only), a 90-minute trip from **Westminster Pier** (0171/930.4721), or by tube on the **District Line** toward Richmond. Trains leave from **Waterloo Station** for **Kew Bridge** (0345/484950). If driving from London, take the **A4** to the **M4**, Junction 1, then the **A205** south over Kew Bridge.

9 GREENWICH

Under Henry VIII (who was born here) and the Tudor royals, this Thames-side borough was the center of the world, and it still possesses the confidence and grandeur befitting that position. Greenwich Meridian (zero degrees longitude) and Greenwich Mean Time are still the standards by which the world sets its measures, and the vistas, elegant buildings, and parklands recall the long-lost British Empire.

The tall masts of the *Cutty Sark* (King William Walk, off Romney Rd, 858.3445), the last of the great 19th-century tea clippers that could sail 360 miles in a single day, loom over the streets. Now drydocked, the ship has been turned into a museum. Next to it is the smaller *Gipsy Moth IV*, which sailed around the world in 1966-1967 with Sir Francis Chichester alone at the helm. Both ships are in the care of the Maritime Trust, but only the *Cutty Sark* can be visited. ◆ Admission. M-Sa; Su, noon-6PM, Apr-Sept; noon-5PM, Oct-May

The domes and colonnades of the **Royal Naval College** (King William Walk, off Romney Rd, 858.2154), the triumphant achievement of three great architects—**Wren, Vanbrugh,** and **Hawksmoor**—preside magnificently over the River Thames. Inside, the paintings of Sir James Thornhill line the walls of the **Painted Hall**. The Chapel was redone with intricate detailing after a fire in the late 18th century. Only the Painted Hall and the Chapel are open to visitors. ◆ Free. M-W, F-Su, 2:30-5PM

The **National Maritime Museum** (Romney Rd, at Park Row, 858.4422), farther back from the river, houses the finest collection of globes in the world, along with marine paintings, navigational instruments, memorabilia about Lord Nelson, and more than 2,000 model ships. The centerpiece of the museum is the purely classical **Queen's House**, designed by Inigo Jones in 1616-1635. The great hall—a perfect cube—and the tulip staircase are both stunning. From the Queen's House, pass through **Greenwich Park**, with its delightful flower garden, to the buildings of the **Old Royal Observatory**, designed by **Sir Christopher Wren** for Charles II in 1675-1676. Inside is a fascinating collection of telescopes and astronomical instruments. The park is free; one admission allows entry to the museum, house, and observatory. ◆ Daily

A riverside walk from the **Naval College** takes you to the extraordinary **Thames Flood Barrier** (**Thames Barrier Visitors' Centre**, Unity Way, off Eastmoor St, Woolwich, 305.4188), constructed between 1975 and 1982 to the tune of £500 million and comprising 10 enormous movable gates between river piers and abutments on either bank. ◆ Admission. Daily. It is possible to catch a boat to the Thames Flood Barrier from Greenwich pier. Or, if you go by train from London to **Charlton Rail Station**, it's a 20-minute walk.

Two restored early Georgian town houses contain a collection of more than 2,000 fans that date from the 17th century onward. The **Fan Museum** (12 Crooms Hill, at Burney St, 858.7879) hosts changing exhibitions on related themes. The fan motif even extends to the museum's café, the **Orangery**—you can gaze on a fan-shaped parterre while enjoying tea or a snack here. ◆ Admission. Tu-Sa; Su, noon-4:30PM

Despite its grand buildings, Greenwich has a raffish air, never more so than on Sunday, when there are several antiques and crafts markets. The **Greenwich Tourist Information Centre** (46 Greenwich Church St, between Nelson Rd and College Approach, 858.6376) is open daily. ◆ The best way to reach Greenwich is by riverboat. Boats depart from **Westminster Pier** (Victoria Embankment, just north of Westminster Bridge, 0207/930.4097/9003) every 30 minutes between 10:30AM and 5PM; the trip takes 45 minutes. The last boat leaves Greenwich at 5:45PM June-Aug and 3:45PM the rest of the year. Trains run from **Charing Cross** to **Maze Hill** every half hour and take 20 minutes. Bus **No. 188** runs between Greenwich and **Waterloo Station**, making the journey in 35 minutes. If traveling by car, take the **A200** southeast. Oh, and if you wanted to get into the Dome, you've missed it.

10 CANTERBURY

This important ancient city in the county of Kent is the "cradle of Christianity" in England. It was here that St. Augustine landed in 597 to convert the locals and was welcomed by King Ethelbert, whose wife, Bertha, was already a Christian. The king and the local population duly became converts. Today the spiritual head of the Church of England is the Archbishop of Canterbury.

The interior of **Canterbury Cathedral** has an awesome beauty and a wealth of medieval stained glass. A site in a corner of the cathedral marks the martyrdom of St. Thomas à Beckett in 1170 when King Henry II's knights took too literally his outburst "Who will rid me of this troublesome priest?" The Beckett shrine attracted pilgrims for centuries, their journeys immortalized in Geoffrey Chaucer's *Canterbury Tales.*

The compact little town of Canterbury, nestled by the River Stour, still has substantial medieval stone walls with a walkway that allows visitors to stroll along the top. There are plenty of shops and restaurants, and the picturesque streets, with a wealth of thatch-roofed, half-timbered buildings, get quite busy, particularly as the town is close to Ramsgate, Dover, and Folkestone, the ferry ports for the Continent. Folkestone is also where the **Eurostar** train goes under the Channel Tunnel.

A large ruin just outside the town wall, **St. Augustine's Abbey** (Longport, at Lower Chantry La, 01227/767345) is now a museum with artifacts that were unearthed during excavations, and a free interactive tour. Visitors push the buttons of display panels throughout the abbey ruins that activate such sound effects as choral music, Gregorian chants, and anecdotes told by characters from its history. There's also a computer image that re-creates the abbey as it might have appeared at the various stages of its construction over the centuries. ♦ Admission. Daily

In the center of town you'll find **The Canterbury Tales** (St. Margaret's St, between Watling and High Sts, 01227/479227), a display of tableaux with figures re-creating the stories told by Chaucer's famous characters. ♦ Admission. Daily

The **Canterbury Tourist Information Centre** (34 St. Margaret's St, between Watling and High Sts, 01227/766567) is open Monday through Saturday; it's also open Sunday between Easter and September.
♦ Canterbury, 60 miles southeast of London, can be reached direct by trains from **Victoria** and **Charing Cross Stations** in 1.5 hours or by bus from **Victoria Station** in just over 1 hour. To drive, take the **A2/M2**; it takes just over 1 hour.

11 FOREST GREEN

Should you want to blow the London cobwebs out of your hair while you are here, the traditional English way to do it is with a lovely country walk. And the more sensible English way to do it is with a lovely country walk that has at the end of it a fabulous country pub with wood-burning stove and real ales and fine wines and really good food. So one excellent option is to get yourselves down to **The Parrot** at Forest Green (about an hour from London),

park up in its generous parking facilities, and set off on a nice long walk in the gorgeous Sussex Hills. There are thousands of acres of National Trust and Forestry Commission land here, so you can be assured it is beautiful and well looked after. All manner of wildlife, both running and flying, is to be spotted, and the fresh air and the undulating countryside will work up a huge appetite. Which is when you get yourselves back to The Parrot. Charles and Linda Gotto have for years run London's best (and best loved) gastropubs—pubs like The Ship and The Alma in Wandsworth, famous for good food and great atmosphere. Now they have moved out to the country, to be nearer their farm, where happy, naturally reared cattle, rare breed pigs, and sheep live an outdoor, high-quality life before ending up on your plate in the pub's restaurant.

♦ The Parrot at Forest Green (near Dorking). Take **A24** out of London to Dorking, then continue on the **A24** to Beare Green. Turn right onto the **A29** for three miles to Ockley, and then turn right onto the **B2161** to Forest Green. Trains will take you to Dorking (from Waterloo), from where it is a medium-length taxi ride.

12 SALISBURY

The country town of Salisbury in Wiltshire, 83 miles from London, rests on a plain where the Rivers Nadder and Bourne flow into the Avon, quietly expressing the calm beauty of this medieval town and its famous cathedral. The community is lucky: Because it's too far from London for commuters and bypassed by major roads, its old city center is virtually intact, utterly charming, and worth a wander around. Salisbury's other major asset is its convenient location—just 10 miles from **Stonehenge**, one of the most important prehistoric monuments in Europe.

Immortalized by John Constable (whose painting can be seen at the **National Gallery** if you can't make this trip), classic **Salisbury Cathedral** (The Close, off North Walk), consecrated in 1258, is the pinnacle of English cathedral architecture. It was made even more beautiful by the addition of a majestic spire (circa 1320) rising above the water meadows beside the Avon. At 404 feet high, it is the tallest spire in England, enchanting the eye with its deceptively light appearance—in reality, the 6,400 tons of stonework have put such a strain on the four load-bearing columns that they are slightly bent. The Avon marks the western side of the cathedral's grounds, and a 14th-century wall of stone from Old Sarum, part of the city that was razed in 1331 to provide building materials for the Cathedral Close, borders the other three sides.

The interior of the cathedral is not as breathtaking as the exterior, due in part to the ruthlessness of **James Wyatt**'s renova-

---

Restaurants/Clubs: Red | Hotels: Purple | Shops: Orange | Outdoors/Parks: Green | Sights/Culture: Blue

tions (1788–1789), in which he removed the screens and chapels and rearranged the monuments in rows. Happily, the restoration by **Sir George Gilbert Scott** in 1859 minimized the damage. The cathedral contains tombs of the Crusaders and those who fought at Agincourt. Other treasures include exquisite lancet windows with patchworks of glass from the 13th and 15th centuries and a 14th-century wrought-iron clock that was restored to working order in 1956 and is now possibly the oldest working clock in the world. The **Cloisters** and the beautiful, octagonal **Chapter House**, built between 1364 and 1380, were modeled after those of Westminster Abbey. Many of the cathedral's treasures are displayed in the Chapter House, including one of four existing copies of the Magna Carta, brought here for safekeeping shortly after 1265. The **Cathedral Close** contains the medieval **Bishop's Palace and Deanery**. ♦ Admission. Daily

Also in the Close and open to the public are **Malmesbury House**, built in 1327 and restored in 1749, and the 18th-century **Mompesson House**. Malmesbury House (01722/327027) features a Queen Anne façade and several rooms decorated with period furnishings, including a grand hall, a music room, and a drawing room. Part of the structure dates as far back as 1399. ♦ Admission. Tu–Sa, Apr–Oct

Mompesson House (01722/335659), operated by the National Trust, boasts an elegant oak staircase, antiques, a collection of china and glassware from the 18th century, and a lovely walled garden. ♦ Admission. M–W; Sa, Su

The **Salisbury Tourist Information Centre** (Fish Row, at Queen St, 01722/334956) is open Monday through Saturday; it's also open Sunday between May and September.

In **Wilton Village**, easily reached by bus or car, is the splendid **Wilton House** (**A30**, three miles west of Salisbury, 01722/746720). The home of the Earl of Pembroke for more than 400 years, it features 17th-century staterooms by **Inigo Jones**. The incomparable art collection includes 16 works by Van Dyck, which are hung in the famous double-cube room (60 feet long by 30 feet high and 30 feet wide) where General Eisenhower viewed plans of the Normandy invasion. ♦ Admission. Daily, Apr–Oct. Buses take the 18-minute journey from the station (Windsor Rd, off Fisherton St) to Wilton House every half hour; if you're driving, take the **A30**.

♦ Salisbury is 83 miles from London and can be reached by way of a picturesque, 90-minute railway journey, which leaves from **Waterloo Station** every hour. There are at least two bus trips daily from **Victoria Coach Station** that take three hours, but the bus service in the afternoon from Salisbury is often at awkward times—take the train! The station is a 10-minute walk from the center of Salisbury. If you're driving, take the **M3** and then the **A36**.

Near Salisbury:

STONEHENGE

This great historic structure is one of the oldest and most important megalithic monuments in Europe, dating from between 1850 BC and 1400 BC, although the earliest signs of the Stone Circle date back to the Bronze Age, circa 3500 BC. Though the fence around the monument, added in modern times for its own protection, makes it look like a captive animal and takes away the initial impact, the sight of the long, eerie collection of stones is still breathtaking, and the way **Stonehenge** interacts with the sun on certain days of the year is astounding.

The stones are arranged in four series within a circular ditch 300 feet in diameter. The outer ring, with a diameter of 97 feet, is a circle of 17 sandstones connected on top by a series of lintel stones. The second ring is of bluestones, the third is horseshoe shaped, and the inner ring is ovoid. Within the ovoid ring lies the **Altar Stone**, made of micaceous sandstone. The great upright **Heelstone** is along the Avenue, the broad road leading to the monument. Some of the stones, weighing up to four tons each, have been shown to come from the Preseli Mountains in Wales, a distance of some 135 miles.

Stonehenge was at one time believed to be a druid temple, a theory contradicted by the fact that the druids didn't arrive in Britain until circa 500 BC. In 1963, British astronomer Gerald Hawkins theorized that the collection of stones was a huge astronomical instrument used to accurately measure solar and lunar movements as well as eclipses. Avoid visiting during the two weeks preceding Midsummer's Day (21 June), as security around the area is tightened because of the latter-day hippies and would-be druids who try to perform rituals at the monument at that time. ♦ Admission. Daily. Located 10 miles northwest of Salisbury. Take the **A345**, then the **A303**. 01980/624715

13 WINCHESTER

This is the ancient capital of England, graceful and unspoiled, and a perfect trip to combine with **Salisbury** and **Stonehenge**, only 20 miles away. Winchester was England's capital city for nearly 250 years, from 829 until after the Norman Conquest, when the Normans decided to move the capital to London. King Alfred the Great reigned here between 871 and 899, during the invasion of the Danes, and helped the city evolve into a great center of learning. The picturesque High Street, in the center of town, is lined with a charming medley of buildings dating from the 13th century. Near the end of the street is the **Great Hall** (1235), all that remains of **Winchester Castle**, which was demolished in 1644–1645. An early fake **Round Table** (probably made in Henry VIII's time) of the legendary King Arthur stands in the hall, which was the scene of many medieval parliaments and notable trials, including that of Sir Walter Raleigh for conspiring against Elizabeth I.

The beautiful early Norman **Winchester Cathedral** (The Close, at Colebrook St) has the longest Perpendicular-Gothic-style nave in Europe (556 feet)—and it's made to seem even longer by its height (78 feet). The best view of the cathedral, emphasizing its setting in the city, is from Magdalen Hill, the road approaching Winchester from the east. Begun in 1079, consecrated in 1093, and partially rebuilt in 1346-1366, it contains a wealth of treasures, most striking of which are the seven richly carved chantry chapels. **Bishop Wykeham's Chantry**, in the west end of the nave, contains an effigy of William of Wykeham, the great builder, statesman, and founder of nearby **Winchester College**, one of the oldest public schools in England (it dates from 1382), and of **New College, Oxford**. On the opposite wall are a brass tablet and window dedicated to Jane Austen (1775-1817), who is buried here. The bronze statues of James I and Charles I are by Hubert Le Sueur (1685).

Under the organ loft in the north transept is the **Chapel of the Holy Sepulchre** (12th century), with superb wall paintings (circa 1170-1205) of the *Life and Passion of Christ*. The oak screen separating the choir from the nave is by Sir Gilbert Scott, and the magnificent stalls (1305-1310), with their misericords carved with human, animal, and monster motifs, are the oldest cathedral stalls in England, except for some fragments at Rochester. The **Library**, over the passage between the south transept and the old **Chapter House**, was built in the 12th century and reconstructed in 1668. It contains 4,000 printed books and rare manuscripts, the most important of which is the *Winchester Bible* (12th century), one of the finest existing medieval manuscripts.

If you walk about a mile south of the cathedral, you will come upon the ancient **St. Cross Hospital**, where the "wayfarer's dole" of a horn of beer and a portion of bread—once a handout to the needy—is still offered to visitors.

The **Winchester Tourist Information Centre** (Guildhall, Broadway, between Bridge and High Sts, 01962/8405001) is open Monday through Saturday; it's also open Sunday between April and September.

♦ Winchester, 65 miles southwest of London, can be reached by train from **Waterloo Station** in 60 minutes, or by buses leaving **Victoria Coach Station** every hour for the two-hour journey. To get here by car from London, take the **M3**; from Salisbury, take the **A30** to the **A272**.

14 BRIGHTON

The first place to stop in this seaside community 53 miles south of London is the **Royal Pavilion** (Pavilion Parade, between Old Steine and Grand Parade, 01273/290900). Originally a modest 18th-century structure, the pavilion was rebuilt in grand fashion between 1815 and 1822 by **John Nash** for the prince regent, who later became George IV; the project cost £500,000 (a huge sum at the time). Its great onion-shaped dome, huge tentlike roofs, and small ornate pinnacles and minarets are so reminiscent of a fairy-tale Indian mogul's palace that you almost expect to see elephants filing past you carrying a rajah. Inside, it's pure chinoiserie, filled with ornate furniture and paintings that were chosen especially for this palace. A series of spectacular suites culminates in the **Banquet Room**, with brilliantly colored, gilt-painted walls and a ceiling like a huge palm tree with a bedragonned chandelier. ♦ Admission. Daily

The rest of the town echoes the elegant proportions of Regency days with frequent and unexpected onion domes and roofs. For yet more inspiration, just behind the pavilion is the **Brighton Museum and Art Gallery** (Church St, at Marlborough Pl, 01273/290900) with its Art Nouveau and Art Deco collections. ♦ Free. M, Tu, Th-Sa; Su, 2-5PM

Brighton has two piers, but only the **Victorian Palace Pier** is open to the public. This center of entertainment with amusement arcades and slot machines is well worth visiting during the week, but avoid it on weekends when it's crowded with day-trippers. Also, be sure to stroll through **The Lanes**—17th-century redbrick streets full of tiny shops selling every kind of antique imaginable. The area is heaven for browsers and connoisseurs alike, and there are even more restaurants than antiques shops. The **Brighton Tourist Information Centre** (10 Bartholomew Sq, in The Lanes, 01273/711.2255) is open daily. ♦ The nicest (and quickest) way to get to Brighton is by a 52-minute rail trip from **Victoria Station**. You also can go by coach from **Victoria Coach Station**, which will take 105 minutes. If driving, take the **M23**, then the **A23**; the journey takes about 1.5 hours.

Brighton has many terrific restaurants, one of which has a chef recently voted Best Italian Chef in the UK by both *Which* and *Italia Magazine*. His name is Francesco Furiello, and his restaurant (which he runs with his lovely wife) is **One Paston Place**. ♦ Tu-Sa, lunch and dinner. 1 Paston Place. 01273/606933. www.onepastonplace.co.uk

---

Restaurants/Clubs: Red | Hotels: Purple | Shops: Orange | Outdoors/Parks: Green | Sights/Culture: Blue

HISTORY

The dates given in parentheses after the names of the British monarchs are the years of their reigns.

55–54 BC   Julius Caesar makes two expeditions into Britain, but following armed resistance, he agrees to a peace settlement.

AD 43   The Romans, led by Emperor Claudius, conquer Britain and establish Londinium (London).

61   In a revolt against Roman rule, Boadicea, queen of the Iceni tribe, destroys London before her final defeat.

CA. 100   The first **London Bridge** is built.

200   The Romans build the first wall around London.

410   The Roman army withdraws from Britain to defend Rome against the Goths.

597   Christianity is introduced to Britain by the Benedictine monk Augustine.

829   Egbert King of Wessex (802–839) establishes the House of Wessex as the supreme ruling dynasty of England.

842   The Viking Danes invade Britain, sacking London.

886   Alfred the Great (871–899) defeats the Viking Danes and establishes himself and the royal court in London.

991   With renewed threats from the Vikings, Ethelred the Unready (979-1016) introduces a tax to buy off the invading armies.

1016   After Ethelred's death, Canute, the king of Denmark, marries Ethelred's widow and becomes king of England (1016-1035).

1042   Edward the Confessor reestablishes the House of Wessex (1042-1066).

1065   Edward's great building, the first **Westminster Abbey**, is consecrated at Christmas; he dies a few days later.

1066   The House of Normandy is established under William the Conqueror after he defeats Harold II at the Battle of Hastings. He is crowned at **Westminster Abbey**, establishing a tradition (1066-1087).

1085–1086   The *Domesday Book* is compiled, providing William with a complete record of his kingdom for taxation purposes.

1087   Fire destroys most of the **City** and **St. Paul's Cathedral**.

1097   William II (1087-1100) begins to build **Westminster Hall**, now the oldest part of the **Houses of Parliament**.

1135   After the death of Henry I (1100-1135), his nephew Stephen of Blois becomes king (1135-1154) but is challenged by Henry's daughter, Matilda. Civil war breaks out and lasts throughout his reign.

1154   Matilda's son, Henry II, is crowned king (1154-1189) and establishes the Plantagenets.

1167   The expulsion of English students from Paris leads to the establishment of universities at **Oxford** (and a few decades later, at **Cambridge**).

1170   Thomas à Beckett, Archbishop of Canterbury, is murdered at **Canterbury Cathedral** after his allegiance to the church causes disagreements with King Henry II (1154-1189).

1176   Construction begins on **London Bridge**, the first stone bridge, which is completed in 1290.

1192   London establishes mayoral rule; Henry FitzAilwin is elected the first lord mayor.

1215   King John (1199-1216) signs the Magna Carta at Runnymede.

1269   The present **Westminster Abbey** is consecrated.

1280   Old **St. Paul's Cathedral** is completed; it is half as tall as the present building.

1337   Edward III (1327-1377) claims the French throne, and the Hundred Years War begins.

1338   **Westminster** becomes the regular meeting place of Parliament.

1348   Black death strikes Europe; about half of London's 50,000 citizens die.

1381   London bears the brunt of the Peasant Revolt, led by Wat Tyler against high taxes. It is quelled by Richard II (1377-1399), and Tyler is stabbed to death.

1399   Henry IV (1399-1413) accedes to the throne, establishing the House of Lancaster.

1415 As the Hundred Years War continues, Henry V (1413–1422) has a great victory at Agincourt.

1455 The War of the Roses begins.

1461 King Edward IV establishes the House of York.

1476 William Caxton's printing press is set up near **Westminster Abbey**. The first books in English are printed.

1483 The Little Princes disappear, probably murdered in the **Tower of London**. Their uncle, Richard III, becomes king (1483–1485).

1485 Richard III is killed in battle, and with the accession of Henry Tudor as Henry VII (1485–1509), the House of Tudor is established.

1509 Henry VIII (1509–1547) accedes to the throne and marries Catherine of Aragon. He starts to build **St. James's Palace**.

1530 The fall of Cardinal Thomas Wolsey occurs after he fails to secure an annulment of the king's marriage. Arrested for treason, Wolsey dies en route to London. Henry VIII moves into **York Place** (renaming it **Whitehall**) and takes over Wolsey's palatial home, **Hampton Court**.

1533 Henry VIII's marriage to Catherine of Aragon is declared void by the king's new archbishop, Thomas Cranmer. The king breaks with Rome, declaring himself the head of the Church of England. He marries Anne Boleyn.

1536 Anne Boleyn is executed for adultery at the **Tower of London**. Henry begins the dissolution of the monasteries (which continues until 1540).

1537 Jane Seymour dies while giving birth to Edward VI.

1540 Henry VIII marries Anne of Cleves. They divorce six months later, and the king marries Catherine Howard.

1542 Catherine Howard is executed in the **Tower** for adultery. Henry VIII proclaims himself king of Ireland.

1543 Henry VIII marries Catherine Parr, who outlives him.

1547 Henry's son, Edward VI, age 9, succeeds him but lives only six years.

1553 Mary I (1553–1558) marries Philip II of Spain and reinstates Catholicism. Citizens are martyred at **Smithfield**.

1558 Elizabeth I (1558–1603) accedes to the throne, restores Protestantism, and the Elizabethan Age begins.

1568 Mary, Queen of Scots, flees to England (executed 1587). The Royal Exchange is set up.

1585 Shakespeare arrives in London.

1588 The Spanish Armada fails to invade Britain after being defeated in its coastal waters.

1598 Timber beams from England's first theater in Shoreditch are taken apart and used to construct the **Globe Theatre** in **Southwark**.

1603 Elizabeth I dies without an heir. James VI of Scotland becomes James I of England (1603–1625) and establishes the House of Stuart.

1605 The Gunpowder Plot, a Roman Catholic conspiracy to blow up the **Houses of Parliament**, fails. The participants, including Guy Fawkes, are executed.

1620 Pilgrims sail on the *Mayflower* from Plymouth and settle in New England.

1625 **Inigo Jones's Banqueting House** is completed.

1631 **Covent Garden** is laid out by **Inigo Jones**.

1642–1646 Quarrels between Charles I and Parliament lead to Civil War between the Royalists and Parliament. The king is forced to leave London and headquarters himself in **Oxford**. Civil war battles take place throughout England until the king is captured and imprisoned.

1649 Charles I is executed at **Banqueting House**, the monarchy and the House of Lords are abolished, and the country is declared a republic.

1653 The republic (Commonwealth) is headed by Oliver Cromwell, Protector (1653–1658), and then by his son Richard Cromwell, Protector (1658–1659).

1660 The House of Stuart is restored when Charles II returns from exile in France.

1665 In the year of the Great Plague, 100,000 die.

1666 The Great Fire destroys half of London. It is described in the *Diary* of Samuel Pepys.

1670–1723 **Sir Christopher Wren** designs and erects **St. Paul's Cathedral** and 52 other London churches during the rebuilding of London.

1688 James II is deposed and exiled during the Glorious Revolution led by his daughter, Mary, and her husband, William of

Orange. They reign as joint monarchs until her death in 1694; William reigns until 1702.

1694   The Bank of England is founded.

1698   **Whitehall Palace** is destroyed by fire.

1701   The Act of Settlement bars Roman Catholics (and anyone marrying a Roman Catholic) from the throne.

1714   The House of Hanover is established with the accession of George I (1714-1727).

1721   Sir Robert Walpole leads the Whigs in Parliament until 1742. He is known as the first prime minister.

1735   An act of Parliament is passed to purchase the extensive collections of Sir Hans Sloane to display to the public; this is the beginning of the **British Museum**.

1768   The **Royal Academy of Arts** is founded.

1772   The **Adelphi** is built by **Robert** and **John Adam**.

1776   America declares its independence from Britain.

1805   Lord Nelson dies at the Battle of Trafalgar and is buried in **St. Paul's Cathedral**.

1814   Gas lighting is installed in Piccadilly.

1815   The Duke of Wellington defeats Napoleon at Waterloo.

1816   **John Nash** lays out **Regent's Park**, **Portland Place**, **Regent Street**, and **The Mall**.

1824   The **National Gallery** is founded.

1829   The first police force is founded. The first London bus appears; it holds 18 passengers.

1835   **Charles Barry** and **Augustus Pugin** begin building the **Houses of Parliament**; they are completed in 1860.

1836   The **University of London** receives a Royal Charter.

1837   Victoria (1837-1901) accedes to the throne; **Buckingham Palace** becomes the permanent residence of the sovereign.

1838   London's first passenger railway opens, running from Southwark to **Greenwich**.

1843   Nelson's statue is erected in **Trafalgar Square**. **Isambard Kingdom Brunel**'s **Rotherhithe Tunnel** (the first under the **Thames**) is built.

1851   The Great Exhibition in the **Crystal Palace** at **Hyde Park** shows off the masterpieces that can be created by machines.

1855   The first mailbox appears on the corner of **Fleet** and **Farringdon Streets**.

1861   The **Tooley Street** fire, the worst in London since 1666, destroys the whole waterfront south of the Thames.

1863   The first underground railway, from **Paddington** to Farringdon Street station, opens.

1877   Victoria is proclaimed empress of India.

1888   Jack the Ripper strikes for the first time in **Whitechapel**.

1889   The creation of the London County Council gives the city a comprehensive government for the first time.

1890   The first electric railway tube runs from the **City** to **Stockwell**.

1894   The **Tower Bridge**, with its double drawbridge, is opened.

1895   **Westminster Cathedral** is built.

1897   Queen Victoria's Diamond Jubilee is celebrated.

1914–1918   During World War I, London is damaged by Zeppelin air raids.

1917   George V (1910-1936) renounces all German titles and adopts the name of Windsor for the royal family.

1918   The right to vote is given to all men over 21 and all women over 30.

1922   The British Broadcasting Corporation (BBC) is founded.

1929   The right to vote is given to all women over 21.

1936   Edward VIII abdicates because of his relationship with Wallis Simpson, an American divorcée. His brother, the Duke of York, becomes George VI (1936-1952).

1939–1945   World War II puts England under siege. The Blitz destroys much of the City of London; **St. Paul's** stands among the ruins.

1945   The election of a Labour government brings about the nationalization of public service and major industries. The rebuilding of bomb-ravaged London begins.

1951   The Festival of Britain is staged as a symbol of its recovery from the war. **South Bank** is built as a cultural center.

1952   Elizabeth II accedes to the throne on the death of her father, George VI.

1953   The coronation of Elizabeth II is the first to be televised.

1971   Decimal currency is introduced, replacing the old pounds, shillings, and pence.

1972   The new **Stock Exchange** opens and the new **London Bridge** is completed.

1973   Britain joins the European Community.

1976   The (**Royal**) **National Theatre** opens.

1977   The Silver Jubilee of Queen Elizabeth II's reign is celebrated.

1979   Margaret Thatcher becomes the first female prime minister.

1981   The royal wedding of Prince Charles and Lady Diana Spencer takes place in **St. Paul's**.

1982   The **Thames Flood Barrier** is completed.

1984   The government establishes the London Development Docklands Corporation to regenerate the derelict docks in east London.

1986   The Greater London Council is abolished, leaving the capital without a central governing body. The *Times* is the first newspaper to move from Fleet Street to **Docklands**.

1989   The *Daily Express* is the last newspaper to leave Fleet Street.

1990   The Poll Tax is introduced. Prime Minister Margaret Thatcher is ousted from office by her own party in favor of John Major.

1992   **Windsor Castle** catches fire. The **Canary Wharf Tower** is completed—Britain's tallest building at 800 feet. The Conservative Party wins the general election for the third time in a row. Betty Boothroyd becomes the first female Speaker of the House of Commons. The queen volunteers to pay income tax on her personal property and revenue.

1993   Women are ordained as priests in the Church of England for the first time. The Irish Republican Army (IRA) attacks London's financial district.

1994   The **Channel Tunnel** (nicknamed the Chunnel) is opened, linking Britain and France by a train route under the **English Channel**. In a TV interview, Prince Charles confirms that he had an affair with Camilla Parker-Bowles. A cease-fire is declared between Britain and the IRA.

1996   Terrorist bombings in London bring to an end the shaky peace between the IRA and the British government.

1997   Prince William is confirmed into the Church of England. The Royal Yacht *Britannia* goes on her last voyage prior to being sold.

Britain continues a lone battle against the introduction of a single currency for the countries within the European Community. The Labour Party wins the election with its biggest ever triumph and a majority of 179 in the House of Commons. Tony Blair, at 43, becomes the youngest prime minister since 1812. John Major steps down as leader of the Conservative Party in the wake of the party's most humiliating setback since 1832.

Princess Diana is killed in a car accident in Paris. Millions watch the funeral procession in London, from **Kensington Palace** to **Westminister Abbey**.

2000   London kicks off the 21st century by unveiling a series of stunning celebratory attractions, most notably the **London Eye**, and the refurbished **Globe Theatre** on the South Bank.

The **Tate Modern** opens in a disused power station on the south bank of the Thames.

2001   Mayday in Central London erupts into the worst violence ever as protesters, including 40 dressed as Wombles, riot, smashing windows and bringing the city to a halt.

2002   The deaths of both Princess Margaret and Queen Elizabeth, the Queen Mother. The Queen Mother's body lay in state in Westminster Abbey and hundreds of thousands of people filed past. Prince Charles himself kept a vigil over her body through the night before her burial.

2003   At the behest of Mayor Ken Livingstone, London becomes the largest city to impose a congestion charge on cars entering the city. Starting at £5, the charge has now risen to £8.

2004   Norman Foster collects a skyscraperful of awards with a revolutionary office building described as "the first environmentally progressive work environment" or, more affectionately, "The Gherkin." At 180 meters tall, it is the equivalent of three Niagara Falls, and its lounge and bar are the highest in London.

2005   Four suicide bombers attack the **London Underground**, killing 52 people and injuring over 700.

2006   On 6 July, London learns that it will be the venue for the 2012 Olympic Games.

2007   On 6 November, HRH Queen Elizabeth opens the £80 million new **Eurostar Terminal** at St. Pancras. London and Paris are now officially just 135 minutes apart.

INDEX

W

Y

Z

RESTAURANTS

Only restaurants with star ratings are listed below. All restaurants are listed alphabetically in the main (preceding) index. Always call in advance to ensure a restaurant has not closed, changed its hours, or booked its tables for a private party. The restaurant price ratings are based on the average cost of an entrée for one person, excluding tax and tip.

★★★★ An Extraordinary Experience
★★★ Excellent
★★ Very Good
★ Good

$$$$ Big Bucks ($21 and up)
$$$ Expensive ($17–$20)
$$ Reasonable ($12–$16)
$ The Price is Right (less than $12)

★★★★

Angelus $$$ **117**
Arbutus $$$ **175**
China Tang $$$$ **83**
The Fat Duck at Bray $$$$ **234**
J Sheekeys $$$ **185**

HOTELS

The hotels listed below are grouped according to their price ratings; they are also listed in the main index. The hotel price ratings reflect the base price of a standard room for two people for one night during the peak season.

$$$$ Big Bucks ($255 and up)
$$$ Expensive ($180–$250)
$$ Reasonable ($105–$175)
$ The Price is Right (less than $100)

$$$$